Math.
Get in the Game.™

Now you and your friends can play cool video games that help you master math.

1 Go to:
PearsonSchool.com/DimensionM

2 Download the Mission

3 Choose Your Avatar

4 Game On!™

DIMENSION M™
Powered By
PEARSON

Prentice Hall

COURSE 2
MATHEMATICS
Common Core

Charles
Illingworth
McNemar
Mills
Ramirez
Reeves

PEARSON

Boston, Massachusetts • Chandler, Arizona • Glenview, Illinois • Upper Saddle River, New Jersey

Acknowledgments appear on p. 766, which constitutes an extension of this copyright page.

ISBN-13: 978-0-13-319668-9
ISBN-10:   0-13-319668-2
2 3 4 5 6 7 8 9 10 V063 15 14 13 12 11

Authors

Series Author

Randall I. Charles, Ph.D., is Professor Emeritus in the Department of Mathematics and Computer Science at San Jose State University, San Jose, California. He began his career as a high school mathematics teacher, and he was a mathematics supervisor for five years. Dr. Charles has been a member of several NCTM committees and is the former Vice President of the National Council of Supervisors of Mathematics. Much of his writing and research has been in the area of problem solving. He has authored more than 75 mathematics textbooks for kindergarten through college. *Scott Foresman-Prentice Hall Mathematics Series Author Kindergarten through Algebra 2*

Program Authors

Mark Illingworth has taught in both elementary and high school math programs for more than twenty years. During this time, he received the Christa McAuliffe sabbatical to develop problem solving materials and projects for middle grades math students, and he was granted the Presidential Award for Excellence in Mathematics Teaching. Mr. Illingworth's specialty is in teaching mathematics through applications and problem solving. He has written two books on these subjects and has contributed to math and science textbooks at Prentice Hall.

Bonnie McNemar is a mathematics educator with more than 30 years' experience in Texas schools as a teacher, administrator, and consultant. She began her career as a middle school mathematics teacher and served as a supervisor at the district, county, and state levels. Ms. McNemar was the director of the Texas Mathematics Staff Development Program, now known as TEXTEAMS, for five years, and she was the first director of the Teachers Teaching with Technology (T^3) Program. She remains active in both of these organizations as well as in several local, state, and national mathematics organizations, including NCTM.

Darwin Mills, an administrator for the public school system in Newport News, Virginia, has been involved in secondary level mathematics education for more than fourteen years. Mr. Mills has served as a high school teacher, a community college adjunct professor, a department chair, and a district level mathematics supervisor. He has received numerous teaching awards, including teacher of the year for 1999–2000, and an Excellence in Teaching award from the College of Wooster, Ohio, in 2002. He is a frequent presenter at workshops and conferences. He believes that all students can learn mathematics if given the proper instruction.

Alma Ramirez is co-director of the Mathematics Case Project at WestEd, a nonprofit educational institute in Oakland, California. A former bilingual elementary and middle school teacher, Ms. Ramirez has considerable expertise in mathematics teaching and learning, second language acquisition, and professional development. She has served as a consultant on a variety of projects and has extensive experience as an author for elementary and middle grades texts. In addition, her work has appeared in the 2004 NCTM Yearbook. Ms. Ramirez is a frequent presenter at professional meetings and conferences.

Andy Reeves, Ph.D., teaches at the University of South Florida in St. Petersburg. His career in education spans 30 years and includes seven years as a middle grades teacher. He subsequently served as Florida's K–12 mathematics supervisor, and more recently he supervised the publication of The Mathematics Teacher, Mathematics Teaching in the Middle School, and Teaching Children Mathematics for NCTM. Prior to entering education, he worked as an engineer for Douglas Aircraft.

Contributing Author

Denisse R. Thompson, Ph.D., is a Professor of Mathematics Education at the University of South Florida. She has particular interests in the connections between literature and mathematics and in the teaching and learning of mathematics in the middle grades. Dr. Thompson contributed to the Guided Problem Solving features.

Reviewers

Course 1 Reviewers

Donna Anderson
Math Supervisor, 7–12
West Hartford Public Schools
West Hartford, Connecticut

Nancy L. Borchers
West Clermont Local Schools
Cincinnati, Ohio

Kathleen Chandler
Walnut Creek Middle School
Erie, Pennsylvania

Jane E. Damaske
Lakeshore Public Schools
Stevensville, Michigan

Frank Greco
Parkway South Middle School
Manchester, Missouri

Rebecca L. Jones
Odyssey Middle School
Orlando, Florida

Marylee R. Liebowitz
H. C. Crittenden Middle School
Armonk, New York

Kathy Litz
K. O. Knudson Middle School
Las Vegas, Nevada

Don McGurrin
Wake County Public School System
Raleigh, North Carolina

Ron Mezzadri
K–12 Mathematics Supervisor
Fair Lawn School District
Fair Lawn, New Jersey

Sylvia O. Reeder-Tucker
Prince George's County Math
    Department
Upper Marlboro, Maryland

Julie A. White
Allison Traditional Magnet
    Middle School
Wichita, Kansas

Charles Yochim
Bronxville Middle School
Bronxville, New York

Course 2 Reviewers

Cami Craig
Prince William County Public Schools
Marsteller Middle School
Bristow, Virginia

Donald O. Cram
Lincoln Middle School
Rio Rancho, New Mexico

Pat A. Davidson
Jacksonville Junior High School
Jacksonville, Arkansas

Yvette Drew
DeKalb County School System
Open Campus High School
Atlanta, Georgia

Robert S. Fair
K–12 District Mathematics Coordinator
Cherry Creek School District
Greenwood Village, Colorado

Michael A. Landry
Glastonbury Public Schools
Glastonbury, Connecticut

Nancy Ochoa
Weeden Middle School
Florence, Alabama

Charlotte J. Phillips
Wichita USD 259
Wichita, Kansas

Mary Lynn Raith
Mathematics Curriculum Specialist
Pittsburgh Public Schools
Pittsburgh, Pennsylvania

Tammy Rush
Consultant, Middle School
    Mathematics
Hillsborough County Schools
Tampa, Florida

Judith R. Russ
Prince George's County Public Schools
Capitol Heights, Maryland

Tim Tate
Math/Science Supervisor
Lafayette Parish School System
Lafayette, Louisiana

Dondi J. Thompson
Alcott Middle School
Norman, Oklahoma

Candace Yamagata
Hyde Park Middle School
Las Vegas, Nevada

Course 3 Reviewers

Linda E. Addington
Andrew Lewis Middle School
Salem, Virginia

Jeanne Arnold
Mead Junior High School
Schaumburg, Illinois

Sheila S. Brookshire
A. C. Reynolds Middle School
Asheville, North Carolina

Jennifer Clark
Mayfield Middle School
Putnam City Public Schools
Oklahoma City, Oklahoma

Nicole Dial
Chase Middle School
Topeka, Kansas

Christine Ferrell
Lorin Andrews Middle School
Massillon, Ohio

Virginia G. Harrell
Education Consultant
Hillsborough County, Florida

Jonita P. Howard
Mathematics Curriculum Specialist
Lauderdale Lakes Middle School
Lauderdale Lakes, Florida

Patricia Lemons
Rio Rancho Middle School
Rio Rancho, New Mexico

Susan Noce
Robert Frost Junior High School
Schaumburg, Illinois

Carla A. Siler
South Bend Community School Corp.
South Bend, Indiana

Kathryn E. Smith-Lance
West Genesee Middle School
Camillus, New York

Kathleen D. Tuffy
South Middle School
Braintree, Massachusetts

Patricia R. Wilson
Central Middle School
Murfreesboro, Tennessee

Patricia Young
Northwood Middle School
Pulaski County Special School District
North Little Rock, Arkansas

Content Consultants

Ann Bell
Mathematics
Prentice Hall Consultant
Franklin, Tennessee

Blanche Brownley
Mathematics
Prentice Hall Consultant
Olney, Maryland

Joe Brumfield
Mathematics
Prentice Hall Consultant
Altadena, California

Linda Buckhalt
Mathematics
Prentice Hall Consultant
Derwood, Maryland

Andrea Gordon
Mathematics
Prentice Hall Consultant
Atlanta, Georgia

Eleanor Lopes
Mathematics
Prentice Hall Consultant
New Castle, Delaware

Sally Marsh
Mathematics
Prentice Hall Consultant
Baltimore, Maryland

Bob Pacyga
Mathematics
Prentice Hall Consultant
Darien, Illinois

Judy Porter
Mathematics
Prentice Hall Consultant
Raleigh, North Carolina

Rose Primiani
Mathematics
Prentice Hall Consultant
Harbor City, New Jersey

Jayne Radu
Mathematics
Prentice Hall Consultant
Scottsdale, Arizona

Pam Revels
Mathematics
Prentice Hall Consultant
Sarasota, Florida

Barbara Rogers
Mathematics
Prentice Hall Consultant
Raleigh, North Carolina

Michael Seals
Mathematics
Prentice Hall Consultant
Edmond, Oklahoma

Margaret Thomas
Mathematics
Prentice Hall Consultant
Indianapolis, Indiana

Dear Student,

We have designed this unique mathematics program with you in mind. We hope that Prentice Hall Mathematics will help you make sense of the mathematics you learn. We want to enable you to tap into the power of mathematics.

Examples in each lesson are broken into steps to help you understand how and why math works. Work the examples so that you understand the concepts and the methods presented. Then do your homework. Ask yourself how new concepts relate to old ones. Make connections! As you practice the concepts presented in this text, they will become part of your mathematical power.

The many real-world applications will let you see how you can use math in your daily life and give you the foundation for the math you will need in the future. The applications you will find in every lesson will help you see why it is important to learn mathematics. In addition, the Dorling Kindersley Real-World Snapshots will bring the world to your classroom.

This text will help you be successful on the tests you take in class and on high-stakes tests required by your state. The practice in each lesson will prepare you for the format as well as for the content of these tests.

Ask your teacher questions! Someone else in your class has the same question in mind and will be grateful that you decided to ask it.

We wish you the best as you use this text. The mathematics you learn this year will prepare you for your future as a student and your future in our technological society.

Sincerely,

Randy Charles.

Andy Reeves

Darwin E. Mills

Mark Illingworth

Bonnie McNemar

Alma Beatriz Ramirez

Contents in Brief

About the Common Core State Standards

In 2009, members of the National Governors Association agreed to work together to develop standards for mathematics and English language arts that many states would adopt. Having the same standards from one state to the next would make it much easier when students and their families move to a new school in a different state. The governors agreed to work with the National Governors' Association Center for Best Practices and the Council for Chief State School Officers to develop these standards.

The **Common Core State Standards for Mathematics** (CCSSM) were released in June 2010. Over 40 states have already adopted them. Schools and school districts are now working on plans to implement these standards. Teachers and administrators are developing curricula that teach the concepts and skills required at each grade level.

The CCSSM consist of two sets of standards, the Standards for Mathematical Practice and the Standards for Mathematical Content. The **Standards for Mathematical Practice** describe the processes, practices, and dispositions of mathematicians. These eight Standards for Mathematical Practice are the same across all grade levels, K–12 to emphasize that students are developing these processes, practices, and dispositions throughout their school career.

The **Standards for Mathematical Practice** are shown below.

1. Make sense of mathematics and persevere in solving them.
2. Reason abstractly and quantitatively.
3. Construct viable arguments and critique the reasoning of others.
4. Model with mathematics.
5. Use appropriate tools strategically.
6. Attend to precision.
7. Look for and make use of structure.
8. Look for and express regularity in repeated reasoning.

The **Standards for Mathematical Content** outline the concepts and skills that are important at each grade level. At Grade 6, these standards focus on these areas:

- Ratios and Proportional Relationships
- The Number System
- Expressions and Equations
- Geometry
- Statistics and Probability

These are many of the same topics that middle grade students have been studying for many years. One big difference, however, is that the Standards for Mathematical Content contain fewer standards and fewer topics to study at each grade level. With fewer topics, you can spend more time on concepts and achieve greater mastery of these concepts.

Assessing the Common Core State Standards

You will not only be learning concepts and skills based on a new set of standards, you will also likely be taking a new test to measure how well you are meeting these new standards. Two different groups are developing new assessment that you will soon be taking. Here's some information about the two groups.

Partnership for Assessment of Readiness for College and Careers (PARCC)

The PARCC assessment system will be made up of three Through-Course Assessments and one End-of-Year Comprehensive Assessment.

- The Through-Course Assessments will be given at the end of the first, second, and third quarters and will focus on the critical areas for each grade. The first and second Through-Course Assessment will require one class period to complete; the third Through-Course Assessment may require more than one class period to complete. You will take these assessments primarily on computers or other digital devices. The types of items on the assessment will range from multiple choice to performance tasks and computer-enhanced items.

- The End-of-Year Assessment will sample all of the standards at the grade level. You'll take this assessment online during the last month of the school year. Each test will have 40 to 65 items, with a range of item types (i.e., selected-response, constructed-response, performance tasks).

Your final score will be based on your scores on the three Through-Course Assessments and the End-of-Year Assessment.

SMARTER Balanced Assessment Consortium (SBAC)

The SBAC summative assessment system consists of performance tasks and one End-of-Year Adaptive Assessment.

- Performance tasks: You will complete two performance tasks during the last 12 weeks of the school year. These tasks will measure your ability to integrate knowledge and skills from the CCSSM. You will take these assessments primarily on computers or other digital devices.

- The End-of-Year Assessment will also be administered during the last 12 weeks of the school year. It will be made up of 40 to 65 items, with a range of item types (i.e., selected-response, constructed-response, performance tasks). Some items will be computer-scored while others will be human-scored.

Your summative score will be based on your scores on the Performance Tasks and the End-of-Year Adaptive Assessment.

Supplemental Common Core Lessons

Throughout *Prentice Hall Course 2,* you will find many opportunities to develop and build on both the Standards for Mathematical Practice and the Standards for Mathematical Content. In the **Problem Solving Handbook,** found on pages xxxii through xlix, you will find strategies to help you make sense of problems, persevere in solving them, reason abstractly and quantitatively, and use tools appropriately. With the **Guided Problem Solving** exercises, you can strengthen these same practices. The **More than One Way** activities offer you the opportunity to look at and critique the reasoning and thinking of others and to defend your solutions. The **Take Note** boxes model proper mathematical language to help you be more precise in your speaking, writing, and thinking. Many of the exercises also help you develop mathematical models to represent real-life situations. With this program, you're well on your way to becoming a proficient student of mathematics!

You'll also find in the program that the lessons align well to the Standards for Mathematical Content. To ensure in-depth and comprehensive coverage of all of the Standards for Mathematical Content, Pearson developed these supplemental Common Core lessons. Each lesson addresses a particular content standard, shown on the first page of the lesson, and was developed to be studied with existing lessons. In the left margin of the lesson, you'll find that lesson listed.

You'll notice that some exercises have a small ⊚ logo next to them. This logo indicates that these exercises are *particularly* focused on helping you become more proficient with Standards for Mathematical Practice. All of the exercises help you master the Standards for Mathematical Content.

Listing of Supplemental Common Core Lessons

Addition and Subtraction of Rational Numbers

CONTENT STANDARDS

7.NS.1 Apply and extend previous understandings of addition and subtraction to add and subtract rational numbers; represent addition and subtraction on a horizontal or vertical number line diagram.

7.NS.1.c Understand subtraction of rational numbers as adding the additive inverse, $p - q = p + (-q)$. Show that the distance between two rational numbers on the number line is the absolute value of their difference, and apply this principle in real-world contexts.

7.NS.1.d Apply properties of operations as strategies to add and subtract rational numbers.

You already know how to add and subtract integers. The table shows the rules, where a, b, c, and d are positive integers and $a > b$.

	Same Sign	Different Sign
Add: The sum has the sign of the addend with greater absolute value.	$a + b = c$ $-a + (-b) = c$	$a + (-b) = d$ $-a + b = -d$
Subtract: Rewrite as adding the additive inverse.	$a - b = a + (-b) = d$ $-a - (-b) = -a + b = -d$	$a - (-b) = a + b = c$ $-a - b = -a + (-b) = -c$

You also know how to add positive decimals, fractions, and mixed numbers. Use these skills to add and subtract any rational numbers.

ACTIVITY　　© **MATHEMATICAL PRACTICES**

1. The sum $\frac{1}{2} + \left(-\frac{3}{4}\right)$ can be represented on a horizontal number line diagram.

　Copy the number line diagram and label the parts that represent $\frac{1}{2}$ and $\left(-\frac{3}{4}\right)$.

2. What is the sum of these two fractions?

3. Can you use the same number line diagram to represent $\frac{1}{2} - \frac{3}{4}$?

4. Represent each sum or difference on a horizontal number line. Then find each sum or difference.

　a. $-\frac{3}{4} + \frac{5}{8}$

　b. $\frac{1}{4} - \left(-\frac{3}{4}\right)$

　c. $\frac{3}{4} + \left(-\frac{1}{2}\right)$

　d. $-\frac{1}{4} - \frac{5}{8}$

5. Use a horizontal number line like the one below to represent the sum of $-2.25 + 1.75$.

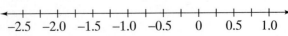

GO for Help
to Lesson 1-7

Use after Lesson 3-3.

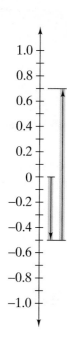

6. The vertical number line at the left represents $-0.5 - (-1.2)$.
   a. How else could you write this expression?
   b. What is the value of this expression?

7. Represent $-1\frac{1}{4} - 5\frac{1}{2}$ on a vertical number line diagram and find the difference.

ACTIVITY   **MATHEMATICAL PRACTICES**

The altitude at sea level is 0 meters. A scuba diver is standing on a platform 3.1 meters above sea level on a boat in the ocean.

1. Draw a diagram. At what altitude are the diver's feet?

2. The diver jumps into the water and stops at the top of a kelp plant 8.25 meters below sea level. Add this information to your diagram.

3. Find the absolute value of the difference between 3.1 and –8.25 to determine the distance the diver descended.

4. The diver follows the kelp plant down to its base at 21.3 meters below sea level. Complete your diagram.

5. Simplify the expression $3.1 - (-21.3)$ to find the total distance the diver descended.

Exercises

Represent each sum or difference on a horizontal or vertical number line diagram. Then find each sum or difference.

1. $3.5 + (-2.8)$

2. $-\frac{3}{4} + \left(-\frac{7}{8}\right)$

3. $-2.8 + 3.5$

4. $2.1 - (-1.7)$

5. $-1\frac{5}{8} - \left(-4\frac{3}{8}\right)$

6. $1\frac{1}{4} - 2\frac{7}{8}$

Add or subtract the following rational numbers.

7. $-16 - 26.6$

8. $-15.2 + 15.2$

9. $-9\frac{4}{5} - 4\frac{3}{5}$

10. $15\frac{1}{5} - \left(-15\frac{1}{5}\right)$

11. $-9.7 - (-8.8)$

12. $8\frac{3}{8} + \left(-6\frac{1}{4}\right)$

13. What is the temperature difference between $120°C$ and $-50°C$?

14. It was $75.5°F$ at 2 P.M. and then the temperature dropped $15.1°F$ in an hour. What was the temperature at 3 P.M.?

15. It was $-20.5°F$ at 6 A.M. and $22°F$ at noon. How much did the temperature change?

16. **Writing in Math** Explain why $p - q = p + (-q)$ is true for all rational numbers.

Multiplication of Rational Numbers

CONTENT STANDARDS

7.NS.2 Apply and extend previous understandings of multiplication and division and of fractions to multiply and divide rational numbers.

7.NS.2.a Understand that multiplication is extended from fractions to rational numbers by requiring that operations continue to satisfy the properties of operations, particularly the distributive property, leading to products such as $(-1)(-1) = 1$ and the rules for multiplying signed numbers. Interpret products of rational numbers by describing real-world contexts.

7.NS.2.c Apply properties of operations as strategies to multiply and divide rational numbers.

GO for Help
to Lesson 1-8.

You already know how to multiply integers. You also know how to multiply positive decimals, fractions, and mixed numbers. Use these skills to multiply rational numbers.

ACTIVITY   **MATHEMATICAL PRACTICES**

1. The model below shows the product $\left(2\frac{1}{2}\right) \cdot \left(-1\frac{1}{2}\right)$.

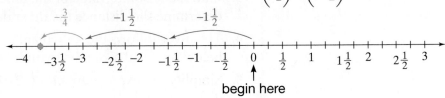
begin here

   a. Explain which property justifies why $2\frac{1}{2} \cdot \left(-1\frac{1}{2}\right)$ is equal to
   $2 \cdot \left(-1\frac{1}{2}\right) + \frac{1}{2} \cdot \left(-1\frac{1}{2}\right).$

   b. Explain how the number line above illustrates
   $2 \cdot \left(-1\frac{1}{2}\right) + \frac{1}{2} \cdot \left(-1\frac{1}{2}\right).$

   c. What is the sum of $2\frac{1}{2}$ groups of $-1\frac{1}{2}$?

   d. What is the product $\left(2\frac{1}{2}\right) \cdot \left(-1\frac{1}{2}\right)$?

2. How does this model show $\left(1\frac{1}{2}\right) \cdot \left(-2\frac{1}{2}\right)$?

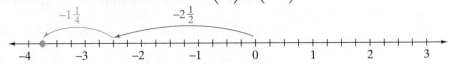

3. Compare $2\frac{1}{2} \cdot \left(-1\frac{1}{2}\right)$ and $1\frac{1}{2} \cdot \left(-2\frac{1}{2}\right)$.

   a. What is true about the product of these expressions?

   b. Is $2\frac{1}{2} \cdot \left(-1\frac{1}{2}\right)$ the same as $(1) \cdot \left(2\frac{1}{2}\right) \cdot (-1) \cdot \left(1\frac{1}{2}\right)$? Explain.

   c. Why does each expression equal $(1) \cdot (-1) \cdot \left(1\frac{1}{2}\right) \cdot \left(2\frac{1}{2}\right)$?

   d. What is the sign of $(1)(-1)$?

   e. Why is the product of a positive rational number and a negative rational number negative?

Use after Lesson 3-4.

4. a. Write the expression $(-2.2)(-0.45)$ as a product of four factors that includes $(-1)(-1)$.

b. What is the product of $(-2.2)(-0.45)$?

c. Explain how finding the sign of the product of two rational numbers is similar to finding the sign of the product of two integers.

ACTIVITY   Ⓒ **MATHEMATICAL PRACTICES**

Jolene graduated from college last year and is repaying her student loan. Every month she makes a payment of $124.18 from her checking account.

1. Does each payment increase or decrease her checking account balance?

2. Jolene has paid 7 months of her loan so far. Simplify the expression $(-124.18) \times 7$ to determine the change to her checking account balance caused by these seven loan payments.

3. Jolene gets a promotion and decides to pay 4.5 months of loan payments in advance. Write an expression to represent the change this will make to her checking account balance.

4. How much will she pay in advance toward the loan?

5. What is the sign of your answer? Explain why.

Exercises

Describe the product each number line models.

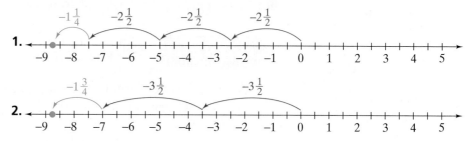

1.

2.

Ⓒ **3.** **Writing in Math** Use properties of mathematics to explain why the products in Exercises 1 and 2 have the same value.

4. For the past three months, Arturo's phone bill was $58.93 each month. He made each payment from the same checking account. How much did these payments change his account balance?

Phone Bill

Total: $58.93

Find each product.

5. $3.5 \cdot (-2.4)$

6. $-16 \cdot 6.6$

7. $-1\frac{5}{8} \cdot \left(-3\frac{1}{7}\right)$

8. $-2\frac{1}{3} \cdot -1\frac{3}{4}$

9. $-5.2 \cdot (-5.2)$

10. $3\frac{2}{5} \cdot -3\frac{1}{3}$

CC-3 Division of Rational Numbers

CONTENT STANDARDS

7.NS.2 Apply and extend previous understandings of multiplication and division and of fractions to multiply and divide rational numbers.

7.NS.2.b ...Interpret quotients of rational numbers by describing real-world contexts.

7.NS.2.c Apply properties of operations as strategies to multiply and divide rational numbers.

You already know how to divide integers.

Two Numbers	Sign of Quotient	Examples
Same Sign	Quotient is positive.	$16 \div 2 = 8$ $-16 \div (-2) = 8$
Opposite Signs	Quotient is negative.	$-16 \div 2 = (-8)$ $16 \div (-2) = (-8)$

You also know how to divide positive decimals, fractions, and mixed numbers. Use these skills to divide rational numbers.

ACTIVITY  MATHEMATICAL PRACTICES

1. Write the division problem $-3\frac{1}{3} \div 2\frac{1}{3}$. Will the sign of the quotient be positive or negative? Why?
2. Rewrite each mixed number as an improper fraction.
3. Rewrite the division problem as a multiplication problem. To divide by a fraction, multiply by its reciprocal.
4. What is the product? Write your answer as a mixed number.
5. When dividing two numbers with opposite signs, does it matter which number is negative and which number is positive? Use properties of operations to justify your answer.

ACTIVITY  MATHEMATICAL PRACTICES

Denise takes her father's old bicycle to a mechanic to have it restored. Afterwards, the mechanic sends her a bill with the charges shown.

Repair Bill

Tune-up	$50.00
Brake Shoes	$15.42
Tires	$34.19
Drive Train	$105.50

1. Find the sum of the charges on the bill.
2. From Denise's point of view, money that she receives is a positive number, and money that she owes is a negative number.
   To Denise, is the sum of the charges on the bill positive or negative? Explain.

Use after Lesson 3-5.

3. The mechanic wants full payment of the bill in four and a half months. Write an expression for how Denise's checking account will change each month.

4. What does the sign of the quotient represent?

5. What does the quotient tell Denise about paying her bill?

6. Next year, Denise has two more parts replaced. She uses a $25 gift card to pay for part of the work. Her expenses are shown below.

$$-\$54.50$$
$$-\$62.75$$
$$+\$25.00$$

What is the sum?

7. If Denise pays off the bill in 15 weeks, or 3.75 months, how much will her checking account change per month?

Exercises

Find each quotient.

1. $-14.28 \div 4.2$

2. $14.28 \div 4.2$

3. $14.28 \div (-4.2)$

4. $-2\frac{3}{4} \div 11$

5. $2\frac{3}{4} \div 11$

6. $2\frac{3}{4} \div (-11)$

7. $-\frac{3}{8} \div \left(-1\frac{1}{10}\right)$

8. $-10.5 \div (-0.5)$

9. $-12.96 \div (-10.8)$

10. $3\frac{1}{2} \div -2\frac{2}{3}$

11. How does the quotient $10.8 \div (-2.4)$ compare to the quotient $-10.8 \div 2.4$?

12. A spreadsheet program uses rational numbers to keep track of income and expenses for a business.

Business Expenses and Income

	Phone	Supplies	Wages	Income
Monday	−$4.32	$0.00	−$135.50	$0.00
Tuesday	−$4.32	−$17.25	−$135.50	$782.00
Wednesday	−$4.32	$0.00	−$135.50	$525.00
Thursday	−$4.32	−$25.00	−$135.50	$782.00
Friday	−$4.32	−$9.25	−$135.50	$0.00

a. What is the total balance for Monday?

b. Find the total balance for each other day of the week.

c. What is the average daily balance?

Simplifying Expressions

CONTENT STANDARDS

7.EE.1 Apply properties of operations as strategies to add, subtract, factor, and expand linear expressions with rational coefficients.

You evaluate algebraic expressions by substituting values for variables. To simplify algebraic expressions, use properties of operations.

Like terms are terms that have the same variable factors. For example, $12x$ and $3x$ are like terms, but $4a$ and $5b$ are not like terms. You can use the properties of operations to order, group, and combine like terms.

EXAMPLE **Using Properties to Add and Subtract**

1 Simplify $5x + 9 + 2x - 4$.

$5x + 9 + 2x - 4$ ← Identify which parts of the expression are like terms.
$= 5x + 2x + 9 - 4$ ← Commutative Property of Addition
$= (5 + 2)x + 9 - 4$ ← Distributive Property
$= 7x + 9 - 4$ ← Simplify the coefficient.
$= 7x + 5$ ← Simplify.

The simplified expression is $7x + 5$.

✓ Quick Check

1. Simplify each expression.
   a. $2x + 8 + 4x - 5$ b. $6 + 7y - 4y + 1$ c. $10r - 5 + 3 + r$

Sometimes an expression should be expanded before it can be simplified.

Test Prep Tip 🖊️

The model illustrates the Distributive Property.

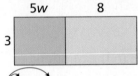

$3(5w + 8) = 15w + 24$

EXAMPLE **Expanding Expressions**

2 Simplify $3(5w + 8) - 6$.

$3(5w + 8) - 6$
$= (15w + 24) - 6$ ← Distributive Property
$= 5w + (24 + (-6))$ ← Associative Property of Addition
$= 15w + 18$ ← Simplify.

The simplified expression is $15w + 18$.

✓ Quick Check

2. Simplify each expression.
   a. $6(2x + 3) - 4$ b. $2(1 - 8v) + 5$ c. $9 - 4(3z + 2)$

Use after Lesson 4-1.

You can use the Distributive Property to rewrite an addition expression as a product of two factors. Use the greatest common factor (GCF) so the expression is factored completely.

EXAMPLE **Factoring Expressions**

3 Factor $4x + 14$.

GCF of 4 and 14 is 2.   ← Identify the GCF.

$4x + 14 = 2 \cdot 2x + 2 \cdot 7$ ← Factor each term by the GCF.

$\qquad\quad = 2(2x + 7)$ ← Distributive Property

The factored expression is $2(2x + 7)$.

✅ Quick Check

3. Factor each expression completely.
   a. $9x + 15$ **b.** $36 + 24t$ **c.** $8c - 20$

Homework Exercises

GO for Help

For Exercises	See Examples
1–9	1–2
10–12	3

Simplify each expression.

1. $9x + 3 + 2x - 2$ **2.** $6y + 7 - 3y + 3$ **3.** $12w - 7 + 1 + 4w$

4. $4 - 6x + 8 + 3x$ **5.** $3a + 8 + a - 9 - 2a$ **6.** $4(5x + 2) - 6$

7. $10 + 3(2v - 3)$ **8.** $4 - 5(3t + 3)$ **9.** $6(y + 2) - 6 + 5y$

Factor each expression completely.

10. $6x + 10$ **11.** $30 + 20y$ **12.** $12x - 28$

GPS

ⓒ **13. Guided Problem Solving** Simplify $\frac{6x + 4}{2}$.

• **Make a Plan** Rewrite the quotient as a product. Apply the Distributive Property. Write all fractions in simplest form.

• **Carry Out the Plan**

$$\frac{6x + 4}{2} = \frac{\square}{\square}(6x + 4) = \frac{\square}{\square}x + \frac{\square}{\square} = \square\, x + \square$$

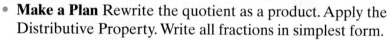

Simplify each expression.

14. $\frac{24x + 16}{8}$ **15.** $\frac{15 + 36y}{3}$ **16.** $\frac{96b - 24}{12}$

ⓒ **17.** **Writing in Math** The expression $3x - 6 + 2x + 4$ is modeled with algebra tiles as shown.

Explain how to use the model to simplify the expression.

Simplify each expression.

18. $8.4x + 10.2 + 4.3x - 2.9$ **19.** $5y + 4.7 + 2.08 - 0.6y$

20. $\frac{2}{3}(8x + 12) - \frac{4}{3}$ **21.** $1 + \frac{1}{2}x - \frac{3}{4}\left(\frac{1}{6} - \frac{2}{9}x\right)$

ⓒ **22. Error Analysis** Jane did the work shown. Explain her error.

$9y - 2 + 4y$
$9y - 4y + 2$
$5y + 2$

CC-5 Solving Equations of the Form $p(x + q) = r$

CONTENT STANDARDS

7.EE.4.a Solve word problems leading to equations of the form $px + q = r$ and $p(x + q) = r$, where p, q, and r are specific rational numbers. Solve equations of these forms fluently. Compare an algebraic solution to an arithmetic solution, identifying the sequence of the operations used in each approach.

You can use the Distributive Property to solve equations in the form $p(x + q) = r$.

EXAMPLE   Solve Using the Distributive Property

Solve $10(a - 6) = -25$.

$$10(a) + 10(-6) = -25 \quad \leftarrow \text{Use the Distributive Property.}$$
$$10a - 60 = -25 \quad \leftarrow \text{Simplify.}$$
$$10a = 35 \quad \leftarrow \text{Add 60 to both sides.}$$
$$a = 3.5 \quad \leftarrow \text{Divide both sides by 10.}$$

✓ Quick Check

Solve these equations.

1. $-4.5 = -3(b + 15)$ **2.** $8\frac{1}{2}(c - 16) = 340$

MATHEMATICAL PRACTICES

● More Than One Way

Each of 4 workers in a gourmet bakery makes $2\frac{1}{2}$ pounds of cranberry granola every day. The workers also make almond granola. Together, they make 24 pounds of granola every day. How many pounds of almond granola does each worker make daily?

Sarah's Method

I can use number sense. The amount of cranberry granola made daily is $4 \times 2\frac{1}{2}$ or 10 pounds. Since $24 - 10 = 14$ and $14 \div 4 = 3\frac{1}{2}$, each worker makes $3\frac{1}{2}$ pounds of almond granola daily.

Ryan's Method

I can write an equation. Let b represent the pounds of almond granola that each worker makes. Together, the workers make $4(2\frac{1}{2} + b)$ pounds of granola.

$$4\left(2\frac{1}{2} + b\right) = 24$$

$$10 + 4b = 24 \quad \leftarrow \text{Use the Distributive Property.}$$
$$4b = 14 \quad \leftarrow \text{Subtract 10 from both sides.}$$
$$b = 3\frac{1}{2} \quad \leftarrow \text{Divide both sides by 4.}$$

Each worker makes $3\frac{1}{2}$ pounds of almond granola daily.

Use after Lesson 4-6.

Compare the Methods

1. Compare the sequence of operations in Ryan's and Sarah's methods. Explain how they are alike and how they differ.
© 2. Which method do you prefer? Can you improve on that method?

Homework Exercises

GO for Help

For Exercises	See Example
1–10	1

Solve.

1. $-8(x + 2) = -10$

2. $10(2.2 - b) = 15.2$

3. $10\left(c + 6\frac{1}{5}\right) = -102$

4. $3\frac{2}{3}(12 - a) = 43$

5. $17\frac{5}{8} = -2(x + 15)$

6. $4(m + 2.5) = 7.5$

7. $14(0.5 + k) = -14$

8. $3(0.2 + y) = 9.6$

9. $100(a - 4.5) = 350$

10. $138.75 = 9.25(-6 + t)$

GPS

© 11. **Guided Problem Solving** Sandra buys a kit that has exactly enough material to replace the seats and backs of two antique chairs. The seats and backs are woven from cane. Each seat uses $83\frac{1}{3}$ yards of cane. If the kit has $416\frac{2}{3}$ yards of cane, how much is provided for each back?

- Each chair seat is made from $83\frac{1}{3}$ yards of cane. Write an expression that represents the amount of cane for one chair.
- Write an expression that represents the cane for both chairs.
- Write an equation that represents the situation and solve it.

12. **Food Preparation** Annie made fruit punch for 12 people. The punch contains sparkling water and $\frac{2}{3}$ pint of fruit juice per person. If there are $10\frac{2}{5}$ pints of fruit punch, how many pints of sparkling water did Annie add per person?

13. **Algebra** Write and solve an equation using the distributive property modeled by the algebra tiles below.

14. **Cell Phone** Paulo pays $45.99 per month for unlimited calls, with additional charges for text messages. His bill for 4 months is $207.96 If he sends 100 texts each month, how much is he charged per text?

© 15. **Writing in Math** Is it possible to solve the equation $5(b - 2) = 20$ by first dividing each side by 5? Explain.

CC-6 Solving Inequalities

CONTENT STANDARDS

7.EE.4.b Solve word problems leading to inequalities of the form $px + q > r$ or $px + q < r$, where p, q, and r are specific rational numbers.

Test Prep Tip ✏️

Reverse the direction of the inequality symbol when you multiply or divide each side of an inequality by a negative number.

To solve two-step inequalities you follow the same steps as solving two-step equations. The solution can be graphed on a number line.

EXAMPLE Solving Two-Step Inequalities

1 Solve $-3.5x + 6 > 10.2$. Graph the solution.

$-3.5x + 6 > 10.2$	← **Write the inequality.**
$-3.5x + 6 - 6 > 10.2 - 6$	← **Subtract 6 from each side.**
$-3.5x > 4.2$	← **Simplify.**
$\dfrac{-3.5x}{-3.5} < \dfrac{4.2}{-3.5}$	← **Divide each side by -3.5.**
$x < -1.2$	← **Simplify.**

A number line from -3 to 3 with an open circle at -1.2 and shading to the left.

✓ Quick Check

  1. Solve $-\frac{1}{3}a + \frac{1}{2} \leq \frac{1}{5}$. Graph the solution on a number line.

EXAMPLE Application: Music Downloads

2 A music club charges $0.75 per song download plus a membership fee of $5.70. Diego can spend at most $15. Write and graph the inequality for the number of songs Diego can download.

Words $0.75 times number of songs plus monthly fee is at most $15

Let s = the number of songs

Expression $0.75 \cdot s + 5.7 \leq 15$

$0.75s + 5.7 \leq 15$	← **Write the inequality.**
$0.75s + 5.7 - 5.7 \leq 15 - 5.7$	← **Subtract 5.7 from each side.**
$0.75s \leq 9.3$	← **Simplify.**
$\dfrac{0.75s}{0.75} \leq \dfrac{9.3}{0.75}$	← **Divide each side by 0.75.**
$s \leq 12.4$	← **Simplify.**

A number line from 10 to 14 with a closed circle at 12.4 and shading to the left.

Only whole-number solutions are reasonable in this context, so Diego can download at least 0 songs and no more than 12 songs.

Use after Lesson 4-9.

✓ Quick Check

2. A phone plan charges $0.20 per text message plus a monthly fee of $42.50. Lin can spend at most $50. Write an inequality for the number of text messages Lin can send. Graph and describe the solutions.

Homework Exercises

GO for Help

For Exercises	See Examples
1–9	1
10	2

Solve each inequality. Graph the solution.

1. $-1.6x + 5 > 7.4$

2. $3.7y + 2.8 \geq 25$

3. $-5.6c - 7.2 \leq 6.8$

4. $2.4w - 7.1 < 8.5$

5. $-\frac{5}{7} - \frac{6}{7}z < -\frac{2}{7}$

6. $-9.4x + 6 > -8.1$

7. $\frac{x}{5} + \frac{1}{2} \geq \frac{1}{10}$

8. $-\frac{3}{4}y - \frac{3}{8} < \frac{1}{8}$

9. $\frac{d}{3} - \frac{1}{6} > \frac{1}{12}$

10. Tricia receives a $5 allowance every week. She also earns $6.50 for every hour that she baby-sits. Next week she wants to earn at least $21.25 to buy a present. Write an inequality to find the number of hours she needs to baby-sit. Graph and describe the solutions.

© 11. Guided Problem Solving Kate sells bracelets at a craft fair and earns $9.60 per bracelet. She pays a rental fee of $35.20 for her booth. She wants to earn at least $200. Write an inequality to find the number of bracelets Kate needs to sell. Graph and describe the solutions.

- **Make a Plan** Complete the chart below:

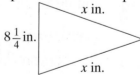

Words: ___ times [number of bracelets] minus [rental fee] [is at least] ___

Let b = the number of bracelets

Expression: ___ · ___ − ___ ▊ ___

- **Carry Out the Plan** Solve the inequality. Graph and describe the solutions.

12. Darrell wants to make a pennant with the pattern shown.

$8\frac{1}{4}$ in. x in. x in.

He has 4 feet of gold trim. Write an inequality for the value of x so that there is enough gold trim to go around all three edges of the pennant. Graph and describe the solutions.

© 13. **Writing in Math** Randy wants a snack with no more than 200 calories. He includes some cherries that have 5 calories each and a banana that has 121 calories. Randy writes the inequality $5c + 121 \leq 200$ to describe the number of cherries c he can eat. Describe the steps Randy must take to determine the value of c.

CC-7 Unit Rates and Ratios of Fractions

CONTENT STANDARDS

7.RP.1 Compute unit rates associated with ratios of fractions, including ratios of lengths, areas and other quantities measured in like or different units.

You know how to find unit rates using whole numbers and decimals. You can also find unit rates from data expressed as fractions.

EXAMPLE — Determining Unit Rates

1 Cindy walks $\frac{6}{10}$ mile in $\frac{1}{4}$ hour. Over that distance, what is her speed in miles per hour?

$$\text{miles} \div \text{hour} = \frac{6}{10} \div \frac{1}{4} \qquad \leftarrow \textbf{Divide miles by hours.}$$

$$= \frac{6}{10} \cdot \frac{4}{1} \qquad \leftarrow \textbf{Multiply by } \frac{4}{1}, \textbf{ the reciprocal of } \frac{1}{4}.$$

$$= \frac{6}{\underset{5}{10}} \cdot \frac{\overset{2}{4}}{1} \qquad \leftarrow \textbf{Divide 10 and 4 by their GCF, 2.}$$

$$= \frac{12}{5} \qquad \leftarrow \textbf{Multiply.}$$

$$= 2\frac{2}{5} \qquad \leftarrow \textbf{Write as a mixed number.}$$

Cindy walks $2\frac{2}{5}$ miles per hour.

✓ Quick Check

1. Find the unit rate.

    a. $\frac{3}{10}$ mile in $\frac{3}{4}$ hour   **b.** $\frac{7}{8}$ container in $\frac{1}{2}$ minute

Unit rates can be used for many comparisons.

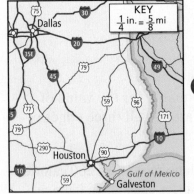

KEY
$\frac{1}{4}$ in. $= \frac{5}{8}$ mi

EXAMPLE — Scale Factors

2 How many inches on the map equal 1 mile?

Think: How many inches per mile? Set up a division expression.

$$\text{inches} \div \text{mile} = \frac{1}{4} \div \frac{5}{8} \qquad \leftarrow \textbf{Divide inches by miles.}$$

$$= \frac{1}{4} \cdot \frac{8}{5} \qquad \leftarrow \textbf{Multiply by } \frac{8}{5}, \textbf{ the reciprocal of } \frac{5}{8}.$$

$$= \frac{1}{\underset{1}{4}} \cdot \frac{\overset{2}{8}}{5} \qquad \leftarrow \textbf{Divide 4 and 8 by their GCF, 4.}$$

$$= \frac{2}{5} \qquad \leftarrow \textbf{Multiply.}$$

So, $\frac{2}{5}$ inch on the map equals 1 mile.

Use after Lesson 5-2.

Quick Check

2. A map scale is $\frac{1}{4}$ inch $= \frac{2}{5}$ mile. How many inches represent 1 mile?

Homework Exercises

GO for Help

For Exercises	See Examples
1–4	1
5–8	2

Find the unit rate.

1. $\frac{1}{2}$ dozen pencils in $\frac{1}{3}$ box

2. $\frac{4}{5}$ chapter in $\frac{1}{4}$ hour

3. $\frac{3}{5}$ page in $\frac{3}{4}$ minute

4. $\frac{7}{12}$ gallon in $\frac{3}{10}$ kilometer

Convert the scale to a unit rate. Label your answer.

5. $\frac{1}{4}$ in. $= \frac{3}{4}$ mi

6. $\frac{3}{8}$ in. $= \frac{3}{4}$ yd

7. $\frac{7}{10}$ cm $= \frac{5}{6}$ km

8. $\frac{3}{10}$ cm $= \frac{2}{5}$ km

9. **Guided Problem Solving** In a science experiment, $16\frac{1}{2}$ grams of a powdered substance must be added to a liquid uniformly during exactly 1 minute 45 seconds. What is this rate in grams per minute?
   - Write 1 minute 45 seconds as a mixed number of minutes.
   - Write both numbers as improper fractions.

10. **Equestrian** Rayelle's horse can run $2\frac{1}{2}$ laps in 3 minutes 6 seconds. What is this rate in laps per minute?

11. How many centimeters equal 1 kilometer on the map?

KEY
$1\frac{1}{2}$ cm $= 1\frac{1}{5}$ km

Find the unit rate.

12. $2\frac{1}{2}$ miles in $11\frac{1}{2}$ minutes

13. $2\frac{1}{5}$ sandwiches in $4\frac{2}{5}$ minutes

14. $3\frac{1}{4}$ baskets in $2\frac{1}{2}$ days

15. $3\frac{3}{8}$ cups in $1\frac{1}{2}$ servings

16. Oren is tiling a bathroom. He uses $72\frac{1}{4}$ tiles in $8\frac{1}{2}$ rows to complete the floor. What is the unit rate in tiles per row?

17. **Landscaping** A landscaper used $\frac{1}{10}$ pound of fertilizer in the soil for every $22\frac{1}{3}$ square feet of lawn. What is the unit rate in pounds per square foot?

18. Maxine can peel, core, and cut $\frac{3}{4}$ pound of apples in $2\frac{1}{2}$ minutes. What is Maxine's unit rate in pounds per hour?

19. **Writing in Math** Arturo can paint $\frac{1}{2}$ of a room in $2\frac{1}{2}$ hours. Explain how to calculate two different unit rates using this data.

20. **Open-Ended** Write a scenario and find the unit rate:

$$1\frac{2}{3} \text{ pint in } \frac{1}{6} \text{ square meter}$$

CC-7 Unit Rates and Ratios of Fractions **CC19**

CONTENT STANDARDS

7.G.2 Draw (freehand, with ruler and protractor, and with technology) geometric shapes with given conditions. Focus on constructing triangles from three measures of angles or sides, noticing when the conditions determine a unique triangle, more than one triangle, or no triangle.

Every triangle has three measures of angles and three measures of sides. A triangle is unique if there is exactly one triangle that can be determined from given measures.

ACTIVITY

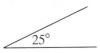

MATHEMATICAL PRACTICES

1. **a.** Use a ruler to draw a line segment. Measure and draw a 25° angle at one end of the line segment such as the one below.

25°

Complete your triangle by drawing a line segment that intersects the other two line segments at 50° and 105°.
   b. Compare triangles with a classmate. Are your triangles the same?
   c. Do three angle measures determine a unique triangle? Explain.

2. **a.** Construct a triangle with angle measures of 30°, 40°, and 110° and a 2-inch side length. Describe the steps you followed.
   b. Compare your triangle with the triangle below. Are the triangles the same or different? Explain.

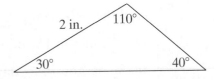

2 in. 110°

30° 40°

   c. Do three angle measures and a side measure determine a unique triangle? Explain.

3. **a.** One student started constructing a triangle, as shown below, with side lengths of 7.5 cm, 10 cm, and 12.5 cm. What information is not given? Why is this construction challenging?

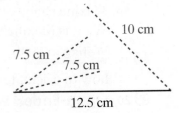

10 cm

7.5 cm

7.5 cm

12.5 cm

   b. Choose available tools and try to construct the triangle.
   c. Describe the strategy you used, explaining why you chose the tools that you did for the construction.

Use after Lesson 7-3.

d. Can triangles with the same three side measures have different shapes? Explain your reasoning.

e. Is a triangle unique when only three side measures are given?

ACTIVITY © **MATHEMATICAL PRACTICES**

1. Cut straws to lengths of 2 cm, 3 cm, 4 cm, 5 cm, and 6 cm. For each combination of 3 straws, identify the type of a triangle you can make using three straws: unique, more than one, or none. Make a table to list the combinations.

Lengths	Type of Triangle
2 cm, 3 cm, and 4 cm	Unique
2 cm, 3 cm, and 5 cm	None

2. Is it possible to construct two different triangles using the same set of three straws? Explain.

3. Do you notice any similarities about the lengths of the straws when you cannot make a triangle?

Exercises

1. The table shows three measures for five triangles. Tell whether each determines a unique triangle, more than one triangle, or no triangle.

Triangle	Measure 1	Measure 2	Measure 3
A	75°	70°	35°
B	10 cm	6 cm	3 cm
C	7 cm	7 cm	9 cm
D	6 in.	5 in.	40°
E	36°	49°	4 in.

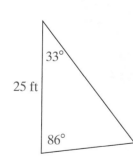

2. The triangle at the left has 25-foot side and angle measures of 33° and 86°. How many different triangles also have a side measuring 25 feet and angle measures of 33° and 86°? Explain.

3. Draw each shape.
   a. a parallelogram with angle measures of 45° and 135°
   b. a hexagon with sides that all have a measure of 1 inch
   c. a rhombus with a side length of 3 cm and an 80° angle
   d. a trapezoid with one side 2 inches long and two 90° angles

© 4. **Writing in Math** Write directions telling how to use a ruler and a protractor to construct a unique triangle that has a side measuring 4 centimeters that connects two angles with measures of 50° and 95°.

CC-9 **Cross Sections**

A **cross section** is the two-dimensional shape that you see after slicing through a three-dimensional object.

cross section of an apple

cross section of a tree trunk

ACTIVITY  **MATHEMATICAL PRACTICES**

1. Jim made a clay model of a square pyramid. He shows the cross section of the pyramid by slicing the pyramid with a string.

Vertical Slice   Horizontal Slice

 a. Sketch the two-dimensional shape that will result if Jim slices the pyramid vertically. Tell how you determined the shape.
 b. Sketch the two-dimensional figure that will result if Jim slices the pyramid horizontally. Tell how you determined the shape.

2. Ripping refers to cutting wood with the grain of the wood, and crosscutting refers to cutting wood across the grain of the wood.

Ripping   Crosscutting

 a. Identify the two-dimensional shape of the cross section for each type of cut and compare them.
 b. Would any other cuts produce a cross section in the same geometric shape? If so, describe how the cut would be made.

3. You have a block of cheese in the shape shown at the left.
 a. What shape will the slice of cheese be if the cheese is sliced horizontally?
 b. What shape will the slice of cheese be if the cheese is sliced vertically?
 c. Does it matter where the cuts are made? Explain your reasoning.

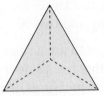

Use after Lesson 8-8.

4. Jorge and Patti both bought sushi rolls for lunch. The sushi rolls were shaped like cylinders. Jorge cut his sushi roll vertically, and Patti cut her sushi roll horizontally as shown below.

Jorge

Patti

 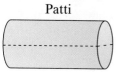

They compared the shapes of the cross sections that resulted from the cuts. Describe what they saw.

5. Sasha cut an orange shaped like a sphere through the center. What shape is the cross section that she sees?

Exercises

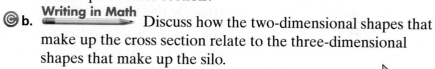

1. Parallel vertical slices are made through a rectangular pyramid as shown below.

What are the shapes of the cross sections? Describe how the cross sections will change as additional cuts are made.

2. A barn silo has the shape of the figure shown at the left.
   a. If it is sliced in half with a vertical cut, what geometric shapes make up the cross section?

   ⓒ b. **Writing in Math** Discuss how the two-dimensional shapes that make up the cross section relate to the three-dimensional shapes that make up the silo.

3. What three-dimensional figure can have a cross section in the same shape as the triangle shown at the right? Explain your reasoning.

4. A three-dimensional figure has a rectangular vertical cross section and a horizontal cross section in the shape of a hexagon.

vertical cross section   horizontal cross section

What is the three-dimensional figure?

ⓒ 5. **Reasoning** A cross section of a rectangular prism is a rectangle with sides measuring 5 cm and 7 cm. Can the exact dimensions of the prism be determined? Explain your reasoning.

Graphs and Proportional Relationships

You can use tables and graphs to decide whether or not two quantities have a proportional relationship.

ACTIVITY  **MATHEMATICAL PRACTICES**

The tables below show a person's earnings at the end of each year at two different banks on a deposit of $100 over a five-year period. For each bank, earnings include simple interest paid annually at the same rate each year. In addition, Bank B gives depositors a $5 bonus when an account is first opened.

Bank A

Years	1	2	3	4	5
Earnings	$2	$4	$6	$8	$10

Bank B

Years	1	2	3	4	5
Earnings	$7	$9	$11	$13	$15

1. For each bank, find the ratio comparing years to earnings for all pairs of values in the table. What do you notice about the ratios?

2. Make a graph for each bank, plotting all the values in each table on a coordinate grid.

3. Extend the lines. What are the earnings at each bank for year 0?

4. How are the graphs different?

5. For each bank, determine if years and earnings are proportional. Explain your answer using the tables and the graphs from Step 2.

6. Information for earnings at Banks C and D is given below.

Bank C

Years	1	2	3	4	5
Earnings	$3	$6	$9	$12	$15

Bank D

Years	1	2	3	4	5
Earnings	$7	$10	$13	$16	$19

   How much does Bank D give as a bonus for opening an account?

7. Find the ratio comparing years to earnings for all pairs of values in each table.

8. Make a graph for Bank C and Bank D.

9. Look for patterns between the tables for all four banks. Give a general rule for using a table to decide if two quantities are proportional.

10. Look for patterns between the graphs for all four banks. Give a general rule for using a graph to decide if two quantities are proportional.

Use after Lesson 10-3.

  **MATHEMATICAL PRACTICES**

Keisha and Dave are riding in a bike-a-thon. The tables below show distances they traveled.

Keisha

Hours	0	2	4	5	7
Miles	0	13	26	32.5	45.5

Dave

Hours	0	3	6	8	9
Miles	0	18.6	37.2	49.6	55.8

1. For each cyclist, graph the relationship between distance and time.
2. Is there a proportional relationship between time and distance for either or both cyclists? Explain.
3. What does the point $(4, 26)$ represent?
4. What is the meaning of the point $(0, 0)$ in this situation?
5. Where $x = 1$ on each graph, what does the y value represent?
6. In the graph of any proportional relationship, what is represented by r at the point $(1, r)$?
7. How does r compare with the unit rate for each cyclist?

Exercises

For Exercises 1–6, determine whether there is a proportional relationship. Explain your reasoning.

1.

x	1	2	4	7	9
y	5	9	17	29	37

2.

x	2	4	6	8	10
y	1.5	3	4.5	6	7.5

3.

x	1	3	5	7	9
y	$\frac{7}{2}$	$\frac{21}{2}$	$\frac{35}{2}$	$\frac{49}{2}$	$\frac{63}{2}$

4.

x	1	2	3	4	5
y	2	8	16	32	64

5.
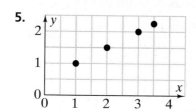

6.
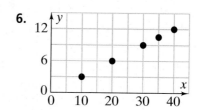

For Exercises 7–8, explain what the point with x-coordinate 3 represents. Then find the unit rate, r.

7. **Walking**

8. **Hot Air Balloon**
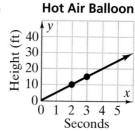

CONTENT STANDARDS

7.RP.2.b Identify the constant of proportionality (unit rate) in tables, graphs, equations, ... and verbal descriptions of proportional relationships.

7.RP.2.c Represent proportional relationships by equations.

When the ratio of two quantities is always the same, the quantities are proportional. The value of the ratio is called the **constant of proportionality**. This value is also equivalent to the unit rate.

The graph of a proportional relationship is a straight line through the origin with a slope equal to the constant of proportionality.

EXAMPLE Identifying Unit Rate

1 The table at the left shows a proportional relationship between the number of minutes and the amount the customer pays for cell phone service. Identify the constant of proportionality.

Step 1: Use one data point to find the constant of proportionality c.

$$\frac{\text{price}}{\text{minutes}} = \frac{10}{100} \quad \leftarrow \text{ Find the price per minute by dividing the price by the number of minutes.}$$

$$= 0.1 \quad \leftarrow \text{ Simplify.}$$

Step 2: Check by multiplying c times the first quantity.

$100 \times 0.1 = 10 \checkmark \qquad 500 \times 0.1 = 50 \checkmark$

$1{,}000 \times 0.1 = 100 \checkmark \qquad 1{,}500 \times 0.1 = 150 \checkmark$

The constant of proportionality is 0.1.

This unit rate represents a payment of $0.10 per minute.

Minutes, m	Price, p (dollars)
100	$10
500	$50
1,000	$100
1,500	$150

✓ Quick Check

1. Find the constant of proportionality for each table of values.
   a. yards of cloth per blanket
   b. pay per hour

Yards (y)	16	32	40
Blankets (b)	8	16	20

Hours (h)	2	10	16
Pay (p)	$11	$55	$88

EXAMPLE Representing Proportional Relationships

2 A ruler shows 12 inches on one edge and 30.48 centimeters on the other. The graph shows the relationship of inches to centimeters. Write a formula to find the number of centimeters c in n inches.

Step 1: Use one data point to find the constant of proportionality.

$$\frac{\text{centimeters}}{\text{inches}} = \frac{30.48}{12} \quad \leftarrow \text{ To find the number of centimeters per inch, write a rate with inches in the denominator.}$$

$$= 2.54 \quad \leftarrow \text{ Divide.}$$

Step 2: Write an equation for c in terms of n.

$$c = 2.54n$$

Inches to Centimeters

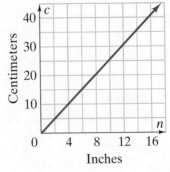

Use after Lesson 10-3.

✓ Quick Check

2. Write an equation to describe the relationship.
   a. An inn uses 3,500 gallons of water each week. Predict the number of gallons used for d days.
   b. Tim is paid $58 for 8 hours. Find his wage for h hours.

Homework Exercises

GO for Help

For Exercises	See Examples
1–4	1
5–7	2

Pecks per Bushel

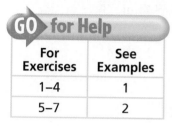

Find the constant of proportionality for each table of values.

1. profit per shirt sold

Shirts	5	10	15
Profit	$7.50	$15.00	$22.50

2. wages per day

Days	5	10	15
Wages	$51.25	$102.50	$153.75

3. price per pound

Apples (lb)	4	5	6
Price	$7.96	$9.95	$11.94

4. pounds per bag

Bags	3	8	11
Dog Food (lb)	7.5	20	27.5

Write an equation using the constant of proportionality to describe the relationship.

5. The graph at left shows the relationship between bushels and pecks. Find the number of pecks p in b bushels.

6. A horse that is 16 hands tall is 64 inches tall. Find the number of hands h in n inches.

7. One day, 16 U.S. dollars was worth 10 British pounds. Find the number of dollars d in p pounds.

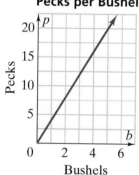

ⓒ **8. Guided Problem Solving** Distance traveled d is proportional to the travel time t at a constant rate r. Write an equation that describes the relationship between d and t.
   • What is r in terms of d and t?
   • What equation tells how to find d given r and t?

9. The ratio of the circumference C of a circle to its diameter d is π. Write an equation that describes the relationship between C and d.

Orange Prices

$	$8	$10	$20
lbs	4	6	10

ⓒ **10. Error Analysis** A salesperson showed the table on the left while explaining that oranges are the same price per pound, no matter what size bag they come in. Why is the salesperson wrong?

Art Sales

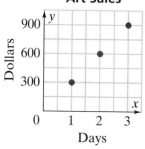

Use the graph for questions 11–13.

11. What is the constant of proportionality, dollars per day?

12. Make a table of values to show the data in the graph.

13. Write an equation to find the amount for any number of days.

ⓒ **14.** **Writing in Math** Explain how to identify the constant of proportionality from a graph of any proportional relationship.

CC-12 Data Variability

CONTENT STANDARDS

7.SP.3 Informally assess the degree of visual overlap of two numerical data distributions with similar variabilities, measuring the difference between the centers by expressing it as a multiple of a measure of variability.

GO for Help
Activity 1-10b

Data displays can be used to assess the visual overlap of two data sets. You can compare their centers, such as mean or median, and their **variability**, the way data is spread out.

ACTIVITY  **MATHEMATICAL PRACTICES**

A veterinarian collects data about the weights of dogs she treats.

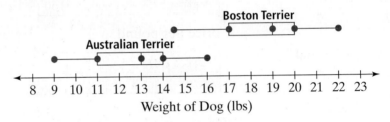

1. Do the two data sets overlap? Explain your reasoning.

2. The interquartile range (IQR) measures variability. The IQR is the difference between the upper and lower quartiles. Determine the IQR for each breed.

3. The difference between the median weights of these two breeds is 6 pounds. What number multiplied by the IQR equals 6?

4. These plots show data for Australian terriers and border terriers.

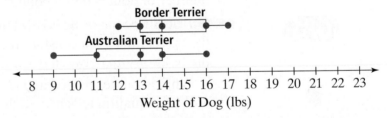

   Describe the visual overlap between the two data sets.

5. Express the difference between medians as a multiple of the IQR.

6. Can you use this multiple to assess the amount of visual overlap between two data sets? Explain.

7. Box-and-whisker plots for two other breeds are shown below.

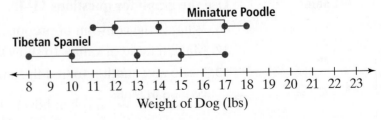

Use after Lesson 11-3.

What multiple of the IQR is the difference of medians?

CC28   CC-12   Data Variability

ACTIVITY · MATHEMATICAL **PRACTICES**

1. Describe the overlap of the two data sets below.

Dog Weights (lbs)

Pug		Dachshund
✗ ✗	13	✗
✗ ✗	14	
✗ ✗ ✗	15	
✗	16	✗ ✗
✗	17	✗ ✗ ✗
✗	18	✗ ✗
	19	✗ ✗

2. Calculate the mean of each data set.

3. You can use the mean absolute deviation (MAD) to measure variability of a data set. The MAD measures the average distance from the mean to each data point. The MAD of pug weights is calculated in this table.

Weight (lbs)	13	13	14	14	15	15	15	16	17	18
Mean	15	15	15	15	15	15	15	15	15	15
Distances	2	2	1	1	0	0	0	1	2	3
MAD = **Total Distances/# Weights**					$\frac{12}{10} = \frac{6}{5} = 1.2$					

Copy the table below to calculate the MAD of dachshund weights.

Weight (lbs)										
Mean										
Distances										
MAD = **Total Distances/# Weights**										

Dog Weights (lbs)

Pug		Miniature Dachshund
	6	✗
	7	✗
	8	✗
	9	✗ ✗ ✗
	10	✗ ✗ ✗
	11	
	12	✗
✗ ✗	13	
✗ ✗	14	
✗ ✗ ✗	15	
✗	16	
✗	17	
✗	18	

4. Can you verify that the variability for both sets is the same by looking at the shape of the data? Explain your reasoning.

5. What number multiplied by the MAD equals the difference between the means?

6. The line plots at the left show the weights of pugs and miniature dachshunds. Describe the overlap of these two sets.

7. Calculate the mean of the miniature dachshund weights. Then find the MAD.

8. How does the MAD of the miniature dachshund weights compare with the MAD of pug weights?

9. What number multiplied by the MAD equals the difference between these two means?

10. Can you use this multiple to assess the amount of visual overlap between two data sets? Explain.

A random sample of a population is used to make predictions about an entire population. These predictions are called **inferences**.

ACTIVITY **MATHEMATICAL PRACTICES**

1. A deck of 100 cards has either a circle or a square on it, and the shape on the card is shaded either red or blue. Kris chose this sample of five cards:

   Explain why you can use the proportion $\frac{3}{5} = \frac{x}{100}$ to predict the number of red cards in the deck.

2. Make an inference about the number of red cards in the whole deck.

3. Kris returned the cards, shuffled the deck, and chose five new cards.

   Based on the results of this sample, use a proportion to make an inference about the number of red cards in the deck.

4. Kris repeated this three more times and recorded the results.

Sample	1	2	3	4	5
Red Cards	3	4	2	4	4
Blue Cards	2	1	3	1	1

   Make separate predictions for the number of red cards in the whole deck based on Samples 3, 4, and 5.

5. What are the highest and lowest predictions?

6. Describe the variation of all your predictions.

7. Which of your predictions do you think is most accurate?

8. Make an inference on the number of red cards that are in the whole deck based on all six samples combined.

9. Kris also recorded the shapes on the cards.

Sample	1	2	3	4	5
Squares	2	3	4	4	3
Circles	3	2	1	1	2

   Make an inference about the number of circles in the deck.

Use after Lesson 11-5.

1. Make a deck of 20 cards. Each card should have a blue circle, a blue square, a red circle, or a red square. Trade decks with a partner, shuffle, and choose five cards. How many circles did you choose?

2. Return the cards to the deck, shuffle, pick five new cards, and record the results four more times. Record the results in a table.

Sample	1	2	3	4	5
Squares					
Circles					

3. For each sample, estimate the number of cards in the full deck that are circles.

4. Describe the variations in your estimates.

5. Make an inference about the number of squares and the number of circles that are in the deck after looking at all five samples.

6. How do your final results compare to your first estimate?

7. Repeat the experiment and record the color of each card. Predict the number of red and blue cards in the deck.

8. Sort the cards. How do your inferences compare to the population?

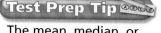

Test Prep Tip

The mean, median, or mode of the predictions can be used to make an inference that is in the center of the predictions.

The principal asked the four student council officers to survey samples of the student body about after-school activities.

Favorite After-School Activity

	Sports	Band	Clubs	Tutoring	No Activity
Bo	15	10	13	8	4
Mel	15	8	12	7	8
Lea	14	7	12	8	9
Zoe	19	8	13	2	8

1. How many observations are in each student's sample?

2. Five hundred students are enrolled are in the whole school. Make four separate predictions for the number of students who favor tutoring based on the results of each survey.

3. Gauge the variation in the predictions.

4. Make an inference about the number of students who favor tutoring based on the median of your predictions.

5. **Writing in Math** Is it advantageous to make inferences based on multiple samples instead of just one sample? Explain.

Simulating Compound Events

7.SP.8.c Design and use a simulation to generate frequencies for compound events.

GO for Help

Lesson 12-2

Vocabulary Tip

A *compound event* consists of two or more events.

A **simulation** is a model used to calculate probabilities for an experimental situation. A compound event consists of two or more simple events. These events may have different probabilities of occurring.

ACTIVITY   **MATHEMATICAL PRACTICES**

One half of the students enter projects in the science fair and two fifths of the students compete in the annual spelling bee.

1. Jemal wants to find the experimental probability that a student enters the science fair and also participates in the spelling bee. The available tools are shown below.

Coins   Number Cubes   Spinner

a. Which tools can Jemal use to simulate a student entering the science fair? Explain how he can use them.

b. Which tools can Jemal use to simulate a student participating in the spelling bee? Explain how he can use them.

2. Jemal decides to use a coin and a five-section spinner.

a. Jemal lets tails (T) represent a student entering the science fair, and sections 1 and 2 on the spinner represent a student participating in the spelling bee. What does the result below mean?

b. Jemal records the result as H4 and repeats the simulation 23 more times. He records the results in a table.

H4	T4	T3	H2	T3	H5	H2	T4
T2	H2	H1	H4	H1	T1	T4	T5
H3	H1	H4	T1	T1	H2	T2	H5

Which compound events represent a student participating in the science fair and competing in the spelling bee?

c. What is the experimental probability that a student enters the science fair and participates in the spelling bee?

Use after Lesson 12-4.

ACTIVITY © MATHEMATICAL PRACTICES

GO for Help
Activity 12-2b

At an art school, 30% of the students are left-handed. Denise wants to know the probability that in a group of 4 students, at least 1 is left-handed.

1. Denise generates random digits from 0 to 9 and lets the digits 0, 1, and 2 represent a left-handed student. Is this a good tool to simulate the event that a student is left-handed?

2. The table below shows randomly generated 4-digit numbers.

7982	5839	4965	8814	3900
3933	6042	9397	4856	8373
3890	2305	3601	8174	4919
6022	6107	7903	9409	8271

Use the first 4-digit number in the table to simulate the results of asking one group of 4 students. How many are left-handed?

3. Identify all of the 4-digit numbers in the table that represent the event *at least 1 of the 4 students is left-handed*.

4. What is the experimental probability that in a group of 4 students, at least 1 is left-handed?

5. If you did not have this table of random numbers, would a coin or a number cube be a good tool to simulate this event? Explain.

6. How can you simulate asking 30 groups of 5 students if they are left-handed?

Exercises

1. a. At Perlina's school, 30% of the students prefer folk music, 10% prefer country, 20% prefer rock, and 40% prefer hip-hop. Describe how to use a random number table with digits 0-9 to simulate finding the probability that in a group of 3 students, at least 2 prefer hip-hop.

   b. Use the random number table below to find the probability that in a group of 3 students, at least 2 like hip-hop.

165	108	952	944	542
661	827	647	333	457
950	593	087	169	813
614	869	738	027	284

© 2. **Writing in Math** One third of students walk to school, and 80% buy hot lunch. You want to know the probability that a student walks to school but does not buy hot lunch. Describe how you could simulate 25 trials to determine how many students walk to school but do not buy hot lunch.

CHAPTER 1

Decimals and Integers

Student Support

Vocabulary 🔊

Vocabulary Review 4, 8, 14, 20, 26, 31, 38, 44, 48, 53

New Vocabulary 4, 8, 14, 31, 38, 48, 53

Vocabulary Builder 35

Vocabulary Tip 15, 20, 48

Exercises 6, 10, 16, 22, 28, 33, 41, 50, 55

GO Online

Video Tutor Help 8, 53

Active Math 32, 40

Homework Video Tutor 7, 11, 17, 22, 30, 34, 42, 47, 51, 57

Lesson Quiz 7, 11, 17, 23, 29, 33, 41, 47, 51, 57

Vocabulary Quiz 60

Chapter Test 62

Math at Work 18

GPS Guided Problem Solving

Exercises 6, 10, 16, 22, 29, 33, 41, 46, 50, 56

Choosing Operations 24

DK Applications: Applying Integers, 64–65

Assessment and Test Prep

CHAPTER 2

Exponents, Factors, and Fractions

Assessment and Test Prep

CHAPTER 3

Operations With Fractions

Student Support

Vocabulary 🔊

Vocabulary Review 120, 126, 130, 136, 141, 148, 154
New Vocabulary 120, 141, 154
Vocabulary Builder 124
Vocabulary Tip 121, 148, 154
Exercises 122, 156

GO Online

Video Tutor Help 126, 141
Active Math 137, 142
Homework Video Tutor 123, 128, 133, 139, 144, 151, 157
Lesson Quiz 123, 129, 133, 139, 145, 151, 157
Vocabulary Quiz 160
Chapter Test 162
Math at Work 134

GPS Guided Problem Solving

Exercises 122, 128, 132, 138, 144, 150, 156
Practice Solving Problems 146
DK Applications: Applying Fractions, 164–165

Assessment and Test Prep

CHAPTER 4

Equations and Inequalities

Assessment and Test Prep

CHAPTER

5

Ratios, Rates, and Proportions

Student Support

Vocabulary 🔊

GO Online

GPS Guided Problem Solving

Assessment and Test Prep

CHAPTER 6

Percents

Assessment and Test Prep

CHAPTER 7

Geometry

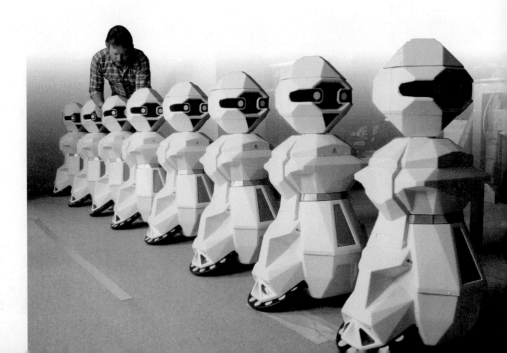

CHAPTER 8

Measurement

Student Support

Vocabulary 🔊

Vocabulary Review 374, 380, 384, 388, 394, 400, 405, 410, 414, 421

New Vocabulary 374, 380, 384, 388, 394, 400, 405, 410, 414, 421

Vocabulary Tip 380, 385, 388, 401, 411, 417

Exercises 376, 382, 386, 391, 402, 407, 412, 416, 424

GO Online

Video Tutor Help 380, 421

Active Math 405, 423

Homework Video Tutor 378, 383, 387, 392, 397, 403, 408, 413, 418, 425

Lesson Quiz 377, 383, 387, 391, 397, 403, 407, 413, 417, 425

Vocabulary Quiz 428

Chapter Test 430

GPS Guided Problem Solving

Exercises 377, 382, 386, 391, 396, 402, 407, 412, 417, 424

Areas of Irregular Figures 398

DK Applications: Applying Volume, 432–433

Assessment and Test Prep

CHAPTER 9

Patterns and Rules

Student Support

Assessment and Test Prep

CHAPTER

10

Algebra

Graphing in the Coordinate Plane

Student Support

Vocabulary 🔊

Vocabulary Review 486, 491, 498, 504, 510, 514, 519
New Vocabulary 486, 491, 498, 504, 510, 514, 519
Vocabulary Builder 508
Vocabulary Tip 492, 499, 511, 519
Exercises 488, 493, 500, 506, 512, 516, 521

GO Online

Video Tutor Help 492, 505
Active Math 498, 520
Homework Video Tutor 489, 494, 501, 507, 513, 517, 522
Lesson Quiz 489, 493, 501, 507, 513, 517, 521
Vocabulary Quiz 524
Chapter Test 526

GPS Guided Problem Solving

Exercises 488, 493, 500, 506, 512, 516, 521
Practice Solving Problems 496
DK Applications: Applying Coordinates, 528–529

Assessment and Test Prep

CHAPTER 11

Displaying and Analyzing Data

Assessment and Test Prep

Student Support

Vocabulary 🔊

GO Online

GPS Guided Problem Solving

Using Probability

Student Support

Vocabulary ◀))

Vocabulary Review 580, 586, 591, 598, 606, 610
New Vocabulary 580, 586, 591, 598, 606, 610
Vocabulary Builder 603
Vocabulary Tip 580, 610
Exercises 582, 588, 593, 600, 608, 611

GO Online

Video Tutor Help 581, 586
Active Math 599, 606
Homework Video Tutor 582, 589, 594, 602, 609, 612
Lesson Quiz 583, 589, 595, 601, 609, 613
Vocabulary Quiz 616
Chapter Test 618

GPS Guided Problem Solving

Exercises 582, 588, 594, 601, 608, 612
Practice With Probability 604
DK Applications: Applying Probability, 622–623

Assessment and Test Prep

Connect Your Learning

through problem solving, activities, and the Web

Applications: Real-World Applications

Activity Labs: Data Analysis

Activity Labs: Data Collection

Activity Labs: Algebra Thinking

Activities: Chapter Projects

Problem Solving Strategies

Guided Problem Solving Features

Go Online

Throughout this book you will find links to the Prentice Hall Web site. Use the Web Codes provided with each link to gain direct access to online material. Here's how to *Go Online*:

1. **Go to PHSchool.com**
2. **Enter the Web Code**
3. **Click Go!**

Lesson Web Codes

Lesson Quiz Web Codes: There is an online quiz for every lesson. Access these quizzes with Web Codes ara-0101 through ara-1206 for Lesson 1-1 through Lesson 12-6. See page 89.

Homework Video Tutor Web Codes: For every lesson, there is additional support online to help students complete their homework. Access the Homework Video Tutors with Web Codes are-0101 through are-1206 for Lesson 1-1 through Lesson 12-6. See page 297.

Lesson Quizzes
Web Code format: ara-0204 02 = Chapter 2   04 = Lesson 4

Homework Video Tutor
Web Code format: are-0605 06 = Chapter 6   05 = Lesson 5

Chapter Web Codes

Chapter	Vocabulary Quizzes	Chapter Tests	Chapter Projects
1	arj-0151	ara-0152	ard-0161
2	arj-0251	ara-0252	ard-0261
3	arj-0351	ara-0352	ard-0361
4	arj-0451	ara-0452	ard-0461
5	arj-0551	ara-0552	ard-0561
6	arj-0651	ara-0652	ard-0661
7	arj-0751	ara-0752	ard-0761
8	arj-0851	ara-0852	ard-0861
9	arj-0951	ara-0952	ard-0961
10	arj-1051	ara-1052	ard-1061
11	arj-1151	ara-1152	ard-1161
12	arj-1251	ara-1252	ard-1261
End-of-Course		ara-1254	

Additional Web Codes

Video Tutor Help:
Use Web Code are-0775 to access engaging online instructional videos to help bring math concepts to life. See page 126.

Data Updates:
Use Web Code arg-9041 to get up-to-date government data for use in examples and exercises. See page 541.

Math at Work:
For information about each Math at Work feature, use Web Code arb-2031. See page 345.

Using Your Book for Success

Welcome to *Prentice Hall Course 2*. There are many features built into the daily lessons of this text that will help you learn the important skills and concepts you will need to be successful in this course. Look through the following pages for some study tips that you will find useful as you complete each lesson.

Getting Ready to Learn

Check Your Readiness

Complete the *Check Your Readiness* exercises to see what topics you may need to review before you begin the chapter.

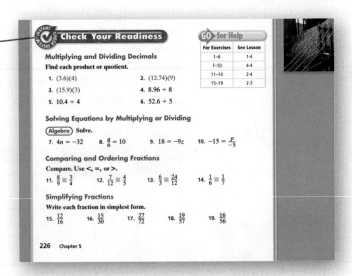

Check Skills You'll Need

Complete the *Check Skills You'll Need* exercises to make sure you have the skills needed to successfully learn the concepts in the lesson.

New Vocabulary

New Vocabulary is listed for each lesson, so you can pre-read the text. As each term is introduced, it is highlighted in yellow.

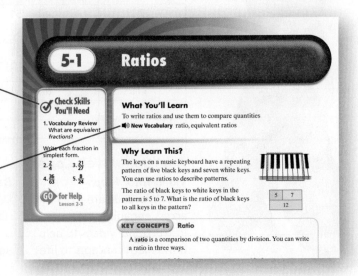

Built-In Help

Go for Help

Look for the green labels throughout your book that tell you where to "Go" for help. You'll see this built-in help in the lessons and in the homework exercises.

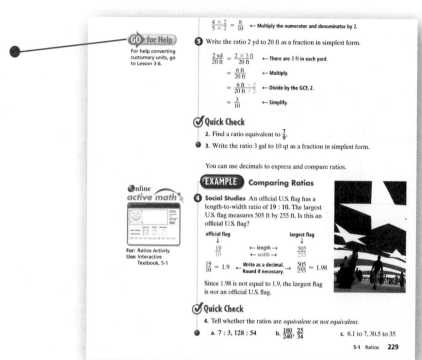

Video Tutor Help

Go online to see engaging videos to help you better understand important math concepts.

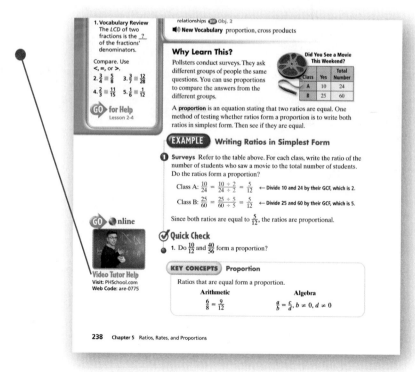

Understanding the Mathematics

Quick Check

Every lesson includes numerous examples, each followed by a *Quick Check* question that you can do on your own to see if you understand the skill being introduced. Check your progress with the answers at the back of the book.

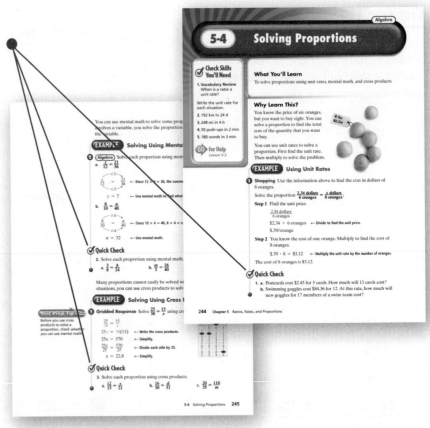

Understanding Key Concepts

Frequent *Key Concept* boxes summarize important definitions, formulas, and properties. Use these to review what you've learned.

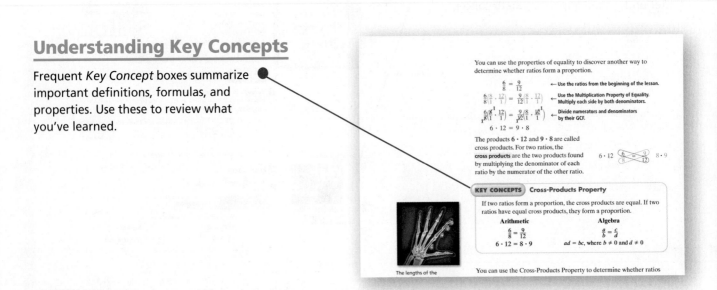

Online Active Math

Make math come alive with these online activities. Review and practice important math concepts with these engaging online tutorials.

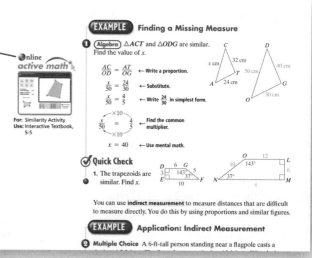

Vocabulary Support

Understanding mathematical vocabulary is an important part of studying mathematics. *Vocabulary Tips* and *Vocabulary Builders* throughout the book help focus on the language of math.

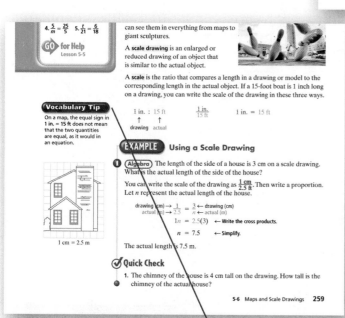

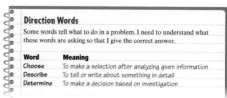

Understanding the Mathematics

Guided Problem Solving

These features throughout your Student Edition provide practice in problem solving. Solved from a student's point of view, this feature focuses on the thinking and reasoning that goes into solving a problem.

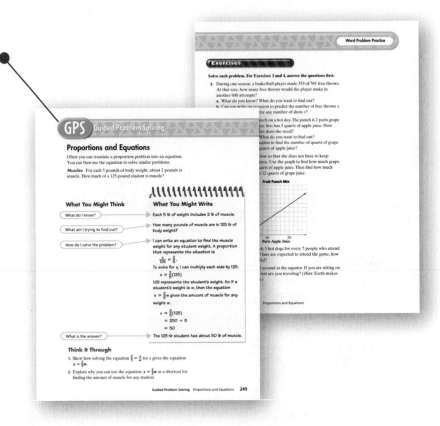

Activity Labs

Activity Labs throughout the book give you an opportunity to explore a concept. Apply the skills you've learned in these engaging activities.

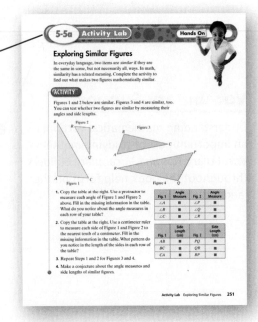

Practice What You've Learned

There are numerous exercises in each lesson
that give you the practice you need to master
the concepts in the lesson. The following
exercises are included in each lesson.

Check Your Understanding

These exercises help you prepare for the
Homework Exercises.

Practice by example

These exercises refer you back to the Examples
in the lesson, in case you need help with
completing these exercises.

Apply your skills

These exercises combine skills from earlier
lessons to offer you richer skill exercises
and multi-step application problems.

Homework Video Tutor

These interactive tutorials provide you
with homework help for *every lesson*.

Challenge

This exercise gives you an opportunity
to extend and stretch your thinking.

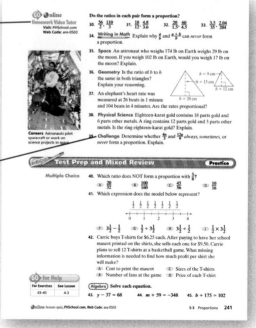

Beginning-of-Course Diagnostic Test

1. Write the value of the underlined digit in 523.6<u>5</u>4.

2. Write the value of the underlined digit in 402.<u>6</u>59.

3. Write a number for fifty-one and six thousandths.

4. Write 7.325 in words.

Use < or > to compare the whole numbers.

5. 2,648 ■ 264

6. 625 ■ 6,250

7. 42,509 ■ 42,709

8. Round 75,845 to the nearest thousand.

9. Round 256.24 to the nearest whole number.

10. Round 546.256 to the nearest tenth.

11. Round 2.5879 to the nearest hundredth.

Multiply.

12. $\begin{array}{r} 4.6 \\ \times\, 0.7 \\ \hline \end{array}$

13. $\begin{array}{r} 0.421 \\ \times\, 5.6 \\ \hline \end{array}$

14. 3.08×12.4

15. $\begin{array}{r} 0.7 \\ \times\, 0.02 \\ \hline \end{array}$

16. 0.032×0.06

17. 0.28×0.07

18. 0.06×0.2

Divide.

19. $5\overline{)10.16}$

20. $13\overline{)34.918}$

21. $27.05 \div 2$

22. $0.036 \div 24$

Multiply.

23. $0.07 \times 1,000$

24. 478.24×0.01

25. 0.001×0.04

26. $0.9 \times 1,000$

27. 6.04×0.01

Divide.

28. $0.832 \div 0.26$

29. $0.5031 \div 0.039$

30. $0.42\overline{)0.273}$

31. $0.03\overline{)0.144}$

32. $0.00027 \div 0.18$

33. $0.018 \div 0.9$

Add or subtract. Write the answer in simplest form.

34. $\frac{5}{9} + \frac{2}{9}$ **35.** $\frac{7}{12} - \frac{3}{12}$

36. $5\frac{4}{8} + 4\frac{6}{8}$ **37.** $4\frac{8}{10} - 2\frac{6}{10}$

USING THE Problem Solving Plan

One of the most important skills you can have is the ability to solve problems. An integral part of learning mathematics is how adept you become at unraveling problems and looking back to see how you found the solution. Maybe you don't realize it, but you solve problems every day—some problems are easy to solve, and others are challenging and require a good plan of action. In this Problem Solving Handbook you will learn how to work though mathematical problems using a simple four-step plan:

THE 4-STEP PLAN

1. **Understand** **Understand the problem.**
   Read the problem. Ask yourself, "What information is given? What is missing? What am I being asked to find or to do?"

2. **Plan** **Make a plan to solve the problem.**
   Choose a strategy. As you use problem solving strategies throughout this book, you will decide which one is best for the problem you are trying to solve.

3. **Carry Out** **Carry out the plan.**
   Solve the problem using your plan. Organize your work.

4. **Check** **Check the answer to be sure it is reasonable.**
   Look back at your work and compare it against the information and question(s) in the problem. Ask yourself, "Is my answer reasonable? Did I check my work?"

Problem Solving Strategies

Creating a good plan to solve a problem means that you will need to choose a strategy. What is the best way to solve that challenging problem? Perhaps drawing a diagram or making a table will lead to a solution. A problem may seem to have too many steps. Maybe working a simpler problem is the key. There are a number of strategies to choose from. You will decide which strategy is most effective.

As you work through this book, you will encounter many opportunities to improve your problem solving and reasoning skills. Working through mathematical problems using this four-step process will help you to organize your thoughts, develop your reasoning skills, and explain how you arrived at a particular solution.

Putting this problem solving plan to use will allow you to work through mathematical problems with confidence. Getting in the habit of planning and strategizing for problem solving will result in success in future math courses and high scores on those really important tests!

Good Luck!

THE STRATEGIES

Here are some examples of problem solving strategies. Which one will work best for the problem you are trying to solve?

- Draw a Picture
- Look for a Pattern
- Systematic Guess and Check
- Act It Out
- Make a Table
- Work a Simpler Problem
- Work Backward
- Write an Equation

Draw a Picture

When to Use This Strategy You can *Draw a Picture* to show a problem visually. A picture often helps you understand a problem better.

A worm is trying to escape from a well 10 ft deep. The worm climbs up 2 ft per day, but each night it slides back 1 ft. How many days will the worm take to climb out of the well?

Understand

The total distance to travel is 10 ft. The worm gains 2 ft during the day, but loses 1 ft each night. The goal is to find out how many days the worm will take to get out of the well.

Plan

Draw a picture to track the worm's position from day to day.

Carry Out

The worm reaches 10 ft and climbs out of the well at the end of the ninth day.

Worm's Progress

Number of Feet Climbed vs. Days

Check

You might think that the worm progresses 1 ft each day and so needs 10 days to escape. The worm does move a total of 1 ft each day, except on the ninth day. On the ninth day, it climbs 2 ft to the edge of the well.

● Practice

1. Suppose the worm in the example above climbs up 3 ft per day and slides back 2 ft per night. How many days will it take for the worm to climb out of the 10-ft well?

2. **Multiple Choice** You schedule the games for your basketball league's tournament. If a team loses a game, it is eliminated. There are 32 teams. How many games do you need to schedule to determine the league champion?

   A. 30 games
   B. 31 games
   C. 32 games
   D. 64 games

3. There are 10 girlcs and 8 boys in a club. The club advisor can send one boy and one girl to a conference. How many different pairs of students can go to the conference?

4. A bricklayer is removing a square section of a rectangular patio. The patio is 12 feet long by 20 feet wide. She needs to remove a section 5 ft long × 5 ft wide What is the area of the patio without the square section?

5. Use the pattern below:

   How many dots will make up the 12th pattern?

6. A pizza party is having pizzas with pepperoni, pineapple chunks and green pepper slices. How many different pizzas can be made with these toppings? *Hint: A pizza with all the toppings is shown in the picture.*

Look for a Pattern

When to Use This Strategy Certain problems allow you to look at similar cases. You can *Look for a Pattern* in the solutions of these cases to solve the original problem.

Geometry What is the sum of the measures of the angles of a 12-sided polygon?

Understand

The goal is to find the sum of the measures of the angles of a 12-sided polygon. The sum of the measures in a triangle is 180°

Plan

Draw polygons with 3, 4, 5, and 6 sides. Divide each polygon into triangles by drawing diagonals from one vertex.
Look for a pattern.

Carry Out

The diagrams below show polygons divided into triangles.

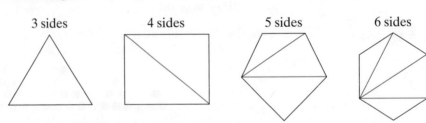

| 3 sides | 4 sides | 5 sides | 6 sides |

The number of triangles formed is two less than the number of sides of the polygon. This means that the sum of the measures of the angles of each polygon is the number of triangles times 180° For a 12-sided polygon, the number of triangles is $12 - 2 = 10$. The sum of the measures of the angles is $10 \times 180° = 1,800°$.

Check

Draw a diagram to check that exactly ten triangles are formed when you draw diagonals from one vertex of a 12-sided polygon.

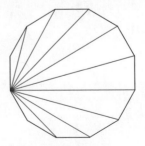

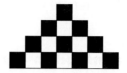

1. The figure below shows a pattern of black and white tiles. How many black tiles will you need for nine rows?

2. The figure below has four rows of small triangles. How many small triangles will you need for eight rows?

3. In a 3 × 3 grid, there are 14 squares of different sizes. There are nine 1 × 1 squares, four 2 × 2 squares, and one 3 × 3 square. How many squares of different sizes are in a 5 × 5 grid?

4. Your sister's new jobs pays $150 per week. After the first week, she decides to put $37.50 in a new savings account. After the second week, she puts $45.00 in the savings account. After the third week, she puts $52.50 in savings.

   a. If the pattern continues, how much will she put in the account after the fourth and fifth weeks?
   b. What will be the total amount in the savings account after the fifth week?

5.

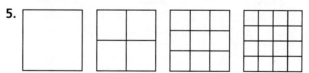

   Which series of numbers best describe the next two shapes in the pattern?

Systematic Guess and Check

When to Use This Strategy The strategy *Systematic Guess and Check* works well when you can start by making a reasonable estimate of the answer.

Construction A group of students is building a sailboat. The students have 48 ft^2 of material to make a sail. They design the sail in the shape of a right triangle as shown below. Find the length of the base and the height.

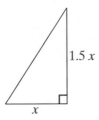

$1.5\,x$

x

Understand

The diagram shows that the height is 1.5 times the length of the base.

Plan

Test possible dimensions of the triangle formed by the boom (base), the mast (height), and the sail. Check to see if they produce the desired area. Organize your results in a table.

Carry Out

Boom	Mast	Area	Conclusion
6	9	$\frac{1}{2} \cdot 6 \cdot 9 = 27$	Too low
10	15	$\frac{1}{2} \cdot 10 \cdot 15 = 75$	Too high
8	12	$\frac{1}{2} \cdot 8 \cdot 12 = 48$	✔

Check

A triangle with a base length of 8 ft and a height of 12 ft has an area of 48 ft^2.

Practice

1. The width of a rectangle is 4 cm less than its length. The area of the rectangle is 96 cm^2. Find the length and width of the rectangle.

2. **Multiple Choice** A dance floor is a square with an area of 1,444 ft^2. What are the dimensions of the dance floor?

   A. 38 ft $\times$ 38 ft
   B. 38 ft^2 $\times$ 38 ft^2
   C. 361 ft $\times$ 361 ft
   D. 361 ft^2 $\times$ 361 ft^2

3. You are building a rectangular tabletop for a workbench. The perimeter of the tabletop is 22 ft. The area of the tabletop is 24 ft^2. What are the dimensions of the tabletop?

4. You want to put up a fence around a rectangular garden. The length of the garden is twice its width. If the garden has an area of 2,450 ft^2, how much fencing material do you need?

5. The owner of the hot dog stand made $64.50 from selling 18 items from the menu. How many hot dogs did he sell?

Act It Out

When to Use This Strategy You can use the strategy *Act It Out* to simulate a problem.

A cat is expecting a litter of four kittens. The probabilities of having male and female kittens are equal. What is the probability that the litter contains three females and one male?

Understand

Your goal is to find the experimental probability that the litter of four kittens contains three females and 1 male.

Plan

Act out the problem by tossing a coin. Let heads represent a male and tails represent a female. Toss the coin 100 times. Separate the results into groups of 4 to represent the four kittens in a litter.

Carry Out

The table below shows 25 "litters" of 4.

T T H H	(H T T T)	H T H H	(H T T T)	T H T H
T T H H	H H H T	H H T T	(T H T T)	H H H H
H H T T	(T T T H)	T H T H	H T H H	H T H T
(T H T T)	H T H T	T H H T	H H H H	H H H H
T H H H	T T T T	T H H T	H T H H	(T T T H)

Six groups out of twenty-five contain three females and one male. So $P(\text{3 females and 1 male}) = \frac{6}{25}$. The experimental probability is 0.24.

Check

Make a list of all 16 possible outcomes for having male and female kittens. Of these outcomes, only 4 have three females and one male. So the theoretical probability is $\frac{4}{16}$, or 0.25. This is close to the experimental value.

M M M M	F M M M	F M M F	M M F F
M M M F	F F M M	M F F M	(F M F F)
M M F M	(F F F M)	M F M F	(F F M F)
M F M M	F F F F	F M F M	(M F F F)

● Practice

1. A sports jersey number has two digits. Even and odd digits are equally likely. Use a simulation to find the probability that both digits are even.

2. You are taking a 4-question true-or-false quiz. You do not know any of the answers. Use a simulation to find the probability that you guess exactly 3 out of 4 answers correctly.

3. A restaurant gives away a model car with each meal. You are equally likely to get any of the five cars. Use a simulation to find the probability that you get two of the same car after two meals.

4. Three friends are going bowling. Use a simulation to determine how many bowling orders are possible.

5. Conduct a simulation using a game spinner divided into 10 equal sections and numbered 1 to 10 to determine the probability of the spinner landing on an odd number three times in a row.

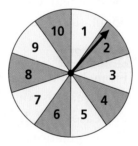

6. A bag of marbles contains 10 red marbles and 8 blue marbles. Some marbles spill out as shown.

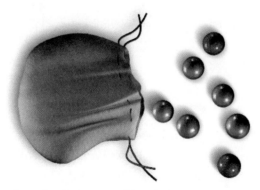

You randomly select two marbles from the marbles remaining in the bag. Use a simulation to determine the probability of selecting one red marble and one blue marble.

Make a Table

When to Use This Strategy A real-world problem may ask you to examine a set of data and draw a conclusion. In such a problem, you can *Make a Table* to organize the data.

Biology A wildlife preserve surveyed its wolf population in 1996 and counted 56 wolves. In 2000, there were 40 wolves. In 2002, there were 32 wolves. If the wolf population changes at a constant rate, in what year will there be fewer than 15 wolves?

Understand

Given the wolf population in 1996, 2000, and 2002, you want to find the year in which there will be fewer than 15 wolves.

Plan

Find the rate of change. *Make a Table* to organize the information in the problem. Use the rate of change to extend the table until the wolf population is less than 15.

Carry Out

From 2000 to 2002, the wolf population decreased by 8. Since the rate of decrease is constant, you can say that every 2 years, the population decreases by 8. In the beginning of 2006, there will be about 16 wolves. The population will be less than 15 later that year.

Year	Wolves
2000	40
2002	$40 - 8 = 32$
2004	$32 - 8 = 24$
2006	$24 - 8 = 16$

Check

Step 1 → For there to be 15 wolves, the population must decrease by $56 - 15$ wolves, or 41 wolves.

Step 2 → The population decreases by 4 wolves per year. Let x represent the number of years until there are 15 wolves.

Step 3 → Solve $4x = 41$. The value of x is about 10 years. So $1996 + 10 = 2006$.

Practice

1. **Multiple Choice** You are starting a business selling lemonade. You know that it costs $6 to make 20 c of lemonade and $7 to make 30 c of lemonade. How much will it cost to make 50 c of lemonade?

   A. $8
   B. $9
   C. $10
   D. $12

2. You have $10 saved and plan to save an additional $2 each week. How much will you have after 7 weeks?

3. A driver of a car slows to a stop. The decrease in speed is constant. When the driver first applies the brakes, the car is going 50 mi/h. After 5 s, the car is traveling 30 mi/h. About how long does it take the car to stop?

4. A family drives 127 miles on their first day of vacation. They drive an additional 35 miles each day after that.

   a. On what day will they have driven a total of 372 miles?
   b. How many total miles did they drive after the first 5 days?

5. A house plant starts at 13 in. and grows 4 in. each week. How tall will it be at the end of 7 weeks?

6. How many different groups of letters can be made with the following letter tiles?

Work a Simpler Problem

When to Use This Strategy If a problem seems to have many steps, you may be able to *Work a Simpler Problem* first. The result may give you a clue about the solution of the original problem.

When you simplify 3^{50}, what number is in the ones place?

Understand

You know that 3^{50} is a large number to calculate. You need to find the number in the ones place.

Plan

It is not easy to simplify 3^{50} with paper and pencil. Simplify easier expressions such as 3^2, 3^3, and 3^4, to see what number is in the ones place.

Carry Out

The table shows the values of the first 10 powers of 3.

Power	Value
3^1	3
3^2	9
3^3	27
3^4	81
3^5	243
3^6	729
3^7	2,187
3^8	6,561
3^9	19,683
3^{10}	59,049

Notice that the ones digits in the value column repeat in the pattern 3, 9, 7, and 1. Every fourth power of 3 has a ones digit of 1. Since 4 is divisible by 4, 3^{48} has a ones digit of 1. Then the ones digit of 3^{49} is 3 and the ones digit of 3^{50} is 9.

Check

When the exponent of 3 is 2, 6, or 10, the ones digit is 9. The numbers 2, 6, and 10 are divisible by 2 but not by 4. Since 50 is divisible by 2 but not by 4, the ones digit of 3^{50} is 9.

Practice

1. a. What is the pattern for the ones digit of any power of 8?
   b. When you simplify 8^{63}, what number is in the ones place?

2. a. What is the pattern for the ones digit of any power of 7?
   b. When you simplify 7^{21}, what number is in the ones place?

3. The table shows the values of powers of 2 with even exponents from 10 to 20.

Power	Value
2^{10}	1,024
2^{12}	4,096
2^{14}	16,384
2^{16}	65,536
2^{18}	262,144
2^{20}	1,048,576

   What is the ones digit of 2^{80}?

4. What is the value of $(-1)^{427}$? Explain.

5. When you simplify 10^{347}, what digit is in the ones place?

6. Find the sum of the first 10 powers of 10, that is, the sum of $10^1 + 10^2 + 10^3 + \ldots 10^{10}$.

7. How many minutes are there in one week?

June						
1	2	3	4	5	6	7
8	9	10	11	12	13	14
15	16	17	18	19	20	21
22	23	24	25	26	27	28
29	30					

Work Backward

When to Use This Strategy You can use the strategy *Work Backward* when a problem asks you to find an initial value.

You and your friends are going to dinner and then to a concert that starts at 8:00 P.M., It will take $\frac{3}{4}$ h to drive to the restaurant and $1\frac{1}{4}$ h to eat and drive to the theater. You want to arrive at the theater 15 min before the concert starts. At what time should you leave?

Understand

Your goal is to find out what time you should leave home to arrive 15 min early for the 8:00 P.M. concert. It takes $\frac{3}{4}$ h to drive to the restaurant and $1\frac{1}{4}$ h to eat and drive to the theater.

Plan

You know that the series of events must end at 8:00 P.M. It makes sense to *Work Backward* to find when you must leave your house.

Carry Out

Concert starts.
8:00 P.M.

Arrive at theater.
7:45 P.M.

Arrive at dinner.
6:30 P.M.

Leave home.
5:45 P.M.

Working backward shows that when you leave at 5:45 P.M., you will get to the concert 15 min early.

Check

Find the total time it takes for the series of events to happen.

$\frac{3}{4} + 1\frac{1}{4} + \frac{1}{4} = 2\frac{1}{4}$.

Subtract $2\frac{1}{4}$ h from 8:00 P.M., and you get 5:45 P.M.

 Practice

1. After school today, you spent $1\frac{3}{4}$ h at band practice and then a half hour in the library. It took you 15 min to get home at 6:00 P.M. What time did you start practice?

2. Your friend spends one third of her money on lunch. You then give her $2.50 to repay a loan. After school, your friend spends $4.00 for a movie and $2.50 for a snack. She has $4.90 left. How much money did she have before lunch?

3. If you start with a number, add 5, and then multiply by 7, the result is 133. What was the original number?

4. A bakery uses 12 bags of flour on Monday, 8 bags on Tuesday, 14 bags on Wednesday, and half of the remaining bags on Thursday. After Thursday there are 3 bags of flour left. How many bags of flour did the bakery start with on Monday?

5. A concert begins at 7:00 P.M. The walk to the bus station will take 20 minutes. The bus ride to a friend's house is 30 minutes. From there it is a 17-minute walk to the concert. The opening act is set to perform for 45 minutes. What time should you leave if you want to make it to the concert after the opening act is finished?

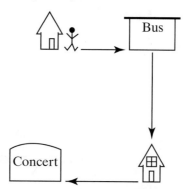

6. A delivery driver used $\frac{1}{3}$ of a tank of gas on his way to his first stop. He used $\frac{1}{8}$ of a tank from there to his second stop. He got $\frac{1}{2}$ a tank at the gas station and used another $\frac{1}{8}$ of a tank on the drive to the warehouse. His final gas gauge is shown.

How much gas did the driver start with?

Write an Equation

When to Use This Strategy You can *Write an Equation* to represent a real-world situation that involves two variables.

The cost of materials needed to make one toboggan is $8. A craftsman has a budget of $2,000. How many toboggans can he make?

Understand

Your goal is to find the number of toboggans the craftsman can make given his budget and the cost of materials.

Plan

Write an Equation to model the situation. Then solve the equation.

Carry Out

Write an equation to represent the number of toboggans.

Words	amount budgeted	divided by	cost of materials	is the	number of toboggans

Equation

Let b = amount budgeted. Let n = number of toboggans.

$$b \quad \div \quad \$8 \quad = \quad n$$

$$\frac{b}{8} = n$$

$$\frac{2,000}{8} = n \quad \leftarrow \text{Substitute } b \text{ for 2,000.}$$

$$250 = n \quad \leftarrow \text{Simplify.}$$

The craftsman can make 250 toboggans.

Check

The total cost of making 250 toboggans is 250 · $8, or $2,000. This equals the craftsman's budget. The answer checks.

Practice

1. Family membership at a science museum costs $89 per year. The shows at the museum theater cost $22.50 per family each visit. How many shows can a family see if its yearly budget is $300?

2. **Multiple Choice** A pair of boots costs $10 more than twice the cost of a pair of shoes. The boots cost $76.50. How much do the shoes cost?
   A. $33.25
   B. $38.25
   C. $44.25
   D. $70.50

3. Your family's car can travel 23 mi using 1 gal of gas. To the nearest gallon, how many gallons of gas will your car need for a 540-mi trip?

4. An oven preheats at 15 degrees per minute. How long will it take for the oven to heat up to 375 degrees?

5. A courier service ships packages for $50 for the first 40 pounds. It costs an additional $.79 for each additional pound. The weight of a package is shown below.

How much will it cost to ship the package?

What You've Learned

- In a previous course, you compared and ordered whole numbers.
- You used the properties of addition and multiplication to add, subtract, multiply, and divide whole numbers.
- You used the order of operations and the Distributive Property to simplify expressions with whole numbers.

 Check Your Readiness

Comparing and Ordering Whole Numbers

Use > or < to compare the whole numbers.

1. 72 ■ 720

2. 3,972 ■ 3,927

Dividing Whole Numbers

Find each quotient.

3. 8)296 **4.** 9)684 **5.** 11)2,376 **6.** 68)14,552

Place Value and Decimals

Write the value of the underlined digit.

7. 24.3<u>5</u> **8.** 4.08<u>6</u> **9.** 17<u>9</u>.8 **10.** 59.0<u>3</u> **11.** 1.046<u>7</u>

Reading and Writing Decimals

Write each number in words. Use *tenths*, *hundredths*, or *thousandths*.

12. 421.5 **13.** 5,006.25 **14.** 15.004 **15.** 0.329 **16.** 710.413

Rounding Decimals

Round to the nearest hundredth.

17. 34.124 **18.** 278.786 **19.** 3.602 **20.** 81.796 **21.** 16.999

GO for Help

For Exercises	See Skills Handbook
1–2	p. 654
3–6	p. 657
7–11	p. 658
12–16	p. 659
17–21	p. 660

What You'll Learn Next

- In this chapter, you will compare and order integers.
- You will use the properties of addition and multiplication to add, subtract, multiply, and divide decimals and integers.
- You will use the order of operations and the Distributive Property to simplify expressions with decimals and integers.

 Key Vocabulary

- absolute value (p. 31)
- additive inverses (p. 38)
- compatible numbers (p. 5)
- integers (p. 31)
- mean (p. 53)
- median (p. 54)
- mode (p. 54)
- opposites (p. 31)
- order of operations (p. 48)
- outlier (p. 53)
- range (p. 55)

 Problem Solving Application On pages 64 and 65, you will work an extended activity on integers.

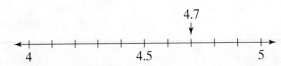

1-1 Using Estimation Strategies

Check Skills You'll Need

1. **Vocabulary Review**
   How is an estimate different from a guess?

Round to the place of the underlined digit.

2. 82,729   **3.** 449

4. 24,106   **5.** 3,528

GO for Help
Skills Handbook
p. 655

What You'll Learn

To estimate using rounding, front-end estimation, and compatible numbers

🔊 **New Vocabulary** compatible numbers

Why Learn This?

You can estimate an answer before you calculate it. Sometimes an estimate is all you need.

You can use rounding to estimate sums, differences, and products. You can use a number line to help you round decimals.

```
                              4.7
                               ↓
   ←—+—+—+—+—+—+—+—+—+—+—+→
     4           4.5           5
```
4.7 is between 4.0 and 5.0.
You can round 4.7 to 5.0.

When you estimate, use the symbol ≈, which means "is approximately equal to."

EXAMPLE Estimating by Rounding

1 **Biology** The span of an eagle ray's fins is 3.27 m. The span of her baby's fins is 0.88 m. Estimate the difference between the spans. Round to the nearest whole number before you find the difference.

$$3.27 - 0.88 \approx 3 - 1 \quad \leftarrow \textbf{Round to the nearest whole number.}$$
$$= 2 \quad \leftarrow \textbf{Subtract.}$$

The difference in spans is about 2 m.

GO for Help
For help with rounding decimals, go to Skills Handbook p. 660.

✓ Quick Check

1. Estimate. First round to the nearest whole number.
   a. 1.75 + 0.92   **b.** 14.34 − 7.8   **c.** 4.90 × 6.25

You can use front-end estimation when you want to find the sum of several numbers. First add the front numbers. Then estimate the sum of the lesser numbers and adjust the estimate.

EXAMPLE · Estimating by Front-End Estimation

② **Shopping** You have $10 and want to purchase several gift items. You select a kaleidoscope for $4.39, gift wrap for $1.49, and a card for $2.95. Estimate the total cost to determine whether you have enough money.

Step 1 Add the front-end digits.

$$
\begin{array}{r}
\$4.39 \\
\$1.49 \\
+\ \$2.95 \\
\hline
\$7
\end{array}
$$

Step 2 Estimate the sum of the cents to the nearest dollar.

$$
\begin{array}{r}
\$4.39 \\
\$1.49
\end{array}\Big\} \leftarrow \text{about } \$1
$$

$$
\$2.95 \quad \leftarrow \text{about } \$1
$$

$$
+ \qquad\qquad \$2 = \$9
$$

The total cost is about $9. You have enough money.

✓ Quick Check

2. Estimate to the nearest dollar the total cost of a dog collar for $5.79, a dog toy for $2.48, and a dog dish for $5.99.

Compatible numbers are numbers that are easy to compute mentally. You can use compatible numbers to estimate. Simply adjust the numbers in the problem to ones that are close to make the calculation easier. Compatible numbers are particularly useful for finding quotients.

EXAMPLE · Estimating Using Compatible Numbers

③ **Movies** Suppose you have saved $50.25. About how many DVDs can you buy from category D in the table?

$50.25 \div 7.95$ ← Use division.

$48 \div 8$ ← Choose compatible numbers such as 48 and 8.

6 ← Simplify.

DVD Price List	
Category	**Price**
A	$23.95
B	$15.95
C	$12.95
D	$7.95

You can buy about six DVDs from category D.

✓ Quick Check

3. Your friend says you can buy about twice as many DVDs from category D as from category B. Is your friend correct? Explain.

1. **Vocabulary** Explain the difference between rounded numbers and compatible numbers.

2. **Error Analysis** A student estimated the cost of three shirts. What error was made?

$$\$17.99 + \$23.45 + \$20.15 \approx 18 + 23 + 2$$
$$= 43$$

Match each problem with the method you would use to estimate.

3. $22.4 \div 3.21$

4. $7.3 + 22.4 + 6.5 + 13.6$

5. $21.8 - 17.4$

A. front-end estimation
B. rounding
C. compatible numbers

Homework Exercises

For more exercises, see Extra Skills and Word Problems.

GO for Help

For Exercises	See Examples
6–11	1
12–17	2
18–24	3

Estimate. First round to the nearest whole number.

6. $5.82 - 1.76$

7. $10.13 + 1.46$

8. 6.07×3.29

9. 9.86×9.13

10. $21.18 - 17.92$

11. $11.53 + 7.23$

Use front-end estimation to estimate each sum.

12. $5.43 + 2.67$

13. $8.09 + 11.24$

14. $7.18 + 5.89$

15. $4.39 + 9.57$

16. $24.21 + 16.03$

17. $3.62 + 2.31$

Use compatible numbers to estimate each quotient.

18. $76.5 \div 8.8$

19. $19.45 \div 4.92$

20. $27.36 \div 3.14$

21. $103.6 \div 9.72$

22. $32.2 \div 7.56$

23. $3.963 \div 1.79$

24. **Trains** The world's fastest train travels about 162 mi/h. Estimate how far the train travels in 4.75 h.

25. **Guided Problem Solving** A giant burrito required 75.75 lb of cheese. About how many 12-lb boxes of cheese did the cooks use?
    • Which operation will you use to solve the problem?
    • Which numbers will you use to make your estimate?

26. You can buy 12 magnets for $34.68, or 3 magnets for $9.57. Estimate to decide which is the better buy. Explain your reasoning.

27. **Reasoning** When you estimate to determine if you have enough money, why should you underestimate the amount you have?

Estimate the cost of each group of items.

28.
97¢ per lb
2.35 LB

29.
$1.36 per lb
1.48 LB

30.
79¢ per lb
4.16 LB

31. **Writing in Math** When is an estimate *not* as useful as an exact answer? Give an example.

32. On vacation, you wish to send eight postcards to friends at home. You find cards costing $.59 each. Eight postcard stamps cost about $2 total. About how much will it cost to buy and mail the cards?

33. **Challenge** Your family is going to visit a relative who lives 389.2 mi from your home. The family car gets 29.6 miles per gallon of gasoline. If the price of a gallon of gas is $2.16, about how much will the gasoline for the trip cost?

Test Prep and Mixed Review
Practice

Multiple Choice

34. The table shows the number of students at Stewart Middle School who belong to several groups. Which conclusion is reasonable?

Stewart Middle School Groups

Group	Number of Students
Pep Club	123
Band	68
Drama Club	32
Student Council	54

Ⓐ Student Council has twice as many members as Drama Club.
Ⓑ Pep Club has about 4 times as many members as Drama Club.
Ⓒ Band has about twice as many members as Pep Club.
Ⓓ Student Council has the fewest members.

35. Carrie earned $612 in a year at a part-time job. Which is the best estimate of her weekly earnings?

Ⓕ $18　　Ⓖ $16　　Ⓗ $14　　Ⓙ $12

For Exercises	See Skills Handbook
36–37	p. 654

Order the numbers from least to greatest.

36. 4.0 4,004 40 403

37. 761.8 768.1 768.0 706.8

Adding and Subtracting Decimals

What You'll Learn

To add and subtract decimals and to do mental math using the properties of addition

🔊 **New Vocabulary** Identity Property of Addition, Commutative Property of Addition, Associative Property of Addition

Why Learn This?

Sometimes an estimate is not good enough. You can add and subtract decimals to find an exact answer.

When you add decimals, you must align the decimal points so that corresponding place values are added. You may need to insert, or "annex," zeros so you have the same number of decimal places in each number.

EXAMPLE **Adding Decimals**

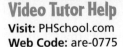 **Online**

Video Tutor Help
Visit: PHSchool.com
Web Code: are-0775

① **Music** A marching band has 6.5 minutes to perform at a football game. Does the band have enough time to play "America the Beautiful" and "Yankee Doodle Dandy"?

Estimate $3.63 + 2.5 \approx 4 + 3$, or 7

Align the decimal points.

```
   3.63       Insert a zero so both addends
 + 2.50    ←  have the same number of
   6.13       decimal places.
```

The band will play for 6.13 minutes. The band will have enough time.

Check for Reasonableness Since 6.13 is close to 7, the answer is reasonable.

Band Selections

Title	Min
"76 Trombones"	3.12
"Stars and Stripes Forever"	3.52
"Born in the U.S.A."	4.65
"America the Beautiful"	3.63
"Yankee Doodle Dandy"	2.5
"The Star-Spangled Banner"	4.5

✓ Quick Check

1. How long will the band take to play "Stars and Stripes Forever" and "The Star-Spangled Banner"?

When you subtract decimals, you may need to regroup.

EXAMPLE Subtracting Decimals

2 Find $89.9 - 46.78$.

Align the decimal points.	Regroup.	Subtract.
$\begin{array}{r} 89.90 \\ -\ 46.78 \end{array}$ ← Insert a zero.	$\begin{array}{r} {\overset{8}{}\overset{10}{}} \\ 89.\cancel{9}0 \\ -\ 46.78 \end{array}$	$\begin{array}{r} {\overset{8}{}\overset{10}{}} \\ 89.\cancel{9}0 \\ -\ 46.78 \\ \hline 43.12 \end{array}$

✓ **Quick Check**

● **2.** Find $26.7 - 14.81$.

You can use the properties of addition to add mentally.

> **KEY CONCEPTS** Properties of Addition
>
> **Identity Property of Addition** The sum of 0 and a is a.
>
> **Arithmetic** $5.6 + 0 = 5.6$ **Algebra** $a + 0 = a$
>
> **Commutative Property of Addition** Changing the order of the addends does not change the sum.
>
> **Arithmetic** $1.2 + 3.4 = 3.4 + 1.2$ **Algebra** $a + b = b + a$
>
> **Associative Property of Addition** Changing the grouping of the addends does not change the sum.
>
> **Arithmetic** **Algebra**
> $(2.5 + 6) + 4 = 2.5 + (6 + 4)$ $(a + b) + c = a + (b + c)$

EXAMPLE Using Properties of Addition

3 **Mental Math** Find $0.7 + 12.5 + 1.3$.

What You Think

I should look for compatible numbers. The sum of 0.7 and 1.3 is 2. Then I can add 2 and 12.5 for a total of 14.5.

Why It Works

$$0.7 + 12.5 + 1.3 = 0.7 + 1.3 + 12.5 \quad \leftarrow \text{Commutative Property of Addition}$$
$$= (0.7 + 1.3) + 12.5 \quad \leftarrow \text{Associative Property of Addition}$$
$$= 2 + 12.5 = 14.5$$

Test Prep Tip

Look for compatible numbers when you add several numbers.

✓ **Quick Check**

● **3.** Use mental math to find $4.4 + 5.3 + 0.6$.

1. **Vocabulary** Which property allows you to regroup addends?

2. **Number Sense** Which pair of addends forms compatible numbers in the expression $6.1 + 8.4 + 1.6$?

Mental Math Find each sum.

3. $23 + 17$

4. $0.8 + 1.2$

5. $16.9 + 2.1$

Find each missing number.

6. $2.7 + \blacksquare = 1.5 + 2.7$

7. $144.98 + \blacksquare = 144.98$

Homework Exercises

For more exercises, see Extra Skills and Word Problems.

GO for Help

For Exercises	See Examples
8–17	1
18–26	2
27–32	3

Find each sum.

8. $4.56 + 2.9$

9. $102.8 + 3$

10. $3.061 + 1.8$

11. $0.582 + 7$

12. $3.29 + 2 + 6.71$

13. $1.913 + 0.08 + 3$

14. $1.4 + 3.75 + 6$

15. $7.58 + 2.4 + 0.101$

16. $0.005 + 0.5 + 5$

17. The average length of a king cobra is 3.7 m. The record length is 1.88 m longer than the average. How long is the record holder?

Find each difference.

18. $5.3 - 0.12$

19. $12.46 - 7.2$

20. $3.102 - 0.89$

21. $0.1305 - 0.066$

22. $0.08 - 0.002$

23. $100 - 31.93$

24. $2.101 - 1.22$

25. $46.2 - 38.25$

26. $0.15 - 0.015$

Use mental math to find each sum.

27. $16.2 + 23.5 + 3.8$

28. $24.4 + (5.6 + 11)$

29. $27.4 + 0 + 12.1$

30. $9.2 + 1.8 + 0$

31. $(4.7 + 10.6) + 0.3$

32. $8.5 + 6.3 + 1.5$

33. **Guided Problem Solving** A band can play as much as 8 minutes of music in a competition. If the band plays a 2.33-minute song and a 4.25-minute song, how many minutes does it have left?
    - **Make a Plan** First find the total number of minutes in the two songs. Then subtract the total from the maximum time allowed.
    - **Carry Out the Plan** The total time is ■. The time remaining is ■.

34. <u>Writing in Math</u> How can you use the Identity Property of Addition to find $51.23 - 51.23 + 97.9$?

GO **Online**
Homework Video Tutor
Visit: PHSchool.com
Web Code: are-0102

Use <, =, or > to complete each statement.

35. $3.45 + 2.9$ ■ $8.9 - 2.75$

36. $15 - 6.82$ ■ $32.18 - 24$

37. Architecture Find the difference in the heights of the Empire State Building and the Eiffel Tower.

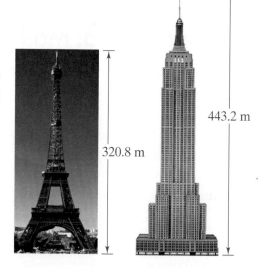

443.2 m

320.8 m

38. You decide to save some money. In week 1 you save $4.20, in week 2 you save $3.85, and in week 3 you save $2.50. Estimate your total savings. Then find the exact amount you saved.

39. Weather During a 3-day storm, 8.91 in. of rain fell in Tallahassee and 4.24 in. fell in St. Augustine. How much more rain fell in Tallahassee than in St. Augustine?

40. The original price for a jacket is $79.95. How much do you save if you buy the jacket on sale for $62.79?

41. Challenge The fastest mammal, the cheetah, can run as fast as 67.912 mi/h. The fastest fish, the sailfish, can swim as fast as 1.132 mi/min. Which animal is faster? How much faster is it?

Test Prep and Mixed Review

Practice

Multiple Choice

42. You receive $50 for your birthday. You buy a book for $14.95 and a baseball cap for $24.95. How much money do you have left?
　Ⓐ $60.10　　Ⓑ $39.90　　Ⓒ $29.90　　Ⓓ $10.10

43. The average rainfall for Houston, Texas, is 4.5 inches in October, 4.2 inches in November, and 3.7 inches in December. Find the total average rainfall for the last three months of the year.
　Ⓕ 11.4 in.　　Ⓖ 11.9 in.　　Ⓗ 12.4 in.　　Ⓙ 12.9 in.

44. Carla bought a CD for $12.99 and a book for $7.29. She also rented a movie for $3.99. Which expression can be used to find the best estimate of the total amount Carla spent, not including tax?
　Ⓐ $12 + 7 + 3$　　　　　Ⓒ $13 + 7 + 3$
　Ⓑ $12 + 7 + 4$　　　　　Ⓓ $13 + 7 + 4$

GO **for Help**

For Exercises	See Skills Handbook
45–47	p. 656

Find each product.

45. 17×8　　　　**46.** 15×0　　　　**47.** 4×56

Using Mental Math

Compensation allows you to adjust the numbers and make the expressions easier to calculate mentally. You can use compensation to find sums and differences.

The sum of two numbers remains the same if you add a number to one addend and subtract the same number from the other addend.

The difference between two numbers remains the same if you add (or subtract) the same number from both numbers.

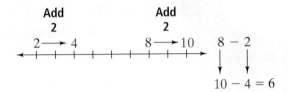

Subtract 3   **Add 3**

$2 \leftarrow 5 \quad 7 \rightarrow 10 \quad 7 + 5$

$10 + 2 = 12$

Add 2   **Add 2**

$2 \rightarrow 4 \quad 8 \rightarrow 10 \quad 8 - 2$

$10 - 4 = 6$

EXAMPLE   **Using Compensation**

Find each sum or difference using compensation.

a. $4.96 + $3.79

$$4.96 + $3.79$$

$$+ 0.04 - 0.04$$ Add 0.04 to one addend ← and subtract 0.04 from the other addend.

$$5.00 + $3.75 = $8.75$$

b. $6.1 - 1.3$

$$6.1 - 1.3$$

$$+ 0.7 + 0.7$$ Add 0.7 to both numbers ← so that you subtract a whole number.

$$6.8 - 2 = 4.8$$

Exercises

Find each sum or difference using compensation.

1. $\begin{array}{r} 0.95 \\ + 1.45 \end{array}$

2. $\begin{array}{r} 2.54 \\ + 8.16 \end{array}$

3. $\begin{array}{r} 3.89 \\ + 1.73 \end{array}$

4. $\begin{array}{r} 72.2 \\ + 14.9 \end{array}$

5. $\begin{array}{r} 38.0 \\ - 11.1 \end{array}$

6. $\begin{array}{r} 9.3 \\ - 6.8 \end{array}$

7. $\begin{array}{r} 102 \\ - 77 \end{array}$

8. $\begin{array}{r} 41.6 \\ - 0.7 \end{array}$

9. $0.4 + 7.8$

10. $117 + 96$

11. $74.6 - 35.8$

12. $12.4 - 8.3$

13. $11.7 - 6.9$

14. $2.9 + 10.5$

15. $984 - 852$

16. $72.3 + 8.1$

17. Money You have five items to purchase at the grocery store. The prices are $.98, $3.95, $2.08, $4.99, and $1. Use compensation to determine the amount you owe at the checkout.

Modeling Decimal Multiplication

You can use models to multiply decimals. The grid below is divided into 10 columns and 10 rows. Each column or row represents one tenth of the whole, or 0.1. Each square represents one hundredth of the whole, or 0.01.

ACTIVITY

You can use three grids to construct a model to find 0.7×0.4.

Step 1 Model 0.7 by shading 7 columns in one color. Model 0.4 by shading 4 rows in a different color.

Step 2 Shade 0.7 and 0.4 on the same grid. Count the number of squares that are shaded in both colors.

● There are 28 squares shaded in both colors, so $0.7 \times 0.4 = 0.28$.

Exercises

Draw a model to find each product.

1. 0.2×0.9

2. 0.5×0.3

3. 0.4×0.4

Write the product represented by each decimal grid.

4.

5.

6.

7. Use Exercises 1–3. Multiply each factor by 10. Find the new products. How do the new products compare to the original products?

Check Skills You'll Need

1. **Vocabulary Review** How is estimating different from finding an exact answer?

Estimate.

2. 2.7×5.3
3. 4.09×6.8
4. 1.134×9.76

 **for Help**

Lesson 1-1

What You'll Learn

To multiply decimals and to do mental math using the properties of multiplication

🔊 **New Vocabulary** Properties of Multiplication: Identity Property, Zero Property, Commutative Property, Associative Property

Why Learn This?

Multiplying decimals can help you find how much money you will earn working at a part-time job.

To multiply decimals, treat the factors as whole numbers. Then multiply. Count the decimal places in both factors. Use the total to locate the decimal point in the product.

EXAMPLE Multiplying Decimals

① At your part-time job, you earn $7.30 per hour. You work for two and a half hours. How much money do you earn?

Estimate $7.30 \times 2.5 \approx 7 \times 3 = 21$.

Step 1 Multiply as if the numbers are whole numbers.

$$
\begin{array}{r}
730 \\
\times\ 25 \\
\hline
3650 \\
1460 \\
\hline
18250
\end{array}
$$

Step 2 Locate the decimal point in the product by adding the decimal places of the factors.

$$
\begin{array}{r}
7.30 \\
\times\ 2.5 \\
\hline
3650 \\
1460 \\
\hline
18.250
\end{array}
$$

7.30 ← two decimal places (hundredths)
× 2.5 ← one decimal place (tenths)

hundredths × tenths = thousandths
← Use three decimal places.

You earn $18.25.

Check for Reasonableness The product 18.25 is close to the estimate of 21. The answer is reasonable.

✓ Quick Check

● **1.** Estimate 14.3×0.81. Then find the product.

Four ways to write "3 times 5" using different symbols are shown below.

$$3 \times 5 \qquad 3 \cdot 5 \qquad 3(5) \qquad (3)(5)$$

> **KEY CONCEPTS** **Properties of Multiplication**
>
> **Identity Property of Multiplication** The product of 1 and a is a.
>
> | Arithmetic | Algebra |
> |---|---|
> | $5 \cdot 1 = 5$ | $a \cdot 1 = a$ |
> | $1 \cdot 5 = 5$ | $1 \cdot a = a$ |
>
> **Zero Property** The product of 0 and any number is 0.
>
> | Arithmetic | Algebra |
> |---|---|
> | $5 \cdot 0 = 0$ | $a \cdot 0 = 0$ |
> | $0 \cdot 5 = 0$ | $0 \cdot a = 0$ |
>
> **Commutative Property of Multiplication** Changing the order of factors does not change the product.
>
> | Arithmetic | Algebra |
> |---|---|
> | $5 \cdot 2 = 2 \cdot 5$ | $a \cdot 2 = 2 \cdot a$ |
>
> **Associative Property of Multiplication** Changing the grouping of factors does not change the product.
>
> | Arithmetic | Algebra |
> |---|---|
> | $(3 \cdot 2) \cdot 5 = 3 \cdot (2 \cdot 5)$ | $(a \cdot b) \cdot c = a \cdot (b \cdot c)$ |

Vocabulary Tip

To *commute* means "to change places." A commutative property lets numbers change places.

To *associate* means "to gather in groups." An associative property forms groups of numbers.

You can use the properties of multiplication to multiply mentally.

EXAMPLE **Using Multiplication Properties**

2 **Mental Math** Use mental math to find $0.25 \cdot 3.58 \cdot 4$.

What you think

I should look for compatible numbers. The product of 0.25 and 4 is 1. Then the product of 1 and 3.58 is 3.58.

Why it works

$$
\begin{aligned}
0.25 \cdot 3.58 \cdot 4 &= 0.25 \cdot 4 \cdot 3.58 && \leftarrow \text{Commutative Property of Multiplication} \\
&= (0.25 \cdot 4) \cdot 3.58 && \leftarrow \text{Associative Property of Multiplication} \\
&= 1 \cdot 3.58 && \leftarrow \text{Simplify.} \\
&= 3.58 && \leftarrow \text{Identity Property of Multiplication}
\end{aligned}
$$

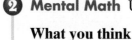 **Quick Check**

2. Use mental math to find $2.5 \cdot 6.3 \cdot 4$.

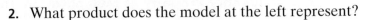
1. **Vocabulary** Which property of multiplication allows you to switch the order of the factors?

2. What product does the model at the left represent?

3. **Number Sense** The product of 4 and 25 is 100. What happens to the product when you change one factor from 25 to 2.5?

Multiply.

4. 0.5×6

5. $0.25 \cdot 8$

6. 1.5×2

Find the missing numbers. Name the property of multiplication shown.

7. $3.6 \cdot \blacksquare = 0$

8. $\blacksquare \cdot 1 = 25.5$

9. $\blacksquare \cdot 4 = 4 \cdot 3$

10. $(5 \cdot \blacksquare) \cdot 2.3 = 5 \cdot (1.4 \cdot 2.3)$

Homework Exercises

For more exercises, see Extra Skills and Word Problems.

Estimate. Then find each product.

GO for Help

For Exercises	See Examples
11–19	1
20–29	2

11. 0.2×0.7

12. 0.4×0.6

13. 0.3×0.5

14. 1.02×3.6

15. 8.7×0.45

16. 1.45×2.6

17. 41×7.5

18. 1.3×0.05

19. 1.1×1.1

Mental Math Find each product.

20. $0.2 \cdot 3.41 \cdot 5$

21. $1.09 \cdot 23.6 \cdot 0$

22. $(2.3 \cdot 0.5) \cdot 4$

23. $5 \cdot (4.3 \cdot 1)$

24. $0 \cdot 2.78 \cdot 1$

25. $0.4 \cdot 3.29 \cdot 25$

26. $0.4 \cdot (0.5 \cdot 0.2)$

27. $3.6 \cdot 2.5 \cdot 2$

28. $7.1 \cdot 6.2 \cdot 3.5 \cdot 0$

29. **Biking** If your speed is 3.5 mi/h, how far will you bike in 1.2 h?

30. **Guided Problem Solving** You have 17 pennies, 31 nickels, 22 dimes, and 14 quarters. How much money will you have if you lend $6.50 to a friend?
    - How much money do you have in each type of coin?
    - What is the total amount of money you have?

31. **Money** A penny weighs about 0.1 oz. How much is a pound of pennies worth? (1 lb = 16 oz)

32. A cubic foot of water weighs 62.4 lb. A water storage tank can hold 89.5 cubic feet of water. How much will the water in the storage tank weigh when the tank is full?

GO Online

Homework Video Tutor

Visit: PHSchool.com
Web Code: are-0103

Find each product.

33. $0.36 \cdot 1.2$ **34.** $3.6 \cdot 0.12$ **35.** $0.36 \cdot 0.012$ **36.** $0.036 \cdot 0.12$

37. <u>**Writing in Math**</u> How are the identity properties of multiplication and addition similar? How are they different?

38. New tennis balls must bounce back to no less than 0.53 and no more than 0.58 of the starting height. A ball is dropped from 200 cm. Within what range of heights should it bounce?

39. One year, Texas had about 2.6 times as many head of cattle as Oklahoma. Oklahoma had 5.2 million. How many head of cattle did Texas have?

40. **Reasoning** You multiply two decimals that are both less than 1. How does the size of the product compare to each factor? Explain.

41. **Challenge** White flour costs $1.30/kg, and whole wheat flour costs $1.10/kg. Flour is sold in bags of 1.2 kg and 3.4 kg. A chef buys 4 bags of flour. If each bag of flour the chef buys is different, how much must the chef pay?

Test Prep and Mixed Review
Practice

Multiple Choice

42. Which model represents the expression 0.3×0.6?

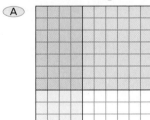 A

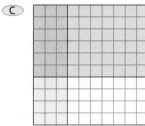 C

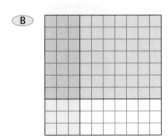 B

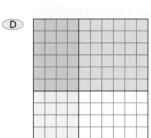 D

43. Mr. Porter bought 24 bagels at 6 for $2.49 and 12 cartons of juice at 6 for $1.98. What was the total cost of the bagels and juice Mr. Porter bought, not including tax?

   Ⓕ $8.84   Ⓖ $9.96   Ⓗ $11.88   Ⓙ $13.92

GO for Help

For Exercises	See Lesson
44–47	1-2

Find each sum or difference.

44. $8.56 + 3.11$ **45.** $9.843 - 8.2$ **46.** $9.4 - 7.024$ **47.** $17.1 + 3.09$

Use each strategy to estimate $3.07 + $3.48 + $4.24.

1. rounding to the nearest dollar first

2. front-end estimation

Use compatible numbers to estimate each answer.

3. $129.4 \div 23$

4. $37.6 \div 3.05$

Find each sum or difference.

5. $2.99 + 3.08 + 18.5$ **6.** $9.718 + 4.603$ **7.** $11.64 - 8.72$ **8.** $22.4 - 0.54$

Find each product.

9. $1.36 \cdot 8.94$ **10.** 2.4×0.04 **11.** 12.16×4.2 **12.** $5.45 \cdot 2.04$

13. Use $<$, $=$, or $>$ to complete $61.25 - 30.17$ ▪ 14.8×2.1.

14. Eduardo can type 65 words per minute. How many words can he type in 7.5 minutes?

15. **Crafts** A box of supplies contains 0.8 lb of red clay, 1.3 lb of green clay, and 2.1 lb of white clay, as well as three cans of paint that weigh 0.75 lb each. What is the total weight of the supplies?

MATH AT WORK

Detective

Most people think of a detective as a person in a trench coat, looking for clues. In reality, detectives dress like anyone else. They can work for lawyers, government agencies, and businesses. Detectives may gather information to trace debtors or conduct background investigations.

Detectives use mathematics to locate stolen funds, develop financial profiles, or monitor expense accounts.

Go Online
PHSchool.com   **For:** Information about detectives
Web Code: arb-2031

Modeling Decimal Division

You can use models to divide decimals. Follow the steps
in the activity to model the quotient 0.6 ÷ 0.2.

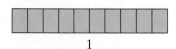

Step 1 Cut out a rectangular strip of paper that is 10 in. long. This strip
represents 1 whole. Mark each inch of the strip. Notice that you
now have 10 equal parts, each representing 0.1, or one tenth, of
the whole.

1

Step 2 Cut the strip so that you have 2 segments. One segment
should represent 0.6 of the whole.

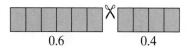

0.6   0.4

Step 3 Use another piece of paper and repeat Step 1.

Step 4 Cut this strip into 5 equal segments, so that each segment
represents 0.2 of the whole.

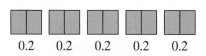

0.2   0.2   0.2   0.2   0.2

Step 5 Align the segments that represent 0.2 under the segment
that represents 0.6 of the whole.

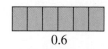

0.6

Step 6 Count the number of 0.2 segments needed to equal the
length of the 0.6 segment.

0.2   0.2   0.2

● You used 3 segments, each representing 0.2 unit, so 0.6 ÷ 0.2 = 3.

Exercises

Use a model to find each quotient.

1. 0.3 ÷ 0.1

2. 0.4 ÷ 0.2

3. 0.8 ÷ 0.4

Write the quotient represented by each model.

4.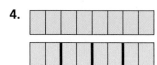

5.

6.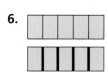

7. Reasoning The quotient of 0.6 and 0.2 is 3. What happens to the
quotient when you multiply the dividend and divisor by 10? Explain.

What You'll Learn

To divide decimals and to solve problems by dividing decimals

Why Learn This?

You may need to divide decimals to plan how many items you can buy with the money you have.

Suppose you have $1.20 and you want to buy pencils that cost $.30 each. How many pencils can you buy? Three ways to write "1.2 divided by 0.3" appear below.

$$1.2 \div 0.3 \qquad 0.3\overline{)1.2} \qquad \frac{1.2}{0.3}$$

To divide decimals, multiply both the divisor and the dividend by the power of 10 that makes the divisor a whole number. Then divide.

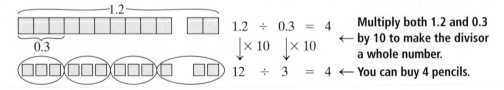

$$1.2 \div 0.3 = 4$$
$$\downarrow \times 10 \quad \downarrow \times 10$$
$$12 \div 3 = 4$$

Multiply both 1.2 and 0.3 ← by 10 to make the divisor a whole number.

← You can buy 4 pencils.

EXAMPLE   **Dividing a Decimal by a Decimal**

1 Find $2.064 \div 0.24$.

Place the decimal point in the
← quotient above the decimal
point in the dividend.

$$0.24\overline{)2.064} \qquad \rightarrow \qquad \begin{array}{r} 8.6 \\ 24\overline{)206.4} \\ \underline{192} \\ 144 \\ \underline{144} \\ 0 \end{array}$$

↑
Multiply the divisor and the
dividend by 100 to make the
divisor a whole number.

✓ Quick Check

1. Find each quotient.

    a. $12.42 \div 5.4$ **b.** $67.84 \div 0.64$ **c.** $144.06 \div 9.8$

When you divide by a decimal, sometimes you need to annex extra zeros in the dividend.

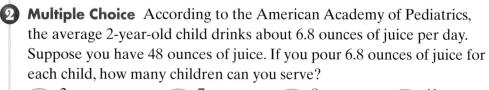 **EXAMPLE** **Annexing Zeros to Divide**

② **Multiple Choice** According to the American Academy of Pediatrics, the average 2-year-old child drinks about 6.8 ounces of juice per day. Suppose you have 48 ounces of juice. If you pour 6.8 ounces of juice for each child, how many children can you serve?

Ⓐ 2 Ⓑ 7 Ⓒ 8 Ⓓ 41

Step 1 Estimate to eliminate unreasonable answers.

$48 \div 6.8 \approx 49 \div 7 = 7$ ← Use compatible numbers 49 and 7.

Since the estimate is 7, only choices B and C are reasonable. You can eliminate choices A and D.

Step 2 Calculate to decide which answer is correct.

$$6.8\overline{)48.0} \quad \rightarrow \quad 68\overline{)480.}$$

Annex the zero in the dividend.
← Multiply the divisor and dividend by 10 to make the divisor a whole number.

$$
\begin{array}{r}
7. \\
68\overline{)480.} \\
\underline{476} \\
4
\end{array}
\quad \rightarrow \quad
\begin{array}{r}
7.05 \\
68\overline{)480.00} \\
\underline{476} \\
400 \\
\underline{340} \\
60
\end{array}
$$

Annex two zeros and divide. The quotient is
← about 7.05, which is only slightly more than 7. Only 7 children can be served.

You can serve 7 children with 48 oz of juice. The answer is B.

 **Test Prep Tip**

To eliminate unreasonable choices, estimate the answer to a multiple-choice question before calculating.

✓ Quick Check

2. You use 0.6 lb of bananas in each smoothie. How many smoothies can you make with 3.12 lb of bananas?

Notice the patterns in the divisors and the quotients at the right. As the divisors decrease by a factor of 10, the quotients increase by a factor of 10.

What happens when you try to divide by zero? Consider these related problems.

$3 \cdot 2 = 6 \rightarrow 6 \div 3 = 2$

$0 \cdot \blacksquare = 12 \rightarrow 12 \div 0 = \blacksquare$

No value for ■ makes sense! So, division by zero is undefined.

Dividend		Divisor		Quotient
50	÷	100	=	0.5
50	÷	10	=	5
50	÷	1	=	50
50	÷	0.1	=	500
50	÷	0.01	=	5,000
50	÷	0.001	=	50,000
50	÷	0.0001	=	500,000

1. **Vocabulary** The number being divided in a division problem is called the   ? .

2. **Estimation** Use compatible numbers to estimate 22.54 ÷ 3.99.

Find each quotient.

3. $75\overline{)300}$

4. $7.5\overline{)300}$

5. $0.75\overline{)300}$

6. **Patterns** Look at the divisors in Exercises 3–5. Notice that the decimal point moves one place to the left from one exercise to the next. Describe what happens to the quotients.

Homework Exercises

For more exercises, see Extra Skills and Word Problems.

GO for Help

For Exercises	See Examples
7–15	1
16–22	2

Find each quotient.

7. $19.2 \div 3.2$

8. $1.8\overline{)7.74}$

9. $\dfrac{56.4}{4.7}$

10. $\dfrac{17.8}{8.9}$

11. $83.7 \div 2.7$

12. $5.4\overline{)43.2}$

13. $9\overline{)641.7}$

14. $\dfrac{0.0882}{6}$

15. $325.28 \div 30.4$

Annex zeros to find each quotient.

16. $0.04\overline{)10}$

17. $5.4 \div 7.2$

18. $\dfrac{126}{1.2}$

19. $592 \div 0.8$

20. $0.21 \div 0.6$

21. $\dfrac{0.003}{0.5}$

22. **Food** Nuts cost $1.75 per jar. How many jars can you buy with $14?

23. **Guided Problem Solving** A store buys 12 pens for $11.28. The store sells each pen for $1.99. What is the store's profit per pen?
    - **Make a Plan** Divide to find the cost of one pen. Then subtract the store's cost from the selling price to find the profit.
    - **Carry Out the Plan** A single pen costs ■.
      The profit per pen is ■.

24. You spend $13.92 for fabric. Each yard costs $4.35. How many yards of fabric do you buy?

25. **Movies** You buy five movie tickets for a total of $23.75. Your friend gives you $5 for one ticket. How much change should you give your friend?

GO Online
Homework Video Tutor
Visit: PHSchool.com
Web Code: are-0104

26. A car travels 360.25 mi. It uses 13.1 gal of gas. How many miles per gallon of gas does the car travel?

Find each quotient.

27. $224.5 \div 0.05$

28. $1.25\overline{)0.21}$

29. $4.5\overline{)13.59}$

30. $654 \div 0.12$

31. $1.25\overline{)3.85}$

32. $5.95\overline{)7.3423}$

33. **Landscaping** After digging up lilac bushes in a garden, a landscape architect uses sod to cover the ground. The sod costs $2.25/yd. He pays $31.50. How much sod does he buy?

34. You have a dog-walking business. Last week you worked 7.5 hours and you earned $41.25. How much do you earn per hour?

35. **Reasoning** When you divide a whole number by a decimal divisor less than 1, how does the size of the quotient relate to the divisor? Explain.

36. **Writing in Math** Do you think there is a commutative property of division? Explain why or why not. Give examples.

37. You are making a homework planner that is 8.5 in. wide. The first column is 1.25 in. wide and lists the subjects. The next five columns are equally wide and represent the five school days. How many inches wide is the column for Monday?

38. **Challenge** You want to cover a square floor that measures 127.2 in. on a side with square tiles. Each tile measures 2.4 in. on a side. How many tiles do you need?

Test Prep and Mixed Review   **Practice**

Multiple Choice

39. Which expression does the model represent?

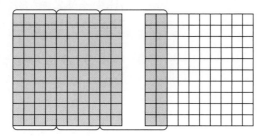

Ⓐ $1.2 \div 4$ Ⓑ $1.2 \div 3$ Ⓒ $0.2 \div 4$ Ⓓ $0.2 \div 3$

40. At Tony's Shoppe, the turkey sandwich contains 5.5 ounces of sliced turkey. Tony has a boneless turkey breast weighing 154 ounces. How many turkey sandwiches can Tony make?

Ⓕ 2   Ⓖ 3   Ⓗ 28   Ⓙ 29

GO for Help

For Exercises	See Lesson
41–43	1-3

Mental Math Find each product.

41. $0.5 \cdot 6.7 \cdot 2$

42. $5.3 \cdot 4.9 \cdot 0$

43. $8.2 \cdot 2.5 \cdot 4$

Choosing Operations

Gas Up! The odometer of a motor scooter with a full tank of gas read 15 miles. It took 1.2 gallons of gas to refill the tank when the odometer read 126.4 miles. How many miles per gallon did the scooter get?

What You Might Think

What do I know? What do I want to find out?

How do I show the main idea?

Can I estimate the answer?

How do I solve the problem? What is the answer?

Is the answer reasonable?

What You Might Write

The scooter went 126.4 − 15, or 111.4, miles using 1.2 gallons of gas. I want to find how far the scooter goes on 1 gallon.

Draw a diagram.

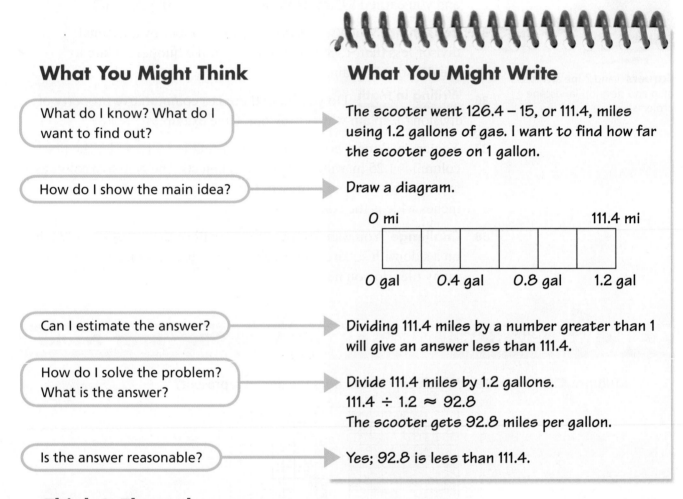

Dividing 111.4 miles by a number greater than 1 will give an answer less than 111.4.

Divide 111.4 miles by 1.2 gallons.
$111.4 \div 1.2 \approx 92.8$
The scooter gets 92.8 miles per gallon.

Yes; 92.8 is less than 111.4.

Think It Through

1. The diagram above shows the number of gallons used on the same vertical line as the number of miles traveled. Explain why.

2. **Reasoning** Explain how you know that dividing 111.4 by a number greater than 1 will give an answer less than 111.4.

3. **Number Sense** Suppose the scooter had used 0.95 gallons of gas instead of 1.2 gallons to travel the same distance. Would the mileage have been better or worse? Explain.

Exercises

Solve each problem. For Exercises 4 and 5, answer the questions first.

4. At an amusement park, Tanya finds a poster for $3.75 and a shirt for $14.95. She has $20. Can she buy both items and still have enough money for a bus ticket home that costs $1.75? Explain.
   a. What do you know? What do you want to find out?
   b. How can you use the diagram below to help find the answer?

$20		
$14.95	$3.75	■

5. In May, 1860, the longest run in the history of the Pony Express was made using four horses. The table at the right shows the distances run by the horses. What was the average distance?
   a. What do you know? What do you want to find out?

Horse	Distance (miles)
1	60
2	35
3	37
4	30

   b. How can you use the diagram below to help find the answer?

60	35	37	30

6. Early settlers often sold their furniture to lighten their wagons. Suppose a settler sold furniture for 0.2 times the amount he paid. If he sold a chair for $3.80, what did he pay for it?

7. In the 1850s, a wind wagon was invented that was half sailboat and half wagon. The wind wagon took about 133 days to travel 1,968 mi. About how many miles did the wind wagon travel each day?

8. The Mississippi River is 3.2 times longer than the Platte-South Platte River. The Mississippi River is 2,340 mi long. How long is the Platte-South Platte River?

1-5 Measuring in Metric Units

Check Skills You'll Need

1. **Vocabulary Review**
   $4 \cdot 8 = 8 \cdot 4$ is an example of the ? Property of Multiplication.

Simplify.

2. $0.25 \cdot 10$

3. $4.567 \cdot 1,000$

4. $0.03 \cdot 100$

5. $0.07 \cdot 1,000$

 **for Help**
Lesson 1-3

What You'll Learn

To use and convert metric units of measure

Why Learn This?

Countries around the world use the metric system for measurement. Measurements are easy to convert in the metric system because it is a decimal system.

The table below is a guide for choosing an appropriate metric unit.

Type	Unit	Reference Example
Length	millimeter (mm)	about the thickness of a dime
	centimeter (cm)	about the width of your little finger
	meter (m)	about the distance from a doorknob to the floor
	kilometer (km)	about the length of 11 football fields
Capacity	milliliter (mL)	a small spoon holds about 5 mL
	liter (L)	a little more than 1 quart
Mass	milligram (mg)	about the mass of a mosquito
	gram (g)	about the mass of a paper clip
	kilogram (kg)	about the mass of a bunch of bananas

EXAMPLE   Choosing a Reasonable Estimate

1 Choose a reasonable estimate. Explain your choice.

   a. height of a classroom: 3 cm   3 m   3 km

      3 m; a classroom is about 3 times as high as the distance from a doorknob to the floor.

   b. mass of a bag of flour: 2.3 mg   2.3 g   2.3 kg

      2.3 kg; a bag of flour is much heavier than a few paper clips.

Quick Check

1. Choose a reasonable estimate. Explain your choice.
     a. capacity of a soup bowl: 180 mL   180 L   180 kL
     b. mass of a butterfly: 500 mg   500 g   500 kg

The basic unit for length in the metric system is the meter (m). The prefixes *deci-*, *centi-*, and *milli-* describe measures that are less than one basic unit. The prefixes *deca-*, *hecto-*, and *kilo-* describe measures that are greater than one basic unit.

Each unit in the table is 10 times the value of the unit to its right.

Unit	kilo-meter	hecto-meter	deca-meter	meter	deci-meter	centi-meter	milli-meter
Symbol	km	hm	dam	m	dm	cm	mm
Value	1,000 m	100 m	10 m	1 m	0.1 m	0.01 m	0.001 m

The basic unit of mass is the gram. The basic unit of capacity is the liter.

You can change a measurement from one unit to another by finding the relationship between the two units and multiplying.

EXAMPLES Multiplying to Change Units

2 Change 245 milliliters to liters.

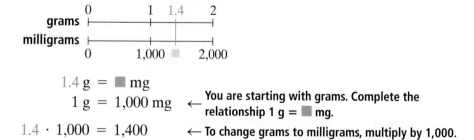

$$245 \text{ mL} = \blacksquare \text{ L}$$
$$1 \text{ mL} = 0.001 \text{ L} \quad \leftarrow \text{You are starting with milliliters. Complete the relationship 1 mL} = \blacksquare \text{ L.}$$
$$245 \cdot 0.001 = 0.245 \quad \leftarrow \text{To change milliliters to liters, multiply by 0.001.}$$

245 milliliters equals 0.245 liters.

3 Change 1.4 grams to milligrams.

$$1.4 \text{ g} = \blacksquare \text{ mg}$$
$$1 \text{ g} = 1,000 \text{ mg} \quad \leftarrow \text{You are starting with grams. Complete the relationship 1 g} = \blacksquare \text{ mg.}$$
$$1.4 \cdot 1,000 = 1,400 \quad \leftarrow \text{To change grams to milligrams, multiply by 1,000.}$$

1.4 grams equals 1,400 milligrams.

Check for Reasonableness A gram is greater than a milligram, so the number of grams should be less than the number of milligrams. Since $1.4 < 1,400$, the answer is reasonable.

Test Prep Tip

Pay attention to the prefixes when you convert metric units.

✓ **Quick Check**

2. Change 34 liters to milliliters.

3. Change 4,690 grams to kilograms.

● More Than One Way

A fruit punch recipe calls for 1 L of orange juice, 400 mL of pineapple juice, 60 mL of lemon juice, 2 L of apple juice, and 840 mL of water. Can you make a batch of this punch in a 5-L punch bowl?

Anna's Method

I can start by subtracting 1 L of orange juice and 2 L of apple juice from the 5 L available. That leaves 2 L of capacity in the punch bowl.

400 mL + 60 mL + 840 mL = 1,300 mL ← **Add the ingredients in milliliters.**

2 · 1,000 = 2,000; 2 L = 2,000 mL ← **Change remaining capacity to milliliters.**

Since 1,300 mL is less than 2,000 mL, I can make the punch in the bowl.

Ryan's Method

I can convert all the measures in milliliters to liters by multiplying each measure by 0.001.

400 · 0.001 = 0.4;   400 mL = 0.4 L

60 · 0.001 = 0.06;   60 mL = 0.06 L   ← **Change milliliters to liters.**

840 · 0.001 = 0.84;   840 mL = 0.84 L

1 L + 0.4 L + 0.06 L + 2 L + 0.84 L = 4.3 L   ← **Add all ingredients.**

The capacity of the punch bowl is 5 L. I can make a full batch of the punch in the punch bowl.

Choose a Method

For a craft project, you need ribbon in lengths of 3 m, 25 cm, 4 m, 58 cm, 1.5 m, and 70 cm. You have 10 m of ribbon. Is that enough? Explain why you chose the method you used.

✓ Check Your Understanding

1. **Vocabulary** In the metric system, the prefix *kilo-* means that the unit is ■ times the basic unit of measure.

What number should you multiply by to change each unit?

2. grams to kilograms   3. centiliters to liters   4. liters to decaliters

Write the number that makes each statement true.

5. 64 g = ■ kg   6. ■ L = 302 mL   7. 8,490 mm = ■ km

For more exercises, see Extra Skills and Word Problems.

GO for Help

For Exercises	See Examples
8–10	1
11–17	2–3

Choose a reasonable estimate.

8. capacity of a small bottle   250 mL   250 L   250 kL

9. height of an oak tree   22 cm   22 m   22 km

10. mass of an adult bullfrog   0.5 mg   0.5 g   0.5 kg

Complete each statement. You may find a number line helpful.

11. $0.9 \text{ kg} = \blacksquare \text{ g}$ 12. $\blacksquare \text{ L} = 90 \text{ mL}$ 13. $58 \text{ m} = \blacksquare \text{ mm}$

14. $7{,}800 \text{ g} = \blacksquare \text{ kg}$ 15. $7 \text{ m} = \blacksquare \text{ km}$ 16. $\blacksquare \text{ L} = 240 \text{ kL}$

17. The capacity of a plastic cup is 350 mL. How many cups can you fill from a 2.1-L bottle of juice?

18. **Guided Problem Solving** You are making a drawing of a family crest from a book. You have a piece of paper that is 21.5 cm wide and want to leave a 35-mm margin on each side. How wide can you draw the crest?
    - What is the width in centimeters of the margin on one side?
    - What is the combined width of the margins on the two sides?
    - How can you find the maximum width of the crest?

19. **Nutrition** You need 1.3 g of calcium per day. You get 290 mg of calcium per glass of milk. If you drink 4 glasses of milk, how much more calcium do you need from other sources?

20. **Geography** Antarctica averages 2,400 meters in elevation. What is the average elevation of Antarctica in kilometers?

21. The world's tallest man was 272 cm tall. Find his height in meters.

22. **Choose a Method** A bag of birdseed mix contains 400 g of sunflower seed, 300 g of thistle seed, and 0.5 kg of mixed seeds. You order six bags of birdseed mix. How many grams of birdseed is your order? Explain why you chose the method you used.

Match each measurement in the first column with an equivalent measurement in the second column.

23. 25 mL

24. 2.5 km

25. 0.25 L

26. 250 mm

27. 25,000 mg

    A. 0.025 kg
    B. 25 cm
    C. 0.025 L
    D. 25 cL
    E. 2,500 m

Write the metric unit that makes each statement true.

28. 2,034 mg = 2.034 __?__

29. 3.456 cm = 34.56 __?__

30. 9,023 mL = 90.23 __?__

31. 0.1347 m = 134.7 __?__

32. Writing in Math Explain how to change units in the metric system.

33. **Money** A roll of 50 pennies has a mass of 125 g. Find the mass of $5 in pennies.

34. The mass of a basketball is 620 g. The mass of a soccer ball is 0.45 kg. How much greater is the mass of a basketball in grams?

35. **Food** The capacity of a coffee mug is 350 mL. How many coffee mugs can you fill from a 2 L container?

36. **Reasoning** Suppose you want to change 125 kg 84 g to a single unit. Would you choose kilograms or grams? Explain your choice.

37. **Challenge** A recipe for modeling clay requires 470 mL of baking soda, 240 mL of cornstarch, and 300 mL of water. Can you make a double batch in a 1.9-L pan? Explain.

Test Prep and Mixed Review

Practice

Multiple Choice

38. A company is manufacturing a sports water jug that holds 1,350 mL. What is the capacity of the jug in liters?

Ⓐ 1,350,000 L

Ⓒ 1.305 L

Ⓑ 1.35 L

Ⓓ 1.035 L

39. Tina lives 350 m from school. She walks to school and home again each day. During a 5-day school week, how far does she walk?

Ⓕ 1750 km Ⓖ 70 km Ⓗ 3.5 km Ⓙ 1.75 km

40. A diagram of a bike path is shown below. Shawn biked all the way around the path once. How far did Shawn ride?

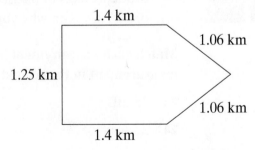

Ⓐ 3.71 km Ⓑ 5.6 km Ⓒ 6.17 km Ⓓ 6.27 km

For Exercises	See Lesson
41–43	1-4

Find each quotient.

41. 15.621 ÷ 2.46

42. 0.17595 ÷ 1.035

43. 5.58 ÷ 9.3

1-6 Comparing and Ordering Integers

Check Skills You'll Need

1. **Vocabulary Review**
   You know that
   $5 \cdot (b \cdot 2) =$
   $(5 \cdot b) \cdot 2$, because
   of the ? Property
   of Multiplication.

Find each product.

2. $530.6 \cdot 8$

3. $0.0771 \cdot 7$

4. $214.17 \cdot 30$

 **for Help**

Lesson 1-3

What You'll Learn

To compare and order integers and to find absolute values

 New Vocabulary integers, opposites, absolute value

Why Learn This?

Most shipwrecks lie under water. You can use integers to describe distances above and below sea level.

Integers are the set of positive whole numbers, their opposites, and zero. The wreck of *La Belle*, a ship from the 1600s, lies 12 feet below sea level off the coast of Texas. You can use -12 to describe the wreck's depth.

Two numbers that are the same distance from 0 on a number line, but in opposite directions, are **opposites**. You can use integers to find opposites.

EXAMPLE Finding an Opposite

1 Find the opposite of -12.

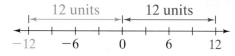

The opposite of -12 is 12, because -12 and $+12$ are both twelve units from 0, but in opposite directions.

 **for Help**

For help with ordering whole numbers, see Skills Handbook p. 654.

Quick Check

1. Find the opposite of each number.
   a. -8 **b.** 13   **c.** -22

The **absolute value** of a number is its distance from 0 on a number line. You write "the absolute value of -3" as $|-3|$.

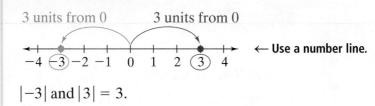

EXAMPLE **Finding Absolute Value**

② Find $|-3|$ and $|3|$.

3 units from 0   3 units from 0

← Use a number line.

-4 ⊖3 -2 -1 0 1 2 ③ 4

$|-3|$ and $|3| = 3$.

✅ Quick Check

● **2.** Find $|-8|$.

You can compare and order integers by graphing.

EXAMPLE **Comparing Integers**

Test Prep Tip

Of two integers on a
number line, the one
farther to the right is
greater.

③ Compare -7 and 1 using $<$, $=$, or $>$.

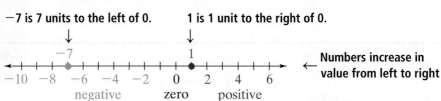

−7 is 7 units to the left of 0.   1 is 1 unit to the right of 0.

-7 1

Numbers increase in
value from left to right

-10 -8   -6   -4   -2   0   2   4   6
     negative   zero   positive

Since -7 is to the left of 1 on the number line, $-7 < 1$.

✅ Quick Check

● **3.** Compare -8 and -2 using $<$, $=$, or $>$.

EXAMPLE **Ordering Integers**

④ **Climate** Order the cities on the map
from coldest to warmest by graphing.

Lowest October Temperatures

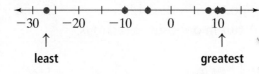

-30   -20   -10   0   10

↑   ↑
least   greatest

Coldest to warmest:
Fairbanks, Nome, Anchorage,
Valdez, Kodiak, Juneau.

ALASKA

Nome (−10°F)
Fairbanks (−27°F)
Anchorage (−5°F)
Valdez (8°F)
Juneau (11°F)
Kodiak (10°F)

SOURCE: National Weather Service

✅ Quick Check

● **4.** Order the numbers 3, −1, −4, and 2
from least to greatest.

1. **Vocabulary** How are integers different from whole numbers?

2. **Number Sense** Which two numbers have an absolute value of 1?

3. **Reasoning** Decide if each of the following is *always true,* *sometimes true,* or *never true* for all integer values of *x*.

   a. $|x| = x$ **b.** $|-x| = x$ **c.** $-|x| = x$ **d.** $|x| = -x$

Find the opposite of each number.

   4. 2   **5.** 4   **6.** 3   **7.** −2

Which number in each pair is farther away from zero?

   8. 4, −5   **9.** 2, 5   **10.** −1, −3   **11.** −12, 11

Homework Exercises

For more exercises, see Extra Skills and Word Problems.

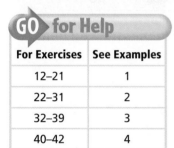

For Exercises	See Examples
12–21	1
22–31	2
32–39	3
40–42	4

Find the opposite of each number. You may find a number line helpful.

   12. −1   **13.** −8   **14.** 15   **15.** 11   **16.** 90

   17. −45   **18.** 20   **19.** −20   **20.** −123   **21.** 160

Find each absolute value.

   22. $|10|$ **23.** $|-11|$ **24.** $|-16|$ **25.** $|-1|$ **26.** $|4|$

   27. $|7|$ **28.** $|-3|$ **29.** $|-5|$ **30.** $|6|$ **31.** $|-10|$

Compare using <, =, or >.

   32. 0 ■ −2   **33.** −6 ■ −3   **34.** −14 ■ 14   **35.** −23 ■ 0

   36. −4 ■ −5   **37.** 17 ■ −18   **38.** 7 ■ −12   **39.** 5 ■ −1

Order the numbers from least to greatest.

   40. −4, 8, −2, −6, 3   **41.** −2, 0, 7, −1, −5   **42.** 2, −3, −7, 1, 10

43. **Guided Problem Solving** Scores in a golf tournament are reported by the number of strokes each player is above or below par. The scores for five players are −12, +2, −7, +4, and −3. Order the scores from the lowest under par to the greatest over par.
   ● Which score is farthest to the left on a number line?
   ● Which score is the next-farthest to the left?

44. **Writing in Math** A friend does not know how to order integers. Explain how to order 12, −4, and −5 from least to greatest.

45. a. Which city has the highest normal temperature?
   b. Which city has the greatest difference between its normal high and normal low temperatures?

Normal Temperatures for January (°F)

City	High	Low
Barrow, Alaska	−8	−20
Bismarck, N. Dak.	21	−1
Caribou, Maine	19	0
Duluth, Minn.	18	−1
Omaha, Nebr.	32	13

Source: National Climatic Data Center.
Go to **PHSchool.com** for a data update.
Web Code: arg-9041

Order from least to greatest.

46. $-14, -15, |-14|, 12, |-16|$

47. $-3551, -3155, -3151, -3515$

48. Sports In golf, the person with the lowest score is the winner. Rank the players at the right by ordering their scores from lowest to highest.

Player	Score
T. Woods	−12
V. Singh	−4
E. Els	+10
P. Mickelson	−3
R. Goosen	−5

49. Reasoning Write three numbers that are between −3 and −4. Are the numbers you wrote integers? Explain.

50. Challenge The number −5 is 5 units away from 0. This means that $|-5| = 5$. How far away is −3 from 2? What is $|-3 - 2|$?

Test Prep and Mixed Review

Practice

Multiple Choice

51. The table shows the lowest altitudes on four continents. Which continent has the lowest altitude?
   Ⓐ Africa
   Ⓑ Asia
   Ⓒ Europe
   Ⓓ North America

Lowest Altitudes

Continent	Altitude (ft below sea level)
Africa	−512
Asia	−1,348
Europe	−92
N. America	−282

52. Three friends have a 2.79-liter bottle of water to share. About how much water will each person receive?
   Ⓕ 950 mL   Ⓖ 95 mL   Ⓗ 760 mL   Ⓙ 76 mL

Write a number that makes each statement true.

53. 45.3 cm = ▦ mm   **54.** 26.78 mL = ▦ L   **55.** 256 mg = ▦ g

Find each quotient.

1. $4.2 \div 3.5$

2. $6.93 \div 2.2$

3. $3.1\overline{)5.27}$

Write the number that makes each statement true.

4. $5{,}000 \text{ mL} = \blacksquare \text{ cL}$

5. $410 \text{ cm} = \blacksquare \text{ m}$

6. $1.7 \text{ kg} = \blacksquare \text{ g}$

Compare using <, =, or >.

7. $-4 \; \blacksquare \; -5$

8. $-2 \; \blacksquare \; 0$

9. $|-7| \; \blacksquare \; |7|$

10. Baking A bread recipe calls for 0.24 L of milk. Your measuring cup is marked in milliliters. How many milliliters of milk do you need?

Vocabulary Builder

Learning New Math Terms

Your textbook has many features designed to help you as you read. When you aren't sure what a word means, keep these hints in mind.

- **Look for new vocabulary.** New vocabulary words are listed at the beginning of lessons. The first time vocabulary words are used in a lesson they look like **these words.**
- **Review the key concepts.** Important mathematical terms are explained in Key Concepts boxes.
- **Look for vocabulary tips.** They help you remember what a word means.
- **Use the glossary.** This book contains a glossary, which defines words and refers you to the page where the word is explained.
- **Read carefully.** If necessary, reread a section with new vocabulary until you understand all the information.

Exercises

Look through Lessons 1-1 to 1-3. Write down the page numbers where these items appear.

1. Vocabulary Tip

2. Key Concepts

3. New Vocabulary

Modeling Integer Addition and Subtraction

You can use models to add and subtract integers. Use chips of two different colors. Let one color represent positive integers and the other color represent negative integers.

ACTIVITY

1. Find 5 + 2.

Show 5 "+" chips.
Then add 2 "+" chips.

There are 7 "+" chips.
So 5 + 2 = 7.

 →

2. Find −5 + (−2).

Show 5 "−" chips.
Then add 2 "−" chips.

There are 7 "−" chips.
So −5 + (−2) = −7.

 →

To add integers with different signs, use zero pairs. These chips ⊕ ● are a *zero pair* because ⊕ ● = 0. Removing a zero pair does not change the sum.

3. Find 5 + (−2).

Show 5 "+" chips.
Then add 2 "−" chips.

Pair the "+" and "−" chips.
Remove the pairs.

There are 3 "+" chips left.
So 5 + (−2) = 3.

 → 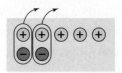 →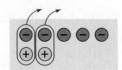

4. Find −5 + 2.

Show 5 "−" chips.
Then add 2 "+" chips.

Pair the "+" and "−" chips.
Remove the pairs.

There are 3 "−" chips left.
So −5 + 2 = −3.

 →

ACTIVITY

1. Find $5 - 2$.

Show 5 "+" chips.

Take away 2 "+" chips.

There are 3 "+" chips left. So $5 - 2 = 3$.

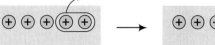

2. Find $-5 - (-2)$.

Show 5 "−" chips.

Take away 2 "−" chips.

There are 3 "−" chips left. So $-5 - (-2) = -3$.

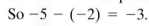

Sometimes you need to insert zero pairs in order to subtract.

3. Find $5 - (-2)$.

Show 5 "+" chips.

Insert two zero pairs. Then take away 2 "−" chips.

There are 7 "+" chips left. So $5 - (-2) = 7$.

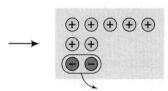

4. Find $-5 - 2$.

Show 5 "−" chips.

Insert two zero pairs. Then take away 2 "+" chips.

There are 7 "−" chips left. So $-5 - 2 = -7$.

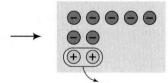

Exercises

Use chips or mental math to add or subtract the following integers.

1. $4 + 9$ **2.** $9 + (-3)$ **3.** $13 + (-8)$ **4.** $-14 + 6$

5. $-7 + (-12)$ **6.** $8 + (-11)$ **7.** $11 - 3$ **8.** $-4 - (-6)$

9. $5 - 12$ **10.** $-13 - 7$ **11.** $5 - (-9)$ **12.** $-8 - (-13)$

13. Write a rule for adding: (a) two positive integers, (b) two negative integers, and (c) two integers with different signs.

Algebra

1-7 Adding and Subtracting Integers

Check Skills You'll Need

1. Vocabulary Review
On a number line, how far from zero is the opposite of a number?

Find the opposite of each number.

2. 73   **3.** −49

4. 22   **5.** 13

6. −424   **7.** −13

 **for Help**
Lesson 1-6

What You'll Learn

To add and subtract integers and to solve problems involving integers

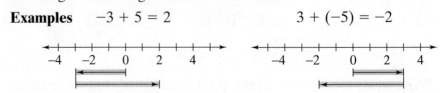 **New Vocabulary** additive inverses

Why Learn This?

You can add and subtract integers to keep track of money.

Suppose you start the week with no money. You borrow $10, and then you earn $10 babysitting to pay back the money you borrowed. You can add integers on a number line to see how much money you have.

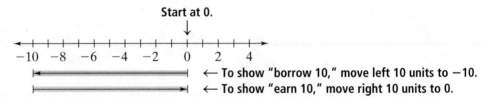

Start at 0.

← To show "borrow 10," move left 10 units to −10.
← To show "earn 10," move right 10 units to 0.

The number line shows that the sum of −10 and 10 is 0. You are back at zero where you started the week. Two numbers whose sum is 0 are **additive inverses.** You can use the following rules to add integers.

KEY CONCEPTS   **Adding Integers**

Same Sign The sum of two positive numbers is positive. The sum of two negative numbers is negative.

Examples $3 + 5 = 8$ $-3 + (-5) = -8$

Different Signs Find the absolute value of each number. Subtract the lesser absolute value from the greater. The sum has the sign of the integer with the greater absolute value.

Examples $-3 + 5 = 2$ $3 + (-5) = -2$

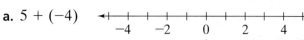

EXAMPLE **Adding Integers With a Number Line**

1 Use a number line to find each sum.

  a. $5 + (-4)$

The sum is 1.

  b. $-5 + (-2)$

The sum is -7.

✓ Quick Check

1. Use a number line to find each sum.
   a. $-8 + 1$ **b.** $-1 + (-7)$ **c.** $-6 + 6$

You can also add integers by using the absolute value of an integer.

EXAMPLE **Adding Integers**

2 Find each sum.

  a. $-18 + (-16) = -34$ ← Both integers are negative. The sum is negative.

  b. $-23 + 8$

   $|-23| = 23$ and $|8| = 8$ ← Find the absolute value of each integer.
   $23 - 8 = 15$ ← Subtract 8 from 23 because $|8| < |-23|$.
   $-23 + 8 = -15$ ← The sum has the same sign as -23.

✓ Quick Check

2. Find each sum.
   a. $-97 + (-65)$ **b.** $21 + (-39)$ **c.** $22 + (-22)$

You can subtract integers, too. The number line shows that $9 - 5 = 4$ and $9 + (-5) = 4$. Subtracting 5 is the same as adding -5.

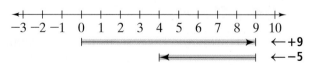

Subtract 5.   Add the opposite of 5.
$9 - 5 = 4$ $9 + (-5) = 4$
        └─────── The answer is 4. ───────┘

This result suggests a rule for subtracting integers.

> **KEY CONCEPTS** Subtracting Integers
>
> To subtract an integer, add its opposite.

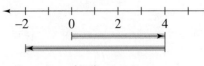 **EXAMPLES** Subtracting Integers

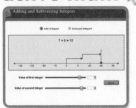
3 Find $4 - 6$.

Start at 0. Move 4 units right.
Then add the opposite of 6,
which is -6.

$$4 - 6 = 4 + (-6) = -2$$

4 Find $-2 - (-5)$.

Start at 0. Move 2 units left.
Then add the opposite of -5,
which is 5.

$$-2 - (-5) = -2 + 5 = 3$$

✓ Quick Check

3. Find $-6 - 1$.   4. Find $14 - (-7)$.

You can subtract integers to find differences between measurements.

EXAMPLE Application: Weather

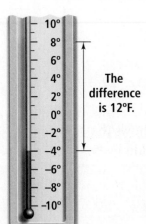

5 The temperature in Caribou, Maine, was 8°F at noon. By 10:00 P.M. the
temperature had dropped to -4°F. Find the change in the temperatures.

$8 - (-4)$ ← Subtract to find the difference.

$8 + 4$ ← Add the opposite of -4, which is 4.

12

The change in the temperatures is 12°F.

✓ Quick Check

5. **a.** During the biggest drop of the Mean Streak roller coaster in Ohio,
your altitude changes by -155 ft. The Texas Giant™ in Texas has a
-137 ft change. You want to know how much farther you drop on the
Mean Streak. Which expression can you use to solve this problem:
$-155 - (-137)$, or $-137 - (-155)$?

b. How much farther do you drop on the Mean Streak?

1. **Vocabulary** The absolute values of two numbers that are additive inverses will __?__ be the same.
   A always   B sometimes   C never

2. The sum of a number and −20 is 40. What is the number?

3. **Reasoning** When you add a positive number and a negative number, the positive addend will __?__ be less than the sum.
   A always   B sometimes   C never

Find each missing number.

4. $-7 + \blacksquare = -15$ 5. $7 - \blacksquare = -1$ 6. $-15 - \blacksquare = 15$

Homework Exercises

For more exercises, see Extra Skills and Word Problems.

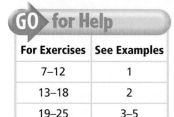

For Exercises	See Examples
7–12	1
13–18	2
19–25	3–5

Use a number line to find each sum.

7. $-5 + 4$ 8. $2 + (-8)$ 9. $-6 + 7$

10. $7 + 3$ 11. $-2 + (-3)$ 12. $-5 + (-5)$

Find each sum.

13. $-99 + 137$ 14. $27 + (-24)$ 15. $-42 + 42$

16. $-15 + 20$ 17. $-28 + (-32)$ 18. $126 + (-92)$

Find each difference. You may find a number line helpful.

19. $29 - 16$ 20. $-3 - (-3)$ 21. $17 - (-8)$

22. $-14 - 14$ 23. $12 - (-4)$ 24. $-15 - 2$

25. In the game of billiards called 14.1, players lose points if they receive penalties. Find the difference in the scores of the winner with 50 points and the opponent with −17 points.

GPS 26. **Guided Problem Solving** On Friday, Rosa borrowed $10 from her sister. The next day she paid back $5. Then on Monday she borrowed $4 more. How much did Rosa owe then?
   • How much money did Rosa owe before Monday?
   • How much money did Rosa still need to repay?

27. **Temperature** The highest temperature ever recorded in the United States was 134°F, measured at Death Valley, California. The coldest temperature, −80°F, was recorded at Prospect Creek, Alaska. What is the difference between these temperatures?

Write an addition expression for each model. Then find the sum.

28.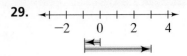

29.

30. $-7 + 6 = x$ 31. $x + 2 = 0$ 32. $x - 3 = -6$

The continental United States has four time zones. Consider time changes as positive when going east and negative when going west. The time is given in your zone. Find the time in the indicated time zone.

33. 6:00 A.M.; 2 time zones east

34. 9:00 P.M.; 3 time zones west

35. midnight; 2 time zones west

36. 12:00 A.M.; 1 time zone east

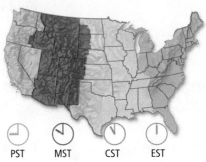

PST   MST   CST   EST

37. **Writing in Math** Your friend has trouble simplifying $20 - (-38)$. Write an explanation to help your friend.

38. **Challenge** You earn $5.25 an hour at your job in a restaurant but pay for any food you eat. On Friday, you receive a check for 7 hours of work, minus $8.90 for food. What is the amount on your check?

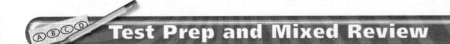

Test Prep and Mixed Review   Practice

Multiple Choice

39. Which expression is represented by the model below?

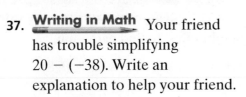

$$\begin{array}{c}
\text{A} \quad -5 + 0 \qquad\qquad \text{C} \quad -5 + 3 \\
\text{B} \quad -5 + 2 \qquad\qquad \text{D} \quad -5 + 5
\end{array}$$

40. The Fred Hartman Bridge in Baytown, Texas, is 381 m long. The Clark Bridge in Alton, Illinois, is 1.408 km. Which method can you use to find the difference in length of the bridges in meters?
    F Subtract 140.8 from 0.381.   H Subtract 381 from 1,408.
    G Divide 381 by 1,408.   J Multiply 1,408 by 100.

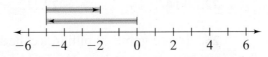

For Exercises	See Lesson
41–43	1-6

Compare. Use <, =, or >.

41. $-4 \; \blacksquare \; -10$ 42. $|-3| \; \blacksquare \; |3|$ 43. $16 \; \blacksquare \; |-23|$

Modeling Integer Multiplication

To remember the rules for multiplying integers, you can think of the effects that different operations would have on your bank account. The algebra tiles in the diagrams below show groups of integers added to or taken away from a bank account. Think about whether each action would make you feel positive or negative.

ACTIVITY

1. Use algebra tiles to make a "bank account" like the one at the right. Using tiles, add two groups of 3 to your account. Does adding the tiles make you feel positive or negative? Write an equation to represent this operation.

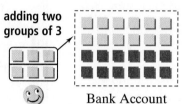

adding two groups of 3

Bank Account

2. Suppose you have to pay two video-rental late fees of $3 each. This is an example of adding negative integers to your account. Would this make you feel positive or negative? Use algebra tiles to model adding two groups of −3 to your account. Use the diagram below to write an equation for the operation.

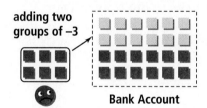

adding two groups of −3

Bank Account

3. Take away two groups of 4 from your account. Use the diagram below to write an equation representing this operation. Describe a situation that this operation might represent.

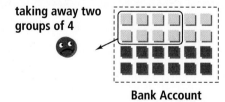

taking away two groups of 4

Bank Account

4. Suppose you have two library fines for $4 each. You *owe* this money, so you can use the integer −4 to represent each fine. If the librarian told you that you did not have to pay the fines, how would you feel? Use the diagram at the right to write an equation representing this operation.

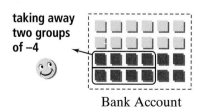

taking away two groups of −4

Bank Account

5. Use a table to summarize the rules for multiplying integers. Include all four possibilities. Describe any patterns you notice.

1-8 Multiplying and Dividing Integers

Check Skills You'll Need

1. Vocabulary Review
Two numbers that are *additive inverses* always have a sum of _?_ .

Find each sum.

2. 7 + (−3)

3. −4 + 9

4. −22 + (−13)

5. −17 + 17

for Help
Lesson 1-7

What You'll Learn

To multiply and divide integers and to solve problems involving integers

Why Learn This?

Balloonists watch their altitude when they fly. You can multiply integers to find change in altitude.

A balloon descends at a rate of 4 ft/min for 3 min. To multiply integers, think of multiplication as repeated addition.

$3(-4) = (-4) + (-4) + (-4) = -12$ ← **The balloon descends 12 ft.**

You can use number lines to multiply integers.

3(2) means three groups of 2.

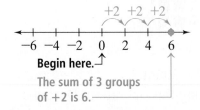

3(−2) means three groups of −2.

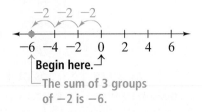

−3(2) is the opposite of three groups of 2.

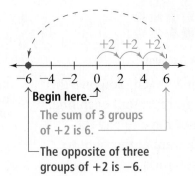

−3(−2) is the opposite of three groups of −2.

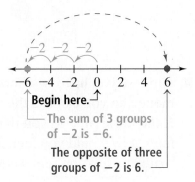

This pattern suggests the rules for multiplying integers.

Multiplying Integers

The product of two integers with the same sign is positive. The product of two integers with different signs is negative.

Examples $-3(-2) = 6$ $3(-2) = -6$

EXAMPLE Multiplying Integers

1 Find each product.

a. $5(3) = 15$ ← same signs; positive product → **b.** $-5(-3) = 15$

c. $5(-3) = -15$ ← different signs; negative product → **d.** $-5(3) = -15$

✓ Quick Check

1. Simplify the expression $-4(-7)$.

Since $-2(5) = -10$, you know that $-10 \div (-2) = 5$. The rules for dividing integers are similar to the rules for multiplying.

Dividing Integers

The quotient of two integers with the same sign is positive. The quotient of two integers with different signs is negative.

Examples $-10 \div (-2) = 5$ $10 \div (-2) = -5$

EXAMPLE Dividing Integers

2 A rock climber is at an elevation of 10,100 feet. Five hours later, she is at 7,340 feet. Use the formula below to find the climber's vertical speed.

$$\text{vertical speed} = \frac{\text{final elevation} - \text{initial elevation}}{\text{time}}$$

$$= \frac{7{,}340 - 10{,}100}{5}$$ ← Substitute 7,340 for final elevation, 10,100 for initial elevation, and 5 for time.

$$= \frac{-2{,}760}{5} = -552$$ ← Simplify. The negative sign means the climber is descending.

The climber's vertical speed is -552 feet per hour.

✓ Quick Check

2. Find the vertical speed of a climber who goes from an elevation of 8,120 feet to an elevation of 6,548 feet in three hours.

1. **Number Sense** A cave explorer descends at a rate of 6 m/min. Which expression CANNOT be used to find her depth after 4 min.?
   - Ⓐ $-6 + (-6) + (-6) + (-6)$
   - Ⓑ $\dfrac{-6}{4}$
   - Ⓒ $-6(4)$
   - Ⓓ $-6 - 6 - 6 - 6$

2. **Reasoning** The product of two integers is zero. What do you know about the value of at least one of the integers? Explain.

Find each missing number.

3. $-7 \times \blacksquare = -28$ 4. $-48 \div \blacksquare = 6$ 5. $\dfrac{\blacksquare}{-4} = -20$

Find each product or quotient.

6. $-2(-13)$ 7. $22 \div (-11)$ 8. $-4(9)$ 9. $-25 \div 5$

For more exercises, see Extra Skills and Word Problems.

GO for Help

For Exercises	See Examples
10–18	1
19–28	2

Find each product.

10. -5×4 11. $12(3)$ 12. $6(-6)$

13. $-7 \cdot (-3)$ 14. $-21 \times (-4)$ 15. $3(-33)$

16. $-12(-17)$ 17. $-35 \cdot 24$ 18. $-102(6)$

Find each quotient.

19. $\dfrac{36}{12}$ 20. $\dfrac{14}{-2}$ 21. $-42 \div 3$

22. $-80 \div -20$ 23. $-8\overline{)64}$ 24. $\dfrac{-27}{-9}$

25. $96 \div (-12)$ 26. $\dfrac{-195}{13}$ 27. $\dfrac{-242}{-1}$

28. **Hiking** In four hours, a hiker in a canyon goes from 892 ft to 256 ft above the canyon floor. Find the hiker's vertical speed.

29. **Guided Problem Solving** A submarine takes 6 min to dive from a depth of 29 m below the water's surface to 257 m below the surface. Find the submarine's vertical speed.

$$\text{vertical speed} = \frac{\text{final depth} - \text{initial depth}}{\text{time}} = \frac{\blacksquare - (-29)}{\blacksquare}$$

30. **Birds** A hawk soars at an altitude of 1,800 ft. If the hawk descends to the ground in 45 min, what is its vertical speed?

Algebra Find each value of *x*.

31. $x \cdot 9 = -9$ **32.** $x \div 3 = -5$ **33.** $\dfrac{-8}{x} = 4$

34. **Writing in Math** Explain how you would decide whether the product of three numbers is positive or negative.

35. **Hobbies** A scuba diver is 180 ft below sea level and rises to the surface at a rate of 30 ft/min. How long will the diver take to reach the surface?

36. **Open-Ended** Describe a situation that can be represented by the expression $4(-2)$.

37. In July, a sporting goods store offers a bike for $278. Over the next five months, the store reduces the price of the bike $15 each month.
 a. Write an expression for the total change in price after the months of discounts.
 b. What is the price of the bike at the end of five months?

38. **Challenge** A bank customer has $172 in a bank account. She withdraws $85 per month for the next 3 months. She also writes 4 checks for $45.75 each. How much money should she deposit to ensure that her balance is at least $25 at the end of the 3 months?

Test Prep and Mixed Review

Practice

Multiple Choice

39. Which model best represents the expression $2 \times (-4)$?

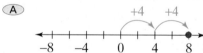
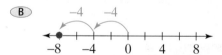
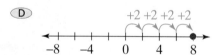

40. One day in January, five different cities had temperatures of $-12°F$, $5°F$, $-16°F$, $0°F$, and $73°F$. Which list shows the temperatures from least to greatest?
 F $-16°F, 5°F, -12°F, 0°F, 73°F$
 G $0°F, 5°F, -12°F, -16°F, 73°F$
 H $-16°F, -12°F, 0°F, 5°F, 73°F$
 J $73°F, -16°F, -12°F, 0°F, 5°F$

GO **for Help**

For Exercises	See Lesson
41–43	1-5

Write the number that makes each statement true.

41. $142 \text{ cm} = \blacksquare \text{ m}$ **42.** $0.67 \text{ L} = \blacksquare \text{ mL}$ **43.** $\blacksquare \text{ kg} = 3{,}400 \text{ g}$

Check Skills You'll Need

1. Vocabulary Review
Which property is illustrated by the statement
$1.6 + 4 = 4 + 1.6$?

Use mental math to simplify.

2. $2.5 + 7.1 + 2.5$

3. $6.4 + 6.2 + 5.6$

4. $8.1 + 3.8 + 8.1$

 **for Help**
Lesson 1-2

What You'll Learn

To use the order of operations and the Distributive Property

◀)) **New Vocabulary** order of operations, Distributive Property

Why Learn This?

Cash registers calculate the total price when a customer buys several items. You can use order of operations to be sure the total is correct.

Suppose you want to find the total price of one shirt and two hats. You can simplify $\$20 + \$5 \times 2$. If you add first, the price is $50. If you multiply first, then the price is $30.

To avoid confusion, mathematicians have agreed upon a particular **order of operations.**

HATS
$5.00
EACH

SHIRTS
$20.00
EACH

KEY CONCEPTS **Order of Operations**

Work inside grouping symbols.

1. Multiply and divide in order from left to right.

2. Add and subtract in order from left to right.

EXAMPLE **Using the Order of Operations**

1 Find the value of each expression.

a. $30 \div 3 + 2 \cdot 6$

$10 + 12$ ← Divide and multiply.

22 ← Add.

b. $30 \div (3 + 2) \cdot 6$

$30 \div 5 \cdot 6$ ← Work inside grouping symbols.

$6 \cdot 6$ ← Divide.

36 ← Multiply.

Vocabulary Tip

Grouping symbols include parentheses, ( ), brackets, [ ], and fraction bars, $\frac{3+5}{2}$.

✓ Quick Check

1. Find the value of each expression.

a. $7(-4 + 2) - 1$

b. $\frac{-40}{4} + 2 \cdot 5$

c. $\frac{8+4}{6} - 11$

EXAMPLE Application: Shopping

2 You want to buy two magazines and three greeting cards from the rack shown at the left. What is the total cost of the items?

Words   2 magazines   plus   3 greeting cards

Expression $2 \cdot 3.99$ + $3 \cdot 1.99$

$$2 \cdot 3.99 + 3 \cdot 1.99 = 7.98 + 5.97 \qquad \leftarrow \textbf{First multiply.}$$
$$= 13.95 \qquad\qquad \leftarrow \textbf{Then add.}$$

The total cost is $13.95.

✓ Quick Check

2. What is the total cost of 5 magazines and 2 greeting cards?

Note that $3(5 + 4) = 3(9)$, or 27. Note also that $3(5) + 3(4) = 15 + 12$, or 27. This is an example of the Distributive Property.

KEY CONCEPTS Distributive Property

Arithmetic	Algebra
$9(4 + 5) = 9(4) + 9(5)$	$a(b + c) = a(b) + a(c)$
$5(8 - 2) = 5(8) - 5(2)$	$a(b - c) = a(b) - a(c)$

You can use the Distributive Property to multiply numbers mentally.

EXAMPLE The Distributive Property in Mental Math

Look for opportunities for using mental math to make calculations easier.

3 **Mental Math** Use the Distributive Property to find $7(59)$.

What You Think

If I think of 59 as $(60 - 1)$, then $7(59)$ is the same as $7(60 - 1)$. I know that $7(60) - 7(1) = 420 - 7 = 413$.

Why It Works $7(59) = 7(60 - 1)$
$$= 7(60) - 7(1) \quad \leftarrow \textbf{Use the Distributive Property.}$$
$$= 420 - 7 \qquad\quad \leftarrow \textbf{Multiply.}$$
$$= 413 \qquad\qquad\; \leftarrow \textbf{Subtract.}$$

✓ Quick Check

3. Use the Distributive Property and mental math to find $9(14)$.

1. **Vocabulary** The Distributive Property combines which operation with addition or subtraction?

2. **Reasoning** Does $6(50 + 3) = (50 + 3)6$? Explain.

3. **Error Analysis** A classmate used the Distributive Property to find $11(9.2)$. What error did your classmate make?

> $11(9.2) = 11(9) + 11(2)$
> $= 99 + 22$
> $= 121$

Use the order of operations to fill in the blanks.

4. $4 \times 5 + 7 = \blacksquare + 7 = \blacksquare$

5. $20 - 2 \cdot 8 = \blacksquare - 16 = \blacksquare$

Use mental math to find the missing numbers. Then simplify.

6. $\blacksquare(4.8) = 6(5) - 6(\blacksquare)$

7. $5(32) = 5(\blacksquare) + 5(\blacksquare)$

Homework Exercises

For more exercises, see Extra Skills and Word Problems.

GO for Help

For Exercises	See Examples
8–16	1-2
17–25	3

Find the value of each expression.

8. $6 + 1 \cdot 5$

9. $-4 \div 2 + 9$

10. $5 - 8 \div 4$

11. $3 - 0 \cdot 11$

12. $18 \div 3 \cdot 2$

13. $100 - 7 \cdot 9$

14. $-12 \div 6 - (1 + 4)$

15. $48 \div (-4 \cdot 3) + 2$

16. **Coins** You buy some items at a store and pay with a $5 bill. You receive two quarters, two dimes, and three pennies as change. How much money do you receive?

Use the Distributive Property and mental math to find each product.

17. $5(29)$

18. $6(3.9)$

19. $9 \cdot 2.2$

20. $5(42)$

21. $7 \cdot 2.6$

22. $8(87)$

23. $4 \cdot 10.2$

24. $11.6(9)$

25. $1.1(22)$

26. **Guided Problem Solving** The sheet of plywood at the right has a piece cut from one corner. What is the area of the plywood?
   - What are the dimensions of the original piece of plywood?
   - What are the dimensions of the missing piece?

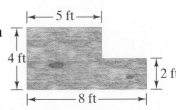

Copy each statement. Add parentheses to make it true.

27. $4 + 4 \div 4 - 4 = -2$

28. $4 \cdot 4 \div 4 + 4 = 2$

29. Architecture Use the floor plan at the right. Find the area of the floor.

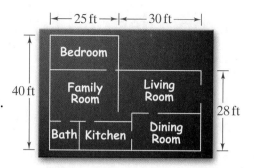

30. Business A florist is buying flowers to use in centerpieces. Each centerpiece has 3 lilies. There are 10 tables in all. Each lily costs $.98. Use mental math to find the cost of the lilies.

31. A freight train has 62 cars and a locomotive that is 65 ft long. Each car is 50 ft long. There is 3 ft of space between the locomotive and the first car and between each pair of cars. How long is the train?

32. Geometry Write two expressions to find the total area of the figure. Then find the area.

3 cm

5 cm   5 cm

33. Writing in Math Explain how you can use the Distributive Property in two different ways to calculate 4(110.5).

34. Challenge You go with five friends to an amusement park. The tickets originally cost $36.50 each, but you receive a group discount. The total cost is $198. What discount does each person receive?

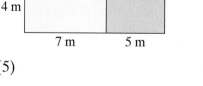
Test Prep and Mixed Review
Practice

Multiple Choice

35. What is the value of the expression $3 \times (-2) + 6 \div (-2) - 5$?
  Ⓐ −14   Ⓑ −9   Ⓒ −5   Ⓓ 4

36. Which expression does NOT represent the total area of the figure?
  Ⓕ 4(7 + 5)   Ⓗ 4(7) + 5
  Ⓖ 28 + 20   Ⓙ 4(7) + 4(5)

4 m

7 m   5 m

37. At 8 P.M., the wind-chill temperature was −9°F. One hour later, the wind-chill temperature had fallen to −29°F. Which number sentence shows this change?
  Ⓐ −29 − (−9) = −20   Ⓒ −9 − (−29) = 20
  Ⓑ 29 + (−9) = 20   Ⓓ 29 + (−9) = −20

GO for Help

For Exercises	See Lesson
38–41	1-8

Find each product.

38. −6(8)   **39.** 12(−5)   **40.** −7(−9)   **41.** 11(13)

Properties and Equality

Understanding number properties and equality will
help you solve algebraic equations.

EXAMPLE Understanding Number Properties

1 Use a number property or number sense to determine whether the
equation $8.86 + 12.51 + 1.23 = 1.23 + 8.86 + 12.51$ is true or false.
Justify your reasoning.

$$8.86 + 12.51 + 1.23 = 8.86 + 1.23 + 12.51 \quad \leftarrow$$ The order of the numbers has changed. This is an
example of the Commutative Property of Addition.

● True; the Commutative Property of Addition is being used.

EXAMPLE Understanding Equality

2 Use number properties, mental math, or number sense to determine
whether the scales are balanced. Justify your reasoning.

| 4.75 | 13.8 | 14.75 | 3.8 | **14.75 on the right is 10 more than 4.75 on the left. 13.8 on the left is 10 more than 3.8 on the right.** |

Each side has one block that is 10 more than a block on the other side.
● So the scale is balanced.

Exercises

**Determine whether each equation is true or false. Justify your
reasoning.**

1. $25.97 - (13 - 10) = (25.97 - 13) - 10$ **2.** $603 \times 9.5 = 603 \times 10 - 603 \times 0.5$

3. $530 \div 5 = 500 \div 5 + 30 \div 5$ **4.** $530 \div 5 = 530 \div 4 + 530 \div 1$

Determine whether each scale is balanced. Justify your reasoning.

5.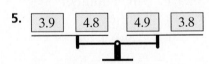

6.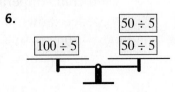

7. Make a balance-scale puzzle like those above. Write the solution.

1-10 Mean, Median, Mode, and Range

Check Skills You'll Need

1. **Vocabulary Review**
   When you simplify $2 + 6 \div 3$, which operation should you use first?

Find the value of each expression.

2. $(7 + 19) \div 2$

3. $\dfrac{-14 + 6}{2}$

4. $-9 + 4 \cdot 2 - 1$

for Help
Lesson 1-9

What You'll Learn

To describe data using mean, median, mode, and range

🔊 **New Vocabulary** mean, outlier, median, mode, range

Why Learn This?

You can use data to model the past and predict the future.

School officials use averages to predict how many new students will enroll next year. One average is the **mean,** which is the sum of the data divided by the number of data items.

New Students

22 20 23 5 25
Year 1 Year 2 Year 3 Year 4 Year 5

EXAMPLE Finding the Mean

1 Use the data in the graph above to find the mean number of new students per year.

$$\frac{22 + 20 + 23 + 5 + 25}{5} \quad \leftarrow \text{Divide the sum by the number of items.}$$

$$\frac{95}{5} = 19 \quad \leftarrow \text{Simplify.}$$

The mean is 19 students.

✔ Quick Check

1. Find the mean of 216, 230, 198, and 252.

An **outlier** is a data item that is much higher or lower than the other items in a set of data. In the data set in Example 1, 5 is an outlier.

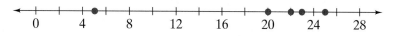

Since 5 is far less than the other values, the outlier decreases the mean. When a set of data has outliers, the mean may not be the best measure for describing the data.

The **median** of a data set is the middle value when the data are arranged in numerical order. The median of a set always separates the data into two groups of equal size. The median for an even number of data items is the mean of the two middle values.

EXAMPLE Finding the Median

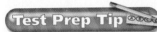

The median for an odd number of data items is the middle value.

2 **Multiple Choice** The table at the right shows data collected from student responses. What is the median number of times that students drank from the water fountain?

Ⓐ 2   Ⓑ 2.5   Ⓒ 3   Ⓓ 3.5

20 Responses to "How many times a day do you drink from the water fountain?"				
0	1	1	5	2
10	2	3	5	1
5	2	2	3	4
3	5	5	2	2

First write the data in order from least to greatest.

0 1 1 1 2 2 2 2 2 3 3 3 4 5 5 5 5 5 10

↑ ↑   **The two middle values are 2 and 3.**

$$\frac{2 + 3}{2} = 2.5 \quad \leftarrow \text{Find the mean of the two middle values.}$$

The median is 2.5. The answer is B.

✓ Quick Check

2. Find the median in the set of data: −5   −1   3   −18   −2   2.

The **mode** of a data set is the item that occurs with the greatest frequency. A set of data may have more than one mode. There is no mode when all the data items occur the same number of times. The mode is a useful measure for data with values that are repetitive or nonnumerical.

EXAMPLE Finding the Mode

3 Find the mode of the data at the left.

Make a table to organize the data.

There are two modes, rose and daisy.

Favorite Flowers of Ten People Surveyed

rose	rose
pansy	peony
pansy	daisy
daisy	rose
daisy	orchid

Rose	Pansy	Peony	Daisy	Orchid
///	//	/	///	/

✓ Quick Check

3. Find the mode(s).
   a. 17   16   18   17   16   17   **b.** 3.2   3.7   3.5   3.7   3.5   3.2
   c. pen, pencil, marker, marker, pen, pen, pen, pencil, marker

The **range** of a data set is the difference between the greatest and the least values. The range describes the spread of the data. You find the range by subtracting the least value from the greatest value.

> **EXAMPLE** **Finding Range**

4 **Climate** Temperatures at Verkhoyansk, Russia, have ranged from a low of −90°F to a high of 98°F. Find the temperature range in Verkhoyansk.

$$98 - (-90) = 98 + 90 \quad \leftarrow \text{Add the opposite of } -90, \text{ which is } 90.$$
$$= 188 \quad \leftarrow \text{Simplify.}$$

The temperature range in Verkhoyansk is 188°F.

✓ Quick Check

4. Record temperatures in Texas set in the 1930s were a low of −23°F and a high of 120°F. Find the temperature range.

✓ Check Your Understanding

1. **Vocabulary** A data item that can greatly affect the mean of a set of data is called a(n) _?_ .

2. If you increase every number in a data set by 2, what will happen to the mean?

3. **Mental Math** A data set consists of the integers 1 to 9. What is the median of this data set?

4. A data set has a mean of 3, a median of 4, and a mode of 5. Which number *must be* in the data set—3, 4, or 5? Explain.

5. **Choose a Method** Is mean or median the better way to describe the data below? Explain your choice.
   2 4 5 5 5 6 8 10 45

Find the mean, median, mode, and range of each set of data.

6. 1 2 3 5 5   7. 3 3 3 4 4 4

8. **Error Analysis** Each day your tennis team practices for at least one hour and for at most five hours. Your teammate does the calculation shown. What mistake does your teammate make?

> Times (hours): 1, 3, 4, 5, 3
> Mean: 1 + 3 + 4 + 5 + 3
> Mean = 16 hours

For more exercises, see Extra Skills and Word Problems.

GO for Help

For Exercises	See Examples
9–12	1
13–16	2
17–19	3
20–23	4

Find the mean of each set of data.

9. 8   12   6   9   5

10. 3.4   0.53   1.3   2.9   1.47   0.24

11. −6   3   −2   6   7   −3   −5   8

12. −17   32   −9   0   52   12   −14

Find the median of each set of data.

13. 5   10   18   3   6   2   9   1   8   15   10

14. 23   18   67   32   54   41   70   11   56   33   41   58

15. −4   −1   −8   −5   −6   −2   7   2   0   −1   −7   2

16. 2.1   −41.2   0.13   −7.1   −1.68   8.32   2.45   7.89   3.19

Find the mode(s).

17. 51   58   54   58   51   57   55   58   51   54

18. 1   12   2   21   22   1   13   31   32   31   12

19. red, blue, white, white, red, red, red, blue, white, blue

Find the range.

20. from 24 to −2   **21.** from −3 to 7   **22.** from −145 to 234

23. Video game scores vary from 6 to −6. What is the range?

24. Guided Problem Solving A city has kept records on cloud cover for 47 years. The mean number of cloudless days in October is 13. How many cloudless days occurred in October during that time?

mean number of cloudless days in October   ■
number of years of records   ×   ■
total number of cloudless days   ■

25. There are eight dogs in a kennel. Each of the two small dogs needs 1 cup of dry food per day. Each of the three medium-sized dogs needs 2 cups per day. Each of the remaining three large dogs needs 4 cups per day. What is the mean number of cups of food required per dog each day?

26. Find the mean, median, and mode for the hours of practice before a concert: 2   1   0   1   5   3   4   2   0   3   1   2.

27. Estimation A company's mean weekly profit is $30,021. Estimate how much profit the company will make in a year.

28. The table at the right shows the average life expectancy for several animals.
  a. Find the mean, median, mode, and range of the data.
  b. Choose a Method Which measure best describes the data? Explain.

Make a data set for each condition.

29. mode > median   **30.** median = mean

31. Writing in Math Explain how it is possible for two sets of data to consist of different numbers but have the same mean, the same median, and the same mode. Give an example.

32. Music When you join a music club, you get six CDs for 1 cent each. You buy eight more CDs at $7.99 each. What is the mean price you pay for a CD?

33. Challenge According to the U.S. Department of Agriculture, the mean annual egg consumption in the United States is 258.2 eggs per person. Find the number of cartons of eggs needed in a year for an average family of four. Each carton holds one dozen eggs.

Average Life Expectancy

Animal	Years
Bison	15
Cow	15
Deer	8
Donkey	12
Elk	15
Goat	8
Horse	20
Moose	12
Pig	10
Sheep	12

SOURCE: *The World Almanac*

Test Prep and Mixed Review **Practice**

Multiple Choice

34. The table shows Tammy's times in the 100-meter dash. Which number could be added to make the median and mode of the set equal?
  Ⓐ 11.6   Ⓒ 12
  Ⓑ 11.8   Ⓓ 12.25

35. In a golf tournament, five players had scores of −6, +5, +1, −2, and −8. Which expression can be used to find the average score?
  Ⓕ $(6 + 5 + 1 + 2 + 8) \div 5$
  Ⓖ $6 + 5 + 1 + 2 + 8 \div 5$
  Ⓗ $[-6 + 5 + 1 + (-2) + (-8)] \div 5$
  Ⓙ $-6 + 5 + 1 + (-2) + (-8) \div 5$

Tammy's Times in the 100-meter Dash

Trial	Time (seconds)
1	12.8
2	11.96
3	12.4
4	11.6
5	12.25
6	■

Order each set of numbers from least to greatest.

36. 32   35   −21   −42   29   **37.** 213   231   312   123   321

For Exercises	See Lesson
36–37	1-6

Box-and-Whisker Plots

A **box-and-whisker plot** is a graph that summarizes a data set along a number line.

ACTIVITY

Points Scored per Player

Team A	Team B
6	5
2	9
8	7
10	9
3	13
15	11
4	13
20	15
7	14
4	10

Step 1 Arrange the data for Team A from least to greatest. Find the median. This value is called the middle quartile.

2   3   4   4   6   7   8   10   15   20
The median is 6.5.

Step 2 Find the median of the lower half of the data. This value is the lower quartile.

2   3   4   4   6
The median is 4.

Step 3 Find the median of the upper half of the data. This value is the upper quartile.

7   8   10   15   20
The median is 10.

Step 4 Identify the least and greatest values of the full data set.

least value = 2   greatest value = 20

Step 5 Draw a number line. Plot the points of the 5 values you found in Steps 1–4 above the number line.

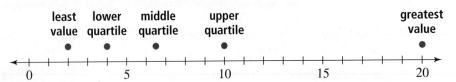

Step 6 Draw a box using the lower and upper quartile points as the ends of the box. Then draw lines, or whiskers, from the ends of the box to the least and greatest values.

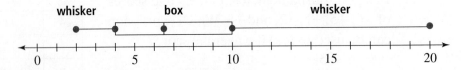

Exercises

1. Make a box-and-whisker plot using the data for Team B.

2. Compare your graph to the one in the activity. What do the two graphs tell you about how the players on each team score?

Writing Gridded Responses

Some tests call for gridded responses. You find a numerical answer. Then you write the answer at the top of the grid and fill in the corresponding bubbles below. You must use the grid correctly.

EXAMPLES

1 The mean of 0.2, 0.4, 0.6, and 0.8 is 0.5. Record this answer.

You can write the answer as 0.5 or .5. Here are the two ways to enter these answers.

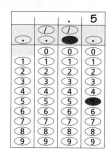

2 Cindy had $19.25 before she went shopping. She spent $18.50 on purchases that day. How much money, in dollars, did she have left?

$$\begin{array}{r} 19.25 \\ -\ 18.50 \\ \hline 0.75 \end{array}$$

The answer is 0.75. You grid this as 0.75 or .75.

Exercises

Write the number you would grid for each answer. If you have a grid, complete it.

1. A bottle of apple juice holds 3.79 L. A bottle of orange juice holds 1.89 L. How many more liters does the bottle of apple juice hold?

2. You are organizing a pet show. On the first morning, 40 dogs will be shown. For each dog, you will allow one minute to set up and four minutes for showing. How many minutes will the morning session last?

3. A student scores 88, 93, 79, and 68 on four quizzes. What is the mean of the scores?

Chapter 1 Review

Vocabulary Review

◀))) absolute value (p. 31)
additive inverses (p. 38)
Associative Property of
  Addition (p. 9)
Associative Property of
  Multiplication (p. 15)
Commutative Property of
  Addition (p. 9)

Commutative Property of
  Multiplication (p. 15)
compatible numbers (p. 5)
Distributive Property (p. 49)
Identity Property of Addition
  (p. 9)
Identity Property of
  Multiplication (p. 15)
integers (p. 31)

mean (p. 53)
median (p. 54)
mode (p. 54)
opposites (p. 31)
order of operations (p. 48)
outlier (p. 53)
range (p. 55)
Zero Property (p. 15)

Choose the correct term to complete each sentence.

1. The __?__ combines multiplication with sums and differences.

2. The statement $3 + (5 + 7) = (3 + 5) + 7$ demonstrates the __?__.

3. The __?__ of a number is its distance from 0 on a number line.

4. To find the __?__, take the data item that occurs most often.

5. By the __?__, you know that $4 + 7 \cdot 3$ equals 25 and not 33.

Go **O**nline
PHSchool.com
For: Online vocabulary quiz
Web Code: arj-0151

Skills and Concepts

Lesson 1-1
• To estimate using rounding, front-end estimation, and compatible numbers

You can estimate decimals using rounding, front-end estimation, or **compatible numbers.**

Use any estimation strategy to calculate. Name the strategy you used.

6. $50.3 \div 6.9$ 7. $98.52 - 46.91$ 8. 6.9×8.92 9. $1.46 + 4.38$

Lessons 1-2, 1-3, 1-4
• To add and subtract decimals and to do mental math using the properties of addition
• To multiply decimals and to do mental math using the properties of multiplication
• To divide decimals and to solve problems by dividing decimals

To add or subtract decimals, align the decimal points. To multiply decimals, use the sum of the number of decimal places in the factors. To divide decimals, rewrite the problem so the divisor is a whole number.

Use the **commutative properties** to change the order in an expression. Use the **associative properties** to change the grouping.

Simplify.

10. $23.68 \div 6.4$ 11. $0.54 + 0.027$ 12. $4.6 - 3.87$ 13. 2.7×6.25

14. **Shopping** At a grocery store, you buy hamburger weighing 1.42 lb, sausage weighing 2.16 lb, and chicken weighing 3.73 lb. How many pounds of meat do you buy?

Lesson 1-5
- To use and convert metric units of measure

To change a measure from one unit to another, find a relationship between the two units and then multiply.

Write the number that makes each statement true.

15. 4.56 mm = ▦ cm   **16.** 14.2 L = ▦ mL   **17.** 0.34 kg = ▦ g

18. You have three lengths of kite string measuring 18.2 m, 927 cm, and 0.044 km. What is the total length of kite string in meters?

Lesson 1-6
- To compare and order integers and to find absolute values

Opposites are two numbers that are the same distance from 0 on a number line, but in opposite directions. **Integers** are the set of positive whole numbers, their opposites, and zero. The **absolute value** of an integer is its distance from 0 on a number line.

Compare. Use <, =, or >.

19. -7 ▦ 7 **20.** $|-3|$ ▦ $|3|$ **21.** 9 ▦ $|-4|$ **22.** $|8|$ ▦ -15

Lessons 1-7, 1-8
- To add and subtract integers and to solve problems involving integers
- To multiply and divide integers and to solve problems involving integers

The sum of two positive integers is positive. The sum of two negative integers is negative. To find the sum of two integers with different signs, find the absolute value of each integer. Subtract the lesser absolute value from the greater. The sum has the sign of the integer with the greater absolute value. To subtract an integer, add its opposite.

The product or quotient of two integers with the same sign is positive. The product or quotient of two integers with different signs is negative.

Simplify.

23. $14 + (-8)$ **24.** $17 - (-12)$ **25.** $-5 \cdot 6$ **26.** $125 \div (-5)$

Lessons 1-9, 1-10
- To simplify numerical expressions involving order of operations
- To describe data using mean, median, mode, and range

Use the **order of operations** to simplify an expression. The **Distributive Property** combines multiplication with addition or subtraction. The **mean, median, mode,** and **range** of a set of data, along with any **outliers,** reflect the characteristics of the data.

Find the value of each expression.

27. $(7.3 + 4) \div 4 + 0.3 \cdot 2$ **28.** $8 - 6.2 \div 5 + 7(0.91)$

29. $20 + 24 \div 2 - (8 + 5)$ **30.** $8(20.3)$

31. Pets The data set below gives the weights, in ounces, of one-month-old hamsters. Find the mean, median, mode, and range of the data set.
4, 1, 3, 2, 2, 2, 1, 1, 2, 1, 2, 3

Chapter 1 Test

Go Online For: Online chapter test
PHSchool.com Web Code: ara-0152

Estimate using any estimation strategy.

1. $289.76 - 52$
2. $7.532 + 2.19$
3. $97.6 \cdot 3.4$
4. $68.5 \div 7.02$

5. Use front-end estimation to estimate the sum of the following grocery items to the nearest dollar: $7.99, $2.79, $4.15, $2.09.

Simplify.

6. $9.53 + 3.29$
7. $8 - 6.17$
8. $10.5 - 9.67$
9. $0.57 + 1.825$

10. **Money** You have a balance of $213.15 in a savings account. You make withdrawals of $68.94 and $128.36. Find your new balance.

11. **Decorations** For a class party, the student council purchases 42 balloons at $1.85 each. Estimate the total cost of the balloons.

Identify each property shown.

12. $9.5 + 6.1 + 2.3 = 9.5 + 2.3 + 6.1$

13. $7.2 \times (1.6 \times 3.9) = (7.2 \times 1.6) \times 3.9$

14. $5.1(7.4 - 3.1) = 5.1(7.4) - 5.1(3.1)$

Find each quotient. Round to the nearest tenth.

15. $1.2 \div 0.3$
16. $1.58 \div 1.1$

Find the value of each expression.

17. $9.5 - 7.1 + 2.4 \cdot 0.5 - 1.3$

18. $\frac{8.25}{4} \cdot (0.6 - 0.54) + 8.3$

Change each measurement to the given unit.

19. $4.2 \text{ cm} = \blacksquare \text{ m}$
20. $5.17 \text{ kL} = \blacksquare \text{ L}$
21. $6 \text{ kg } 14 \text{ g} = \blacksquare \text{ g}$
22. $2 \text{ km } 7 \text{ m} = \blacksquare \text{ km}$

Compare. Use <, =, or >.

23. $-12 \blacksquare 12$
24. $-9 \blacksquare -5$
25. $|-7| \blacksquare -8$
26. $|-6| \blacksquare 6$

Mental Math Find each product mentally using the Distributive Property.

27. $6(10.5)$
28. $3(98)$

Write an expression for each model. Then find the sum.

29.

30.

31. Write these integers in order from least to greatest: 2 5 0 −7 −3.

Simplify.

32. $-3 + 5$
33. $-2 + (-2)$
34. $-4 - 9$
35. $-8 \cdot (-9)$
36. $48 \div (-3)$
37. $-6(11)$

38. **Produce** The weights of four bags of apples are 3.5 lb, 3.8 lb, 4.2 lb, and 3.5 lb. What is the median weight?

39. **Fitness** Suppose you plan to ride your bicycle a total of 257.5 mi in a benefit ride. How many miles must you average each day to finish the ride in 4.5 days?

40. **Writing in Math** When you calculate a mean, the sign of the quotient always depends on the sign of the dividend. Why?

41. **Sports** On successive plays, the home football team gains 12 yd, loses 3 yd, loses 5 yd, gains 15 yd, and runs 16 yd for a touchdown. What is the average gain or loss in yards per play?

42. Find the mean, median, and mode for the following junior league bowling scores: 45, 56, 134, 55, 78, 121, 38, 66, 56, 41.

Reading Comprehension

Read each passage and answer the questions that follow.

> **Big Shows** Successful films earn large amounts of money for movie studios. Five movies that have earned particularly large amounts of money in the United States, and their approximate total receipts, are: *TITANIC* (1997), $600 million; *Star Wars* (1977), $460 million; *Star Wars: The Phantom Menace* (1999), $430 million; *E.T.* (1982), $400 million; and *Jurassic Park* (1993), $360 million.

1. What are the mean total box office receipts of the five films?
   - (A) $400 million
   - (B) $430 million
   - (C) $450 million
   - (D) $460 million

2. *Star Wars: The Phantom Menace* sold about $64,811,000 worth of tickets on its opening weekend. Which is the best estimate of the portion of its total sales that took place the first weekend?
   - (F) 0.1
   - (G) 0.15
   - (H) 0.35
   - (J) 0.5

3. What is the median earnings of the films?
   - (A) $400 million
   - (B) $430 million
   - (C) $450 million
   - (D) $460 million

4. Between which pair of films is the range in total receipts the greatest?
   - (F) *Star Wars* and *Jurassic Park*
   - (G) *TITANIC* and *Star Wars*
   - (H) *Star Wars* and *E.T.*
   - (J) *E.T.* and *Jurassic Park*

> **Parity** We say that two integers have the same *parity* if they are both even or both odd. So 2 and 12 have the same parity, and 51 and 139 have the same parity. If one number is even and the other number is odd, then we say they have different or opposite parities. 2 and 51 have opposite parities.

5. Two integers have the same parity. Describe the parity of their sum.
   - (A) same as the two numbers
   - (B) opposite of the two numbers
   - (C) same if the numbers are odd
   - (D) opposite if the numbers are odd

6. Two integers have the same parity. Describe the parity of their difference.
   - (F) same as the two numbers
   - (G) opposite of the two numbers
   - (H) same only if the numbers are even
   - (J) same only if the numbers are odd

7. Two integers have the same parity. Describe the parity of their product.
   - (A) same as the two numbers
   - (B) opposite of the two numbers
   - (C) same only if the numbers are odd
   - (D) opposite only if the numbers are odd

8. Two integers have different parity. Describe their product.
   - (F) always even
   - (G) always odd
   - (H) sometimes even
   - (J) odd if the smaller number is odd

Applying Integers

Energy Field Too hot? Open a window. Too cold? Put on a sweater. Sound familiar? Heating and air-conditioning systems can let you live more comfortably in a wide range of weather conditions, but they cost money. The cost of heating or cooling a home depends on many things, including the outdoor air temperature, the indoor air temperature, and the cost of fuel.

Ancient Thermometer
In this thermometer, changing temperatures cause the colored glass balls to rise and fall in the water inside the glass tubes.

Put It All Together

Data File Use the data on these two pages and on page 673 to answer these questions.

1. Use the heating cost formula to estimate the cost of heating a house to 68°F for one day when the average outside temperature is 20°F.

2. **a. Open-Ended** Choose three places from the table on page 673. Use the heating cost formula to estimate the cost of heating a house to 68°F in each place on the coldest day.

   b. Use a number line to display your answers to part (a). Include the location and the outdoor temperature.

3. You can use the equation below to calculate the cost of changing the indoor temperature from 68°F to 66°F.

   $$\frac{\text{change}}{\text{in cost}} = \text{new cost} - \text{old cost} = \text{cost at 66°F} - \text{cost at 68°F}$$

   a. Use the low temperature for Indianapolis, Indiana. Calculate the cost of changing the temperature to 68°F.

   b. Reasoning Explain why your answer to part (a) is a negative number.

4. **Writing in Math** Where do you think changing the indoor temperature from 68°F to 70°F will cost the most? Explain. Check your prediction by calculating the increased cost in several locations. Explain your results.

Heating Cost Formula (°F)

$$\frac{\text{daily heating}}{\text{cost (\$)}} = 0.15 \times \left(\frac{\text{indoor}}{\text{temperature}} - \frac{\text{outdoor}}{\text{temperature}}\right)$$

Weather Around the World
Photographs from space show giant swirls of clouds around Earth. These swirls show the constant movement of gases that gives us our weather.

Forms of Precipitation

Water droplets less than 0.5 mm in diameter fall as drizzle.

Water droplets combine to form raindrops 0.5–5.0 mm in diameter.

Rising air

Rain From Clouds Not Reaching Freezing Level

Water droplets fall as rain.

Snowflakes melt to fall as rain.

Snowflakes from ice crystals fall as snow.

Rising air

Rain and Snow From Clouds Reaching Freezing Level

Vertical air currents toss frozen water droplets up and down.

Alternate freezing and melting builds up layers of ice.

Ice falls as hailstones.

Rising air

Hail

Go Online
PHSchool.com
For: Information about weather
Web Code: are-0153

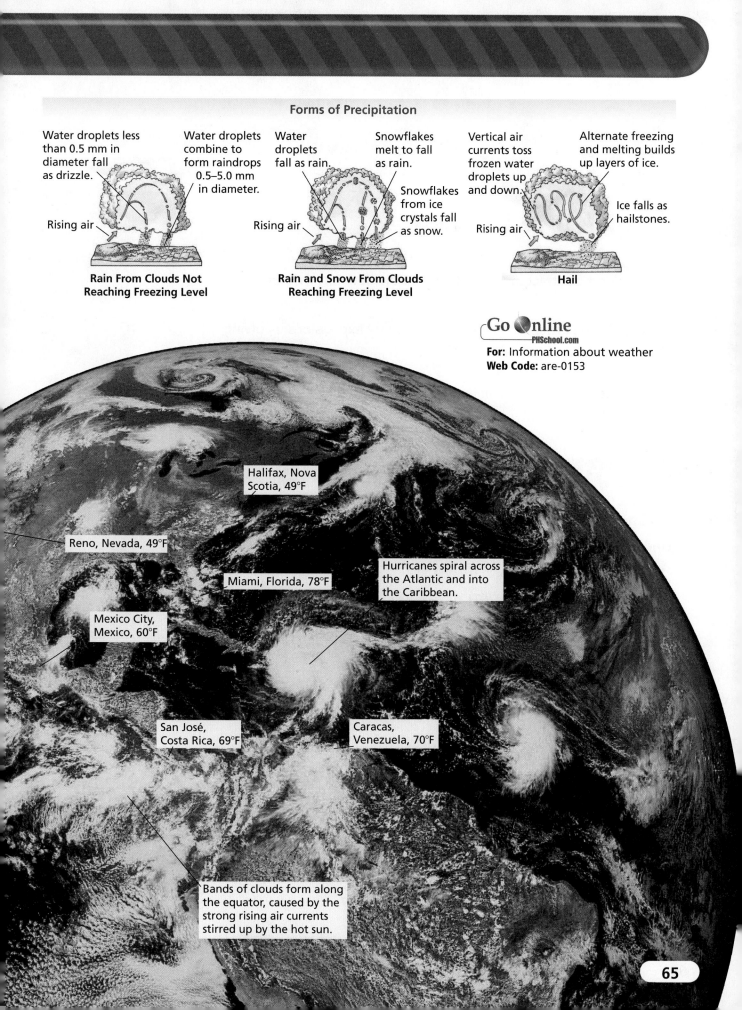

Halifax, Nova Scotia, 49°F

Reno, Nevada, 49°F

Hurricanes spiral across the Atlantic and into the Caribbean.

Miami, Florida, 78°F

Mexico City, Mexico, 60°F

San José, Costa Rica, 69°F

Caracas, Venezuela, 70°F

Bands of clouds form along the equator, caused by the strong rising air currents stirred up by the hot sun.

CHAPTER 2

Exponents, Factors, and Fractions

What You've Learned

- In Chapter 1, you compared and ordered integers.
- You added, subtracted, multiplied, and divided decimals and integers.
- You used the order of operations to simplify expressions involving decimals and integers.

 Check Your Readiness

GO for Help

For Exercises	See Lesson
1–4	1-2
5–10	1-6
11–14	1-8
15–17	1-9

Adding and Subtracting Decimals

Find each sum or difference.

1. $2.1 + 3.4$ **2.** $6.02 - 4.597$

3. $7.0 - 3.11$ **4.** $671.02 + 6.427$

Comparing Integers

Compare. Use $<$, $=$, or $>$.

5. $|-2| \ \blacksquare \ |-5|$ **6.** $|11| \ \blacksquare \ |-13|$ **7.** $10 \ \blacksquare \ |-10|$

8. $-8 \ \blacksquare \ |-8|$ **9.** $|9| \ \blacksquare \ |-14|$ **10.** $|-1| \ \blacksquare \ 0$

Multiplying and Dividing Integers

Find each product or quotient.

11. $-9 \cdot 3$ **12.** $-3 \cdot (-3)$ **13.** $27 \div (-3)$ **14.** $-16 \div (-4)$

Order of Operations and the Distributive Property

Find the value of each expression.

15. $12 + 4(16 \div 4)$ **16.** $30 \div 3 - 4 \cdot 2$ **17.** $(8 + 4) \div 4 - 2$

What You'll Learn Next

- In this chapter, you will compare and order rational numbers.

- You will convert between fractions and decimals.

- You will use the order of operations to simplify expressions with exponents.

 Problem Solving Application On pages 116 and 117, you will work an extended activity on fractions.

◀)) Key Vocabulary

- base (p. 68)
- composite number (p. 75)
- equivalent fraction (p. 82)
- exponent (p. 68)
- greatest common factor (GCF) (p. 75)
- improper fraction (p. 91)
- least common denominator (LCD) (p. 87)
- least common multiple (LCM) (p. 74)
- mixed number (p. 91)
- prime number (p. 75)
- rational number (p. 102)

✓ Check Skills You'll Need

1. **Vocabulary Review** Using the *order of operations,* do you multiply factors before or after you add?

Find the value of each expression.

2. $5 - 1 \cdot 3$

3. $(5 - 1) \cdot 3$

4. $10 \div 2 - 3 \cdot 5$

5. $(1 + 99) \div 10 - 9$

GO for Help
Lesson 1-9

What You'll Learn

To write and simplify expressions with exponents

🔊 **New Vocabulary** exponent, base, power

Why Learn This?

Googol is a large number written as the digit one followed by 100 zeros. Writing out the number takes a long time. You can use exponents to write googol and other large numbers in a easier way. For example, you can write googol as 10^{100}.

An **exponent** tells you how many times a number, or **base,** is used as a factor.

$$\underbrace{5^3}_{\substack{\text{exponent} \\ \text{base}}} = \underbrace{5 \cdot 5 \cdot 5}_{\text{The base is used as a factor three times.}} = \overbrace{125}^{\text{value of the expression}}$$

A number that can be expressed using an exponent is called a **power.** The number 125 is a power of 5 because it can be written as 5^3.

EXAMPLE Writing Expressions Using Exponents

1 Write $3 \cdot 3 \cdot 3 \cdot 3 \cdot 3$ using an exponent.

$3 \cdot 3 \cdot 3 \cdot 3 \cdot 3 = 3^5$ ← 3 is the base. 5 is the exponent.

✓ Quick Check

1. Write each product using exponents.
   a. $44 \cdot 44 \cdot 44 \cdot 44$ **b.** $(-2) \cdot (-2)$

You can find the value of an expression with exponents by writing it as the product of repeated factors. You can also use a scientific calculator.

Video Tutor Help

Visit: PHSchool.com
Web Code: are-0775

EXAMPLE   Application: Geography

2 Gibraltar is at the mouth of the Mediterranean Sea. Its area is about the same as the area of a square 1.5 mi on a side. Find Gibraltar's area.

Method 1 Since $A = s^2$, compute to find 1.5^2.

$$1.5^2 = (1.5)(1.5) \quad \leftarrow \text{Write as a product of repeated factors.}$$
$$= 2.25 \quad \leftarrow \text{Multiply.}$$

Method 2 Use a geometric model. In the model, each side of the blue square has a length of 1.5. The total area in blue equals one whole square plus two half squares plus one quarter square. The total is 2.25 squares. The area of Gibraltar is about 2.25 mi^2.

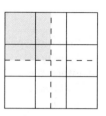

▣ Calculator Tip

You can use the ∧ or y^x key to find a power.

To find 1.5^2, use 1.5 ∧ 2 ▤ 2.25 or 1.5 y^x 2 ▤ 2.25.

If your calculator does not have an exponent key, use 1.5 ✕ 1.5 ▤ 2.25.

✅ Quick Check

2. Simplify. Use paper and pencil, a model, or a calculator.
   a. 3^5 **b.** 10^9 **c.** 3.1^2

The order of operations includes expressions with exponents.

> **KEY CONCEPTS**   Order of Operations
>
> **1.** Do all operations within grouping symbols first.
>
> **2.** Evaluate any term(s) with exponents.
>
> **3.** Multiply and divide in order from left to right.
>
> **4.** Add and subtract in order from left to right.

The expressions -2^4 and $(-2)^4$ are not equivalent. The expression -2^4 means the opposite, or the negative, of 2^4. The base of -2^4 is 2, not -2.

Vocabulary Tip

The phrase *Please Excuse My Dear Aunt Sally* can help you remember the order of operations. The first letter of each word in the phrase stands for *Parentheses, Exponents, Multiplication, Division, Addition,* and *Subtraction.*

EXAMPLE   Simplifying Using Order of Operations

3 Simplify $-2^4 + (3 - 5)^4$.

$$-2^4 + (3 - 5)^4 = -2^4 + (-2)^4 \quad \leftarrow \text{Do operations in parentheses.}$$
$$= -16 + 16 \quad \leftarrow \text{Find the values of the powers.}$$
$$= 0 \quad \leftarrow \text{Add.}$$

✅ Quick Check

3. Simplify.
   a. $(-3)^3$ **b.** -3^3 **c.** $(3 + 5)^2 - 2$

Check Your Understanding

For: Order of Operations
Activity
Use: Interactive
Textbook, 2-1

1. **Vocabulary** How is an exponent different from a base?

2. Write an expression for *the opposite of the fourth power of 2.*

Simplify each expression.

3. $-1 \cdot 5^4$　　4. $(-5)^4$　　5. $2^4 \cdot (7-6)^3$

Science **Match each fact with the appropriate power.**

6. number of moons orbiting Earth

7. planets in the solar system

8. freezing point of water in degrees Fahrenheit

A. 2^5
B. 3^2
C. 1^1

Homework Exercises

For more exercises, see Extra Skills and Word Problems.

For Exercises	See Examples
9–14	1
15–23	2
24–29	3

Write using an exponent.

9. $2 \cdot 2 \cdot 2 \cdot 2 \cdot 2 \cdot 2$　10. $7 \cdot 7 \cdot 7 \cdot 7 \cdot 7$　11. $6 \cdot 6 \cdot 6$

12. $-5 \cdot -5 \cdot -5 \cdot -5$　13. $9 \cdot 9 \cdot 9 \cdot 9 \cdot 9 \cdot 9$　14. $12 \cdot 12 \cdot 12 \cdot 12$

Simplify. Use paper and pencil, a model, or a calculator.

15. 9^2　　16. 10^8　　17. 0.2^6　　18. 1.7^3

19. -3^4　　20. $(-3)^4$　　21. $(-2)^3$　　22. $(-4)^3$

23. Each side of a sugar cube is 0.6 in. long. Find the volume of the sugar cube.

Simplify using the order of operations.

24. $2^3 \cdot (6-3)^2$　　25. $(2^3 \cdot 6) - 3^2$　　26. $2^3 \cdot 6 - 3^2$

27. $-3^2 + 2^3 \cdot 6$　　28. $3^2 - 2^3$　　29. $(2+1)^3 \div 3^2$

30. **Guided Problem Solving** Suppose you have a part-time job. Your boss offers to pay you $2 the first day, with the amount to double each day. How much will you be paid for the tenth day?
    - **Make a Plan** Find the amounts you will be paid on the second, third, and fourth days. Write each amount using exponents.
    - **Carry Out the Plan** On each day, you will earn ■ dollars, which can be written using exponents as $2^{■}$. Identify the pattern.

31. Write two equivalent expressions for the number of seconds in 60 hours. Use exponents in only one of the expressions.

32. (**Algebra**) Suppose a is a nonzero number. How would you write $a \cdot a \cdot a$ using an exponent?

For Exercises 33–35, refer to the table.

33. Copy the table. Fill in the missing values.

34. Patterns What patterns do you notice?

35. Reasoning Predict the number of zeros in 10^{12}.

Power of 10	Value	Number of Zeros
10^1	■	1
10^2	■	■
10^3	■	■
10^4	■	■
10^5	■	■

36. A scanning electron microscope (SEM) can magnify an image to as much as 10^5 times the actual size. How many times is this?

37. Without calculating, decide whether the value of $(-672)^2 - 192$ is positive or negative. Explain your reasoning.

38. What exponent completes the table below? Use your answer to find $2^0, 3^0, 4^0, 5^0,$ and 10^0.

Value	16	8	4	2	1
Power of 2	2^4	2^3	2^2	2^1	$2^{■}$

39. Writing in Math Write a general rule to find the value of a nonzero expression with an exponent of 0.

40. a. Geometry How many small squares line up on one edge of the larger square?

   b. How many small squares fit in the large square?
   c. Explain why 5^2 is read as "5 squared."

41. Challenge Evaluate $g^2(f + h)$ for $f = -2$, $g = -3$, and $h = -4$.

This dust mite has been magnified 1.5×10^5 times.

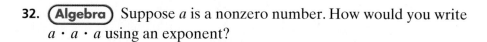
Test Prep and Mixed Review
Practice

Multiple Choice

42. What is the value of the expression $(4 - 1)^3 - 3 \times 8 \div 6$?
   Ⓐ 0.5   Ⓑ 5   Ⓒ 21   Ⓓ 23

43. The table shows a plant's growth each week for four weeks. If the plant grew 4.75 cm in all, how much did it grow in week 4?
   Ⓕ 0.65 cm   Ⓗ 1.65 cm
   Ⓖ 1.35 cm   Ⓙ 4.75 cm

Week	Growth (cm)
1	0.25
2	1.5
3	1.35
4	

GO for Help

For Exercises	See Lesson
44–47	1-8

Find the value of each expression.

44. $12(-2)$ **45.** $-4(-10)$ **46.** $-8 \div (-4)$ **47.** $49 \div (-7)$

Using a Scientific Calculator

Many calculators use the order of operations. To test your calculator, try to compute $3 + 5 \cdot 2$. If the answer is 13, your calculator uses the order of operations.

You can use a scientific calculator to simplify expressions that contain more than one operation.

EXAMPLE **Simplifying Expressions**

1 Find $6 + 18 \div 2$.

$6\ \boxed{+}\ 18\ \boxed{\div}\ 2\ \boxed{=}\ 15$

The expression $6 + 18 \div 2$ simplifies to 15.

You can use a scientific calculator to simplify expressions that have grouping symbols.

EXAMPLE **Using Grouping Symbols**

2 Find $(5.5 - 9) \div 2$.

$\boxed{(}\ 5\ \boxed{\cdot}\ 5\ \boxed{-}\ 9\ \boxed{)}\ \boxed{\div}\ 2\ \boxed{=}\ -1.75$

The expression simplifies to -1.75.

You can simplify expressions by inserting grouping symbols.

EXAMPLE **Inserting Parentheses**

3 Find $\dfrac{-7 - 5}{-6 + 3}$.

$\boxed{(}\ \boxed{(-)}\ 7\ \boxed{-}\ 5\ \boxed{)}\ \boxed{\div}\ \boxed{(}\ \boxed{(-)}\ 6\ \boxed{+}\ 3\ \boxed{)}\ \boxed{=}\ 4$ ← Use the $\boxed{(-)}$ key for negative numbers.

The quotient is 4.

Exercises

Use a calculator to find the value of each expression.

1. $9 + 4 \cdot 2$

2. $5.6 - 9 \div 2.5$

3. $(5 - 14.9) \div 3$

4. $\dfrac{8.2 - 16.3}{4.5}$

5. $7.2 \div (4.3 - 3.7)$

6. $\dfrac{-9 - 6.2}{2.1 + 2.9}$

Divisibility Tests

One whole number is **divisible** by a second whole number if the remainder is 0 when you divide the first number by the second number. The table below shows tests to determine if a number is divisible by 2, 3, 4, 5, 8, 9, or 10.

EXAMPLES

1 Is 567 divisible by 3?

Yes, 5 + 6 + 7 = 18; 18 is divisible by 3.

2 Is 934 divisible by 4?

No it is not, since 34 is not divisible by 4.

3 Is 29,640 divisible by 8?

Yes it is, because 640 is divisible by 8.

4 Is 3,016 divisible by 9?

No, 3 + 0 + 1 + 6 = 10; 10 is not divisible by 9.

Number	Test for Divisibility
2	Number ends in 0, 2, 4, 6, or 8.
3	Sum of the digits is divisible by 3.
4	The number formed by the last two digits is divisible by 4.
5	Number ends in 0 or 5.
8	The number formed by the last three digits is divisible by 8.
9	Sum of the digits is divisible by 9.
10	Number ends in 0.

Exercises

Tell whether each number is divisible by 2, 3, 4, 5, 8, 9, or 10. Some numbers may be divisible by more than one number.

1. 324　　　　**2.** 840　　　　**3.** 2,724　　　　**4.** 81,816　　　　**5.** 7,848

6. Games In an adventure game, you can open the door to a treasure room if you have the correct key. The number of the correct key is divisible by 3 and 4, but not 5. Which color key will open the door?

413,270　　267,528　　326,340　　135,480　　640,905

7. A *conjecture* is a prediction that suggests what can be expected to happen. Make a conjecture for the divisibility tests of 12 and 15.

2-2 Prime Factorization

Check Skills You'll Need

1. **Vocabulary Review**
A whole number is divisible by a second whole number if the remainder after division is ■.

Use mental math to find the quotient.

2. 48 ÷ 2

3. 63 ÷ 3

4. 72 ÷ 6

 **for Help**

Skills Handbook, page 657

What You'll Learn

To find multiples and factors and to use prime factorization

🔊 **New Vocabulary** multiple, least common multiple, factor, composite, prime, prime factorization, greatest common factor

Why Learn This?

You can use factors and multiples to solve problems involving scheduling.

Suppose you volunteer every third day at an animal shelter, and your friend volunteers every fourth day. You can use multiples to find the next day when you both will be at the shelter.

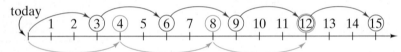

A **multiple** of a number is the product of that number and any nonzero whole number. The diagram above shows multiples of 3 and 4. The **least common multiple (LCM)** of two or more numbers is the least multiple that is common to all of the numbers.

EXAMPLE Finding the LCM

❶ **Scheduling** A fish sandwich is on a school's lunch menu every 6 school days. Spaghetti with meat sauce is on the menu every 9 school days. If both items are on the menu today, when will both be served again?

Find the least common multiple of 6 and 9.

Multiples of 6: 6, 12, 18, 24, 30, 36, . . . ⎤
                                                  ⎬ ← List the first several
Multiples of 9: 9, 18, 27, 36, . . .   ⎦   multiples of 6 and 9.

The LCM of 6 and 9 is 18. Both will be served again in 18 school days.

✔ Quick Check

1. Find the LCM of each pair of numbers.
  a. 4, 10   **b.** 5, 7   **c.** 12, 15

A **factor** is a whole number that divides another whole number with a remainder of 0. Any number is always divisible by all of its factors.

A **composite number** is a whole number that has more than two factors. A **prime number** is a whole number with exactly two factors, 1 and the number itself. The number 1 is neither prime nor composite.

EXAMPLE Prime Numbers and Composite Numbers

2 Determine whether each number is prime or composite.

a. 12

Look for pairs of numbers with a product of 12:

  1 · 12   2 · 6   3 · 4

Then list the factors in order: 1, 2, 3, 4, 6, 12.

Since 12 has factors other than 1 and itself, 12 is a composite number.

b. 13

Look for pairs of numbers with a product of 13: 1 · 13.

Since 13 has no factors other than 1 and itself, 13 is a prime number.

✓ Quick Check

2. Is 15 prime or composite? Explain.

Writing a composite number as the product of its prime factors shows its **prime factorization.** This product is unique except for the order of the factors. You can use a factor tree to find prime factors.

EXAMPLE Writing Prime Factorization

For help with writing expressions involving exponents, go to Lesson 2-1, Example 1.

3 Use a factor tree to write the prime factorization of 60.

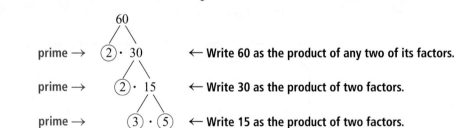

$60 = 2 \cdot 2 \cdot 3 \cdot 5$. Using exponents, you can write $60 = 2^2 \cdot 3 \cdot 5$.

✓ Quick Check

3. Write the prime factorization of 72. Use exponents where possible.

The **greatest common factor (GCF)** of two or more numbers is the greatest number that is a factor of all the numbers.

Finding the GCF

4 Find the GCF of 24 and 36.

$24 = 2 \cdot 2 \cdot 2 \cdot 3 \quad 36 = 2 \cdot 2 \cdot 3 \cdot 3$ ← **Write the prime factorizations.**

$GCF = 2 \cdot 2 \cdot 3 = 12$ ← **Find the product of the common factors.**

The GCF of 24 and 36 is 12.

✓ Quick Check

4. Find the GCF of 16 and 24.

● More Than One Way

Two different teams are marching in rows that all contain the same number of people. One team has 32 members and the other has 40. If the rows are as long as possible, how many people are in each row?

Carlos's Method

I'll write the prime factorizations of 40 and 32. Then I'll find the GCF.

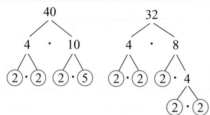

← **Write as products of two factors.**

← **Write as products of two factors.**

← **Write as a product of two factors.**

$40 = 2 \cdot 2 \cdot 2 \cdot 5$
$32 = 2 \cdot 2 \cdot 2 \cdot 2 \cdot 2$ ← **Write the prime factorizations.**

$GCF = 2 \cdot 2 \cdot 2 = 8$ ← **Multiply the common factors.**

There are 8 people in each row.

Anna's Method

First I'll list the possible sizes of rows. Then I'll choose the greatest number in both lists.

The factors of 32 are 1, 2, 4, 8, 16, and 32.
The factors of 40 are 1, 2, 4, 5, 8, 10, 20, and 40.

The greatest common factor is 8. There are 8 people in each row.

Choose a Method

Teams of 36 and 60 will march in rows of equal length. How many marchers will be in the longest row possible?

1. **Vocabulary** How is a factor different from a multiple?

2. **Number Sense** Which numbers are factors of all even numbers?

3. What is the only even prime number?

Is the number prime or composite? Explain.

4. 29   5. 28   6. 27   7. 26

Homework Exercises

For more exercises, see Extra Skills and Word Problems.

GO for Help

For Exercises	See Examples
8–16	1
17–24	2
25–32	3
33–40	4

Find the LCM of each pair of numbers.

8. 4, 6   9. 9, 12   10. 8, 5   11. 2, 5

12. 6, 7   13. 5, 10   14. 10, 6   15. 24, 8

16. **Fitness** You have aerobics classes every 3 days and soccer practice every 7 days. Today you had both aerobics and soccer. When will you next have both activities on the same day?

Find the factors of each number.

17. 20   18. 23   19. 32   20. 62

Determine whether each number is prime or composite.

21. 37   22. 50   23. 1   24. 63

Write the prime factorization of each number. Use exponents.

25. 45   26. 64   27. 84   28. 111

29. 52   30. 75   31. 60   32. 132

Find the GCF of each pair of numbers.

33. 18, 32   34. 12, 15   35. 16, 80   36. 10, 85

37. 38, 76   38. 75, 90   39. 54, 80   40. 52, 26

41. **Guided Problem Solving** In his art class, Raul made two rectangular mosaics with 1-cm tiles. He used 48 tiles for one mosaic and 56 tiles for the other. Both mosaics have the same length, measured in whole centimeters. What is the greatest possible length of each mosaic?
    • What are the possible lengths of each mosaic?
    • What are the corresponding widths for each mosaic?

Homework Video Tutor
Visit: PHSchool.com
Web Code: are-0202

Mental Math **Find the GCF of each pair of numbers.**

42. 3, 10   **43.** 7, 12   **44.** 4, 20   **45.** 50, 1000

46. Find two composite numbers with a GCF of 1.

47. Choose a Method You can buy juice boxes in packs of 12 or 30. Both packs contain the same number of boxes in each row. What is the greatest possible number of boxes per row? Describe your method and explain why you chose it.

48. A movie theater just added two rooms. One room is large enough for 125 people, and the other can seat up to 350 people. In each room, the seating is arranged in horizontal rows with the same number of seats in each row. What is the greatest number of seats that can make up each row?

49. Error Analysis Two students made factor trees of the prime factors of 24. Are both correct? Explain.

50. You can express 100 as 10^2 using exponents. Is 10^2 the same as the prime factorization of 100? Explain.

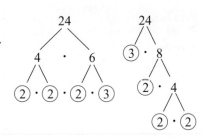

51. 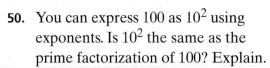 Describe the relationships among 3, 5, and 15 using the words *factor* and *multiple*.

52. Challenge Let *n* be any prime number. Tell whether the statement "$2n + 1$ is prime" is *sometimes*, *always*, or *never* true.

Test Prep and Mixed Review   **Practice**

Multiple Choice

53. The Stillwater High School library is arranging 108 books. Each shelf can hold as many as 10 books, and the librarian wants to place the same number of books on each shelf. What is the greatest number of books that can be placed on each shelf?

   Ⓐ 2   Ⓑ 9   Ⓒ 10   Ⓓ 12

54. The table shows how far model cars traveled after rolling down an incline. How many centimeters farther did car 2 travel than car 4 and car 5 combined?

   Ⓕ 16.71   Ⓗ 42.19
   Ⓖ 17.88   Ⓙ 58.9

Car	Distance (cm)
1	52.64
2	83.21
3	66.86
4	24.31
5	41.02

GO for Help

For Exercises	See Lesson
55–57	1-6

Order from least to greatest.

55. 3, −4, −5, 6   **56.** −7, −10, −13   **57.** 20, −21, 21, 0

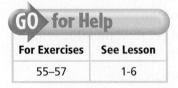

Simplify each expression.

1. $8^2 + 11$
2. $(-1)^4$
3. $5 + (3^2 - 2)^2$

Find the LCM of each pair of numbers.

4. 3, 4
5. 7, 10
6. 5, 12

Find the factors of each number.

7. 39
8. 52
9. 110
10. 200

Write the prime factorization of each number. Use exponents where possible.

11. 96
12. 150
13. 225
14. 333

15. Two pieces of rope have lengths 72 ft and 96 ft. A woodcutter needs to cut the two pieces into smaller pieces all of equal lengths. What is the greatest possible length of each smaller piece?

MATH GAMES

Factor Cards

What You'll Need

- 40 index cards, numbered from 1 to 40

How To Play

- Form two teams.
- Team A chooses a card at random.
- Team B removes the cards from the deck that are factors of Team A's card. For example, if Team A picks 10, Team B takes cards 1, 2, and 5.
- Teams switch places until all of the cards are taken. No points are given for cards that have already been chosen. The team whose cards have the highest sum wins.

Using LCM and GCF

Movie Rentals   To boost sales, a video rental store offered a free bag of microwave popcorn to every sixth customer and a free movie rental to every eighth customer. What customer was the first to win both popcorn *and* a free movie rental?

What You Might Think

What do I know?

What am I trying to find out?

How do I show the main idea?

How do I solve the problem?

What is the answer?

What You Might Write

Every sixth person in line won popcorn and every eighth person won a free movie rental.

I want to know which person was the first to win both popcorn and a free movie rental.

Draw a diagram.

Find the least common multiple (LCM) of 6 and 8. This means I need to find the smallest number that is a multiple of both 6 and 8.

The multiples of 8 are 8, 16, 24, 32, 40, . . .

The smallest number that is also a multiple of 6 is 24.

The 24th person in line was the first to win both the popcorn and a free movie rental.

Think It Through

1. Explain how the diagram shows multiples of 6 *and* multiples of 8.

2. Explain why it makes sense to look first at the multiples of the larger number when finding the LCM.

3. What is the number of the second person in line to win both prizes? The third person in line to win both prizes?

Exercises

For Exercises 4 and 5, answer the questions first. Then solve the problem.

4. As a promotion, a "hot wings" restaurant gave away free boxes according to the sign below.

   HOT WING BOXES   FREE to this customer
       6 wings   every 6th in line
      10 wings   every 10th in line
      15 wings   every 15th in line

   Which person in line was the first to get boxes of all three sizes?
   a. What do you know?
   b. What do you want to find out?
   c. Draw a diagram that shows people winning different boxes.
   d. How will finding the LCM of three numbers help you?

5. Southside Middle School held a tug-of-war contest. Seventy-eight seventh graders and seventy-two eighth graders signed up. Each grade was divided into several teams. If both grades had the same number of people on each team, what was the greatest possible number of people on a team?
   a. What do you know?
   b. What do you want to find out?
   c. How will finding the GCF of 72 and 78 help you?

6. Jeremiah wants to make a square pattern for an art project using tiles 8 cm by 12 cm. What is the smallest square he can design using whole tiles?

7. There are 252 beats in one passage of a musical composition. In this passage, the triangle player plays once every 12 beats. The timpani player plays once every 9 beats. How many times will they play at the same time during this passage?

8. All the school lockers are closed at the beginning of the school day. Wayne is the first person to come into school, and he opens every tenth locker. Jake comes in after Wayne and switches every eighth locker from open to closed, or vice versa. Which locker is the first to be opened and then closed?

What You'll Learn

To write equivalent fractions and to simplify fractions

◀》 **New Vocabulary** equivalent fractions, simplest form

Why Learn This?

Suppose you have three identical chocolate bars. You break one bar into 4 pieces and give away 3 of them. You break the second bar into 8 pieces and give away 6. You break the third bar into 12 pieces and give away 9. The model below shows that you give away the same fraction of each bar.

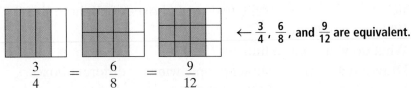

← $\frac{3}{4}$, $\frac{6}{8}$, and $\frac{9}{12}$ are equivalent.

$$\frac{3}{4} = \frac{6}{8} = \frac{9}{12}$$

Fractions that name the same amount are **equivalent fractions.** You can write equivalent fractions by multiplying or dividing the numerator and the denominator by the same nonzero number.

EXAMPLE Using Multiples

1 Use a table of multiples to write three fractions equivalent to $\frac{7}{8}$.

	×2	×3	×4
7	14	21	28
8	16	24	32

← Multiples in the same column form fractions equivalent to $\frac{7}{8}$.

Three fractions equivalent to $\frac{7}{8}$ are $\frac{14}{16}$, $\frac{21}{24}$, and $\frac{28}{32}$.

✓ Quick Check

1. Use multiples to write two fractions equivalent to $\frac{4}{5}$.

A fraction is written in **simplest form** when the numerator and the denominator have no common factors other than 1. For example, $\frac{1}{3}$ and $\frac{3}{9}$ are equivalent, but only $\frac{1}{3}$ is written in simplest form.

EXAMPLE Using Factors

② Write three fractions equivalent to $\frac{24}{30}$.

Factors of 24: 1, 2, 3, 4, 6, 8, 12, 24

Factors of 30: 1, 2, 3, 5, 6, 10, 15, 30

List the factors of each number. Look for common factors.

$$\frac{24}{30} \overset{\div 2}{\underset{\div 2}{=}} \frac{12}{15} \qquad \frac{24}{30} \overset{\div 3}{\underset{\div 3}{=}} \frac{8}{10} \qquad \frac{24}{30} \overset{\div 6}{\underset{\div 6}{=}} \frac{4}{5}$$

Three fractions equivalent to $\frac{24}{30}$ are $\frac{12}{15}$, $\frac{8}{10}$, and $\frac{4}{5}$.

✓ Quick Check

● 2. Use common factors to write two fractions equivalent to $\frac{18}{30}$.

EXAMPLE Simplifying by Dividing

Vocabulary Tip

Another term for *simplest form* is *lowest terms*.

③ Simplify $\frac{12}{24}$.

$$\frac{12 \div 2}{24 \div 2} = \frac{6}{12} \quad \leftarrow \textbf{Divide the numerator and denominator by a common factor.}$$

$$\frac{6 \div 6}{12 \div 6} = \frac{1}{2} \quad \leftarrow \textbf{If necessary, divide again by another common factor.}$$

In simplest form, $\frac{12}{24}$ is $\frac{1}{2}$.

✓ Quick Check

● 3. Write $\frac{8}{12}$ in simplest form.

EXAMPLE Using the GCF to Simplify a Fraction

④ In the United States, there are 48 types of road signs. Of these, 16 are instructional, such as speed limit or stop signs. What fraction of road signs are instructional? Write your answer in simplest form.

$$\frac{16}{48} = \frac{16 \div 16}{48 \div 16} = \frac{1}{3} \quad \leftarrow \textbf{Divide both numerator and denominator by the GCF, 16.}$$

The fraction of road signs that are instructional is $\frac{1}{3}$.

✓ Quick Check

4. Your class ordered 45 calculators. Of these, 18 were solar powered. What fraction of the calculators were solar powered?

1. **Vocabulary** Can two equivalent fractions both be fractions written in simplest form? Explain.

2. Are $\frac{2}{4}$ and $\frac{8}{8}$ equivalent? Explain.

3. **Error Analysis** A teacher asked students to find a fraction equivalent to $\frac{5}{6}$. One answer is below. Is it correct? Explain.

$$\frac{5}{6} = \frac{5+4}{6+4} = \frac{9}{10}$$

For each term, write three equivalent fractions, one in simplest form.

4. $\frac{3}{9}$

5. $\frac{36}{48}$

6. $\frac{16}{36}$

For more exercises, see Extra Skills and Word Problems.

GO for Help

For Exercises	See Examples
7–14	1
15–22	2
23–28	3–4

Use multiples to write two fractions equivalent to each fraction.

7. $\frac{5}{6}$

8. $\frac{3}{8}$

9. $\frac{2}{9}$

10. $\frac{7}{10}$

11. $\frac{4}{7}$

12. $\frac{3}{5}$

13. $\frac{6}{11}$

14. $\frac{1}{5}$

Use common factors to write two fractions equivalent to each fraction.

15. $\frac{8}{24}$

16. $\frac{18}{36}$

17. $\frac{27}{81}$

18. $\frac{60}{140}$

19. $\frac{30}{42}$

20. $\frac{45}{90}$

21. $\frac{24}{84}$

22. $\frac{36}{80}$

Write each fraction in simplest form.

23. $\frac{24}{32}$

24. $\frac{18}{27}$

25. $\frac{33}{39}$

26. $\frac{8}{18}$

27. **Biology** An adult's body has 206 bones. Of these, 106 are in the feet, ankles, wrist, and hands. What fraction of an adult's bones are in the feet, ankles, wrists, and hands?

28. **Weather** The city of Houston, Texas, typically has 90 clear days out of the 365 days in a year. Houston's clear days represent what fraction of a year? Write your answer in simplest form.

GPS 29. **Guided Problem Solving** A school offers two summer sports: lacrosse and tennis. There are 438 students in all. Of this number, 52 participate in lacrosse and 94 participate in tennis. Nobody does both. What fraction of the students participate in a sport?
   - The number of students who participate in a summer sport is ■.
   - The total number of students at the school is ■.

Write two equivalent fractions for each model.

30.

31.

32.

33. Which square does *not* have the same fraction shaded as the others?

A. **B.** **C.** **D.**

34. **Writing in Math** Are the fractions $\frac{9}{16}$, $\frac{10}{24}$, and $\frac{15}{35}$ in simplest form? Explain.

35. The circle graph shows a student's daily activities. Write a fraction in simplest form to represent the time spent on each activity.

36. Draw models to show that the fractions $\frac{2}{3}$ and $\frac{10}{15}$ are equivalent.

37. **Challenge** The variables a and b represent positive integers. Name two fractions equivalent to $\frac{a}{b}$.

Test Prep and Mixed Review
Practice

Multiple Choice

38. If only one thousand people lived on Earth, the population would be distributed according to the table below. What fraction of the people live in Africa?

Asia	Africa	Europe	South America	Australia	North America
607	132	120	57	5	79

Ⓐ $\frac{3}{25}$ Ⓑ $\frac{33}{250}$ Ⓒ $\frac{7}{50}$ Ⓓ $\frac{4}{25}$

39. Pablo spent half of his birthday money on concert tickets and one third of the remaining amount on food. After he used $12.35 on a train ticket, he had $8.25 left. How much money did Pablo begin with?

Ⓕ $20.60 Ⓖ $41.20 Ⓗ $61.80 Ⓙ $123.60

Find each sum or difference.

40. $14.02 + 3.06$ **41.** $25.98 - 8.89$ **42.** $10.132 - 6.7$

2-4a **Activity Lab**

Hands On

Comparing Fractions

You can use a number line to compare two integers such as 3 and −5. You know 3 is greater because it lies to the right of −5. In this activity, you will use paper strips and a number line to compare two fractions.

You can compare $\frac{3}{5}$ and $\frac{7}{10}$ using two strips of paper, each 10 cm long, and a number line that is 10 cm long. On your number line, mark the points 0, $\frac{1}{2}$, and 1.

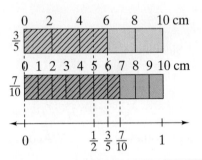

← Divide one strip into 5 equal parts. Shade in 3 parts to represent $\frac{3}{5}$.

← Divide the other strip into 10 equal parts. Shade in 7 parts to represent $\frac{7}{10}$.

← Use the strips to mark the two fractions on a number line.

Since $\frac{7}{10}$ is to the right of $\frac{3}{5}$ on the number line, you know that $\frac{7}{10} > \frac{3}{5}$.

ACTIVITY

Step 1 Using paper strips, compare the five pairs of fractions listed in the table at the right. For each pair, cut two strips of paper to the given length. Then use a number line and an inequality to show your comparison.

Step 2 Use 15-cm strips of paper to compare $\frac{7}{10}$ and $\frac{6}{9}$. Explain why this comparison is more difficult than the others. What would be a better length for the paper strips? Explain.

Step 3 Explain how the paper lengths shown in the table relate to the fractions being compared. Why do you think those lengths were chosen?

Step 4 List several fraction pairs that could be compared using paper strips that are 32 cm long.

Step 5 How long would you make the paper strips to compare $\frac{6}{8}$, $\frac{4}{5}$, and $\frac{7}{10}$? Explain.

Step 6 Use what you have learned to compare $\frac{7}{9}$ and $\frac{4}{5}$ without making paper strips. Explain your reasoning.

Fractions	Paper Length
$\frac{3}{4}$ and $\frac{7}{12}$	12 cm
$\frac{2}{5}$ and $\frac{1}{4}$	20 cm
$\frac{6}{8}$ and $\frac{2}{3}$	24 cm
$\frac{3}{4}$ and $\frac{5}{7}$	28 cm
$\frac{3}{10}$ and $\frac{2}{6}$	30 cm

✓ **Check Skills You'll Need**

1. **Vocabulary Review** What is the name for the smallest multiple common to two numbers?

Find the LCM of each pair of numbers.

2. 3, 4

3. 4, 10

4. 2, 8

5. 9, 15

**for Help**
Lesson 2-2

What You'll Learn

To compare and order fractions

 **New Vocabulary** least common denominator (LCD)

Why Learn This?

Camera exposure times are given as fractions of a second. Knowing how to compare fractions can help you choose the correct exposure times and take better pictures.

The exposure times below are listed in order of greatest to least. If the numerators of two fractions are the same, the fraction with the lesser denominator has the greater value. For example, $\frac{1}{125} > \frac{1}{500}$, because 1 divided into 125 parts is greater than 1 divided into 500 parts.

Camera Exposure Times

$$\frac{1}{4} \quad \frac{1}{30} \quad \frac{1}{60} \quad \frac{1}{125} \quad \frac{1}{250} \quad \frac{1}{500} \quad \frac{1}{1000}$$

Longer time— lets in more light   Shorter time— lets in less light

If the denominators are the same, the numerators show which fraction is greater. Use the "is greater than" (>) or the "is less than" (<) symbol.

You can use a number line to compare fractions. Any number to the right of any other number on a number line is the greater of the two.

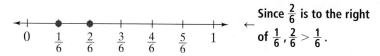

Since $\frac{2}{6}$ is to the right of $\frac{1}{6}$, $\frac{2}{6} > \frac{1}{6}$.

You can also use models to compare fractions. The fraction models show that $\frac{7}{12} > \frac{3}{8}$. To compare fractions with different denominators, rewrite each with a common denominator.

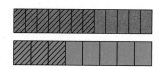

The **least common denominator (LCD)** of two or more fractions is the least common multiple (LCM) of their denominators.

GO Online

Video Tutor Help

Visit: PHSchool.com
Web Code: are-0775

EXAMPLE Comparing Fractions

Test Prep Tip

Draw a number line to help you visualize the order of the fractions.

1 Compare $\frac{3}{4}$ and $\frac{7}{10}$.

The denominators are 4 and 10. Their LCM is 20. So 20 is the LCD.

$$\frac{3}{4} = \frac{3 \times 5}{4 \times 5} = \frac{15}{20}$$

Write the equivalent fractions with a denominator of 20.

$$\frac{7}{10} = \frac{7 \times 2}{10 \times 2} = \frac{14}{20}$$

$$\frac{14}{20} < \frac{15}{20} \quad \leftarrow \text{Compare the numerators.}$$

So $\frac{7}{10} < \frac{3}{4}$.

✓ Quick Check

1. Compare each pair of fractions. Use $<$, $=$, or $>$.
   a. $\frac{3}{4} \blacksquare \frac{5}{6}$ b. $\frac{1}{6} \blacksquare \frac{2}{9}$ c. $\frac{4}{10} \blacksquare \frac{3}{8}$

You can use the LCD to order more than two fractions.

EXAMPLE Application: Construction

2 Multiple Choice A construction company uses plywood sheets in the following thicknesses: $\frac{3}{8}$ in. for roofing, $\frac{1}{2}$ in. for flooring, $\frac{1}{4}$ in. for countertop surfaces, and $\frac{1}{8}$ in. for filling gaps. Which list shows the fractions in order from least to greatest?

Ⓐ $\frac{1}{4}, \frac{3}{8}, \frac{1}{2}, \frac{1}{8}$ Ⓑ $\frac{1}{2}, \frac{1}{4}, \frac{1}{8}, \frac{3}{8}$ Ⓒ $\frac{1}{8}, \frac{1}{4}, \frac{1}{2}, \frac{3}{8}$ Ⓓ $\frac{1}{8}, \frac{1}{4}, \frac{3}{8}, \frac{1}{2}$

Order $\frac{3}{8}, \frac{1}{2}, \frac{1}{4}$, and $\frac{1}{8}$. The LCM of 8, 2, and 4 is 8. So 8 is the LCD.

Roofing: $\frac{3}{8}$

Flooring: $\frac{1}{2} = \frac{1 \times 4}{2 \times 4} = \frac{4}{8}$

Countertop: $\frac{1}{4} = \frac{1 \times 2}{4 \times 2} = \frac{2}{8}$ $\leftarrow$ **Use the LCD to write equivalent fractions.**

Filling: $\frac{1}{8}$

$\frac{1}{8} < \frac{2}{8} < \frac{3}{8} < \frac{4}{8}$. So $\frac{1}{8} < \frac{1}{4} < \frac{3}{8} < \frac{1}{2}$. $\leftarrow$ **Compare the numerators.**

The order is $\frac{1}{8}, \frac{1}{4}, \frac{3}{8}$, and $\frac{1}{2}$. The correct answer is choice D.

✓ Quick Check

2. A carpenter uses four screws with diameters of $\frac{1}{4}$ in., $\frac{3}{8}$ in., $\frac{5}{16}$ in., and $\frac{5}{32}$ in. Order the diameters from least to greatest.

1. **Vocabulary** How are the least common multiple (LCM) and least common denominator (LCD) related?

2. **Reasoning** To order $\frac{4}{10}$, $\frac{3}{5}$, and $\frac{5}{25}$, it is helpful to write each fraction in simplest form first, before finding the LCD. Explain why.

Find the LCD of each pair of fractions.

3. $\frac{5}{7}$, $\frac{2}{9}$

4. $\frac{3}{11}$, $\frac{2}{5}$

5. $\frac{7}{8}$, $\frac{1}{3}$

Compare each pair of fractions. Use <, =, or >.

6. $\frac{1}{7}$ ■ $\frac{3}{8}$

7. $\frac{3}{12}$ ■ $\frac{1}{6}$

8. $\frac{2}{10}$ ■ $\frac{3}{5}$

Homework Exercises

For more exercises, see **Extra Skills and Word Problems.**

GO for Help

For Exercises	See Examples
9–17	1
18–27	2

Compare each pair of fractions. Use <, =, or >.

9. $\frac{5}{12}$ ■ $\frac{7}{12}$

10. $\frac{5}{6}$ ■ $\frac{3}{6}$

11. $\frac{1}{3}$ ■ $\frac{3}{4}$

12. $\frac{5}{6}$ ■ $\frac{3}{5}$

13. $\frac{3}{8}$ ■ $\frac{2}{3}$

14. $\frac{4}{7}$ ■ $\frac{4}{5}$

15. $\frac{2}{3}$ ■ $\frac{5}{8}$

16. $\frac{5}{6}$ ■ $\frac{5}{10}$

17. $\frac{1}{8}$ ■ $\frac{3}{16}$

Order from least to greatest.

18. $\frac{1}{3}$, $\frac{5}{6}$, $\frac{3}{8}$

19. $\frac{1}{8}$, $\frac{1}{6}$, $\frac{1}{9}$

20. $\frac{3}{15}$, $\frac{3}{10}$, $\frac{3}{5}$

21. $\frac{5}{8}$, $\frac{7}{9}$, $\frac{2}{1}$

22. $\frac{6}{10}$, $\frac{7}{12}$, $\frac{5}{8}$

23. $\frac{2}{5}$, $\frac{3}{20}$, $\frac{4}{5}$

24. 1, $\frac{4}{6}$, $\frac{1}{3}$

25. $\frac{10}{15}$, $\frac{6}{10}$, $\frac{1}{3}$

26. $\frac{1}{8}$, $\frac{3}{12}$, $\frac{4}{10}$

27. **Languages** At an international school, $\frac{1}{3}$ of the languages spoken are Romance languages, $\frac{2}{15}$ are Germanic, and $\frac{8}{15}$ are Balto-Slavic. Order the language categories from least to greatest.

28. **Guided Problem Solving** A bank offers three types of interest-bearing accounts. One account increases by $\frac{1}{2}$ percent annually, another increases by $\frac{3}{5}$ percent, and a third increases by $\frac{7}{12}$ percent. In which account would you prefer to invest your money? Explain.
    • What is the least common denominator of the three fractions?
    • Is it better to earn more interest or less interest?

29. **Carpentry** You want to nail a board that is $\frac{1}{2}$ in. thick onto a wall. You can choose between nails that are $\frac{3}{8}$ in. long and $\frac{3}{4}$ in. long. Which size nail is the better choice? Explain.

Compare each pair of fractions. Use <, =, or >.

30. $\frac{7}{12} \blacksquare \frac{5}{9}$ **31.** $\frac{10}{15} \blacksquare \frac{16}{24}$ **32.** $\frac{8}{16} \blacksquare \frac{15}{32}$ **33.** $\frac{22}{26} \blacksquare \frac{10}{13}$

Use the table at the right.

34. Do people remember more of what they say or what they do?

35. Do people remember more of what they hear or what they say?

Memory Facts

People remember . . .	of . . .
three fourths	what they say.
one tenth	what they hear.
nine tenths	what they do.

Write two fractions for the models and compare them. Use <, =, or >.

36.
37.

38. Patterns Copy the table. Compare the fractions and fill in your answers. Use <, =, or >.

39. Writing in Math Describe an easy way to compare fractions that have the same numerator, such as $\frac{4}{5}$ and $\frac{4}{7}$. Explain why your method works.

40. Challenge The variable n represents a positive integer. Which is greater, $\frac{1}{n}$ or $\frac{1}{n+1}$?

$\frac{1}{2}$	$\blacksquare$	$\frac{1}{3}$
$\frac{1}{3}$	$\blacksquare$	$\frac{1}{4}$
$\frac{1}{4}$	$\blacksquare$	$\frac{1}{5}$
$\frac{1}{5}$	$\blacksquare$	$\frac{1}{6}$

Test Prep and Mixed Review

Practice

Multiple Choice

41. Which fraction is found between $\frac{7}{12}$ and $\frac{5}{6}$ on a number line?

Ⓐ $\frac{13}{24}$ Ⓑ $\frac{11}{12}$ Ⓒ $\frac{5}{12}$ Ⓓ $\frac{17}{24}$

42. Eddie bought 12.9 gallons of gas that cost $2.89 per gallon. About how much did he pay for the gas?

Ⓕ Less than $23   Ⓗ Between $30 and $36
Ⓖ Between $23 and $30   Ⓙ More than $36

43. Which expression is represented by the model below?

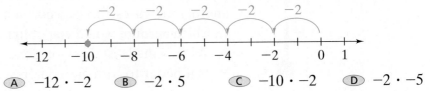

Ⓐ $-12 \cdot -2$ Ⓑ $-2 \cdot 5$ Ⓒ $-10 \cdot -2$ Ⓓ $-2 \cdot -5$

GO for Help

For Exercises	See Lesson
44–46	2-1

Simplify.

44. $4^2 + 2^3 \cdot 3$ **45.** $(4^2 + 2^3) \cdot 3$ **46.** $4^2 \cdot (2^3 + 3)^2$

Mixed Numbers and Improper Fractions

Check Skills You'll Need

1. Vocabulary Review What does it mean when a fraction is in *simplest form*?

Write each fraction in simplest form.

2. $\frac{12}{20}$ **3.** $\frac{15}{18}$

4. $\frac{45}{60}$ **5.** $\frac{20}{48}$

 **for Help**
Lesson 2-3

What You'll Learn

To write mixed numbers and improper fractions

🔊 **New Vocabulary** improper fraction, mixed number

Why Learn This?

Suppose you are trying to share the extra pies left over from a pie eating contest. You can use improper fractions to find the number of equal-sized parts you can make from the leftovers.

The models below show that $1\frac{2}{3} = \frac{5}{3}$.

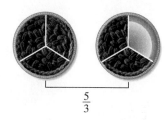

$$1\frac{2}{3} \qquad\qquad \frac{5}{3}$$

The fraction $\frac{5}{3}$ is an improper fraction. An **improper fraction** is a fraction that has a numerator that is greater than or equal to its denominator.

The number $1\frac{2}{3}$ is a mixed number. A **mixed number** is the sum of a whole number and a fraction.

A number line can also help you understand improper fractions and mixed numbers.

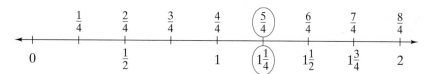

The number line shows that $1\frac{1}{4} = \frac{5}{4}$.

One way to write a mixed number as an improper fraction is to write the mixed number as a sum. Write a fraction that is equivalent to the whole number and then find the sum of the fractions.

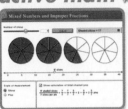

For: Fractions Activity
Use: Interactive
Textbook, 2-5

EXAMPLE Writing an Improper Fraction

1 Write $4\frac{2}{3}$ as an improper fraction.

Method 1 Using addition

$$4\frac{2}{3} = 4 + \frac{2}{3} \qquad \leftarrow \text{Write the mixed number as a sum.}$$

$$= \frac{12}{3} + \frac{2}{3} \qquad \leftarrow \begin{array}{l} \text{Change 4 to a fraction with the same denominator as } \frac{2}{3}. \\ \text{Substitute. } 4 = 4 \times \frac{3}{3} = \frac{12}{3} \end{array}$$

$$= \frac{12 + 2}{3} = \frac{14}{3} \qquad \leftarrow \text{Add the numerators.}$$

Method 2 Using multiplication

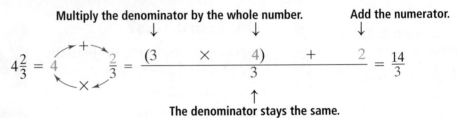

Multiply the denominator by the whole number.   Add the numerator.

$$4\frac{2}{3} = 4 \quad \frac{2}{3} = \frac{(3 \quad \times \quad 4) \quad + \quad 2}{3} = \frac{14}{3}$$

The denominator stays the same.

✓ Quick Check

1. Choose a Method Write $2\frac{5}{8}$ as an improper fraction.

To write an improper fraction as a mixed number, divide and write the remainder as a fraction of the denominator. Then simplify the fraction.

EXAMPLE Writing a Mixed Number

2 You are planning a party and estimate that you will need 30 slices of pie for your guests. If each pie contains 8 slices, how many pies should you buy?

To find the number of pies, write $\frac{30}{8}$ as a mixed number.

$$\text{denominator} \to \quad 8\overline{)30} \quad \leftarrow \text{whole number}$$
$$\underline{-24}$$
$$6 \quad \leftarrow \text{remainder}$$

$$3\frac{6}{8} = 3\frac{3}{4} \quad \leftarrow \text{Write the remainder as a fraction, } \frac{\text{remainder}}{\text{denominator}}. \text{ Simplify.}$$

Since you cannot buy $3\frac{3}{4}$ pies, you should buy 4 pies.

✓ Quick Check

2. A bakery sells a jumbo pie with 12 slices. If you need 30 slices, how many jumbo pies should you buy?

1. **Vocabulary** How are mixed numbers and improper fractions related?

2. Write 7 as an improper fraction.

Label each as an *improper fraction, mixed number,* or *proper fraction.*

3. $\frac{7}{11}$

4. $4\frac{1}{2}$

5. $\frac{15}{6}$

Fill in the blank.

6. $7 = \frac{\blacksquare}{2}$

7. $2\frac{2}{3} = \frac{\blacksquare}{3}$

8. $\blacksquare = \frac{18}{3}$

9. **Mental Math** Without calculating, decide whether the value of $\frac{72}{12}$ is a whole number or a mixed number. Explain your reasoning.

Homework Exercises

For more exercises, see Extra Skills and Word Problems.

GO for Help

For Exercises	See Examples
10–19	1
20–30	2

Write each mixed number as an improper fraction. You may find a model helpful.

10. $2\frac{3}{8}$

11. $5\frac{3}{4}$

12. $1\frac{1}{12}$

13. $4\frac{3}{5}$

14. $1\frac{3}{7}$

15. $4\frac{5}{8}$

16. $3\frac{2}{5}$

17. $2\frac{11}{12}$

18. $5\frac{2}{3}$

19. $9\frac{1}{4}$

Write each improper fraction as a mixed number in simplest form. You may find a model helpful.

20. $\frac{16}{3}$

21. $\frac{25}{3}$

22. $\frac{42}{4}$

23. $\frac{31}{12}$

24. $\frac{28}{6}$

25. $\frac{49}{6}$

26. $\frac{40}{6}$

27. $\frac{45}{10}$

28. $\frac{48}{11}$

29. $\frac{15}{8}$

30. A recipe calls for $\frac{1}{4}$ c of flour. You need $\frac{11}{4}$ c to make 11 servings. Write $\frac{11}{4}$ as a mixed number.

31. **Guided Problem Solving** 101 faculty members attended a breakfast, and each member was served $\frac{1}{4}$ loaf of banana bread. If each loaf contains eight slices, about how many slices of bread were served? About how many loaves were baked?
    - *Draw a diagram.* If eight slices make one loaf, how many slices are in $\frac{1}{4}$ loaf?
    - 101 people were served $\frac{1}{4}$ loaf. How many whole loaves is that?

32. Marisa is sewing an outfit. She uses $2\frac{5}{6}$ yards of fabric for her blouse, 3 yards of fabric for her skirt, and $\frac{20}{3}$ yards of fabric for her jacket. Write these values in order from least to greatest.

Online
Homework Video Tutor
Visit: PHSchool.com
Web Code: are-0205

(Algebra) In Exercises 33–35, evaluate each expression for $a = 6$, $b = 3$, $c = 2$, and $d = 5$. Write your answer in simplest form.

33. $\dfrac{b}{a^2}$

34. $\dfrac{a^2 + b}{c}$

35. $\dfrac{a + c}{b + d}$

Write each length as a mixed number and as an improper fraction.

36.

37.

38. A tailor designs a skirt that is $25\frac{1}{4}$ in. long. What is the length in eighths of an inch? Write your answer as an improper fraction.

39. The distance around a track is $\frac{1}{8}$ mi. A wheelchair racer completes 35 laps around the track. Write the distance he travels in miles as a mixed number.

40. **Writing in Math** Which is longer, $\frac{9}{4}$ miles or $1\frac{1}{2}$ miles? Explain.

41. Write two mixed numbers and an improper fraction for the model.

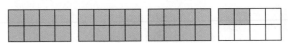

42. **Challenge** Using each of the digits 2, 5, and 9 exactly once, write a fraction with the greatest possible value. Then write the fraction as a mixed number.

Test Prep and Mixed Review

Practice

Multiple Choice

43. The table below shows the distances a football team ran each day last week. On which day did the team run the least?

Football Practice

Day	Monday	Tuesday	Wednesday	Thursday
Distance Run	$\frac{7}{10}$ mile	$\frac{5}{8}$ mile	$\frac{3}{4}$ mile	$\frac{2}{3}$ mile

Ⓐ Monday   Ⓑ Tuesday   Ⓒ Wednesday   Ⓓ Thursday

44. A 1-cup serving of mashed potatoes with whole milk and butter has 634 milligrams of sodium. How many grams of sodium are in 3 cups of mashed potatoes?

Ⓕ 0.1902 g   Ⓖ 1.902 g   Ⓗ 190.2 g   Ⓙ 1,902 g

Find each difference.

45. $-3 - 9$

46. $(-10) - (-18)$

47. $21 - (-7)$

GO for Help

For Exercises	See Lesson
45–47	1-7

Comparing Fractions and Decimals

A baseball player's batting average is the number of hits divided by the number of times at bat. You can tell which player has the best record by comparing batting averages.

ACTIVITY

1. Copy the table below.

Name of Player	Number of Hits	Times at Bat	Batting Average	
			Fraction	Decimal
Allan	43	195	■	■
Belinda	8	127	■	■
Char	43	183	■	■
Denise	47	183	■	■
Emil	29	174	■	■
Farik	45	135	■	■

2. Write each batting average as a fraction.

3. Use a calculator to write each batting average as a decimal. Round to the nearest thousandth.

Exercises

1. **a.** Which players had averages that are decimals with a repeating block of digits?
   b. List the players in order, from highest to lowest batting averages.

2. Is it easier to compare and order batting averages using fractions or decimals? Explain.

3. A student thought that Belinda's average was 0.630. What error do you think she made?

4. How can you tell, without using decimals, that Denise has a higher average than Char?

5. Can a player get 132 hits in 125 times at bat? How is your answer related to the highest possible batting average of 1.000?

What You'll Learn

To convert between fractions and decimals

🔊 **New Vocabulary** terminating decimal, repeating decimal

Why Learn This?

When you order sandwich meat at a delicatessen, you may ask for half a pound. The scales at a deli often use decimal measures. You can convert between fractions and decimals to make sure you are receiving the correct amount.

You write a fraction as a decimal by dividing the numerator by the denominator. A decimal that stops, or terminates, is a **terminating decimal.**

EXAMPLE Writing a Terminating Decimal

1 Gridded Response The pull of gravity is weaker on the moon than on Earth. The fraction $\frac{4}{25}$ represents the ratio of the moon's gravity to Earth's gravity. Write this fraction as a decimal.

$$\frac{4}{25} \text{ or } 4 \div 25 = 25\overline{)4.00} \quad \begin{array}{r} 0.16 \\ \hline 4.00 \end{array} \leftarrow \text{quotient}$$

$$\begin{array}{r} -25 \\ \hline 150 \\ -150 \\ \hline 0 \end{array} \leftarrow \text{The remainder is 0.}$$

The ratio of the moon's gravity to Earth's gravity as a decimal is 0.16. This is a terminating decimal because the division process stops when the remainder is 0.

✓ Quick Check

1. The fraction of nitrogen in a chemical sample is $\frac{5}{8}$. Write the fraction as a decimal.

Vocabulary Tip

The symbol for a repeating decimal is a bar over the repeated digit(s), for example, $0.\overline{17}$.

If the same block of digits in a decimal repeats without end, the decimal is a **repeating decimal.** The repeating block can include one or more digits.

$$5.355555555555\ldots = 5.3\overline{5} \quad \leftarrow \text{The digit 5 repeats.}$$
$$0.171717171717\ldots = 0.\overline{17} \quad \leftarrow \text{The digits 17 repeat.}$$

EXAMPLE Writing a Repeating Decimal

2 Write $\frac{3}{11}$ as a decimal.

Method 1 Paper and Pencil

$$\frac{3}{11} \text{ or } 3 \div 11 = 11\overline{)3.00000} \quad \begin{array}{r} 0.27272 \\ \end{array} \quad \leftarrow \text{The digits 27 repeat.}$$

$$\begin{array}{r} -22 \\ \hline 80 \\ -77 \\ \hline 30 \\ -22 \\ \hline 80 \\ -77 \\ \hline 30 \end{array} \quad \leftarrow \begin{array}{l} \text{There will always be a remainder} \\ \text{of 30 or 80.} \end{array}$$

Calculator Tip

Most calculators display as many digits as possible of a repeating decimal and round off the final digit. For example, $0.\overline{27}$ might be shown as 0.272727273.

Method 2 Calculator

$$3 \boxed{\div} 11 \boxed{=} 0.27272727273$$

So $\frac{3}{11} = 0.\overline{27}$.

✓ Quick Check

2. Write $\frac{5}{9}$ as a decimal.

You can write a terminating decimal as a fraction or a mixed number by writing the digits to the right of the decimal point as a fraction.

EXAMPLE Writing a Decimal as a Fraction

3 Write 1.325 as a mixed number with a fraction in simplest form.

Since $0.325 = \frac{325}{1,000}$, $1.325 = 1\frac{325}{1,000}$.

$$1\frac{325}{1,000} = 1\frac{325 \div 25}{1,000 \div 25} \quad \leftarrow \text{Use the GCF to write the fraction in simplest form.}$$

$$= 1\frac{13}{40}$$

✓ Quick Check

3. Write each decimal as a mixed number in simplest form.
   a. 1.364   b. 2.48   c. 3.6

To compare fractions and decimals, you can write the decimals as fractions or the fractions as decimals. You can decide which is easier for different numbers.

For help with place value and decimals, go to Skills Handbook p. 658

EXAMPLE Ordering Fractions and Decimals

4 Order from greatest to least: 2, 2.55, $2\frac{6}{18}$.

$2\frac{6}{18} = 2\frac{1}{3} = 2.\overline{3}$ ← **Use a calculator to change the mixed number to a decimal.**

Use a number line to find each decimal number's relative position.

```
                              2      2.3  2.55
  ←—+—+—+—+—+—+—+—+—●—+—+—●—+—●+—+—→
    1.0  1.2  1.4  1.6  1.8  2.0  2.2  2.4  2.6  2.8
```

So the order of the numbers from greatest to least is 2.55, $2\frac{6}{18}$, and 2.

☑ **Quick Check**

4. Order from greatest to least: $1\frac{3}{8}$, $1\frac{7}{15}$, 1.862.

You can order rational numbers to analyze data results.

EXAMPLE Application: Surveys

Careers Journalists gather information, analyze data, and write reports.

5 For a survey naming four animals, adults were asked to choose the animal they thought was the most endangered species. Of the adults surveyed, 0.25 chose black rhinoceros, $\frac{10}{48}$ chose tiger, $\frac{5}{12}$ chose giant panda, and 0.125 chose mako shark. List their choices in order of frequency.

First write all 4 ratios as decimals.

black rhinoceros: 0.25

tiger: $\frac{10}{48} = \frac{5}{24} = 0.208\overline{3}$ ⎫
                                                                ⎬ ← **Use a calculator to change the fractions to decimals.**
giant panda: $\frac{5}{12} = 0.41\overline{6}$ ⎭

mako shark: 0.125

Since $0.41\overline{6} > 0.25 > 0.208\overline{3} > 0.125$, the order of frequency was giant panda, black rhinoceros, tiger, and mako shark.

☑ **Quick Check**

5. In a survey about pets, $\frac{2}{5}$ of students prefer cats, 0.33 prefer dogs, $\frac{3}{25}$ prefer birds, and 0.15 prefer fish. List the choices in order of preference.

1. **Vocabulary** What is the difference between a terminating decimal and a repeating decimal?

2. **Reasoning** Is a remainder of 0 the same as no remainder? Explain.

Write each decimal as a mixed number or a fraction in simplest form.

3. 1.375   4. 0.44   5. 3.99

6. **Reasoning** Is 3.03003000300003 . . . a repeating decimal? Explain.

7. Order the following numbers from least to greatest: $1.\overline{9}$, $1\frac{1}{3}$, 2, 0.5.

Homework Exercises

For more exercises, see Extra Skills and Word Problems.

GO for Help

For Exercises	See Examples
8–15	1–2
16–23	3
24–28	4–5

Write each fraction as a decimal.

8. $\frac{2}{5}$ 9. $\frac{4}{5}$ 10. $\frac{3}{8}$ 11. $\frac{2}{3}$

12. $\frac{3}{4}$ 13. $\frac{1}{8}$ 14. $\frac{7}{11}$ 15. $\frac{3}{16}$

Write each decimal as a mixed number or a fraction in simplest form.

16. 0.125   17. 0.66   18. 2.5   19. 3.75

20. 0.32   21. 0.19   22. 0.8   23. 0.965

Order from greatest to least.

24. $\frac{9}{22}$, 0.83, $\frac{7}{8}$, 0.4, $\frac{44}{44}$ 25. 3.84, 3.789, 3, $3\frac{41}{50}$

26. $\frac{2}{3}$, 0.67, $\frac{5}{9}$, 0.58, $\frac{7}{12}$ 27. $0.1\overline{2}$, 0.1225, $\frac{3}{25}$, $\frac{7}{125}$

28. **Biology** DNA content in a cell is measured in picograms (pg). A sea star cell has $\frac{17}{20}$ pg of DNA, a scallop cell has $\frac{19}{20}$ pg, a red water mite cell has 0.19 pg, and a mosquito cell has 0.24 pg. Order the DNA contents from greatest to least.

GPS 29. **Guided Problem Solving** On an adventure trail, you biked 12 mi, walked 4 mi, ran 6 mi, and swam 2 mi. What fraction of the total distance did you bike? Write this number as a decimal.
   • The total distance of the adventure trail is ■ mi.
   • You biked ■ mi. As a fraction, this is ■ of the total distance.

30. **Music** To compose music on a computer, you can write notes as decimals. What decimals should you enter for a half note, a quarter note, an eighth note, and a sixteenth note?

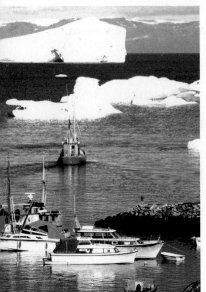
Greenland is the world's largest island.

(**Algebra**) Compare. Use <, =, or >. (*Note: n* is a value greater than 1.)

31. $\dfrac{1}{n}$ ■ $\dfrac{n}{n}$ **32.** 1 ■ $\dfrac{n}{1}$ **33.** n ■ $\dfrac{1}{n}$ **34.** $\dfrac{n}{n^2}$ ■ $\dfrac{1}{n}$

35. Number Sense Examine the fractions $\frac{2}{3}$, $\frac{3}{3}$, $\frac{4}{3}$, $\frac{5}{3}$, and $\frac{6}{3}$. Explain when a denominator of 3 will result in a repeating decimal.

36. Geography About 12,500 icebergs break away from Greenland each year. Of these, about 375 float into the Atlantic Ocean.
   a. What fraction of the icebergs float into the Atlantic Ocean?
   b. Write your answer for part (a) as a decimal.
   c. What fraction of the icebergs do *not* float into the Atlantic?

For Exercises 37–39, use the table at the right.

37. For each state, write a fraction that shows the ratio $\dfrac{\text{number of people under age 18}}{\text{total population}}$.

38. For most of the states, would $\frac{1}{2}$, $\frac{1}{3}$, or $\frac{1}{4}$ best describe the fraction of the population that is under age 18?

39. Calculator Order the states from least to greatest fraction under age 18.

40. Writing in Math Describe some everyday situations in which you need to change fractions to decimals.

41. Challenge Divide 50 by these numbers: 100, 10, 1, 0.1, 0.01, 0.001. Explain how the quotient changes as the divisor approaches 0.

Population (thousands)

State	Total	Under Age 18
N.Y.	19,227	4,572
Texas	22,490	6,267
Calif.	33,893	9,596
Fla.	17,397	4,003
Ohio	11,459	2,779

SOURCE: U.S. Census Bureau. Go to PHSchool.com for a data update. Web Code: arg-9041

Test Prep and Mixed Review

Practice

Gridded Response

42. Bennie's teacher gave him a score of $\frac{34}{40}$ on his quiz. What decimal is equivalent to the score Bennie received?

43. When Rahmi was 11 years old, he was 150.25 centimeters tall. For the next 4 years, he grew 6.5 centimeters a year. To the nearest centimeter, how tall was Rahmi when he was 15 years old?

44. Serena has a part-time job at a supermarket. Her boss tells her to find last week's average number of smoothies sold per day. He gives her the printout of sales in the past seven days: 14, 23, 42, 22, 15, 28, and 31. Serena correctly finds the average number of smoothies sold per day. What is the number?

Find each product.

45. $0.4 \cdot 0.9$ **46.** $1.7 \cdot 0.5$ **47.** $3.06 \cdot 0.3$ **48.** $9.013 \cdot 1.0$

GO for Help

For Exercises	See Lesson
45–48	1-3

Using Tables to Compare Data

Analyzing data is easier if the data are organized. You can rearrange a table to organize and display data.

An experiment with seeds resulted in the data recorded in the table. Analyze the data and redraw the table to show which seed types sprouted most frequently.

Seed Type	A	B	C	D	E	F	G	H	I
Number Sprouted	15	5	22	17	18	21	14	18	8
Number Planted	48	20	44	35	52	63	55	35	15

1. For each seed type, find the fraction $\dfrac{\text{number sprouted}}{\text{number planted}}$.

2. Compare the fractions. Order the seed types from most frequently sprouted to least frequently sprouted. (*Hint:* Convert to decimals.)

3. Redraw the table showing the seed types in order from most frequently sprouted to least frequently sprouted.

Checkpoint Quiz 2

Lessons 2-3 through 2-6

Simplify each fraction.

1. $\dfrac{18}{36}$

2. $\dfrac{42}{60}$

3. $\dfrac{35}{56}$

Compare. Use <, =, or >.

4. $\dfrac{1}{8}$ ■ $\dfrac{2}{100}$

5. $\dfrac{5}{12}$ ■ $\dfrac{7}{9}$

6. $\dfrac{12}{20}$ ■ $\dfrac{3}{5}$

Write each improper fraction as a mixed number and each mixed number as an improper fraction.

7. $\dfrac{29}{6}$

8. $4\dfrac{1}{9}$

9. $\dfrac{82}{5}$

10. Twins are born once in every 89 births. Identical twins are born 4 times in every 1,000 births. Triplets are born once in every 6,900 births. Write each birth frequency as a decimal and order the decimals from least to greatest frequency.

Rational Numbers

✓ Check Skills You'll Need

1. Vocabulary Review Is 1.234 a repeating decimal or a terminating decimal? Explain.

Write each fraction as a decimal.

2. $\frac{3}{4}$ **3.** $-\frac{7}{9}$

4. $1\frac{1}{3}$ **5.** $\frac{12}{48}$

 **for Help**

Lesson 2-6

What You'll Learn

To compare and order rational numbers

🔊 **New Vocabulary** rational number

Why Learn This?

Rational numbers are part of everyday life. You see them on price tags, highway signs, and charts. Rational numbers can be written in different forms. To compare rational numbers, it is easier to convert them into the same form.

A **rational number** is a number that can be written as a quotient of two integers, where the divisor is not 0. Examples are $\frac{2}{5}$, $0.\overline{3}$, -6, and $3\frac{1}{2}$.

EXAMPLE **Comparing Rational Numbers**

❶ Compare $-\frac{1}{2}$ and $-\frac{3}{4}$.

Method 1

← Since $-\frac{3}{4}$ is farther to the left on the number line, it is the lesser number.

So $-\frac{3}{4} < -\frac{1}{2}$.

GO for Help

For help with writing equivalent fractions, go to Lesson 2-3, Example 1.

Method 2

$-\frac{1}{2} = \frac{-1}{2}$ ← Rewrite $-\frac{1}{2}$ with -1 in the numerator.

$= \frac{-1 \times 2}{2 \times 2}$ ← The LCD is 4. Write an equivalent fraction.

$= \frac{-2}{4} = -\frac{2}{4}$ ← The fraction $-\frac{2}{4}$ is equivalent to $\frac{-2}{4}$.

Since $-\frac{3}{4} < -\frac{2}{4}$, $-\frac{3}{4} < -\frac{1}{2}$.

✓ Quick Check

1. Compare $-\frac{2}{3}$ and $-\frac{1}{6}$. Use $<$, $=$, or $>$.

EXAMPLE Comparing Decimals

2 **a.** Compare -4.4 and 4.7.

$-4.4 < 4.7$ ← Any negative number is less than a positive number.

b. Compare -4.4 and -4.7.

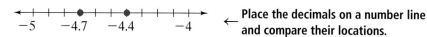

← Place the decimals on a number line and compare their locations.

$-4.4 > -4.7$ since -4.4 is to the right of -4.7.

✓ Quick Check

2. Compare -4.2 and -4.9. Use $<, =,$ or $>$.

When you compare and order decimals and fractions, it is often helpful to write the fractions as decimals.

EXAMPLE Ordering Rational Numbers

3 **Multiple Choice** The peaks of four mountains or seamounts are located either below or above sea level as follows: $\frac{1}{4}$ mi, -0.2 mi, $-\frac{2}{9}$ mi, 1.1 mi. Which list shows the order of numbers from least to greatest?

Ⓐ $\frac{1}{4}, -0.2, -\frac{2}{9}, 1.1$

Ⓒ $-\frac{2}{9}, -0.2, \frac{1}{4}, 1.1$

Ⓑ $\frac{1}{4}, -\frac{2}{9}, 1.1, -0.2$

Ⓓ $-0.2, -\frac{2}{9}, 1.1, \frac{1}{4}$

Test Prep Tip ⒶⒷⒸⒹ

Sometimes it is easier to order rational numbers when they are all written as decimals.

Order these numbers from least to greatest: $\frac{1}{4}, -0.2, -\frac{2}{9}, 1.1$.

$\frac{1}{4} = 1 \div 4 = 0.250$ ← Write as a decimal.

$-\frac{2}{9} = -2 \div 9 = -0.22222\ldots = -0.\overline{2}$ ← Write as a repeating decimal.

You can use a number line to order the numbers.

$-0.\overline{2} < -0.2 < 0.25 < 1.1$ ← Compare the decimals.

In order, the numbers are $-\frac{2}{9}, -0.2, \frac{1}{4},$ and 1.1. The answer is C.

✓ Quick Check

3. The following temperatures were recorded during a science project: $12\frac{1}{2}°C, -4°C, 6.55°C,$ and $-6\frac{1}{4}°C$. Order the temperatures from least to greatest.

✓ Check Your Understanding

1. **Vocabulary** In your own words, define *rational number*.

Compare. Use <, =, or >.

2. $2\frac{1}{5}$ ■ $3\frac{1}{3}$

3. $-3\frac{1}{2}$ ■ $-3\frac{3}{4}$

4. -6.1 ■ -6

Order from least to greatest.

5. $-236, -7\frac{1}{7}, 0, \frac{41}{99}, -3.\overline{3}$

6. $-8, -5\frac{1}{3}, -8.22, -8\frac{1}{3}, \frac{16}{42}$

Homework Exercises

For more exercises, see Extra Skills and Word Problems.

GO for Help

For Exercises	See Examples
7–12	1
13–18	2
19–22	3

Compare. Use <, =, or >.

7. $-\frac{1}{7}$ ■ $-\frac{6}{7}$

8. $-\frac{3}{4}$ ■ -3

9. $-\frac{1}{2}$ ■ $-\frac{2}{10}$

10. $-\frac{3}{4}$ ■ -1

11. $-\frac{1}{2}$ ■ $-\frac{5}{6}$

12. $-\frac{4}{5}$ ■ $-\frac{1}{3}$

13. 5.2 ■ -8.3

14. -6.5 ■ 6.2

15. -4.9 ■ -4.3

16. 1.09 ■ -1.90

17. -1.22 ■ -6.5

18. -10.2 ■ -10.23

Order from least to greatest.

19. $\frac{3}{2}, 0.25, -\frac{3}{4}, -1.0$

20. $\frac{7}{3}, 2.4, -\frac{6}{25}, -1.34$

21. $\frac{6}{11}, -1.5, 0.545, \frac{1}{2}$

22. $\frac{7}{6}, \frac{11}{12}, \frac{14}{24}, 1$

23. **Guided Problem Solving** You are skier A, the first skier in a skiing event with three other skiers. Compared to your time, skier B is slower, by a time of +00:28. Skier C has a time of +02:13, and skier D has a time of −01:24. Who is the fastest skier?
    - Since all times are compared to yours, what is your time?
    - What is the order of times, from fastest to slowest?

24. The table below shows melting points of four elements. Which element has the highest melting point?

Melting Points

Chemical Solid	Krypton	Argon	Xenon	Helium
Melting Point (°C)	−157.36	−189.35	−111.79	−272.2

SOURCE: Encyclopædia Brittanica

Compare. Use <, =, or >.

25. -5.8 ▪ $-5\frac{9}{10}$ **26.** $-6\frac{11}{50}$ ▪ -6.21 **27.** -10.42 ▪ $-10.4\overline{2}$

28. **Writing in Math** Compare $-\frac{5}{8}$ and $-\frac{3}{4}$. Is it easier to find common denominators or to write decimal equivalents? Explain.

29. **Animals** About $\frac{1}{25}$ of a toad's eggs survive to adulthood. About 0.25 of a frog's eggs and $\frac{1}{5}$ of a green turtle's eggs survive to adulthood. Which animal's eggs have the highest survival rate?

30. **Money** Here is part of Mr. Lostcash's checkbook register. Order his balances from greatest to least.

Description	Debits (−)	Credits (+)	Balance
Paycheck		122.18	122.18
Sneakers	95.00		27.18
Two outfits	68.09		−40.91
Paycheck		122.18	81.27
Insufficient funds fee	25.00		56.27
Three CDs	59.97		−3.70

31. **Challenge** Evaluate $\frac{m - n}{-12}$ for $m = -3$ and $n = 6$.

Test Prep and Mixed Review   **Practice**

Multiple Choice

32. Harry's class wants to buy one slice of pie for each person in the class. The table below shows prices from a local bakery. What additional information is needed to estimate the total cost?

Rainbow Bakery Pies

Pie Size	Price	Number of Pieces
Small	$8	2
Medium	$10	3

    Ⓐ The cost of each piece for each pie size
    Ⓑ The number of students in Harry's class
    Ⓒ The number of pieces in each pie
    Ⓓ The flavors of the pies

33. Eight photo albums contain equal numbers of photos. Which of the following could be the total number of photos in all the albums?

    Ⓕ 1,821   Ⓖ 1,218   Ⓗ 1,182   Ⓙ 1,128

For Exercises	See Lesson
34–37	2-3

Write each fraction in simplest form.

34. $\frac{36}{38}$ **35.** $\frac{14}{28}$ **36.** $\frac{12}{56}$ **37.** $\frac{18}{48}$

Check Skills You'll Need

1. **Vocabulary Review**
An exponent tells you how many times a number, or base, is used as a   ?   .

Simplify.

2. 3^3 **3.** 4^2

4. 10^5 **5.** 2^4

 **for Help**
Lesson 2-1

What You'll Learn

To write numbers in both scientific notation and standard form

◀)) **New Vocabulary** scientific notation

Why Learn This?

Some numbers are so large that they are difficult to write. You can use scientific notation to express large numbers, such as distances and speeds in space. Scientists use scientific notation to calculate with large numbers.

In Lesson 2-1, you learned about exponents. When the base is 10, the exponent tells you the number of zeros the number will have in standard form.

Powers of 10

Exponential Form	10^1	10^2	10^3	10^4	10^5	10^6
Number of Zeros in Standard Form	1	2	3	4	5	6
Standard Form	10	100	1,000	10,000	100,000	1,000,000

When you multiply a factor by a power of 10, you can find the product by moving the decimal point in the factor to the right. The exponent tells you how many places to move the decimal point. When you divide by a power of 10, you move the decimal point to the left.

Multiplying and Dividing by Powers of 10

Standard Form	$3.5 \div 100$	$3.5 \div 10$	3.5×10	3.5×100	$3.5 \times 1,000$
Exponential Form	$3.5 \div 10^2$	$3.5 \div 10^1$	3.5×10^1	3.5×10^2	3.5×10^3
Number	0.035	0.35	35	350	3,500

Scientific notation is a shorter way to write numbers using powers of 10.

Scientific Notation

A number in **scientific notation** is written as the product of two factors, one greater than or equal to 1 and less than 10, and the other a power of 10.

$$7,500,000,000,000 = 7.5 \times 10^{12}$$

EXAMPLE Writing in Scientific Notation

1 Science The moon orbits Earth at a distance of 384,000 km. Write this number in scientific notation.

   3.84000.   ← Move the decimal point to get a factor greater than 1 but less than 10.

$$384,000 = 3.84 \times 100,000 \quad \leftarrow \text{Write as a product of 2 factors.}$$
$$= 3.84 \times 10^5 \quad \leftarrow \text{Write 100,000 as a power of 10.}$$

The moon orbits Earth at a distance of 3.84×10^5 km.

✓ Quick Check

1. NASA's Hubble Telescope took pictures of a supernova that is 169,000 light years away. Write this number in scientific notation.

You can change expressions from scientific notation to standard form by simplifying the product of the two factors.

EXAMPLE Writing in Standard Form

2 Science The mean distance from the sun to Mars is approximately 2.3×10^8 km. Write this number in standard form.

Method 1

$$2.3 \times 10^8 = 2.3 \times 100,000,000 \quad \leftarrow \text{Write as a product of 2 factors.}$$
$$= 230,000,000 \quad \leftarrow \text{Multiply the factors.}$$

Method 2

$$2.3 \times 10^8 = 2.30000000 \quad \leftarrow \begin{array}{l}\text{The exponent is 8. Move the decimal} \\ \text{8 places to the right.}\end{array}$$
$$= 230,000,000$$

The mean distance is approximately 230,000,000 km.

✓ Quick Check

2. A large telescope gathers about 6.4×10^5 times the amount of light your eye receives. Write this number in standard form.

Check Your Understanding

1. **Vocabulary** Describe how to write a number in scientific notation.

2. **Reasoning** Is 107×10^4 written in scientific notation? Explain.

Fill in the blank.

3. $1{,}700 = 1.7 \times 10^{\blacksquare}$

4. $2{,}850{,}000 = \blacksquare \times 10^6$

Match the equivalent numbers.

5. 3.96×10^6

6. 3.96×10^7

7. 3.96×10^5

   A. 396,000
   B. 3,960,000
   C. 39,600,000

Homework Exercises

For more exercises, see Extra Skills and Word Problems.

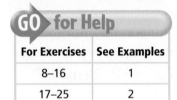

For Exercises	See Examples
8–16	1
17–25	2

Write in scientific notation.

8. 7,500   9. 75,000,000   10. 1,250   11. 44,000

12. 149,000,000   13. 34,025   14. 11,020   15. 120,000

16. One light year is 5,880,000,000,000 mi. Write in scientific notation.

Write in standard form.

17. 3.4×10^3 18. 5.9×10^2 19. 8.21×10^3 20. 6.678×10^2

21. 7.45×10^4 22. 9.9673×10^2 23. 5×10^{11} 24. 7.02×10^1

25. The normal red blood cell count for adult males is about 4.5×10^{12} per liter. Write this number in standard form.

26. **Guided Problem Solving** The Folsom Dam in California holds back 319 billion gallons of water. Write this in scientific notation.
    - How can you rewrite 319 billion in standard form?
    - How do you write 319 billion in scientific notation?

27. **Ballooning** The first balloon to carry passengers weighed 1.6×10^3 lb. Write the number of pounds in standard form.

28. A scientist observes two colonies of bacteria. The first grows at a rate of 2.2×10^6 bacteria per hour. The other grows at a rate of 6.3×10^5 bacteria per hour. Which grows faster? How do you know?

29. **Writing in Math** Explain how you would find the power of 10 needed to write 725,000,000 in scientific notation.

Planet	Mass (kg)
Mercury	3.303×10^{23}
Venus	4.869×10^{24}
Earth	5.976×10^{24}
Mars	6.421×10^{23}
Jupiter	1.900×10^{27}
Saturn	5.688×10^{26}
Uranus	8.686×10^{25}
Neptune	1.024×10^{26}
Pluto	1.290×10^{22}

30. **Science** The table at the left shows the planets in the solar system and their masses. List the masses in order from least to greatest.

31. **Plants** There are about 350,000 species of plants on Earth. Write this number in scientific notation.

Math in the Media Use the cartoon below for Exercises 32 and 33.

FOX TROT

by Bill Amend

32. How many minutes was the warning? Write in standard form.

33. Convert the time to hours. Write in scientific notation.

34. **Challenge** An astronomical unit (AU) is approximately 9.3×10^7 mi. Pluto is about 39 AU from the sun. Write the distance in miles using both scientific notation and standard form.

Test Prep and Mixed Review

Practice

Multiple Choice

35. Population density is a measure of how crowded a place is. The table below shows the population density of several states in 1990 and in 2000. Based on the information in the table, which of the following is NOT a reasonable assumption?

   Ⓐ Texas had the same population density in 1990 that Alabama had in 2000.

   Ⓑ Alabama was more crowded in 1990 than West Virginia was in 2000.

   Ⓒ In 1990, West Virginia was more crowded than Texas.

   Ⓓ All of the states had a greater population density in 2000 than they did in 1990.

Population Density

State	Persons per Square Mile	
	1990	2000
Alabama	$79\frac{3}{5}$	87.6
Missouri	$74\frac{3}{10}$	81.2
Texas	$64\frac{9}{10}$	79.6
W. Virginia	$74\frac{1}{2}$	75.1

Find the LCM of each pair of numbers.

36. 7, 8   37. 6, 20   38. 11, 3   39. 9, 15

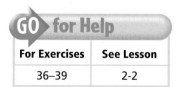

For Exercises	See Lesson
36–39	2-2

Negative Exponents

To write a number between 0 and 1 in scientific
notation, you use a negative exponent.

EXAMPLE   **Writing in Scientific Notation**

1   Write 0.0084 in scientific notation.

     0.008.4   ← Move the decimal point to obtain a factor greater than 1 but less than 10.

      $0.0084 = 8.4 \times 0.001$ ← Write as the product of 2 factors.
           $= 8.4 \times 10^{-3}$ ← The decimal point was moved 3 places to the right. Use -3 as the exponent.

In scientific notation, 0.0084 is written as 8.4×10^{-3}.

EXAMPLE   **Writing in Standard Form**

2   Write 3.52×10^{-5} in standard form.

Method 1

     $3.52 \times 10^{-5} = 3.52 \times 0.00001$ ← Write as the product of 2 factors.
            $= 0.0000352$ ← Multiply the factors.

Method 2

     $3.52 \times 10^{-5} = 0.00003.52$ ← The exponent of 10 is -5.
                         Move the decimal 5 places to the left.

          $= 0.0000352$

The value of 3.52×10^{-5} is 0.0000352.

Exercises

Write each number in scientific notation.

1. 0.0008   **2.** 0.00000691   **3.** 0.5   **4.** 0.049562

Write each number in standard form.

5. 8.55×10^{-1} **6.** 2.005×10^{-2} **7.** 6.079×10^{-5}

8. The width of a hair is about 3×10^{-7} meters.   **9.** A flea weighs 4.9×10^{-3} grams.

Writing Extended Responses

An extended response question is usually worth a maximum of 4 points and has multiple parts. To get full credit, you need to answer each part and show all your work or justify your reasoning.

EXAMPLE

Without performing the division, test whether 15,534 is divisible by 3, 4, 9, and 12. Justify each response.

Below are four responses and the amount of credit each received.

4 points

Divisible by 3?
$1 + 5 + 5 + 3 + 4 = 18$
Yes, since 18 is divisible by 3.

Divisible by 4? $34 \div 4 = 8.5$
No, since 34 is not divisible by 4.

Divisible by 9? $18 \div 9 = 2$
Yes, since 18 is divisible by 9.

Divisible by 12?
No, since 15,534 is not divisible by 4.

The 4-point response shows the correct answers and justifies each one.

3 points

Divisible by 3?
$1 + 5 + 5 + 3 + 4 = 17$
No, since 17 is not divisible by 3.

Divisible by 4? $34 \div 4 = 8.5$
No, since 34 is not divisible by 4.

Divisible by 9? $17 \div 9 = 1.8$
No, since 17 is not divisible by 9.

Divisible by 12?
No, since 15,534 is not divisible by 4.

The 3-point response has a computational error, but the student completed both parts.

2 points

Divisible by 3?
$1 + 5 + 5 + 3 + 4 = 18$
Yes, since 18 is divisible by 3.

Divisible by 4? $34 \div 4 = 8$
Yes, since 34 is divisible by 4.

Divisible by 9? $18 \div 2 = 9$

Divisible by 12?
Yes, since 15,534 is divisible by 3 and 4.

1 point

Yes, 15,534 is divisible by 3.

No, 15,534 is not divisible by 4.

Yes, 15,534 is divisible by 9.

No, 15,534 is not divisible by 12.

The 1-point response shows correct answers but with no work or justification.

A 0-point response has incorrect answers and no work shown.

The 2-point response has a computational error and is missing an answer.

Vocabulary Review

🔊 base (p. 68)
composite number (p. 75)
equivalent fractions (p. 82)
exponent (p. 68)
factor (p. 75)
greatest common factor (GCF)
(p. 75)

improper fraction (p. 91)
least common denominator
(LCD) (p. 87)
least common multiple (p. 74)
mixed number (p. 91)
multiple (p. 74)
power (p. 68)

prime factorization (p. 75)
prime number (p. 75)
rational number (p. 102)
repeating decimal (p. 97)
scientific notation (p. 107)
simplest form (p. 82)
terminating decimal (p. 96)

Choose the correct term to complete each sentence.

1. In the expression 6^3, 3 represents the (power, exponent).

2. A (composite, prime) number has exactly two factors, 1 and itself.

3. (Multiples, Factors) of 28 are 1, 2, 4, 7, 14, and 28.

4. At a class party, you and two friends eat $\frac{6}{8}$ of a pizza. This can also be written as the (improper fraction, equivalent fraction) $\frac{3}{4}$.

Go **Online**
PHSchool.com
For: Online vocabulary quiz
Web Code: arj-0251

5. The (GCF, LCM) of 24 and 36 is 12.

Skills and Concepts

Lesson 2-1
• To write and simplify expressions with exponents

An **exponent** tells you how many times a number, or base, is used as a factor. A number expressed with an exponent is a **power**.

Simplify.

6. -2^4 7. $(-4)^3$ 8. $5^2 + 10^2$ 9. $4(5^2 - 10)$

Lesson 2-2
• To find multiples and factors and to use prime factorization

A **multiple** is the product of a number and any nonzero whole number. A **factor** is a whole number that divides another whole number with a remainder of 0. A whole number greater than 1 is **composite** if it has more than two factors and is **prime** if its only factors are 1 and itself.

Write the prime factorization. Use exponents where possible.

10. 84   11. 78   12. 90   13. 92   14. 125

15. A grocer buys food from three suppliers. The suppliers deliver every 5 days, 6 days, and 7 days. All three came today. In how many days will they all deliver on the same day again?

Lessons 2-3, 2-4
- To write equivalent fractions and to simplify fractions
- To compare and order fractions

A fraction is in **simplest form** when the numerator and denominator have no common factors other than 1. To compare and order fractions, you can use the **least common denominator (LCD),** which is the least common multiple of the fractions' denominators.

Order from least to greatest.

16. $\frac{1}{4}, \frac{1}{3}, \frac{1}{6}$ **17.** $\frac{1}{4}, \frac{2}{5}, \frac{3}{8}$ **18.** $\frac{3}{8}, \frac{5}{6}, \frac{1}{2}$ **19.** $\frac{5}{9}, \frac{2}{3}, \frac{7}{12}$

20. Martha saw the same item on sale at two stores. Store A's sign read "Sale! $\frac{1}{3}$ off!" Store B's sign read "Sale! $\frac{2}{5}$ off!" Which store offered a greater discount?

Lesson 2-5
- To write mixed numbers and improper fractions

An **improper fraction** has a numerator that is greater than or equal to its denominator. A **mixed number** is the sum of a whole number and a fraction.

21. Tracey worked a total of 345 min. on a project. Use mixed numbers to write the time in hours.

Write each improper fraction as a whole or mixed number. Simplify.

22. $\frac{42}{7}$ **23.** $\frac{27}{12}$ **24.** $\frac{20}{3}$ **25.** $\frac{125}{5}$ **26.** $\frac{84}{12}$

Lessons 2-6, 2-7
- To convert between fractions and decimals
- To compare and order rational numbers

To write a fraction as a decimal, you divide the numerator by the denominator. When the division ends with a remainder of 0, the quotient is a **terminating decimal.** When the same block of digits in a decimal repeats without end, the quotient is a **repeating decimal.** A **rational number** can be written as the quotient of two integers, where the denominator is not zero.

Write each fraction as a decimal.

27. $\frac{1}{3}$ **28.** $\frac{5}{9}$ **29.** $\frac{5}{2}$ **30.** $\frac{16}{20}$ **31.** $\frac{4}{50}$

Order from least to greatest.

32. $\frac{3}{4}, 0.\overline{3}, -\frac{7}{8}$ **33.** $2.7, -0.3, -\frac{4}{11}$ **34.** $-\frac{5}{6}, 2.2, -0.5$

Lesson 2-8
- To write numbers in both scientific notation and standard form

A number in **scientific notation** is written as a product of a factor greater than or equal to 1 but less than 10, and another factor that is a power of 10.

Write in scientific notation or in standard form.

35. 7,123,000   **36.** 9.06×10^5 **37.** 81,900   **38.** 6.015×10^8

Go Online For: Online chapter test
PHSchool.com **Web Code:** ara-0252

Find the value of each expression.

1. $(3^2 - 4) + 5$ 2. $5^2 - 7^2$

3. $(6 - 9)^3$ 4. $54 + 3^2$

Write using an exponent.

5. $3 \cdot 3 \cdot 3 \cdot 3$ 6. $11 \cdot 11 \cdot 11$

Write the prime factorization. Use exponents where possible.

7. 48   8. 60   9. 121

List 3 factors and 3 multiples of each number.

10. 27   11. 36   12. 100   13. 25

Find the GCF of each pair of numbers.

14. 32, 40   15. 55, 15   16. 36, 57   17. 24, 68

18. **Reasoning** Tell whether each statement is true or false.
    a. 2 is a composite number.
    b. Any factor of a whole number is greater than any multiple of a whole number.
    c. A number is divisible by 3 if its last digit is divisible by 3.
    d. 1 is neither composite nor prime.

19. Use a factor tree to write the prime factorization of 42.

Write two fractions equivalent to each fraction.

20. $\frac{1}{3}$ 21. $-\frac{15}{24}$ 22. $-\frac{4}{5}$ 23. $\frac{16}{28}$

Write each fraction in simplest form.

24. $\frac{12}{18}$ 25. $\frac{27}{54}$ 26. $\frac{36}{96}$ 27. $\frac{7}{42}$

28. **Writing in Math** Explain how you can use prime factorization to write a fraction in simplest form.

29. **Modeling** Draw models to represent $\frac{3}{4}$ and $2\frac{3}{5}$.

30. What fraction does the shaded part of the model represent?

Compare. Use <, =, or >.

31. $\frac{2}{9} \blacksquare \frac{8}{9}$ 32. $\frac{5}{16} \blacksquare \frac{3}{8}$ 33. $\frac{7}{18} \blacksquare \frac{2}{5}$

34. **Ships** A crew finds a treasure chest with 168 gold coins and 200 silver coins. Each crew member gets the same share of gold coins and of silver coins, with none left over.
    a. What is the greatest possible number of crew members?
    b. How many of each type of coin does each crew member get?

Write as an improper fraction.

35. $5\frac{2}{3}$ 36. $4\frac{5}{6}$ 37. $8\frac{7}{10}$ 38. $3\frac{2}{5}$

Write as a whole number or a mixed number.

39. $\frac{12}{5}$ 40. $\frac{30}{9}$ 41. $\frac{48}{12}$ 42. $\frac{42}{30}$

Write each fraction as a decimal.

43. $\frac{2}{16}$ 44. $\frac{6}{15}$ 45. $\frac{5}{4}$ 46. $\frac{8}{25}$

Write each decimal as a mixed number or fraction in simplest form.

47. 0.2   48. 1.3   49. 0.35   50. 3.62

Write using scientific notation.

51. 12,300,000   52. 75,462

Write in standard form.

53. 2.1×10^4 54. 8×10^9

55. Order from least to greatest:
    $2.56, -2.\overline{5}, -2\frac{1}{5}, \frac{24}{10}, -2.4$

Reading Comprehension

Read each passage and answer the questions that follow.

Prime Construction Jackie says, "If I multiply the first two prime numbers together and add 1, I get a new prime number." Amit says, "If I multiply the first three prime numbers and add 1, I also get a prime number." Carl says, "I bet the same will happen if I multiply the first four prime numbers and add 1." "It seems to me," says Maria, "that if I multiply any two or more prime numbers, the product is never prime."

1. What prime number does Jackie get?
   - A 8
   - B 6
   - C 7
   - D 11

2. What prime number does Amit get?
   - F 16
   - G 31
   - H 41
   - J 43

3. What number would Carl get?
   - A 107
   - B 181
   - C 210
   - D 211

4. Which numbers could NOT be used to test Maria's statement?
   - F 3, 13
   - G 2, 5, 11
   - H 31, 33
   - J 17, 29

Light Reading Light travels very quickly—at about 1.86×10^5 mi/s. This is fast enough that we do not notice any delay when we flip a light switch. However, light from distant objects in space does not arrive instantaneously. The sun is about 9.3×10^7 mi from Earth. The next nearest star system, Alpha Centauri, is about 2.5×10^{13} mi away.

5. About how far away would a lamp have to be for its light to take 2 s to reach our eyes?
   - A 37,000 mi
   - B 370,000 mi
   - C 3,700,000 mi
   - D 37,000,000 mi

6. About how long does it take light from the sun to reach Earth?
   - F 5 s
   - G 5×10 s
   - H 5×10^2 s
   - J 500 min

7. Which does NOT express the time in seconds it takes light from Alpha Centauri to reach Earth?
   - A $\dfrac{2.5 \times 10^{13}}{186 \times 10^3}$
   - B $\dfrac{2.5 \times 10^{13}}{186,000}$
   - C $\dfrac{1.86}{2.5 \times 10^8}$
   - D $\dfrac{2.5}{1.86} \cdot \dfrac{10^{13}}{10^5}$

8. About how many times farther is Alpha Centauri from Earth than the sun is from Earth?
   - F 4
   - G 23
   - H 2.6×10^3
   - J 270,000

Applying Fractions

Photographic Memory You've probably seen pictures of athletes, animals, or cars that "freeze" the subject's motion but show all the excitement of the moment. A good photographer chooses the best shutter speed for the action. If the shutter stays open too long, the camera records too much movement, and the picture is blurry.

Cameras Then and Now

In the 1850s, leather bellows folded a camera into a protective case, making it easier to carry. Zoom lenses on digital cameras fold into the camera for protection.

Capturing Movement

For this photograph, the photographer used a very slow shutter speed and a strobe light. The shutter stayed open while the dancer moved.

Light Trail

For this photograph, the photographer used a very slow shutter speed and no flash. The shutter stayed open while traffic moved along the upper and lower levels of Interstate 5 in Seattle, Washington.

Put It All Together

Data File Use the data on these two pages and the exposure times on page 87 to answer these questions.

1. The image of the runner is blurry because the runner moved a visible amount during the $\frac{1}{15}$ of a second that the shutter was open.
   a. The blur for $\frac{1}{15}$ s is 1 in. long. How long would the blur be for 1 s?
   b. How long would the blur be for each exposure time on page 87?
   c. **Reasoning** At what shutter time do you think the length of the blur would be small enough that it would not show in the photo?

2. **a.** How many times would the blur length fit into the space between the two cones in the photo? What fraction of the distance between the cones is the blur?
   b. Use your answer to part (a) to find the distance the runner moved while the shutter was open.
   c. Maintaining the same speed, how far would the runner go in 1 s? In 1 min?

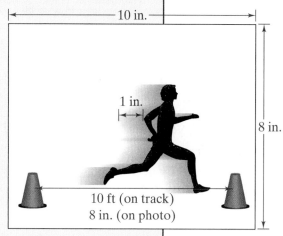

10 in.

1 in.

8 in.

10 ft (on track)
8 in. (on photo)

Go Online
PHSchool.com
For: Information about photography
Web Code: are-0253

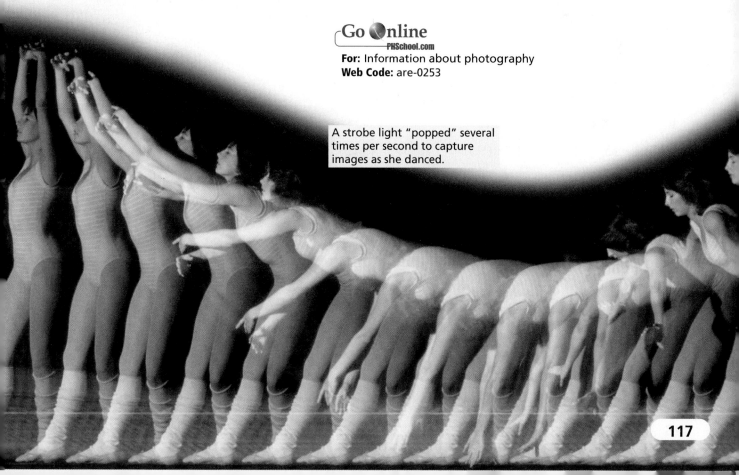

A strobe light "popped" several times per second to capture images as she danced.

Operations With Fractions

What You've Learned

- In Chapter 1, you estimated with decimals. You changed units in the metric system.

- In Chapter 2, you simplified fractions and wrote mixed numbers and improper fractions.

Check Your Readiness

GO for Help

For Exercises	See Lesson
1–4	1-7
5–8	1-8
9–12	2-2
13–20	2-3

Adding and Subtracting Integers

Find each sum or difference.

1. $-55 + 15$ **2.** $-3 + (-21)$

3. $58 - (-42)$ **4.** $-7 - (-25)$

Multiplying and Dividing Integers

Find each product or quotient.

5. $-3 \cdot 15$ **6.** $-12 \cdot (-5)$ **7.** $39 \div (-13)$ **8.** $-60 \div (-3)$

Finding the Greatest Common Factor

Use prime factorization to find the GCF of each pair of numbers.

9. $18, 27$ **10.** $21, 42$ **11.** $24, 36$ **12.** $45, 36$

Simplifying Fractions

Write each fraction in simplest form.

13. $\frac{12}{16}$ **14.** $\frac{15}{30}$ **15.** $\frac{42}{48}$ **16.** $\frac{27}{72}$

17. $\frac{19}{57}$ **18.** $\frac{25}{45}$ **19.** $\frac{34}{51}$ **20.** $\frac{16}{56}$

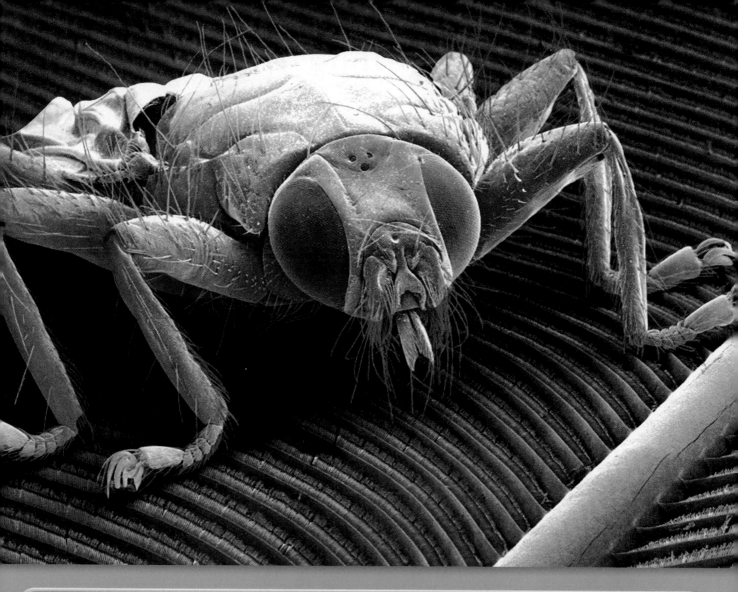

What You'll Learn Next

- In this chapter, you will estimate with fractions and mixed numbers.

- You will change units in the customary system.

- You will add, subtract, multiply, and divide fractions and mixed numbers.

 Problem Solving Application On pages 164 and 165, you will work an extended activity on fractions.

🔊 **Key Vocabulary**

- benchmark (p. 120)
- precision (p. 154)
- reciprocal (p. 141)

Estimating With Fractions and Mixed Numbers

Check Skills You'll Need

1. **Vocabulary Review** How is estimating with *compatible numbers* different from estimating by *rounding*?

Use compatible numbers to estimate each quotient.

2. $49.8 \div 6.8$

3. $21.05 \div 5.29$

4. $25.27 \div 2.99$

5. $52.6 \div 8.8$

6. $19.4 \div 10.1$

GO for Help
Lesson 1-1

What You'll Learn

To estimate sums, differences, products, and quotients of fractions

◀ᴺ **New Vocabulary** benchmark

Why Learn This?

Estimation can help you find amounts that are not whole numbers.

At the right, $\frac{7}{12}$ of one pie and $\frac{3}{8}$ of the other pie remain. You can estimate that a total of about one full pie remains.

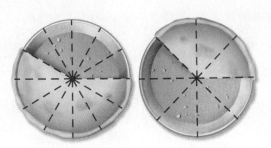

A **benchmark** is a convenient number used to replace fractions less than 1. You can use the benchmarks 0, $\frac{1}{2}$, and 1 to estimate fractions.

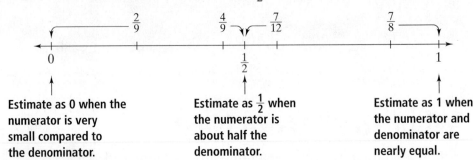

Estimate as 0 when the numerator is very small compared to the denominator.

Estimate as $\frac{1}{2}$ when the numerator is about half the denominator.

Estimate as 1 when the numerator and denominator are nearly equal.

EXAMPLE Using Benchmarks With Fractions

1 A family bought a plot of land last year that was $\frac{4}{9}$ acre. They plan to buy an adjoining plot this year that is $\frac{7}{8}$ acre. Estimate the total amount of land the family will have.

$$\frac{4}{9} + \frac{7}{8} \approx \frac{1}{2} + 1 = 1\frac{1}{2} \quad \leftarrow \text{Use benchmarks to estimate each fraction. Then add.}$$

The family will have about $1\frac{1}{2}$ acres of land.

✓ Quick Check

1. Use benchmarks to estimate $\frac{3}{5} - \frac{1}{8}$.

To estimate a sum, difference, or product of mixed numbers, you can first round each mixed number to the nearest whole number. Then compute.

EXAMPLES **Estimating With Mixed Numbers**

2 A skysurfer falls 500 feet in about $2\frac{4}{5}$ seconds. A skydiver wearing a wing suit falls 500 feet in about $4\frac{1}{6}$ seconds. Approximately how many more seconds than the skysurfer does the skydiver take to fall 500 feet?

$$4\frac{1}{6} - 2\frac{4}{5} \qquad \leftarrow \text{Use subtraction.}$$
$$\downarrow \qquad \downarrow$$
$$4 \;-\; 3 = 1 \qquad \leftarrow \text{Round each mixed number. Then subtract.}$$

The skydiver takes about 1 more second than the skysurfer to fall 500 ft.

3 Estimate the product $2\frac{2}{5} \cdot 6\frac{1}{10}$.

$$2\frac{2}{5} \;\cdot\; 6\frac{1}{10}$$
$$\downarrow \qquad \downarrow$$
$$2 \;\cdot\; 6 = 12 \qquad \leftarrow \text{Round each mixed number. Then multiply.}$$

✓ Quick Check

2. **Science** For an experiment on plant growth, you recorded the height of a plant every day. On Monday, the plant was $5\frac{1}{4}$ in. tall. A week later, it was $10\frac{7}{8}$ in. tall. About how many inches did the plant grow?

3. Use rounding to estimate each product.

   a. $3\frac{5}{6} \cdot 5\frac{1}{8}$ **b.** $8\frac{1}{8} \cdot 5\frac{11}{12}$ **c.** $7\frac{1}{3} \cdot 1\frac{13}{16}$

To estimate a quotient of mixed numbers, you can use compatible numbers. Choose numbers that are easy to divide.

EXAMPLE **Estimating With Compatible Numbers**

Vocabulary Tip

Compatible numbers are numbers that are easy to compute mentally.

4 Estimate the quotient $43\frac{1}{4} \div 5\frac{7}{8}$.

$$43\frac{1}{4} \div 5\frac{7}{8}$$
$$\downarrow \qquad \downarrow$$
$$42 \;\div\; 6 = 7 \qquad \leftarrow \begin{array}{l}\text{Use compatible numbers.} \\ \text{Use 42 for } 43\frac{1}{4} \text{ and use 6 for } 5\frac{7}{8}.\end{array}$$

✓ Quick Check

4. Use compatible numbers to estimate each quotient.

   a. $35\frac{3}{4} \div 5\frac{11}{12}$ **b.** $22\frac{7}{8} \div 3\frac{5}{6}$ **c.** $46\frac{2}{5} \div 5\frac{1}{10}$

1. **Vocabulary** What is a benchmark?

2. **Reasoning** How can you tell whether a fraction is greater than, less than, or equal to $\frac{1}{2}$? Explain.

Choose a benchmark for each fraction. Use 0, $\frac{1}{2}$, or 1.

3. $\frac{15}{16}$ 4. $\frac{1}{10}$ 5. $\frac{5}{8}$ 6. $\frac{2}{9}$

Round each mixed number to the nearest whole number.

7. $1\frac{1}{3}$ 8. $10\frac{3}{4}$ 9. $6\frac{7}{12}$ 10. $8\frac{2}{5}$

Homework Exercises

For more exercises, see Extra Skills and Word Problems.

GO for Help

For Exercises	See Examples
11–19	1
20–28	2–3
29–32	4

Use benchmarks to estimate each sum or difference.

11. $\frac{1}{7} + \frac{3}{8}$ 12. $\frac{3}{5} - \frac{1}{2}$ 13. $\frac{5}{11} - \frac{1}{5}$ 14. $\frac{8}{9} - \frac{5}{6}$

15. $\frac{1}{6} + \frac{5}{8}$ 16. $\frac{3}{4} + \frac{1}{5}$ 17. $\frac{3}{4} - \frac{5}{6}$ 18. $\frac{9}{10} + \frac{7}{16}$

19. Suppose it rains $\frac{4}{5}$ inch in the morning and $\frac{6}{7}$ inch in the afternoon. About how many inches of rain fall during the day?

Use rounding to estimate.

20. $9\frac{1}{11} - 3\frac{7}{9}$ 21. $5\frac{3}{5} + 3\frac{2}{3}$ 22. $4\frac{1}{2} - \frac{24}{25}$ 23. $7\frac{2}{3} - 2\frac{11}{12}$

24. $2\frac{1}{8} \cdot 3\frac{6}{7}$ 25. $5\frac{2}{9} \cdot 4\frac{9}{10}$ 26. $3\frac{3}{8} \cdot 5\frac{1}{6}$ 27. $1\frac{7}{10} \cdot 8\frac{1}{12}$

28. Marsha bought $1\frac{3}{8}$ lb of snow peas and $3\frac{1}{10}$ lb of carrots at the market. About how many more pounds of carrots did she buy?

Use compatible numbers to estimate each quotient.

29. $10\frac{7}{8} \div 3\frac{1}{9}$ 30. $36\frac{1}{3} \div 4\frac{2}{5}$ 31. $7\frac{3}{5} \div 1\frac{1}{2}$ 32. $8\frac{2}{12} \div 8\frac{2}{7}$

 33. **Guided Problem Solving** You want to make three kinds of pasta salad. The recipes call for $\frac{2}{3}$ c, $\frac{3}{4}$ c, and $1\frac{2}{3}$ c of pasta. You have 4 c of pasta. Do you have enough? Explain.
   • About how many cups of pasta do you need for each recipe?
   • About how many cups of pasta do you need for all 3 recipes?

34. **Number Sense** $30\frac{1}{7} \div 1\frac{4}{5}$ is about $30 \div 2 = 15$. Is the estimate of 15 for the quotient high or low? Explain.

Use benchmarks to estimate each sum or difference.

35. $6\frac{5}{6} + 8\frac{2}{12} + 14\frac{1}{7}$

36. $19\frac{9}{11} - 4\frac{5}{14} - 3\frac{7}{8}$

37. A teacher's school day is $8\frac{1}{4}$ h long. The teacher has six classes every day. Each class is $\frac{5}{6}$ h long. About how many hours of the school day is the teacher not in class?

Music The table below shows the weight of the bells of Boston's Old North Church. Use the table for Exercises 38–42.

Tone	F	E	D	C	B-flat	A	G	Low F
Weight in Tons	$\frac{3}{10}$	$\frac{3}{10}$	$\frac{7}{20}$	$\frac{2}{5}$	$\frac{11}{25}$	$\frac{19}{40}$	$\frac{3}{5}$	$\frac{3}{4}$

38. Estimate the total weight of the two heaviest bells.

39. Estimate the weight difference of the F bell and the Low F bell.

40. Which bells weigh less than $\frac{1}{2}$ ton?

41. Estimate the total weight of all eight bells.

42. Estimate the average weight of the four heaviest bells.

43. **Writing in Math** You need $9\frac{9}{16}$ lb of chicken. The store sells chicken in half-pound quantities. How much chicken should you order? Explain.

44. Challenge Estimate the median of $9\frac{3}{5}$, $5\frac{1}{4}$, $7\frac{5}{10}$, $1\frac{7}{8}$, $6\frac{3}{4}$, and $3\frac{2}{8}$.

Test Prep and Mixed Review

Practice

Multiple Choice

45. Jade needs $2\frac{2}{3}$ yards of fabric to make one tablecloth. She has $11\frac{2}{3}$ yards of fabric. What is the greatest number of tablecloths Jade can make?

    Ⓐ 3   Ⓑ 4   Ⓒ 5   Ⓓ 6

46. The length of a piece of fabric measures between 3 and $3\frac{1}{4}$ feet. Which length could it be?

    Ⓕ $\frac{72}{25}$ ft   Ⓖ $\frac{25}{8}$ ft   Ⓗ $\frac{18}{5}$ ft   Ⓙ $\frac{26}{7}$ ft

47. Brian bought 4 burritos for $15. He later bought another burrito for $2.50. What was the mean cost of all the burritos?

    Ⓐ $3.15   Ⓑ $3.50   Ⓒ $3.75   Ⓓ $12.50

GO for Help

For Exercises	See Lesson
48–51	2-6

Write each decimal as a mixed number or fraction in simplest form.

48. 0.04   **49.** 11.125   **50.** 0.0625   **51.** 3.408

Vocabulary Builder

High-Use Academic Words

High-use academic words are words that you will see often in textbooks and on tests. These words are not math vocabulary terms, but knowing them will help you to succeed in mathematics.

Direction Words

Some words tell what to do in a problem. I need to understand what these words are asking so that I give the correct answer.

Word	Meaning
Explain	To give details that make an idea easy to understand
Find	To obtain an answer by solving a problem
Order	To arrange or organize information in a sequence

Exercises

Fill in the blank with *order, explain,* or *find*.

1. Question: What is the correct ? of a U.S. student's education?

    Answer: elementary school, middle school, high school

2. In many middle schools, students must ? the classroom for each subject they take.

3. On the first day of school, many teachers ? the rules of the class.

4. Explain how you know that the sum of $\frac{4}{5}$ and $\frac{14}{15}$ will be greater than 1.

5. Find compatible numbers for $80\frac{5}{6}$ and $9\frac{2}{9}$ and estimate the quotient.

6. Order the fractions $\frac{4}{8}$, $\frac{2}{6}$, $-\frac{10}{12}$, $\frac{4}{4}$, $-\frac{1}{3}$ from least to greatest.

7. **Word Knowledge** Think about the word *reasonable*.
    a. Choose the letter for how well you know the word.
        A. I know its meaning.
        B. I've seen it, but I don't know its meaning.
        C. I don't know it.
    b. **Research** Look up and write the definition of *reasonable*.
    c. Use the word in a sentence involving mathematics.

Using Fraction Models

You can use models to add and subtract fractions.

EXAMPLES Using Fraction Models

1 Find $\frac{3}{10} + \frac{1}{10}$.

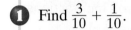

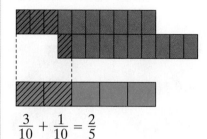

← To add, align the right side of the shaded part of the first model with the left side of the second one.

← Find a model that represents the sum of the shaded parts. If you have more than one model to choose from, use the one with the largest sections.

$\frac{3}{10} + \frac{1}{10} = \frac{2}{5}$

2 Find $\frac{3}{4} - \frac{1}{3}$.

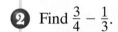

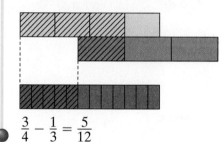

← To subtract, align the right ends of the shaded part of each model.

← Find the model that represents the difference.

$\frac{3}{4} - \frac{1}{3} = \frac{5}{12}$

Exercises

Write a number sentence for each model.

1.

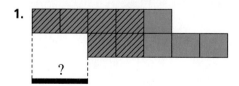

?

2.

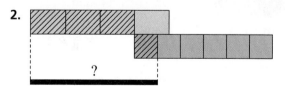

?

Use models to find each sum or difference.

3. $\frac{3}{8} + \frac{3}{8}$ **4.** $\frac{5}{6} - \frac{1}{6}$ **5.** $\frac{2}{5} + \frac{1}{2}$ **6.** $\frac{7}{10} - \frac{1}{5}$

7. You need 1 lb of sugar. You have $\frac{3}{8}$ lb and $\frac{2}{5}$ lb of sugar. Do you have enough?

Adding and Subtracting Fractions

✓ Check Skills You'll Need

1. Vocabulary Review
Two fractions that name the same amount are called ___?___.

Find each missing number.

2. $\dfrac{8}{16} = \dfrac{\blacksquare}{8}$

3. $\dfrac{\blacksquare}{10} = \dfrac{4}{5}$

4. $\dfrac{1}{6} = \dfrac{4}{\blacksquare}$

GO for Help
Lesson 2-3

What You'll Learn

To add and subtract fractions and to solve problems involving fractions

Why Learn This?

Sometimes you want an exact answer when you add or subtract fractions.

When you are sewing, you should leave extra material to make a hem. You can add fractions to find how much extra material you need to make a hem of $\dfrac{5}{8}$ in. when you make clothing.

When you add or subtract fractions that have common denominators, keep the denominator the same. Add or subtract the numerators.

GO Online

Video Tutor Help

Visit: PHSchool.com
Web Code: are-0775

EXAMPLE Common Denominators

① Find $\dfrac{1}{8} + \dfrac{5}{8}$.

Estimate $\dfrac{1}{8} + \dfrac{5}{8} \approx 0 + \dfrac{1}{2}$, or $\dfrac{1}{2}$

$$\dfrac{1}{8} + \dfrac{5}{8} = \dfrac{1+5}{8} \qquad \leftarrow \text{Keep the denominator the same.}$$

$$= \dfrac{6}{8} \qquad \leftarrow \text{Add the numerators.}$$

$$= \dfrac{3}{4} \checkmark \qquad \leftarrow \text{Simplify. The answer is close to the estimate.}$$

✓ Quick Check

1. Find each sum or difference.

    a. $\dfrac{3}{5} + \dfrac{1}{5}$ **b.** $\dfrac{13}{16} - \dfrac{9}{16}$ **c.** $\dfrac{1}{4} + \dfrac{3}{4}$

Sometimes you add or subtract fractions with different denominators. You can use models to help you find the sum or the difference.

This model shows $\frac{1}{4} + \frac{1}{3} = \frac{7}{12}$.

This model shows $\frac{1}{2} - \frac{1}{3} = \frac{1}{6}$.

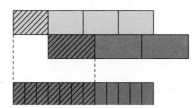

To add or subtract fractions with different denominators, first find the Least Common Denominator (LCD).

EXAMPLE **Different Denominators**

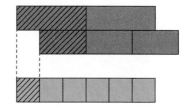

Test Prep Tip

The LCD of two fractions is the least common multiple of their denominators.

2 Find $\frac{4}{5} + \frac{2}{3}$.

Estimate $\frac{4}{5} + \frac{2}{3} \approx 1 + \frac{1}{2}$, or $1\frac{1}{2}$

$\frac{4}{5} = \frac{4 \cdot 3}{5 \cdot 3} = \frac{12}{15}$ ← The LCD is 15. Write an equivalent fraction.

$+\frac{2}{3} = \frac{2 \cdot 5}{3 \cdot 5} = +\frac{10}{15}$ ← Write an equivalent fraction.

$\frac{22}{15}$ ← Add the numerators.

$1\frac{7}{15}$ ← Write as a mixed number. This is close to the estimate.

✓ Quick Check

2. a. Find $\frac{3}{4} - \frac{1}{6}$.

b. Find $\frac{3}{7} + \frac{5}{14}$.

EXAMPLE **Application: Carpentry**

3 A cabinetmaker needs a board that is $\frac{9}{16}$ in. thick. By how much must he reduce the thickness of a board that is $\frac{7}{8}$ in. thick?

Estimate $\frac{7}{8} - \frac{9}{16} \approx 1 - \frac{1}{2} = \frac{1}{2}$

$\frac{7}{8} = \frac{7 \cdot 2}{8 \cdot 2} = \frac{14}{16}$ ← The LCD is 16. Write an equivalent fraction.

$-\frac{9}{16} = -\frac{9}{16} = -\frac{9}{16}$ ← Write an equivalent fraction.

$\frac{5}{16}$ ← Subtract the numerators.

The cabinetmaker should reduce the thickness of the board by $\frac{5}{16}$ in.

Check for Reasonableness The answer $\frac{5}{16}$ is close to the estimate $\frac{1}{2}$.

✓ Quick Check

3. You hiked $\frac{5}{8}$ mi and $\frac{1}{4}$ mi in the afternoon. How far did you hike?

1. Why do you need common denominators to add or subtract fractions?

Find the least common denominator of the fractions.

2. $\frac{1}{5}, \frac{3}{4}$ 3. $\frac{5}{8}, \frac{1}{16}$ 4. $\frac{7}{10}, \frac{1}{4}$ 5. $\frac{1}{2}, \frac{2}{3}$

Find each sum or difference.

6. $\frac{1}{8} + \frac{5}{8}$ 7. $\frac{1}{2} + \frac{1}{2}$ 8. $\frac{3}{5} - \frac{2}{5}$ 9. $\frac{5}{6} - \frac{1}{6}$

10. $\frac{1}{2} + \frac{5}{16}$ 11. $\frac{1}{5} + \frac{3}{8}$ 12. $\frac{9}{10} - \frac{2}{5}$ 13. $\frac{3}{6} - \frac{4}{9}$

For more exercises, see Extra Skills and Word Problems.

GO for Help

For Exercises	See Examples
14–25	1
26–34	2–3

Find each sum or difference. You may find a model helpful.

14. $\frac{1}{7} + \frac{4}{7}$ 15. $\frac{3}{4} + \frac{3}{4}$ 16. $\frac{6}{8} + \frac{3}{8}$ 17. $\frac{1}{10} + \frac{3}{10}$

18. $\frac{4}{5} - \frac{1}{5}$ 19. $\frac{7}{10} - \frac{1}{10}$ 20. $\frac{5}{12} - \frac{1}{12}$ 21. $\frac{7}{8} - \frac{5}{8}$

22. $\frac{3}{4} + \frac{1}{4}$ 23. $\frac{11}{16} - \frac{1}{16}$ 24. $\frac{8}{9} - \frac{2}{9}$ 25. $\frac{3}{32} + \frac{1}{32}$

Find each sum or difference by writing equivalent fractions.

26. $\frac{7}{12} + \frac{1}{6}$ 27. $\frac{3}{3} + \frac{5}{8}$ 28. $\frac{4}{5} + \frac{7}{8}$ 29. $\frac{1}{2} + \frac{4}{5}$

30. $\frac{5}{6} - \frac{1}{3}$ 31. $\frac{3}{5} - \frac{1}{4}$ 32. $\frac{5}{6} - \frac{1}{2}$ 33. $\frac{2}{3} - \frac{1}{4}$

34. The gas tank in your family's car was $\frac{7}{8}$ full when you left your house. When you arrived at your destination, the tank was $\frac{1}{4}$ full. What fraction of a tank of gas did you use during the trip?

GPS 35. **Guided Problem Solving** One third of the students in your class got an A on a test. One fourth of them got a B. What fraction of the students got an A or a B on the test?
  • **Make a Plan** Determine the correct operation to use. Find the LCD and write equivalent fractions.
  • **Carry Out the Plan** The correct operation is __?__. The LCD of the two fractions is ■.

GO Online
Homework Video Tutor
Visit: PHSchool.com
Web Code: are-0302

36. Suppose you are using nails $\frac{5}{6}$ in. long to nail plywood $\frac{1}{4}$ in. thick to a post. How much of the nail extends into the post?

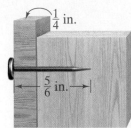

Mental Math Will each sum be *positive*, *negative*, or *zero*?

37. $-\frac{2}{3} + \frac{5}{6}$ **38.** $-\frac{4}{5} + \frac{8}{10}$ **39.** $-\frac{7}{8} + \frac{3}{4}$

40. You rowed $\frac{2}{3}$ mi. Your friend rowed $\frac{8}{10}$ mi. Who rowed farther? How much farther?

41. What fraction, when added to $\frac{1}{6}$, results in a sum of $\frac{2}{3}$?

42. Error Analysis A student added $\frac{2}{8} + \frac{3}{8}$ and got $\frac{5}{16}$. What was the student's mistake? What is the correct answer?

Use the circle graph for Exercises 43–45.

43. Data Analysis What fraction of takeout food is eaten at home or in a car?

44. How much greater is the fraction of takeout food eaten at home than the fraction eaten at work?

45. What fraction of the food is eaten at home, in a car, or at work?

Where Is Takeout Food Eaten?

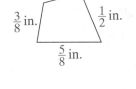

46. Challenge Find the perimeter of the figure at the left.

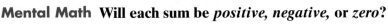

Test Prep and Mixed Review   **Practice**

Multiple Choice

47. Rolf has a math test. He plans to study $\frac{5}{6}$ hour tonight and $\frac{3}{4}$ hour tomorrow. How many hours does Rolf plan to study in all?

Ⓐ $1\frac{3}{4}$ h   Ⓑ $1\frac{7}{12}$ h   Ⓒ $\frac{4}{5}$ h   Ⓓ $\frac{9}{10}$ h

48. To make a noodle casserole, Jack uses $\frac{1}{3}$ cup of cream cheese, Myra uses $\frac{2}{5}$ cup, Donna uses $\frac{3}{4}$ cup, and Ernesto uses $\frac{1}{2}$ cup. Who uses the most cream cheese?

Ⓕ Jack   Ⓖ Myra   Ⓗ Donna   Ⓙ Ernesto

49. Which expression can be used to find the maximum number of 0.5-inch lengths of wire that can be cut from a wire 10.2 inches long?

Ⓐ $0.5 \div 10.2$ Ⓒ $10.2 \div 0.5$
Ⓑ 0.5×10.2 Ⓓ 10.2×0.5

GO for Help

For Exercises	See Lesson
50–51	2-6

Order from least to greatest.

50. $\frac{4}{3}, 0.52, -\frac{3}{4}, 1.0$ **51.** $1.34, \frac{25}{6}, -2.4, \frac{7}{3}$

Adding and Subtracting Mixed Numbers

Check Skills You'll Need

1. **Vocabulary Review** How does the *LCD* of two fractions help you compare the fractions?

Compare each pair of fractions. Use $<$, $=$, or $>$.

2. $\frac{3}{12}$ ■ $\frac{5}{12}$

3. $\frac{1}{6}$ ■ $\frac{1}{4}$

 **for Help**
Lesson 2-4

What You'll Learn

To add and subtract mixed numbers and to solve problems involving mixed numbers

Why Learn This?

Adding mixed numbers can help you find the total distance you travel, such as the number of miles you run while training for a race.

To find the sum of two mixed numbers with fraction parts that have the same denominator, you can first add the fractions and then add the whole numbers.

EXAMPLE   Same Denominators

1 **Cross Country** You are training for a race. On Monday you run $2\frac{3}{4}$ mi, and on Tuesday you run $4\frac{3}{4}$ mi. What is your total mileage?

Estimate $2\frac{3}{4} + 4\frac{3}{4} \approx 3 + 5$, or 8

$$2\frac{3}{4} + 4\frac{3}{4} = 6\frac{6}{4} \qquad \leftarrow \text{Add the fractions. Add the whole numbers.}$$

$$= 6 + 1\frac{2}{4} \qquad \leftarrow \text{Write as a sum. Write } \frac{6}{4} \text{ as } 1\frac{2}{4}.$$

$$= 6 + 1\frac{1}{2} \qquad \leftarrow \text{Simplify.}$$

$$= 7\frac{1}{2} \qquad \leftarrow \text{Add the whole numbers.}$$

Your total mileage is $7\frac{1}{2}$ mi.

Check for Reasonableness The answer $7\frac{1}{2}$ is close to the estimate 8.

Quick Check

1. Find each sum or difference.

   a. $1\frac{2}{3} + 2\frac{2}{3}$ **b.** $1\frac{2}{5} + 3\frac{2}{5}$ **c.** $5\frac{1}{2} - 4\frac{1}{2}$

Fractions in mixed numbers may have different denominators. You can use the LCD to rewrite them as fractions with common denominators.

EXAMPLE **Different Denominators**

2 Find $4\frac{1}{4} + 3\frac{2}{3}$.

Estimate $4\frac{1}{4} + 3\frac{2}{3} \approx 4 + 4$, or 8

$$4\frac{1}{4} = \quad 4\frac{3}{12} \quad \leftarrow \text{The LCD is 12. Write an equivalent fraction.}$$
$$+3\frac{2}{3} = +3\frac{8}{12} \quad \leftarrow \text{Write an equivalent fraction.}$$
$$= \quad 7\frac{11}{12} \quad \leftarrow \text{Add the fractions. Add the whole numbers.}$$

Check for Reasonableness The answer $7\frac{11}{12}$ is close to the estimate 8. The answer is reasonable.

When you add or subtract fractions, use the least common multiple of the denominators.

✓**Quick Check**

2. Find each sum or difference.

   a. $2\frac{3}{4} - 1\frac{3}{4}$ b. $3\frac{1}{6} + 8\frac{7}{8}$ c. $6\frac{1}{2} - 2\frac{1}{5}$

When you subtract mixed numbers, you may need to rename one of the numbers before subtracting.

EXAMPLE **Subtracting With Renaming**

3 **Multiple Choice** You bought $6\frac{1}{9}$ yd of ribbon and used $2\frac{2}{3}$ yd to make a pillow. How many yards of ribbon did you have left?

Ⓐ $8\frac{7}{9}$ Ⓑ $4\frac{5}{9}$ Ⓒ $3\frac{2}{9}$ Ⓓ $3\frac{4}{9}$

Find $6\frac{1}{9} - 2\frac{2}{3}$.

Estimate $6\frac{1}{9} - 2\frac{2}{3} \approx 6 - 3$, or 3

$$6\frac{1}{9} = \quad 5\frac{10}{9} \quad \leftarrow \text{Rename: } 6\frac{1}{9} = 5 + 1\frac{1}{9} = 5 + \frac{10}{9}.$$
$$-2\frac{2}{3} = -2\frac{6}{9} \quad \leftarrow \text{The LCD is 9. Write an equivalent fraction.}$$
$$= \quad 3\frac{4}{9} \quad \leftarrow \text{Subtract.}$$

You have $3\frac{4}{9}$ yards of ribbon left. The correct answer is D.

Check for Reasonableness The answer $3\frac{4}{9}$ is close to the estimate 3.

✓**Quick Check**

3. Your friend bought $4\frac{1}{3}$ ft of gift-wrap and used $2\frac{5}{6}$ ft to wrap a gift. How many feet of gift-wrap did your friend have left?

Rewrite each mixed number so that the fraction part is a proper fraction.

1. $2\frac{7}{4}$

2. $3\frac{6}{5}$

3. $1\frac{14}{10}$

4. Reasoning Do you use the skill you practiced in Exercises 1–3 when you *add* or when you *subtract* mixed numbers? Explain.

Rewrite each mixed number so that the whole-number part is less by 1.

5. $4\frac{1}{2}$

6. $2\frac{3}{8}$

7. $1\frac{9}{10}$

8. Number Sense Suppose you want to find the difference $6 - 3\frac{2}{5}$. How would you rewrite 6 as a mixed number?

For more exercises, see Extra Skills and Word Problems.

GO for Help

For Exercises	See Examples
9–13	1
14–17	2
18–22	3

Find each sum.

9. $6\frac{2}{5} + 1\frac{4}{5}$

10. $9\frac{3}{7} + 1\frac{2}{7}$

11. $3\frac{3}{8} + 4\frac{5}{8}$

12. $1\frac{7}{10} + 5\frac{1}{10}$

13. To make lemonade, you use $3\frac{1}{3}$ cups of lemon concentrate and $1\frac{1}{3}$ cups of water. How many cups of lemonade do you make?

Find each sum by writing equivalent fractions.

14. $6\frac{2}{5} + 1\frac{4}{10}$

15. $9\frac{1}{2} + 9\frac{1}{3}$

16. $7\frac{1}{6} + 8\frac{1}{8}$

17. $6\frac{1}{2} + 4\frac{5}{6}$

Find each difference.

18. $7\frac{2}{3} - 1\frac{1}{6}$

19. $15 - 3\frac{3}{4}$

20. $12\frac{1}{8} - 8\frac{3}{8}$

21. $14 - 5\frac{1}{5}$

22. Cooking You have 4 cups of flour, and you need to use $1\frac{3}{4}$ cups for a cookie recipe. How much flour will you have left?

GPS **23. Guided Problem Solving** Is a 6-quart punch bowl large enough to hold all the ingredients called for in the recipe? Explain.
- Using mental math, what is $1\frac{1}{2} + \frac{1}{2}$?
- What is the LCM of 3 and 4?
- Is the sum of all the ingredients greater than or less than 6 qt?

Lemon Raspberry Fizz

$2\frac{1}{4}$ qt ginger ale • $1\frac{2}{3}$ qt lemon sherbet

$1\frac{1}{2}$ qt lemonade • $\frac{1}{2}$ qt raspberry juice

Find each sum or difference.

24. $17\frac{3}{4} + 3\frac{3}{8}$ **25.** $17\frac{2}{5} + 11\frac{3}{4}$ **26.** $15\frac{1}{3} - 9\frac{1}{2}$ **27.** $6\frac{3}{8} - 2\frac{3}{4}$

28. Error Analysis A student subtracted $10\frac{1}{7} - 3\frac{5}{7}$ and got $6\frac{6}{7}$. Find the correct answer. What mistake do you think the student made?

29. On Saturday you hiked $4\frac{3}{8}$ mi. On Sunday, you hiked $3\frac{1}{2}$ mi. How far did you hike during the weekend?

30. A bolt must go through a sign and a support that together are $2\frac{1}{8}$ in. thick. You need an additional $\frac{1}{16}$ in. for a washer and $\frac{1}{4}$ in. for a nut. How long should the bolt be?

31. Geometry Figures A and B have a total area of $5\frac{3}{4}$ in.² The area of Figure A is $1\frac{1}{4}$ in.² Find the area of Figure B.

32. Calculator Use a calculator to find $5\frac{1}{2} + 4\frac{3}{4}$.

33. Challenge A newspaper has the following advertising spaces available: $2\frac{7}{8}$ c.i. (column inches), $3\frac{1}{2}$ c.i., and $4\frac{1}{4}$ c.i. What is the total number of column inches available?

Test Prep and Mixed Review   **Practice**

Multiple Choice

34. How much heavier is $28\frac{1}{2}$ pounds than $15\frac{11}{16}$ pounds?

   Ⓐ $12\frac{3}{4}$ lb   Ⓑ $12\frac{13}{16}$ lb   Ⓒ $12\frac{7}{8}$ lb   Ⓓ $13\frac{13}{16}$ lb

35. The table shows the number of runs Jason's baseball team, the Tigers, scored each game. What is the median number of runs the Tigers scored per game?

Tigers Runs Scored

5	8	4	1	7	10	5
6	3	4	0	6	3	5

   Ⓕ 4   Ⓖ 4.5   Ⓗ 4.8   Ⓙ 5

36. A submarine is located at 250 ft below sea level. At the end of the day, the submarine rises 140 ft. Which expression represents the movement of the submarine?

   Ⓐ $250 + 140$ Ⓒ $-250 + (-140)$
   Ⓑ $-250 + 140$ Ⓓ $250 - (-140)$

GO for Help

For Exercises	See Lesson
37–39	1-9

Mental Math **Find each product using the Distributive Property.**

37. $5(23)$ **38.** $7(18)$ **39.** $4(62)$

The table below shows the average rainfall from July through December for a city in Florida. Use benchmarks and the table to answer Exercises 1–3.

Month	July	August	September	October	November	December
Inches	$7\frac{7}{10}$	$6\frac{4}{5}$	$6\frac{3}{5}$	$3\frac{2}{5}$	$1\frac{9}{10}$	$2\frac{1}{10}$

1. Estimate the difference between rainfall in July and in December.

2. Estimate the sum of rainfall in August and in September.

3. Estimate the average rainfall for the six months.

Simplify.

4. $\frac{12}{18} - \frac{9}{18}$

5. $\frac{4}{3} + \frac{2}{3}$

6. $10\frac{7}{10} - 4\frac{4}{5}$

7. $6\frac{3}{4} + 2\frac{1}{5}$

8. $\frac{5}{9} - \frac{1}{3}$

9. $17 - 5\frac{3}{8}$

10. **Measurement** Five years ago, Tyler's height was $43\frac{7}{8}$ in. Now his height is $65\frac{1}{2}$ in. How many inches has he grown in 5 years?

MATH AT WORK

Songwriter

Songwriters need to know what types of music are "in" to compose a song that will sell. Then a songwriter must find an artist to record the song. Producers and record companies decide whether they will promote a song as a potential hit.

Songwriters use mathematics to make complex rhythms. Many hip-hop or rap beats use rhythms that follow a pattern. Songwriters write musical notes that have fractional names to create the pattern. Some common musical notes are half notes and quarter notes.

Go Online
PHSchool.com **For:** Information on songwriters **Web Code:** arb-2031

Modeling Fraction Multiplication

You can fold paper to model multiplication of fractions.
Use paper folding to find $\frac{1}{3}$ of $\frac{1}{4}$, or $\frac{1}{3} \cdot \frac{1}{4}$.

ACTIVITY

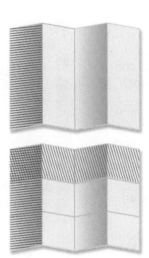

Step 1 Fold a sheet of paper into fourths as shown in the drawing at the right. Shade $\frac{1}{4}$ of it.

Step 2 Fold the same paper lengthwise into thirds as shown in the lower drawing. Shade $\frac{1}{3}$ of it.

Step 3 Count the total number of rectangles made by the folds. How many rectangles did you shade twice? What fraction of all the rectangles did you shade twice?

Step 4 Use the model to complete the equation: $\frac{1}{3} \cdot \frac{1}{4} = \blacksquare$. Explain how you found the product.

Step 5 Choose two fractions from $\frac{1}{3}$, $\frac{2}{3}$, and $\frac{3}{4}$. Use modeling to find the product of the two fractions.

Step 6 Suggest a rule for multiplying fractions.

Exercises

Complete each equation using the model shown below.

1. $\frac{1}{2} \cdot \blacksquare = \frac{1}{6}$

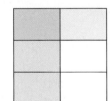

2. $\frac{2}{3} \cdot \frac{2}{3} = \blacksquare$

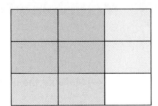

3. $\blacksquare \cdot \frac{3}{4} = \frac{3}{20}$

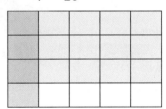

Make a model to represent each expression. Then find the product.

4. $\frac{1}{3} \cdot \frac{2}{5}$ **5.** $\frac{5}{6} \cdot \frac{1}{2}$ **6.** $\frac{1}{2} \cdot \frac{1}{4}$ **7.** $\frac{3}{4} \cdot \frac{2}{3}$ **8.** $\frac{3}{8} \cdot \frac{1}{3}$

9. Reasoning In the exercises above, compare the product to each of its factors. Make a conjecture about the product of two numbers between 0 and 1.

3-4

Check Skills You'll Need

1. Vocabulary Review
In an *improper fraction,* how does the numerator compare to the denominator?

Write each mixed number as an improper fraction.

2. $2\frac{3}{5}$ **3.** $6\frac{1}{2}$

4. $1\frac{2}{3}$ **5.** $4\frac{3}{4}$

 **for Help**
Lesson 2-5

What You'll Learn

To multiply fractions and mixed numbers and to solve problems by multiplying

Why Learn This?

You multiply fractions to find part of a quantity, which is useful when you cook.

A baker makes a batch of bread dough and splits it into three parts. Then she takes half of one part for one loaf. You can multiply $\frac{1}{3} \cdot \frac{1}{2}$ to find the fraction of the batch she uses for one loaf of bread.

When multiplying fractions, you do *not* need a common denominator. You multiply the numerators and multiply the denominators.

KEY CONCEPTS **Multiplying Fractions**

Arithmetic	Algebra
$\frac{1}{3} \cdot \frac{1}{2} = \frac{1 \cdot 1}{3 \cdot 2} = \frac{1}{6}$	$\frac{a}{b} \cdot \frac{c}{d} = \frac{ac}{bd}, b \neq 0 \text{ and } d \neq 0$

EXAMPLE **Multiplying Fractions**

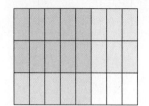

The model represents the product in Example 1.

1 Find $\frac{5}{8} \cdot \frac{2}{3}$.

$\frac{5}{8} \cdot \frac{2}{3} = \frac{5 \cdot 2}{8 \cdot 3}$ ← Multiply the numerators. Multiply the denominators.

$= \frac{10}{24}$ ← Find the two products.

$= \frac{5}{12}$ ← Simplify.

Quick Check

1. Find each product.

a. $\frac{3}{5} \cdot \frac{1}{4}$ **b.** $\frac{5}{6} \cdot \frac{4}{5}$ **c.** $\frac{2}{3} \cdot \frac{4}{5}$

To multiply a fraction by a whole number, you can write the whole number as a fraction with a denominator of 1. When a numerator and a denominator have a common factor, you can simplify before multiplying.

EXAMPLE Multiplying by a Whole Number

Test Prep Tip

Read the question carefully and make sure you are answering the question that is asked.

2 **Gridded Response** On Friday, $\frac{3}{7}$ of the 28 students in a class went to a music competition. How many students were still in class?

Find $\frac{3}{7}$ of the 28 students, or $\frac{3}{7} \cdot 28$.

$\frac{3}{7} \cdot 28 = \frac{3}{7} \cdot \frac{28}{1}$ ← Write 28 as $\frac{28}{1}$.

$= \frac{3}{\underset{1}{7}} \cdot \frac{\overset{4}{28}}{1}$ ← Simplify before multiplying.

$= \frac{12}{1}$ ← Multiply the numerators.
  ← Multiply the denominators.

$= 12$ ← Simplify. There were 12 students absent.

$28 - 12 = 16$ ← Subtract.

There were 16 students still in class on Friday.

✓ Quick Check

2. There are 168 members in an orchestra, and $\frac{3}{8}$ of them play the violin. How many members play the violin?

To multiply mixed numbers, first write them as improper fractions, and then multiply as you do with fractions.

EXAMPLE Multiplying Mixed Numbers

Online active math

For: Multiplying Fractions Activity
Use: Interactive Textbook, 3-4

3 Find $2\frac{3}{5} \cdot 4\frac{1}{2}$.

Estimate $2\frac{3}{5} \cdot 4\frac{1}{2} \approx 3 \cdot 5$, or 15

$2\frac{3}{5} \cdot 4\frac{1}{2} = \frac{13}{5} \cdot \frac{9}{2}$ ← Write the mixed numbers as improper fractions.

$= \frac{13 \cdot 9}{5 \cdot 2}$ ← Multiply numerators. Multiply denominators.

$= \frac{117}{10}$ ← Simplify.

$= 11\frac{7}{10}$ ← Write as a mixed number.

Check for Reasonableness $11\frac{7}{10}$ is close to the estimate 15.

✓ Quick Check

3. Find each product.

a. $2\frac{1}{3} \cdot 4\frac{5}{8}$ b. $3\frac{3}{5} \cdot 1\frac{3}{10}$ c. $5\frac{3}{4} \cdot 2\frac{5}{8}$

Complete the first step in finding each product.

1. $\dfrac{2}{5} \cdot \dfrac{3}{4} = \dfrac{2 \cdot \blacksquare}{5 \cdot \blacksquare}$

2. $\dfrac{5}{6} \cdot 18 = \dfrac{5}{6} \cdot \dfrac{18}{\blacksquare}$

3. $2\dfrac{1}{4} \cdot 1\dfrac{2}{3} = \dfrac{\blacksquare}{4} \cdot \dfrac{\blacksquare}{3}$

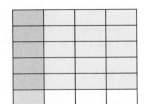

4. What product does the model at the left represent?

5. **Reasoning** When you multiply two fractions, do you need to find a common denominator first? Explain why or why not.

6. **Number Sense** Is $\dfrac{5}{7}$ of 28 *more* or *less* than 28? Explain how you know without actually multiplying.

Homework Exercises

For more exercises, see Extra Skills and Word Problems.

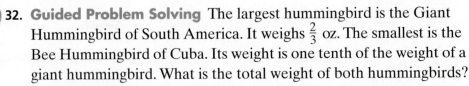

GO for Help

For Exercises	See Examples
7–14	1
15–23	2
24–31	3

Find each product. Write your result in simplest form. You may find a model helpful.

7. $\dfrac{1}{2} \cdot \dfrac{2}{3}$

8. $\dfrac{1}{4} \cdot \dfrac{3}{5}$

9. $\dfrac{1}{3} \cdot \dfrac{5}{6}$

10. $\dfrac{9}{10} \cdot \dfrac{2}{3}$

11. $\dfrac{1}{6} \cdot \dfrac{3}{5}$

12. $\dfrac{1}{8} \cdot \dfrac{4}{5}$

13. $\dfrac{2}{3} \cdot \dfrac{2}{5}$

14. $\dfrac{2}{3} \cdot \dfrac{4}{9}$

Find each product.

15. $\dfrac{3}{4} \cdot 16$

16. $9 \cdot \dfrac{1}{3}$

17. $52 \cdot \dfrac{1}{2}$

18. $\dfrac{2}{5} \cdot 10$

19. $\dfrac{1}{4}$ of 12

20. $\dfrac{3}{5}$ of 15

21. $\dfrac{2}{3}$ of 18

22. $\dfrac{5}{8}$ of 64

23. To make a fruit punch drink, you use $\dfrac{1}{3}$ cup of water. You want to make 6 drinks. How many cups of water do you need?

Find each product. Write your answer as a mixed number.

24. $2\dfrac{2}{5} \cdot 3\dfrac{3}{8}$

25. $5\dfrac{1}{4} \cdot 2\dfrac{2}{7}$

26. $1\dfrac{3}{10} \cdot 6\dfrac{2}{3}$

27. $1\dfrac{3}{8} \cdot 2\dfrac{2}{3}$

28. $3\dfrac{1}{3} \cdot 1\dfrac{1}{4}$

29. $2\dfrac{1}{2} \cdot 1\dfrac{3}{5}$

30. $4\dfrac{2}{3} \cdot \dfrac{3}{4}$

31. $\dfrac{1}{4} \cdot 3\dfrac{1}{5}$

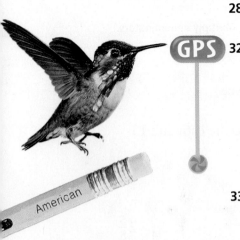

GPS 32. **Guided Problem Solving** The largest hummingbird is the Giant Hummingbird of South America. It weighs $\dfrac{2}{3}$ oz. The smallest is the Bee Hummingbird of Cuba. Its weight is one tenth of the weight of a giant hummingbird. What is the total weight of both hummingbirds?
   - **Make a Plan** Find the weight of the smallest hummingbird. Then add its weight to the weight of the largest hummingbird.
   - **Carry Out the Plan** The weight of both hummingbirds is $\blacksquare$ oz.

33. **Baking** A recipe calls for $2\dfrac{3}{4}$ cups of flour. You want to triple the recipe and add another $\dfrac{1}{4}$ cup. How much flour will you need?

American

(Algebra) **Find the value of x using mental math.**

34. $\frac{1}{4}x = \frac{1}{4}$ **35.** $\frac{2}{3}x = 0$ **36.** $2 + \frac{3}{5}x = 2$

37. <u>Writing in Math</u> How does multiplying two fractions differ from adding two fractions? Give an example.

38. **Science** As a roller coaster car reaches the bottom of a slope and begins to go up the next slope, its acceleration, combined with the downward pull of gravity, can make you feel $3\frac{1}{2}$ times as heavy as you really are. This sensation is called "supergravity." How heavy would a 120-lb person experiencing supergravity feel?

39. The length of a track around a field is $\frac{1}{4}$ mi. You jog $3\frac{1}{2}$ times around the track. How far do you jog?

40. **Error Analysis** A student multiplies two mixed numbers, $2\frac{3}{5}$ and $1\frac{1}{3}$, and finds the product to be $2\frac{3}{15}$. Explain the student's mistake. What is the correct answer?

41. Mark has 224 board games. He bought $\frac{3}{4}$ of his games on the Internet. Of the games he bought on the Internet, $\frac{1}{6}$ are card games. How many card games did he buy on the Internet?

42. **Calculator** Use a calculator to find $10\frac{2}{5} \cdot 4\frac{1}{2}$.

43. **Challenge** A farmer built a fence around a rectangular lot. The lot's length is $2\frac{1}{2}$ mi, and its width is $\frac{4}{5}$ its length. What is the area of the lot? How long is the fence?

Test Prep and Mixed Review **Practice**

Gridded Response

44. The Dancemania dancing studio sent $\frac{2}{3}$ of its dancers to a competition. If there are 36 dancers, how many dancers did the studio send to the competition?

45. Damien designed a thin border for his rectangular painting. The perimeter of the painting is 22 ft. The width of the painting is 4.75 ft. What is the length of the painting, in feet?

46. Helen received a gift certificate for her birthday. She spent $\frac{1}{3}$ of the gift certificate on lunch, and $\frac{1}{4}$ of the remaining amount on dessert. After she spent $3.50 for the tip, she had $4.00 left. What was the amount of Helen's gift certificate, in dollars?

Estimate. Round to the nearest whole number before you calculate.

47. $19.5 + 56.13$ **48.** $34.3 - 18.9$ **49.** $26.7 \cdot 9.9$

For Exercises	See Lesson
47–49	1-1

3-5a | Activity Lab | Hands On

Modeling Fraction Division

How many times does 2 go into 14? You know the
answer is 7. When you divide with fractions, the answer
may not be so obvious. You can use a model to help you
find the answer.

EXAMPLE

Alfinio finds $2\frac{1}{4}$ pizzas left after his birthday party. If he decides
to eat $\frac{1}{2}$ pizza per meal, how many meals does he have left?

Step 1 Cut out 3 congruent circles. Then cut $\frac{1}{4}$ of one circle. You
now have $2\frac{1}{4}$ circles that represent the leftover pizza.

Step 2 Cut your circles into meals for Alfinio. Remember that
Alfinio wants to eat $\frac{1}{2}$ pizza per meal.

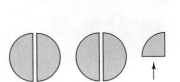

Step 3 How many $\frac{1}{2}$-pizza meals can Alfinio make from
$2\frac{1}{4}$ pizzas?

Your model shows that   So there are 4 full meals
he had $2\frac{1}{4}$ pizzas.   plus $\frac{1}{2}$ meal left.

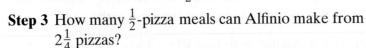

This shows that $2\frac{1}{4} \div \frac{1}{2} = 4\frac{1}{2}$.

Exercises

1. Identify the division problem shown in the model. Find the quotient.

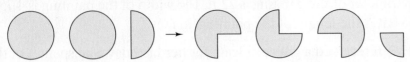

Make a model to represent each expression. Then find the quotient.

2. $1\frac{2}{3} \div \frac{1}{3}$ 3. $1\frac{1}{2} \div \frac{1}{4}$ 4. $3\frac{1}{2} \div \frac{3}{4}$

5. a. In the example above, how does the number of meals relate to the
   number of pizzas?
   b. **Number Sense** Dividing by $\frac{1}{2}$ is the same as multiplying by
   what number?

Dividing Fractions and Mixed Numbers

Check Skills You'll Need

1. Vocabulary Review Which operation do you use to find a *product*?

Find each product.

2. $\frac{3}{7} \cdot \frac{2}{3}$

3. $\frac{5}{9} \cdot \frac{1}{2}$

4. $50 \cdot \frac{9}{10}$

5. $2\frac{2}{9} \cdot 1\frac{4}{5}$

 **for Help**
Lesson 3-4

What You'll Learn

To divide fractions and mixed numbers and to solve problems by dividing

🔊 **New Vocabulary** reciprocals

Why Learn This?

When you work with measurements, you will often need to divide fractions and mixed numbers. The ruler below shows there are four $\frac{3}{4}$'s in 3 wholes. So $3 \div \frac{3}{4} = 4$. Notice that $3 \cdot \frac{4}{3}$ also equals 4. The numbers $\frac{3}{4}$ and $\frac{4}{3}$ are reciprocals. Two numbers are **reciprocals** if their product is 1. To divide by a fraction, you multiply by its reciprocal.

KEY CONCEPTS Dividing by Fractions

Arithmetic	Algebra
$3 \div \frac{3}{4} = 3 \cdot \frac{4}{3} = 4$	$\frac{a}{b} \div \frac{c}{d} = \frac{a}{b} \cdot \frac{d}{c}$ for b, c, and $d \neq 0$

GO **Online**

Video Tutor Help

Visit: PHSchool.com
Web Code: are-0775

EXAMPLE Dividing by a Fraction

1 Find $\frac{2}{3} \div \frac{5}{6}$.

$$\frac{2}{3} \div \frac{5}{6} = \frac{2}{3} \cdot \frac{6}{5} \quad \leftarrow \text{Multiply by } \frac{6}{5}, \text{ the reciprocal of } \frac{5}{6}.$$

$$= \frac{2 \cdot \overset{2}{\cancel{6}}}{\underset{1}{\cancel{3}} \cdot 5} \quad \leftarrow \text{Divide 6 and 3 by their GCF, 3.}$$

$$= \frac{4}{5} \quad \leftarrow \text{Simplify.}$$

✓ Quick Check

1. a. Find $\frac{7}{8} \div \frac{1}{4}$.   **b.** Find $\frac{5}{8} \div \frac{3}{4}$.   **c.** Find $14 \div \frac{7}{10}$.

To divide mixed numbers, rewrite them as improper fractions.

EXAMPLE Dividing Mixed Numbers

For: Dividing Fractions Activity
Use: Interactive Textbook, 3-5

2 **Measurement** You have a space of $9\frac{1}{2}$ in. on a poster for a row of photos. Each photo is $2\frac{3}{4}$ in. wide. How many photos can you fit?

To find how many photos you can fit, divide $9\frac{1}{2}$ by $2\frac{3}{4}$.

$$9\frac{1}{2} \div 2\frac{3}{4} = \frac{19}{2} \div \frac{11}{4} \quad \leftarrow \text{Write the mixed numbers as improper fractions.}$$

$$= \frac{19}{2} \cdot \frac{4}{11} \quad \leftarrow \text{Multiply by } \frac{4}{11}, \text{ the reciprocal of } \frac{11}{4}.$$

$$= \frac{19}{\cancel{2}_1} \cdot \frac{\cancel{4}^2}{11} \quad \leftarrow \text{Divide 4 and 2 by their GCF, 2.}$$

$$= \frac{38}{11} \quad \leftarrow \text{Multiply.}$$

$$= 3\frac{5}{11} \quad \leftarrow \text{Write as a mixed number.}$$

You can fit 3 photos.

✓ Quick Check

2. **a.** Find $5\frac{3}{4} \div 3\frac{2}{3}$. **b.** Find $4\frac{1}{8} \div 5\frac{1}{2}$. **c.** Find $3\frac{9}{16} \div 3$.

EXAMPLE Application: Meal Planning

3 How many $1\frac{1}{2}$-oz servings of cereal are in the larger cereal box at the right?

To find how many $1\frac{1}{2}$-oz servings are in $19\frac{1}{2}$ oz, divide $19\frac{1}{2}$ by $1\frac{1}{2}$.

Estimate $19\frac{1}{2} \div 1\frac{1}{2} \approx 20 \div 2$, or 10

$$19\frac{1}{2} \div 1\frac{1}{2} = \frac{39}{2} \div \frac{3}{2} \quad \leftarrow \text{Write the mixed numbers as improper fractions.}$$

$$= \frac{39}{2} \cdot \frac{2}{3} \quad \leftarrow \text{Multiply by } \frac{2}{3}, \text{ the reciprocal of } \frac{3}{2}.$$

$$= \frac{\cancel{39}^{13} \cdot \cancel{2}^{1}}{\cancel{2}_1 \cdot \cancel{3}_1} \quad \leftarrow \text{Divide 39 and 3 by their GCF. Divide 2 by itself.}$$

$$= \frac{13}{1} = 13 \quad \leftarrow \text{Simplify.}$$

There are thirteen $1\frac{1}{2}$-oz servings in the larger cereal box.

Check for Reasonableness 13 is close to 10. The answer is reasonable.

✓ Quick Check

3. One can of iced tea holds 12 fl oz. A 2-liter bottle holds $67\frac{3}{5}$ fl oz. How many cans of iced tea will you need to fill a 2-liter bottle?

You want to put 4 lb of raisins in bags so that each bag contains $\frac{2}{3}$ lb. How many bags do you need?

● More Than One Way

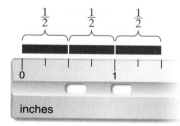

Kayla's Method

I can use number sense. $\frac{2}{3} + \frac{2}{3} + \frac{2}{3} = \frac{6}{3} = 2$, so three times $\frac{2}{3}$ lb is 2 lb. That means six times $\frac{2}{3}$ lb is 4 lb.

I need six bags.

Will's Method

I can divide 4 by $\frac{2}{3}$.

$$4 \div \frac{2}{3} = \frac{4}{1} \div \frac{2}{3} \quad \leftarrow \text{Write the whole number as a fraction.}$$

$$= \frac{4}{1} \cdot \frac{3}{2} \quad \leftarrow \text{Multiply by } \frac{3}{2} \text{, the reciprocal of } \frac{2}{3}.$$

$$= \frac{\overset{2}{4} \cdot 3}{1 \cdot \underset{1}{2}} \quad \leftarrow \text{Divide 4 and 2 by their GCF, 2.}$$

$$= \frac{6}{1} = 6 \quad \leftarrow \text{Simplify.}$$

I need six bags.

Choose a Method

You want to bike 12 miles in $1\frac{1}{3}$ hours. What should your average speed be? Describe your method and explain why you chose it.

✓ Check Your Understanding

inches

1. What quotient does the model at the left represent?

Find the reciprocal of each number.

2. $\frac{5}{8}$　　　　3. $\frac{1}{4}$　　　　4. 9　　　　5. $3\frac{1}{2}$

Mental Math Match each expression to the correct quotient.

6. $6 \div \frac{1}{2}$　　　　**A.** 25

　　　　　　　　B. 12

7. $5 \div \frac{1}{5}$　　　　**C.** 90

8. $9 \div \frac{1}{10}$

Homework Exercises

For more exercises, see Extra Skills and Word Problems.

GO for Help

For Exercises	See Examples
9–20	1
21–33	2–3

Find each quotient. You may find a model helpful.

9. $\frac{4}{5} \div \frac{1}{10}$
10. $\frac{4}{5} \div \frac{1}{5}$
11. $\frac{5}{16} \div \frac{1}{2}$

12. $\frac{7}{10} \div \frac{1}{5}$
13. $\frac{2}{7} \div \frac{1}{9}$
14. $\frac{1}{9} \div \frac{5}{6}$

15. $\frac{3}{4} \div \frac{2}{3}$
16. $\frac{1}{4} \div \frac{3}{8}$
17. $\frac{3}{8} \div \frac{1}{4}$

18. $\frac{1}{2} \div \frac{2}{7}$
19. $\frac{3}{5} \div \frac{2}{3}$
20. $\frac{9}{10} \div \frac{1}{5}$

Find each quotient. Write your answer as a mixed number.

21. $1\frac{1}{2} \div 3\frac{1}{4}$
22. $2\frac{1}{6} \div 3\frac{5}{6}$
23. $5\frac{1}{4} \div 3\frac{1}{2}$

24. $5\frac{1}{3} \div 4\frac{2}{3}$
25. $2\frac{2}{3} \div 5\frac{1}{9}$
26. $6\frac{2}{3} \div 1\frac{1}{4}$

27. $3\frac{3}{4} \div 4\frac{1}{2}$
28. $11\frac{1}{2} \div 3\frac{1}{2}$
29. $12\frac{3}{4} \div 4\frac{1}{2}$

30. $11\frac{1}{3} \div 4\frac{1}{2}$
31. $8\frac{1}{3} \div 2\frac{1}{2}$
32. $1\frac{5}{9} \div 2\frac{1}{3}$

33. You can jog $\frac{1}{4}$ mi in 2 min. How long will it take you to jog 2 mi?

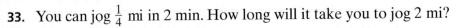

34. Guided Problem Solving Telephone cable is being installed along a $6\frac{3}{4}$-mi-long street. Workers install $\frac{9}{16}$ mi in the morning and $\frac{9}{16}$ mi in the afternoon. How long will they take to install all of the cable?
  - How many miles of cable can they install in one day?
  - How many miles of cable do they have to install?
  - What should you divide by to find how long the project will take?

35. Error Analysis Your friend wrote the reciprocal of $5\frac{3}{8}$ as $5\frac{8}{3}$. Explain why your friend is incorrect. What is the correct reciprocal?

36. Estimate $8\frac{2}{5} \div 3\frac{1}{2}$. Compare your estimate to the exact quotient.

37. A nail weighs about $\frac{1}{10}$ oz. How many nails are in a 5-lb box?

38. Choose a Method Ranchers in the American West often wear what is called a ten-gallon hat. However, a ten-gallon hat actually holds only $\frac{3}{4}$ gallon. How many ten-gallon hats would be needed to hold 10 gallons? Describe your method and explain why you chose it.

39. Joanne has $13\frac{1}{2}$ yd of material to make costumes. Each complete costume requires $1\frac{1}{2}$ yd for the top and $\frac{3}{4}$ yd for the bottom. How many complete costumes can she make?

40. Reasoning Can you use the rule for multiplying by the reciprocal to divide whole numbers such as $10 \div 2$? Explain.

GO Online
Homework Video Tutor
Visit: PHSchool.com
Web Code: are-0305

41. $\frac{1}{4} \div x = \frac{1}{4}$ **42.** $x \div \frac{33}{100} = 0$ **43.** $x \div \frac{2}{5} = 1$

44. Biology A manatee can swim 5 mi in $1\frac{1}{4}$ h. If the manatee swims at the same average speed, how far can it swim in 1 h?

45. Writing in Math What positive number is its own reciprocal? What number has no reciprocal? Explain.

46. A one-serving recipe calls for $\frac{1}{3}$ c of vegetable oil for a marinade and $\frac{1}{6}$ c of oil for the sauce. You have $3\frac{1}{2}$ c of vegetable oil. How many servings can you make?

47. The area of a rectangle is 117 ft². The length of the rectangle is $9\frac{3}{4}$ ft. What is the width of the rectangle?

48. Challenge A rectangular floor measures 9 ft by 6 ft. You use $1\frac{1}{2}$-ft-square tiles to cover the floor. How many tiles will you need?

Careers Marine biologists collect and analyze data on marine life.

Test Prep and Mixed Review

Practice

Multiple Choice

49. Which model best represents the expression $4 \div \frac{2}{3}$?

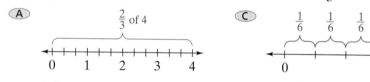

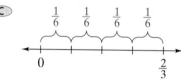

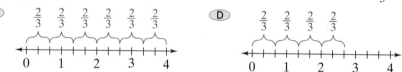

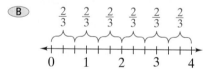

50. Eliza's grades on her daily math homework were 8, 10, 7, 9, 9, 4, 8, 2, 10, 8, 3, 7, 9, 8, 6, and 4. Which measure of the data is NOT represented by a score of 8?
  Ⓕ Mean   Ⓖ Median   Ⓗ Mode   Ⓙ Range

51. At an animal adoption center, $\frac{3}{8}$ of the animals are dogs, and $\frac{5}{16}$ are cats. How would you find the fraction of animals that are neither dogs nor cats?
  Ⓐ Add the fraction of dogs and the fraction of cats.
  Ⓑ Subtract the fraction of cats from the fraction of dogs.
  Ⓒ Subtract the fraction of dogs from 1 and add the fraction of cats.
  Ⓓ Add both fractions and then subtract the result from 1.

GO for Help

For Exercises	See Lesson
52–54	2-8

Write in standard form.

52. 5.5×10^4 **53.** 2.564×10^3 **54.** 5.6302×10^1

GPS Guided Problem Solving

Practice Solving Problems

SALE! $\frac{3}{2}$ of regular price

An employee plays a joke and posts the wrong sale sign to see if anyone notices. Freddy enters the store and buys a suit on sale. The regular price of the suit is $200. What does he pay for the suit after $21 for sales tax is added?

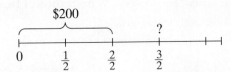

What You Might Think

What do I know?
What am I trying to find out?

How do I show the main idea?

How do I estimate the answer?

How do I solve the problem?

What is the answer?

Is the answer reasonable?

What You Might Write

Freddy must pay $\frac{3}{2}$ of $200 and $21 for sales tax. I want to find the total after tax is added.

Draw a diagram.

$200

0    $\frac{1}{2}$ $\frac{2}{2}$ $\frac{3}{2}$?

$\frac{3}{2}$ is $1\frac{1}{2}$. So the suit costs $1\frac{1}{2}$ times the original price.

$1\frac{1}{2} \times \$200 = \$300$

With sales tax, the price will be over $300.

$\$300 + \$21 = \$321$

$321 is the exact answer.

Yes, it is reasonable. The answer is close to the estimate of $300.

Think It Through

1. **a.** In the diagram, what does it mean for $200 to be equivalent to $\frac{2}{2}$?
   b. What does the $\frac{3}{2}$ mark represent? Explain.

2. How do you know that $1\frac{1}{2} \times \$200 = \$300$?

Exercises

For Exercises 3 and 4, answer the questions first and then solve the problem.

3. Your friend bought a shirt at the $\frac{3}{2}$-price sale. The regular price for the shirt was $60, and $4.20 for sales tax was added. If your friend paid with a $100 bill, how much change did he get?
   a. What do you know?
   b. What do you want to find out?
   c. Finish drawing the diagram below to help you find the answer.

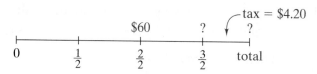

   d. Estimate the answer.

4. Harriet bought her father a tie at the $\frac{3}{2}$-price sale. The sale price was $24, not including tax. What was the regular price?
   a. What do you know?
   b. What do you want to find out?
   c. Make a drawing to show the main idea.
   d. Estimate the answer.

For Exercises 5–7, use the sale sign shown below.

SALE!
Belts : $\frac{1}{3}$ off   Hats : $\frac{1}{4}$ off
Jewelry : $\frac{1}{2}$ off   Dresses : $\frac{1}{5}$ off

5. Mary buys a hat at the sale. The hat's regular price is $24. She will pay $1.26 for sales tax. How much change should she get from a $20 bill?

6. Juanita buys a dress at the sale. The regular price of the dress is $45. She will pay $2.52 for sales tax. What will be the total cost?

7. Xavier buys a belt at the sale. The cost was $16 before tax was added. What was the regular price of the belt?

Changing Units in the Customary System

✓ Check Skills You'll Need

1. **Vocabulary Review**
Why is $1\frac{3}{8}$ called a *mixed number*?

Find each sum or difference.

2. $\frac{2}{3} + \frac{5}{12}$

3. $\frac{15}{16} - \frac{5}{16}$

4. $5\frac{1}{2} + 6\frac{3}{4}$

5. $8 - 3\frac{3}{4}$

 **for Help**

Lesson 3-3

What You'll Learn

To change units of length, capacity, and weight in the customary system

Why Learn This?

Most people in the United States use the customary system of measurement for length, capacity, and weight. Changing units allows you to compare measures and compute with them, as carpenters do.

Customary Units of Measure

Type	Length	Capacity	Weight
Unit	inch (in.) foot (ft) yard (yd) mile (mi)	fluid ounce (fl oz) cup (c) pint (pt) quart (qt) gallon (gal)	ounce (oz) pound (lb) ton (t)
Equivalents	1 ft = 12 in. 1 yd = 3 ft 1 mi = 5,280 ft	1 c = 8 fl oz 1 pt = 2 c 1 qt = 2 pt 1 gal = 4 qt	1 lb = 16 oz 1 t = 2,000 lb

EXAMPLE Changing Units of Length

Vocabulary Tip

The customary system is sometimes called the "English system," even though it is no longer used in England.

1 **Carpentry** A carpenter has a board 10 ft long. He cuts a piece 5 ft 3 in. long from the board. What is the length in feet of the remaining piece?

You need to subtract 5 ft 3 in. from 10 ft.

$5 \text{ ft } 3 \text{ in.} = 5\frac{3}{12} \text{ ft} = 5\frac{1}{4} \text{ ft}$ ← Write 3 in. as a fraction of a foot.

$10 - 5\frac{1}{4} = 9\frac{4}{4} - 5\frac{1}{4}$ ← Rename 10 as $9\frac{4}{4}$.

$= 4\frac{3}{4}$ ← Subtract.

The remaining piece is $4\frac{3}{4}$ ft long.

✓ Quick Check

1. How much shorter than a board 10 ft long is a board 8 ft 5 in. long?

To change from a smaller unit to a larger unit, you *divide*. To change from a larger unit to a smaller unit, you *multiply*.

EXAMPLE **Changing Units of Capacity**

2. **Multiple Choice** Jonah has 30 fluid ounces of juice. How many $1\frac{1}{2}$-cup servings does he have altogether?

Ⓐ $2\frac{1}{2}$ Ⓑ 18   Ⓒ 20   Ⓓ $28\frac{1}{2}$

First you need to find the number of fluid ounces in $1\frac{1}{2}$ cups. Since there are 8 fluid ounces in 1 cup, you know that there are 12 fluid ounces in $1\frac{1}{2}$ cups.

Next you need to find the number of groups of 12 fluid ounces that are in 30 fluid ounces. You need to divide 30 by 12.

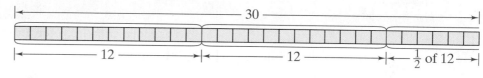

$$30 \div 12 = 2.5 = 2\frac{1}{2} \quad \leftarrow \text{Write as a mixed number.}$$

There are $2\frac{1}{2}$ servings in 30 fl oz of juice. The correct answer is choice A.

Test Prep Tip
Some questions require two steps to find the answer. Read carefully, and tackle one step at a time.

✓ Quick Check

● **2.** How many 1-cup servings are in 50 fluid ounces of juice?

EXAMPLE **Changing Units of Weight**

3. **Cycling** The lighter the frame of a mountain bike, the easier it is to ride. In the ad shown at the left, Mountain Master weighs 76 oz and Super Cycle weighs $4\frac{1}{4}$ lb. Which bike will be easier to ride?

Think of the relationship between pounds and ounces. A pound is a larger unit of measure than an ounce. There are 16 ounces in one pound.

$$1 \text{ lb } = 16 \text{ oz}$$
$$\searrow \times 16 \nearrow$$

To change $4\frac{1}{4}$ lb to ounces, multiply $4\frac{1}{4}$ by 16.

$$4\frac{1}{4} \cdot 16 = \frac{17}{4} \cdot \frac{16}{1} \quad \leftarrow \text{Write } 4\frac{1}{4} \text{ as an improper fraction.}$$
$$= 68 \quad \leftarrow \text{Multiply.}$$

The Super Cycle will be easier to ride because it is lighter.

✓ Quick Check

● **3.** Find the number of ounces in $4\frac{5}{8}$ lb.

Tell whether you would *multiply* or *divide* to change from one unit of measure to the other.

1. gallons to quarts   **2.** ounces to pounds   **3.** yards to feet

4. pints to cups   **5.** feet to miles   **6.** tons to pounds

7. Number Sense Why do you *multiply* to change from a larger unit to a smaller unit?

8. Why do you *divide* to change from a smaller unit to a larger unit?

Homework Exercises

For more exercises, see Extra Skills and Word Problems.

GO for Help

For Exercises	See Examples
9–15	1
16–22	2
23–29	3

Change each unit of length.

9. 4 ft 6 in. = ■ ft   **10.** 1 ft 9 in. = ■ ft   **11.** 6 ft 2 in. = ■ ft

12. 4 yd 2 ft = ■ yd   **13.** 1 yd 1 ft = ■ yd   **14.** 10 yd 3 ft = ■ yd

15. A carpenter cuts 2 ft 9 in. off a board that was 4 ft long. How long is the piece that is left, in feet and inches?

Change each unit of capacity.

16. 48 fl oz = ■ c   **17.** 6 c = ■ p   **18.** 40 qt = ■ gal

19. 1 c = ■ p   **20.** 9 pt = ■ qt   **21.** 12 c = ■ qt

22. How many cups are in a 12-fl oz can of lemonade?

Change each unit of weight.

23. $\frac{3}{4}$ lb = ■ oz   **24.** $2\frac{1}{4}$ lb = ■ oz   **25.** $2\frac{1}{2}$ t = ■ lb

26. 32 oz = ■ lb   **27.** 80 oz = ■ lb   **28.** 1,000 lb = ■ t

29. Which is lighter, 12 oz of cheese or 1 lb of cheese?

30. Guided Problem Solving People in the United States discard an average of 75,000 t of food per day. If a garbage truck can hold 12,000 lb, how many trucks are needed to haul all of the food?
- How many tons is 12,000 lb?
- What operation should you use to find the number of garbage trucks needed?

31. You are hiking a 2-mi trail. A sign shows that you have hiked 1,000 ft. How many feet do you have left to hike?

Complete.

32. 500 lb = ■ t   **33.** $1\frac{1}{5}$ t = ■ lb   **34.** $5\frac{1}{4}$ gal = ■ qt

35. 7 pt = ■ qt   **36.** 69 in. = ■ ft   **37.** 16 ft = ■ yd

38. Sam bought three packages of low-salt pretzels weighing 12 oz, 32 oz, and $1\frac{1}{2}$ lb. How many pounds of pretzels did Sam buy all together?

39. **Biology** Baby crocodiles are about 8 in. long when they hatch, and they grow about 10 in. each year. How many feet long is a crocodile that is 4 years old?

40. How are the rates "6 pounds per day" and "6 days per pound" different? When would each be useful?

41. **Error Analysis** Your friend says that a quarter-pound burger is heavier than a six-ounce burger. Is your friend correct? Explain.

42. The length of the Amazon River in South America is about 4,000 mi. How many feet is this?

43. **Writing in Math** Explain how fluid ounces and ounces differ.

44. **Challenge** Three students recorded their heights as 64 in., $5\frac{1}{6}$ ft, and $1\frac{2}{3}$ yd. Find the average height in feet of the three students.

Test Prep and Mixed Review   Practice

Multiple Choice

45. An assortment of cheeses is weighed on a scale. What is the best estimate of the total weight of the 8 cheeses listed at the right?
  Ⓐ Less than 5 pounds
  Ⓑ Between 5 and 10 pounds
  Ⓒ Between 10 and 15 pounds
  Ⓓ More than 15 pounds

Cheese Assortment

Quantity	Weight
1	1.1 lb
2	2 lb 4 oz
5	$\frac{1}{2}$ lb

46. Mr. Paik started an 18-week training program to prepare for a marathon. The first week he jogged $1\frac{1}{2}$ mi each day, the second week he jogged 3 mi each day, and the third week he jogged $4\frac{1}{2}$ mi each day. If the pattern continues, how far will he jog each day of the sixth week?
  Ⓕ 6 mi   Ⓗ 9 mi
  Ⓖ $7\frac{1}{2}$ mi   Ⓙ $10\frac{1}{2}$ mi

GO for Help

For Exercises	See Lesson
47–49	3-5

Find each quotient.

47. $\frac{3}{7} \div \frac{1}{7}$ **48.** $\frac{4}{5} \div \frac{4}{10}$ **49.** $\frac{3}{11} \div \frac{9}{22}$

Solving Puzzles

People often describe real-world situations using language that can be translated into numerical expressions. A class made some puzzles about the number of relatives who are coming to their family outings. Solve the puzzles below.

EXAMPLE

Sandra has a total of 12 aunts and cousins coming to her family outing. Two thirds are cousins, and half as many aunts as cousins are coming. How many aunts and how many cousins are coming to Sandra's outing?

Step 1 List what you know:

- $\frac{2}{3}$ cousins
- $\frac{1}{2}$ as many aunts as cousins
- 12 aunts and cousins all together

Step 2 Find the number of cousins:

$$\frac{2}{3} \cdot 12 = \frac{24}{3} \quad \leftarrow \text{Multiply } \frac{2}{3} \text{ by 12.}$$

$$\frac{24}{3} = 8 \quad \leftarrow \text{Simplify. There are 8 cousins.}$$

Step 3 Find the number of aunts:

$$\frac{1}{2} \cdot 8 = 4 \quad \leftarrow \text{Multiply } \frac{1}{2} \text{ by 8. There are 4 aunts.}$$

● Sandra has 8 cousins and 4 aunts coming to her outing.

Exercises

1. Mark has 16 people coming to his outing. $\frac{3}{8}$ are his nieces, $\frac{1}{4}$ are his nephews, and the rest are his cousins. How many nieces, nephews, and cousins are coming to Mark's outing?

2. Phil has 24 guests in all. Two thirds are cousins. The rest are aunts and uncles, and there are the same number of aunts as uncles. How many cousins, aunts, and uncles are coming to the outing?

3. Create your own puzzle like the ones above. Your first clue should be the number of relatives who will come to a reunion. Then write clues using fractions, like the ones above, to describe the situation.

Find each product.

1. $\dfrac{1}{3} \cdot \dfrac{6}{7}$ 2. $\dfrac{3}{4} \cdot 4\dfrac{1}{3}$ 3. $\dfrac{2}{5} \cdot \dfrac{1}{2}$ 4. $3\dfrac{1}{4} \cdot 2\dfrac{7}{8}$ 5. $1\dfrac{1}{10} \cdot \dfrac{2}{3}$

6. What is the area of a courtyard that is $2\dfrac{2}{3}$ yd by $4\dfrac{1}{6}$ yd?

Find each quotient.

7. $\dfrac{5}{9} \div \dfrac{5}{6}$ 8. $12\dfrac{1}{2} \div 1\dfrac{7}{8}$ 9. $3\dfrac{1}{7} \div \dfrac{11}{7}$ 10. $\dfrac{8}{25} \div \dfrac{2}{5}$ 11. $5\dfrac{1}{5} \div \dfrac{4}{10}$

12. You have a leaking bucket with $15\dfrac{1}{4}$ liters of water. Water drains out of the bucket at a rate of $\dfrac{1}{3}$ liter per minute. In how many minutes will the bucket be empty?

Change each unit of length.

13. 3 ft 4 in. = ■ ft   14. 2 ft 3 in. = ■ ft   15. 8 ft 6 in. = ■ ft

3-7a   Activity Lab

Choosing Appropriate Units

When you measure an object, you should measure in an appropriate unit. For example, you would measure the length of a stapler in inches, not in miles.

Number Sense Choose the more appropriate unit of measure.

1. the mass of a horse   kilograms   grams

2. the length of a marathon road race   miles   feet

3. the capacity of a car's gas tank   ounces   gallons

4. the length of an eyelash   meters   millimeters

5. the weight of a baseball   ounces   pounds

6. **Writing in Math** Choose one of your answers from Questions 1–5. Explain why you chose that unit of measure.

Precision

Check Skills You'll Need

1. **Vocabulary Review**
   What are the basic metric units for *length, capacity,* and *mass*?

Complete.

2. 1 m = ■ cm

3. 1 m = ■ km

4. 1 cm = ■ mm

5. 1 kg = ■ g

6. 1 mL = ■ L

 **for Help**
Lesson 1-5

What You'll Learn

To find and compare the precision of measurements

◀)) **New Vocabulary** precision

Why Learn This?

Every measurement has a unit. Some units are more appropriate to use than others, and some units give a more precise measurement than others.

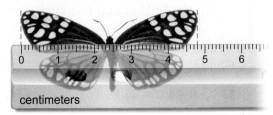
centimeters

If you measure the butterfly above to the nearest centimeter, the length is 5 cm. If you measure the butterfly to the nearest millimeter, the length is 48 mm. The measurement 48 mm is more precise than 5 cm.

The **precision** of a measurement refers to its exactness. When you compare measurements, the more precise measurement is the one that uses the smaller unit of measure.

EXAMPLES Precision in Measurement

Vocabulary Tip

Precise is the adjectival form of *precision.*

❶ Choose the more precise measurement: 12 fl oz or 2 c.

A fluid ounce is a smaller unit than a cup. So the measurement 12 fl oz is more precise than 2 c.

❷ Choose the more precise measurement: 3 L or 2.5 L

One tenth of a liter is a smaller unit than a liter. So the measurement 2.5 L is more precise than 3 L.

❸ Choose the more precise measurement: 8 in. or 21 in.

Both measurements use the inch as a unit. So neither measurement is more precise than the other.

✓ Quick Check

Choose the more precise measurement.

1. 2 ft, 13 in.   **2.** 12.5 g, 11 g   **3.** $3\frac{1}{2}$ mi, $10\frac{1}{5}$ mi

There are many different measuring tools, such as rulers, scales, and thermometers. The marks on a measuring tool tell you the precision that is possible with that tool.

EXAMPLE Finding Precision

④ **Cooking** Oven thermometers measure cooking temperatures. What is the greatest precision possible with the thermometer shown at the right?

The interval from any red dot to the next black dot is 25°F. Measurements made with this thermometer are precise to the nearest 25°F.

✅ Quick Check

4. What is the greatest precision possible with each ruler below?

a.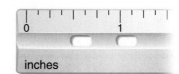

b.

A calculation is only as precise as the least precise measurement used in the calculation. When you add or subtract measurements with the same unit, round your answer to match the least precise measurement.

EXAMPLES Precision and Rounding

⑤ Find $8\frac{2}{5}$ mi + 5 mi. Round your answer appropriately.

$8\frac{2}{5} + 5 = 13\frac{2}{5}$

Since 5 is less precise than $8\frac{2}{5}$, round to the nearest whole number. The sum is 13 mi.

⑥ Find 9.97 cm − 5.9 cm. Round your answer appropriately.

$9.97 - 5.9 = 4.07$

Since 5.9 is less precise than 9.97, round to the nearest tenth. The difference is 4.1 cm.

✅ Quick Check

Find each sum or difference. Round your answer appropriately.

5. 11.4 g + 2.65 g   6. 45 m − 0.9 m

1. Measure the pencil below to the nearest inch, to the nearest $\frac{1}{2}$ inch, and to the nearest $\frac{1}{8}$ inch.

2. **Vocabulary** Which measurement in Exercise 1 is the most precise?

3. **Number Sense** Can you use the ruler in Exercise 1 to measure the pencil to the nearest $\frac{1}{16}$ inch? Explain.

Choose the more precise measurement.

4. 13 cm, 13 mm
5. 9 ft, $4\frac{1}{2}$ ft
6. 8.5 kg, 2.25 kg

Homework Exercises

For more exercises, see Extra Skills and Word Problems.

GO for Help

For Exercises	See Examples
7–15	1–3
16–17	4
18–23	5–6

Choose the more precise measurement.

7. 16 in., $11\frac{15}{16}$ in.
8. 30 g, 2.5 kg
9. 37 t, 56 lb

10. 25 qt, 38 pt
11. 21 L, 35 mL
12. $6\frac{1}{10}$ lb, 6.37 lb

13. 12 mo, 1 yr
14. 0.25 g, 101 mg
15. 12 days, 2 wk

Find the greatest precision possible for each scale shown.

16.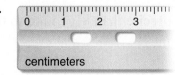

17.

Find each sum or difference. Round your answer appropriately.

18. $19 \text{ m} + 4\frac{9}{10} \text{ m}$
19. $6 \text{ ft} - 2\frac{1}{4} \text{ ft}$
20. $7.4 \text{ L} + 1.16 \text{ L}$

21. $6.53 \text{ oz} + 2\frac{2}{5} \text{ oz}$
22. $18 \text{ g} - 3.8 \text{ g}$
23. $6.52 \text{ in.} - 5.8 \text{ in.}$

24. **Guided Problem Solving** You have 81 ft² of fabric. You cut a square of fabric with side length $4\frac{1}{2}$ ft. How much fabric is left?
   • How many square feet of fabric did you cut out?
   • What operation tells you how much fabric is left?
   • What should you round to?

Find the length of each segment to the greatest precision possible.

25.
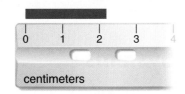

26.
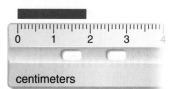

27. **Biology** The length of a chicken egg can be $2\frac{3}{16}$ in. The length of an ostrich egg can be $6\frac{3}{8}$ in. What is the difference between the lengths of the eggs? Round your answer appropriately.

28. **Writing in Math** Your friend says that 5.25 kg is a more precise measurement than 6.2 g because a hundredths unit is smaller than a tenths unit. Do you agree? Explain.

Choose the more precise unit of measure.

29. foot, meter

30. gallon, liter

31. centimeter, inch

32. deciliter, gallon

33. kilometer, mile

34. kilogram, pound

35. A climber ascends 2,458.75 ft up a 3,000-ft mountainside. How much farther does the climber have to go to reach the top? Round your answer appropriately.

36. **Challenge** Three students measured the width of a bulletin board. The three measurements were 1 yd, 3 ft, and 36 in. Compare the measurements and the precision of the measurements.

Test Prep and Mixed Review   **Practice**

Multiple Choice

37. The fraction $\frac{3}{8}$ is found between which pair of fractions on a number line?

Ⓐ $\frac{4}{16}$ and $\frac{13}{32}$ Ⓑ $\frac{5}{16}$ and $\frac{10}{32}$ Ⓒ $\frac{6}{16}$ and $\frac{20}{32}$ Ⓓ $\frac{7}{16}$ and $\frac{24}{32}$

38. Hector bought two bags of apples. The larger bag weighed $3\frac{3}{4}$ lb. The smaller bag weighed $\frac{5}{8}$ lb less than the larger bag. Which expression can be used to find the weight, in pounds, of the smaller bag?

Ⓕ $3\frac{3}{4} + \frac{5}{8}$ Ⓖ $3\frac{3}{4} \cdot \frac{5}{8}$ Ⓗ $3\frac{3}{4} - \frac{5}{8}$ Ⓙ $3\frac{3}{4} \div \frac{5}{8}$

39. What is the value of the expression $4 + (12 \div 4)^2 - 3 \cdot 5$?

Ⓐ -10 Ⓑ -2 Ⓒ 20 Ⓓ 50

GO for Help

For Exercises	See Lesson
40–43	3-1

Estimate each answer.

40. $12\frac{1}{10} - 5\frac{7}{8}$ 41. $2\frac{2}{9} + 4\frac{1}{8}$ 42. $3\frac{1}{3} \cdot 10\frac{4}{5}$ 43. $16\frac{1}{9} \div 3\frac{6}{7}$

Estimating in Different Systems

Every day you see measurements in both the customary system and the metric system. You can use estimates to help you compare measurements in the two systems.

A liter is a little more than a quart.
An inch is about 2.5 cm.
A kilometer is about 0.6 mi.
A kilogram is about 2.2 lb.

You may be more familiar with temperatures measured in Fahrenheit than in Celsius. You can use the table at the right to help you relate to Celsius temperatures.

Celsius Temperature	How It Feels
30°	hot
20°	nice
10°	cold
0°	freezing

EXAMPLE

Which measurement is longer, 15 cm or 10 in.?

One inch is about 2.5 cm.

$10 \cdot 2.5 = 25$ ← **Multiply by 10 to find the number of centimeters in 10 in.**

There are about 25 cm in 10 in. So 10 in. is longer than 15 cm.

Exercises

Which of the two measurements is greater?

1. 600 km or 200 mi

2. 0°C or 0°F

3. 80 L or 40 gal

4. 50 cm or 25 in.

5. 30 lb or 20 kg

6. 10°F or 20°C

7. **Travel** A sign reads "Austin, 200 km." About how many miles would you have to drive to get to Austin?

8. **Clothing** A sign shows that the temperature is 27°C. Would you be more comfortable in a short-sleeved shirt or in a ski parka?

9. A student tells you that he is 175 cm tall and weighs 72 kg.
   a. About how many feet tall is the student?
   b. About how many pounds does the student weigh?

10. You need to bring about a gallon of water for a hike. Bottled water is sold in liter bottles. How many liter bottles should you buy?

Reading for Understanding

Reading-comprehension questions are based on a passage that gives you facts and information. First read the question carefully. Make sure you understand what is being asked. Then read the passage. Look for the information you need to answer the question.

EXAMPLE

Recycling Math The United States produces more than 4 pounds of trash per person each day, and recycles about one fourth of it. Canada produces about $3\frac{1}{2}$ pounds of trash per person each day, and recycles about one tenth of it. Japan produces about $2\frac{1}{2}$ of trash per person each day, and recycles about one fifth of it.

In one week, a family living in the United States produced 112 pounds of trash. About how many pounds of the trash were recycled?

What is being asked? How many pounds of trash were recycled?

Identify the information you need. The United States recycles about one fourth of the trash it produces.

Solve the problem. Pounds of recycled trash $= \frac{1}{4} \cdot 112 = 28$. About 28 pounds of the American family's trash were recycled.

Exercises

Use the passage in the example to complete Exercises 1–4.

1. a. About how many pounds of trash will a Canadian family of four produce in one week?
   b. About how many pounds of the trash will be recycled?

2. In one week, a family living in Japan produces 85 pounds of trash. About how many pounds of the trash will be recycled?

3. Suppose your family recycles one third of its trash. How much more trash does your family recycle than an average U.S. family?

4. In one month, a school recycled two fifths of its paper and produced 25 pounds of paper. How many pounds were *not* recycled?

Chapter 3 Review

Vocabulary Review

🔊 **benchmark** (p. 120)

precision (p. 154)

reciprocals (p. 141)

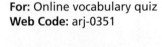

Go Online
PHSchool.com
For: Online vocabulary quiz
Web Code: arj-0351

Choose the correct vocabulary term to complete each sentence.

1. The number $\frac{7}{8}$ is the __?__ of the number $\frac{8}{7}$.

2. A __?__ is a number used to replace fractions that are less than 1.

3. The __?__ of a measurement refers to its degree of exactness.

4. When you use a __?__ to estimate a sum, your answer has less __?__ than the exact answer.

Skills and Concepts

Lesson 3-1
• To estimate sums, differences, products, and quotients involving fractions

You can use the **benchmarks** $0, \frac{1}{2}$, and 1 to estimate sums and difference of fractions. To estimate sums, differences, products, and quotients of mixed numbers, round to the nearest whole number or use compatible numbers.

Estimate each answer.

5. $\frac{3}{4} + \frac{1}{8}$

6. $\frac{5}{6} - \frac{1}{3}$

7. $\frac{2}{5} + \frac{3}{8}$

8. $\frac{4}{9} - \frac{2}{18}$

Use rounding to estimate.

9. $4\frac{11}{12} - 2\frac{1}{10}$

10. $5\frac{2}{5} \cdot 4\frac{7}{9}$

11. $8\frac{4}{5} + 4\frac{7}{8}$

12. $24\frac{1}{6} - 13\frac{2}{3}$

13. **Maps** A map shows three hiking trails of lengths $2\frac{1}{2}$ mi, $1\frac{4}{5}$ mi, and $3\frac{3}{10}$ mi. You want to hike the entire length of each trail. Estimate the total distance.

Lessons 3-2, 3-3
• To add and subtract fractions and to solve problems involving fractions
• To add and subtract mixed numbers and to solve problems involving mixed numbers

To add or subtract fractions, you first find a common denominator and then add or subtract the numerators. To add or subtract mixed numbers, you add or subtract the fractions first, and then the whole numbers. You may need to rename a mixed number before subtracting.

Find each sum or difference.

14. $2\frac{1}{3} - \frac{3}{4}$

15. $16\frac{2}{3} - 9\frac{4}{5}$

16. $8\frac{1}{6} + 7\frac{3}{12}$

17. $2\frac{1}{6} + 3\frac{3}{8}$

18. Rich walks to school in $10\frac{1}{5}$ minutes. John walks in $21\frac{1}{4}$ minutes. How many more minutes does it take John to get to school?

Lessons 3-4, 3-5

- To multiply fractions and mixed numbers and to solve problems by multiplying
- To divide fractions and mixed numbers and to solve problems by dividing

To multiply fractions, you multiply their numerators and multiply their denominators. To divide by a fraction, you multiply by its reciprocal.

Find each product.

19. $\frac{2}{3} \cdot \frac{3}{8}$ **20.** $\frac{3}{5} \cdot 1\frac{1}{2}$ **21.** $2\frac{2}{3} \cdot 3\frac{3}{8}$ **22.** $8\frac{5}{6} \cdot 10\frac{3}{4}$

23. What is the area of a room that is $12\frac{2}{3}$ m long and $3\frac{1}{8}$ m wide?

Find each quotient.

24. $\frac{2}{3} \div \frac{4}{3}$ **25.** $5\frac{1}{4} \div \frac{7}{8}$ **26.** $4\frac{4}{5} \div 1\frac{1}{3}$ **27.** $1\frac{1}{3} \div 4\frac{4}{5}$

28. The area of Sally's garden is $17\frac{1}{2}$ square feet. If Sally's garden is $5\frac{1}{2}$ ft long, how wide is her garden?

Lesson 3-6

- To change units of length, capacity, and weight in the customary system

To change from a smaller unit to a larger unit, you *divide*. To change from a larger unit to a smaller unit, you *multiply*.

Complete.

29. 42 in. = ▓ ft   **30.** 12 fl oz = ▓ c   **31.** 80 oz = ▓ lb

32. 10,560 ft = ▓ mi   **33.** 2 t = ▓ lb   **34.** $3\frac{1}{2}$ qt = ▓ pt

35. The highest annual rainfall on record for the state of Texas was about 109 in., in 1873. How many feet of rain did Texas receive that year?

Lesson 3-7

- To find and compare the precision of measurements

The **precision** of a measurement refers to its degree of exactness. The smaller the units on a measuring instrument, the more precise a measurement is. When you add or subtract measurements with the same unit, round your answer to match the precision of the least precise measurement.

Choose the more precise measurement.

36. 12 c, 8 pt   **37.** 5.5 L, 2 L   **38.** 8.5 m, 8.75 m

39. 1 day, 23 h   **40.** 25 g, 3.5 kg   **41.** $11\frac{3}{16}$ in., 5 in.

Find each sum or difference. Round your answer appropriately.

42. 17.3 g − 10 g   **43.** $5\frac{1}{3}$ yd + 8 yd   **44.** 7.75 cm + 3.8 cm

45. 5.25 lb + 15.75 lb   **46.** 8 L − 3.005 L   **47.**
       12.175 m − 7.05 m

Estimate each answer.

1. $\frac{7}{8} + \frac{15}{16}$
2. $\frac{3}{5} - \frac{1}{2}$

3. $7\frac{1}{8} + 2\frac{3}{4}$
4. $8\frac{3}{8} - 5\frac{1}{3}$

5. $4\frac{5}{8} \cdot 2\frac{1}{10}$
6. $43\frac{1}{2} \div 5\frac{1}{5}$

7. **Tutoring** You tutored for $2\frac{1}{2}$ h on Monday, $2\frac{1}{6}$ h on Wednesday, and $1\frac{3}{4}$ h on Friday. Estimate the total number of hours you tutored during the week.

Find each sum or difference.

8. $\frac{15}{16} - \frac{3}{16}$
9. $\frac{1}{4} + \frac{2}{3}$

10. $\frac{1}{2} - \frac{3}{8}$
11. $\frac{2}{3} + \frac{5}{6}$

12. $8\frac{2}{5} + 5\frac{3}{5}$
13. $1\frac{2}{3} - \frac{3}{4}$

14. $4\frac{3}{4} + 5\frac{1}{5}$
15. $9\frac{3}{8} - 5\frac{1}{4}$

16. At birth, a baby weighed $7\frac{3}{8}$ lb. The baby now weighs $8\frac{13}{16}$ lb. How much weight has the baby gained?

17. You ride your bike $1\frac{3}{10}$ mi to school. At the end of the day, you stop at a park on the way home. The park is $\frac{2}{5}$ mi from school. How far is the park from your house?

Find each product or quotient.

18. $\frac{4}{5} \cdot \frac{1}{4}$
19. $\frac{4}{5} \div \frac{1}{4}$

20. $\frac{3}{4} \cdot \frac{2}{3}$
21. $\frac{1}{4} \div \frac{4}{5}$

22. $1\frac{2}{3} \cdot 1\frac{1}{4}$
23. $1\frac{2}{3} \div 1\frac{1}{4}$

24. $150 \div 2\frac{2}{3}$
25. $5\frac{3}{8} \cdot 3\frac{3}{4}$

26. **Masonry** A brick is $1\frac{7}{8}$ in. high. Mortar that is $\frac{3}{8}$ in. thick is spread on each row of bricks. How many rows of bricks are needed to reach the top of a $7\frac{1}{2}$-ft doorway?

Find each answer.

27. $10\frac{3}{4} + \frac{5}{8}$
28. $6\frac{1}{2} - 4\frac{3}{5}$

29. $10 \div \frac{1}{4}$
30. $2\frac{1}{2} \cdot 12$

31. $16 \div \frac{1}{3}$
32. $8\frac{3}{5} + \frac{1}{7}$

33. $2\frac{3}{10} - 1\frac{1}{2}$
34. $7\frac{3}{4} + \frac{3}{8}$

35. **Earnings** You have a part-time job at a deli and work $12\frac{1}{2}$ hours in one week. You earn $6.50 per hour. How much money do you earn that week?

36. **Discounts** A store is having a $\frac{1}{3}$-off sale. You want to buy a jacket that originally cost $60. What is the sale price of the jacket?

Complete.

37. 38 in. = ▪ ft
38. 60 oz = ▪ lb

39. $3\frac{3}{4}$ qt = ▪ c
40. $1\frac{2}{3}$ mi = ▪ ft

41. $5\frac{1}{2}$ yd = ▪ in.
42. 50 fl oz = ▪ c

43. **Writing in Math** About how heavy should an object be before you start to measure the object in tons instead of pounds? Explain.

44. You have $1\frac{1}{2}$ lb of fish. How many 6-oz servings can you make?

45. You jog $8\frac{1}{2}$ times around a block. The distance around the block is 770 yd. About how many miles have you jogged? (Hint: 1 mi = 1,760 yd)

Choose the more precise measurement.

46. 36 min, $1\frac{1}{4}$ h

47. 1 t, 500 lb

48. 100.5 mg, 10.67 g

49. 18 months, 1 year

Multiple Choice
Read each question. Then write the letter of the correct answer on your paper.

1. Using estimation, which sum is between 21 and 22?
   - (A) $13.71 + 1.5 + 8.2$
   - (B) $6.75 + 9.02 + 5.838$
   - (C) $5.99 + 2.69 + 15.49$
   - (D) $3.772 + 12.04 + 4.009$

2. Which of the following statements is true?
   - (F) $-23 \geq 23$
   - (H) $-14 < -3$
   - (G) $14 < -21$
   - (J) $7 < 0$

3. Which of the following expressions is equal to 10?
   - (A) $4 + 2 - 5 \div 2$
   - (B) $4 + 2 \div 2$
   - (C) $4 + 3 - 2 \cdot 2$
   - (D) $(4 + 3 - 2) \cdot 2$

4. Karin received the following scores on her last four math tests: $87, 92, 80, 85$. What was her mean test score?
   - (F) 86
   - (H) 90
   - (G) 88
   - (J) 92

5. What is the value of the expression $2^3 + 3 \cdot 4$?
   - (A) 18
   - (C) 28
   - (B) 20
   - (D) 44

6. How is $73,460,000,000$ written in scientific notation?
   - (F) $73.46 + 10^4$
   - (G) 73.46×10^9
   - (H) 7.346×10^9
   - (J) 7.346×10^{10}

7. Which of the following is NOT written in order from least to greatest?
   - (A) $\frac{1}{9}, \frac{1}{8}, \frac{1}{7}$
   - (C) $\frac{1}{2}, \frac{2}{3}, \frac{3}{4}$
   - (B) $\frac{2}{3}, \frac{1}{2}, \frac{3}{4}$
   - (D) $\frac{2}{5}, \frac{1}{2}, \frac{7}{8}$

8. A student measured his height and found that it is between 5 ft and $5\frac{1}{3}$ ft. Which height could it be?
   - (F) $\frac{51}{8}$ ft
   - (H) $\frac{28}{5}$ ft
   - (G) $\frac{25}{4}$ ft
   - (J) $\frac{62}{12}$ ft

9. Which unit is the most appropriate unit for the length of a pencil?
   - (A) mL
   - (C) kg
   - (B) cm
   - (D) m

10. To get to your friend's house, you must travel $\frac{1}{3}$ mile down one street, $\frac{3}{4}$ mile down another street, and $1\frac{1}{2}$ mile down a third street. How many miles must you travel in all to get to your friend's house?
    - (F) $1\frac{5}{9}$ mi
    - (H) $2\frac{5}{9}$ mi
    - (G) $1\frac{7}{12}$ mi
    - (J) $2\frac{7}{12}$ mi

Gridded Response
Record your answer in a grid.

11. You want to buy some helium balloons for a birthday party. A store charges $3.35 per balloon. You spend $16.75. How many balloons do you buy?

Short Response

12. Is 54.5 g or 54.5 kg a more reasonable estimate for a person's weight? Explain.

Extended Response

13. One goaltender makes 72 saves on 78 shots. Another makes 52 saves on 56 shots.
    a. Write two fractions in simplest form to express the numbers of saves per shot.
    b. Which goaltender has the greater number of saves per shot?
    c. Explain how you found your answer to part (b).

Applying Fractions

Into the Earth With Integers Millions of people come to Arizona each year to stand at the edge of the Grand Canyon and look down at the Colorado River, a mile below. If you're one of them, you might decide to hike the winding trail to the canyon floor.

two black bands

Collared Lizard

Adult collared lizards typically grow up to 10–13 in. long and can travel at speeds over 10 mi/h. To escape predators, they can run bipedally (on two legs).

colorful dotted back

long tail

Put It All Together

Materials 10 index cards, markers, two boxes

What You'll Need

- Number four of the index cards -2, -1, $+1$, and $+2$. Put them in one of the boxes and label it "numerators."

- Number the remaining index cards 3, 4, 5, 6, 7, and 8. Put them in the other box and label it "denominators."

How To Play

- The goal of the game is to move from the canyon rim (0) to the canyon floor (-1).

- Draw one card from each box. Write down the fraction it represents. (For example, -2 from the numerator box and 5 from the denominator box represent $-\frac{2}{5}$, or descending $\frac{2}{5}$ mi into the canyon.) *To leave the canyon rim, you must draw a negative numerator.*

- Replace the cards and draw again. Add the fractions. Repeat until one of the players reaches -1 (or beyond). If your total rises above 0, you are back on the rim. *Start again at 0!*

1. Write an equation to show how far you go toward the bottom in your first two moves. *Use zero for each positive move before your first negative move.*

2. a. Reasoning How would you calculate the total distance you hiked? Explain.

   b. How far did you hike?

3. a. Writing in Math Choose whichever numerator and whichever denominator you want for your first move. Explain your choice.

   b. Reasoning Suppose you can choose for each move, but you cannot use the same denominator twice. How many moves will it take for you to get to the bottom? Explain, using a fraction sentence.

Riding Down

Mules are one form of transportation in the Grand Canyon.

The Pinyon Jay

Pinyon jays live in the Grand Canyon, and among the Pinyon and Juniper pines throughout the southwest.

blue throat with white streaks

long pointed black bill

blue tail

Go Online
PHSchool.com
For: Information about canyons
Web Code: are-0353

CHAPTER 4 — Equations and Inequalities

What You've Learned

- In Chapter 1, you added, subtracted, multiplied, and divided decimals and integers.
- You used number lines to model operations with integers.

Check Your Readiness

GO for Help

For Exercises	See Lesson
1–4	1-2
5–8	1-8
9–14	1-9
15–18	2-4

Adding and Subtracting Decimals

Find each sum or difference.

1. $5.304 - 0.89$ **2.** $2.35 + 1.8 + 4.45$

3. $2.15 - 1.36$ **4.** $3.14 + 2.67 + 9.4$

Multiplying and Dividing Integers

Find each product or quotient.

5. $-12 \cdot 3$ **6.** $-3 \div (-3)$ **7.** $-6 \cdot (-7)$ **8.** $-54 \div 9$

Order of Operations

Find the value of each expression.

9. $14 + 2(15 \div 5)$ **10.** $20 \div 2 - 3 \cdot 3$ **11.** $(5 + 4) \cdot 4 \div 36$

12. $(9 - 4) \div 5 \cdot 6$ **13.** $9 \div (18 - 15) + 4$ **14.** $6 + 8 \cdot 7 - 24$

Comparing Fractions

Compare each pair of fractions. Use <, =, or >.

15. $\frac{20}{24}$ ■ $\frac{28}{36}$ **16.** $\frac{15}{27}$ ■ $\frac{5}{9}$ **17.** $\frac{6}{7}$ ■ $\frac{18}{22}$ **18.** $\frac{8}{9}$ ■ $\frac{9}{10}$

What You'll Learn Next

- In this chapter, you will solve equations and inequalities by adding, subtracting, multiplying, or dividing.

- You will write inequalities and graph their solutions on number lines.

 Problem Solving Application On pages 224 and 225, you will work an extended activity on inequalities.

◀)) Key Vocabulary

- Addition Property of Equality (p. 180)
- algebraic expression (p. 169)
- Division Property of Equality (p. 186)
- equation (p. 174)
- inequality (p. 205)
- inverse operations (p. 181)
- Multiplication Property of Equality (p. 188)
- open sentence (p. 174)
- solution of an equation (p. 174)
- solution of an inequality (p. 205)
- Subtraction Property of Equality (p. 180)
- variable (p. 169)

Describing Patterns

You can identify and describe patterns to make predictions.

ACTIVITY

During part of its flight, an airplane rises 12 feet in altitude each second. Use this information to find a pattern.

Time (s)	Distance (ft)
1	12
5	60
10	120
20	■
25	■
50	■
100	■
200	■

1. Look at the table at the right. Explain how to find the distance the plane rises for each amount of time.

2. Copy and complete the table at the right.

3. At t seconds, how many feet has the plane risen?

You can use different scales to measure temperature. The Celsius and Kelvin scales have a special relationship.

Celsius (C)	Kelvin (K)
0	273
1	274
5	278
10	■
20	■
30	■
75	■
100	■

4. Look at the table of temperatures at the right. Explain how to find the temperature in Kelvin for each temperature in degrees Celsius.

5. Copy and complete the table.

6. At c degrees Celsius, what is the temperature in Kelvin?

Exercises

Copy and complete each table. Describe the pattern you find.

1.

A	B
1	8
2	9
5	12
10	■
30	■
50	■
n	■

2.

C	D
1	−4
2	−3
5	0
10	■
25	■
45	■
n	■

3.

E	F
1	40
2	80
5	200
10	■
100	■
500	■
n	■

4. **Reasoning** What does the letter n represent in each table above? How is it used to describe the pattern in the table?

4-1

Evaluating and Writing Algebraic Expressions

✓ Check Skills You'll Need

1. **Vocabulary Review**
The set of rules for simplifying an expression is called the _?_ .

Find the value of each expression.

2. $3 + 4 \cdot 2$

3. $12 - 6 \div 3$

4. $6 \cdot (5 - 7) + 2$

5. $(4 + 3) \cdot 2 - 11$

 **for Help**
Lesson 1-9

What You'll Learn

To write and evaluate algebraic expressions

◀)) **New Vocabulary** variable, algebraic expression

Why Learn This?

You can use algebraic expressions to help you make predictions based on patterns. If you know how far you can swim in 1 minute, you can estimate how far you can swim in 5 minutes.

A **variable** is a symbol that represents one or more numbers. Variables are usually letters. An **algebraic expression** is a mathematical phrase with at least one variable.

Diagrams and algebraic expressions can represent word phrases.

Word Phrase	Diagram	Algebraic Expression
a temperature of t degrees increased by 5 degrees	t | 5	$t + 5$
five cats fewer than c cats	c / ? | 5	$c - 5$
the product of 5 and n nickels	n|n|n|n|n	$5n$
a dinner bill of d dollars divided among five friends	d / $\frac{d}{5}$|$\frac{d}{5}$|$\frac{d}{5}$|$\frac{d}{5}$|$\frac{d}{5}$	$\frac{d}{5}$

EXAMPLE Writing Algebraic Expressions

Test Prep Tip ⊕⊗⊙⊝⊚

You can use diagrams to represent algebraic expressions.

1 Write an algebraic expression for each word phrase.

a. swimming m meters per minute for 3 minutes → $3m$

b. 12 heartbeats more than x heartbeats → $x + 12$

✓ Quick Check

1. Write an algebraic expression for a price p decreased by 16.

You can use algebraic expressions to represent real-world situations.

EXAMPLE Application: Public Service

② The Environmental Club is making posters. The materials for each poster cost $4. Write an algebraic expression for the cost of p posters.

Words $4 per poster   times   the number of posters

Expression   4   · p

An algebraic expression for the cost of the posters is $4p$.

✅ **Quick Check**

2. Nine students will hang t posters each. Write an algebraic expression for the total number of posters the students will hang.

You can translate algebraic expressions into word phrases.

EXAMPLE Writing Word Phrases

③ Write three different word phrases for $x + 2$.

A number plus two

A number increased by two

Two more than a number

For: Expressions Activity
Use: Interactive
      Textbook, 4-1

✅ **Quick Check**

3. Write three different word phrases for $c - 50$.

You can substitute for a variable to evaluate an algebraic expression.

EXAMPLE Evaluating Algebraic Expressions

④ Evaluate each expression. Use the values $p = 2$, $n = 3$, and $s = 5$.

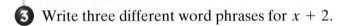

a. $2p + 7$

$$2p + 7 = 2(2) + 7 \quad \leftarrow \textbf{Substitute.} \rightarrow$$
$$= 4 + 7 \quad \leftarrow \textbf{Multiply.} \rightarrow$$
$$= 11 \quad \leftarrow \ \textbf{Add.} \ \rightarrow$$

b. $p + (n \cdot s)$

$$p + (n \cdot s) = 2 + (3 \cdot 5)$$
$$= 2 + (15)$$
$$= 17$$

✅ **Quick Check**

4. Use the values $n = 3$, $t = 5$, and $y = 7$ to evaluate $(n + t) \cdot y$.

1. **Vocabulary** A numerical expression is a mathematical phrase that uses numbers. What is the difference between an *algebraic* expression and a *numerical* expression?

Tell which operation you would use for each word phrase.

2. six goals fewer than *g* goals

3. *p* people increased by two

Write a word phrase for each algebraic expression.

4. $w - 3$

5. $5 \cdot w$

6. $12 + w$

7. $\frac{w}{4}$

Evaluate each expression. Use the value $p = 2$.

8. $p + 8$

9. $3 \cdot p$

10. $16 - p$

11. $\frac{12}{p}$

Homework Exercises

For more exercises, see Extra Skills and Word Problems.

GO for Help

For Exercises	See Examples
12–16	1–2
17–24	3
25–30	4

Write an algebraic expression for each word phrase. You may find a diagram helpful.

12. four more than *s* shirts

13. the quotient of *p* and 5

14. the sum of *t* TVs and 11 TVs

15. five times your quiz score *q*

16. Your job pays $7 per hour. Write an algebraic expression for your pay in dollars for working *h* hours.

Write a word phrase for each algebraic expression.

17. $d + 2$

18. $\frac{4}{n}$

19. $c - 9.1$

20. $6.5 - h$

21. $1.3 \cdot p$

22. $10 + q$

23. $\frac{w}{10}$

24. $3.5v$

Evaluate each expression. Use the values $p = 4$, $n = 6$, and $s = 2$.

25. $7n$

26. $-6.1p$

27. $5 - s$

28. $\frac{n}{2}$

29. $8s - 6$

30. $1.5(p + n)$

31. **Guided Problem Solving** A student mows one lawn each week day after school and two lawns on Saturday. She earns $15.75 per lawn. Write an algebraic expression for the amount of money she makes in *w* weeks.
    - How many lawns does she mow in one week?
    - *Draw a picture* to represent the amount of money she makes in one week.

Homework Video Tutor
Visit: PHSchool.com
Web Code: are-0401

Write an algebraic expression for the nth term of each table.

32.

A	0	1	2	3	5	10	n
B	5	6	7	8	10	15	?

33.

C	0	1	2	3	5	10	n
D	0	10	20	30	50	100	?

34. Write an algebraic expression to find the number of seconds in n minutes. Evaluate the expression for $n = 20$.

35. Birds The blue-throated hummingbird has a heart rate of about 1,260 beats per minute. Explain how you would calculate the number of times the hummingbird's heart beats in a 24-hour day. Then find the number of beats in a 24-hour day.

36. Describe a situation that the expression $10n$ can model.

37. Writing in Math You can write "twelve less than a number" as $n - 12$, but not as $12 - n$. Explain why.

38. Estimation This section of a page from a telephone directory shows a column with 11 names in 1 inch. Each page has four 10-inch columns. Write an algebraic expression for the approximate number of names in p pages of the directory.

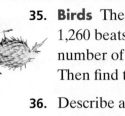

```
6-4462   Daalling V 8 Everett All..........
2-3302   Daavis K 444 Greeley R.........
4-1775   Dabady V 94 Burnside All.......
2-0014   Dabagh L 13 Lancaster R......
6-3356   Dabagh W Dr 521 Weston All..
4-7322   Dabar G 98 River All.............
6-1530   Dabarera F 34 Roseland All..
2-2279   Dabas M 17 Riverside R........
4-9978   D'Abate D 86 Moss Hill Rd All..
2-6745   D'Abate G 111 South Central R
4-5456   Dabbous H 670 Warren Dr All.
6-3064   Dabbraccio F 151 Century All..
6-2257   Dabby D 542 Walnut All.........
2-9987   Dabcovich M G 219 Green R..
6-5643   Dabcovich M 72 Main All.......
```

39. Challenge A student baby-sitting for $5 per hour writes the expression $5n$ to represent the money he makes for n hours. Another student writes $3n + 15$ to represent the amount in dollars she makes. What is the second student's hourly rate? What does the number 15 represent?

Test Prep and Mixed Review

Practice

Multiple Choice

40. In ancient Greece, a measurement called a cubit equaled 18.3 inches. Which expression represents the number of inches in c cubits?

 Ⓐ $c - 18.3$ Ⓑ $c \div 18.3$ Ⓒ $18.3 + c$ Ⓓ $18.3c$

41. Which expression does the model represent?

 Ⓕ $\frac{2}{3} \times \frac{3}{4}$ Ⓗ $\frac{1}{2} \times \frac{2}{3}$

 Ⓖ $\frac{1}{3} \times \frac{3}{4}$ Ⓙ $\frac{1}{2} \times \frac{3}{4}$

Find the value of each expression.

42. $7(1.2) + 7(0.5)$ **43.** $3(4 + 5) + 2(4 + 5)$ **44.** $5(0.25 \cdot 40)$

GO for Help

For Exercises	See Lesson
42–44	1-9

Using Spreadsheets

You can use a computer spreadsheet to keep track of the balance in a checking account. You add deposits and subtract checks. Using the formulas you supply, the spreadsheet computes values in cells.

EXAMPLE **Using Spreadsheets**

Use the spreadsheet. Find the balance after each entry.

	A	B	C	D
1	Date	Deposits	Checks	Balance
2				$350
3	4/29	$100		▦
4	4/30		$400	▦

Use the formula "= D2 + B3".
← The computer finds 350 + 100 = 450.
← Use the formula "= D3 − C4".
The computer finds 450 − 400 = 50.

● The first balance is $450. The second balance is $50.

Exercises

Use the spreadsheet at the right.

1. Find the account balance after each entry. Write the formulas you used.

2. Which formula can you use to find the balance in cell D9, whether or not a check has been written or a deposit has been made?

   Ⓐ = D8 − B9 + C9   Ⓒ = D8 + B9 + C9
   Ⓑ = D8 − B9 − C9   Ⓓ = D8 + B9 − C9

3. **Reasoning** Suppose the balance in cell D9 is $130.34. Was the amount of a deposit entered into cell B9, or was the amount of a check entered into cell C9? Support your answer.

4. **Writing in Math** Consider your answer to Exercise 2. Explain why the formula you chose works. Give examples.

5. **Reasoning** Suppose the balance in cell D8 is $250 and you do not know the original balance. Explain how would you calculate the original balance in cell D2. Then find the original balance.

	A	B	C	D
1	Date	Deposits	Checks	Balance
2				$250
3	11/3		$25.98	▦
4	11/9		$239.40	▦
5	11/10	$122.00		▦
6	11/13		$54.65	▦
7	11/20	$350.00		▦
8	11/29		$163.80	▦

Using Number Sense to Solve Equations

Algebra

4-2

✓ Check Skills You'll Need

1. Vocabulary Review
A __?__ is a symbol that represents one or more numbers.

Write an algebraic expression for each word phrase.

2. four more than y

3. six less than v

4. k divided by 9

 **for Help**
Lesson 4-1

What You'll Learn

To solve one-step equations using substitution, mental math, and estimation

🔊 **New Vocabulary** equation, open sentence, solution of an equation

Why Learn This?

Solving equations can help you find amounts that are not easy to measure on their own. For example, if you know the weight of the bucket, you can use an equation to find the weight of the panda.

An **equation** is a mathematical sentence with an equal sign. An equation with one or more variables is an **open sentence**. The open sentence $p + 2 = 16$ is neither true nor false until p is replaced.

You can substitute a number for the variable in an equation to see if the value makes the equation true. A **solution of an equation** is a value for a variable that makes an equation true.

$$p + 2 = 16 \qquad 20 + 2 = 16 \qquad 14 + 2 = 16$$
$$\text{false} \qquad\qquad \text{true}$$

Since 14 makes the equation true, 14 is a solution of the equation.

EXAMPLE Solving Equations Using Substitution

1 Find the solution of $12m = 108$ from the numbers 4, 7, and 9. You can test each number by substituting for m in the equation.

$$12(4) \stackrel{?}{=} 108 \qquad\quad 12(7) \stackrel{?}{=} 108 \qquad\quad 12(9) \stackrel{?}{=} 108$$
$$48 = 108 \; \text{✗ False} \quad 84 = 108 \; \text{✗ False} \quad 108 = 108 \; \text{✔ True}$$

Since the equation is true when you substitute 9 for m, the solution is 9.

✓ Quick Check

1. Find the solution of each equation from the given numbers.
 a. $24n = 120$; 3, 5, or 11   **b.** $124p = 992$; 4, 6, or 8

Sometimes you can solve an equation by using mental math.

EXAMPLE Solving Equations Using Mental Math

 Use mental math to solve each equation.

a. $4y = 20$ **b.** $m + 7 = 15.5$

What you think

What number times 4 equals 20?

Since $4 \cdot 5 = 20$, $y = 5$.

What you think

What number plus 7 equals 15.5?

Since $7 + 8.5 = 15.5$, $m = 8.5$.

✅ Quick Check

2. Use mental math to solve each equation.
   a. $t - 3 = 7$ **b.** $n + 6 = -10.1$
   c. $\dfrac{h}{4} = 2.2$ **d.** $7x = -63$

You can solve problems by using equations and estimation.

EXAMPLE Estimating Solutions

Careers A veterinarian is a health-care provider for animals.

3 **Multiple Choice** A veterinarian holds a puppy and steps on a scale. The scale reads 134.5 lb. The veterinarian weighs 125.3 lb alone. Which is the best estimate of the weight of the puppy?
   Ⓐ Between 3 and 5 lb   Ⓒ Between 9 and 11 lb
   Ⓑ Between 6 and 8 lb   Ⓓ Between 12 and 15 lb

Words   weight   plus   puppy's weight   equals   total weight

      Let   w   = the weight of the puppy.

Equation   125.3   +   w   =   134.5

$$125.3 + w = 134.5$$
$$125.3 \approx 125 \quad 134.5 \approx 135 \quad \leftarrow \text{Choose compatible numbers.}$$
$$125 + w = 135 \quad\quad\quad \leftarrow \text{What number added to 125 is 135?}$$
$$w = 10 \quad\quad\quad\quad\quad \leftarrow \text{Use mental math.}$$

The puppy weighs about 10 lb. The correct answer is choice C.

Test Prep Tip

When writing an algebraic expression, choose a letter for the variable that will remind you of what the variable represents.

✅ Quick Check

3. A box of machine parts weighs 14.7 lb. A forklift has a maximum weight limit of 390 lb. About how many boxes of parts can the forklift carry at one time?

1. **Vocabulary** The value of a variable that makes an equation true is called the __?__ of the equation.

2. **Number Sense** The open sentence $14k = 0$ has __?__ solution(s).
   Ⓐ no   Ⓑ one   Ⓒ infinitely many

Tell whether each value of the variable is a solution of the equation.

3. $5x = -35$; $x = -7$ 4. $8 - y = 2$; $y = 6$ 5. $-7 + b = 4$; $b = 3$

Use mental math to solve each equation.

6. $10m = -90$ 7. $6 + w = 3$ 8. $\dfrac{40}{z} = 8$ 9. $-5p = 20$

For more exercises, see Extra Skills and Word Problems.

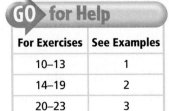

For Exercises	See Examples
10–13	1
14–19	2
20–23	3

Find the solution of each equation from the given numbers.

10. $p + 17 = 56$; 29, 39, or 49   11. $\dfrac{y}{9} = 32$; 261, 279, or 288

12. $6d = -36.6$; -6.1, 0, or 6.1   13. $n - 27 = 38$; 11, 51, or 65

Use mental math to solve each equation.

14. $n + 4 = 7.9$ 15. $4d = -32$ 16. $\dfrac{p}{5} = 3.1$

17. $24 = -6w$ 18. $\dfrac{c}{-3} = 8$ 19. $z - 8.4 = 0$

Estimate the solution of each equation to the nearest whole number.

20. $3.1g = 20.9$ 21. $h - 4.9 = 13.8$ 22. $7.8 + n = 38.2$

23. A bowling ball has a mass of 5.54 kg. A bowling pin has a mass of 1.58 kg. About how many pins are equal in mass to one ball?

24. **Guided Problem Solving** Your class has collected 84.5 lb of canned food. The school record is 103.25 lb. Write an equation and use it to estimate the amount of canned food the class still needs to collect to match the record.
    - Estimate 84.5 and 103.25 by rounding.
    - Choose a variable for the amount of food the class still needs.
    - Write an equation using your variable and your estimates.

25. An elevator has a maximum lift of 2,000 lb. You are moving 55-lb boxes of books. Write an equation and estimate how many boxes you can safely place on the elevator.

26. Describe a situation that can be represented by $4.5 + t = 30$.

Solve using mental math or estimation. If you estimate, round to the nearest whole number before you add or subtract.

27. $p - 7.35 = 46.71$ **28.** $a - 20 = 17$ **29.** $28.71 + t = 49.43$

30. $n - 11 = 33$ **31.** $k - 99.9 = 463.04$ **32.** $17 + p = -3$

33. Baseball The total distance around a baseball diamond is 360 ft. Write an equation to represent the distance from first base to second base.

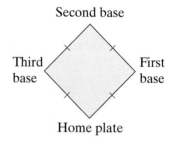

Second base

Third base

First base

Home plate

34. Writing in Math Equations can be true or false. Can an expression like $2a + 7$ be true or false? Explain.

Data Analysis Use the table below for Exercises 35 and 36.

35. The average precipitation for Houston is 1.5 times the average for Detroit. Find the average precipitation for Detroit.

36. The average precipitation for Raleigh is 4.3 times the average for San Diego. Find the average precipitation for San Diego.

Average Annual Precipitation

City	Precipitation (in.)
Detroit, Mich.	■
Houston, Tex.	47.84
Raleigh, N.C.	43.05
San Diego, Calif.	■

SOURCE: National Climatic Data Center.
Go to **PHSchool.com** for a data update.
Web Code: arg-9041

37. Challenge You want to buy 4 candles that cost $12.95 each. A clerk tells you that the total, including sales tax, is $67.80. Is the clerk's total reasonable? Explain.

Test Prep and Mixed Review   **Practice**

Multiple Choice

38. Jane had $22.25 before baby-sitting on Saturday. After baby-sitting, she had $48.75. Which equation can be used to find b, the amount of money Jane earned from baby-sitting?

　Ⓐ $22.25 - b = $48.75   Ⓒ $48.75 - b = $22.25
　Ⓑ $22.25 + $48.75 = b   Ⓓ $48.75 + b = $22.25

39. The table shows the points the Cougars scored during their last 4 games. Which measure of data is represented by 64.5?

　Ⓕ mean   Ⓗ median
　Ⓖ mode   Ⓙ range

Cougars Points Scored

Game	Points
1	72
2	60
3	47
4	69

GO for Help

For Exercises	See Lesson
40–42	1-7

Use a number line to find each sum.

40. $-5 + 9$ **41.** $-9 + 10$ **42.** $-2 + -8$

Keeping the Balance

You can use a balance-scale model to solve equations.
The scales below are balanced. Use them for the activity.
Objects that look identical have the same weight. Objects
that look different have different weights.

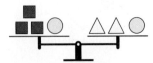 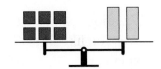

ACTIVITY

1. Decide whether each scale is balanced. Explain your reasoning.

a.

b.
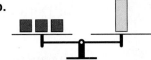

c.
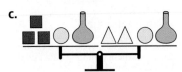

d.
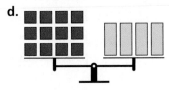

Exercises

Tell whether each statement is true or false. Explain.

1. A balanced scale will stay balanced if I add the same amount to each side.

2. A balanced scale will stay balanced if I remove the same amount from each side.

3. A balanced scale will stay balanced if I multiply each side by the same amount.

4. A balanced scale will stay balanced if I divide each side by the same amount.

Decide whether each scale is balanced. Explain your reasoning.

5.
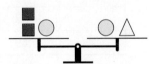

6.
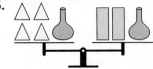

7.
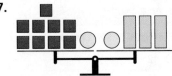

Modeling Equations

You can model and solve equations using algebra tiles.

EXAMPLE **Solving Addition Equations**

1 Use algebra tiles to solve $x + 4 = 12$.

$x + 4 = 12$  ← Model the equation. Use yellow tiles for positive integers.

$x + 4 - 4 = 12 - 4$ 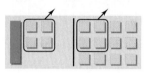 ← Remove 4 tiles from each side.

$x = 8$  ← Simplify.

EXAMPLE **Solving Multiplication Equations**

2 Use algebra tiles to solve $3x = -21$.

$3x = -21$  ← Model the equation. Use red tiles for negative integers.

$\dfrac{3x}{3} = \dfrac{-21}{3}$  ← Divide each side into three equal groups.

$x = -7$  ← Simplify.

Exercises

Use algebra tiles to solve each equation.

1. $x + 12 = 18$ **2.** $x + 3 = 16$ **3.** $x + 8 = 17$ **4.** $x + (-7) = 13$

5. $x + (-2) = -7$ **6.** $x + (-7) = -11$ **7.** $3x = 18$ **8.** $5x = -25$

9. $7x = 21$ **10.** $2x = -18$ **11.** $4x = 28$ **12.** $2x = 24$

4-3 Solving Equations by Adding or Subtracting

What You'll Learn

To solve equations by adding or subtracting

🔊 **New Vocabulary** Addition Property of Equality, Subtraction Property of Equality, inverse operations

Why Learn This?

If you can solve equations, you can use known information to find unknown information.

You can think of an equation as a balance scale. When you do something to one side of an equation, you must do the same thing to the other side of the equation to keep it balanced.

You can find the value of the unknown weight above by removing four weights from each side of the scale. The result is the scale on the right.

This illustrates the Subtraction Property of Equality. You can use this property and the Addition Property of Equality to solve equations.

KEY CONCEPTS Properties of Equality

Addition Property of Equality
If you add the same value to each side of an equation, the two sides remain equal.

Arithmetic	Algebra
$\frac{20}{2} = 10$, so $\frac{20}{2} + 3 = 10 + 3$.	If $a = b$, then $a + c = b + c$.

Subtraction Property of Equality
If you subtract the same value from each side of an equation, the two sides remain equal.

Arithmetic	Algebra
$\frac{12}{2} = 6$, so $\frac{12}{2} - 4 = 6 - 4$.	If $a = b$, then $a - c = b - c$.

To solve an equation, you want to get the variable alone on one side of the equation. You can use **inverse operations,** operations that undo each other, to get the variable alone.

Addition and subtraction are inverse operations. You can use addition to undo subtraction.

EXAMPLE Solving Equations by Adding

Test Prep Tip

You can represent the equation in Example 1 with this model.

x	
34	−46

1 Solve $x - 34 = -46$.

$$x - 34 = -46$$
$$x - 34 + 34 = -46 + 34 \quad \leftarrow \text{Addition Property of Equality: Add 34 to each side.}$$
$$x + 0 = -12 \quad \leftarrow \text{The numbers −34 and 34 are additive inverses.}$$
$$x = -12 \quad \leftarrow \text{Identity Property of Addition}$$

Check $\quad x - 34 = -46 \quad \leftarrow \text{Check the solution in the original equation.}$
$$-12 - 34 = -46 \quad \leftarrow \text{Substitute −12 for } x.$$
$$-46 = -46 \ ✔ \quad \leftarrow \text{Subtract.}$$

✓ **Quick Check**

1. Solve the equation $x - 104 = 64$.

Just as addition undoes subtraction, subtraction undoes addition.

EXAMPLE Solving Equations by Subtracting

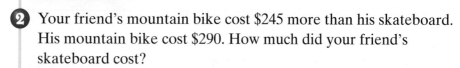

2 Your friend's mountain bike cost $245 more than his skateboard. His mountain bike cost $290. How much did your friend's skateboard cost?

Words cost of bike is $245 more than cost of skateboard

Let s = the cost of the skateboard.

Equation   290   = 245   + s

$$290 = 245 + s$$
$$290 - 245 = 245 - 245 + s \quad \leftarrow \text{Subtract 245 from each side.}$$
$$45 = s \quad \leftarrow \text{Simplify.}$$

The skateboard cost $45.

✓ **Quick Check**

2. A hardcover book costs $19 more than its paperback edition. The hardcover book costs $26.95. How much does the paperback cost?

Writing Problem Situations

3 Describe a problem situation that matches the equation $s - 286 = 74$.

Step 1 Translate the symbols into words. The equation represents 286 subtracted from some original amount. The result of the subtraction is 74.

Step 2 Choose a context to describe the numbers and symbols.

original amount s	minus	286	is	74
↓		↓		↓
s songs	minus	286 songs	is	74 songs

Rita deleted 286 songs from her audio player. She had 74 songs left. How many songs did Rita have on her audio player before she deleted 286 songs?

You can find a solution to your equation by solving for s.

$$s - 286 = 74$$
$$s - 286 + 286 = 74 + 286 \qquad \leftarrow \textbf{Add 286 to each side.}$$
$$s = 360 \qquad \leftarrow \textbf{Simplify.}$$

Rita had 360 songs on her audio player.

✓ Quick Check

3. a. Describe a problem situation that matches the equation $n + 41 = 157$.

b. Solve the equation $n + 41 = 157$.

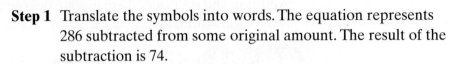 **Check Your Understanding**

1. **Vocabulary** ? operations are operations that undo each other.

2. **Error Analysis** Dylan and Jean tried to solve the equation $x + 4 = -9$. Who solved the equation correctly? Explain.

Dylan
$$x + 4 = -9$$
$$x + 4 + 4 = -9 + 4$$
$$x = -5$$

Jean
$$x + 4 = -9$$
$$x + 4 - 4 = -9 - 4$$
$$x = -13$$

 **Vocabulary Tip**

When you get the variable alone on one side of the equation, you are "isolating the variable."

Fill in the missing numbers to solve each equation.

3.
$$b + 12 = 39$$
$$b + 12 - \blacksquare = 39 - \blacksquare$$

4.
$$y - 8 = 35$$
$$y - 8 + \blacksquare = 35 + \blacksquare$$

For more exercises, see Extra Skills and Word Problems.

GO for Help

For Exercises	See Examples
5–10	1
11–17	2
18–21	3

Solve each equation. Check your answer. You may find a model helpful.

5. $x - 6 = -55$

6. $n - 255 = -455$

7. $-83.4 + m = 122$

8. $t - 32.8 = -27$

9. $h - 37 = -42$

10. $q - 16 = 40$

11. $k + 17 = 29$

12. $d + 261.9 = -48$

13. $x + 34 = 212$

14. $253 + c = 725$

15. $89 + y = 100$

16. $62.5 + t = -77$

17. Invisible braces cost $500 more than metal braces. Metal braces cost $4,800. How much do invisible braces cost?

Describe a problem situation that matches each equation. Then solve.

18. $t - 3.5 = 8$

19. $34 = g + 25$

20. $q + 12 = 100$

21. $63.8 = p - 17$

22. **Guided Problem Solving** A runner's heart rate is 133 beats per minute. This is 62 beats per minute more than his resting heart rate. Write and solve an equation to find the runner's resting heart rate.
   • Choose a variable to represent the resting heart rate.
   • Write an equation that represents the information provided.
   • Check your answer. Does it fit the details of the problem?

23. A basketball player scores 15 points in one game and p points in a second game. Her two-game total is 33 points. Write and solve an equation to find the number of points scored in the second game.

24. **Biology** A student collects 12 ladybugs for a science project. This is 9 fewer than the number of ladybugs the student collected yesterday. Write and solve an equation to find the number of ladybugs the student collected yesterday.

Match each equation with the graph of its solution.

25. $t + 14 = 18$

26. $x - 5 = -3$

27. $w + 4 = 2$

28. $y - 7 = -10$

A. ◄─┼─●─┼─┼─┼─┼─┼─►
     −2   0   2

B. ◄─┼─┼─┼─┼─┼─●─┼─►
      0   2   4

C. ◄─┼─●─┼─┼─┼─┼─┼─►
   −4 −2   0   2

D. ◄─┼─┼─┼─┼─┼─●─┼─►
     −2   0   2

29. **Physics** At 20°C, the speed of sound in air is 343 m/s. This is 1,166 m/s slower than the speed of sound in water. Write and solve an equation to find the speed of sound in water.

30. **Reasoning** How can you transform the equation $5 + x = 4$ into $3 + x = 2$? Support your answer with a property of equality.

Use a calculator, paper and pencil, or mental math. Solve each equation.

31. $n - 35 = 84$

32. $\frac{5}{6} = m + \frac{2}{9}$

33. $x + 2.5 = 1.6$

34. $-\frac{1}{7} = x + 1\frac{2}{3}$

35. $\frac{3}{16} = c - \frac{7}{8}$

36. $3\frac{1}{4} = 2\frac{1}{3} + r$

37. Money Use the advertisement at the right. Write and solve an equation to find the original price of the sweater.

38. Writing in Math A student is saving money for field hockey camp. Her savings are modeled by the equation $135 + d = 250$. Explain what each part of the equation represents.

SALE $21.50
SAVE $8.45

39. Challenge During five baseball games, your team scores 3, 4, 2, 6, and 8 runs. How many more runs must your team score to have a total of 30 runs? Write and solve an equation.

Test Prep and Mixed Review

Practice

Multiple Choice

40. The model represents the equation $x - 4 = 2$. What is the value of x?

  Ⓐ 2   Ⓒ 3
  Ⓑ 4   Ⓓ 6

Key
⊕ = +1
⊖ = −1

41. Which problem situation matches the equation $7.50 + x = 100$?

  Ⓕ Roberto bought a box of 100 baseball cards for $7.50. What is x, the price for each baseball card?

  Ⓖ Will works 7.5 hours a day. He will get a pay raise when he works 100 hours. What is x, the number of days he works to get a raise?

  Ⓗ Mr. Midas bought a case of fruit for $7.50. He paid the cashier with a $100 bill. What is x, the amount of change he received?

  Ⓙ Jennifer walks for 7.5 minutes. What is x, the number of miles she can walk in 100 minutes?

42. The U.S. Mint made 1,303,384,000 nickels at the Denver and Philadelphia mints one year. The algebraic expression for the value in dollars of n nickels is $0.05n$. What is the value of this expression, in dollars, for the number of nickels made that year?

  Ⓐ 651,792,000   Ⓑ 65,179,200   Ⓒ 65,169,200   Ⓓ 6,516,920

GO for Help

For Exercises	See Lesson
43–44	2-1

Simplify each expression.

43. $3 - 4 + 5 \cdot 6 - (-4)$

44. $4 \cdot 5 - 6 + (5 - 2)^2$

Vocabulary Builder

High-Use Academic Words

High-use academic words are words that you will see often in textbooks and on tests. These words are not math vocabulary terms, but knowing them will help you succeed in mathematics.

Direction Words

Some words tell what to do in a problem. I need to understand what these words are asking so that I give the correct answer.

Word	Meaning
Choose	To make a selection after analyzing given information
Describe	To tell or write about something in detail
Determine	To make a decision based on investigation

Exercises

1. Choose the colors that represent the United States of America.
   - Ⓐ red, blue, green
   - Ⓑ red, orange, yellow
   - Ⓒ white, blue, red
   - Ⓓ green, purple, orange

2. Describe the design of the American flag. Determine whether there are more red stripes or white stripes on the American flag.

3. Determine whether 2 is a solution of $8 + x = 12$.

4. Describe a situation that $x - 2 = 5$ can represent.

5. Choose the model that represents "3 more than a number p."

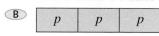
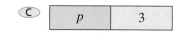

6. **Word Knowledge** Think about the word *substitute*.
   a. Choose the letter for how well you know the word.
      - **A.** I know its meaning.
      - **B.** I've seen it, but I don't know its meaning.
      - **C.** I don't know it.
   b. **Research** Look up and write the definition of *substitute*.
   c. Use the word in a sentence involving mathematics.

4-4 Solving Equations by Multiplying or Dividing

Check Skills You'll Need

1. **Vocabulary Review**
   When the GCF of a numerator and denominator is one, the fraction is in __?__.

Write each expression in simplest form.

2. $\frac{6}{24}$ 3. $\frac{8(4)}{8}$

4. $\frac{7(3)}{21}$ 5. $\frac{3a}{3}$

 **for Help**
Lesson 2-5

What You'll Learn

To solve equations by multiplying or dividing

🔊 **New Vocabulary** Division Property of Equality, Multiplication Property of Equality

Why Learn This?

If you know how to solve equations by multiplying or dividing, you can solve everyday problems such as sharing the cost of a meal with friends.

You and three friends go out for pizza. An extra-large pizza and four bottles of water cost $22.68 (including tax and a $2 coupon). How much does each person owe if you split the bill equally?

You can represent the problem with the model below. Let p represent the amount of money each person owes.

```
CHECK # 325   TABLE # 12
==================
ITEMS ORDERED    AMOUNT
X-LG PIZZA        18.60
$2 COUPON         -2.00
BOT WTR            1.25
BOT WTR            1.25
BOT WTR            1.25
BOT WTR            1.25
$$$$$$$$$$$$$$$$$$$$$$$$$$$$$
TAX                1.08
-----
TOTAL             22.68
```

total bill	→	22.68
p | p | p | p	→	4p

The model shows that you can use the equation $4p = 22.68$. To solve this equation, you can use the Division Property of Equality.

KEY CONCEPTS **Division Property of Equality**

If you divide each side of an equation by the same nonzero number, the two sides remain equal.

Arithmetic	**Algebra**
Since $3(2) = 6$, $\frac{3(2)}{2} = \frac{6}{2}$.	If $a = b$ and $c \neq 0$, then $\frac{a}{c} = \frac{b}{c}$.

Division is the inverse operation of multiplication. When a variable is multiplied by a number, you can use division to undo the multiplication.

Division Undoes Multiplication

$(4 \cdot 9) \div 4 = 9$ $\qquad\qquad$ $5x \div 5 = x$

Video Tutor Help

Visit: PHSchool.com
Web Code: are-0775

Test Prep Tip

The words *each* and *per* are frequently used in problems that involve solving an equation by multiplying or dividing.

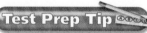

EXAMPLE Solving Equations by Dividing

1 Solve $4p = 22.68$.

$$4p = 22.68 \quad \leftarrow \text{Notice } p \text{ is being } multiplied \text{ by 4.}$$
$$\frac{4p}{4} = \frac{22.68}{4} \quad \leftarrow \text{Divide each side by 4 to get } p \text{ alone.}$$
$$p = 5.67 \quad \leftarrow \text{Simplify.}$$

Check $\quad 4p = 22.68 \quad \leftarrow$ Check your solution in the original equation.

$\quad 4(5.67) \stackrel{?}{=} 22.68 \quad \leftarrow$ Replace p with 5.67.

$\quad 22.68 = 22.68 \; ✔ \quad \leftarrow$ The solution checks.

✓ Quick Check

1. Solve each equation. Check your answer.
   a. $3x = -21.6$ b. $-12y = -108$ c. $104x = 312$

You can use the Division Property of Equality and inverse operations to solve real-world applications.

EXAMPLE Application: Telephone Charges

2 **Gridded Response** Your cellular telephone bill shows that you were charged an extra $8.58 this month for going over your allotted minutes. The company charges $.39 for each extra minute. How many extra minutes did you use?

Words $0.39 times number of minutes equals extra charge

Let n = the number of extra minutes.

Equation   0.39   · n =   8.58

$$0.39n = 8.58$$
$$\frac{0.39n}{0.39} = \frac{8.58}{0.39} \quad \leftarrow \text{Divide each side by 0.39.}$$
$$n = 22 \quad \leftarrow \text{Simplify.}$$

You used 22 extra minutes.

Check The charge for each extra minute is $.39. If you use 22 extra minutes, then the total charge is 22 · $.39, or $8.58. The answer checks.

✓ Quick Check

2. Suppose you and four friends go to a baseball game. The total cost for five tickets is $110. Write and solve an equation to find the cost of one ticket.

Another property you can use to solve equations is the Multiplication Property of Equality.

KEY CONCEPTS **Multiplication Property of Equality**

If you multiply each side of an equation by the same number, the two sides remain equal.

Arithmetic

$\frac{12}{2} = 6$, so $\frac{12}{2} \cdot 2 = 6 \cdot 2$.

Algebra

If $a = b$, then $a \cdot c = b \cdot c$.

Multiplication is the inverse operation of division. When a variable is divided by a number, you can use multiplication to undo the division.

Multiplication Undoes Division

$$\frac{3}{5} \cdot 5 = 3$$

$$\frac{n}{3} \cdot 3 = n$$

EXAMPLE **Solving Equations by Multiplying**

❸ Solve $\frac{t}{-45} = -5$.

Vocabulary Tip

Read $\frac{t}{-45} = -5$ as "t divided by negative 45 equals negative 5."

$$\frac{t}{-45} = -5 \quad \leftarrow \text{Notice that } t \text{ is divided by } -45.$$

$$(-45) \cdot \left(\frac{t}{-45}\right) = (-45) \cdot (-5) \quad \leftarrow \text{Multiply side by } -45.$$

$$t = 225 \quad \leftarrow \text{Simplify.}$$

✓ Quick Check

3. Solve the equation $\frac{w}{26} = -15$. Check your answer.

✓ Check Your Understanding

1. Vocabulary The __?__ states that if you multiply each side of an equation by the same number, the two sides remain equal.

2. Write and solve the equation modeled at the left.

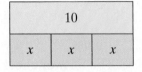

Tell which property you would use to solve each equation.

3. $8g = -25.4$ **4.** $\frac{w}{26} = -15$ **5.** $5 \cdot d = 60$

Match each equation with the correct first step of the solution.

6. $-6y = 12$ **A.** Multiply both sides by -6.

7. $12y = -6$ **B.** Divide both sides by -6.

                   C. Divide both sides by 12.

8. $\frac{y}{-6} = 12$

For more exercises, see **Extra Skills and Word Problems.**

GO for Help

For Exercises	See Examples
9–22	1–2
23–34	3

Solve each equation. Check your answer. You may find a model helpful.

9. $12t = 144$

10. $13e = -52$

11. $35q = -175$

12. $-7n = -294$

13. $0.2x = 4$

14. $-0.5r = -8$

15. $2{,}700 = -900w$

16. $-3k = -18$

17. $8n = 112$

18. $0.4k = -40$

19. $58 = \frac{2}{3}w$

20. $-48 = \frac{1}{2}y$

21. Entertainment A local park rents paddle boats for $5.50 per hour. You have $22 to spend. For how many hours can you rent a boat?

22. A video store charges $2.75 per day for overdue video games. You owe a late fee of $13.75. How many days overdue is the game?

Solve each equation. Check your answer.

23. $\frac{z}{8} = -3$

24. $\frac{n}{3} = 9$

25. $\frac{t}{8} = 12.6$

26. $\frac{q}{2} = -1.4$

27. $\frac{k}{-6} = -5$

28. $\frac{d}{0.5} = 11$

29. $\frac{c}{-6} = -1$

30. $\frac{y}{-12} = -12$

31. $\frac{n}{-5} = 1.1$

32. $\frac{f}{7.9} = 5$

33. $\frac{d}{6} = -4.25$

34. $\frac{m}{-0.5} = -41$

GPS **35. Guided Problem Solving** Julie's car travels 27 miles per gallon of gasoline used. She recently traveled 324 miles. How many gallons of gasoline did her car use?

* **Make a Plan** Choose a variable to represent the number of gallons used. Decide what operation should be used, and write an equation.
* **Carry Out the Plan** Let ▪ represent the number of gallons. The operation to use is __?__ . The equation ▪ can be used to solve the problem.

36. George Adrian of Indianapolis, Indiana, picked 15,830 lb of apples in 8 h. How many pounds of apples per hour is that?

A band with five members is a quintet.

37. Writing in Math Explain why you can use the equation $\frac{m}{5} = 50$ to describe how much money a quintet has to earn for each member to receive $50. What does each part of the equation represent?

38. Estimation What equation would you use to estimate the solution of $12x = -38$? Explain. Estimate the solution.

Solve each equation.

39. $\frac{1}{2}m = 25$ **40.** $\frac{w}{-4.2} = 10.3$ **41.** $\frac{1}{5}t = 17$

42. $\frac{k}{21.45} = 6$ **43.** $\frac{3}{4}x = 16$ **44.** $\frac{y}{-5.22} = -3.11$

45. Trees A growing tree absorbs about 26 lb of carbon dioxide each year. How many years will the tree take to absorb 390 lb of carbon dioxide?

46. The world record for playgoing is held by Dr. H. Howard Hughes of Fort Worth, Texas. He saw 6,136 plays in 31 years. How many plays did Dr. Hughes see in an average year?

47. Reasoning In the equation $ab = 1$, a is an integer. Explain what you know about b.

48. Error Analysis One student's solution for the equation $\frac{n}{-6} = 12$ is $n = -2$. Explain how the student may have found this solution. Then correct the student's mistake.

Open-Ended Write a problem that can be solved using each equation.

49. $3x = 30$ **50.** $\frac{n}{5} = 2$ **51.** $2.5p = 10$

52. Challenge You are starting a savings account. You make an initial deposit of $100. Every week after that, you deposit $20. Your goal is to save $1,000. Write an algebraic equation and find how many weeks you will need to reach your goal.

Gridded Response

53. The table at the right shows the number of cans each student collected for a school food drive. Which number could be added to the set of data in order for the median and the mode of the set to be equal?

54. A recipe calls for 3 lb of potatoes. You have one bag of potatoes that weighs 1.25 lb, and another bag that weighs 0.65 lb. How many more pounds of potatoes do you need for the recipe?

Food Drive Results

Student	Number of Cans
Abel	46
Annie	89
Cris	72
Pedro	63
Sungmee	108
Tasha	■

GO for Help

For Exercises 55–57 See Lesson 4-3

Solve each equation.

55. $p - \frac{4}{7} = \frac{1}{4}$ **56.** $\frac{1}{2} = x - \frac{3}{4}$ **57.** $\frac{1}{2} = w + \frac{5}{12}$

Write an algebraic expression for each word phrase.

1. four less than a number

2. three times a number

3. the quotient of 4 and a number

4. nine more than a number

Solve each equation.

5. $g - 5 = -9.4$

6. $y + 10.2 = 12$

7. $-5x = 45.5$

8. $\frac{h}{6} = 8$

9. **Science** The chemical element aluminum was discovered in 1825 by Hans Christian Oersted. This was 18 years after Sir Humphry Davy discovered the element sodium. Write and solve an equation to find the year that sodium was discovered.

10. Fingernails grow about 1.5 inches per year. How long would it take to grow nails 37 inches long?

MATH GAMES

Evaluating Expressions

What You'll Need

- 24 index cards. Cut them in half so you have 48 smaller cards. On each card, write a different algebraic expression.
- Two number cubes

How to Play

- Deal all the cards. Each player chooses one card from his or her hand and places it face down on the table.
- A player rolls the number cubes. The sum of the numbers is the value of the variable for the first round.
- Each player turns over his or her card, evaluates the expression, and announces its value. Record the value for each player.
- Play continues until all players have rolled the number cubes.
- Find each player's total. The player with the lowest total wins.

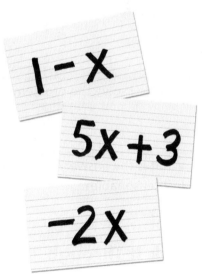

Practice Solving Problems

Big Burgers The world's largest hamburger weighed 8,266 lb. If half of the weight was meat, how many regular quarter-pound hamburgers could have been made from that burger?

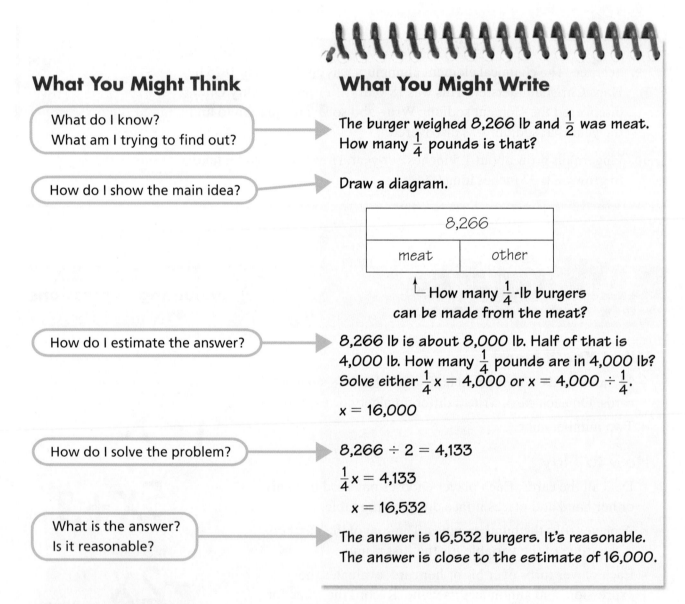

What You Might Think

What do I know?
What am I trying to find out?

How do I show the main idea?

How do I estimate the answer?

How do I solve the problem?

What is the answer?
Is it reasonable?

What You Might Write

The burger weighed 8,266 lb and $\frac{1}{2}$ was meat. How many $\frac{1}{4}$ pounds is that?

Draw a diagram.

8,266	
meat	other

How many $\frac{1}{4}$-lb burgers can be made from the meat?

8,266 lb is about 8,000 lb. Half of that is 4,000 lb. How many $\frac{1}{4}$ pounds are in 4,000 lb? Solve either $\frac{1}{4}x = 4,000$ or $x = 4,000 \div \frac{1}{4}$.

$x = 16,000$

$8,266 \div 2 = 4,133$

$\frac{1}{4}x = 4,133$

$x = 16,532$

The answer is 16,532 burgers. It's reasonable. The answer is close to the estimate of 16,000.

Think It Through

1. In the diagram, why do *meat* and *other* equally share the space under 8,266?

2. Explain why $\frac{1}{4}x = 4,000$ and $x = 4,000 \div \frac{1}{4}$ are equivalent.

Exercises

Solve. For Exercises 3 and 4, answer the questions first.

3. To celebrate National Hot Dog Month, a beef company made a hot dog that measured 16 feet 1 inch. A regular hot dog is $5\frac{1}{2}$ inches long. How many regular hot dogs would you need to make this hot dog?

   a. What do you know? What do you want to find out?

   b. Explain how the diagram below shows the situation. Write an equation.

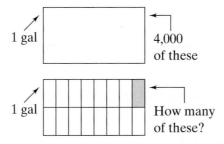

4. The world's largest glass of milk held 4,000 gallons. A gallon holds 16 cups. How many cups were in the world's largest glass of milk?

   a. Explain how the diagram below shows the situation. Write an equation.

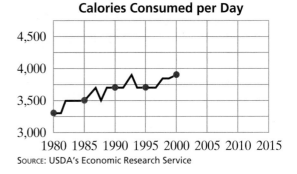

5. a. Look at the graph at the right. Estimate how many more Calories per day an American consumed in 2000 than in 1980.

   b. Suppose the increase in Calories per day was entirely from hamburgers. A quarter-pound hamburger has about 450 Calories. About how many more burgers per week did an American eat in 2000 than in 1980?

Calories Consumed per Day

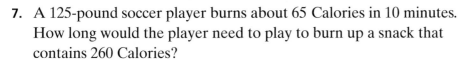

Source: USDA's Economic Research Service

6. Assume the graph at the right keeps climbing at the same rate. Estimate the number of Calories an average American consumes each day this year.

7. A 125-pound soccer player burns about 65 Calories in 10 minutes. How long would the player need to play to burn up a snack that contains 260 Calories?

Exploring Two-Step Problems

What You'll Learn

To write and evaluate expressions with two operations and to solve two-step equations using number sense

Why Learn This?

Suppose you are ordering roses online. Roses cost $5 each, and shipping costs $10. Your total cost depends on how many roses you buy. Two-step equations can help you solve everyday problems.

You can write expressions with variables using one operation. Now you will write algebraic expressions with two operations.

EXAMPLES Writing and Evaluating Expressions

1 Define a variable and write an algebraic expression for the phrase "$10 plus $5 times the number of roses ordered."

Let n = the number of roses ordered   ← **Define the variable.**

$10 + 5 \cdot n$ ← **Write an algebraic expression.**

$10 + 5n$ ← **Rewrite 5 · n as 5n.**

2 Evaluate the expression for 12 roses.

$10 + 5n$

$10 + 5 \cdot 12$ ← **Evaluate the expression for 12 roses.**

$10 + 60$ ← **Multiply.**

70 ← **Simplify.**

If you order 12 roses, you will have to pay $70.

✓ Quick Check

1. Define a variable and write an algebraic expression for "a man is two years younger than three times his son's age."

2. Evaluate the expression to find the man's age if his son is 13.

Suppose your grandmother sends you 5 games for your birthday. Each game has the same weight. The box she mails them in weighs 8 ounces. The total weight is 48 ounces. What is the weight of one game?

You can represent this situation with the diagram below.

Let g represent the weight of a game.

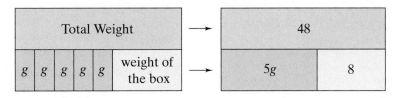

You can solve this problem using the equation $5g + 8 = 48$. Since there is more than one operation in the equation, there will be more than one step in the solution.

EXAMPLE **Using Number Sense**

Test Prep Tip

When solving problems, look for opportunities to use number sense and mental math.

3 Solve $5g + 8 = 48$ by using number sense.

$$5g + 8 = 48$$

$$\blacksquare + 8 = 48 \quad \leftarrow \textbf{Cover } 5g. \textit{ Think}: \textbf{What number added to 8 is 48? Answer: 40}$$

$$5g = 40 \quad \leftarrow \textbf{So } \blacksquare \textbf{, or } 5g \textbf{, must equal 40.}$$

$$5 \cdot \blacksquare = 40 \quad \leftarrow \textbf{Now cover } g. \textit{ Think}: \textbf{What number times 5 is 40? Answer: 8}$$

$$g = 8 \quad \leftarrow \textbf{So } \blacksquare \textbf{, or } g \textbf{, must equal 8.}$$

Check

$$5g + 8 = 48 \qquad \leftarrow \textbf{Check your solution in the original equation.}$$

$$5(8) + 8 \stackrel{?}{=} 48 \qquad \leftarrow \textbf{Substitute 8 for } g.$$

$$40 + 8 \stackrel{?}{=} 48 \qquad \leftarrow \textbf{Simplify.}$$

$$48 = 48 \quad ✔ \quad \leftarrow \textbf{The solution checks.}$$

✓ Quick Check

3. Solve each equation using number sense.

    a. $3m + 9 = 21$ **b.** $8d + 5 = 45$ **c.** $4y - 11 = 33$

EXAMPLE Application: Food

4 Suppose you buy a jumbo lemonade for $1.50 and divide the cost of an order of chicken wings with two friends. Your share of the total bill is $5.50. Write and solve an equation to find the cost of the chicken wings.

| Words | cost of lemonade | plus | (cost of wings ÷ 3) | is | $5.50 |

Let z = the cost of the chicken wings.

| Expression | 1.50 | + | $(z \div 3)$ | = | $5.50 |

$$1.50 + \frac{z}{3} = 5.50$$

$1.50 + \boxed{} = 5.50$ ← Cover $\frac{z}{3}$. *Think*: What number added to 1.50 is 5.50? Answer: 4

$\frac{z}{3} = 4$ ← So $\boxed{}$, or $\frac{z}{3}$, must equal 4.

$\frac{\blacksquare}{3} = 4$ ← Now cover *z*. *Think*: What number divided by 3 is 4? Answer: 12

$z = 12$ ← So ■, or z, must equal 12.

The cost of the chicken wings is $12.

Test Prep Tip

You can represent the relationships in the problem with this model.

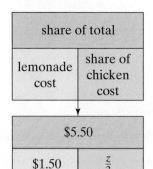

✓ Quick Check

4. **Basketball** During the first half of a game you scored 8 points. In the second half you made only 3-point baskets. You finished the game with 23 points. Write and solve an equation to find how many 3-point baskets you made.

✓ Check Your Understanding

1. **Vocabulary** What is the difference between a one-step expression and a two-step expression?

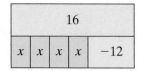

2. Write and solve the equation modeled at the left.

Match each phrase with the correct algebraic expression.

3. 10 centimeters less than twice *x*, your hand length

4. 10 people fewer than half *x*, the town's population

5. 10 more than two times a number *x*

A. $\frac{1}{2}x - 10$
B. $2x - 10$
C. $2x + 10$

Using number sense, fill in the missing number.

6. $4b + 5 = 17$
   $4b = \blacksquare$

7. $7c - 20 = 50$
   $7c = \blacksquare$

For more exercises, see Extra Skills and Word Problems.

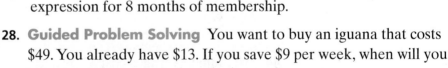

GO for Help

For Exercises	See Examples
8–12	1
13–20	2
21–27	3–4

Define a variable and write an algebraic expression for each phrase.

8. two points fewer than 3 times the number of points scored before

9. one meter more than 6 times your height in meters

10. seven pages fewer than half the number of pages read last week

11. eight pounds less than five times the weight of a chicken

12. twice the distance in miles flown last year, plus 100 miles

Evaluate each expression for the given value of the variable.

13. $4m - 6.5$; $m = 2$ **14.** $5 + 2f$; $f = 6.1$

15. $12 - 3b$; $b = 4.3$ **16.** $6x + 2$; $x = 3$

17. $5y - 5$; $y = 5$ **18.** $7 + 8c$; $c = 7$

19. $2p + 4.5$; $p = 5.1$ **20.** $12 - 2.2s$; $s = 4$

Solve each equation using number sense. You may find a model helpful.

21. $2t + 9.4 = 39.8$ **22.** $4m + 12 = 52$

23. $10h + 14 = 84$ **24.** $7w + 16 = 37$

25. $3y + 13.6 = 40.6$ **26.** $5v + 19 = 24$

27. Money A fitness club advertises a special for new members. Each month of membership is $19, with an initial enrollment fee of $75. Write an expression for the total cost. Then evaluate your expression for 8 months of membership.

GPS **28. Guided Problem Solving** You want to buy an iguana that costs $49. You already have $13. If you save $9 per week, when will you have enough money to buy the iguana?
  • How much money do you already have?
  • How much more money do you need?

29. Writing in Math In addition to her hourly rate, an electrician charges a fee to come to your house. This can be modeled by $40h + 35 = 115$. Explain what each part of the equation represents. Then solve the equation to find the number of hours she works.

30. You order 3 posters advertised on the Internet. Each poster costs the same amount. The shipping charge is $5. The total cost of the posters plus the shipping charge is $41. Find the cost of one poster.

31. Open-Ended Describe a situation that can be modeled by the equation $\frac{b}{2} + 5 = 51$.

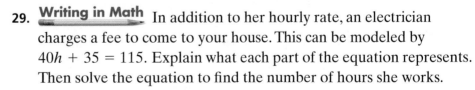

Solve each equation using number sense.

32. $5h + 3 = 18.5$　　**33.** $3m - 7.6 = 26.9$　　**34.** $8y + 17 = 65$

35. $\frac{x}{3} - 3 = 12$　　**36.** $2p - 5 = 15$　　**37.** $\frac{t}{4} + 1 = 6$

38. Telephone A cellular telephone company charges $40 per month plus a $35 activation fee. Write an expression for the total cost. Then evaluate your expression for 10 months of service.

39. Food You are helping to prepare food for a large family gathering. You can slice 2 zucchinis per minute. You need 30 sliced zucchinis. How long will it take you to finish, if you have already sliced 12 zucchinis?

40. Your family rented a car for a trip. The car rental cost $35 per day plus $.30/mile. After a one-day rental, the bill was $74. How many miles did your family drive?

41. Reasoning When you solve an equation, you must do the same operation to both sides. Explain why this is true.

42. Challenge You spend 5 minutes jogging as a warmup. Then you run 4 miles and cool down for 5 minutes. The total time you exercise is 54 minutes. What is your average time for running a mile?

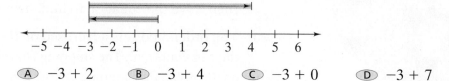

Test Prep and Mixed Review　　**Practice**

Multiple Choice

43. Daniel bought one dozen tennis balls priced at 3 balls for $1.99 and a tennis racquet for $49.99. What is the total amount he spent, not including tax, on tennis balls and a tennis racquet?
　Ⓐ $51.98　　　　　　　　Ⓒ $57.95
　Ⓑ $55.96　　　　　　　　Ⓓ $73.87

44. Medium beverages cost $1.39 and small beverages cost $.89. Which equation can be used to find d, the total cost in dollars of 6 medium drinks?
　Ⓕ $6 = 0.89d$　　　　　　Ⓗ $6 = 1.39d$
　Ⓖ $d = 0.89(6)$　　　　　Ⓙ $d = 1.39(6)$

45. Which expression is represented by the model below?

$$-5\ -4\ -3\ -2\ -1\quad 0\quad 1\quad 2\quad 3\quad 4\quad 5\quad 6$$

　Ⓐ $-3 + 2$　　Ⓑ $-3 + 4$　　Ⓒ $-3 + 0$　　Ⓓ $-3 + 7$

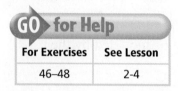

GO **for Help**

For Exercises	See Lesson
46–48	2-4

Compare each pair of fractions. Use <, =, or >.

46. $\frac{7}{9} \,\blacksquare\, \frac{4}{5}$　　　　**47.** $\frac{9}{27} \,\blacksquare\, \frac{1}{3}$　　　　**48.** $\frac{5}{12} \,\blacksquare\, \frac{2}{6}$

Modeling Two-Step Equations

You can use algebra tiles to solve two-step equations.

EXAMPLE Solving Two-Step Equations

Use algebra tiles to solve $2x + 1 = 7$.

$2x + 1 = 7$

← Model the equation. Use yellow tiles for positive integers.

$2x + 1 - 1 = 7 - 1$
$2x = 6$

← Remove 1 yellow tile from each side.

$\dfrac{2x}{2} = \dfrac{6}{2}$

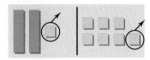

← Divide each side into 2 equal groups.

$x = 3$

← Simplify.

Exercises

Write and solve the equation represented by each model.

1.

2.

3.

Use algebra tiles to solve each equation.

4. $3x - 4 = 2$

5. $2x - 1 = 9$

6. $2x + 4 = 10$

7. $3x + 4 = 7$

8. $2x + 6 = -8$

9. $2x - 6 = -18$

10. At a county fair, an admission ticket costs $5, and each ride costs $2. You have $13. Write an algebraic equation for the number of rides you can go on. Use algebra tiles to solve the equation.

11. **Reasoning** Suppose you have 20 green, 20 red, and 20 yellow algebra tiles. Explain how you could use the tiles to model the equation $500x - 200 = 1,300$.

4-6 Solving Two-Step Equations

✓ Check Skills You'll Need

1. Vocabulary Review
What property states that if $a = b$, then $a \cdot c = b \cdot c$?

Solve each equation.

2. $4b = 24$

3. $-4d = 20$

4. $\frac{k}{4} = -16$

5. $\frac{h}{6} = -3$

 **for Help**
Lesson 4-4

What You'll Learn

To solve two-step equations using inverse operations

Why Learn This?

Detectives often retrace steps to find missing information. You can use the strategy *Work Backward* to solve a two-step equation and find an unknown quantity.

You can solve a two-step equation by using inverse operations and the properties of equality to get the variable on one side of the equation.

For many equations, you can undo addition or subtraction first. Then you can multiply or divide to get the variable alone.

EXAMPLE   Undoing Subtraction First

1 Solve $5n - 18 = -33$.

$$5n - 18 = -33$$
$$5n - 18 + 18 = -33 + 18 \qquad \leftarrow \text{To undo subtraction, add 18 to each side.}$$
$$5n = -15 \qquad \leftarrow \text{Simplify.}$$
$$\frac{5n}{5} = \frac{-15}{5} \qquad \leftarrow \text{To undo multiplication, divide each side by 5.}$$
$$n = -3 \qquad \leftarrow \text{Simplify.}$$

Check $5n - 18 = -33 \qquad \leftarrow$ Check your solution with the original equation.
$$5(-3) - 18 \overset{?}{=} -33 \qquad \leftarrow \text{Substitute } -3 \text{ for } n.$$
$$-15 - 18 \overset{?}{=} -33 \qquad \leftarrow \text{Simplify.}$$
$$-33 = -33 \ \checkmark \qquad \leftarrow \text{The solution checks.}$$

✓ Quick Check

1. Solve the equation $-8y - 28 = -36$. Check your answer.

EXAMPLE Undoing Addition First

2 Solve $\frac{x}{3} + 11 = 16$.

$$\frac{x}{3} + 11 = 16$$

$$\frac{x}{3} + 11 - 11 = 16 - 11 \quad \leftarrow \text{To undo addition, subtract 11 from each side.}$$

$$\frac{x}{3} = 5 \quad \leftarrow \text{Simplify.}$$

$$3\left(\frac{x}{3}\right) = 3(5) \quad \leftarrow \text{To undo division, multiply each side by 3.}$$

$$x = 15 \quad \leftarrow \text{Simplify.}$$

✓ Quick Check

2. Solve the equation $\frac{x}{5} + 35 = 75$. Check your answer.

You can use two-step equations to solve real-world problems.

EXAMPLE Solving Two-Step Equations

3 **Multiple Choice** On weekday afternoons, a local bowling alley offers a special. Each bowling game costs $2.50, and shoe rental is $2.00. You spend $14.50 total. What is the number of games that you bowl?

     A 3   **B** 5   **C** 7   **D** 9

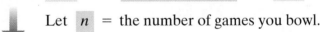

Words   2.50 times number of games plus 2.00 is 14.50

 Let n = the number of games you bowl.

Equation 2.50 · n + 2.00 = 14.50

$$2.5n + 2 = 14.50$$

$$2.5n + 2 - 2 = 14.50 - 2 \quad \leftarrow \text{Subtract 2 from each side.}$$

$$2.5n = 12.50 \quad \leftarrow \text{Simplify.}$$

$$\frac{2.5n}{2.5} = \frac{12.50}{2.5} \quad \leftarrow \text{Divide each side by 2.5.}$$

$$n = 5 \quad \leftarrow \text{Simplify.}$$

You bowled 5 games. The answer is B.

Test Prep Tip ⓐⓑⓒⓓ

You can eliminate answer choices using number sense. Choice D can be eliminated because it is too high. If you played 9 games, your total cost would be greater than $18.

✓ Quick Check

3. Solomon decided to make posters for the student council election. He bought markers that cost $.79 each and a poster board that cost $1.25. The total cost was $7.57. Write and solve an equation to find the number of markers that Solomon bought.

More Than One Way

A family expects 88 people to attend its family reunion. There will be 16 children. Picnic tables seat 8 adults per table. The children will eat on blankets. How many picnic tables does the family need?

Sarah's Method

I can use number sense. First, I know that tables are needed only for adults. There are $88 - 16$, or 72, adults. Each table holds 8 adults. Since $72 \div 8 = 9$, the family needs 9 tables.

Ryan's Method

I can write and solve an equation. Let t represent the number of tables. Then $8t$ is the number of adults.

$$\text{adults} + \text{children} = 88 \text{ people}$$

$$8t + 16 = 88 \quad \leftarrow \textbf{Write the equation.}$$

Each term is divisible by 8. So I will divide first.

$$\frac{8t}{8} + \frac{16}{8} = \frac{88}{8} \quad \leftarrow \textbf{Divide each term by 8.}$$

$$t + 2 = 11 \quad \leftarrow \textbf{Simplify.}$$

I can use mental math to solve the equation. I know that 9 plus 2 is equal to 11. So, the family needs 9 tables.

Choose a Method

You had $25 in your savings account six weeks ago. You deposited the same amount of money each week for five weeks. Your balance is now $145. How much money did you deposit each week? Describe your method and explain why you chose it.

Check Your Understanding

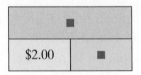

1. Fill in the missing numbers to make the diagram at the left represent the following situation: A taxi charges a flat fee of $2.00 plus $.50 for each mile. Your fare is $5.00. How many miles did you ride?

Solve each equation. Check your answer.

2. $5p - 2 = 18$

3. $7n - (-16) = 100$

4. $\dfrac{y}{4.25} + 15 = -17$

For more exercises, see Extra Skills and Word Problems.

GO for Help

For Exercises	See Examples
5–16	1
17–29	2–3

Solve each equation. Check your answer. You may find a model helpful.

5. $8r - 8 = -32$ **6.** $3w - 6 = -1.5$ **7.** $4g - 4 = 28$

8. $7t - 6 = -104$ **9.** $12x - 14 = -2$ **10.** $10m - \frac{2}{5} = 9\frac{3}{5}$

11. $0.5y - 1.1 = 4.9$ **12.** $-2d - 1.7 = -3.9$ **13.** $-8a - 1 = -23$

14. $2h - \frac{1}{10} = \frac{5}{8}$ **15.** $6t - \frac{1}{6} = 9$ **16.** $5q - 3.75 = 26.25$

17. $\frac{w}{5} + 3 = 6$ **18.** $\frac{n}{4} + 2 = 4$ **19.** $\frac{x}{8} + 4 = 13$

20. $\frac{a}{7} + 10 = 17$ **21.** $\frac{m}{-11} + 1 = -10$ **22.** $\frac{p}{9} + 14 = 16$

23. $\frac{c}{-7} + 3.2 = -2.2$ **24.** $\frac{v}{-3} + \frac{3}{4} = -\frac{1}{8}$ **25.** $\frac{b}{-8} + \frac{5}{7} = \frac{11}{14}$

26. $\frac{c}{2} + 7.3 = 29.3$ **27.** $\frac{m}{-10} + 12 = 67$ **28.** $\frac{y}{-6.5} + 2 = -4$

29. Kristine bought a vase that cost $5.99 and roses that cost $1.25 each. The total cost was $20.99. Write and solve an equation to find how many roses Kristine bought.

30. **Guided Problem Solving** Renting boats on a lake costs $22 per hour plus a flat fee of $10 for insurance. You have $98. Write and solve an equation to find the number of hours you can rent a boat.

  • insurance plus 22 times number of hours = total paid

Write and solve an equation for each situation.

31. A skating rink rents skates at $3.95 for the first hour plus $1.25 for each additional hour. When you returned your skates, you paid $7.70. How many additional hours did you keep the skates?

32. **Jobs** You earn $20 per hour landscaping a yard. You pay $1.50 in bus fare each way. How many hours must you work to earn $117?

33. **Geometry** The sum of the measures of the angles in a triangle is 180 degrees. One angle measures 45 degrees. The measures of the other two angles are equal. What is the measure of each of the other two angles?

34. **Olympics** The first modern Olympic games were held in Greece in 1896. The 2004 Olympic games in Athens had 202 participating countries. The number of countries in the 2004 Olympic games was 6 more than 14 times the number of countries in the 1896 games. How many countries participated in the 1896 Olympic games?

Solve each equation.

35. $\dfrac{x+4}{5}=3$

36. $\dfrac{t-7}{-2}=11$

37. $\dfrac{y+\frac{1}{3}}{4}=2\frac{1}{4}$

38. <u>**Writing in Math**</u> Your class budgets a certain amount of money from the class treasury for a dance. Expenses will include a fixed amount for decorations, plus an hourly wage for the disc jockey. This can be represented by the equation $30x+65=170$. Explain how each number in the equation relates to the problem.

39. **College** In college, you earn credits for courses taken. For one semester, tuition at a local college is $2,400. You have financial aid that will cover $5,160 for the semester. Refer to the information at the left. How many credits can you take?

$2400 plus
$184 per credit

40. The student council sponsored a bake sale to raise money. Kim bought a slice of cake for $1.50 and also bought six cupcakes. She spent $4.20 in all. How much did each cupcake cost?

41. **Open-Ended** Write two different two-step equations that both have a solution of 3.

42. **Challenge** You buy 1.25 lb of apples and 2.45 lb of bananas. The total cost, after using a 75¢-off coupon, is $2.58. Apples and bananas sell for the same price per pound. Find their price per pound.

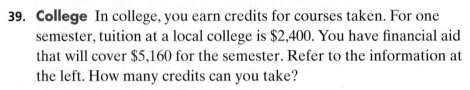

Test Prep and Mixed Review　　　　　　　　**Practice**

Multiple Choice

43. The model below represents the equation $5x+4=14$.

What is the value of x?

Ⓐ $x=\dfrac{18}{5}$　　Ⓑ $x=2$　　Ⓒ $x=-2$　　Ⓓ $x=5$

44. The Dead Sea is 1,345 feet below sea level. What method can be used to find the altitude of the Dead Sea in yards?
Ⓕ Multiply $-1,345$ by 46.　　Ⓗ Divide $-1,345$ by 12.
Ⓖ Multiply $-1,345$ by 3.　　Ⓙ Divide $-1,345$ by 3.

45. What is the value of the expression $2(15-12)^2 \div 6 + 3$?
Ⓐ 12　　Ⓑ 9　　Ⓒ 6　　Ⓓ 2

GO for Help

For Exercises	See Lesson
46–48	4-3

Describe a problem situation that matches each equation. Then solve.

46. $r+11=2$　　47. $h-9=5.5$　　48. $\dfrac{1}{6}q=9$

Check Skills You'll Need

1. **Vocabulary Review**
   Integers are the set of whole numbers and their __?__.

Compare using $<$, $=$, or $>$.

2. 0 ▪ −2

3. 14 ▪ −14

4. −4 ▪ 5

5. −17 ▪ −18

 **for Help**

Lesson 1-6

What You'll Learn

To graph and write algebraic inequalities

 **New Vocabulary** inequality, solution of an inequality

Why Learn This?

When you use an expression such as *at least* or *at most,* you are talking about an inequality. You can use inequalities to represent situations that involve minimum or maximum amounts.

A mathematical sentence that contains $<$, $>$, $\leq$, $\geq$, or $\neq$ is an **inequality.** Sometimes an inequality contains a variable, as in $x \geq 2$.

A **solution of an inequality** is any value that makes the inequality true. For example, 6, 8, and 15 are solutions of $x \geq 6$ because $6 \geq 6$, $8 \geq 6$, and $15 \geq 6$.

EXAMPLE **Identifying Solutions of an Inequality**

① Find whether each number is a solution of $x \leq 2$; −3, 0, 2, 4.5.

Test each value by replacing the variable and evaluating the sentence.

$-3 \leq 2$ ← **−3 is less than or equal to 2: true.** ✔

$0 \leq 2$ ← **0 is less than or equal to 2: true.** ✔

$2 \leq 2$ ← **2 is less than or equal to 2: true.** ✔

$4.5 \leq 2$ ← **4.5 is less than or equal to 2: false.** ✗

The numbers −3, 0, and 2 are solutions of $x \leq 2$. The number 4.5 is not a solution of $x \leq 2$.

Quick Check

1. Which numbers are solutions of the inequality $m \geq -3$; −8, −2, 1.4?

Vocabulary Tip

Read $>$ as "is greater than."

Read $<$ as "is less than."

Read $\geq$ as "is greater than or equal to."

Read $\leq$ as "is less than or equal to."

A graph can show all the numbers in a solution. You use closed circles and open circles to show whether numbers are included in the solution.

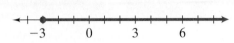 **Graphing Inequalities**

② Graph the solution of each inequality.

a. $n \geq -3$

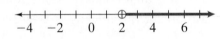 ← Use a closed circle at -3 to show that n can equal -3.

b. $h < 7$

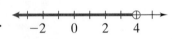 ← Use an open circle at 7 to show that h cannot equal 7.

✓ Quick Check

● **2.** Graph the solution of the inequality $w < -3$.

You can write an inequality by analyzing its graph.

 **Writing Inequalities**

③ Write an inequality for the graph.

← Since the circle at 2 is open, 2 is not a solution.

$x > 2$ ← Since the graph shows values greater than 2, use $>$.

✓ Quick Check

● **3.** Write an inequality for the graph.

You can write inequalities to describe real-world situations.

EXAMPLE **Application: Nutrition**

④ To be labeled sugar free, a food product must contain less than 0.5 g of sugar per serving. Write an inequality to describe this requirement.

Words	amount of sugar	is less than	0.5 g of sugar

Let s = the number of grams of sugar in a serving of food.

Equation	s	$<$	0.5

The inequality is $s < 0.5$.

✓ Quick Check

● **4.** Write an inequality for "To qualify for the race, your time can be at most 62 seconds."

1. **Vocabulary** What is the name of a mathematical sentence that contains the symbols $<$, $>$, $\leq$, $\geq$, or $\neq$?

2. **Reasoning** Is $-4 \geq 4$? Explain.

3. Which inequality does NOT have 8 as a solution?
   Ⓐ $-3 < y$ Ⓑ $13 \geq y$ Ⓒ $y < 8$ Ⓓ $y \geq 8$

Which numbers are solutions of each inequality?

4. $x \geq -5$; $-6, -1, 0$ 5. $x \leq -1$; $-1, 1, 3$ 6. $x > 0$; $-1, 0, 1$

For more exercises, see Extra Skills and Word Problems.

GO for Help

For Exercises	See Examples
7–10	1
11–18	2
19–23	3–4

Which numbers are solutions of each inequality?

7. $x < 1$; $-2, 1, 2$

8. $x > -5$; $-7, -5, -1$

9. $x \leq -9$; $-12, -4, 2$

10. $x < -8$; $-10, -5, 0$

Graph the solution of each inequality.

11. $x \geq 4$ 12. $x \leq -2$ 13. $x < 2$ 14. $x > -4$

15. $x \leq 0$ 16. $h > -5$ 17. $t \geq -5$ 18. $p < -6$

Write an inequality for each graph.

19. ◄─┼─┼─┼─┼─┼─●─┼─►
        0   3   6

20. ◄─┼─┼─┼─┼─⊕─┼─┼─┼─►
     -2 0 2 4 6

21. ◄─┼─┼─●─┼─┼─┼─┼─►
     -2 0 2 4

22. ◄─┼─┼─┼─┼─●─┼─┼─┼─►
     -4 -2 0 2

23. Write an inequality for "Every item costs one dollar or less!"

 24. **Guided Problem Solving** Write an inequality for "The car ride to the park will take at least 30 minutes."
   • Choose a variable: Let x represent how long the car ride will be.
   • Read for key words: Decide whether to use $<$, $>$, $\leq$, or $\geq$.
   • Write the inequality: x ■ 30.

Write an inequality for each statement. Graph the solution.

25. To see the movie, you must be at least 17 years old.

26. The temperature is greater than 100°F.

27. A number p is not positive.

28. The speed limit on the highway is at most 65 mi/h.

Homework Video Tutor
Visit: PHSchool.com
Web Code: are-0407

29. <u>Writing in Math</u> Explain how you know whether to draw an open or closed circle when you graph an inequality.

30. Reasoning Explain why $-17 > -22$.

Use a variable to write an inequality for each situation.

31.

32.

Vocabulary Tip

A *compound inequality* is a number sentence with more than one inequality symbol.

Identify an integer that is a solution for each *compound inequality*.

33. $-3 \le x < 0$ **34.** $-2 < y \le 1$ **35.** $-6 \le p \le -4$

36. Challenge If $a \ge 9$ and $9 \ge b$, then a ■ b. Complete the statement using $<$, $>$, $\le$, or $\ge$.

Test Prep and Mixed Review   **Practice**

Multiple Choice

37. The model below represents the equation $2x + 5 = 9$.

What is the first step in solving the equation?
- Ⓐ Add 5 to each side of the equation.
- Ⓑ Subtract 5 from each side of the equation.
- Ⓒ Divide each side of the equation by 5.
- Ⓓ Subtract 2 from each side of the equation.

38. A recipe calls for 3 pounds of ground turkey. Carmen has one package of ground beef that weighs $1\frac{1}{2}$ pounds, one package of ground turkey that weighs $1\frac{1}{4}$ pound, and another package of ground turkey that weighs $1\frac{5}{8}$ pound. Which information is NOT necessary to find how much more ground turkey Carmen needs?
- Ⓕ Total amount of ground turkey needed for the recipe
- Ⓖ Weight of Carmen's smaller package of ground turkey
- Ⓗ Weight of Carmen's package of ground beef
- Ⓙ Weight of Carmen's larger package of ground turkey

GO for Help

For Exercises	See Lesson
39–41	1-6

Order the numbers from least to greatest.

39. $-2, 4, -4, 2, 7, -1$ **40.** $3, -8, -9, 12, -6$ **41.** $10, 0, -5, -2, 7$

Checkpoint Quiz 2

Solve each equation.

1. $3x + 4 = 19$

2. $\frac{t}{5} - 2 = 6$

3. $-2y - 5 = -9$

4. $\frac{d}{-3} + 7 = 10$

5. $6g + 6 = -6$

6. $\frac{f}{-1} - 8 = -3$

7. A sweater costs $12 more than twice the cost of a skirt. The sweater costs $38. Find the cost of the skirt.

Graph the solution of each inequality.

8. $x > -3$

9. $y \leq -2$

10. $d \geq -1$

4-8a Activity Lab

Data Analysis

Inequalities in Bar Graphs

A class conducted a survey on free time. The standard bar graph shows the average number of hours per week students spend on various activities. The floating bar graph shows the minimum and maximum number of hours students spend on each activity.

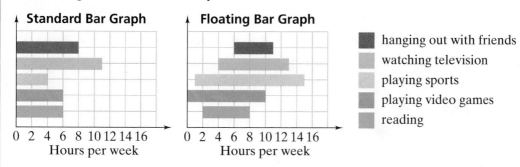

Standard Bar Graph

0 2 4 6 8 10 12 14 16
Hours per week

Floating Bar Graph

0 2 4 6 8 10 12 14 16
Hours per week

 hanging out with friends
watching television
playing sports
playing video games
reading

1. What are the minimum and maximum hours per week that students in the survey spend hanging out with friends?

2. Which activity is not done by all students? Which activity shows the least variety in how students responded to the survey? Explain.

3. Let x represent the number of hours per week spent on an activity. Which activity in the floating bar graph is represented by the inequality $2 \leq x \leq 8$? Write inequalities to represent each activity on the floating bar graph.

4-8 Solving Inequalities by Adding or Subtracting

Check Skills You'll Need

1. **Vocabulary Review** Why are addition and subtraction called *inverse operations*?

Solve each equation.

2. $c + 4 = -2$

3. $x + 9 = 10$

4. $b + (-2) = 7$

5. $m - (-3) = 10$

 **for Help**
Lesson 4-3

What You'll Learn

To solve inequalities by adding or subtracting

 **New Vocabulary** Addition Property of Inequality, Subtraction Property of Inequality

Why Learn This?

Buildings and buses have limits on the number of people they can hold. You can use inequalities to find how many people can fit safely.

You can solve inequalities using properties similar to those you used solving equations.

If you add 3 to each side of the inequality $-3 < 2$, the resulting inequality, $0 < 5$, is also true.

KEY CONCEPTS **Addition Property of Inequality**

You can add the same value to each side of an inequality.

Arithmetic	**Algebra**
Since $7 > 3$, $7 + 4 > 3 + 4$.	If $a > b$, then $a + c > b + c$.
Since $1 < 3$, $1 + 4 < 3 + 4$.	If $a < b$, then $a + c < b + c$.

EXAMPLE **Solving Inequalities by Adding**

 **for Help**

For help with graphing inequalities, see Lesson 4-7, Example 2.

1 Solve $n - 10 > 14$. Graph the solution.

$$n - 10 > 14$$
$$n - 10 + 10 > 14 + 10 \quad \leftarrow \text{Add 10 to each side.}$$
$$n > 24 \quad \leftarrow \text{Simplify.}$$

Quick Check

1. Solve $y - 3 < 4$. Graph the solution.

To solve an inequality involving addition, use subtraction.

> **KEY CONCEPTS** **Subtraction Property of Inequality**
>
> You can subtract the same value from each side of an inequality.
>
> | **Arithmetic** | **Algebra** |
> |---|---|
> | Since $9 > 6$, $9 - 3 > 6 - 3$. | If $a > b$, then $a - c > b - c$. |
> | Since $15 < 20$, $15 - 4 < 20 - 4$. | If $a < b$, then $a - c < b - c$. |
>
> **Note:** The Properties of Inequality also apply to $\leq$ and $\geq$.

EXAMPLE **Solving Inequalities by Subtracting**

2 Solve $y + 7 \geq 12$. Graph the solution.

$$y + 7 \geq 12$$
$$y + 7 - 7 \geq 12 - 7 \quad \leftarrow \text{Subtract 7 from each side.}$$
$$y \geq 5 \quad \leftarrow \text{Simplify.}$$

$$\overset{\xleftarrow{}\!\!+\!\!+\!\!+\!\!+\!\!+\!\!+\!\!+\!\!\bullet\!\!+\!\!+\!\!+\!\!+\!\!\xrightarrow{}}{\underset{-2 \quad 0 \quad 2 \quad 4 \quad 6 \quad 8 \quad 10}{}}$$

✓ Quick Check

2. Solve each inequality. Graph the solution.
   a. $x + 9 > 5$ **b.** $y + 3 < 4$ **c.** $w + 4 \leq -5$

EXAMPLE **Application: Transportation**

3 A school bus can safely carry as many as 76 students. If 19 students are already on the bus, how many more can board the bus?

Words | students already on bus | plus | students remaining | is at most | 76

Let s = the number of students remaining.

Expression | 19 | + | s | $\leq$ | 76

$$19 + s \leq 76$$
$$19 - 19 + s \leq 76 - 19 \quad \leftarrow \text{Subtract 19 from each side.}$$
$$s \leq 57 \quad \leftarrow \text{Simplify.}$$

At most 57 more students can board the bus.

✓ Quick Check

3. To get an A, you need more than 200 points on a two-part test. You score 109 on the first part. How many more points do you need?

1. **Vocabulary** The __?__ states that you can add the same value to each side of an inequality.

2. **Reasoning** What value is a solution of $y + 7 \geq 12$ but is not a solution of $y + 7 > 12$?

Match each inequality with the graph of its solution.

3. $h - 4 < 5$

4. $h + 4 \geq 5$

5. $h - 4 \leq -5$

6. $h + 4 < -5$

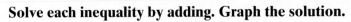

A. [number line: $-12, -9, -6, -3, 0, 3, 6, 9$ with open circle at -9, arrow pointing left]

B. [number line: $-3, -2, -1, 0, 1, 2, 3, 4$ with closed dot at -1, arrow pointing left]

C. [number line: $-9, -6, -3, 0, 3, 6, 9, 12$ with open circle at 9, arrow pointing left]

D. [number line: $-3, -2, -1, 0, 1, 2, 3, 4$ with closed dot at 1, arrow pointing right]

Homework Exercises

For more exercises, see Extra Skills and Word Problems.

GO for Help

For Exercises	See Examples
7–15	1
16–25	2–3

Solve each inequality by adding. Graph the solution.

7. $g - 2 \leq -8$

8. $m - 3 > -24$

9. $y - 5 \geq 11$

10. $x - 7 > -11$

11. $n - 10 \leq 17$

12. $p - 9 < -9$

13. $y - 5 \geq 12$

14. $q - 2 < 4$

15. $b - 4 > -6$

Solve each inequality by subtracting. Graph the solution.

16. $h + 8 < -13$

17. $n + 3 \geq 4$

18. $r + 9 > 4$

19. $p + 10 \leq 6$

20. $b + 22 > -1$

21. $f + 5 \geq 0$

22. $m + 3 > 4$

23. $x + 10 < 11$

24. $k + 4 \leq -7$

25. **Consumer Issues** Your parents give you $35 for a scooter that costs at least $100. How much money do you have to save to buy the scooter?

26. **Guided Problem Solving** The weight of a loaded dump truck is less than 75,000 lb. When empty, the truck weighs 32,000 lb. Write and solve an inequality to find how much the load can weigh.

    words: empty truck   plus   __?__   is less than   75,000 lb

    inequality: 32,000   +   ■   <   75,000

27. **Science** Water boils when the temperature is at least 212°F. A pot of water has a temperature of 109°F. How many degrees must the temperature rise for the water to boil?

Solve each inequality by adding or subtracting.

28. $h - 9 < 1.3$ **29.** $w - \frac{1}{4} > -\frac{3}{4}$ **30.** $x + 5 \geq 98$

31. $j + 6.2 \geq 1.2$ **32.** $k + 42 \geq 36$ **33.** $a - 1\frac{4}{5} < 3\frac{7}{10}$

34. Write an inequality for the sentence "Fifteen plus a number is greater than 10." Solve the inequality.

35. **Reasoning** Are the solutions of the inequalities $x + 5 \leq -2$ and $-2 \leq x + 5$ the same? Explain.

36. **Sports** To win the long jump, you need to jump a distance greater than 2.25 m. Your personal best jump is 2.1 m. Write and solve an inequality to find how much farther you need to jump to win.

37. **Writing in Math** The basketball team needs to score at least 420 points this season in order to set a new school record. It has already scored 82 points. Four players argue about which inequality represents the number of points yet to be scored: $p \geq 338$, $338 \geq p$, $p > 338$, or $338 > p$. Which is correct? Explain.

38. A *compound inequality* is a number sentence with more than one inequality symbol. Solve the compound inequality $-3 \leq x + 4 < 9$.

39. **Challenge** You want to eat no more than 3,000 Calories in a day. You consume 710 Calories for breakfast and have two bowls of soup for lunch. Each bowl contains 535 Calories. How many Calories can you consume at dinner?

Test Prep and Mixed Review   **Practice**

Gridded Response

40. A baby who weighed 7.2 pounds at birth gained about 1.4 pounds each month. How many pounds did the baby weigh when it was 6 months old?

41. Two of the driest cities in the United States are Yuma, Arizona, and Las Vegas, Nevada. Yuma averages 3.01 inches of rain each year and Las Vegas averages 4.49 inches each year. How many more inches of rain does Las Vegas receive each year than Yuma?

42. The table shows record weights of 3 types of sunfish. In decimal form, how many pounds did the redbreast sunfish weigh? Round to the nearest hundredth.

Fish	Weight (lb)
Green sunfish	$\frac{17}{8}$
Redbreast sunfish	$\frac{33}{16}$
Redear sunfish	$\frac{87}{16}$

Write each number as an improper fraction.

43. $3\frac{1}{5}$ **44.** $6\frac{3}{4}$ **45.** $8\frac{1}{4}$ **46.** $7\frac{5}{8}$

GO for Help

For Exercises	See Lesson
43–46	2-5

4-9

Solving Inequalities by Multiplying or Dividing

What You'll Learn

To solve inequalities by multiplying or dividing

🔊 **New Vocabulary** Division Property of Inequality, Multiplication Property of Inequality

Why Learn This?

Inequalities can help you plan. You can solve inequalities to make sure you have enough ingredients when you are cooking.

Look at the pattern when you divide each side of an inequality by an integer.

$$18 > 12$$

$$\frac{18}{6} > \frac{12}{6}$$

$$\frac{18}{3} > \frac{12}{3}$$

← When the integer is positive, the direction of the inequality symbol stays the same.

$$\frac{18}{-2} < \frac{12}{-2}$$

$$\frac{18}{-6} < \frac{12}{-6}$$

← When the integer is negative, the direction of the inequality symbol is reversed.

KEY CONCEPTS **Division Property of Inequality**

If you divide each side of an inequality by the same positive number, the direction of the inequality symbol remains unchanged.

Arithmetic	**Algebra**
$9 > 6$, so $\frac{9}{3} > \frac{6}{3}$	If $a > b$, and c is positive, then $\frac{a}{c} > \frac{b}{c}$.
$15 < 20$, so $\frac{15}{5} < \frac{20}{5}$	If $a < b$, and c is positive, then $\frac{a}{c} < \frac{b}{c}$.

If you divide each side of an inequality by the same negative number, the direction of the inequality symbol is reversed.

Arithmetic	**Algebra**
$16 > 12$, so $\frac{16}{-4} < \frac{12}{-4}$	If $a > b$, and c is negative, then $\frac{a}{c} < \frac{b}{c}$.
$10 < 18$, so $\frac{10}{-2} > \frac{18}{-2}$	If $a < b$, and c is negative, then $\frac{a}{c} > \frac{b}{c}$.

EXAMPLE Solving Inequalities by Dividing

1 Solve $-3y \le -27$. Graph the solution.

$$-3y \le -27$$

$$\frac{-3y}{-3} \ge \frac{-27}{-3} \qquad \leftarrow \text{Divide each side by } -3. \text{ Reverse the direction of the symbol.}$$

$$y \ge 9 \qquad \leftarrow \text{Simplify.}$$

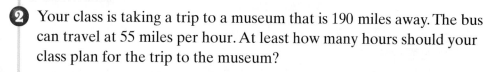

✓ Quick Check

1. Solve each inequality. Graph the solution.
   a. $-4p < 36$ b. $-8m \ge -24$ c. $7n > -21$

You can solve an inequality that involves multiplication by dividing each side of the inequality by the same number.

EXAMPLE Application: Planning

2 Your class is taking a trip to a museum that is 190 miles away. The bus can travel at 55 miles per hour. At least how many hours should your class plan for the trip to the museum?

Words	55 times	number of hours	is at least	total miles

Let h = the number of hours.

Expression	55	$\cdot$	h	$\ge$	190

$$55h \ge 190$$

$$\frac{55h}{55} \ge \frac{190}{55} \qquad \leftarrow \text{Divide each side by 55.}$$

$$h \ge 3.4545 \ldots \qquad \leftarrow \text{Simplify.}$$

$$h \ge 3.5 \qquad \leftarrow \text{Round up to the nearest half hour.}$$

Your class should plan for at least 3 hours and 30 minutes.

✓ Quick Check

2. A long-distance telephone company is offering a special rate of $.06 per minute. Your budget for long-distance telephone calls is $25 for the month. At most how many minutes of long distance can you use for the month with this rate?

The properties of inequality apply to multiplication as well.

Multiplication Property of Inequality

If you multiply each side of an inequality by the same positive number, the direction of the inequality symbol remains unchanged.

Arithmetic	Algebra
$12 > 8$, so $12 \cdot 2 > 8 \cdot 2$	If $a > b$, and c is positive, then $a \cdot c > b \cdot c$.
$3 < 6$, so $3 \cdot 4 < 6 \cdot 4$	If $a < b$, and c is positive, then $a \cdot c < b \cdot c$.

If you multiply each side of an inequality by the same negative number, the direction of the inequality symbol is reversed.

Arithmetic	Algebra
$6 > 2$, so $6(-3) < 2(-3)$	If $a > b$, and c is negative, then $a \cdot c < b \cdot c$.
$3 < 5$, so $3(-2) > 5(-2)$	If $a < b$, and c is negative, then $a \cdot c > b \cdot c$.

EXAMPLE **Solving Inequalities by Multiplying**

Online
active math

For: Inequalities Activity
Use: Interactive
   Textbook, 4–9

3 Solve $\dfrac{y}{-8} \ge 2$.

$$\frac{y}{-8} \ge 2$$

$$-8 \cdot \frac{y}{-8} \le -8 \cdot 2 \quad \leftarrow \begin{array}{l}\textbf{Multiply each side by } -8.\\ \textbf{Reverse the direction of the symbol.}\end{array}$$

$$y \le -16 \quad \leftarrow \textbf{Simplify.}$$

✓ Quick Check

3. Solve $\dfrac{k}{-5} < -4$. Graph the solution.

✓ Check Your Understanding

1. **Vocabulary** What happens when you multiply each side of an inequality by a negative number?

2. If $x > y$, which statement is NOT always true?
   - Ⓐ $y < x$
   - Ⓑ $x + z > y + z$
   - Ⓒ $x - z > y - z$
   - Ⓓ $xz > yz$

Fill in the missing inequality symbol.

3. $3m > 99$

   $\dfrac{3m}{3}$ ▣ $\dfrac{99}{3}$

4. $-8z \le 80$

   $\dfrac{-8z}{-8}$ ▣ $\dfrac{80}{-8}$

5. $\dfrac{d}{-3} < 12$

   $\dfrac{d}{-3} \cdot (-3)$ ▣ $12 \cdot (-3)$

For more exercises, see Extra Skills and Word Problems.

GO for Help

For Exercises	See Examples
6–18	1–2
19–30	3

Solve each inequality by dividing. Graph the solution.

6. $4h < 16$ **7.** $3p > 36$ **8.** $9n \leq -27$

9. $6x < -48$ **10.** $-8b \geq -24$ **11.** $-5w \leq 30$

12. $-10d \geq -70$ **13.** $-2t > 10$ **14.** $5g < -35$

15. $-4.5p \leq 22.5$ **16.** $7y < -42.7$ **17.** $8.3w \geq 53.95$

18. A photo album page can hold six photographs. You have 296 photographs. How many pages do you need?

Solve each inequality by multiplying. Graph the solution.

19. $\dfrac{p}{5} < -3$ **20.** $\dfrac{k}{4} \geq 6$ **21.** $\dfrac{w}{7} \leq -3$

22. $\dfrac{y}{7} > -8$ **23.** $\dfrac{n}{-2} > -5$ **24.** $\dfrac{m}{-6} \leq 5$

25. $\dfrac{x}{10} < -4$ **26.** $\dfrac{c}{-5} \geq -2$ **27.** $\dfrac{x}{4} > -20$

28. $\dfrac{g}{1.2} \geq -7$ **29.** $\dfrac{p}{-8} < 2.1$ **30.** $\dfrac{f}{5} \leq -5.5$

GPS **31. Guided Problem Solving** A forklift can safely carry as much as 6,000 lb. A case of paint weighs 70 lb. At most how many cases of paint can the forklift safely carry at one time?
- Use number sense: How much do 100 cases weigh?
- Try the strategy *Systematic Guess and Check*: How much do 90 cases weigh? 80 cases?

32. Rides A roller coaster can carry 36 people per run. At least how many times does the roller coaster have to run to allow 10,000 people to ride?

33. Baking A recipe for an apple pie calls for 6 apples per pie. You have 27 apples. At most how many apple pies can you make?

Write an inequality for each sentence. Solve the inequality.

34. The product of -3 and a number is greater than 12.

35. A number multiplied by 4 is at most -44.

36. A number divided by -9 is less than 10.

37. The quotient of a number and 5 is at least -8.

38. The product of 2 and a number is less than -10.

39. Writing in Math Explain how solving $-5x < 25$ is different from solving $5x < 25$.

GO Online
Homework Video Tutor
Visit: PHSchool.com
Web Code: are-0409

PEANUTS $1.25
HOT DOGS $4.75

Solve each inequality.

40. $9.9 < -9x$ **41.** $-25.1 > \dfrac{t}{-2}$ **42.** $-5.6 \le -8p$

Use the drawing at the left for Exercises 43–45. You have $15.

43. At most how many hot dogs can you buy?

44. At most how many bags of peanuts can you buy?

45. You buy two hot dogs. How many bags of peanuts can you buy? How much money do you have left?

46. A 1-ton truck can haul 2,000 lb. A refrigerator weighs 302 lb. How many refrigerators can the truck carry?

47. **Error Analysis** A student solves the inequality $5n > -25$. He says the solution is $n < -5$. Explain the student's error.

48. **Reasoning** Solve and graph $-18 \ge -2y$ and $-2y < -18$. Are the solutions the same? Explain.

49. **Challenge** Ten more than -3 times a number is greater than 19. Write and solve an inequality. Graph the solution.

Test Prep and Mixed Review

A B C D

Practice

Multiple Choice

50. Which problem situation matches the equation below?

$$2x + 3 = 21$$

Ⓐ Janice is 3 years more than twice as old as Rashon. Janice is 21 years old. How old is Rashon?

Ⓑ Felicity has scored 2 points more than 3 times as many points as Kendra. Kendra has scored 21 points. How many points has Felicity scored?

Ⓒ Drew paid $2 more than Adam for tickets to a play. Richard's tickets cost him 3 times as much as Drew's tickets. Richard paid $21. How much did Adam pay for his tickets?

Ⓓ Nate worked 2 hours more than 3 times as many hours as Chad. Nate worked 21 hours. How many hours did Chad work?

51. Arnold had a collection of baseball cards that he divided evenly among 5 friends. Each friend received 17 baseball cards. Which equation can be used to find y, the number of baseball cards Arnold had?

Ⓕ $5y = 17$ Ⓗ $17y = 5$

Ⓖ $\dfrac{y}{5} = 17$ Ⓙ $\dfrac{y}{5} - 5 = 17$

For Exercises	See Lesson
52–53	1-10

Find the mean, median, and mode for each set of data.

52. 4 6 3 7 4 7 4 4   **53.** 2.2 6.4 5 2.2 2.2 5

Writing Short Responses

Short-response questions are usually worth a maximum of 2 points. To get full credit, you need to give the correct answer, including appropriate units. You may also need to show your work or justify your reasoning.

EXAMPLE

The cost for using a phone card is 45¢ per call plus 5¢ per minute. A recent call cost $2.05. Write and solve an equation to find the length of the call.

To get full credit you must use a variable to set up an equation, solve the equation, and find the length of the call. Below is a scoring guide that shows the number of points awarded for different answers.

Scoring

[2]   The equation and the solution are correct. The call took 32 minutes.

[1]   There is no equation, but there is a method to show that the call took 32 minutes, OR There is an equation and a solution, both of which may contain minor errors.

[0]   There is no response, or the response is completely incorrect.

Three responses are shown below with the points each one received.

2 points	1 point	0 points
Let m represent the number of minutes. $205 = 45 + 5m$ $160 = 5m$ $32 = m$ The call took 32 minutes.	$\dfrac{2.05 - 0.45}{0.05}$ 32 minutes	30 minutes

Exercises

Use the scoring guide above to answer each question.

1. Explain why each response above received the indicated points.

2. Write a 2-point response that includes the equation $0.05n + 0.45 = 2.05$.

Chapter 4 Review

Vocabulary Review

 **Addition Property of Equality** (p. 180)
Addition Property of Inequality (p. 210)
algebraic expression (p. 169)
equation (p. 174)
Division Property of Equality (p. 186)

Division Property of Inequality (p. 214)
inequality (p. 205)
inverse operations (p. 181)
Multiplication Property of Equality (p. 188)
Multiplication Property of Inequality (p. 216)
open sentence (p. 174)

solution of an equation (p. 174)
solution of an inequality (p. 205)
Subtraction Property of Equality (p. 180)
Subtraction Property of Inequality (p. 211)
variable (p. 169)

Choose the correct term to complete each sentence.

1. A letter that represents a number is called a(n) (equation, variable).

2. If you multiply both sides of an (equation, inequality) by the same negative number, the direction of the inequality symbol is reversed.

3. A mathematical sentence with an equal sign is called a(n) (equation, inverse operation).

4. A mathematical phrase with at least one variable in it is a(n) (algebraic expression, solution of an equation).

5. A(n) (open sentence, solution of an inequality) is a value that makes an inequality true.

Go Online
PHSchool.com
For: Online vocabulary quiz
Web Code: arj-0451

Skills and Concepts

Lesson 4-1
• To write and evaluate algebraic expressions

A **variable** is a letter that stands for a number. An **algebraic expression** is a mathematical phrase that uses variables, numbers, and operation symbols. To evaluate an expression, substitute a given value for each variable and then simplify.

Evaluate each expression for $n = 3$, $p = 5$, and $w = 2$.

6. $3n - 2w$ 7. $\dfrac{4n}{w}$ 8. $p + 4w$ 9. $7w - 2p$

Lesson 4-2
• To solve one-step equations using substitution, mental math, and estimation

An **equation** is a mathematical sentence with an equal sign. An equation with one or more variables is an **open sentence**. A **solution of an equation** is a value for a variable that makes an equation true.

Use number sense to solve each equation.

10. $p + 5 = -2$ 11. $m - 12 = 8$ 12. $7t = 28$ 13. $\dfrac{w}{8} = 9$

Lessons 4-3, 4-4
- To solve equations by adding or subtracting
- To solve equations by mulitplying or dividing

Whatever you do to one side of the equation, you must do the same thing to the other side of the equation. To solve a one-step equation, use **inverse operations.**

Use inverse operations to solve each equation.

14. $y + 14 = 38$ **15.** $p - 12 = 72$ **16.** $\frac{m}{11} = 9$ **17.** $-7b = 84$

18. $x - 8 = 44$ **19.** $12h = 60$ **20.** $k - 14 = 29$ **21.** $\frac{n}{6} = -9$

22. A local band had a concert and made $1,824 from tickets sales. If each ticket cost $16, how many tickets did the band sell?

Lessons 4-5, 4-6
- To write and evaluate expressions with two operations and to solve two-step equations using number sense
- To solve two-step equations using inverse operations

You can also use inverse operations to solve two-step equations.

Solve each equation.

23. $4d + 7 = 11$ **24.** $2m - 21 = 3$ **25.** $-5y + 8 = 23$

26. Savings You save $35 each week. You now have $140. You plan to save enough money for a cruise that costs $1,050. Write and solve an equation to find the number of weeks it will take to save for the cruise.

Lesson 4-7
- To graph and write inequalities

A mathematical sentence that contains $<$, $>$, $\leq$, $\geq$, or $\neq$ is called an **inequality.** A **solution of an inequality** is any number that makes an inequality true. When graphing, use an open circle for $>$ and $<$ and use a closed circle for $\geq$ and $\leq$.

Write an inequality for each statement. Then graph the inequality.

27. The ticket is at most $10. **28.** The race is less than 5 miles.

Lessons 4-8, 4-9
- To solve inequalities by adding or subtracting
- To solve inequalities by multiplying or dividing

You solve inequalities just as you solve equations, but with one exception. When you multiply or divide by a negative number, you must reverse the direction of the inequality symbol.

Solve each inequality. Then graph the inequality.

29. $h + 7 < -15$ **30.** $\frac{p}{5} \geq -3$ **31.** $g - 14 > 3$ **32.** $-4m \leq 28$

33. A farmer needs no less than 20 lb of seeds to plant a crop. Write an inequality for this situation. Then graph the inequality.

Go Online **For:** Online chapter test
PHSchool.com **Web Code:** ara-0452

Evaluate each expression for $n = 3$, $t = -2$, and $y = 4$.

1. $3n + 2t$
2. $5y - 4n$
3. $2(n + 3y)$
4. $ny - 6$
5. $\dfrac{2ny}{t}$
6. $-2t + 6n$

Solve each equation.

7. $x + 7 = 12$
8. $m - \dfrac{1}{3} = \dfrac{1}{6}$
9. $13 + d = 44$
10. $p - 1.8 = 6.2$
11. $5n = 45.5$
12. $\dfrac{h}{7} = 8$
13. $-\dfrac{1}{3}t = 24$
14. $\dfrac{k}{-4} = -12$
15. $14 + 3n = 8$
16. $9h - 21 = 24$
17. $\dfrac{w}{5} - 10 = -4$
18. $14 + \dfrac{y}{8} = 10$

Define a variable. Then write and solve an equation for each problem.

19. **Masonry** A mason is laying a brick foundation 72 in. wide. Each brick is 6 in. wide. How many bricks will the mason need across the width of the foundation?

20. **Groceries** You buy 12 apples. You also buy a box of cereal that costs $3.35. The bill is $8.75. How much does each apple cost?

21. The music boosters sell 322 music buttons and raise $483 for the music department. How much does each button cost?

22. Your family drives from Austin, Texas, to Tampa, Florida. The trip is about 1,145 mi and lasts four days. How many miles must your family drive each day?

23. **Sports** A youth soccer league recently held registration. The number of players was divided into 13 teams of 12 players. How many players registered?

24. Six friends split the cost of a party. Each person also spends $65 for a hotel room. Each person spends $160 on the party and a room. What is the cost of the party?

25. **Open-Ended** Write a problem you can represent with $2k - 10 = 6$. Solve the equation. Show your work.

Define a variable and write an inequality for each statement.

26. The game's duration is at most 3 hours.

27. To rent a car, you must be at least 25 years old.

28. The truck can haul more than 20,000 lb.

29. There are fewer than 10 tickets available for the concert tonight.

Solve each inequality. Graph your solution.

30. $n + 12 \geq 15$
31. $y - 14 > 10$
32. $m - 8 \leq -17$
33. $w + 22 < 14$
34. $12x < -48$
35. $10h \geq 90$
36. $\dfrac{v}{-8} > 6$
37. $\dfrac{p}{11} \leq -6$
38. $-7k \leq -84$
39. $\dfrac{x}{-15} < -4$

Define a variable. Then write and solve an inequality for each problem.

40. **Transportation** A ferry can safely transport at most 220 people. There are already 143 people aboard. How many more people can the ferry take aboard?

41. **Money** A sports drink costs $1.49 per bottle. At most how many bottles can you buy if you have $12?

42. **Shopping** Alex and his mother spent at least $130 while shopping for new clothes. Alex spent $52. How much money did his mother spend?

43. **Writing in Math** Describe the similarities and differences between solving inequalities and equations. Include examples.

Multiple Choice

Read each question. Then write the letter of the correct answer on your paper.

1. Which pair of numbers has a product that is greater than its sum?
   - Ⓐ −2, −5
   - Ⓑ −3, 3
   - Ⓒ 4, −2
   - Ⓓ 0, 1

2. What are the prime factors of 136?
   - Ⓕ 2, 2, 34
   - Ⓖ 2, 2, 2, 17
   - Ⓗ 2, 2, 3, 17
   - Ⓙ 2, 3, 3, 15

3. What is the mean of the temperatures shown below?

   92°   87°   79°   85°   92°
   - Ⓐ 85°
   - Ⓑ 87°
   - Ⓒ 90°
   - Ⓓ 92°

4. You buy a package of socks for $4.89, a T-shirt for $7.75, and a pair of shorts for $14.95. Which is the best estimate of the amount of change you will get back if you give the cashier $30?
   - Ⓕ about $1
   - Ⓖ about $2
   - Ⓗ about $3
   - Ⓙ about $4

5. What is the solution of $5y + 11 = 56$?
   - Ⓐ 8
   - Ⓑ 9
   - Ⓒ 13
   - Ⓓ 10

6. Which list is in order from least to greatest?
   - Ⓕ $\frac{1}{3}, \frac{3}{4}, \frac{1}{5}$
   - Ⓖ $5\frac{1}{8}, 5\frac{1}{4}, 5\frac{2}{3}$
   - Ⓗ $\frac{13}{12}, \frac{4}{5}, \frac{3}{7}$
   - Ⓙ $\frac{8}{9}, \frac{2}{5}, \frac{1}{2}$

7. The average person drinks about 2.5 quarts of water each day. How many pints is this?
   - Ⓐ 2 pt
   - Ⓑ 3 pt
   - Ⓒ 4 pt
   - Ⓓ 5 pt

8. Which variable expression can be described by the word phrase "r increased by 2"?
   - Ⓕ $2r$
   - Ⓖ $r − 2$
   - Ⓗ $r + 2$
   - Ⓙ $r \cdot 2$

9. Which decimal is closest to $\frac{11}{16}$?
   - Ⓐ 0.687
   - Ⓑ 0.69
   - Ⓒ 0.68
   - Ⓓ 0.7

10. Which is the best estimate of $6\frac{3}{4} \cdot 3\frac{1}{5}$?
    - Ⓕ 18
    - Ⓖ 21
    - Ⓗ 24
    - Ⓙ 27

11. Your friend divided 0.56 by 0.7 and got 8 for an answer. This answer is not correct. Which answer is correct?
    - Ⓐ 0.08
    - Ⓑ 0.008
    - Ⓒ 0.8
    - Ⓓ 80

12. Which graph shows the solution of $d + 10 \le 19$?

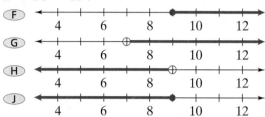

Gridded Response

Record your answer in a grid.

13. During the summer, you work 27 hours per week. Each week, you earn $168.75. How many dollars do you earn per hour?

Short Response

14. Define a variable and write an inequality to model the word sentence "Today's temperature will be at least 55°F."

15. You and four friends are planning a surprise birthday party. Each of you contributes the same amount of money m for the food.
    a. Write a variable expression for the total amount of money contributed for food.
    b. Evaluate your expression for $m = \$7.75$.

Extended Response

16. Eli buys 2 vinyl records each month. He started with 18 vinyl records.
    a. Write an expression to model the number of records Eli has after x months.
    b. How many records will Eli have after 22 months? Justify your answer.

Applying Inequalities

It's a Dog's Life Dogs come in all shapes and sizes. Different breeds have different personalities and sometimes special skills as well. Some make good guard dogs, some hunt or race, and some can pull heavy sleds. Some dogs are very friendly and make great pets. Dogs generally require a lot of attention — exercise, grooming, and, especially, feeding.

Different breeds
More than 200 different breeds of dogs exist. Most scientists believe that dogs are descendants of the wolf.

A German Shepherd's nose is usually black.

Dalmatians are born white, then develop faint smudges that become their distinctive markings.

A Healthy Pet

A healthy diet for a dog includes protein, carbohydrates, fats, fiber, water, vitamins, and minerals. In general, a puppy needs about 100 Cal/lb (Calories per pound of body weight) daily, an adult dog needs about 60 Cal/lb, and a senior dog needs about 25 Cal/lb.

Put It All Together

Data File Use the information on these two pages to answer these questions.

1. **Research** Use your own dog, or find information about a specific dog.
   a. How much does the dog weigh?
   b. Use the dog food label. Find the amount of food the dog will eat in a day.
   c. One cup of dog food weighs about 8 oz. About how many meals will one bag contain?
   d. About how much will it cost to feed the dog for a year?
   e. **Reasoning** Which would cost more to feed for a year: two dogs this size or one dog that is twice as large?

2. A friend decides to start a dog-care business for people who travel.
   a. Use the same dog as for Question 1. How much would it cost to feed the dog for two weeks?
   b. **Writing in Math** Suppose the dog's owners are going on vacation for two weeks. Your friend decides to charge $50/wk, which includes food, grooming, and walking the dog twice a day. Are the dog's owners likely to hire your friend? Why or why not?

GROCERY $3.69

NET WT 4 LB (1.81 kg)

Adult Dog Size	Daily Feeding
(pounds)	Dry (cups)
3–12 lb	1/2 to 1 1/4
13–20 lb	1 1/4 to 1 3/4
21–35 lb	1 3/4 to 2 2/3
36–50 lb	2 2/3 to 3 1/2
51–75 lb	3 1/2 to 4 3/4
76–100 lb	4 3/4 to 5 3/4
Over 100 lb	5 3/4 + 2/3 c for each 10 lb body weight over 100 lb

Go Online
PHSchool.com
For: Information about dogs
Web Code: are-0453

What You've Learned

- In Chapter 2, you compared and ordered rational numbers.
- You converted between fractions and decimals.
- In Chapter 3, you used addition, subtraction, multiplication, and division to solve problems involving fractions.

Check Your Readiness

GO for Help

For Exercises	See Lesson
1–6	1-4
7–10	4-4
11–14	2-4
15–19	2-3

Multiplying and Dividing Decimals

Find each product or quotient.

1. $(3.6)(4)$ **2.** $(12.74)(9)$

3. $(15.9)(3)$ **4.** $8.96 \div 8$

5. $10.4 \div 4$ **6.** $52.6 \div 5$

Solving Equations by Multiplying or Dividing

(Algebra) **Solve.**

7. $4n = -32$ **8.** $\dfrac{a}{6} = 10$ **9.** $18 = -9z$ **10.** $-15 = \dfrac{p}{-5}$

Comparing and Ordering Fractions

Compare. Use <, =, or >.

11. $\dfrac{8}{9} \ \blacksquare \ \dfrac{3}{4}$ **12.** $\dfrac{7}{12} \ \blacksquare \ \dfrac{4}{5}$ **13.** $\dfrac{6}{3} \ \blacksquare \ \dfrac{24}{12}$ **14.** $\dfrac{1}{6} \ \blacksquare \ \dfrac{1}{7}$

Simplifying Fractions

Write each fraction in simplest form.

15. $\dfrac{12}{16}$ **16.** $\dfrac{15}{30}$ **17.** $\dfrac{27}{72}$ **18.** $\dfrac{19}{57}$ **19.** $\dfrac{16}{56}$

What You'll Learn Next

- In this chapter, you will write ratios and unit rates.

- You will write and solve proportions.

- You will use rates and proportions to solve problems involving similar figures, maps, and scale models.

Problem Solving Application On pages 270 and 271, you will work an extended activity on ratios.

🔊)) Key Vocabulary

- cross products (p. 239)
- equivalent ratios (p. 229)
- indirect measurement (p. 253)
- polygon (p. 252)
- proportion (p. 238)
- rate (p. 232)
- ratio (p. 228)
- scale (p. 259)
- scale drawing (p. 259)
- similar polygons (p. 252)
- unit cost (p. 233)
- unit rate (p. 232)

5-1 Ratios

✓ Check Skills You'll Need

1. **Vocabulary Review**
What are *equivalent fractions*?

Write each fraction in simplest form.

2. $\frac{2}{4}$ 3. $\frac{21}{27}$

4. $\frac{36}{63}$ 5. $\frac{8}{24}$

for Help
Lesson 2-3

What You'll Learn

To write ratios and use them to compare quantities

🔊 **New Vocabulary** ratio, equivalent ratios

Why Learn This?

The keys on a music keyboard have a repeating pattern of five black keys and seven white keys. You can use ratios to describe patterns.

The ratio of black keys to white keys in the pattern is 5 to 7. What is the ratio of black keys to all keys in the pattern?

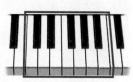

5	7
12	

KEY CONCEPTS Ratio

A **ratio** is a comparison of two quantities by division. You can write a ratio in three ways.

Arithmetic	**Algebra**
5 to 7 5 : 7 $\frac{5}{7}$	a to b $a : b$ $\frac{a}{b}$
	where $b \neq 0$

EXAMPLE Writing Ratios

Video Tutor Help

Visit: PHSchool.com
Web Code: are-0775

1 **Music** Using the pattern shown above, write the ratio of black keys to all keys in three ways.

black keys → 5 to 12 ← all keys

black keys → 5 : 12 ← all keys

$\frac{5}{12}$ ← black keys
    ← all keys

✓ Quick Check

1. Write each ratio in three ways. Use the pattern of keys shown above.
   a. white keys to all keys
   b. white keys to black keys

Two ratios that name the same number are **equivalent ratios.** In Chapter 2, you learned to write equivalent fractions. You can find equivalent ratios by writing a ratio as a fraction and finding an equivalent fraction.

EXAMPLES Writing Equivalent Ratios

2 Find a ratio equivalent to $\frac{4}{5}$.

$$\frac{4 \times 2}{5 \times 2} = \frac{8}{10} \quad \leftarrow \text{ Multiply the numerator and denominator by 2.}$$

GO for Help

For help converting customary units, go to Lesson 3-6.

3 Write the ratio 2 yd to 20 ft as a fraction in simplest form.

$$\frac{2 \text{ yd}}{20 \text{ ft}} = \frac{2 \times 3 \text{ ft}}{20 \text{ ft}} \quad \leftarrow \text{ There are 3 ft in each yard.}$$

$$= \frac{6 \text{ ft}}{20 \text{ ft}} \quad \leftarrow \text{ Multiply.}$$

$$= \frac{6 \text{ ft} \div 2}{20 \text{ ft} \div 2} \quad \leftarrow \text{ Divide by the GCF, 2.}$$

$$= \frac{3}{10} \quad \leftarrow \text{ Simplify.}$$

✓ Quick Check

2. Find a ratio equivalent to $\frac{7}{9}$.

3. Write the ratio 3 gal to 10 qt as a fraction in simplest form.

You can use decimals to express and compare ratios.

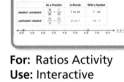

Online active math

For: Ratios Activity
Use: Interactive Textbook, 5-1

EXAMPLE Comparing Ratios

4 **Social Studies** An official U.S. flag has a length-to-width ratio of 19 : 10. The largest U.S. flag measures 505 ft by 255 ft. Is this an official U.S. flag?

official flag		largest flag
↓		↓
$\frac{19}{10}$	← length → ← width →	$\frac{505}{255}$

$$\frac{19}{10} = 1.9 \quad \xleftarrow[\text{Round if necessary.}]{\text{Write as a decimal.}} \quad \frac{505}{255} \approx 1.98$$

Since 1.98 is not equal to 1.9, the largest flag is *not* an official U.S. flag.

✓ Quick Check

4. Tell whether the ratios are *equivalent* or *not equivalent.*

    a. 7 : 3, 128 : 54   **b.** $\frac{180}{240}, \frac{25}{34}$ **c.** 6.1 to 7, 30.5 to 35

Check Your Understanding

1. **Vocabulary** How are equivalent ratios like equivalent fractions?

2. **Number Sense** Do all ratios compare a part to a whole? Explain.

Find an equivalent ratio for each ratio.

3. $\frac{1}{8}$ 4. 2 to 7   5. 10 : 9

Write each ratio as a fraction in simplest form.

6. 2 gal to 14 qt   7. 34 in. to 4 ft   8. $\frac{4 \text{ min}}{90 \text{ s}}$

Tell whether the ratios are *equivalent* or *not equivalent*.

9. $\frac{12}{24}, \frac{50}{100}$ 10. 1 to 3, 2 to 9   11. 2 : 3, 24 : 36

Homework Exercises

For more exercises, see Extra Skills and Word Problems.

GO for Help

For Exercises	See Examples
12–13	1
14–16	2
17–22	3
23–25	4

Write a ratio in three ways, comparing the first quantity to the second.

12. A week has five school days and two weekend days.

13. About 21 out of 25 Texans live in an urban area.

Find an equivalent ratio for each ratio.

14. $\frac{14}{28}$ 15. 6 to 7   16. 4 : 5

Write each ratio as a fraction in simplest form.

17. $\frac{4 \text{ ft}}{8 \text{ ft}}$ 18. 10 s : 1 min   19. $\frac{30 \text{ mL}}{2 \text{ L}}$

20. 12 oz : 3 lb   21. 2 ft to 30 in.   22. $\frac{1 \text{ m}}{300 \text{ cm}}$

Tell whether the ratios are *equivalent* or *not equivalent*.

23. $\frac{18}{24}, \frac{3}{4}$ 24. 6 : 7, 30 : 36   25. 16 to 3, 27 to 5

GPS 26. **Guided Problem Solving** The students in Room 101 and Room 104 have one class together. Write the ratio of girls to boys for the combined class.

	Room 101	Room 104
Girls	12	9
Boys	16	20

   - **Make a Plan** First find the total numbers of girls and boys. Then find the ratio of girls to boys for the combined class.

27. **Cooking** To make pancakes, you need 2 cups of water for every 3 cups of flour. Write an equivalent ratio to find how much water you will need with 9 cups of flour.

28. Error Analysis Your math class includes 15 girls and 10 boys. Two new students, a girl and a boy, join the class. Your friend says the ratio of girls to boys is the same as before. Explain your friend's error.

29. Writing in Math How can you tell when a ratio is in simplest form?

30. Chemistry A chemical formula shows the ratio of atoms in a substance. The formula for carbon dioxide, CO_2, tells you that there is 1 atom of carbon (C) for every 2 atoms of oxygen (O). Write the ratio of hydrogen (H) atoms to oxygen atoms in water, H_2O.

31. Antifreeze protects a car's radiator from freezing. In extremely cold weather, you must mix at least 2 parts antifreeze with every 1 part water.
   a. List all of the ratios in the table that provide the necessary protection.
   b. Reasoning How much antifreeze and how much water should you use to protect a 15-qt radiator?

Mixing Antifreeze

Antifreeze (qt)	Water (qt)
8	4
7.5	3
12	8
3.5	1
9	18

32. Challenge A bag contains colored marbles. The ratio of red marbles to blue marbles is 1 : 4. The ratio of blue marbles to yellow marbles is 2 : 5. What is the ratio of red marbles to yellow marbles?

Test Prep and Mixed Review

Practice

Multiple Choice

33. Maria tossed a coin 20 times and got 12 heads. What is the first step to find the ratio of the number of tails to the total number of tosses?
   Ⓐ Divide 12 by 20.
   Ⓒ Multiply 12 by 20.
   Ⓑ Subtract 12 from 20.
   Ⓓ Add 12 to 20.

34. The model represents the equation $3x - 2 = -8$. What is the value of x?
   Ⓕ $x = -6$
   Ⓖ $x = -3$
   Ⓗ $x = -\frac{10}{3}$
   Ⓙ $x = -2$

Key
$\ominus = -1$

35. Emily ran $4\frac{1}{8}$ miles at track practice one day and $3\frac{3}{4}$ miles the next day. How many miles did she run in those two days?
   Ⓐ $7\frac{1}{2}$ miles   Ⓑ $7\frac{3}{4}$ miles   Ⓒ $7\frac{7}{8}$ miles   Ⓓ $8\frac{1}{8}$ miles

GO for Help

For Exercises	See Lesson
36–38	4-4

Algebra Solve each equation.

36. $72 = 8k$ **37.** $\frac{y}{3} = 15$ **38.** $-5 = \frac{q}{7}$

Unit Rates and Proportional Reasoning

Check Skills You'll Need

1. Vocabulary Review
A *ratio* is a comparison of two quantities by __?__ .

Write each ratio in simplest form.

2. $\frac{15}{25}$ **3.** $\frac{21}{7}$

4. $\frac{22}{16}$ **5.** $\frac{4}{36}$

 **for Help**
Lesson 5-1

What You'll Learn

To find unit rates and unit costs using proportional reasoning

🔊 **New Vocabulary** rate, unit rate, unit cost

Why Learn This?

You make decisions about the foods you eat every day. Looking at rates such as grams of fat per serving can help you stay healthy.

A **rate** is a ratio that compares two quantities measured in different units. There are 15 grams of fat in 5 servings of canned soup. The rate of grams of fat per serving is $\frac{15 \text{ grams of fat}}{5 \text{ servings}}$.

The rate for one unit of a given quantity is the **unit rate.** To find a unit rate, divide the first quantity by the second quantity. For a rate of $\frac{15 \text{ grams of fat}}{5 \text{ servings}}$, the unit rate is 3 grams of fat per serving.

5 servings → | ← 15 grams of fat

1 serving → | ← 3 grams of fat

The model shows that

$$\text{total fat} \div \frac{\text{number of}}{\text{servings}} = \frac{\text{fat per}}{\text{serving}}$$

EXAMPLE **Finding a Unit Rate**

1 A package of cheddar cheese contains 15 servings and has a total of 147 grams of fat. Find the unit rate of grams of fat per serving.

$$\begin{array}{l} \text{grams} \rightarrow \\ \text{servings} \rightarrow \end{array} \frac{147}{15} = 9.8 \quad \leftarrow \text{Divide the first quantity by the second quantity.}$$

The unit rate is $\frac{9.8 \text{ grams}}{1 \text{ serving}}$, or 9.8 grams of fat per serving.

✓ Quick Check

1. Find the unit rate for 210 heartbeats in 3 minutes.

A unit rate that gives the cost per unit is a **unit cost.** Suppose a box of cereal weighs 8 oz and has a unit cost of $.31 per ounce.

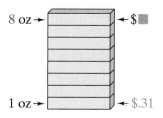

8 oz →   ← $■

1 oz →   ← $.31

The model shows that

unit cost · number of ounces = total cost

EXAMPLE   **Using Unit Cost to Find Total Cost**

2   **Food** Use the information at the right to find the cost of the box of cereal.

Cereal $.31/oz
8 oz

Estimate $.31 · 8 ≈ $.30 · 8, or $2.40

    $.31 · 8 = $2.48   ← unit cost · number of units = total cost

Check for Reasonableness The total cost of $2.48 is close to the estimate of $2.40. So $2.48 is reasonable.

✔ Quick Check

   2. Dog food costs $.35/lb. How much does a 20-lb bag cost?

To find the unit cost, divide the total cost of the item by the number of units in the item.

EXAMPLE   **Using Unit Cost to Compare**

Test Prep Tip
The "better buy" is the item that has the lower unit cost.

3   **Smart Shopping** Two sizes of shampoo bottles are shown. Which size is the better buy? Round to the nearest cent.

shampoo²   shampoo²
16 oz   13.5 oz
$6.19 $3.99

Divide to find the unit cost of each size.

cost → $\dfrac{\$3.99}{13.5 \text{ fl oz}}$ ≈ $.30/fl oz
size →

cost → $\dfrac{\$6.19}{16 \text{ fl oz}}$ ≈ $.39/fl oz
size →

Since $.30 < $.39, the 13.5-fl-oz bottle is the better buy.

✔ Quick Check

   3. Which bottle of apple juice is the better buy: 48 fl oz for $3.05 or 64 fl oz for $3.59?

Check Your Understanding

1. **Vocabulary** What makes a unit rate a unit cost?

Find the unit rate for each situation by filling in the blanks.

2. skating 1,000 m in 200 s: $\dfrac{\text{meters}}{\text{seconds}} \rightarrow \dfrac{1{,}000}{\blacksquare} = 5$ meters per second

3. earning \$147 in 21 h: $\dfrac{\text{dollars}}{\text{hours}} \rightarrow \dfrac{\blacksquare}{21} = \blacksquare$ dollars per hour

4. spending \$89 in 5 h: $\dfrac{\text{dollars}}{\text{hours}} \rightarrow \dfrac{89}{\blacksquare} = \blacksquare$ dollars per hour

5. Use the model at the right to find the total amount of fat in 4 servings.

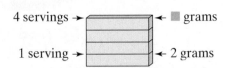

4 servings → ■ grams

1 serving → 2 grams

Homework Exercises

For more exercises, see Extra Skills and Word Problems.

GO for Help

For Exercises	See Examples
6–9	1
10–13	2
14–18	3

Find the unit rate for each situation. Round to the nearest hundredth, if necessary.

6. traveling 1,200 mi in 4 h

7. scoring 96 points in 6 games

8. reading 53 pages in 2 h

9. 592 students in 17 classrooms

Find the total cost using each unit cost.

10. 5 ft at \$3 per foot

11. 15 yd^2 at \$2 per square yard

12. 10 gal at \$2.40 per gallon

13. 26 oz at \$.15 per ounce

Test Prep Tip ⒶⒷⒸⒹ

Drawing a model can help you find unit rates.

Find each unit cost.

14. \$12 for 4 yd^2

15. \$3.45 for 3.7 oz

16. \$9 for 5 L

Which size is the better buy?

17. detergent: 32 fl oz for \$1.99
    50 fl oz for \$2.49

18. crackers: 12 oz for \$2.69
    16 oz for \$3.19

19. **Guided Problem Solving** A school has 945 students and 35 teachers. If the numbers of teachers and students both increase by 5, does the unit rate remain the same? Explain.

    • Find unit rates. $\dfrac{\text{students}}{\text{teachers}} \rightarrow \dfrac{\blacksquare}{\blacksquare} = \blacksquare$ students per teacher

20. **Biking** You bike 18.25 km in 1 h 45 min. What is the unit rate in kilometers per minute? In meters per minute?

21. **Crafts** The costs for three different types of ribbon are \$.79 for 1 yd, \$1.95 for 3 yd, and \$2.94 for 6 yd. Which is the best buy?

Find each unit cost.

22.  2 qt $3.69

23.  2 pt $1.49

24.  11 oz $.99

25.  5 lb $2.99

26. The world record for the women's 3,000-m steeplechase is 9 min 1.59 s. Find the runner's speed in meters per second. Round your answer to the nearest hundredth.

27. **Geography** Population density is the number of people per unit of area.
   a. Alaska has the lowest population density of any state in the United States. It has 626,932 people in 570,374 mi^2. What is its population density? Round to the nearest person per square mile.
   b. **Reasoning** New Jersey has 1,134.5 people/mi^2. Can you conclude that 1,134.5 people live in every square mile in New Jersey? Explain.

28. **Writing in Math** Explain the difference between a rate and a unit rate.

29. **Challenge** A human heart beats an average of 2,956,575,000 times in 75 years. About how many times does a heart beat in one year? In one day? In one minute?

Test Prep and Mixed Review

Practice

Multiple Choice

30. A grocery store sells apple juice in these sizes: 64 ounces for $2.48, 128 ounces for $4.48, and 48 ounces for $1.92. Which size has the lowest unit cost?
   (A) 48-oz only
   (B) 64-oz only
   (C) 128-oz only
   (D) 128-oz and 64-oz

31. There are 12 teams in a soccer league. Each team must play every other team once. How many games will be played in all?
   (F) 60 games (G) 66 games (H) 72 games (J) 132 games

32. Aaron received the following scores on different tests: 98, 79, 85, 92, 88. Which measure of the data is represented by 19 points?
   (A) median (B) range (C) mean (D) mode

GO for Help

For Exercises	See Lesson
33–35	2-1

Use paper and pencil, mental math, or a calculator to simplify.

33. $3^2 + 4 \cdot 5$

34. $(6 - 3)^3 - 1$

35. $2 \cdot 4 - 5^2$

Using Conversion Factors

A conversion factor is a rate that equals 1. For example, since
60 min = 1 h, both $\frac{60\ \text{min}}{1\ \text{h}}$ and $\frac{1\ \text{h}}{60\ \text{min}}$ equal 1. You can use $\frac{60\ \text{min}}{1\ \text{h}}$
as a conversion factor to change hours into minutes.

$$7\ \text{h} = \frac{7\ \cancel{\text{h}}}{1} \cdot \frac{60\ \text{min}}{1\ \cancel{\text{h}}} = 420\ \text{min} \quad \leftarrow \begin{array}{l}\textbf{Divide the common unit, hours (h).}\\ \textbf{The result is in minutes.}\end{array}$$

The table shows some common conversion factors for converting
between the metric system and the customary system.

Conversion Factors
Length
1 in. = 2.54 cm
1 km ≈ 0.62 mi
Capacity
1 L ≈ 1.06 qt
Weight and Mass
1 oz ≈ 28 g
1 kg ≈ 2.2 lb

EXAMPLE **Converting to the Metric System**

1 Convert 15 inches to centimeters.

$$15\ \text{in.} = \frac{15\ \cancel{\text{in.}}}{1} \cdot \frac{2.54\ \text{cm}}{1\ \cancel{\text{in.}}} \quad \leftarrow \begin{array}{l}\textbf{Use } \frac{\textbf{2.54 cm}}{\textbf{1 in.}} \textbf{ since conversion is to}\\ \textbf{centimeters. Divide the common units.}\end{array}$$

$$= (15)(2.54)\ \text{cm} \quad \leftarrow \textbf{Simplify.}$$

$$= 38.1\ \text{cm} \quad \leftarrow \textbf{Multiply.}$$

EXAMPLE **Converting to the Customary System**

2 The mass of a western diamondback rattlesnake is about 6.7 kg.
How many pounds does the snake weigh? Round
to the nearest tenth.

$$6.7\ \text{kg} = \frac{6.7\ \cancel{\text{kg}}}{1} \cdot \frac{2.2\ \text{lb}}{1\ \cancel{\text{kg}}} \quad \leftarrow \textbf{Use } \frac{\textbf{2.2 lb}}{\textbf{1 kg}} \textbf{ since conversion is to pounds.}$$

$$= (6.7)(2.2)\ \text{lb} \quad \leftarrow \textbf{Simplify.}$$

$$= 14.74\ \text{lb} \quad \leftarrow \textbf{Multiply.}$$

$$\approx 14.7\ \text{lb} \quad \leftarrow \textbf{Round to the nearest tenth.}$$

Exercises

Write a conversion factor you can use to convert each measure.

1. kilometers to miles
2. liters to quarts
3. ounces to grams

Use a conversion factor to convert each measure. Round to the nearest tenth.

4. 22 in. ≈ ■ cm
5. 26.4 lb ≈ ■ kg
6. 20.5 oz ≈ ■ g

7. 500 g ≈ ■ oz
8. 5 km ≈ ■ mi
9. 20 L ≈ ■ qt

1. Write the ratio 7 : 52 in two other ways.

Write each ratio in simplest form.

2. $\frac{4}{6}$

3. $\frac{16}{48}$

4. 24 to 14

5. 18 : 27

Write a unit rate for each situation.

6. typing 126 words in 3 min

7. scoring 45 points in 5 games

Find each unit cost. Which is the better buy?

8. 3 for $.79, 4 for $.99

9. 5 for $39, 7 for $46

10. The last time you bought pizza, 3 pizzas were just enough for 7 people. At that rate, how many pizzas should you buy for a party for 35 people?

MATH AT WORK

Automotive Engineer

Automotive engineers design, develop, and test all kinds of vehicles. They also test and evaluate a design's cost, reliability, and safety.

Engineers have many opportunities to use math skills. They use problem-solving skills to find out why cars break down.

Computer-aided design systems help automotive engineers plan the cars of the future. Computer simulations allow them to test for quality and to predict how their designs will work in the real world.

Go Online
PHSchool.com
For: Information on automotive engineers
Web Code: arb-2031

5-3 Proportions

What You'll Learn

To test whether ratios form a proportion by using equivalent ratios and cross products

🔊 **New Vocabulary** proportion, cross products

Why Learn This?

Pollsters conduct surveys. They ask different groups of people the same questions. You can use proportions to compare the answers from the different groups.

Did You See a Movie This Weekend?

Class	Yes	Total Number
A	10	24
B	25	60

A **proportion** is an equation stating that two ratios are equal. One method of testing whether ratios form a proportion is to write both ratios in simplest form. Then see if they are equal.

EXAMPLE Writing Ratios in Simplest Form

1 Surveys Refer to the table above. For each class, write the ratio of the number of students who saw a movie to the total number of students. Do the ratios form a proportion?

Class A: $\frac{10}{24} = \frac{10 \div 2}{24 \div 2} = \frac{5}{12}$ ← **Divide 10 and 24 by their GCF, which is 2.**

Class B: $\frac{25}{60} = \frac{25 \div 5}{60 \div 5} = \frac{5}{12}$ ← **Divide 25 and 60 by their GCF, which is 5.**

Since both ratios are equal to $\frac{5}{12}$, the ratios are proportional.

✓ Quick Check

1. Do $\frac{10}{12}$ and $\frac{40}{56}$ form a proportion?

KEY CONCEPTS Proportion

Ratios that are equal form a proportion.

Arithmetic	**Algebra**
$\frac{6}{8} = \frac{9}{12}$	$\frac{a}{b} = \frac{c}{d}, b \neq 0, d \neq 0$

You can use the properties of equality to discover another way to determine whether ratios form a proportion.

$$\frac{6}{8} = \frac{9}{12}$$ ← Use the ratios from the beginning of the lesson.

$$\frac{6}{8}\left(\frac{8}{1} \cdot \frac{12}{1}\right) = \frac{9}{12}\left(\frac{8}{1} \cdot \frac{12}{1}\right)$$ ← Use the Multiplication Property of Equality. Multiply each side by both denominators.

$$\frac{6}{{}_1\cancel{8}}\left(\cancel{\frac{8}{1}}^1 \cdot \frac{12}{1}\right) = \frac{9}{{}_1\cancel{12}}\left(\frac{8}{1} \cdot \cancel{\frac{12}{1}}^1\right)$$ ← Divide numerators and denominators by their GCF.

$$6 \cdot 12 = 9 \cdot 8$$

The products $6 \cdot 12$ and $9 \cdot 8$ are called cross products. For two ratios, the **cross products** are the two products found by multiplying the denominator of each ratio by the numerator of the other ratio.

$6 \cdot 12$ 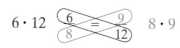 $8 \cdot 9$

KEY CONCEPTS **Cross-Products Property**

If two ratios form a proportion, the cross products are equal. If two ratios have equal cross products, they form a proportion.

Arithmetic

$$\frac{6}{8} = \frac{9}{12}$$
$$6 \cdot 12 = 8 \cdot 9$$

Algebra

$$\frac{a}{b} = \frac{c}{d}$$
$ad = bc$, where $b \neq 0$ and $d \neq 0$

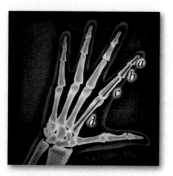

The lengths of the bones in your hands form a proportion.

SOURCE: *Fascinating Fibonaccis*

You can use the Cross-Products Property to determine whether ratios form a proportion.

EXAMPLE **Using Cross Products**

2 Do the ratios in each pair form a proportion?

a. $\frac{5}{9}, \frac{30}{54}$

$$\frac{5}{9} \stackrel{?}{=} \frac{30}{54}$$ ← Test each pair of ratios. →

$$5 \cdot 54 \stackrel{?}{=} 9 \cdot 30$$ ← Write cross products. →

$$270 = 270$$ ← Simplify. →

Yes, $\frac{5}{9}$ and $\frac{30}{54}$ form a proportion.

b. $\frac{7}{8}, \frac{55}{65}$

$$\frac{7}{8} \stackrel{?}{=} \frac{55}{65}$$

$$7 \cdot 65 \stackrel{?}{=} 8 \cdot 55$$

$$455 \neq 440$$

No, $\frac{7}{8}$ and $\frac{55}{65}$ do *not* form a proportion.

✓ Quick Check

2. Determine whether the ratios form a proportion.

a. $\frac{3}{8}, \frac{6}{16}$ **b.** $\frac{6}{9}, \frac{4}{6}$ **c.** $\frac{4}{8}, \frac{5}{9}$

1. **Vocabulary** A proportion states that two __?__ are equal.

2. **Number Sense** Without writing $\frac{3}{5}$ and $\frac{9}{15}$ in simplest form or using the Cross-Products Property, how can you tell whether the ratios form a proportion?

Fill in the blank so that each pair of ratios forms a proportion.

3. $\frac{1}{2}, \frac{4}{\blacksquare}$

4. $\frac{3}{3}, \frac{9}{\blacksquare}$

5. $\frac{3}{4}, \frac{\blacksquare}{12}$

6. $\frac{4}{7}, \frac{8}{\blacksquare}$

7. $\frac{2}{3}, \frac{\blacksquare}{18}$

8. $\frac{\blacksquare}{5}, \frac{6}{10}$

9. **Error Analysis** A student used the Cross-Products Property to determine that $\frac{3}{4}$ and $\frac{12}{16}$ do not form a proportion. His work is shown at the right. Is he correct? Explain.

$$\frac{3}{4} \stackrel{?}{=} \frac{12}{16}$$
$$3 \cdot 12 \stackrel{?}{=} 4 \cdot 16$$
$$36 \neq 64$$

For more exercises, see Extra Skills and Word Problems.

GO for Help

For Exercises	See Examples
10–18	1
19–27	2

Determine whether the ratios can form a proportion.

10. $\frac{1}{2}, \frac{14}{28}$

11. $\frac{6}{8}, \frac{4}{3}$

12. $\frac{8}{18}, \frac{20}{45}$

13. $\frac{21}{24}, \frac{56}{64}$

14. $\frac{15}{45}, \frac{3}{15}$

15. $\frac{45}{9}, \frac{10}{2}$

16. $\frac{19}{76}, \frac{5}{20}$

17. $\frac{17}{34}, \frac{2}{3}$

18. $\frac{40}{12}, \frac{160}{3}$

19. $\frac{6}{10}, \frac{9}{15}$

20. $\frac{4}{5}, \frac{10}{13}$

21. $\frac{7}{8}, \frac{15}{18}$

22. $\frac{6}{14}, \frac{3}{7}$

23. $\frac{7}{22}, \frac{28}{77}$

24. $\frac{12}{15}, \frac{20}{25}$

25. $\frac{6}{10}, \frac{24}{42}$

26. $\frac{5}{9}, \frac{15}{27}$

27. $\frac{3}{10}, \frac{15}{25}$

28. **Guided Problem Solving** Your boat engine needs 5 fl oz of oil mixed with every 2 gal of gas. A gas container has 12 gal of gas mixed with 34 fl oz of oil. Is this the correct mixture? Explain.
    - **Make a Plan** Write the ratio of oil to gas for the boat and for the gas container. Determine whether the ratios form a proportion.
    - **Carry Out the Plan** The ratios of oil to gas are $\frac{\blacksquare \text{ fl oz}}{2 \text{ gal}}$ and $\frac{\blacksquare \text{ fl oz}}{12 \text{ gal}}$.

29. **Decorating** A certain shade of green paint requires 4 parts blue to 5 parts yellow. If you mix 16 quarts of blue paint with 25 quarts of yellow paint, will you get the desired shade of green? Explain.

Do the ratios in each pair form a proportion?

30. $\frac{56}{2}, \frac{110}{3}$ **31.** $\frac{18}{12}, \frac{4.8}{3.6}$ **32.** $\frac{20}{1.5}, \frac{60}{4.5}$ **33.** $\frac{3.5}{35}, \frac{2.04}{204}$

34. <u>**Writing in Math**</u> Explain why $\frac{a}{b}$ and $\frac{a+b}{b}$ can *never* form a proportion.

35. **Space** An astronaut who weighs 174 lb on Earth weighs 29 lb on the moon. If you weigh 102 lb on Earth, would you weigh 17 lb on the moon? Explain.

36. **Geometry** Is the ratio of b to h the same in both triangles? Explain your reasoning.

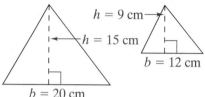
$h = 9$ cm
$h = 15$ cm
$b = 12$ cm
$b = 20$ cm

37. An elephant's heart rate was measured at 26 beats in 1 minute and 104 beats in 4 minutes. Are the rates proportional?

38. **Physical Science** Eighteen-karat gold contains 18 parts gold and 6 parts other metals. A ring contains 12 parts gold and 3 parts other metals. Is the ring eighteen-karat gold? Explain.

39. **Challenge** Determine whether $\frac{4n}{3}$ and $\frac{12n}{9}$ *always*, *sometimes*, or *never* form a proportion. Explain.

Careers Astronauts pilot spacecraft or work on science projects in space.

Test Prep and Mixed Review   Practice

Multiple Choice

40. Which ratio does NOT form a proportion with $\frac{5}{8}$?

   Ⓐ $\frac{20}{32}$ Ⓑ $\frac{100}{160}$ Ⓒ $\frac{45}{56}$ Ⓓ $\frac{10}{16}$

41. Which expression does the model below represent?

$$\frac{1}{2} \quad \frac{1}{2} \quad \frac{1}{2} \quad \frac{1}{2} \quad \frac{1}{2} \quad \frac{1}{2} \quad \frac{1}{2}$$

0   1   2   3   4

   Ⓕ $3\frac{1}{2} - \frac{1}{2}$ Ⓖ $\frac{1}{2} \div 3\frac{1}{2}$ Ⓗ $3\frac{1}{2} \div \frac{1}{2}$ Ⓙ $\frac{1}{2} \times 3\frac{1}{2}$

42. Carrie buys T-shirts for $6.25 each. After paying to have her school mascot printed on the shirts, she sells each one for $9.50. Carrie plans to sell 12 T-shirts at a basketball game. What missing information is needed to find how much profit per shirt she will make?

   Ⓐ Cost to print the mascot   Ⓒ Sizes of the T-shirts

   Ⓑ Number of fans at the game   Ⓓ Price of each T-shirt

GO for Help

For Exercises	See Lesson
43–45	4-3

(**Algebra**) **Solve each equation.**

43. $y - 37 = 68$ **44.** $m + 59 = -348$ **45.** $b + 175 = 102$

Interpreting Rates Visually

You can describe real-world situations using rates.

ACTIVITY

Manny mowed lawns to earn spending money. He charged $10 per hour. Ilene earned money by baby-sitting at $8 per hour, plus a $5 travel fee. Who earned the most for a 3-hour job?

1. Copy and complete the table below to show how much each person earns.

Earnings

	1 hour	2 hours	3 hours	4 hours	5 hours
Manny	■	■	■	■	■
Ilene	■	■	■	■	■

2. Graph the data above on a coordinate system like the one below. Make Manny's line solid and make Ilene's line dashed.

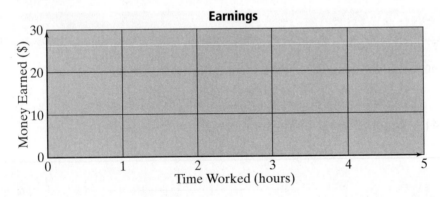

3. Why does the line for Manny's earnings start at $0 for zero hours worked? Why does the line for Ilene's earnings start at $5 for zero hours worked?

4. An expression for Manny's earnings is $10x$, where x is the number of hours worked. Write an expression for Ilene's earnings.

5. Estimate the time at which the lines cross. What does this point represent?

6. According to the graph, who earned more for a 3-hour job?

7. Estimate each person's earnings for a $1\frac{1}{2}$-hour job. Estimate each person's earnings for a $2\frac{1}{2}$-hour job.

Using Proportions With Data

You can use proportions to estimate the number of times your heart beats in one minute, which is called your heart rate.

ACTIVITY

Copy and complete the table below. Use your data from Steps 1–4.

My Heart Rate Data

Ratio: $\dfrac{\text{counted beats}}{\text{10 seconds}}$	■
Resting Heart Rate	■
Minimum Target Value	■
Maximum Target Value	■
Exercising Heart Rate	■

Step 1 Count the number of times your heart beats in 10 seconds. Write this value as a ratio.

Step 2 Let $x =$ your heart rate. Use your data to write a proportion.

$$\frac{\text{counted beats}}{\text{10 seconds}} = \frac{x \text{ beats}}{\text{60 seconds}}$$

Use mental math to find x. This is your resting heart rate.

Step 3 When you exercise, your heart rate should fall within a target zone. Calculate the values for your target zone.

Minimum value $= 0.6(220 - \text{your age})$
Maximum value $= 0.8(220 - \text{your age})$

Step 4 Jog in place for one minute. Repeat Steps 1 and 2 to estimate your exercising heart rate.

Exercises

1. Compare your exercising rate with your target zone.

2. Explain why counting your heartbeats for 10 seconds, rather than for a full minute, gives you a more accurate estimate of your exercising heart rate.

3. Express your resting heart rate as a unit rate and estimate the number of times your heart beats in 24 hours.

5-4 Solving Proportions

✔ Check Skills You'll Need

1. **Vocabulary Review**
   When is a ratio a *unit rate*?

Write the unit rate for each situation.

2. 192 km in 24 d

3. 248 mi in 4 h

4. 50 push-ups in 2 min

5. 180 words in 3 min

 **for Help**
Lesson 5-2

What You'll Learn

To solve proportions using unit rates, mental math, and cross products

Why Learn This?

You know the price of six oranges, but you want to buy eight. You can solve a proportion to find the total cost of the quantity that you want to buy.

6 for $2.34

You can use unit rates to solve a proportion. First find the unit rate. Then multiply to solve the problem.

EXAMPLE   Using Unit Rates

1 **Shopping** Use the information above to find the cost in dollars of 8 oranges.

Solve the proportion $\frac{2.34 \text{ dollars}}{6 \text{ oranges}} = \frac{x \text{ dollars}}{8 \text{ oranges}}$.

Step 1 Find the unit price.

$\frac{2.34 \text{ dollars}}{6 \text{ oranges}}$

$2.34 \div 6 \text{ oranges}$ ← Divide to find the unit price.

$.39/orange

Step 2 You know the cost of one orange. Multiply to find the cost of 8 oranges.

$.39 \cdot 8 = \$3.12$ ← Multiply the unit rate by the number of oranges.

The cost of 8 oranges is $3.12.

✔ Quick Check

1. **a.** Postcards cost $2.45 for 5 cards. How much will 13 cards cost?
   b. Swimming goggles cost $84.36 for 12. At this rate, how much will new goggles for 17 members of a swim team cost?

You can use mental math to solve some proportions. When a proportion involves a variable, you solve the proportion by finding the value of the variable.

EXAMPLE Solving Using Mental Math

2 (**Algebra**) Solve each proportion using mental math.

a. $\dfrac{z}{12} = \dfrac{21}{36}$

$$\overset{\times 3}{\dfrac{z}{12}} = \overset{}{\dfrac{21}{36}}_{\times 3}$$ ← Since 12 × 3 = 36, the common multiplier is 3.

$z = 7$ ← Use mental math to find what number times 3 equals 21.

b. $\dfrac{8}{10} = \dfrac{n}{40}$

$$\overset{\times 4}{\dfrac{8}{10}} = \overset{}{\dfrac{n}{40}}_{\times 4}$$ ← Since 10 × 4 = 40, 8 × 4 = n.

$n = 32$ ← Use mental math.

✓ Quick Check

2. Solve each proportion using mental math.

a. $\dfrac{3}{8} = \dfrac{b}{24}$ b. $\dfrac{m}{5} = \dfrac{16}{40}$ c. $\dfrac{15}{30} = \dfrac{5}{p}$

Many proportions cannot easily be solved with mental math. In these situations, you can use cross products to solve a proportion.

EXAMPLE Solving Using Cross Products

Test Prep Tip
Before you use cross products to solve a proportion, check whether you can use mental math.

3 **Gridded Response** Solve $\dfrac{25}{38} = \dfrac{15}{x}$ using cross products.

$\dfrac{25}{38} = \dfrac{15}{x}$

$25x = 38(15)$ ← Write the cross products.

$25x = 570$ ← Simplify.

$\dfrac{25x}{25} = \dfrac{570}{25}$ ← Divide each side by 25.

$x = 22.8$ ← Simplify.

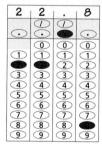

✓ Quick Check

3. Solve each proportion using cross products.

a. $\dfrac{12}{15} = \dfrac{x}{21}$ b. $\dfrac{16}{30} = \dfrac{d}{51}$ c. $\dfrac{20}{35} = \dfrac{110}{m}$

More Than One Way

Nature An oyster bed covers 36 m². Your class studies 4 m² of the oyster bed. In those 4 m² you count 96 oysters. Predict the number of oysters in the entire bed.

Carlos's Method

I will let x represent the number of oysters in the 36-m² bed.

$$\text{oysters} \rightarrow \frac{96}{4} = \frac{x}{36} \leftarrow \text{oysters} \atop \text{area} \rightarrow \qquad \leftarrow \text{area}$$ ← Write a proportion.

$$96(36) = 4x$$ ← Write the cross products.

$$3{,}456 = 4x$$ ← Simplify.

$$\frac{3{,}456}{4} = \frac{4x}{4}$$ ← Divide each side by 4.

$$864 = x$$ ← Simplify.

There are about 864 oysters in the oyster bed.

Brianna's Method

Since $9 \cdot 4\ \text{m}^2 = 36\ \text{m}^2$, the entire bed is 9 times as large as the portion studied. So I know there should be about $9 \cdot 96$, or 864, oysters in the oyster bed.

Choose a Method

You buy a bag of 400 marbles. In a handful of 20 marbles, you find 8 red marbles. About how many red marbles are in the bag? Explain why you chose the method you used.

Check Your Understanding

1. **Writing in Math** How does a unit rate help you solve a proportion?

2. **Number Sense** Does the proportion $\frac{3}{7} = \frac{x}{21}$ have the same solution as $\frac{7}{3} = \frac{21}{x}$? Explain.

Solve each proportion using mental math.

3. $\frac{2}{5} = \frac{m}{10}$

$$\frac{2}{5} \overset{\times 2}{\underset{\times 2}{=}} \frac{m}{10}$$

$m = \blacksquare$

4. $\frac{1}{6} = \frac{4}{y}$

$$\frac{1}{6} \overset{\times 4}{\underset{\times 4}{=}} \frac{4}{y}$$

$y = \blacksquare$

5. $\frac{7}{3} = \frac{28}{b}$

$$\frac{7}{3} \overset{\times 4}{\underset{\times 4}{=}} \frac{28}{b}$$

$b = \blacksquare$

For more exercises, see Extra Skills and Word Problems.

GO for Help

For Exercises	See Examples
6–10	1
11–16	2
17–25	3

Solve each problem by finding a unit rate and multiplying.

6. If 5 goldfish cost $6.45, what is the cost of 8 goldfish?

7. If 12 roses cost $18.96, what is the cost of 5 roses?

8. If 3 onions weigh 0.75 lb, how much do 10 onions weigh?

9. If 13 key chains cost $38.35, what is the cost of 20 key chains?

10. At a telethon, a volunteer can take 48 calls over a 4-hour shift. At this rate, how many calls can 12 volunteers take in a 4-hour shift?

Solve each proportion using mental math.

11. $\frac{2}{7} = \frac{x}{21}$

12. $\frac{18}{32} = \frac{m}{16}$

13. $\frac{c}{10} = \frac{36}{60}$

14. $\frac{c}{35} = \frac{4}{7}$

15. $\frac{16}{38} = \frac{b}{19}$

16. $\frac{9}{w} = \frac{36}{20}$

Solve each proportion using cross products.

17. $\frac{8}{12} = \frac{y}{30}$

18. $\frac{15}{33} = \frac{m}{22}$

19. $\frac{c}{28} = \frac{49}{16}$

20. $\frac{y}{18} = \frac{21}{63}$

21. $\frac{14}{34} = \frac{x}{51}$

22. $\frac{9}{30} = \frac{p}{16}$

23. $\frac{20}{w} = \frac{12}{3}$

24. $\frac{27}{20} = \frac{36}{v}$

25. $\frac{19}{r} = \frac{152}{4}$

 26. **Guided Problem Solving** You received $57.04 for working 8 h. At that rate, how much would you receive for working 11 h?

$$\begin{array}{c} \text{hours} \to \\ \text{pay} \to \end{array} \frac{8}{\blacksquare} = \frac{\blacksquare}{x} \quad \leftarrow \text{You would receive } x \text{ dollars for } \blacksquare \text{ hours.}$$

27. **History** Franklin D. Roosevelt was elected president in 1932 with about 22,800,000 votes. The ratio of the number of votes he received to the number of votes the other candidates received was about 4 : 3. About how many votes did the other candidates receive?

28. There are 450 students and 15 teachers in a school. The school hires 2 new teachers. To keep the student-to-teacher ratio the same, how many students in all should attend the school?

29. **Reasoning** Brian solved the proportion $\frac{18}{45} = \frac{a}{20}$ at the right. His first step was to simplify the ratio $\frac{18}{45}$. Is his answer correct? Explain.

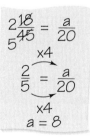

30. A jet takes $5\frac{3}{4}$ h to fly 2,475 mi from New York City to Los Angeles. About how many hours will a jet flying at the same average rate take to fly 5,452 mi from Los Angeles to Tokyo?

President Franklin D. Roosevelt

Solve each proportion using cross products. Round to the nearest tenth, if necessary.

31. $\dfrac{1.7}{2.5} = \dfrac{3.4}{d}$ **32.** $\dfrac{y}{9.3} = \dfrac{12.6}{5.4}$ **33.** $\dfrac{33.1}{x} = \dfrac{6.2}{1.3}$ **34.** $\dfrac{16.9}{13.5} = \dfrac{t}{7.4}$

35. Error Analysis A videocassette recorder uses 2 m of tape in 3 min when set on extended play. To determine how many minutes a tape that is 240 m long can record on extended play, one student wrote the proportion $\frac{2}{3} = \frac{n}{240}$. Explain why this proportion is incorrect. Then write a correct proportion.

36. Health Your heart rate is the number of heartbeats per minute.
   a. What is your heart rate if you count 18 beats in 15 seconds?
   b. Choose a Method How many beats do you count in 15 seconds if your heart rate is 96 beats/min? Explain the method you chose.

37. Writing in Math You estimate you will take 75 min to bike 15 mi to a state park. After 30 min, you have traveled 5 mi. Are you on schedule? Explain.

38. Challenge A recipe for fruit salad serves 4 people. It calls for $2\frac{1}{2}$ oranges and 16 grapes. You want to serve 11 people. How many oranges and how many grapes will you need?

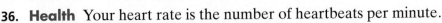
Test Prep and Mixed Review   **Practice**

Gridded Response

39. An antelope ran 237 ft in 3 seconds. If the antelope continued to run at the same rate, how many seconds would it take him to run 790 ft?

40. The table below shows the leaders in punt returns for the National Football Conference during one season.

Punt Return Leaders

Name	Number of Returns	Yards
Brian Westbrook	20	306
Allen Rossum	39	545
Reggie Swinton	23	318
R. W. McQuarters	37	452

What was the unit rate of yards per return for Reggie Swinton? Round to the nearest hundredth.

41. A restaurant bill for four people is $37.80. How much money, in dollars, should each person contribute to share the cost evenly?

Order the numbers from least to greatest.

42. $16, -12, 10, -3$ **43.** $-6, -3, 8, -2, 1$ **44.** $5, 0, -1, 2, -5$

Proportions and Equations

Often you can translate a proportion problem into an equation.
You can then use the equation to solve similar problems.

Muscles For each 5 pounds of body weight, about 2 pounds is
muscle. How much of a 125-pound student is muscle?

What You Might Think

What do I know?

What am I trying to find out?

How do I solve the problem?

What is the answer?

What You Might Write

Each 5 lb of weight includes 2 lb of muscle.

How many pounds of muscle are in 125 lb of
body weight?

I can write an equation to find the muscle
weight for any student weight. A proportion
that represents the situation is

$$\frac{x}{125} = \frac{2}{5}.$$

To solve for x, I can multiply each side by 125.

$$x = \frac{2}{5}(125)$$

125 represents the student's weight. So if a
student's weight is w, then the equation

$x = \frac{2}{5}w$ gives the amount of muscle for any
weight w.

$$x = \frac{2}{5}(125)$$
$$= 250 \div 5$$
$$= 50$$

The 125-lb student has about 50 lb of muscle.

Think It Through

1. Show how solving the equation $\frac{2}{5} = \frac{x}{w}$ for x gives the equation
   $x = \frac{2}{5}w$.

2. Explain why you can use the equation $x = \frac{2}{5}w$ as a shortcut for
   finding the amount of muscle for any student.

Exercises

Solve each problem. For Exercises 3 and 4, answer the questions first.

3. During one season, a basketball player made 353 of 765 free throws. At that rate, how many free throws would the player make in another 600 attempts?
   a. What do you know? What do you want to find out?
   b. Can you write an equation to predict the number of free throws x the player will make for any number of shots s?

4. Jess wants to sell fruit punch on a hot day. The punch is 2 parts grape juice to 3 parts apple juice. Jess has 5 quarts of apple juice. How many quarts of grape juice does she need?
   a. What do you know? What do you want to find out?
   b. Can you write an equation to find the number of quarts of grape juice g needed for a quarts of apple juice?

5. Jess makes the graph below so that she does not have to keep calculating amounts of juice. Use the graph to find how much grape juice is needed for 15 quarts of apple juice. Then find how much apple juice is needed for 12 quarts of grape juice.

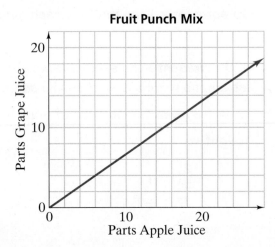

6. A concession stand needs 3 hot dogs for every 7 people who attend a football game. If 1,400 fans are expected to attend the game, how many hot dogs are needed?

7. Earth is about 25,000 mi around at the equator. If you are sitting on the equator, about how fast are you traveling? (*Hint:* Earth makes one rotation in 24 hours.)

Exploring Similar Figures

In everyday language, two items are *similar* if they are the same in some, but not necessarily all, ways. In math, similarity has a related meaning. Complete the activity to find out what makes two figures mathematically similar.

ACTIVITY

Figures 1 and 2 below are similar. Figures 3 and 4 are similar, too. You can test whether two figures are similar by measuring their angles and side lengths.

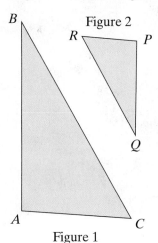

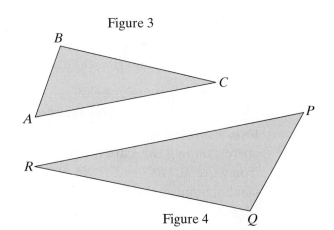

1. Copy the table at the right. Use a protractor to measure each angle of Figure 1 and Figure 2 above. Fill in the missing information in the table. What do you notice about the angle measures in each row of your table?

Fig. 1	Angle Measure	Fig. 2	Angle Measure
∠A	■	∠P	■
∠B	■	∠Q	■
∠C	■	∠R	■

2. Copy the table at the right. Use a centimeter ruler to measure each side of Figure 1 and Figure 2 to the nearest tenth of a centimeter. Fill in the missing information in the table. What pattern do you notice in the length of the sides in each row of the table?

Fig. 1	Side Length (cm)	Fig. 2	Side Length (cm)
AB	■	PQ	■
BC	■	QR	■
CA	■	RP	■

3. Repeat Steps 1 and 2 for Figures 3 and 4.

4. Make a conjecture about the angle measures and side lengths of similar figures.

Using Similar Figures

Check Skills You'll Need

1. Vocabulary Review
An equation stating that two ratios are equal is a ? .

Solve each proportion.

2. $\frac{x}{4} = \frac{12}{8}$ **3.** $\frac{4}{b} = \frac{16}{48}$

4. $\frac{84}{12} = \frac{g}{6}$ **5.** $\frac{6}{3} = \frac{19}{m}$

Lesson 5-4

What You'll Learn

To use proportions to find missing lengths in similar figures

🔊 **New Vocabulary** polygon, similar polygons, indirect measurement

Why Learn This?

The heights of objects such as totem poles may be difficult to measure directly. You can measure indirectly by using figures that have the same shape. When two figures have the same shape, but not necessarily the same size, they are similar.

In the similar triangles below, corresponding angles have the same measure. Since $\frac{40}{60} = \frac{50}{75} = \frac{34}{51}$, the corresponding sides are proportional. You write $\triangle ABC \sim \triangle FGH$. The symbol $\sim$ means "is similar to."

When solving problems involving similar figures, make sure you are working with corresponding angles and sides.

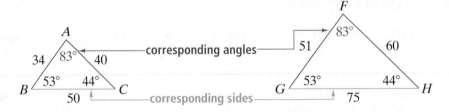

A **polygon** is a closed plane figure formed by three or more line segments that do not cross.

KEY CONCEPTS Similar Polygons

Two polygons are **similar polygons** if
- corresponding angles have the same measure, and
- the lengths of the corresponding sides form equivalent ratios.

You can use proportions to find missing side lengths in similar polygons.

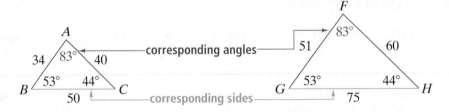

A **polygon** is a closed plane figure formed by three or more line segments that do not cross.

KEY CONCEPTS Similar Polygons

Two polygons are **similar polygons** if
- corresponding angles have the same measure, and
- the lengths of the corresponding sides form equivalent ratios.

You can use proportions to find missing side lengths in similar polygons.

EXAMPLE Finding a Missing Measure

1 (**Algebra**) $\triangle ACT$ and $\triangle ODG$ are similar. Find the value of x.

$$\frac{AC}{OD} = \frac{AT}{OG} \quad \leftarrow \text{Write a proportion.}$$

$$\frac{x}{50} = \frac{24}{30} \quad \leftarrow \text{Substitute.}$$

$$\frac{x}{50} = \frac{4}{5} \quad \leftarrow \text{Write } \frac{24}{30} \text{ in simplest form.}$$

$$\frac{x}{50} \overset{\times 10}{=} \frac{4}{5} \quad \leftarrow \text{Find the common multiplier.}$$

$$x = 40 \quad \leftarrow \text{Use mental math.}$$

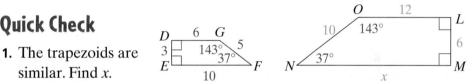

✓ Quick Check

1. The trapezoids are similar. Find x.

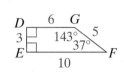

You can use **indirect measurement** to measure distances that are difficult to measure directly. You do this by using proportions and similar figures.

EXAMPLE Application: Indirect Measurement

2 **Multiple Choice** A 6-ft-tall person standing near a flagpole casts a shadow 4.5 ft long. The flagpole casts a shadow 15 ft long. What is the height of the flagpole?

  Ⓐ 11.25 ft   Ⓑ 18 ft   Ⓒ 20 ft   Ⓓ 360 ft

Draw a picture and let x represent the height of the flagpole.

$$\frac{x}{6} = \frac{15}{4.5} \quad \leftarrow \text{Write a proportion.}$$

$$4.5x = 6 \cdot 15 \quad \leftarrow \text{Write the cross products.}$$

$$\frac{4.5x}{4.5} = \frac{6 \cdot 15}{4.5} \quad \leftarrow \text{Divide each side by 4.5.}$$

$$x = 20 \quad \leftarrow \text{Simplify.}$$

The height of the flagpole is 20 ft. The answer is C.

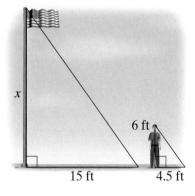

Test Prep Tip
Drawing a picture can help you see what quantities you know and what quantities you are looking for.

✓ Quick Check

2. A 6-ft person has a shadow 5 ft long. A nearby tree has a shadow 30 ft long. What is the height of the tree?

1. **Vocabulary** What must be true about the corresponding angles and the corresponding sides for two polygons to be similar?

△ABC is similar to △RST. Complete each statement.

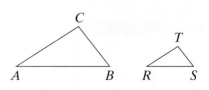

2. ∠B corresponds to __?__ .

3. $\overline{RS}$ corresponds to __?__ .

4. **Geometry** Are the rectangles similar? Explain.

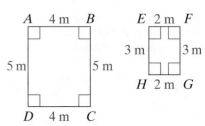

5. **Open-Ended** Think of a distance that is difficult to measure directly. How would you find it indirectly?

Homework Exercises

For more exercises, see Extra Skills and Word Problems.

GO for Help

For Exercises	See Examples
6–9	1
10	2

(Algebra) **△ABC is similar to △PQR. Find each measure.**

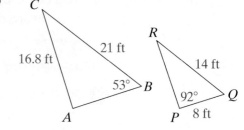

6. length of $\overline{AB}$

7. length of $\overline{RP}$

8. measure of ∠A

9. measure of ∠Q

10. A woman is 5 ft tall and her shadow is 4 ft long. A nearby tree has a shadow 30 ft long. How tall is the tree?

11. **Guided Problem Solving** An image is 16 in. by 20 in. You want to make a copy that is similar. Its longer side will be 38 in. The copy costs $.60 per square inch. Estimate the copy's total cost.
    • What is the approximate length of the shorter side of the copy?
    • What is the approximate area of the copy?

12. **Social Studies** You want to enlarge a copy of the flag of the Philippines that is 4 in. by 8 in. The two flags will be similar. How long should you make the shorter side if the long side is 6 ft?

13. **Geometry** A rectangle with an area of 32 in.² has one side measuring 4 in. A similar rectangle has an area of 288 in.². How long is the longer side in the larger rectangle?

GO Online
Homework Video Tutor
Visit: PHSchool.com
Web Code: are-0505

Each pair of figures below is similar. Find the value of each variable.

14.
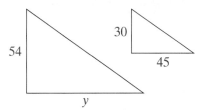

15.
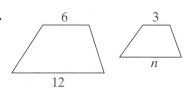

16. A burro is standing near a cactus. The burro is 59 in. tall. His shadow is 4 ft long. The shadow of the cactus is 7 ft long. Estimate the height of the cactus.

17. **Surveying** Surveyors know that $\triangle PQR$ and $\triangle STR$ are similar. They cannot measure the distance d across the lake directly. Find the distance across the lake.

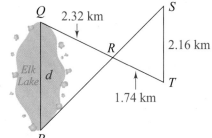

18. **Writing in Math** Give three examples of real-world objects that are similar. Explain why they are similar.

19. **Challenge** The ratio of the corresponding sides of two similar triangles is 4 : 9. The sides of the smaller triangle are 10 cm, 16 cm, and 18 cm. Find the perimeter of the larger triangle.

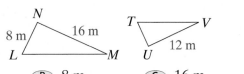

Test Prep and Mixed Review   **Practice**

Multiple Choice

20. In the figure, $\triangle LMN \sim \triangle TVU$. What is the length of $\overline{UT}$?

    N
    8 m   16 m   T   V
    L   M   U   12 m

    Ⓐ 6 m   Ⓑ 8 m   Ⓒ 16 m   Ⓓ 24 m

21. The cost of two pounds of pears is $1.78. How much will five pounds of pears cost?
    Ⓕ $0.71   Ⓖ $2.67   Ⓗ $4.45   Ⓙ $8.90

22. Which algebraic expression represents five inches less than twice last year's rainfall f in inches?
    Ⓐ $5 - 2f$ Ⓑ $2f - 5$ Ⓒ $2 - 5f$ Ⓓ $5f - 2$

GO for Help

For Exercises	See Lesson
23–25	4-6

Algebra Solve each equation.

23. $3x + 2 = 17$ 24. $\frac{x}{5} + 5 = 21$ 25. $2a - 4 = 8$

Drawing Similar Figures

Using a computer is an excellent way to explore similar figures. For this activity you need geometry software.

ACTIVITY

Follow these steps to draw two similar triangles like those at the right.

Step 1 Draw a triangle and label it *ABC*.

Step 2 Draw a point *D* not on the triangle.

Step 3 Draw a triangle similar to △*ABC* using the dilation command. To use this command, you will need to enter a scale factor and name one point as the center of the dilation. Use 2 as a scale factor and name point *D* as the center.

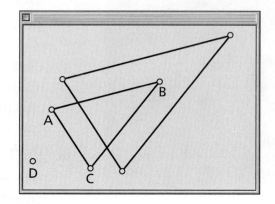

Exercises

1. Change the shape of △*ABC* by dragging point *A*, *B*, or *C*. What happens to the larger triangle each time?

2. Drag point *D* to different locations. Describe what happens in each case below.
   a. *D* is inside △*ABC*.
   b. *D* is on $\overline{AB}$.
   c. *D* is on top of point *C*.

3. Use the software to draw $\overleftrightarrow{AD}$ (line *AD*), $\overleftrightarrow{BD}$, and $\overleftrightarrow{CD}$.
   a. What do you notice about the lines and the larger triangle?
   b. Why do you think that point *D* is called the center of the dilation?

4. Draw a third triangle similar to △*ABC*. This time use 0.5 as the scale factor. Keep *D* as the center. What do you notice about the new triangle?

5. **a. Open-Ended** Draw more triangles similar to △*ABC* by choosing other scale factors. Again keep *D* as the center.
   b. <u>**Writing in Math**</u> Explain how your choice of scale factor affects the final figure.
   c. Use what you have learned to write a definition for scale factor.

Checkpoint Quiz 2

Determine whether the ratios form a proportion.

1. $\dfrac{5}{8}, \dfrac{12}{20}$

2. $\dfrac{4}{10}, \dfrac{2}{5}$

3. $\dfrac{24}{15}, \dfrac{4}{3}$

4. $\dfrac{8}{3}, \dfrac{48}{18}$

5. The last time your family bought hamburgers, 5 hamburgers cost $5.25. At this rate, what is the cost of 8 hamburgers?

6. 7 movie tickets cost $57.75. What is the cost of 2 movie tickets?

$\triangle ABC$ is similar to $\triangle WXY$. Find each measure.

7. $\angle X$

8. $\angle C$

9. length of $\overline{AB}$

10. length of $\overline{WY}$

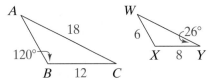

Vocabulary Builder

Learning Vocabulary

You can make your own dictionary of new math vocabulary terms.

EXAMPLE

Write entries for your dictionary for the terms *ratio* and *rate*.

Term	Definition	Example
Ratio	Comparison of two different quantities by division	$\dfrac{20 \text{ people}}{5 \text{ people}}$
Rate	Ratio that compares two quantities measured in different units	$\dfrac{20 \text{ people}}{5 \text{ cars}}$

Make a table with 3 columns.
← Label the columns "Term," "Definition," and "Example."

Write the vocabulary term
← and its definition. Then give an example of the term.

Exercises

Write an entry for your dictionary for each term.

1. proportion

2. similar figures

3. cross products

Scale Drawings and Models

The sketches below show the measurements of Jackie's bedroom. You can use these sketches to make a model of Jackie's bedroom.

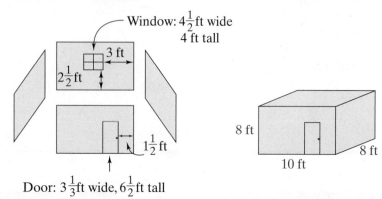

Window: $4\frac{1}{2}$ ft wide
4 ft tall

3 ft

$2\frac{1}{2}$ ft

$1\frac{1}{2}$ ft

Door: $3\frac{1}{3}$ ft wide, $6\frac{1}{2}$ ft tall

8 ft

10 ft

8 ft

ACTIVITY

Step 1 Make a drawing on graph paper of the floor and walls of Jackie's room as shown. Let one unit on the graph paper represent one foot. Include the windows and doors.

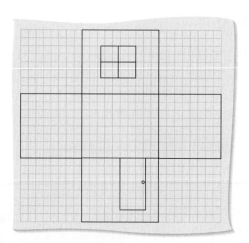

Step 2 Cut around your drawing and tape up the walls to make your model.

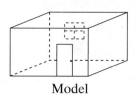

Model

Exercises

1. Jackie's bedroom bureau is shown at the right. Use the same steps as above to make a drawing and a model of the bureau.

2. Measure the heights and lengths of the walls of your classroom. Use graph paper to make an accurate drawing of the floor and walls.

3. Cut around your drawing and make a model of your classroom.

4. Explain how you can use ratios and proportions to find the dimensions of your model.

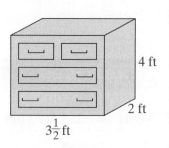

4 ft

2 ft

$3\frac{1}{2}$ ft

What You'll Learn

To use proportions to solve problems involving scale

◀)) **New Vocabulary** scale drawing, scale

Why Learn This?

When you know how scales work, you can see them in everything from maps to giant sculptures.

A **scale drawing** is an enlarged or reduced drawing of an object that is similar to the actual object.

A **scale** is the ratio that compares a length in a drawing or model to the corresponding length in the actual object. If a 15-foot boat is 1 inch long on a drawing, you can write the scale of the drawing in these three ways.

$$1 \text{ in.} : 15 \text{ ft} \qquad \frac{1 \text{ in.}}{15 \text{ ft}} \qquad 1 \text{ in.} = 15 \text{ ft}$$

↑   ↑
drawing actual

EXAMPLE   Using a Scale Drawing

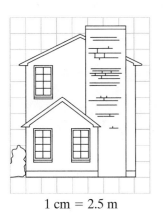

1 cm = 2.5 m

1 **(Algebra)** The length of the side of a house is 3 cm on a scale drawing. What is the actual length of the side of the house?

You can write the scale of the drawing as $\frac{1 \text{ cm}}{2.5 \text{ m}}$. Then write a proportion. Let n represent the actual length of the house.

$$\text{drawing (cm)} \rightarrow \frac{1}{2.5} = \frac{3}{n} \leftarrow \text{drawing (cm)}$$
$$\text{actual (m)} \rightarrow \qquad \qquad \leftarrow \text{actual (m)}$$

$$1n = 2.5(3) \quad \leftarrow \text{Write the cross products.}$$

$$n = 7.5 \qquad \leftarrow \text{Simplify.}$$

The actual length is 7.5 m.

✓ Quick Check

1. The chimney of the house is 4 cm tall on the drawing. How tall is the chimney of the actual house?

EXAMPLE   Application: Geography

2 Find the actual distance from Charlotte to Winston-Salem.

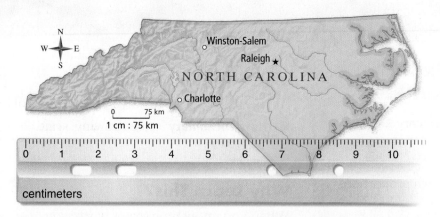

Step 1 Use a centimeter ruler to find the map distance from Charlotte to Winston-Salem. The map distance is about 1.6 cm.

Step 2 Use a proportion to find the actual distance. Let n represent the actual distance.

$$\begin{array}{l} \text{map (cm)} \rightarrow \\ \text{actual (km)} \rightarrow \end{array} \frac{1}{75} = \frac{1.6}{n} \begin{array}{l} \leftarrow \text{map (cm)} \\ \leftarrow \text{actual (km)} \end{array} \quad \leftarrow \textbf{Write a proportion.}$$

$$1n = 75(1.6) \qquad \leftarrow \textbf{Write the cross products.}$$

$$n = 120 \qquad\qquad \leftarrow \textbf{Simplify.}$$

The actual distance from Charlotte to Winston-Salem is about 120 km.

Test Prep Tip

When writing a proportion, make sure each ratio compares the same types of quantities.

✓ Quick Check

2. Find the actual distance from Charlotte to Raleigh.

You can use the GCF to find the scale of a drawing or a model.

EXAMPLE   Finding the Scale

3 **Models** Refer to the model boxcar shown at the right. The actual length of a boxcar is 609 in. What is the scale of the model?

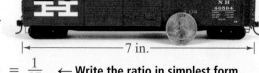
7 in.

$$\begin{array}{l} \text{scale length} \rightarrow \\ \text{actual length} \rightarrow \end{array} \frac{7}{609} = \frac{7 \div 7}{609 \div 7} = \frac{1}{87} \quad \leftarrow \textbf{Write the ratio in simplest form.}$$

The scale is 1 in. : 87 in.

✓ Quick Check

3. The length of a room in an architectural drawing is 10 in. Its actual length is 160 in. What is the scale of the drawing?

Application: Models

4 **Multiple Choice** You want to make a scale model of a sailboat that is 51 ft long and 48 ft tall. You plan to make the model 17 in. long. Which equation can you use to find x, the height of the model?

(A) $\dfrac{48}{51} = \dfrac{17}{x}$ (B) $\dfrac{17}{51} = \dfrac{x}{48}$ (C) $\dfrac{48}{17} = \dfrac{x}{51}$ (D) $\dfrac{x}{17} = \dfrac{51}{48}$

$$\text{model (in.)} \rightarrow \dfrac{17}{51} \leftarrow \text{actual (ft)} = \dfrac{\blacksquare}{\blacksquare} \begin{array}{l}\leftarrow \text{model (in.)}\\ \leftarrow \text{actual (ft)}\end{array} \quad \leftarrow \textbf{Write a proportion.}$$

$$\dfrac{17}{51} = \dfrac{x}{48} \quad \leftarrow \begin{array}{l}\textbf{Fill in the information you know.}\\ \textbf{Use } x \textbf{ for the information you do not know.}\end{array}$$

The correct answer is choice B.

You can solve the proportion to find the height of the model. You can simplify $\dfrac{17}{51}$ to make calculating easier.

GO for Help

For help with simplifying ratios, go to Lesson 5-3, Example 1.

$$\dfrac{\overset{1}{\cancel{17}}}{\underset{3}{\cancel{51}}} = \dfrac{x}{48} \quad \leftarrow \textbf{Simplify } \dfrac{17}{51} \textbf{ by dividing by the GCF, 17.}$$

$$\dfrac{1}{3} = \dfrac{x}{48}$$

$$\underset{\times 16}{\overset{\times 16}{\dfrac{1}{3} = \dfrac{x}{48}}} \quad \leftarrow \textbf{Find the common multiplier, 16.}$$

$$x = 16 \quad \leftarrow \textbf{Use mental math.}$$

The height of the model is 16 inches.

✓ Quick Check

4. If the sailboat is 15 ft wide, how wide should the model be?

✓ Check Your Understanding

1. **Vocabulary** A scale is a _?_ that compares a length in a drawing to the corresponding _?_ in the actual object.

2. **Reasoning** The scale of a drawing is 5 cm : 1 mm. Is the scale drawing larger or smaller than the actual figure? Explain.

3. **Error Analysis** A student wants to write the scale of a statue of President Kennedy, who was 6 ft tall. The statue is 8 ft tall. The student writes the scale as 6 ft : 8 ft. Is the student correct? Explain.

The scale of a map is 1 inch : 5 miles. Find each distance.

4. A road is 3 in. long on the map. Find the actual length of the road.

5. A lake is 35 miles long. Find the length of the lake on the map.

For more exercises, see Extra Skills and Word Problems.

GO for Help

For Exercises	See Examples
6–11	1
12–15	2
16–17	3–4

(Algebra) **A scale drawing has a scale of 1 in. : 11 ft. Find the actual length for each drawing length.**

6. 21 in.   **7.** 15 in.   **8.** 6 in.

9. 45 in.   **10.** 13.5 in.   **11.** 1.5 in.

Geography Find the actual distance between each pair of cities. Use a ruler to measure. Round to the nearest mile.

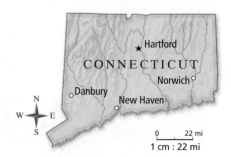

12. Hartford and Danbury

13. Norwich and Hartford

14. New Haven and Norwich

15. New Haven and Danbury

16. In a scale drawing, the width of a sofa is 15 cm. The actual width of the sofa is 150 cm. What is the scale of the drawing?

17. A certain car is about 100 in. long and 60 in. wide. You plan to make a model of this car that is 9 in. wide. How long will your model be?

18. Guided Problem Solving The height of a building on a blueprint is 10 in. Its actual height is 150 ft. What is the scale of the drawing?
- What ratio can you use to find the scale?
- How can finding the GCF help you to simplify your answer?

19. The scale of a model is 0.5 in. : 6 ft. Find the length of the model for an actual length of 204 ft.

20. Geography Dallas is $6\frac{3}{4}$ in. from Houston on a map of Texas with a scale of $\frac{3 \text{ in.}}{100 \text{ mi}}$. What is the actual distance from Dallas to Houston?

21. Architecture The blueprint below is a scale drawing of an apartment. The scale is $\frac{1}{4}$ in. : 4 ft. Sketch a copy of the floor plan. Write the actual dimensions in place of the scale dimensions.

GO Online
Homework Video Tutor
Visit: PHSchool.com
Web Code: are-0506

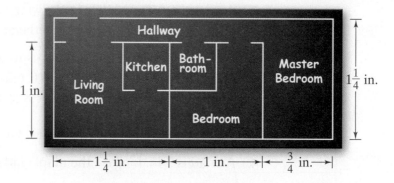

Use a centimeter ruler to measure the length of the segment shown in each figure below. Find the scale of each drawing.

22.
Peach Aphid

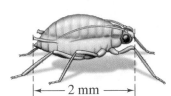

|← 2 mm →|

23.
Killer Whale

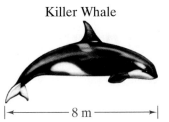

|← 8 m →|

24. <u>Writing in Math</u> You are making a scale drawing with a scale of 2 in. = 17 ft. Explain how you find the length of the drawing of an object that has an actual length of 51 ft.

25. Special Effects A special-effects artist has made a scale model of a dragon for a movie. In the movie, the dragon will appear to be 16 ft tall. The model is 4 in. tall.
  a. What scale has the artist used?
  b. The same scale is used for a model of a baby dragon, which will appear to be 2 ft tall. What is the height of the model?

26. Challenge A building is drawn with a scale of 1 in. : 3 ft. The height of the drawing is 1 ft 2 in. After a design change, the scale is modified to be 1 in. : 4 ft. What is the height of the new drawing?

Ⓐ Ⓑ Ⓒ Ⓓ **Test Prep and Mixed Review** **Practice**

Multiple Choice

27. Doug drew a map with a scale of 1 inch : 5 miles. What distance on Doug's map should represent 4.5 miles?
  Ⓐ 0.45 in.   Ⓑ 0.9 in.   Ⓒ 0.95 in.   Ⓓ 4.5 in.

28. In the figure at the right, $ABCD \sim STUV$. Which of the following statements is NOT true?
  Ⓕ $\overline{UV}$ corresponds to $\overline{CD}$.
  Ⓖ $\overline{AD}$ corresponds to $\overline{SV}$.
  Ⓗ $\angle A$ corresponds to $\angle S$.
  Ⓙ $\angle D$ corresponds to $\angle U$.

29. A cycling route is 56 miles long. There is a water station every $3\frac{3}{4}$ mi. Which equation represents the total number of water stations w?
  Ⓐ $56w = 3\frac{3}{4}$
  Ⓑ $3\frac{3}{4}w = 56$
  Ⓒ $3\frac{3}{4} - w = 56$
  Ⓓ $w + 3\frac{3}{4} = 56$

30. Find the values of x and y in the similar triangles at the right.

GO for Help

For Exercise	See Lesson
30	5-5

Plan a Trip

0 ——————— 85 mi
1 in. : 85 mi

ACTIVITY

Use the map above to plan a trip from Indianapolis to Cleveland.

Located on the shore of Lake Erie, the 150,000-square-foot Rock and Roll Hall of Fame and Museum is a landmark for the city of Cleveland, Ohio.

1. Measure the distances on Routes 69 and 90 from Indianapolis to Fort Wayne, Fort Wayne to Toledo, and Toledo to Cleveland. Add them to get the total map distance.

2. Locate the scale on the map. Use the scale to convert the map distance into the actual distance for your trip.

3. Use an average speed of 50 mi/h. Find the time it will take to drive the total actual distance. If you plan to drive no more than 4 hours per day, how many days will your trip take?

4. Suppose you want to make the same trip, but you want to visit a friend in Columbus. Plan your trip from Indianapolis to Cleveland to pass through Columbus. Compare the two trips.

5. **Research** Now suppose that you are planning a cross-country road trip from Trenton, New Jersey, to San Francisco, California. Locate a map of the United States and plan your trip. Decide which cities you would like to visit along the way. How long will your trip take you?

Using a Variable

You can solve many problems by using a variable to represent an unknown quantity.

EXAMPLE

Purple is a mixture of the primary colors red and blue. A certain shade of purple paint requires 6 parts red paint to 7 parts blue paint. If you have 16 quarts of red paint, how many quarts of blue paint do you need to make the desired shade of purple? How many quart cans of blue paint do you need to buy?

The problem is asking for the amount of blue paint needed to make a shade of purple. You can write and solve a proportion.

Let b represent the number of quarts of blue paint you need.

$$\text{red paint} \rightarrow \frac{6}{7} = \frac{16}{b} \leftarrow \text{red paint} \qquad \leftarrow \textbf{Write a proportion.}$$

$$6b = 112 \qquad \leftarrow \textbf{Write the cross products and simplify.}$$

$$\frac{6b}{6} = \frac{112}{6} \qquad \leftarrow \textbf{Divide each side by 6.}$$

$$b = 18\tfrac{2}{3} \qquad \leftarrow \textbf{Simplify.}$$

● You need $18\tfrac{2}{3}$ quarts of blue paint. You should buy 19 cans.

Exercises

Use a variable to write and solve an equation.

1. To serve 16 people, 96 pieces of fruit are needed. How many pieces of fruit are needed to serve 22 people?

   Ⓐ $18\tfrac{2}{3}$ Ⓑ 11   Ⓒ 132   Ⓓ 144

2. A paper distributor is shipping mailing tubes to an art gallery. The distributor has previously shipped 560 tubes in 16 boxes. At this rate, how many boxes would the distributor need to ship 112 tubes?

   Ⓕ 4   Ⓖ 5   Ⓗ 12   Ⓙ 35

3. A class of 37 students is making origami boxes. Each box requires 8 pieces of origami paper. The class will split into groups of at most 3 students per group. If each group is going to make one box, what is the least number of pieces of paper needed by the class?

   Ⓐ 24   Ⓑ 96   Ⓒ 104   Ⓓ 296

Chapter 5 Review

Vocabulary Review

🔊 cross products (p. 239)
equivalent ratios (p. 229)
indirect measurement (p. 253)
polygon (p. 252)

proportion (p. 238)
rate (p. 232)
ratio (p. 228)
scale (p. 259)

scale drawing (p. 259)
similar polygons (p. 252)
unit cost (p. 233)
unit rate (p. 232)

Choose the correct term to complete each sentence.

1. A street map is an example of (a scale drawing, cross products).

2. Knowing a(n) (indirect measurement, unit cost) is helpful for getting the best buy when you shop.

3. A speed limit of 40 mi/h is an example of a (rate, proportion).

4. A ratio that compares a length in a drawing to the actual length of an object is a (scale, proportion).

Go **Online**
PHSchool.com
For: Online vocabulary quiz
Web Code: arj-0551

5. When two polygons have corresponding angles with equal measures and corresponding sides with proportional lengths, the polygons are (cross products, similar).

Skills and Concepts

Lesson 5-1
• To write ratios and use them to compare quantities

A **ratio** is a comparison of two quantities by division. You can write the same ratio in three ways. To find equal ratios, multiply or divide the numerator and denominator by the same nonzero number.

Write each ratio in simplest form.

6. $\frac{9}{30}$ 7. $\frac{64}{20}$ 8. 99 : 33   9. 75 : 20   10. $\frac{45}{180}$

11. **Sports** During a recent Olympics, the United States won 97 medals, including 39 gold medals. Write the ratio of gold medals to total medals in three ways.

Lesson 5-2
• To find unit rates and unit costs using proportional reasoning

A **rate** is a ratio that compares two quantities measured in different units. A **unit rate** has a denominator of 1. Find a **unit cost** by dividing the price of an item by the size of the item.

Write the unit rate for each situation.

12. 282 passengers in 47 cars   13. 600 Calories in 8 servings

14. 414 students in 18 classrooms   15. $136 for 34 kg

Lesson 5-3

• To test whether ratios form a proportion by using equivalent ratios and cross products

16. Shopping A 10-oz box of cereal costs $2.79. A 13-oz box of the same brand of cereal costs $3.99. Find the unit cost for each item and determine which is the better buy.

17. A carpenter renovating a house is sanding the dining room floor. She sands 300 ft^2 of wood floor in 1 h 40 min. What is the unit rate in square feet per minute?

Lesson 5-4

• To solve proportions using unit rates, mental math, and cross products

A proportion is an equation stating that two ratios are equal. If two ratios form a proportion, the **cross products** are equal.

Solve each proportion.

18. $\frac{3}{7} = \frac{n}{28}$ **19.** $\frac{3}{5} = \frac{15}{x}$ **20.** $\frac{a}{18} = \frac{12}{72}$ **21.** $\frac{32}{c} = \frac{4}{17}$

22. Wood A local lumberyard sells a total of 250,000 board feet of hardwood each year. The ratio of softwood sold to hardwood sold is 5 : 3. Write and solve a proportion to find the amount of softwood sold each year. Round your answer to the nearest thousand.

23. The ratio of the width of a rectangle to its length is 5 : 8. What is the width in feet if the length is 12 ft?

Lesson 5-5

• To use proportions to find missing lengths in similar figures

Two polygons are **similar polygons** if corresponding angles have equal measures and the lengths of corresponding sides form equivalent ratios.

24. A fire hydrant is 30 in. tall and casts a shadow 8 in. long. How tall is a nearby tree that casts a shadow 4 ft long?

Each pair of figures is similar. Find each missing value.

25.

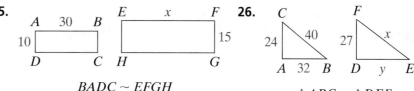

$BADC \sim EFGH$

26.

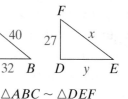

$\triangle ABC \sim \triangle DEF$

Lesson 5-6

• To use proportions to solve problems involving scale

A **scale drawing** is an enlarged or reduced drawing of an object that is similar to the actual object. A **scale** is a ratio that compares a length in a drawing to the corresponding length in an actual object.

27. Maps The scale on a map is 1 in. : 525 mi. The map distance from Chicago to Tokyo is 12 in. Find the actual distance between the cities.

28. Architecture A drawing's scale is 0.5 in. : 10 ft. A room is 15 ft long. How long is the room on the drawing?

Go Online For: Online chapter test
PHSchool.com **Web Code:** ara-0552

1. Write a ratio for the following information in three ways: In the United States, 98 million out of 99.6 million homes have at least one television.

Write each ratio in two other ways.

2. $\frac{9}{7}$ 3. $48 : 100$ 4. 33 to 9

5. $46 : 50$ 6. 19 to 91 7. $6 : 7$

8. **Gas Mileage** Engineers test four cars to find their fuel efficiency. Use the information in the table below. Which car gets the most miles per gallon?

Car	Miles	Gallons Used
A	225	14
B	312	15
C	315	10
D	452	16

Find the unit rate for each situation.

9. running 2.3 km in 7 min

10. earning $36.00 in 4 h

11. **Writing in Math** You need to buy 10 lb of rice. A 2-lb bag costs $1.29. A 10-lb bag costs $6.99. You want to buy a 10-lb bag. Your friend thinks buying five 2-lb bags is a better deal because the unit rate is lower. Is your friend correct? Explain.

Solve each proportion.

12. $\frac{6}{5} = \frac{n}{7}$ 13. $\frac{3}{7} = \frac{8}{x}$ 14. $\frac{k}{4} = \frac{9}{32}$

15. $\frac{3.5}{d} = \frac{14}{15}$ 16. $\frac{80}{35} = \frac{w}{7}$ 17. $\frac{y}{18} = \frac{2.4}{15}$

18. The ratio of teachers to students in a middle school is 2 to 25. There are 350 students in the school. Find the number of teachers.

19. **Maps** A map with a scale of 1 in. : 175 mi shows two cities 5 in. apart. How many miles apart are the cities?

Write each ratio in simplest form.

20. $\frac{7}{49}$ 21. $\frac{12}{4}$ 22. $\frac{8}{2}$

23. $\frac{14}{18}$ 24. $\frac{68}{100}$ 25. $\frac{15}{95}$

26. In the figure below, $\triangle JKL \sim \triangle PQR$. Find x and y.

27. **Utilities** Last month, your electric bill was $25.32 for 450 kilowatt-hours of electricity. At that rate, what would be the bill for 240 kilowatt-hours?

28. A person who is 60 in. tall casts a shadow that is 15 in. long. How tall is a nearby tree that casts a shadow that is 40 in. long?

Use mental math to solve each proportion.

29. $\frac{14}{36} = \frac{7}{x}$ 30. $\frac{40}{16} = \frac{x}{2}$

31. $\frac{x}{1} = \frac{24}{2}$ 32. $\frac{4}{9} = \frac{12}{x}$

33. Suppose you are making a scale drawing of a giraffe that is 5.5 m tall. The drawing is 7 cm tall. Find the scale of the drawing.

34. **Ballooning** A hot-air balloon 2,100 ft above the ground can descend at the rate of 1.5 ft/s. The balloon is scheduled to land at 3:30 P.M. When should the balloonist start descending?

35. **Science** A 380-cubic-centimeter sample of titanium has a mass of 1,170 g. Find the mass of a titanium sample that has a volume of 532 cubic centimeters.

Reading Comprehension

Read each passage and answer the questions that follow.

> **Europe Goes Euro** Until recently, you needed different types of money (francs, marks, punts, etc.) to travel through Europe. Now all you need to get by in most European countries is the new European currency, the euro. One U.S. dollar buys about 0.81 euros. One French franc was worth about 0.15 euros, and an Irish punt was worth about 1.27 euros.

1. About how many euros were 20 French francs worth?
   - (A) 0.15 euros
   - (B) 3.00 euros
   - (C) 20.00 euros
   - (D) 150.00 euros

2. Hsio came home from a trip with currency worth 20 U.S. dollars. She had 10 euros and the rest in U.S. currency. About how many dollars did she have?
   - (F) $12.35
   - (G) $11.90
   - (H) $8.10
   - (J) $7.65

3. About how many U.S. dollars would you get if you exchanged 15 euros?
   - (A) $12.15
   - (B) $18.52
   - (C) $22.50
   - (D) $27.28

4. Which expression shows how many French francs you could get for one Irish punt?
   - (F) 0.15×1.27
   - (G) $\frac{0.15}{1.27}$
   - (H) $0.15 + 1.27$
   - (J) $\frac{1.27}{0.15}$

> **More Money Notes** In the United States, paper money is all the same size: 2.61 inches wide by 6.14 inches long and 0.0043 inch thick. But did you know that American banknotes used to be bigger? Until 1929, they were 3.125 inches wide by 7.4218 inches long. By the way, it costs about 4.2 cents to produce one paper note.

5. What is the current ratio of length to width for U.S. paper money?
   - (A) 0.43 : 1
   - (B) 2.35 : 1
   - (C) 2.61 : 1
   - (D) 6.14 : 1

6. Suppose you make a stack of one thousand $100 bills. How tall is the stack?
   - (F) 0.043 in.
   - (G) 0.43 in.
   - (H) 4.3 in.
   - (J) 43 in.

7. What is the best approximation of the ratio of the current length of U.S. notes to the length before 1929?
   - (A) 1 : 2
   - (B) 3 : 4
   - (C) 5 : 6
   - (D) 9 : 10

8. The government prints about 12 billion paper notes each year. What is the best estimate of how much this costs?
   - (F) $.5 million
   - (G) $5 million
   - (H) $50 million
   - (J) $500 million

Applying Ratios

A Matter of Scale Some movies are about people suddenly shrinking in size. They find themselves in environments both familiar and unfamiliar. A piece of furniture becomes a cliff to climb. Insects become beasts to fear. Although special-effects technicians create many of the visuals on computers, model makers provide scale models for some objects. Using a consistent scale for the models keeps the illusion believable.

Put It All Together

1. You have been sent on a mission to learn as much as you can about a giant and her home.
   a. **Research** Use the clues in the "Giant's World" caption. Research the sizes of things mentioned in the caption. Then find the scale of the giant's world to your world.
   b. Use your scale to find the dimensions of at least three items from the giant's kitchen. Sketch the items and label their dimensions.
   c. Find the height of the giant.

2. Your next trip has brought you to a home inhabited by tiny people.
   a. **Research** Use the clues in the "Miniature World" caption and your research to find the scale of the miniature room to your world.
   b. Use your scale to find the dimensions of at least three items in the miniature living room. Sketch these items and label their dimensions.
   c. Find the height of a person who lives in the tiny house.

3. **Reasoning** Suppose someone in your class is 5 ft 5 in. tall, and another person is 4 ft 10 in. tall. Will these two people get the same answers in Exercises 1 and 2? Explain.

Coffee table

Living room area

Giant's World

When standing on your toes, you can just barely reach the top of a cereal box.

When stood on end, a teaspoon reaches to the bottom of your rib cage.

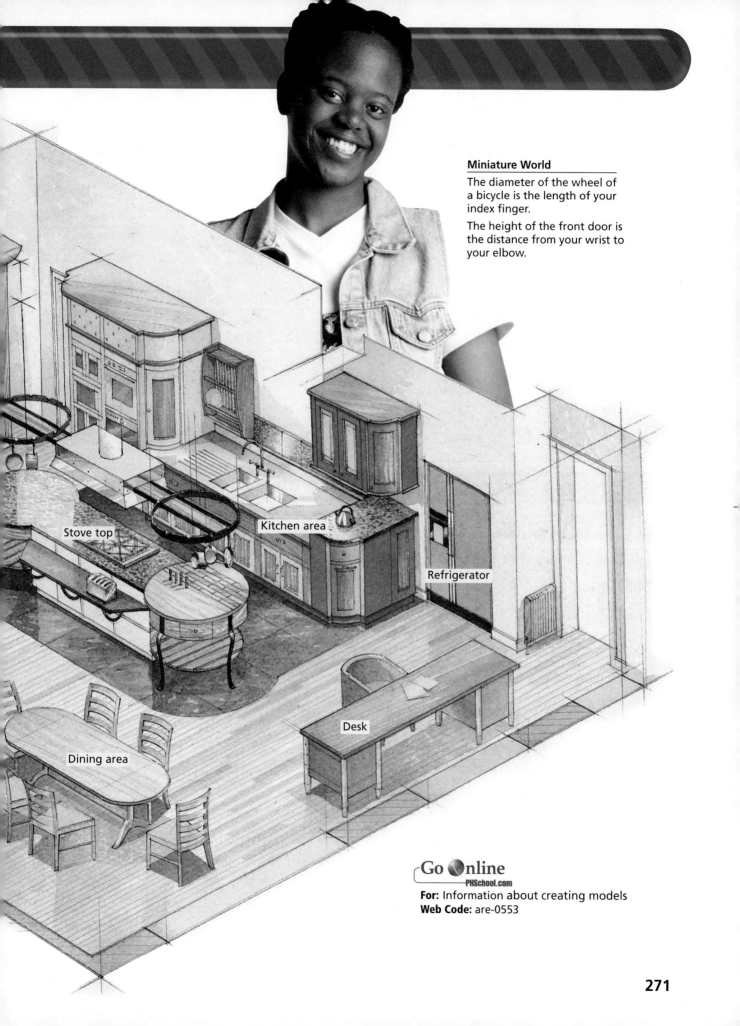

Miniature World

The diameter of the wheel of a bicycle is the length of your index finger.

The height of the front door is the distance from your wrist to your elbow.

Stove top

Kitchen area

Refrigerator

Desk

Dining area

Go Online
PHSchool.com

For: Information about creating models
Web Code: are-0553

What You've Learned

- In Chapter 2, you compared, ordered, and converted between fractions and decimals.
- In Chapter 4, you solved equations.
- In Chapter 5, you solved proportions.

Check Your Readiness

GO for Help

For Exercises	See Lesson
1–4	1-1
5–9	2-6
10–13	4-4
14–16	5-4

Using Estimation Strategies

Use compatible numbers to estimate each quotient.

1. $74.89 \div 14.7$ **2.** $1,409 \div 102.4$

3. $495.89 \div 99.3$ **4.** $1,913 \div 188$

Fractions and Decimals

Write each decimal as a fraction in simplest form.

5. 0.85 **6.** 0.4 **7.** 0.68 **8.** 1.25 **9.** 0.01

Solving Equations by Multiplying or Dividing

(**Algebra**) **Solve each equation.**

10. $0.8t = 24$ **11.** $0.35w = 280$ **12.** $\dfrac{n}{0.6} = 14$ **13.** $\dfrac{z}{0.25} = 12$

Using Proportional Reasoning

Solve each proportion.

14. $\dfrac{4}{5} = \dfrac{n}{100}$ **15.** $\dfrac{x}{8} = \dfrac{27}{100}$ **16.** $\dfrac{6}{a} = \dfrac{3}{100}$

What You'll Learn Next

- In this chapter, you will compare, order, and convert between fractions, decimals, and percents.

- You will solve percent problems using equations and proportions.

 Problem Solving Application On pages 320 and 321, you will work an extended activity on percents.

🔊 Key Vocabulary

- commission (p. 305)
- discount (p. 311)
- markup (p. 311)
- percent (p. 274)
- percent of change (p. 310)

Understanding Percents

Check Skills You'll Need

1. Vocabulary Review
What are *equivalent ratios*?

Find two equivalent ratios for each ratio.

2. $\frac{2}{5}$ **3.** $\frac{13}{50}$

4. $\frac{3}{25}$ **5.** $\frac{1}{10}$

 **for Help**
Lesson 5-1

What You'll Learn

To model percents and to write percents using equivalent ratios

🔊 **New Vocabulary** percent

Why Learn This?

Percents make ratios easier to understand and compare. You can use a percent to represent the floor space needed for each piece of furniture in a room.

A **percent** is a ratio that compares a number to 100. You can use a model to find a percent. You can model a percent using a 10×10 grid.

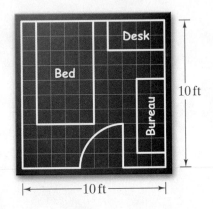

EXAMPLES Using Models With Percents

1 The floor plan above shows a bedroom with an area of 100 ft². Find the percent of floor space needed for each piece of furniture.

Count the number of grid spaces for each piece. Write each number as a ratio to the total number of grid spaces, 100. Then write it as a percent.

Bed $\frac{28}{100} = 28\%$ **Bureau** $\frac{10}{100} = 10\%$ **Desk** $\frac{8}{100} = 8\%$

2 Model 25% on a 10×10 grid.

Shade 25 of the 100 grid spaces. →

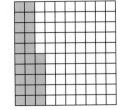

✓ Quick Check

1. Write a ratio and a percent to represent the unused floor space.

2. Model 80% on a 10×10 grid.

Vocabulary Tip

Percent means "per hundred." The root *cent* appears in words such as century, centimeter, and centipede.

For help with finding equivalent fractions, go to Lesson 2-3, Example 1.

The factors of 100 are 1, 2, 4, 5, 10, 20, 25, 50, and 100. Any ratio written as a fraction with a denominator that is a factor of 100 is easy to write as a percent. You can use common multiples to write an equivalent ratio that has a denominator of 100. When you have a fraction with a denominator of 100, look at the numerator to find the percent.

EXAMPLE **Finding Percents Using Models**

3 What percent does each shaded area represent?

a. 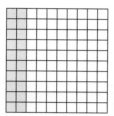 b. 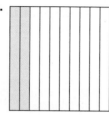 c.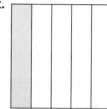

$\frac{20}{100} = 20\%$ $\frac{2}{10} = \frac{20}{100} = 20\%$ $\frac{1}{5} = \frac{20}{100} = 20\%$

✓ Quick Check

3. Write a ratio and a percent for each shaded area.

a.   b.   c.

EXAMPLE **Using Equivalent Ratios**

Test Prep Tip

When answering questions in gridded format, enter only the numerical portion of your answer in the grid.

4 **Gridded Response** You take a quiz that has 20 questions and get only 3 incorrect answers. What is your percent grade on the quiz?

First find the number of correct answers. Then write a ratio.

$\frac{17}{20}$ ← number of correct answers
← total number of answers

$\frac{17 \cdot 5}{20 \cdot 5}$ ← Since 20 · 5 is 100, multiply numerator and denominator by 5.

$\frac{85}{100}$ ← Simplify.

85% ← Write as a percent.

Your percent grade is 85%. Fill in 85 on your answer grid.

✓ Quick Check

4. A tennis team played a total of 25 games and won 20 of them. What percent of the games did the team win?

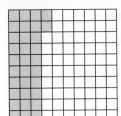

1. Write a ratio and a percent for the shaded area in the diagram.

2. Model 15% on a 10 × 10 grid.

Write each ratio as a percent.

3. $\frac{67}{100}$

4. $\frac{4}{5}$

5. $\frac{9}{10}$

6. **Reasoning** How can you use percents to compare two ratios with different denominators?

Homework Exercises

For more exercises, see Extra Skills and Word Problems.

GO for Help

For Exercises	See Examples
7–9	1
10–14	2
15–18	3–4

Write a ratio and a percent for each shaded figure.

7.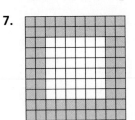

8.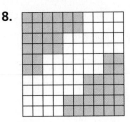

9.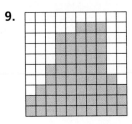

Model each percent on a 10 × 10 grid.

10. 35% 11. 78% 12. 10% 13. 8% 14. 90.5%

Write a ratio and a percent for each shaded area.

15.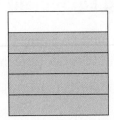

16.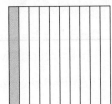

17.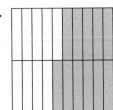

18. **Geography** The area of Argentina is about three tenths the area of the United States. Write this ratio as a percent.

19. **Guided Problem Solving** In a litter of 10 puppies, exactly six puppies are black. What percent of the puppies are not black?
    • How many puppies are not black?
    • How many puppies are in the litter?

20. **Government** An amendment to the U.S. Constitution must be ratified by at least three fourths of the states to become law. Write this ratio as a percent.

Write each ratio as a percent.

21. $\frac{3}{5}$ 22. $\frac{1}{2}$ 23. $\frac{21}{25}$ 24. $\frac{9}{50}$ 25. $\frac{11}{20}$

26. **Writing in Math** Explain how to model 25% two different ways.

Find what percent of a dollar each set of coins makes.

27. 2 quarters and 2 dimes   28. 3 quarters, 1 dime, 3 pennies

29. Your class has 12 boys and 13 girls. What percent of the students in your class are girls?

30. **History** Before the Battle of Tippecanoe, nineteen twentieths of General William Harrison's troops had never before been in a battle. What percent of the troops had previously been in a battle?

Estimate the percent of each figure that is shaded.

31. 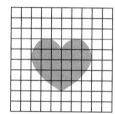   32. 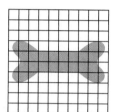   33.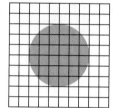

34. **Challenge** You shade four squares in a grid. How many squares are there if the shaded portion represents 20% of the grid?

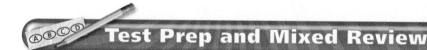
Test Prep and Mixed Review   **Practice**

Gridded Response

35. The table shows the ratios of people who prefer four popular yogurt flavors. What is the percent of people surveyed who prefer blueberry?

Most Popular Yogurt Flavors	
Personal Favorite	**Ratio**
Strawberry	$\frac{2}{5}$
Blueberry	$\frac{3}{25}$
Vanilla	$\frac{3}{50}$
Peach	$\frac{3}{100}$

36. Five students in Ms. Power's class ran for charity. The distances they ran were as follows: 5.8 mi, $4\frac{1}{2}$ mi, 2.4 mi, $3\frac{9}{10}$ mi, and 7 mi. What was the distance, in miles, the students ran altogether?

37. Arthur scored 87 on each of his first three tests. He scored 93 and 95 on his next two tests. What was the mean score of all his tests?

GO for Help

For Exercises	See Lesson
38–40	4-7

Which numbers are solutions of each inequality?

38. $x > -3; -4, 0, 3$ 39. $x \le -2; 0, -2, -3$ 40. $x < 5; 5, 3, -1$

Rational Number Cubes

You can write equivalent rational numbers in several different ways. The table below shows common rational numbers in equivalent forms. The fraction, decimal, and percent in each column are equivalent.

Fraction	$\frac{1}{8}$	$\frac{1}{4}$	$\frac{1}{3}$	$\frac{1}{2}$	$\frac{2}{3}$	$\frac{3}{4}$
Decimal	0.125	0.25	$0.33\overline{3}$	0.5	$0.66\overline{6}$	0.75
Percent	12.5%	25%	$33\frac{1}{3}\%$	50%	$66\frac{2}{3}\%$	75%

ACTIVITY

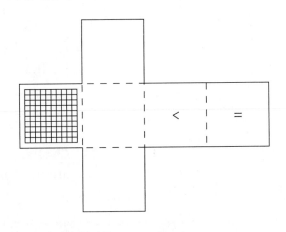

Step 1 A net of a cube is shown at the right. Make six copies of the net.

Step 2 Use the first column from the table above. Fill in the squares of the first net. Write $\frac{1}{8}$ in the first empty square. Write 0.125 and 12.5% in the other two empty squares. Then shade the 10×10 grid to model this rational number.

Step 3 Repeat Step 2 with the other nets and the other columns of the table.

Step 4 Cut out each net. Fold each net along its dotted lines. Tape the edges to form a cube.

Step 5 Work in pairs. Toss the 12 cubes. Use the top views of the cubes. Arrange as many as you can into a chain that reads correctly from left to right. (You can use the inequality symbol as either "less than" or "greater than.")

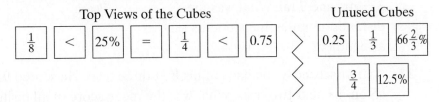

Step 6 Pick up the unused cubes and toss them again. Insert these cubes into the chain wherever they fit. Repeat until you can successfully place all 12 cubes in the chain.

What You'll Learn

To convert between fractions, decimals, and percents

Why Learn This?

The food labels below all use a different form of $\frac{1}{2}$. Any rational number can be written as a fraction, a decimal, or a percent.

50% of the minimum daily amount

Same taste $\frac{1}{2}$ the sugar

This product has 0.5g of fat.

KEY CONCEPTS   **Fractions, Decimals, and Percents**

The model at the right shows 21 out of 100 squares shaded. You can write the shaded part of the model as a fraction, a decimal, or a percent.

Fraction	Decimal	Percent
$\frac{21}{100}$	0.21	21%

To write a decimal as a percent, you can multiply the decimal by 100.

EXAMPLE   **Writing Decimals as Percents**

1 Write 0.759 as a percent.

$$0.759 = \frac{759}{1,000} \quad \leftarrow \text{Write as a fraction.}$$
$$= \frac{75.9}{100} \quad \leftarrow \text{Write an equivalent fraction with 100 in the denominator.}$$
$$= 75.9\% \quad \leftarrow \text{Write as a percent.}$$

Quick Check

1. Write 0.607 as a percent.

To write a percent as a decimal, you can divide it by 100, or move the decimal point two places to the left.

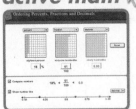

Online
active math

For: Rational Number Activity
Use: Interactive Textbook, 6-2

EXAMPLE **Writing Percents as Decimals**

2 Write 47.5% as a decimal.

$$47.5\% = \frac{47.5}{100} \quad \leftarrow \text{Write the percent as a fraction.}$$

$$= 0.475 \quad \leftarrow \text{Divide.}$$

✅ Quick Check

2. Write each percent as a decimal.
   a. 35%   **b.** 12.5%   **c.** 7.8%

When the denominator of a fraction is a factor of 100, you can easily use equivalent ratios to convert the fraction to a percent. For fractions with other denominators, you can use a calculator to convert the fraction into a decimal, and then rewrite the decimal as a percent.

EXAMPLE **Writing Fractions as Percents**

3 **Nutrition** In a slice of cheese pizza, 45 Calories are from fat. The total number of Calories in each slice is 158. About what percent of the Calories are *not* from fat? Round to the nearest tenth of a percent.

Step 1 Find the number of Calories that are not from fat.

$$158 - 45 = 113$$

Step 2 Estimate.

$$\frac{113}{158} \approx \frac{120}{160}, \text{ which is } \frac{3}{4}, \text{ or } 75\%.$$

Step 3 Write the ratio.

$$\frac{113}{158} \quad \begin{matrix} \leftarrow \text{ Calories from fat} \\ \leftarrow \text{ total Calories} \end{matrix}$$

$$113 \div 158 = 0.71518987 \quad \leftarrow \text{Use a calculator.}$$

$$= 71.518987\% \quad \leftarrow \text{Write as a percent.}$$

$$\approx 71.5\% \quad \leftarrow \text{Round to the nearest tenth of a percent.}$$

About 71.5% of the Calories are not from fat.

Check for Reasonableness Since 71.5% is close to the estimate 75%, the answer is reasonable.

✅ Quick Check

3. Write $\frac{21}{40}$ as a percent. Round to the nearest tenth of a percent.

You can write a percent as a fraction. First write the percent as a fraction with a denominator of 100. Then simplify the fraction.

EXAMPLE **Writing Percents as Fractions**

4 **Science** Behavioral scientists observed an elephant that slept about 12.5% of each day. What fraction of each day did the elephant sleep?

$$12.5\% = \frac{12.5}{100}$$ ← Write 12.5% as a fraction with a denominator of 100.

$$= \frac{12.5 \times 10}{100 \times 10}$$ ← Multiply the numerator and denominator by 10.

$$= \frac{125 \div 125}{1,000 \div 125}$$ ← Divide both numerator and denominator by the GCF, 125.

$$= \frac{1}{8}$$ ← Simplify the fraction.

The elephant slept about $\frac{1}{8}$ of each day.

✓ Quick Check

4. An elephant eats about 6% of its body weight in vegetation each day. Write this as a fraction in simplest form.

To compare rational numbers in different forms, you can write all the numbers in the same form. Then graph each number on a number line.

EXAMPLE **Ordering Rational Numbers**

5 Order 0.52, 37%, 0.19, and $\frac{1}{4}$ from least to greatest.

Write all the numbers as decimals. Then graph them.

$$0.52$$ ← This number is already in decimal form.

$$37\% = 0.37$$ ← Move the decimal point two places to the left.

$$0.19$$ ← This number is already in decimal form.

$$\frac{1}{4} = 0.25$$ ← Divide the numerator by the denominator.

GO for Help

For help converting a fraction to a decimal, go to Lesson 2-6.

From least to greatest, the numbers are 0.19, $\frac{1}{4}$, 37%, and 0.52.

✓ Quick Check

5. Order from least to greatest.

a. $\frac{3}{10}$, 0.74, 29%, $\frac{11}{25}$ **b.** 15%, $\frac{7}{20}$, 0.08, 50%

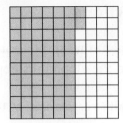

1. Write the shaded part of the model at the left as a percent, a fraction, and a decimal.

2. In each set, find the number that does *not* equal the other two.
   a. 9.9%, $\frac{99}{100}$, 0.99   **b.** 64%, $\frac{16}{50}$, 0.64   **c.** 12%, $\frac{3}{25}$, 1.2

3. **Mental Math** Order 0.54, 55%, and $\frac{1}{2}$ from least to greatest.

4. **Reasoning** When you write a percent as a decimal, why do you move the decimal point 2 units to the left?

Homework Exercises

For more exercises, see Extra Skills and Word Problems.

GO for Help

For Exercises	See Examples
5–9	1
10–14	2
15–20	3
21–26	4
27–29	5

Write each decimal as a percent.

5. 0.57   6. 0.375   7. 0.09   8. 0.155   9. 0.6

Write each percent as a decimal.

10. 32%   11. 88%   12. 19.1%   13. 3%   14. 1.25%

Write each fraction as a percent to the nearest tenth of a percent.

15. $\frac{45}{50}$ 16. $\frac{7}{8}$ 17. $\frac{1}{12}$ 18. $\frac{5}{6}$ 19. $\frac{3}{11}$

20. Out of 49 fish, 31 are goldfish. About what percent are goldfish?

Write each percent as a fraction in simplest form.

21. 15%   22. 6%   23. 20%   24. 37.5%   25. 17%

26. **Computers** A computer screen shows the print on a page at 78% of its actual size. Write 78% as a fraction in simplest form.

Order from least to greatest.

27. $\frac{1}{2}$, 12%, 0.25   28. 68%, 0.37, $\frac{3}{10}$ 29. 0.81, $\frac{4}{5}$, 90%

30. **Guided Problem Solving** In your class, 9 of the 26 students are in the chorus. What percent of your class is in the chorus? Round to the nearest tenth of a percent.
    • What ratio can help to find the percent of students in the chorus?
    • Should you multiply or divide by 100 to find the percent?

31. **Writing in Math** Does 0.4 equal 0.4%? Explain.

32. Compare 0.32 and 3.2%. Use <, =, or >.

33. **Math in the Media** Use the cartoon below to complete the table.

Topping	With Olives	Plain	With Onions and Green Peppers
Percent of the Pizza	■	■	■
Number of Slices	■	■	■

Macaroni & Cheese

Nutrition	
Fat	33 g
Carbohydrates	40 g
Protein	17 g

Spaghetti & Meat Sauce

Nutrition	
Fat	12 g
Carbohydrates	39 g
Protein	19 g

34. **Nutrition** The tables at the left give data on two different foods. A gram of fat has 9 Calories. A gram of carbohydrates and a gram of protein both have 4 Calories. What percent of the Calories in each food are from carbohydrates? Round to the nearest percent.

35. Your teacher uses different methods of grading quizzes. Your quiz grades are 85%, $\frac{9}{10}$, $\frac{16}{20}$, 92%, $\frac{21}{25}$, and 79%.
   a. Write your quiz grades in order from least to greatest.
   b. Find the average percent grade of your quizzes.

36. **Challenge** Write 3.75% as a fraction in simplest form.

Test Prep and Mixed Review **Practice**

Multiple Choice

37. Nathan runs m miles each weekday and $3\frac{1}{4}$ times farther on Saturday. He runs $6\frac{1}{2}$ miles on Saturday. Which equation can be used to find the number of miles Nathan runs each weekday?

 Ⓐ $3\frac{1}{4}m = 6\frac{1}{2}$ Ⓒ $m + 3\frac{1}{4} = 6\frac{1}{2}$

 Ⓑ $6\frac{1}{2}m = 3\frac{1}{4}$ Ⓓ $m \div 3\frac{1}{4} = 6\frac{1}{2}$

38. The prices of 3 different bags of onions are given in the table below. Which size bag has the lowest price per pound?
 Ⓕ The 5-lb bag only
 Ⓖ The 5-lb bag and the 15-lb bag
 Ⓗ The 10-lb bag only
 Ⓙ The 15-lb bag only

Bag (lb)	Price
5	$3.49
10	$6.70
15	$10.33

GO for Help

For Exercises	See Lesson
39–41	4-9

Solve each inequality.

39. $6.3 \geq -7x$ 40. $-12 < \frac{m}{2}$ 41. $-10.2 \leq -0.2y$

What You'll Learn

To convert between fractions, decimals, and percents greater than 100% or less than 1%

Why Learn This?

You can get 110% of one day's Recommended Dietary Allowance of vitamin C by eating one half of a grapefruit.

In a percent, if the number compared to 100 is greater than 100, the percent is greater than 100%. If the number compared to 100 is less than 1, the percent is less than 1%.

You can rewrite these percents as decimals or fractions.

EXAMPLES **Rewriting Percents**

1 Write 110% as a decimal and as a fraction.

$110\% = 1.10$ ← **Move the decimal point two places to the left.**

$110\% = \frac{110}{100} = \frac{11}{10} = 1\frac{1}{10}$ ← **Use the definition of percent. Simplify the fraction.**

110% equals 1.10 in decimal form and $1\frac{1}{10}$ in fraction form.

2 Write 0.7% as a decimal and as a fraction in simplest form.

$0.7\% = 0.007$ ← **Move the decimal point two places to the left.**

$0.7\% = \frac{0.7}{100}$ ← **Use the definition of percent.**

$= \frac{0.7 \cdot 10}{100 \cdot 10} = \frac{7}{1,000}$ ← **Multiply numerator and denominator by 10 to get a whole number numerator. Simplify.**

0.7% equals 0.007 in decimal form and $\frac{7}{1,000}$ in fraction form.

Quick Check

1. Write 125% as a decimal and as a fraction.

2. Write 0.35% as a decimal and as a fraction in simplest form.

A mixed number represents a percent greater than 100%.

EXAMPLE Writing Mixed Numbers as Percents

3 **Entertainment** A movie ticket costs $1\frac{7}{8}$ times as much as renting a video. Write this mixed number as a percent.

$$1\frac{7}{8} = 1 \boxed{+} 7 \boxed{\div} 8 \boxed{=} 1.875 \quad \leftarrow \text{Use a calculator.}$$

$$= 1.87.5 = 187.5\% \quad \leftarrow \begin{array}{l}\text{Move the decimal point two} \\ \text{places to the right.}\end{array}$$

A movie ticket costs 187.5% of the cost of renting a video.

✓ Quick Check

3. You plan to run $2\frac{4}{5}$ times the distance you ran yesterday. Write this number as a percent.

A proper fraction represents a percent less than 100%.

EXAMPLE Application: Government

Test Prep Tip ◈◈◈◈

A fraction less than $\frac{1}{100}$ represents a percent less than 1%. You can use percents less than 1% to describe small numbers.

4 **Multiple Choice** West Virginia has 3 members in the U.S. House of Representatives. There are 432 other representatives who are not from West Virginia. What percent of the representatives are from West Virginia?

Ⓐ 70%   Ⓑ 7%   Ⓒ 0.7%   Ⓓ 0.007%

The total number of representatives is 432 + 3, or 435.

Estimate Round 435 to 400. 4 is close to 3. Then $\frac{4}{400} = 0.01$, or 1%.

$$\frac{\text{West Virginia representatives}}{\text{total number of representatives}} = \frac{3}{435} \quad \leftarrow \text{Write the fraction.}$$

$$= 0.0068965517 \quad \leftarrow \text{Use a calculator.}$$

$$\approx 0.7\% \quad \leftarrow \text{Write as a percent and round.}$$

About 0.7% of the representatives are from West Virginia. The correct answer is choice C.

Check for Reasonableness Since 0.7% is close to the estimate 1%, the answer is reasonable.

✓ Quick Check

4. Idaho has 2 members in the U.S. House of Representatives. What percent of the representatives are from Idaho? Round to the nearest hundredth of a percent.

Write each percent as a decimal and as a fraction in simplest form.

1. 150%

2. 0.2%

Write each decimal or fraction as a percent.

3. 8.25

4. $\frac{1}{160}$

5. **Mental Math** Write 400% as a whole number.

6. **Number Sense** Compare the numerator and denominator of a fraction that is greater than 100%.

7. How can you decide whether a decimal is less than 1%? More than 100%? Give an example for each case.

Homework Exercises

For more exercises, see Extra Skills and Word Problems.

GO for Help

For Exercises	See Examples
8–13	1
14–19	2
20–32	3–4

Write each percent as a decimal and as a fraction in simplest form.

8. 180%
9. 130%
10. 175%
11. 345%

12. 240%
13. 452%
14. 0.1%
15. 0.75%

16. 0.09%
17. 0.16%
18. 0.5%
19. 0.05%

Write each number as a percent to the nearest hundredth of a percent.

20. $4\frac{3}{4}$
21. $1\frac{3}{5}$
22. $1\frac{1}{100}$
23. $2\frac{29}{50}$

24. $3\frac{7}{20}$
25. $2\frac{3}{8}$
26. $\frac{5}{684}$
27. $\frac{2}{329}$

28. $\frac{7}{1,000}$
29. $\frac{1}{400}$
30. $\frac{3}{500}$
31. $\frac{7}{998}$

32. **Social Studies** About 4 of every 804 people in the world are citizens of Canada. Write this number as a percent. Round to the nearest hundredth of a percent.

33. **Guided Problem Solving** Interlibrary loans of reference books have increased to $1\frac{9}{10}$ of what they were 15 years ago. If a library loaned 100 books 15 years ago, how many would it loan today?
    • What is $1\frac{9}{10}$, written as a decimal?
    • How do you write a decimal as a percent?

34. **Geography** The world's total land area is about 57.9 million square miles. Luxembourg has an area of 999 square miles. What percent of the world's total land area does Luxembourg occupy?

Write each mixed number as a percent.

35. $2\frac{7}{10}$ **36.** $5\frac{6}{100}$ **37.** $10\frac{1}{100}$ **38.** $10\frac{3}{20}$

Write each percent as a decimal and as a fraction in simplest form.

39. Jewelry sales in December were 166% of sales in November.

40. Weather On March 1, the snowpack in the Northern Great Basin of Nevada was 126% of the average snowpack.

Model each percent using one or more 10 × 10 grids.

41. 175%   **42.** 120%   **43.** 200%   **44.** 0.5%

45. Science The number of known living species is about 1.7 million. About 4,500 species are mammals. What percent of known living species are mammals? Round to the nearest hundredth of a percent.

46. <u>Writing in Math</u> What does it mean to reach 120% of a savings goal?

Decide whether each percent is reasonable. Explain why or why not.

47. Buttermilk is 105% milk fat.

48. Rainfall in Oregon this year is reported to be 160% of the average.

49. A scientific study concluded that 0.5% of the seeds will not grow.

50. Challenge Recently, a near-mint copy of the Baltimore Orioles 1966 Yearbook was auctioned for $15. The yearbook cost $.50 in 1966. Write a ratio of the auction price to the original price. Find the percent.

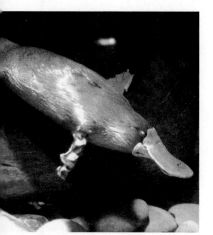

The male platypus has a poisonous spur to use against attackers.

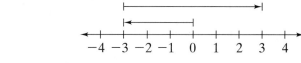
Test Prep and Mixed Review   **Practice**

Multiple Choice

51. The arctic and antarctic icecaps and glaciers make up about 2.3% of the world's water. Which fraction equals 2.3%?

    Ⓐ $\frac{23}{100}$ Ⓑ $\frac{1}{5}$ Ⓒ $\frac{23}{1,000}$ Ⓓ $\frac{23}{10,000}$

52. Which expression is represented by the model below?

    Ⓕ $-3 + 6$ Ⓖ $-3 + 3$ Ⓗ $6 - 3$ Ⓙ $3 + 3$

Write each percent as a fraction in simplest form.

For Exercises	See Lesson
53–56	6-2

53. 28%   **54.** 37.5%   **55.** 80%   **56.** 74%

Write each percent as a decimal and as a fraction in simplest form.

1. 45%

2. 135%

3. 0.98%

4. Write $\frac{14}{25}$ as a percent.

5. Order 0.245, $\frac{1}{6}$, 20%, and $\frac{1}{4}$ from least to greatest.

6. Write a ratio and a percent for the shaded area below.

7. Model 47% on a 10 × 10 grid.

8. One hour is what percent of one week? Round to the nearest tenth of a percent.

9. A club has 100 members. Five of the members are officers. Each officer gets six other members to help them decorate for a club party. What percent of the club members help decorate?

10. You walked to school on 135 days out of 180 days. What percent of the days did you walk? Round to the nearest tenth of a percent.

MATH GAMES

Order, Please!

What You'll Need

- 30 pieces of construction paper, each with a fraction, decimal, or a percent written on it. Include mixed numbers or the equivalent decimals and percents.

How To Play

- Select two teams of five players. Each player receives one piece of construction paper.
- When play begins, team members must order their numbers from the least to the greatest number.
- The first team to order their numbers correctly is the winner.

Using Percent Data in a Graph

You can use percent data in a graph to interpret and understand the information that is shown.

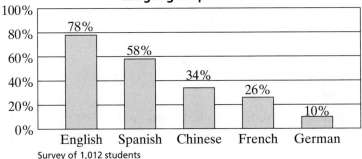

Languages Spoken at GIS

Survey of 1,012 students

The bar graph at the left shows which languages are spoken at Gould International School.

ACTIVITY

Work with a partner to analyze the graph and answer the following questions.

1. What language do most of the students speak?

2. How many students were surveyed?

3. Copy and complete the table at the right. Estimate the number of students who speak each language.

4. What language do about $\frac{1}{3}$ of the students speak?

5. What language do about $\frac{1}{4}$ of the students speak?

6. Why do you think the sum of the percents is greater than 100%?

Language	Percent	Number of Students
English	78%	■
Spanish	■	■
Chinese	■	■
French	■	■
German	10%	~101

Exercises

Based on the graph above, tell whether each of the following statements is reasonable. Explain.

1. More than half of the students at Gould speak English or Spanish.

2. Everyone who speaks French also speaks German.

3. Exactly 20 students speak English but not Spanish.

4. There could be a student at Gould International School who speaks all five languages shown in the bar graph.

 **Finding a Percent of a Number**

What You'll Learn

To find and estimate the percent of a number

Why Learn This?

You can use a percent of a number to help you analyze statistics, such as how many students in each grade participate in school activities.

Suppose your choir has 44 students, and 25% of the students are in eighth grade. Then 25% of 44 is the number of eighth-graders in the choir.

To find 25% of 44, you can write 25% as a decimal or as a fraction, and then multiply by 44.

EXAMPLE **Finding Percent of a Number**

1 Find 25% of 44.

Method 1 Write the percent as a decimal.

$25\% = 0.25$ ← Change 25% to an equivalent form. →

$0.25 \cdot 44 = 11$ ← Multiply. →

25% of 44 is 11.

Method 2 Write the percent as a fraction.

$25\% = \frac{1}{4}$

$\frac{1}{4} \cdot 44 = 11$

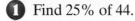
Quick Check

1. Find 75% of 140.

You can use mental math with some percents.

- 100% of a number is the number itself.   100% of 190 is 190.
- 50% of a number is $\frac{1}{2}$ of the number.   50% of 190 is 95.
- 10% of a number is 0.1 of the number.   10% of 190 is 19.
- 1% of a number is 0.01 of the number.   1% of 190 is 1.9.

EXAMPLE   **Using Mental Math**

2. Find 11% of 840.

What You Think

$11\% = 10\% + 1\%$.

10% of 840 is $0.1 \cdot 840$, or 84.

1% of 840 is $0.01 \cdot 840$, or 8.4.

So $84 + 8.4 = 92.4$.

Why It Works

$$11\% \text{ of } 840 = 0.11 \cdot 840 \quad \leftarrow \text{Write 11\% as a decimal.}$$
$$= (0.10 + 0.01) \cdot 840 \quad \leftarrow \text{Substitute } 0.10 + 0.01 \text{ for } 0.11.$$
$$= (0.10 \cdot 840) + (0.01 \cdot 840) \quad \leftarrow \text{Use the Distributive Property.}$$
$$= 84 + 8.4 \quad \leftarrow \text{Multiply.}$$
$$= 92.4 \quad \leftarrow \text{Add.}$$

✓ Quick Check

2. Use mental math to find 40% of 2,400.

For help with estimating using compatible numbers, go to Lesson 1-1, Example 3.

You can use compatible numbers to estimate a percent.

EXAMPLE   **Estimating a Percent**

3. **Elections** The candidate you voted for received 32% of the votes in an election. If 912 votes were counted, about how many votes did your candidate receive?

$$32\% \cdot 912 \quad \leftarrow \text{Write an expression.}$$
$$\downarrow \qquad \downarrow$$
$$\frac{1}{3} \cdot 900 = 300 \quad \leftarrow \text{Use compatible numbers such as } \frac{1}{3} \text{ and 900.}$$

Your candidate received about 300 votes.

✓ Quick Check

3. Estimate each answer.
   a. 24% of 238   **b.** 19% of 473   **c.** 82% of 747

Check Your Understanding

Use mental math, paper and pencil, or a calculator to find each answer.

1. 58% of 50   **2.** 8% of 400   **3.** 48% of 121   **4.** 10% of 70

Estimation Write an expression and estimate each answer.

5. 19% of 63   **6.** 73% of 80   **7.** 15% of 39

8. What is 12% of 100? What is *n*% of 100?

9. **Reasoning** When would you use a decimal to find a percent of a number? When would you use a fraction instead of a decimal?

Homework Exercises

For more exercises, see Extra Skills and Word Problems.

For Exercises	See Examples
10–18	1
19–27	2
28–34	3

Find each answer.

10. 6% of 90   **11.** 20% of 80   **12.** 27% of 120

13. 12% of 230   **14.** 75% of 240   **15.** 15% of 45

16. 3% of 12   **17.** 150% of 17   **18.** 7% of 300

Mental Math Find each answer using mental math.

19. 11% of 520   **20.** 9% of 780   **21.** 50% of 948

22. 40% of 216   **23.** 51% of 840   **24.** 100% of 194

25. 60% of 520   **26.** 49% of 150   **27.** 90% of 345

Estimate each answer.

28. 27% of 162   **29.** 33% of 88   **30.** 53% of 721

31. 19% of 399   **32.** 98% of 65   **33.** 73% of 522

34. There are 75 students at tryouts for the basketball team. Of this number, about 65% are in the seventh grade. About how many seventh-grade students are trying out for the team?

 **35.** **Guided Problem Solving** Of 90 coins in a piggy bank, 20% are quarters. What is the least possible amount of money in the bank?
- How many coins in the bank are quarters?
- What is the value of the coins that are quarters?
- What is the least possible value of the coins that are not quarters?

36. **Sales** The regular price of a calculator is $15.98. Today you can buy it on sale for 70% of the regular price. Estimate the sale price.

First estimate. Then check your estimate by finding the answer.

37. 66% of 243   **38.** 48% of 658   **39.** 13% of 326

40. A nurse earning an annual salary of $39,235 gets a 4% raise. What is the amount of the raise?

41. **Forestry** Russia had 17,000 forest fires in 2001. Aircraft put out 40% of the fires. How many of the fires were put out by aircraft?

42. You take a test with 25 questions on it. Your grade on the test is 84%. How many questions do you get right?

43. **Writing in Math** Is 3% of 96 the same value as 96% of 3? Explain.

44. **Data Analysis** At a high school, 150 students are surveyed about their electives.
  a. Find the percent of the students surveyed taking each elective.
  b. **Estimation** The school population is about 2,500. Estimate the number of students taking each elective.

What Elective Do You Take?

Elective	Number of Students
Ceramics	35
Typing	17
Cooking	68
Others	30

Number of Students: 0 10 20 30 40 50 60 70

45. **Challenge** The number of students in this year's class is 110% of the number in last year's class. If last year's class had 260 students, how many more students are in this year's class?

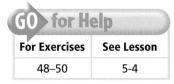

Test Prep and Mixed Review   **Practice**

Multiple Choice

46. At a sale, everything is 70% of the original price. Marc bought a jacket originally priced at $58.90 and a pair of jeans originally priced at $29.95. Which is the best estimate of the total cost?
  Ⓐ $30   Ⓑ $60   Ⓒ $90   Ⓓ $120

47. Which model best represents the expression $\frac{1}{2} \times \frac{2}{5}$?

   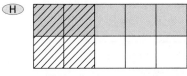

   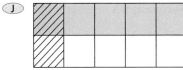

Algebra **Solve each proportion.**

48. $\frac{13}{39} = \frac{n}{60}$ **49.** $\frac{7}{15} = \frac{28}{m}$ **50.** $\frac{21}{x} = \frac{5}{8}$

GO **for Help**

For Exercises	See Lesson
48–50	5-4

6-5 Solving Percent Problems Using Proportions

What You'll Learn

To use proportions to solve problems involving percent

Why Learn This?

Survey and poll results are often reported using percents.

In a survey of 2,000 people in the United States, 204 said they are left-handed. You can use this information to find the percent of people who are left-handed.

You can use a model to help find this percent.

```
              part           whole
               ↓               ↓
Number  0    204            2,000
        ▭▬▬▬▭▭▭▭▭▭▭▭▭▭▭▭▭▭▭▭▭
Percent 0%  n%              100%
```

$\dfrac{204}{2,000} = \dfrac{n}{100}$ ← The part, 204, corresponds to n in the model.
← The whole, 2,000, corresponds to 100.

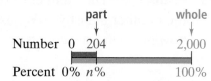 **EXAMPLE** **Finding a Percent**

1 What percent of 2,000 is 204?

Using the model above, you can write and solve a proportion.

$\dfrac{204}{2,000} = \dfrac{n}{100}$ ← Write a proportion.

$2000n = 204(100)$ ← Write cross products.

$\dfrac{2,000n}{2,000} = \dfrac{204(100)}{2,000}$ ← Divide each side by 2,000.

$n = 10.2$ ← Simplify.

204 is 10.2% of 2,000.

✓ Quick Check

1. What percent of 92 is 23?

EXAMPLES **Finding a Part and the Whole**

2 20% of 55 is what number?

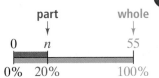

part   whole
↓   ↓
0   n 55
━━━━┿━━━━━━━━━
0%   20%   100%

$$\frac{n}{55} = \frac{20}{100}$$ ← **Write a proportion.**

$$\frac{n}{55} = \frac{1}{5}$$ ← **Simplify the fraction.**

$$\frac{n}{55} = \frac{1}{5}$$ ← **Use the common multiplier, 11.**
(×11)

$$n = 11$$ ← **Simplify.**

11 is 20% of 55.

3 **Budgets** Suppose your entertainment budget is 30% of your weekly wages from a job. You plan to spend $10.50 on a movie night. How much will you need to earn at your job in order to stay within your budget?

part   whole
↓   ↓
0   $10.50 n
━━━━┿━━━━━━━━━
0%   30%   100%

$$\frac{10.50}{n} = \frac{30}{100}$$ ← **Write a proportion.**

$$30n = 10.50(100)$$ ← **Write cross products.**

$$\frac{30n}{30} = \frac{10.50(100)}{30}$$ ← **Divide.**

$$n = 35$$ ← **Simplify.**

You need to earn $35 to stay within your budget.

✓ Quick Check

2. 85% of 20 is what number?

3. Your math teacher assigns 25 problems for homework. You have done 60% of them. How many problems have you done?

KEY CONCEPTS **Percents and Proportions**

Finding a Percent	**Finding a Part**	**Finding a Whole**
What percent of 25 is 5?	What is 20% of 25?	20% of what is 5?

Finding a Percent:
0   5   25
━━┿━━━━━━━━
0% n%   100%

$$\frac{5}{25} = \frac{n}{100}$$
$$n = 20$$

20% of 25 is 5.

Finding a Part:
0   n 25
━━┿━━━━━━━━
0% 20%   100%

$$\frac{n}{25} = \frac{20}{100}$$
$$n = 5$$

5 is 20% of 25.

Finding a Whole:
0   5 n
━━┿━━━━━━━━
0% 20%   100%

$$\frac{5}{n} = \frac{20}{100}$$
$$n = 25$$

20% of 25 is 5.

Tell whether the answer to the question is a *percent*, a *part*, or a *whole*. Then answer the question.

1. What percent of 200 is 50?

2. 12 is 80% of what?

3. 50% of what number is 8?

4. What is 30% of 90?

Match each question with the proportion you could use to answer it.

5. What is 40% of 15?

6. 15 is what percent of 40?

7. 40% of what number is 15?

A. $\dfrac{15}{40} = \dfrac{n}{100}$

B. $\dfrac{15}{n} = \dfrac{40}{100}$

C. $\dfrac{n}{15} = \dfrac{40}{100}$

Homework Exercises

For more exercises, see Extra Skills and Word Problems.

GO for Help

For Exercises	See Examples
8–13	1
14–19	2
20–24	3

Use a proportion to find the percent.

8. 24 is what percent of 32?

9. What percent of 230 is 23?

10. What percent of 25 is 23?

11. 8 is what percent of 400?

12. What percent of 600 is 84?

13. 21 is what percent of 168?

Use a proportion to find the part.

14. What is 4% of 350?

15. 1% of 500 is what number?

16. What number is 62% of 50?

17. 15% of 15 is what number?

18. 40% of 25 is what number?

19. What is 37.5% of 8?

Test Prep Tip ⊘⊙⊙⊙

You can use a model to help you solve percent problems.

Use a proportion to find the whole.

20. 36 is 72% of what number?

21. 80% of what number is 15?

22. 21 is 84% of what number?

23. 28 is 35% of what number?

24. A sweater is on sale for $33. This is 75% of the original price. Find the original price.

25. **Guided Problem Solving** In a market, 44 of the 80 types of vegetables are grown locally. What percent of the vegetables are grown locally?
    • Identify the part. Identify the whole.
    • Complete and solve the proportion: $\dfrac{\blacksquare}{\blacksquare} = \dfrac{\blacksquare}{100}$.

26. A school holds classes from 8:00 A.M. to 2:00 P.M. For what percent of a 24-hour day does this school hold classes?

Write a proportion for each model. Solve for *n*.

27.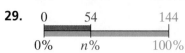

28.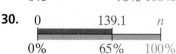

29.
0	54	144
0%	*n*%	100%

30.
0	139.1	*n*
0%	65%	100%

31. **Music** In a school band of 24 students, 9 students play brass instruments. What percent of the members play brass instruments?

32. You purchase a telescope in a state with a 5% sales tax. You pay $14.85 in tax. Estimate the price of the telescope.

33. **Open-Ended** Write a percent problem that compares the number of boys to the number of girls in your class.

34. At the library, you find 9 books on a certain topic. The librarian tells you that 55% of the books on this topic have been signed out. How many books does the library have on the topic?

35. **Writing in Math** A proportion that models a percent problem has four numbers. One of the numbers is always the same. Explain why.

36. **Challenge** A car dealer advertises "All cars 19% off sticker price!" A buyer pays $15,930.95 for a car. Estimate the sticker price.

Test Prep and Mixed Review   **Practice**

Multiple Choice

37. Out of 45 students, 29 go on a field trip. Which best represents the percent of the students who do NOT go on the trip?
    Ⓐ 16%   Ⓑ 36%   Ⓒ 64%   Ⓓ 84%

38. In 2001, 56.5% of households in the United States had a computer. Which expression provides the best estimate for the number of households with computers in a survey of 621 households in 2001?
    Ⓕ 60% of 650   Ⓗ 60% of 600
    Ⓖ 50% of 600   Ⓙ 50% of 650

39. The model below represents $4n + 6 = 18$. What is the value of *n*?

    | *n* | *n* | *n* | *n* |

    Ⓐ $n = 24$ Ⓑ $n = 6$ Ⓒ $n = 3$ Ⓓ $n = -3$

For Exercises	See Lesson
40–43	2-3

Write each fraction in simplest form.

40. $\dfrac{8}{10}$ 41. $\dfrac{4}{12}$ 42. $\dfrac{5}{100}$ 43. $\dfrac{16}{24}$

6-6 Solving Percent Problems Using Equations

Check Skills You'll Need

1. Vocabulary Review
State the *Division Property of Equality.*

Solve each equation.

2. $3n = 51$

3. $\frac{x}{4} = 12$

 **for Help**
Lesson 4-4

Video Tutor Help

Visit: PHSchool.com
Web Code: are-0775

What You'll Learn

To use equations to solve problems involving percent

Why Learn This?

Suppose a ski resort reports that 60% of its trails are open. If you know how many trails are open, you can solve an equation to find the total number of trails in the park.

You can translate percent problems into equations to find parts, wholes, or percents.

EXAMPLE Finding a Whole

1 **Multiple Choice** A ski resort in New Hampshire begins the season with 60% of its trails open. There are 27 trails open. How many trails does the ski resort have?

Ⓐ 5 Ⓑ 16 Ⓒ 22 Ⓓ 45

Words 60% of the number of trails is 27

Let x = the number of trails at this ski resort.

Equation 0.60 · x = 27

$$0.60x = 27 \qquad \leftarrow \textbf{Write the equation.}$$
$$\frac{0.60x}{0.60} = \frac{27}{0.60} \qquad \leftarrow \textbf{Divide each side by 0.60.}$$
$$x = 45 \qquad \leftarrow \textbf{Simplify.}$$

The ski resort has 45 trails. The correct answer is choice D.

✓ Quick Check

1. A plane flies with 54% of its seats empty. If 81 seats are empty, what is the total number of seats on the plane?

You can use an equation to find a whole, a part, or a percent.

EXAMPLE Finding a Part

Test Prep Tip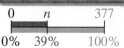

0   n   377

0%   39%   100%

Remember that you can draw a model to help you. This model shows that n is 39% of 377.

② What number is 39% of 377?

Words   A number is 39% of 377

⬇

Let n = the number.

Equation n = 0.39 · 377

$n = 0.39 \cdot 377 = 147.03$ ← Simplify.

✅ Quick Check

● **2.** 27% of 60 is what number?

EXAMPLE Finding a Percent

③ **Recreation** Of 3,072 teens surveyed, 2,212 say they read for fun. What percent of the teens surveyed say they read for fun?

Estimate About 2,000 of 3,000 teens read for fun.

$\frac{2,000}{3,000} = \frac{2}{3} \approx 0.67 = 67\%$

$3,072p = 2,212$ ← Write an equation. Let p = the percent of teens who read for fun.

$\frac{3,072p}{3,072} = \frac{2,212}{3,072}$ ← Divide each side by 3,072.

$p \approx 0.7200520833$ ← Use a calculator.

$p \approx 72\%$ ← Write the decimal as a percent.

About 72% of the teens surveyed say they read for fun.

Check for Reasonableness 72% is close to the estimate 67%.

✅ Quick Check

● **3.** It rained 75 days last year. About what percent of the year was rainy?

KEY CONCEPTS   Percents and Equations

Finding a Percent	**Finding a Part**	**Finding a Whole**
What percent of 25 is 5?	What is 20% of 25?	20% of what is 5?
$n \cdot 25 = 5$	$n = 0.2 \cdot 25$	$0.2 \cdot n = 5$
$n = 0.2$	$n = 5$	$n = 25$
5 is 20% of 25.	5 is 20% of 25.	20% of 25 is 5.

Check Your Understanding

1. Do the following questions mean the same thing? Explain. *What is 20% of 40? 20 is what percent of 40? 20 is 40% of what number?*

Match each question with the equation you could use to answer it.

2. What is 16% of 200?

3. 16 is what percent of 200?

4. 16% of what number is 200?

A. $0.16n = 200$
B. $n = 0.16(200)$
C. $16 = 200n$

Write an equation for each question. Then answer the question.

5. What percent of 625 is 500?

6. What number is 5% of 520?

Homework Exercises

For more exercises, see Extra Skills and Word Problems.

GO for Help

For Exercises	See Examples
7–11	1
12–15	2
16–20	3

Use an equation to find the whole.

7. 96% of what number is 24?

8. 40% of what number is 30?

9. 50.4 is 36% of what number?

10. 12.8 is 32% of what number?

11. You answered 22 questions correctly and scored 88% on a test. How many questions were on the test in all?

Use an equation to find a part.

12. 18% of 90 is what number?

13. What number is 41% of 800?

14. What number is 56% of 48?

15. 70% of 279 is what number?

Use an equation to find the percent.

16. What percent of 496 is 124?

17. 18 is what percent of 48?

18. 39 is what percent of 260?

19. What percent of 620 is 372?

20. A sports team has won 21 out of the 40 games it has played. About what percent of the games has the team won?

21. **Guided Problem Solving** Suppose 24% of a 1,500-Calorie diet is from protein. How many Calories are *not* from protein?
    - **Make a Plan** Find the number of Calories that are from protein. Subtract that number from the daily total number of Calories.
    - **Carry Out the Plan** 24% of 1,500 is ■. Subtract ■ from 1,500.

22. A water tank containing 496 gallons is 62% full. How many more gallons are needed to fill the tank?

Use the table at the right. Find the percent of days in a 365-day year that are school days in each country. Round to the nearest percent.

23. China   **24.** Israel   **25.** Russia

26. Scotland   **27.** United States

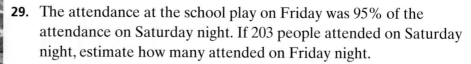

Length of School Year

Country	Days
China	251
Israel	215
Russia	210
Scotland	200
United States	180

Source: *The Top 10 of Everything*

28. Food You make 72 cookies for a bake sale. This is 20% of the cookies at the bake sale. How many cookies are at the bake sale?

29. The attendance at the school play on Friday was 95% of the attendance on Saturday night. If 203 people attended on Saturday night, estimate how many attended on Friday night.

30. Writing in Math If 25% of a number is 45, is the number greater than or less than 45? If 150% of a number is 45, is the number greater than or less than 45? Explain how you can tell.

31. Of the 60 members of a choir, 30% sing alto and 45% sing soprano. How many members of the choir sing alto or soprano?

32. Challenge You plant 40 pots with seedlings. Eight of the pots contain tomato plants. What percent of your seedlings are *not* tomato plants?

Test Prep and Mixed Review
Practice

Multiple Choice

33. About 12% of an iceberg's mass is above water. If the mass above water is 9,000,000 kg, what is the mass of the entire iceberg?
- Ⓐ 108,000 kg
- Ⓑ 1,080,000 kg
- Ⓒ 75,000,000 kg
- Ⓓ 120,000,000 kg

34. On average, a group of 25 college students contains 14 females. Which equation can be used to find x, the percent of females in a typical group of college students?
- Ⓕ $\frac{x}{100} = \frac{14}{25}$
- Ⓖ $\frac{x}{25} = \frac{14}{100}$
- Ⓗ $\frac{x}{25} = \frac{14}{39}$
- Ⓙ $\frac{x}{14} = \frac{25}{100}$

35. The model at the right represents which expression?
- Ⓐ $\frac{1}{5} \times \frac{3}{5}$
- Ⓑ $\frac{1}{3} \times \frac{3}{5}$
- Ⓒ $\frac{1}{2} \times \frac{3}{5}$
- Ⓓ $\frac{2}{3} \times \frac{7}{10}$

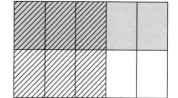

GO **for Help**

For Exercises	See Lesson
36–39	5-3

Determine whether the ratios in each pair can form a proportion.

36. $\frac{4}{12}, \frac{140}{360}$ **37.** $\frac{7}{9}, \frac{35}{45}$ **38.** $\frac{12}{28}, \frac{3}{7}$ **39.** $\frac{45}{60}, \frac{3}{4}$

Solving Percent Problems

Braces are cool! A recent survey of 406 mothers by the American Association of Orthodontists reported that 69% felt that wearing braces makes their children feel cool. If each mother had only one child with braces, how many children would that be?

What You Might Think

What do I know?

What am I trying to find out?

How do I show the main idea?

How can I estimate the answer?

How do I solve the problem?

Is the answer reasonable?

What You Might Write

69% of 406 mothers said their children felt cool. Each mother had 1 child, so that's 69% of 406 children.

The number of children who felt cool.

Make a diagram.

Number of Mothers

0 n 406

0%   50%   69%   100%

69% is close to 75%, which is $\frac{3}{4}$.

406 is close to 400.

$\frac{3}{4}$ and 400 are compatible; $\frac{3}{4}$ of 400 is 300.

69% is 0.69.

$0.69 \times 406 = n$

$280.14 = n$

280.14 can be rounded to 280.

280 is close to the estimate of 300. The answer is reasonable.

Think It Through

1. What percent of 406 mothers did not say their children "felt cool?" How many children is that?

2. How does the diagram above help show the main idea?

Exercises

For Exercises 3 and 4, answer the questions first, and then solve the problem.

3. A solo guitarist received a royalty payment of 9% based on the sales of her CD. If she received a check for $5,238, what were the total sales of her CD?
   a. What do you know?
   b. What do you want to find out?
   c. How can the diagram below help you write an equation?

   $0 $5,238   *n*
   0% 9%   50%   100%

4. The human body is about 67% water. A student weighs 130 pounds. How much of his weight is water?
   a. What do you know?
   b. What do you want to find out?
   c. What diagram would help you show the main idea?

5. Teenagers were asked how many hours per week they worked. The data are shown below. Assume they were paid $5.50 per hour. About how much per week would the largest category of students make? The second-largest?

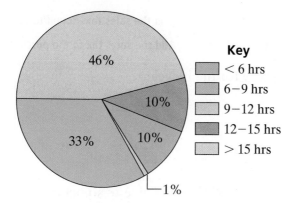

Key
- < 6 hrs
- 6−9 hrs
- 9−12 hrs
- 12−15 hrs
- > 15 hrs

46%
33%
10%
10%
1%

6. When water freezes, its volume increases by 9%. If you freeze one gallon of water to make ice for a party, how many cubic inches of ice will you have? (*Hint*: 1 gallon = 231 in.^{3})

7. Research says that humans learn through listening 11% of the time and through observing 83% of the time. In a 50-minute math class, how much of the time would you be learning by listening? By observing?

6-7 Applications of Percent

 **Check Skills You'll Need**

1. Vocabulary Review
To write a *percent* as a decimal, move the decimal point two places to the __?__.

Write each percent as a decimal.

2. 6.5% **3.** 4.25%

4. 15% **5.** 20%

 **for Help**
Lesson 6-2

What You'll Learn

To find and estimate solutions to application problems involving percent

🔊 **New Vocabulary** commission

Why Learn This?

You use percents to calculate taxes, tips, and commissions.

In many states, you must pay a sales tax on items you buy. The sales tax is a percent of the purchase price. A tax percent is also called a tax rate.

To find sales tax, you can use the formula
sales tax = tax rate · purchase price.

EXAMPLE **Finding Sales Tax**

1 **Shopping** The price of a bicycle you plan to buy is $159.99. The sales tax rate is 6%. How much will you pay for the bicycle?

$0.06 \cdot 159.99 \approx 9.60$ ← **Find the sales tax. Round to the nearest cent.**

$159.99 + 9.60 = 169.59$ ← **Add the sales tax to the purchase price.**

You will pay $169.59 for the bicycle.

✔ **Quick Check**

1. Find the total cost for a purchase of $185 if the sales tax rate is 5.5%.

A tip is a percent of a bill that you give to someone who provides a service. You can use estimation and mental math to find a 15% tip.

Step 1 Round the bill to the nearest dollar.

Step 2 Find 10% of the bill by moving the decimal point one place to the left.

Step 3 Find 5% of the bill by taking one half of the result of Step 2.

Step 4 Add the amounts of Step 2 and Step 3 together to find 15%.

EXAMPLE Estimating a Tip

2 Your family takes a taxi to the train station. The taxi fare is $17.85. Estimate a 15% tip to give the driver.

$$17.85 \approx 18 \quad \leftarrow \textbf{Round to the nearest dollar.}$$

$$0.1 \cdot 18 = 1.8 \quad \leftarrow \textbf{Find 10\% of the bill.}$$

$$\frac{1}{2} \cdot 1.8 = 0.9 \quad \leftarrow \textbf{Find 5\% of the bill. 5\% is } \frac{1}{2} \textbf{ of the 10\% amount.}$$

$$1.8 + 0.9 = 2.7 \quad \leftarrow \textbf{Add the 10\% and 5\% amounts to get 15\%.}$$

For a $17.85 taxi fare, a 15% tip is about $2.70.

✅ Quick Check

2. Estimate a 15% tip for each amount.
   a. $58.20   b. $61.80   c. $49.75

Some sales jobs pay you a **commission**, a percent of the amount of your sales. To find a commission, use *commission = commission rate · sales.*

EXAMPLES Finding a Commission

3 Find the commission on a $500 sale with a commission rate of 12.5%.

$$0.125 \cdot 500 = 62.5 \quad \leftarrow \textbf{Write 12.5\% as 0.125 and multiply.}$$

The commission on the sale is $62.50.

Video Tutor Help

Visit: PHSchool.com
Web Code: are-0775

4 A sales agent earns a weekly salary of $650, plus a commission of 4% on all sales. His sales this week are $1,250. How much does he earn?

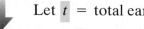

Words total earnings = salary + commission

Let t = total earnings.

Equation t =   650   +   0.04 · 1,250

$$t = 650 + 0.04 \cdot 1{,}250 \quad \leftarrow \textbf{Write the equation.}$$
$$= 650 + 50 \quad \leftarrow \textbf{Multiply.}$$
$$= 700 \quad \leftarrow \textbf{Simplify.}$$

The sales agent earns $700 this week.

✅ Quick Check

3. Find the commission on a $3,200 sale with a commission rate of 6%.

4. Suppose you earn a weekly salary of $800 plus a commission of 3.5% on all sales. Find your earnings for a week with total sales of $1,400.

1. **Vocabulary** What does it mean to earn an 8% commission?

2. **Number Sense** Is 4% sales tax on a $250 item *greater than, less than,* or *equal to* 4% commission on a $250 sale?

3. **Mental Math** Calculate a 15% tip on a restaurant bill of $24.

Find the sales tax for each item. The tax rate is 6%.

4. a CD priced at $12.99   5. a $450 TV

Find each commission, given the sale.

6. 5% on a $900 sale   7. 2% on a $35.50 sale

Homework Exercises

For more exercises, see Extra Skills and Word Problems.

GO for Help

For Exercises	See Examples
8–10	1
11–14	2
15–19	3–4

Find the total cost.

8. $35.99 with a 5% sales tax   9. $72.75 with a 6% sales tax

10. The price of a coat is $114 before sales tax. The sales tax is 7%. Find the total cost of the coat.

Estimate a 15% tip for each amount.

11. $68.50   12. $30.80   13. $9.89   14. $27.59

Find each commission, given the sale and the commission rate.

15. $800, 12%   16. $2,500, 8%   17. $2,000, 7.5%   18. $600, 4.5%

19. Suppose your boss owes you $800, plus a commission of 2.5% on a sale of $1,000. How much does your boss owe you?

20. **Guided Problem Solving** Your lunch bill is $19.75. A 5% sales tax will be added, and you want to give a tip of about 20% of $19.75. Estimate how much you will pay for lunch.
    • To what number should you round the bill?
    • About how much tip should you give?

21. Your neighbor pays $40 to have her lawn mowed and always adds a 15% tip. You and your friend decide to mow the lawn together and split the earnings evenly. How much will each of you make?

GO Online

Homework Video Tutor
Visit: PHSchool.com
Web Code: are-0607

22. **Writing in Math** Explain how you can use estimation and mental math to calculate a 20% tip.

23. A purchase costs $25.79 with a tax of $1.29. Find the sales tax rate.

24. **Art** For a craft project, you select the four packages of modeling clay and the set of tools shown at the right. If there is a 6% sales tax, what is the total cost?

$2.79 ea. plus tax

$1.79 plus tax

25. A real estate agent earns a weekly salary of $200. This week, the agent sold a home for $120,000 and was paid a 5.5% commission. Find the agent's earnings for the week.

26. **Sales** A store pays a 6% commission on the first $500 in sales and 8% on sales over $500. Find the commission on an $800 sale.

27. **Open-Ended** If your employer gave you a choice between earning a fixed salary and earning a commission based on your sales, how would you choose? Explain your reasoning and give an example.

28. **Challenge** Find the commission rate if the total earnings are $970, including a salary of $350 and a commission on sales of $12,400.

Test Prep and Mixed Review **Practice**

Multiple Choice

29. Laundry workers can expect a tip between 15% and 20%. Which is closest to the amount Diane should offer in order to give the minimum tip for a laundry service of $11.50?
    Ⓐ $4.00   Ⓑ $2.50   Ⓒ $2.00   Ⓓ $1.75

30. A surveyor drew this diagram to find the distance across a small lake. If $\triangle RSV$ is similar to $\triangle UST$, what is the width w?
    Ⓕ 44 m   Ⓗ 41.25 m
    Ⓖ 21.8 m   Ⓙ 11.7 m

U, w, T, 30 m, S, V, 16 m, 22 m, R

31. Raul bought 3 posters for $2.59 each and 2 posters for $1.98 each. He paid 59 cents tax. What other information is necessary to find Raul's correct change?
    Ⓐ The amount of money Raul gave the cashier
    Ⓑ Whether the posters were on sale
    Ⓒ The total amount of money Raul spent
    Ⓓ How Raul got to the store

For Exercises	See Lesson
32–33	5-2

Write each unit rate.

32. 408 mi on 12 gal of gasoline   33. $16.45 for 7 lb of fish

Percent Equations

When you have a multiple-choice question with an equation using percent, you can quickly eliminate some of the choices. Use benchmark numbers for percents to help you. Here are some benchmarks:

EXAMPLE

Which statement is true for $49\% \times x = 30$? Explain.

(A) $x \approx 30$ (B) x is negative.   (C) $x < 60$ (D) $x > 30$

Choice A is not true.   ← 49% is about $\frac{1}{2}$ and $\frac{1}{2}$ of 30 is 15. So $x \approx 30$ isn't close.

Choice B is not true.   ← That would make the left side a negative number.

Choice C is not true.   ← 49% is a little less than $\frac{1}{2}$, and $\frac{1}{2}$ of 60 is 30.

Choice D is true.   ← x must be big enough that half of it is 30. x must be about twice 30.

The correct answer is choice D.

Exercises

Reasoning Which choice is true for the equation? Use benchmark numbers to explain. Check each answer choice. Do not compute.

1. $31\% \times x = 23.1$
   (A) $x < 23.1$ (B) $x < 100$ (C) $x \approx 90$ (D) $x \approx \frac{2}{3}$

2. $90 \times x\% = 8.9$
   (F) $x \approx 10$ (G) $x > 30$ (H) $x \approx 50$ (J) $x > 10$

3. $251 \div 500 = x\%$
   (A) $x < 0$ (B) $x \approx 50$ (C) $x \approx 2$ (D) $x < 45$

Write three statements about the variable for each equation. Make some statements true and some false. Circle the ones that are true.

4. $26\% \times x = 101$ **5.** $500 \div 1007 = x\%$ **6.** $20 \times x\% = 10.5$

Find each answer using a proportion.

1. 35 is what percent of 60?　　2. 14.4 is 90% of what number?　3. What percent of 75 is 63?

Find each answer using an equation.

4. What percent of 120 is 54?　　5. What is 72% of 95?　　　6. What is 120% of 185?

Find the price of each item.

7. originally $299; 5% markup　8. originally $97; 15% discount　9. price $32.79; 8.25% tax

10. **Sales** Find the commission for a rate of 5.5% and $1,400 in sales.

6-8a　Activity Lab

Data Analysis

Exploring Percent of Change

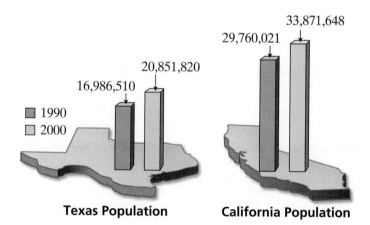

Texas Population　　　California Population

Use the graph above to complete the following exercises.

1. Find the population change from 1990 to 2000 for each state.

2. Which state had the greater change in population?

3. For each state, write the ratio $\frac{\text{change in population}}{\text{1990 population}}$. Write each as a percent.

4. Which state had the greater population change in terms of percent?

5. **Reasoning** Why are your answers to 2 and 4 above different?

309

6-8 Finding Percent of Change

Check Skills You'll Need

1. **Vocabulary Review** What are the *cross products* in the proportion $\frac{5}{16} = \frac{n}{100}$?

Solve each proportion.

2. $\frac{2}{20} = \frac{n}{100}$

3. $\frac{1}{8} = \frac{n}{100}$

4. $\frac{6.5}{13} = \frac{n}{100}$

GO for Help

Lesson 5-4

What You'll Learn

To find percents of increase and percents of decrease

◀)) **New Vocabulary** percent of change, markup, discount

Why Learn This?

You can use percent of change to describe how much an amount increases or decreases over time. For example, every 10 years, the number of U.S. representatives for a state may change, based on the change in the state's population.

A **percent of change** is the percent a quantity increases or decreases from its original amount. Use a proportion to find a percent of change.

$$\frac{\text{amount of change}}{\text{original amount}} = \frac{\text{percent of change}}{100}$$

EXAMPLE Finding a Percent of Increase

1 **Government** North Carolina had 12 seats in the U.S. House of Representatives in the 1990s. After the 2000 census, North Carolina had 13 seats. Find the percent of increase in the number of representatives.

$13 - 12 = 1$ ← Find the amount of change.

$\frac{1}{12} = \frac{n}{100}$ ← Write a proportion. Let n = percent of change.

$100 \cdot \frac{1}{12} = \frac{n}{100} \cdot 100$ ← Multiply each side by 100.

$\frac{100}{12} = n$ ← Simplify.

$8.3 \approx n$ ← Divide.

The number of North Carolina representatives increased by about 8%.

Quick Check

1. In 2000, California went from 52 to 53 representatives. Find the percent of increase in the number of representatives.

To make a profit, stores charge more for items than they pay for them. The difference between the selling price and the store's cost of an item is called the **markup.** The percent of markup is a percent of increase.

$$\frac{\text{amount of markup}}{\text{original cost}} = \frac{\text{percent of markup}}{100}$$

EXAMPLE Finding a Percent of Markup

2 An electronics store orders sets of walkie-talkies for $14.85 each. The store sells each set for $19.90. What is the percent of markup?

$19.90 - 14.85 = 5.05$ ← Find the amount of markup.

$\dfrac{5.05}{14.85} = \dfrac{n}{100}$ ← Write a proportion. Let *n* be the percent of markup.

$14.85n = 5.05(100)$ ← Write cross products.

$\dfrac{14.85n}{14.85} = \dfrac{5.05(100)}{14.85}$ ← Divide each side by 14.85.

$n \approx 34$ ← Simplify.

The percent of markup is about 34%.

Quick Check

2. Find the percent of markup for a $17.95 headset marked up to $35.79.

The difference between the original price and the sale price of an item is called a **discount.** The percent of discount is a percent of decrease.

$$\frac{\text{amount of discount}}{\text{original cost}} = \frac{\text{percent of discount}}{100}$$

EXAMPLE Finding a Percent of Discount

Test Prep Tip ●●●●

Before you find the percent of change, decide whether the change is an increase or a decrease.

3 **Music** During a clearance sale, a keyboard that normally sells for $49.99 is discounted to $34.99. What is the percent of discount?

$49.99 - 34.99 = 15.00$ ← Find the amount of discount.

$\dfrac{15}{49.99} = \dfrac{n}{100}$ ← Write a proportion. Let *n* be the percent of discount.

$49.99n = 15(100)$ ← Write cross products.

$\dfrac{49.99n}{49.99} = \dfrac{15(100)}{49.99}$ ← Divide each side by 49.99.

$n \approx 30$ ← Simplify.

The percent of discount for the keyboard is about 30%.

Quick Check

3. Find the percent of discount of a $24.95 novel on sale for $14.97.

More Than One Way

A jacket goes on sale with a discount of 40% off the original price. The original price of the jacket is $42.95. What is the sale price of the jacket?

Anna's Method

I can find the amount of the discount by multiplying $42.95 by 40%. Then I will subtract the discount from the original price.

$42.95 \cdot 0.40 = 17.18$ ← **Find the amount of the discount.**

$42.95 - 17.18 = 25.77$ ← **Subtract the discount from the original price.**

The sale price of the jacket is $25.77.

Chris's Method

The jacket is discounted by 40%, so I will pay 60% of the original price. I can multiply the original price of $42.95 by the percent I need to pay.

$42.95 \cdot 0.60 = 25.77$ ← **Find the discounted price.**

The sale price of the jacket is $25.77.

Choose a Method
You get a discount of 20% on a $27.50 ticket. How much will your ticket cost? Describe your method and explain why it is appropriate.

Check Your Understanding

1. **Vocabulary** How are percent of markup and percent of discount similar? How are they different?

2. **Number Sense** Is it possible for a markup to be 200%? Give an example and explain.

Write the proportion to find percent of change.

3. $35 to $50

4. 98 to 72

5. 748 to 374

Matching Match each situation with the correct percent of change.

6. Boots first priced at $110 go on sale for $88.

7. A radio costs a store $88 but sells for $110.

A. 25% markup

B. 20% discount

For more exercises, see **Extra Skills and Word Problems.**

GO for Help	
For Exercises	**See Examples**
8–16	1
17–21	2
22–26	3

Find each percent of increase. Round to the nearest percent.

8. 60 to 75 **9.** 88 to 99 **10.** 135 to 200 **11.** 12 to 18

12. 2 to 7 **13.** 12 to 63 **14.** 120 to 240 **15.** 15 to 35

16. Business A worker earning $5.15/h receives a raise. She now earns $6/h. Find the percent of increase in her hourly rate of pay.

Find each percent of markup. Round to the nearest percent.

17. $22 marked up to $33 **18.** $15 marked up to $60

19. $13.50 marked up to $25 **20.** $40 marked up to $59.75

21. Clothing Find the percent of markup for a shirt that a store buys for $3.25 and sells for $7.50.

Find each percent of discount. Round to the nearest percent.

22. $70 discounted to $63 **23.** $9 discounted to $4

24. $10 discounted to $7 **25.** $480 discounted to $300

26. Crafts A package of poster board usually sells for $8.40. This week the package is on sale for $6.30. What is the percent of discount?

27. Guided Problem Solving The annual precipitation for a city dropped from 65 cm to 47 cm over the course of 5 years. What is the average percent of change in the amount of precipitation for 1 year?
- What was the amount of change in the precipitation over 5 years?
- What was the percent of change over 5 years?

28. A scientist earning an annual salary of $49,839 gets a 4% raise. Estimate the new annual salary for this scientist.

29. Sports A football player gained 1,200 yd last season and 900 yd this season. Find the percent of change. State whether the change is an increase or a decrease.

30. Error Analysis The number of students enrolled in a school has increased from 1,938 to 2,128. A student calculates the percent of increase. His work is shown at right. Explain the student's mistake.

$$2{,}128 - 1{,}938 = 190$$
$$190 \div 2{,}128 \approx 0.089$$
$$0.089 = 8.9\%$$

31. Writing in Math Describe how you can find the percent of change in the number of students in your school from last year to this year.

Careers Scientists develop vaccines and treatments.

Find the price of each item.

32. originally $35.75; 65% markup   33. originally $82; 35% discount

34. **Choose a Method** A TV goes on sale with a discount of 28%. The original price of the TV is $942. What is the sale price of the TV?

35. **Business** A toy store opened five years ago. The owner uses a computer to track sales. She uses a program that prints @@@ in some cells instead of numbers. Copy and complete the spreadsheet.

	A	B	C	D	
1	Year	Sales ($)	Change From Last Year ($)	Change From Last Year (%)	
2	1	200,000	(not open last year)	(not open last year)	
3	2	240,000	40,000	@@@	
4	3	300,000	@@@	@@@	
5	4	330,000	@@@	@@@	

36. **Challenge** A storeowner buys a case of 144 pens for $28.80. Tax and shipping cost an additional $8.64. He sells the pens for $.59 each. What is the markup per pen? What is the percent of markup?

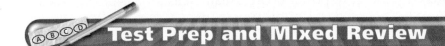

Test Prep and Mixed Review   **Practice**

Multiple Choice

37. Which of the following represents the least percent of change?
    Ⓐ A child grew from 40 inches to 46 inches in one year.
    Ⓑ Internet service costs increased from $21 to $25 per month.
    Ⓒ An after-school program enrollment was 72 and is now 84.
    Ⓓ A child's weekly allowance is changed from $5 to $6.

38. Mr. Chun earns a salary of $150 a week plus 8% commission on all sales. How much will he earn if his sales in one week are $2,990?
    Ⓕ $3,002   Ⓖ $389.20   Ⓗ $251.20   Ⓙ $239.20

39. Julie took a taxi from school to her home. The taxi rate started at $2.00 and then $0.50 was added for every $\frac{1}{4}$ mile traveled. What information is needed to find the cost of the taxi ride?
    Ⓐ Number of minutes she rode in the taxi
    Ⓑ Number of miles Julie's home is from the school
    Ⓒ Number of gallons of gasoline used for the trip
    Ⓓ Average speed of the taxi

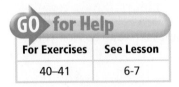

GO for Help

For Exercises	See Lesson
40–41	6-7

Algebra **Find each payment.**

40. $218 with a 6.25% sales tax   41. $451 with a 4.5% sales tax

Working Backward

A useful problem solving strategy for answering multiple-choice questions is to *Work Backward*. Check to see which choice results in a correct answer by substituting the answers into the problem.

EXAMPLE

In a pile of dimes and quarters, there are twice as many dimes as quarters. The total value of the coins is $9.45. How many quarters are in the pile?

    (A) 11   (B) 18   (C) 21   (D) 24

Check each answer to see whether it works.

Choice A   11 quarters: 2.75   22 dimes: 2.20   2.75 + 2.20 = 4.95 ✗
Choice B   18 quarters: 4.50   36 dimes: 3.60   4.50 + 3.60 = 8.10 ✗
Choice C   21 quarters: 5.25   42 dimes: 4.20   5.25 + 4.20 = 9.45 ✔
Choice D   24 quarters: 6.00   48 dimes: 4.80   6.00 + 4.80 = 10.80 ✗

● The correct answer is choice C.

Exercises

Solve each problem by working backward.

1. What is the greatest number of movie tickets you can buy if you have $33.48 and each movie ticket costs $6.75?

    (A) 3   (B) 4   (C) 5   (D) 6

2. Your grades on four math tests are 97, 88, 79, and 92. What grade do you need on the fifth test to have a mean of 90?

    (F) 90   (G) 92   (H) 94   (J) 96

3. If you start with a number, add 5, and then multiply by 7, the result is 133. What is the number?

    (A) 12   (B) 14   (C) 15   (D) 21

4. For your birthday, you receive $48 and a $15 gift certificate to a department store. The store is having a sale that takes 40% off the price of all items. What is the total value of the merchandise you can buy and still have $7.50 left for lunch?

    (F) $70.50   (G) $88.20   (H) $92.50   (J) $100

Chapter 6 Review

Vocabulary Review

commission (p. 305)
discount (p. 311)
markup (p. 311)
percent (p. 274)
percent of change (p. 310)

Choose the vocabulary term from the column on the right that completes the sentence.

1. The difference between the selling price and a store's cost is the __?__.

2. A __?__ can be an increase or a decrease.

3. A __?__ is a ratio that compares a number to 100.

4. The difference between the original price and the sale price is the __?__.

5. A __?__ is a percent of the sales made by a salesperson.

A. commission
B. discount
C. markup
D. percent
E. percent of change

Go Online
PHSchool.com
For: Online vocabulary quiz
Web Code: arj-0651

Skills and Concepts

Lessons 6-1, 6-2

- To model percents and to write percents using equivalent ratios
- To convert between fractions, decimals, and percents

A **percent** is a ratio that compares a number to 100.

To write a decimal as a percent, multiply the decimal by 100, or move the decimal point two places to the right. To write a percent as a decimal, divide by 100, or move the decimal point two places to the left.

To write a fraction as a percent, first convert the fraction into a decimal. To write a percent as a fraction, write the percent with a denominator of 100 and simplify.

Write each percent as a decimal and as a fraction in simplest form.

6. 65%   7. 2%   8. 1.8%   9. $62\frac{1}{2}\%$

10. Write $\frac{3}{8}$ as a percent.   11. Write 0.16 as a percent.

Lessons 6-3, 6-4

- To convert between fractions, decimals, and percents greater than 100% or less than 1%
- To find and estimate the percent of a number

A mixed number represents a percent greater than 100%. A proper fraction represents a percent less than 100%. To find a percent of a whole, write the percent as a decimal or fraction and then multiply.

Find each answer.

12. Find 83% of 54.   13. What is 4% of 16?   14. Find 135% of 72.

Lessons 6-5, 6-6
- To use proportions to solve problems involving percent
- To use equations to solve problems involving percent

Percent problems are solved by using a proportion or an equation.

Use a proportion or an equation to solve.

15. What percent of 40 is 28?

16. 38 is 80% of what number?

17. What is 60% of 420?

18. 80% of 15 is what number?

19.

```
0              54    n
├──────────────┤
0%            75% 100%
```

20.

```
0  36              180
├──────────────┤
0% n%            100%
```

21. Technology The price of a new version of a computer game is 120% of the price of the original version. The original version cost $48. What is the cost of the new version?

Lesson 6-7
- To find and estimate solutions to application problems involving percent

A tip is a percent of a bill that you give to the person providing a service. A **commission** is a percent of a sale.

22. You go to a restaurant with four other people. The total for the food is $43.85. You need to add 5% for tax and 15% for tip. If you decide to split the bill evenly, estimate how much you will pay.

23. Diamonds Find the commission on a diamond that is sold for $6,700 when the commission paid is 4%.

Find each commission, given the sale and the commission rate.

24. $700, 9%

25. $3,600, 6%

26. $5,000, 5.5%

27. Insurance An insurance company pays its agents 40% commission on the first year's premium and 5% on the second year's premium for life insurance policies. If the premiums are $500 per year, what is the total commission that will be paid during the two years?

Lesson 6-8
- To find percents of increase and percents of decrease

A **percent of change** is the percent a quantity increases or decreases from its original amount. Use the proportion $\frac{\text{amount of change}}{\text{original amount}} = \frac{\text{percent change}}{100}$.
Markup is an example of a percent of increase. **Discount** is an example of a percent of decrease.

Find each percent of change. Tell whether it is an increase or a decrease.

28. $90 to $75

29. 3.5 ft to 4.2 ft

30. 120 lb to 138 lb

31. 300 cm to 420 cm

32. 80.5 g to 22.5 g

33. 108 kg to 90 kg

34. Shopping The sale price of a game is $24.95. Its original price was $36.00. Find the percent of change. Round to the nearest percent.

Chapter 6 Test

Go Online For: Online chapter test
PHSchool.com Web Code: ara-0652

Write each decimal as a percent and write each percent as a decimal.

1. 5%   **2.** 0.3   **3.** 125%

4. 0.0045   **5.** 0.39%   **6.** 3.4

Write each fraction as a percent. Write each percent as a fraction.

7. 35%   **8.** 125%   **9.** 2%

10. $\frac{7}{8}$ **11.** $\frac{3}{4}$ **12.** $\frac{6}{5}$

13. According to the U.S. Census Bureau, 0.98% of females in the United States in 1990 were named Barbara. Express this percent as a fraction.

Model each percent on a 10 × 10 grid.

14. 34%   **15.** 285%   **16.** $12\frac{1}{2}$%

17. You work 20 hours per week at a grocery store during the summer. Sixty percent of your job is restocking the shelves. How many hours per week do you spend restocking the shelves?

18. Draw a model and write a proportion to find the answer to "25 percent of what number is 30?"

Write an equation for each question. Then solve the equation.

19. What percent of 82 is 10.25?

20. 108% of 47 is what number?

21. 99 is 72% of what number?

22. 12 is what percent of 1,920?

23. What is 62% of 128?

24. 168% of what number is 714?

25. In a grade of 250 students, there are 6 sets of twins. What percent of the students in this grade have a twin?

Write a proportion for each model. Solve for *n*.

26.

| 0 | 50 | 80 |
| 0% | *n*% | 100% |

27.

| 0 | 60 | *n* |
| 0% | 80% | 100% |

28. **Shopping** You buy a sweater for $18.75, which is 25% off the original price. What was the original price?

29. To prepare for competitions, your swimming coach required you to swim 8 lengths in the pool. You swam 10 lengths. What percent of the required practice did you swim?

Find each percent of change. Round to the nearest tenth of a percent. State whether the change is an increase or a decrease.

30. 4.15 to 4.55   **31.** 379 to 302   **32.** 72 to 102

33. **Jobs** According to the U.S. Department of Labor, total employment is expected to increase from 146 million in 2000 to 168 million in 2010. Find the percent of increase.

34. **Restaurants** You order items from a menu that total $7.85. Your bill comes to $8.30, including tax. What is the percent of the tax? Round to the nearest tenth of a percent.

35. A salesperson receives a salary of $300 per week and a 6% commission on all sales. How much does this salesperson earn in a week with $2,540 in sales?

36. A bicycle store pays $29.62 for a helmet. The store sells the helmet for $39.99. Find the percent of markup.

37. **Writing in Math** How do you determine whether you are finding a percent of increase or a percent of decrease between two values? Explain.

Multiple Choice
Read each question. Then write the letter of the correct answer on your paper.

1. Which number is closest to 35% of 1,291?
   Ⓐ 400 Ⓑ 450 Ⓒ 500 Ⓓ 550

2. Which equation is NOT equivalent to $2x - 3 = 5$?
   Ⓕ $2x = 8$ Ⓗ $2x - 4 = 4$
   Ⓖ $4x - 3 = 10$ Ⓙ $x - 1.5 = 2.5$

3. Which expression equals $3 \times 3 \times 3 \times 3$?
   Ⓐ 3^4 Ⓑ 4^3 Ⓒ 4×3 Ⓓ 3^3

4. In which set of numbers is 9 a factor of all the numbers?
   Ⓕ 36, 18, 21   Ⓗ 98, 81, 450
   Ⓖ 108, 252, 45   Ⓙ 120, 180, 267

5. Which point shows the product $\left(1\frac{7}{8}\right)\left(2\frac{1}{5}\right)$?

   ```
         A    B C D
   <—+——+——●——+●—●—●+—>
     0  1  2  3  4  5
   ```

6. Which fraction is closest in value to 0.46?
   Ⓕ $\frac{19}{50}$ Ⓖ $\frac{22}{50}$ Ⓗ $\frac{25}{50}$ Ⓙ $\frac{28}{50}$

7. You buy a sandwich for $3.45, a salad for $2.25, and a drink for $.89. How much change do you receive from a $10 bill?
   Ⓐ $16.59 Ⓑ $4.30 Ⓒ $3.41 Ⓓ $2.59

8. Which statement is NOT true?
   Ⓕ $\frac{12}{16} = \frac{9}{12}$ Ⓗ $\frac{12}{9} = \frac{16}{12}$
   Ⓖ $\frac{12 + 16}{16} = \frac{9 + 12}{12}$ Ⓙ $\frac{12 + 1}{16} = \frac{9 + 1}{12}$

9. What is $\frac{5}{8}$ written as a percent?
   Ⓐ 625% Ⓑ 160% Ⓒ $62\frac{1}{2}$% Ⓓ 16%

10. What is the order of the numbers 0.361×10^7, 4.22×10^7, and 13.5×10^6 from least to greatest?
    Ⓕ 13.5×10^6, 0.361×10^7, 4.22×10^7
    Ⓖ 4.22×10^7, 13.5×10^6, 0.361×10^7
    Ⓗ 0.361×10^7, 13.5×10^6, 4.22×10^7
    Ⓙ 13.5×10^6, 4.22×10^7, 0.361×10^7

11. What is the value of $\frac{2m}{m + 2n}$ when $m = -4$ and $n = 3$?
    Ⓐ -8 Ⓑ -4 Ⓒ 0 Ⓓ 4

12. Which is the best estimate of $92.56 \cdot 37.1$?
    Ⓕ 2,700 Ⓖ 3,600 Ⓗ 4,000 Ⓙ 4,500

13. Which expression has the greatest value?
    Ⓐ $32 - (-12)$ Ⓒ $-32 - (-12)$
    Ⓑ $32 - |-12|$ Ⓓ $|-32 - (-12)|$

14. The mean of six numbers is 9. Five of the numbers are 4, 7, 9, 10, and 11. What is the sixth number?
    Ⓕ 6   Ⓖ 9   Ⓗ 12   Ⓙ 13

Gridded Response
Record your answer in a grid.

15. A map's scale is 1 in. : 15 mi. Two towns are 3.5 in. apart on the map. How many miles apart are the two towns?

16. A video store charges $.75 per day for overdue videos. Your friend has a video that was due on Sunday. She returns it on the following Friday. How much does she owe?

Short Response

17. Eighteen students in a class of 25 students plan to go on a hiking trip. What percent of the students plan to go on the trip? Show your work.

18. A blue shark swims about 2.26 mi in 10 min. What is the speed of the shark in miles per minute and in miles per hour?

Extended Response

19. A movie theater charges $9 for admission and $4.50 for a bucket of popcorn. Write an expression for the total cost for a group of friends to see a movie and split one bucket of popcorn. Then evaluate your expression for five friends.

Applying Percents

Fractal Facts A fractal is a design that repeats itself at smaller and smaller levels. Fractals give us beautiful, intricate pictures of things like ferns and rivers. They also provide a practical way to increase surface area. For example, the circulatory system branches from arteries into smaller and smaller blood vessels called capillaries. Because there are so many of them, capillaries have a much greater surface area than arteries and can absorb nutrients more effectively.

The activity models how the length of a "blood vessel" increases as it branches out into smaller capillaries.

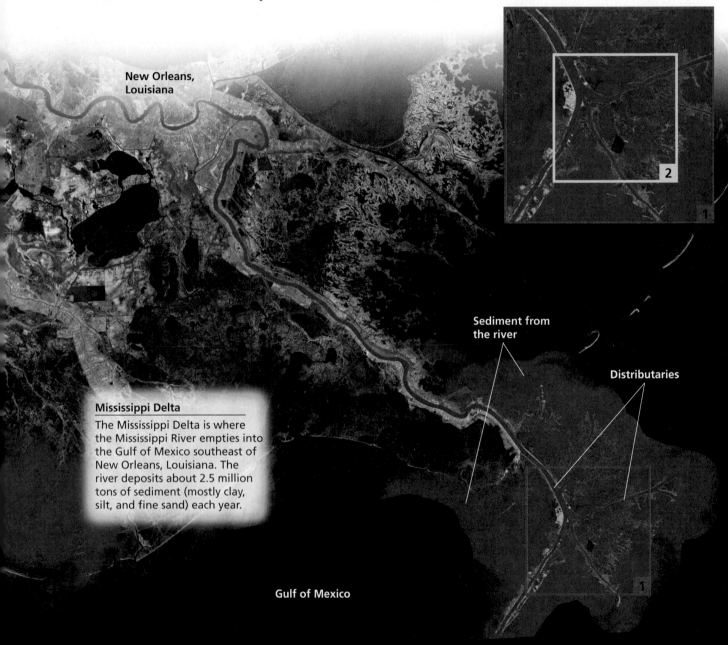

New Orleans, Louisiana

Sediment from the river

Distributaries

Mississippi Delta

The Mississippi Delta is where the Mississippi River empties into the Gulf of Mexico southeast of New Orleans, Louisiana. The river deposits about 2.5 million tons of sediment (mostly clay, silt, and fine sand) each year.

Gulf of Mexico

Fractals in Nature

Each fern leaf (called a "frond") has many small fronds along its main vein. Each of the small fronds also has many even smaller fronds.

Main vein

Fern frond

Smaller fronds

3

2

Fractal Structure

At the delta, the Mississippi River splits into distributaries, or branches. Many of the distributaries split into smaller branches. The smallest branches of the river look the same as the larger ones.

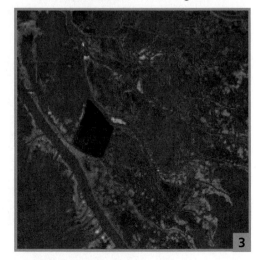

3

Put It All Together

Materials ruler, scissors, tape

1. Cut four thin strips of paper of equal lengths. Choose a length that is easy to divide into thirds. Use one strip to model a simple blood vessel. Mark it to show three equal segments.

   a. How long is your blood vessel?

   b. Fold an unmarked strip into thirds and tape it to form a triangle. Attach this triangle to the center segment of your blood vessel. Measure the total length of the paper blood vessel after you add the triangle. How much did the length increase?

   length

   c. Use your answers to parts (a) and (b). Find the percent of increase.

2. Use the last two strips to make four new triangles with sides that are $\frac{1}{9}$ the length of the marked strip. Attach each triangle to the center of each of the the four segments of your blood vessel.

   a. How long is the blood vessel after you add the four smaller triangles? How much did the length increase?

   b. What is the percent increase?

3. **Patterns** Describe the pattern as a percent increase from one step to the next. Predict the total length if you were to repeat the pattern one more time.

4. Find the percent increase in length of the blood vessel from Exercise 1, part (b) to Exercise 3.

Go Online
PHSchool.com

For: Information about fractals
Web Code: are-0653

321

What You've Learned

- In Chapter 5, you identified similar figures and used proportions to find missing lengths.

- In Chapter 6, you converted between fractions, decimals, and percents.

Check Your Readiness

GO for Help

For Exercises	See Lesson
1–4	1-6
5–10	4-3
11–14	5-4
15–18	6-4

Comparing Integers

Compare using <, =, or >.

1. 83 ■ 90   **2.** 120 ■ 99

3. 0 ■ −47   **4.** −21 ■ −11

Solving One-Step Equations

Solve each equation.

5. $d + 17 = 19$ **6.** $m - 12 = 3$ **7.** $j - 5 = 7$

8. $m - 15 = 90$ **9.** $58 + n = 63$ **10.** $y + 86 = 180$

Solving Proportions

Solve each proportion.

11. $\frac{5}{16} = \frac{25}{w}$ **12.** $\frac{n}{12} = \frac{20}{15}$ **13.** $\frac{18}{k} = \frac{6}{37}$ **14.** $\frac{23}{12} = \frac{x}{24}$

Finding a Percentage of a Number

Find each answer.

15. 30% of 360   **16.** 24% of 360   **17.** 4.5% of 360   **18.** 18% of 360

What You'll Learn Next

- In this chapter, you will classify angles, triangles, and quadrilaterals.

- You will identify congruent figures and find missing measures.

- You will analyze and construct circle graphs.

 Problem Solving Application On pages 370 and 371, you will work an extended activity on geometry.

◀)) Key Vocabulary

7-1 Lines and Planes

Check Skills You'll Need

1. Vocabulary Review
List the five *inequality* symbols.

Graph the solution of each inequality.

2. $x \leq -3$ **3.** $x < 1$

4. $x \leq 2$ **5.** $x \geq 5$

6. $x > 1$ **7.** $x < 4$

 **for Help**
Lesson 4-7

What You'll Learn

To identify segments, rays, and lines

🔊 **New Vocabulary** point, line, ray, segment, plane, intersecting lines, parallel lines, skew lines

Why Learn This?

City maps show parallel and intersecting streets. A statement such as "W. 4th St. runs parallel to W. 3rd St." can help you give and understand directions.

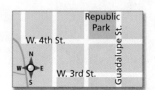

A **point** is a location. A point has no size. You name a point by a capital letter.

• A
point A

• B
point B

A **line** is a series of points that extend in opposite directions without end. You name a line by any two points on the line or by a lowercase letter.

$\overleftrightarrow{AB}, \overleftrightarrow{BA}, n$

A **ray** is part of a line with one endpoint and all the points of the line on one side of the endpoint. You name a ray using two points, starting with the endpoint.

$\overrightarrow{BA}$, ray BA

A **segment** is part of a line with two endpoints and all points in between. You name a segment by its endpoints.

$\overline{AB}, \overline{BA}$

EXAMPLE   Naming Segments, Rays, and Lines

1 Use the points in each diagram to name the figure shown.

a. X — Y
$\overline{XY}$

b. G — R
$\overleftrightarrow{GR}$

c. T — J
$\overrightarrow{JT}$

✓ Quick Check

1. Use the points in each diagram to name the figure shown.

a. P — D →

b. R — S

c. A — V

A **plane** is a flat surface that extends indefinitely in all directions and has no thickness. There are two planes in the diagram below.

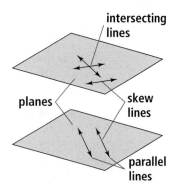

Intersecting lines lie in the same plane. **Intersecting lines** have exactly one point in common. **Parallel lines** are lines in the same plane that never intersect. Parallel segments and rays lie in parallel lines.

Skew lines lie in different planes. They are neither parallel nor intersecting.

Vocabulary Tip

The word *skew* comes from a root word meaning "to avoid."

EXAMPLE **Intersecting, Parallel, and Skew**

2 **Architecture** Use the information in the photograph and diagram below to name a segment with the given description.

a. a segment parallel to $\overline{AB}$

$\overline{GH}$ lies in the same plane as $\overline{AB}$. $\overline{GH}$ does not intersect $\overline{AB}$.

$\overline{GH}$ is parallel to $\overline{AB}$.

b. a segment skew to $\overline{AB}$

$\overline{EF}$ lies in a different plane. $\overline{EF}$ is not parallel to $\overline{AB}$ and does not intersect $\overline{AB}$.

$\overline{EF}$ is skew to $\overline{AB}$.

✓ Quick Check

2. Name the segments in the diagram that fit each description.
   a. parallel to $\overline{BC}$ **b.** intersect $\overline{BH}$ **c.** skew to $\overline{AG}$

1. **Vocabulary** ___?___ are lines that are neither parallel nor intersecting.

2. **Reasoning** Two lines do not intersect. Can you conclude that they are parallel? Explain.

Use the points in each diagram to name the figure shown.

3. *L* ———————————— *C*

4. ◄———— *M* *R* ————►

5. ◄———— *K*   *E* ————►

6. *O* *D* ————————►

Use the diagram for Exercises 7 and 8.

7. Name all the segments parallel to $\overline{AD}$.

8. Name all the segments intersecting $\overline{FG}$.

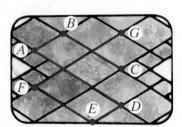

For more exercises, see Extra Skills and Word Problems.

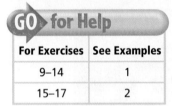

Use the points in each diagram to name the figure shown.

For Exercises	See Examples
9–14	1
15–17	2

9. *L* ———————————— *C*

10. ◄—— *W* ———————— *A*

11. ◄—— *Z* ———————— *V*

12. *P* *F* ————————►

13. *Q* ———————————— *S*

14. ◄—— *G* *H* ————►

Buildings Use the diagram at the right for Exercises 15–17.

15. Name all the segments skew to $\overline{BC}$.

16. Name all the segments intersecting $\overline{AD}$.

17. Name all the segments parallel to $\overline{EH}$.

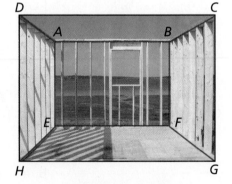

18. **Guided Problem Solving** Describe a route from A to B that includes Main St. and a street parallel to Main St.
    • What street is parallel to Main St.?
    • What street(s) connect Main St. and Lee Ave.?

19. Use the map shown in Exercise 18. Describe a route from A to B that includes Oak St. and a street that intersects Oak St.

Tell whether each figure below contains ray *AB*.

20. 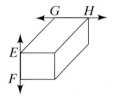 •———•
    A   *B*

21. ◄—•———•—►
    A   *B*

22. ◄—•———•
    A   *B*

23. Are the rungs on a ladder parallel, intersecting, or skew?

Draw each figure.

24. $\overleftrightarrow{AD}$

25. $\overrightarrow{QW}$

26. $\overleftrightarrow{PR}$

27. $\overline{FG}$ intersecting $\overleftrightarrow{TU}$

28. $\overrightarrow{TB}$ and $\overrightarrow{TA}$ on the same line

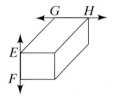

29. **Error Analysis** Jim says that in the box shown at the left $\overleftrightarrow{EF}$ and $\overleftrightarrow{GH}$ are parallel, since they do not intersect. Why is Jim incorrect?

30. **Writing in Math** Describe examples of parallel, intersecting, and skew lines in your classroom.

31. **Challenge** Name each segment, ray, and line in the figure below.

Test Prep and Mixed Review **Practice**

Multiple Choice

32. An advertisement offers you 0.3% off your next purchase. What fraction of the original price does this represent?

    Ⓐ $\frac{3}{10}$ Ⓑ $\frac{3}{100}$ Ⓒ $\frac{3}{1,000}$ Ⓓ $\frac{3}{10,000}$

33. Which expression does the model represent?

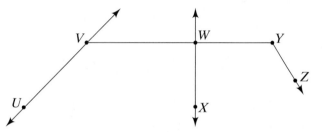

Key
$\bigcirc\!\!\!\!- = -1$

    Ⓕ $3 \times (-2)$ Ⓖ $2 \times (-3)$ Ⓗ $2 \times (-2)$ Ⓙ 3×3

34. Which formula shows *z*, the number of milliliters that result when you add *x* milliliters to *y* liters?

    Ⓐ $z = 100x + y$ Ⓒ $z = 100y + x$
    Ⓑ $z = 1,000x + y$ Ⓓ $z = 1,000y + x$

GO for Help

For Exercises	See Lesson
35–36	6-8

Find the percent of change. Is the change an increase or a decrease?

35. original: $5.75; new: $6.25

36. original: 380 ft; new: 320 ft

Vocabulary Builder

High-Use Academic Words

High-use academic words are words that you will see often in textbooks and on tests. These words are not math vocabulary terms, but knowing them will help you succeed in mathematics.

Direction Words

Some words tell what to do in a problem. I need to understand what these words are asking so that I give the correct answer.

Word	Meaning
Classify	To arrange or group things according to their characteristics
Sketch	To draw something without using a scale
Identify	To recognize and be able to tell what something is

Exercises

1. Identify the sport in which the ball shown at the right is used.

2. Classify each sport as played by a *team* or by an *individual*.
   a. basketball   **b.** golf   **c.** volleyball   **d.** billiards

3. There are six pairs of lines in the diagram at the right. Classify each pair of lines as *intersecting* or *parallel*.

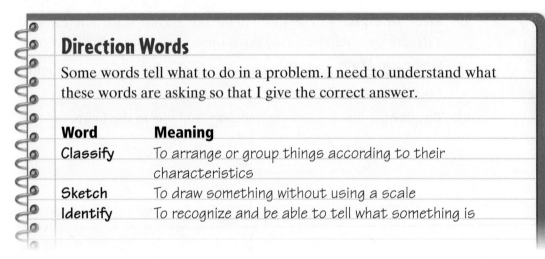

4. Sketch a floor plan of your school's cafeteria.

5. Sketch a line segment and a ray that share endpoint *T*.

6. Identify the ray shown at the right.

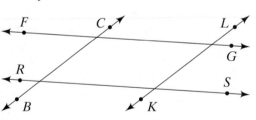

7. **Word Knowledge** Think about the word *justify*.
   a. Choose the letter for how well you know the word.
      A. I know its meaning.
      B. I've seen it, but I don't know its meaning.
      C. I don't know it.
   b. **Research** Look up and write the definition of *justify*.
   c. Use the word in a sentence involving mathematics.

Measuring Angles

An angle (∠) has two sides and a vertex. Angles are measured in degrees (°). You can estimate the measure of an angle before measuring.

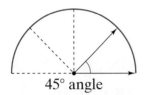

45° angle
(half of a right angle)

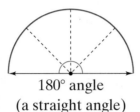

180° angle
(a straight angle)

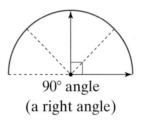

90° angle
(a right angle)

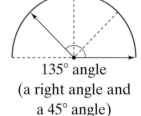

135° angle
(a right angle and
a 45° angle)

EXAMPLE **Measuring Angles**

What is the measure of ∠X at the right?

Estimate ∠X is larger than a 90° angle and smaller than a 135° angle. You can estimate that the measure of ∠X is between 90° and 135°.

Step 1 Place your protractor on the vertex of the angle, as shown.

Step 2 Make sure that one side of the angle passes through zero on one of the protractor's scales.

Step 3 Read the same scale where it intersects the second side of the angle.

The measure of ∠X is 110°. You can write this as $m\angle X = 110°$.

Check for Reasonableness The measure of ∠X is between 90° and 135°. The protractor measure of 110° is reasonable.

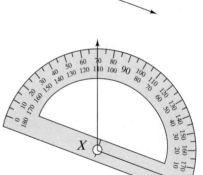

Exercises

Estimate each angle. Then use your protractor to measure each angle.

1.
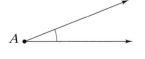

2.
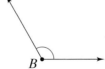

3.
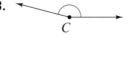

4.
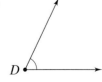

Identifying and Classifying Angles

What You'll Learn

To classify angles and to work with pairs of angles

🔊 **New Vocabulary** angle, vertex, acute angle, right angle, obtuse angle, straight angle, complemetary, supplementary, adjacent angles, vertical angles, congruent angles

Why Learn This?

Architects think about angles in the structures they design. If you can measure angles, you can predict how different geometric figures can fit together.

The design of a geodesic dome requires triangles, because triangles have exactly three angles. They make the dome stable.

An **angle** ($\angle$) is a figure formed by two rays with a common endpoint. You can call the angle below $\angle DCE$, $\angle ECD$, $\angle C$, or $\angle 1$.

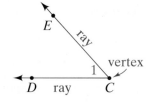

A **vertex** is the point of intersection of two sides of an angle or figure. The plural of *vertex* is *vertices*.

You can classify angles by their measures.

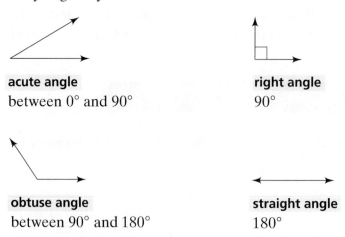

acute angle
between 0° and 90°

right angle
90°

obtuse angle
between 90° and 180°

straight angle
180°

EXAMPLE Identifying Angles

1. **Architecture** Part of a geodesic dome is shown at the right. Identify all the acute angles.

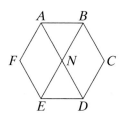

$\angle NEF$, $\angle FAN$, $\angle NAB$, $\angle ABN$, $\angle BNA$, $\angle NBC$, $\angle CDN$, $\angle NDE$, $\angle DEN$, and $\angle END$ are acute.

Quick Check

1. Classify $\angle AFE$ as *acute*, *right*, *obtuse*, or *straight*.

If the sum of the measures of two angles is 90°, the angles are **complementary.** If the sum is 180°, the angles are **supplementary.**

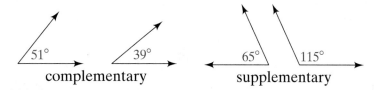

complementary   supplementary

EXAMPLE Finding Complements and Supplements

2. **Multiple Choice** If $\angle A$ and $\angle B$ are supplementary and the measure of $\angle A$ is 37°, what is the measure of $\angle B$?

    Ⓐ 43°   Ⓑ 53°   Ⓒ 143°   Ⓓ 153°

Write an equation. Let $x =$ the measure of $\angle B$.

$$x + 37° = 180°$$ ← The angles are supplementary.
$$x + 37° - 37° = 180° - 37°$$ ← Subtract 37° from each side.
$$x = 143°$$ ← Simplify.

The measure of $\angle B$ is 143°. The answer is C.

Quick Check

2. Find the measure of the complement of $\angle A$ in Example 2.

Adjacent angles share a vertex and a side but have no interior points in common. Angles 1 and 2 are adjacent angles. Adjacent angles formed by two intersecting lines are supplementary.

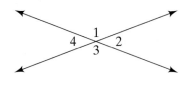

Angles 1 and 3 above are vertical angles. **Vertical angles** are formed by two intersecting lines and are opposite each other. Vertical angles have equal measures. Angles with equal measures are **congruent angles.**

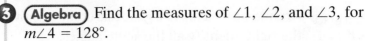

EXAMPLE **Finding Angle Measures**

3 (Algebra) Find the measures of ∠1, ∠2, and ∠3, for
$m\angle 4 = 128°$.

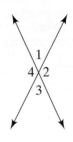

$m\angle 1 = 180° - 128°$ ← **∠1 and ∠4 are supplementary.**

$\qquad = 52°$

$m\angle 2 = 128°$ ← **∠2 and ∠4 are vertical angles.**

$m\angle 3 = 52°$ ← **∠1 and ∠3 are vertical angles.**

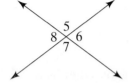

✓ **Quick Check**

3. In the diagram at the left, $m\angle 8 = 72°$. Find the measures of ∠5, ∠6, and ∠7.

● **More Than One Way**

If $m\angle 1 = 140°$ and $m\angle 2 = 40°$, what is $m\angle 3$?

Carlos's Method

∠3 and ∠1 are across from each other, so they are vertical angles. Since vertical angles have the same measure, $m\angle 3 = m\angle 1$.

So $m\angle 3 = 140°$.

Brianna's Method

∠2 and ∠3 together form a straight angle, so their measures add up to 180°. This means that they are supplementary angles.

$$40° + m\angle 3 = 180°$$
$$40° - 40° + m\angle 3 = 180° - 40° \quad \text{← Subtract 40° from each side.}$$
$$m\angle 3 = 140° \quad \text{← Simplify.}$$

So $m\angle 3$ is 140°.

Choose a Method

In the figure at the right, $m\angle BEC = 25°$ and $m\angle CED = 155°$. Find $m\angle AEB$. Explain why you chose the method you used.

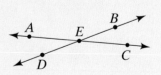

1. **Vocabulary** How are vertical angles and adjacent angles different?

2. **Reasoning** What is the sum of the measures of the four angles formed by intersecting lines?

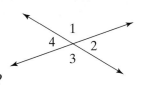

Classify each angle as *acute, right, obtuse,* or *straight.* Then find the measures of the complement and the supplement of each angle.

3. $m\angle A = 45°$ 4. $m\angle B = 105°$ 5. $m\angle C = 75°$

Homework Exercises

For more exercises, see Extra Skills and Word Problems.

GO for Help

For Exercises	See Examples
6–8	1
9–17	2
18–20	3

Classify each angle as *acute, right, obtuse,* or *straight.*

6.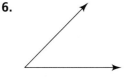

7.   8.

(Algebra) **Find the measures of the complement and the supplement of each angle.**

9. $m\angle G = 79°$ 10. $m\angle H = 67°$ 11. $m\angle J = 12°$

12. $m\angle A = 23.5°$ 13. $m\angle B = 37.6°$ 14. $m\angle C = 47.9°$

15. $m\angle D = 56.4°$ 16. $m\angle E = 75.1°$ 17. $m\angle F = 82.2°$

(Algebra) **In the diagram at the right, $m\angle 2 = 123°$. Find the measure of each angle.**

18. $m\angle 1$ 19. $m\angle 3$ 20. $m\angle 4$

GPS 21. **Guided Problem Solving** Engineers designed a metal support that forms a 65° angle with a dam. Find the measure of the angle's supplement.

$$x + 65° = ■$$
$$x + 65° - ■ = 180° - ■$$
$$x = ■$$

GO Online
Homework Video Tutor
Visit: PHSchool.com
Web Code: are-0702

Find the measures of the supplement and the complement of each angle.

22. $m\angle Q = 48°$ **23.** $m\angle R = 20.2°$ **24.** $m\angle S = 77.7°$

25. Error Analysis A student measured $\angle XYZ$ and said that $m\angle XYZ = 120°$. Explain the student's error.

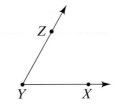

26. Writing in Math Can an angle ever have the same measure as its complement? Explain.

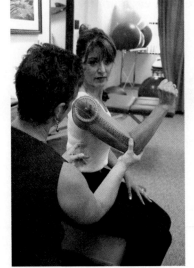

Goniometer

27. Physical Therapy Physical therapists use goniometers to measure the amount of motion a person has in a joint, such as an elbow or a knee. Estimate the measure of the angle shown by the goniometer in the photo at the left.

Use the figure to name the following.

28. two pairs of adjacent supplementary angles

29. two pairs of obtuse vertical angles

30. two pairs of complementary angles

31. an angle congruent to $\angle DCL$

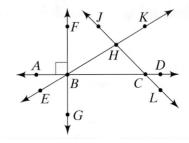

32. Challenge You know that $\angle B$ is the complement of $\angle A$, that $m\angle B = 51°$, and that $m\angle A = (3x - 12)°$. Find x.

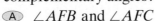
Test Prep and Mixed Review   **Practice**

Multiple Choice

33. In the diagram at the right, which pair of angles form complementary angles?
- Ⓐ $\angle AFB$ and $\angle AFC$
- Ⓑ $\angle BFC$ and $\angle CFD$
- Ⓒ $\angle AFB$ and $\angle CFD$
- Ⓓ $\angle AFB$ and $\angle EFD$

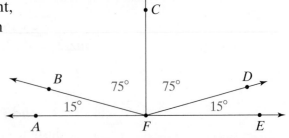

34. The five countries in northern Africa that border the Mediterranean Sea are shown in the table, along with the lowest elevation in each country. Which country contains the lowest point?
- Ⓕ Algeria   Ⓗ Egypt
- Ⓖ Morocco   Ⓙ Tunisia

Country	Elevation
Algeria	−40 m
Egypt	−133 m
Libya	−47 m
Morocco	−55 m
Tunisia	−17 m

GO for Help

For Exercise	See Lesson
35	5-6

35. For a scale of 1 cm : 12 km, find the actual length represented by the length 1.7 cm in a drawing.

Sides and Angles of a Triangle

You need three sides and three angles to form a triangle. Can you make a triangle with *any* three sides? The activity below will help you understand the relationship between the side lengths of a triangle and its angles.

ACTIVITY

Step 1 Cut five straws to the following lengths: 2 in., 4 in., 5 in., 8 in., and 10.5 in.

Step 2 Using any three pieces, try to form a triangle. When you find three lengths that can form a triangle, trace the perimeter of the triangle on a sheet of paper. Label the triangles △A, △B, △C, and so on.

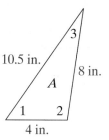

Step 3 Using all possible combinations of three pieces, repeat Step 2 and make as many triangles as you can.

Step 4 Make a list of the side lengths of all the triangles that you made. Record your results in a table like the one below.

Triangle	Shortest Side	Middle Side	Longest Side
A	4 in.	8 in.	10.5 in.
B	■	■	■
C	■	■	■

Step 5 Analyze your table. For each triangle, make a conjecture about the sum of any two side lengths compared to the length of the third side.

Step 6 Now use a protractor to measure the three angles in each triangle. Record your results in a table like the one below.

Triangle	$m \angle 1$	$m \angle 2$	$m \angle 3$	Total
A	■	■	■	■
B	■	■	■	■
C	■	■	■	■

Step 7 Analyze your table. Make a conjecture about the sum of the angles in each triangle.

✓ Check Skills You'll Need

1. **Vocabulary Review**
How does the measure of an *acute angle* compare to 90°?

Classify each angle as *acute*, *right*, *obtuse*, or *straight*.

2.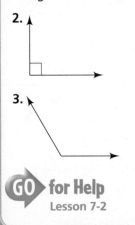

3.

GO for Help
Lesson 7-2

What You'll Learn

To classify triangles and to find the angle measures of triangles

🔊 **New Vocabulary** congruent sides, scalene triangle, isosceles triangle, equilateral triangle, right triangle, acute triangle, obtuse triangle

Why Learn This?

When you can classify triangles, you will recognize them in art and architecture.

Origami is the art of paper folding. At the right is an origami crane. The folds form a variety of triangles.

Congruent sides have the same length. You can classify a triangle by the number of congruent sides it has.

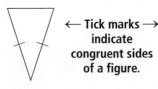

← Tick marks →
indicate
congruent sides
of a figure.

| **scalene triangle** | **isosceles triangle** | **equilateral triangle** |
| no congruent sides | at least two congruent sides | three congruent sides |

EXAMPLE **Classifying Triangles by Sides**

Test Prep Tip ✏️
You can eliminate choice B because it describes the angles of a triangle, not the sides.

1 **Multiple Choice** Which of the following best describes △ABC based on its sides?
- Ⓐ Scalene
- Ⓒ Isosceles
- Ⓑ Right
- Ⓓ Equilateral

△ABC has no congruent sides. Therefore, it is a scalene triangle. The correct answer is A.

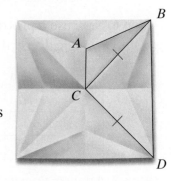

✓ Quick Check

1. Classify △BCD by its sides.

You can also classify a triangle by its angle measures.

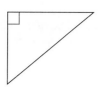 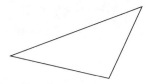

right triangle
one right angle

acute triangle
three acute angles

obtuse triangle
one obtuse angle

EXAMPLE **Classifying Triangles by Angles**

Online
active math

For: Triangle Activity
Use: Interactive
     Textbook, 7-3

2. Classify the triangle shown at the right by its angle measures.

The triangle has one obtuse angle, so it is an obtuse triangle.

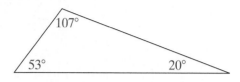

Quick Check

2. Classify each triangle by its angle measures.

  a.   b.

There is a very important property of the angles of a triangle: the sum of the measures of the angles of every triangle is the same.

KEY CONCEPTS **Angle Sum of a Triangle**

The sum of the measures of the angles of any triangle is 180°.

Suppose you know the measures of two of the angles of a triangle. You can write and solve an equation to find the third angle measure.

EXAMPLE **Finding an Angle Measure**

GO for Help

For help solving equations,
go to Lesson 4-3, Example 2.

3. (**Algebra**) Find the value of x in the triangle.

$$x + 53° + 61° = 180°$$
$$x + 114° = 180°$$
$$x + 114° - 114° = 180° - 114°$$
$$x = 66°$$

Quick Check

3. Find the value of x in the triangle.

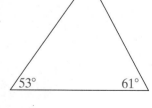

1. **Vocabulary** A scalene triangle has __?__ congruent sides.

2. **Open-Ended** Draw an isosceles right triangle. Label the angle measures and use tick marks to indicate congruent sides.

Classify each triangle by its angle measures and by its sides.

3.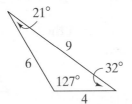

4.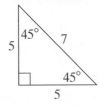

5.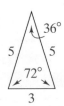

Homework Exercises

For more exercises, see Extra Skills and Word Problems.

GO for Help

For Exercises	See Examples
6–8	1
9–11	2
12–14	3

Classify each triangle by its sides.

6.

7.

8.

Classify each triangle by its angle measures.

9.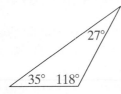

10.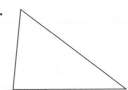

11.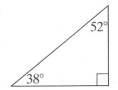

Algebra Find the value of *x* in each triangle.

12.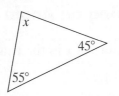

13.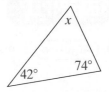

14.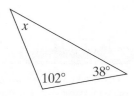

15. **Guided Problem Solving** The angles of a triangle measure *x*°, 2*x*°, and 3*x*°. Classify the triangle by its angles.
   - Use the strategy *Systematic Guess and Check*.
   - Continue until the sum of the measures is 180°.
   - Classify the triangle.

x°	2*x*°	3*x*°	Sum of Angle Measures	Result
10	20	30	60	Too low
▪	▪	▪	▪	▪

(Algebra) **Suppose the sides of a triangle have each of the given measures. Classify each triangle by its sides.**

16. j, j, j **17.** $3a, 3a, 5a$ **18.** $3w, 4w, 6w$

19. <u>**Writing in Math**</u> What is the measure of $\angle E$? Show your work and justify your steps.

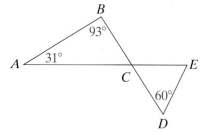

20. The traffic sign at the left is used in Norway. Classify the shape of the sign by its sides.

21. (Algebra) A triangle has two angles that both measure 68°. What is the measure of the third angle?

22. The triangles shown are right triangles.
   a. What is the sum of the measures of the two acute angles in each triangle?
   b. **Reasoning** What is the relationship between the two acute angles in any right triangle? Explain.

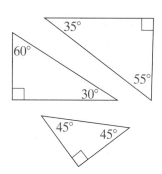

23. **Challenge** Are all equilateral triangles isosceles? Are all isosceles triangles equilateral? Explain.

Test Prep and Mixed Review

Practice

Multiple Choice

24. The side view of a ramp has the shape of a triangle. Which of the following best describes the triangle with the given measures?
   Ⓐ Right isosceles triangle
   Ⓑ Right scalene triangle
   Ⓒ Acute isosceles triangle
   Ⓓ Acute scalene triangle

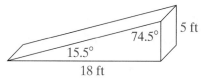

25. On a scale drawing, one side of a box is 2 inches long. The actual length of the box is 6 feet. What is the scale of the drawing?
   Ⓕ 6 in. : 2 ft   Ⓖ 1 in. : 3 ft   Ⓗ 3 in. : 1 ft   Ⓙ 3 ft : 2 in.

26. Three seventh-grade classes go on a camping trip together. The classes have 21, 20, and 19 students. If four students sleep in each tent, how many tents are needed?
   Ⓐ 10   Ⓑ 12   Ⓒ 15   Ⓓ 20

GO for Help

For Exercises	See Lesson
27–30	6-3

Write each percent as a decimal and as a fraction in simplest form.

27. 116%   **28.** 137%   **29.** 155%   **30.** 175%

Quadrilaterals and Other Polygons

Check Skills You'll Need

1. Vocabulary Review What kind of triangle will always have three congruent sides?

Classify each triangle by its sides.

2.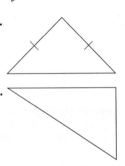

3.

4.

GO for Help
Lesson 7-3

What You'll Learn

To classify polygons and special quadrilaterals

🔊 **New Vocabulary** quadrilateral, pentagon, hexagon, octagon, decagon, regular polygon, irregular polygon, trapezoid, parallelogram, rectangle, rhombus, square

Why Learn This?

Artists and designers use quadrilaterals and other polygons in their work because these shapes are pleasing to the eye. The artist Piet Mondrian is known for painting rectangles.

A polygon is a closed plane figure with sides formed by three or more line segments. The sides meet only at their endpoints.

You classify polygons by their number of sides.

Composition A, 1920 Oil on canvas, 35 1/2 x 35 7/8 inches. © 2006 Mondrian/Holtzman Trust c/o HCR International, Warrenton, VA

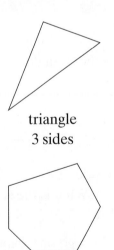

triangle
3 sides

quadrilateral
4 sides

pentagon
5 sides

hexagon
6 sides

octagon
8 sides

decagon
10 sides

A **regular polygon** is a polygon with all sides congruent and all angles congruent. An **irregular polygon** is a polygon with sides that are not all congruent or angles that are not all congruent.

340 Chapter 7 Geometry

EXAMPLE **Identifying Regular Polygons**

Vocabulary Tip

Regular means "consistent" or "the same."

1 Identify each polygon and classify it as *regular* or *irregular*.

a.

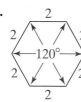

The figure has 6 sides. All sides are congruent. The hexagon is regular.

b.

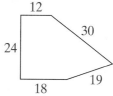

The figure has 5 sides. Not all sides are congruent. The pentagon is irregular.

✓ Quick Check

1. Identify each polygon and classify it as *regular* or *irregular*.

a.

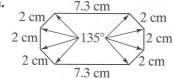

b.

c. **Reasoning** How would you find the perimeter of a regular polygon? Explain.

Some quadrilaterals have special names.

$\overline{AB}$ is parallel to $\overline{CD}$.

A **trapezoid** is a quadrilateral with exactly one pair of parallel sides. The arrows indicate parallel sides.

A **parallelogram** is a quadrilateral with both pairs of opposite sides parallel.

GO for Help

For help with parallel lines, go to Lesson 7-1, Example 2.

There are three special types of parallelograms.

rectangle
four right angles

rhombus
four congruent sides

square
four right angles and four congruent sides

EXAMPLE   Classifying Polygons

② **Architecture** Use the best names to identify the polygons in the window shown at the right.

The outside frame is an octagon. Inside the frame there are triangles, rectangles, trapezoids, and squares.

✓ Quick Check

2. Use the best names to identify the polygons in each pattern.

a.

b.

EXAMPLE   Using Dot Paper

③ Draw each of the following figures on dot paper.

a. a parallelogram that is not a rectangle or a rhombus

b. a rhombus that is not a square

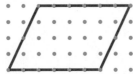

Online active math

For: Quadrilateral Activity
Use: Interactive Textbook, 7-4

✓ Quick Check

3. Draw a trapezoid with a pair of congruent opposite sides.

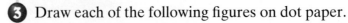

✓ Check Your Understanding

1. **Vocabulary** How do parallelograms and trapezoids differ? Explain.

2. **Reasoning** Can you draw a square that is not a rhombus? Explain.

List all the names that apply to each figure.

3.

4.

5.

For more exercises, see Extra Skills and Word Problems.

GO for Help

For Exercises	See Examples
6–8	1
9–10	2
11–12	3

Identify each polygon and classify it as *regular* or *irregular*. Explain.

6.
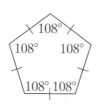

7.

8.
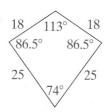

Use the best names to identify the polygons in each pattern.

9.
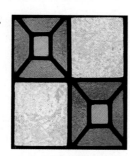

10.

Use dot paper or graph paper to draw each quadrilateral.

11. a trapezoid with vertical sides parallel

12. two squares, the second of which has twice the perimeter of the first

13. **Guided Problem Solving** Find the length of a side of a regular decagon that has a perimeter of 22 ft.
  - How many sides does a decagon have?
  - Can you write a formula for the perimeter of a regular decagon?

Judging by appearance, classify each quadrilateral in the photos below. Then name the parallel sides.

14.
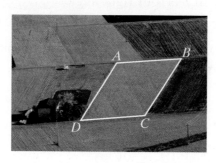

15.
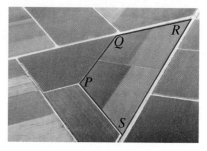

List all side lengths and angle measures you can find for each polygon.

16. rhombus *WXYZ*, *WX* = 4 cm

17. rectangle *JKLN*, *KL* = 5 in.

18. parallelogram *ABCD*, *AB* = 6 cm, $m\angle A = 115°$

Sketch each polygon.

19. pentagon   **20.** octagon   **21.** regular quadrilateral

Math in the Media Use the cartoon for Exercises 22 and 23.

22. <u>**Writing in Math**</u> Can a quadrilateral be both a rhombus and a rectangle? Explain.

23. **Reasoning** Can a trapezoid have three right angles? Draw a diagram to support your answer.

24. a. Use a ruler to draw a trapezoid with opposite sides congruent.
  b. A diagonal joins two vertices that are not endpoints of the same side of a polygon. Draw and measure the diagonals of the figure you drew in part (a). What do you notice?

25. **Challenge** Draw a quadrilateral with exactly one pair of congruent opposite angles.

Test Prep and Mixed Review   **Practice**

Multiple Choice

26. Which statement is always true about a rhombus?
  Ⓐ It has four congruent angles.
  Ⓑ It has four congruent sides.
  Ⓒ It has four right angles.
  Ⓓ It has exactly one pair of parallel sides.

27. A punch recipe calls for 6 cups of pineapple juice. Alicia has 1 quart of pineapple juice. How much more does she need?
  Ⓕ $\frac{1}{2}$ qt   Ⓖ $1\frac{1}{2}$ qt   Ⓗ 3 c   Ⓙ 2 pt

28. An art collector bought five paintings for a total of $3,600. Then he bought another painting for $1,200. What was the mean cost for all of the paintings?
  Ⓐ $720   Ⓑ $800   Ⓒ $960   Ⓓ $4,800

GO for Help

For Exercises	See Lesson
29–32	2-6

Write each fraction as a decimal.

29. $\frac{5}{3}$ **30.** $\frac{7}{16}$ **31.** $\frac{15}{18}$ **32.** $\frac{10}{6}$

Use the points in each diagram to name the figure shown.

1.

X Z

2.

N M

3.

K V

Find the measures of the complement and the supplement of each angle.

4. $m\angle T = 12°$

5. $m\angle R = 47°$

6. $m\angle U = 65°$

7. A triangle has angles that measure 63° and 47°. What is the measure of the third angle?

Classify the triangles in the figure at the right.

8. $\triangle ADE$

9. $\triangle DEC$

10. $\triangle ACD$

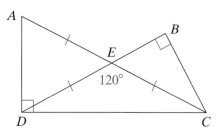

11. In the figure below, all six segments are congruent. Identify the three polygons that are formed by the segments and classify them as *regular* or *irregular*.

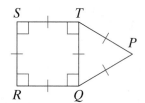

MATH AT WORK

Architect

Do you have an eye for design? If so, then architecture could be a career for you. Architects use creativity, math, science, and art to plan buildings that are beautiful, functional, safe, and economical.

Architects use geometry to understand spatial relationships. They use ratios and percents to plan scale drawings and to build scale models, too.

Architects also must be able to manage projects, supervise people, and communicate complex ideas.

Go Online
PHSchool.com **For:** Information about architects
Web Code: arb-2031

Congruent Figures

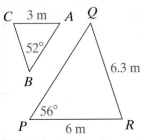
What You'll Learn

To identify congruent figures and to use them to find missing measures

🔊 **New Vocabulary** congruent polygons

Why Learn This?

A manufacturer that makes large quantities of the same item must be sure that the items are all the same shape and size.

Similar polygons have the same shape. **Congruent polygons** are polygons with the same shape *and* the same size. The corresponding parts (sides and angles) of congruent polygons are congruent. The symbol $\cong$ means "is congruent to."

$\overline{AB} \cong \overline{ED}$ $\overline{BC} \cong \overline{DF}$ $\overline{CA} \cong \overline{FE}$

$\angle A \cong \angle E$ $\angle B \cong \angle D$ $\angle C \cong \angle F$

$\triangle ABC \cong \triangle EDF$

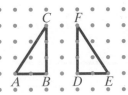

Write the vertices of congruent triangles in corresponding order.

EXAMPLE **Identifying Congruent Figures**

1 Are the figures *congruent* or *not congruent?* Explain.

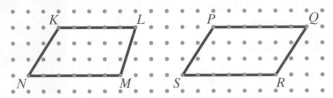

$\overline{KN} \cong \overline{PS}$ and $\overline{NM} \cong \overline{SR}$, but $\overline{LM}$ is not congruent to $\overline{QR}$.

The figures are not congruent.

✓ Quick Check

1. Are the figures *congruent* or *not congruent?* Explain.

EXAMPLE Application: Manufacturing

2️⃣ Assembly-line workers compare manufactured parts to a sample part to see if they are congruent. Is △UVW congruent to the sample triangle, △RST?

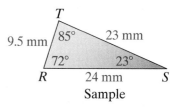

Sample

$\overline{UV} \cong \overline{RS}$, $\overline{VW} \cong \overline{ST}$, $\overline{WU} \cong \overline{TR}$, $\angle U \cong \angle R$, $\angle V \cong \angle S$, and $\angle W \cong \angle T$.

△UVW ≅ △RST

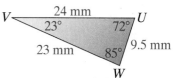

✅ **Quick Check**

2. Is the right figure congruent to the sample figure? Explain.

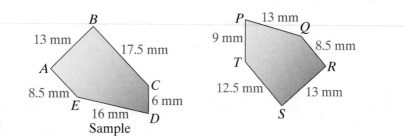

Sample

If you know that figures are congruent, you can use information about one figure to find information about the other.

EXAMPLE Working With Congruent Figures

Test Prep Tip 🔵🔵🔵🔵

If two angles in one triangle are congruent to two angles in another triangle, then both triangles' third angles must also be congruent.

3️⃣ The triangles at the right are congruent.

a. Write six congruences for the corresponding parts of the triangles.

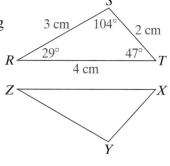

$\angle X \cong \angle T$ $\angle Y \cong \angle S$ $\angle Z \cong \angle R$

$\overline{XY} \cong \overline{TS}$ $\overline{ZY} \cong \overline{RS}$ $\overline{ZX} \cong \overline{RT}$

b. Find ZY and $m\angle X$.

$ZY = 3$ cm   ← $\overline{ZY} \cong \overline{RS}$, so $ZY = RS$

$m\angle X = 47°$ ← $\angle X \cong \angle T$, so $m\angle X = m\angle T$

✅ **Quick Check**

3. The quadrilaterals are congruent.
   a. Write the congruences for the corresponding parts.
   b. Find AD and $m\angle G$.

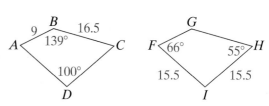

1. **Vocabulary** Is it possible for two similar polygons to be congruent polygons? Explain.

2. **Reasoning** If you know that two polygons are congruent, can you conclude that they are similar? Explain.

Are the figures *congruent* or *not congruent*? Explain.

3.

4.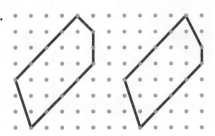

For more exercises, see Extra Skills and Word Problems.

GO for Help

For Exercises	See Examples
5–6	1–2
7–8	3

Are the figures *congruent* or *not congruent*? Explain.

5.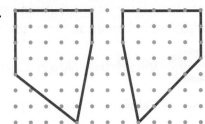

6.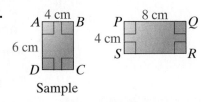

Sample

Each pair of figures is congruent. Write six congruences for the corresponding parts of the figures. Then find the missing side lengths and angle measures.

7.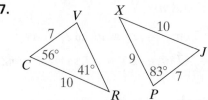

8.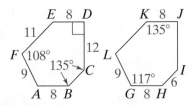

 9. Guided Problem Solving Complete the congruence statement: $\triangle RST \cong \blacksquare$.
 • **Make a Plan** List pairs of congruent corresponding angles to find corresponding vertices.
 • **Carry Out the Plan**
   $\angle R \cong \blacksquare$, $\angle S \cong \blacksquare$, $\angle T \cong \blacksquare$; $\triangle RST \cong \blacksquare$

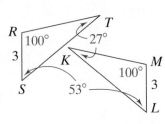

Complete each congruence statement.

10. △ABC ≅ ■

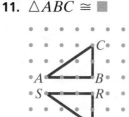

11. △ABC ≅ ■

12. △ABC ≅ ■

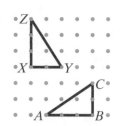

13. **Writing in Math** If you know that corresponding angles in triangles *GHI* and *JKL* are congruent, do you know that the triangles are congruent? Explain.

Architecture **Complete each congruence statement.** △ABC ≅ △ABD

14. $\overline{AC}$ ≅ ■

15. $\overline{BC}$ ≅ ■

16. $\overline{AB}$ ≅ ■

17. ∠D ≅ ■

18. ∠CAB ≅ ■

19. ∠ABC ≅ ■

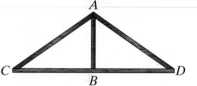

20. **Open-Ended** Draw a pair of congruent triangles. Label the vertices. Then list the pairs of congruent sides and congruent angles.

21. The pair of figures is congruent. Write six congruences for the corresponding parts of the figures. Then find the missing side lengths and angle measures.

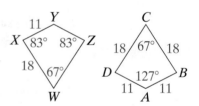

22. **Challenge** Does the statement △JKL ≅ △MNO say the same thing as the statement △JKL ≅ △NOM? Explain.

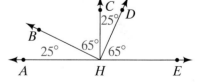
Test Prep and Mixed Review
Practice

Multiple Choice

23. △QRS is similar to △UTS. Which of the following is NOT true about △QRS and △UTS?
Ⓐ $\overline{QS}$ corresponds to $\overline{US}$.
Ⓒ ∠S corresponds to ∠S.
Ⓑ $\overline{RQ}$ corresponds to $\overline{TU}$.
Ⓓ ∠Q corresponds to ∠T.

24. The measure of ∠DHE is 65°. Which angle is supplementary to ∠DHE?
Ⓕ ∠CHD
Ⓗ ∠DHB
Ⓖ ∠CHB
Ⓙ ∠DHA

GO for Help

For Exercises	See Lesson
25–26	6-5

Use a proportion to find the percent.

25. 12 is what percent of 48?

26. 2 is what percent of 100?

Check Skills You'll Need

1. Vocabulary Review
How many endpoints does a *segment* have?

Use the points in each diagram to name the figure shown.

2.
F   R

3.
Z   J

4.
N   K

for Help
Lesson 7-1

What You'll Learn

To identify parts of a circle

◀» **New Vocabulary** circle, radius, diameter, central angle, chord, arc, semicircle

Why Learn This?

In a pizza, each slice is part of a whole pie. In geometry, a central angle is part of a full circle. Just as you can use slices to measure a portion of a pizza, you can use central angles to measure a portion of a circle.

A **circle** is the set of points in a plane that are all the same distance from a given point, called the center. You name a circle by its center. Circle *O* is shown at the right.

•*O*

A **radius** is a segment that connects the center of a circle to the circle.

$\overline{OB}$ is a radius of circle *O*.

B
•*O*

A **diameter** is a segment that passes through the center of a circle and has both endpoints on the circle.

$\overline{AC}$ is a diameter of circle *O*.

C
•*O*
A

A **central angle** is an angle with its vertex at the center of a circle.

∠*AOB* is a central angle of circle *O*.

B
•*O*
A

A **chord** is a segment that has both endpoints on the circle.

$\overline{AD}$ is a chord of circle *O*.

D
•*O*
A

Notice that a central angle is formed by two radii. Two radii lying on the same line form a diameter of a circle. So a radius is half a diameter.

Any two hands of a clock form a central angle on the circular face of the clock.

You can use points on a circle as well as the circle's center to name parts of the circle.

EXAMPLE **Naming Parts Inside a Circle**

1 Name all the radii, diameters, and chords shown for circle O.

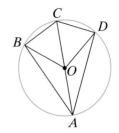

radii: $\overline{OA}$, $\overline{OB}$, $\overline{OC}$, and $\overline{OD}$

diameter: $\overline{AC}$

chords: $\overline{AB}$, $\overline{BC}$, $\overline{CD}$, $\overline{DA}$, and $\overline{AC}$

Vocabulary Tip

The plural of *radius* is *radii* (RAY dee eye).

✓ Quick Check

1. Name all the central angles shown in circle O.

An **arc** is part of a circle. A **semicircle** is half of a circle. In circle P, $\overarc{ST}$ and $\overarc{TW}$ are arcs less than the length of a semicircle. $\overarc{STW}$ is a semicircle. You use three letters to name an arc that is a semicircle or longer.

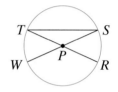

EXAMPLE **Naming Arcs**

2 Name three of the arcs in circle O.

Three arcs are $\overarc{XZ}$, $\overarc{XY}$, and $\overarc{ZXY}$.

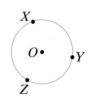

✓ Quick Check

2. Name three other arcs in circle O.

You can use arcs to describe real-world situations involving circles.

EXAMPLE **Application: Amusement Parks**

3 You are in the red car of a Ferris wheel. Your friend is in the green car. Name two different arcs between you and your friend.

The shorter arc is $\overarc{DE}$.

The longer arc is $\overarc{DCE}$.

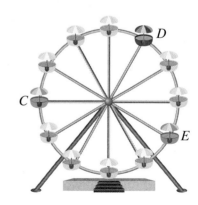

✓ Quick Check

3. Name two different arcs from the blue car to the green car.

1. **Vocabulary** Explain how a radius is different from a diameter.

2. **Reasoning** Must a diameter also be a chord? Explain.

Name each of the following for circle M.

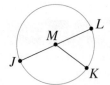

3. center   4. radii   5. chords

6. diameter   7. central angles

Homework Exercises

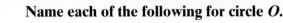

For more exercises, see Extra Skills and Word Problems.

Name each of the following for circle O.

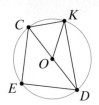

8. center   9. radii   10. chords

11. diameter   12. central angles

GO for Help

For Exercises	See Examples
8–12	1
13–16	2–3

Name the following arcs for circle Q.

13. all arcs shorter than a semicircle

14. all arcs longer than a semicircle

Name the following arcs for circle A.

15. all arcs shorter than a semicircle

16. all arcs longer than a semicircle

17. **Guided Problem Solving** The spoke of the wheel extends from the center of the wheel to the outer edge of the wheel. If a spoke is 26 cm long, what is the diameter of the wheel?
   - What part of a circle does a spoke represent?

Name each of the following for circle D.

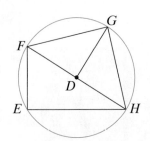

18. two chords   19. two central angles

20. a diameter   21. an isosceles triangle

22. five arcs   23. the longest chord

24. If $m\angle FDG = 90°$, find $m\angle HDG$.

25. **Reasoning** Can a radius also be a chord? Explain.

26. a. **Open-Ended** Draw a design that includes a quadrilateral with vertices on a circle.
   b. **Writing in Math** Describe your design so someone can draw it without looking at your drawing.

Careers Fabric designers use geometric shapes, including circles, to create beautiful patterns on fabrics.

Find each length for radius _r_ and diameter _d._

27. $d = 45.2$ cm, $r = $

28. $r = 2.9$ mm, $d = $ ▮

Draw several diagrams that fit each description. Then make a conjecture.

29. A quadrilateral has vertices that are the endpoints of two diameters.

30. A triangle has all its vertices on a circle. One of its sides is a diameter of the circle.

31. **Challenge** You are running around a circular track. The distance around the track is 200 m. Points _A, B, C, D,_ and _E_ are spaced evenly around the track. If you run along $\overarc{ABD}$, $\overarc{DEB}$, and $\overarc{BCA}$, how far have you run?

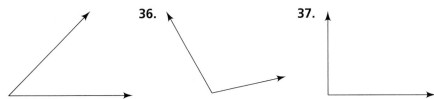

Test Prep and Mixed Review — **Practice**

Multiple Choice

32. Jorge drew the figure shown at the right, with _O_ at the center of the circle. What kind of triangle is $\triangle COB$?
    A. Acute isosceles triangle
    B. Right isosceles triangle
    C. Obtuse scalene triangle
    D. Obtuse isosceles triangle

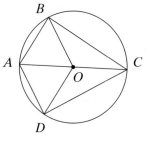

33. Tickets to a sporting event that cost $25 last year cost $32 now. Which equation can be used to find _n_, the percent of increase in the ticket price?
    F. $\frac{25}{32} = \frac{n}{100}$
    G. $\frac{32}{25} = \frac{n}{100}$
    H. $\frac{7}{32} = \frac{n}{100}$
    J. $\frac{7}{25} = \frac{n}{100}$

34. Kiera bought a new computer on sale for $50 less than the original selling price. What other information is necessary to find the percent of the discount?
    A. The store where the computer was purchased
    B. The original price of the computer
    C. The amount of tax charged
    D. The reason for buying a new computer

GO for Help

For Exercises	See Lesson
35–37	7-2

Classify each angle as _acute_, _right_, _obtuse_, or _straight_.

35.

36.

37.

Circle Graphs

Check Skills You'll Need

1. **Vocabulary Review** How is finding the percent of a number like multiplying decimals?

Find each answer.

2. 25% of 360

3. 60% of 360

4. 72% of 360

for Help
Lesson 6-4

What You'll Learn

To analyze and construct circle graphs

New Vocabulary circle graph

Why Learn This?

You can use a circle graph like the one below to display survey or research results. You can see at a glance how the parts compare to one another and to the whole amount.

Music That People Buy

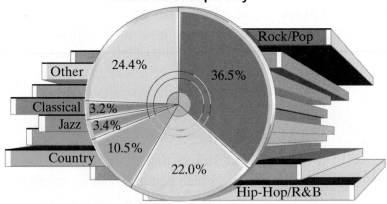

Rock/Pop
24.4%
Other
36.5%
Classical 3.2%
Jazz 3.4%
Country
10.5%
22.0%
Hip-Hop/R&B

SOURCE: Recording Industry Association of America

A **circle graph** is a graph of data in which a circle represents the whole. Each wedge, or sector, is part of the whole. The total must be 100%. You can use a circle graph to see how the whole breaks down into parts.

EXAMPLE Analyzing a Circle Graph

Video Tutor Help
Visit: PHSchool.com
Web Code: are-0775

1. **Gridded Response** In a recent year, consumers spent $13.7 billion on music recordings. Use the circle graph above to find how many dollars, to the nearest tenth of a billion, were spent on country music.

Find 10.5% of $13.7 billion.

0.105 · $13.7 billion ≈ $1.4 billion

Quick Check

1. Approximately how much money was spent on jazz?

	1	.	4
	/	/	
·	·	·	·
0	0	0	0
1	●	1	1
2	2	2	2
3	3	3	3
4	4	4	●
5	5	5	5
6	6	6	6
7	7	7	7
8	8	8	8
9	9	9	9

A circle graph is divided into sectors. Each sector is determined by a central angle. The sum of the measures of the central angles is 360°.

EXAMPLE **Constructing a Circle Graph**

2 **Science** Use the information in the table below to make a circle graph.

NASA Space Shuttle Expenditures

Category	Cost (millions of dollars)
Orbiter	698.8
Propulsion	1,053.1
Operations	738.8
Upgrades	488.8

SOURCE: *Statistical Abstract of the United States*
Go to **PHSchool.com** for a data update.
Web Code: arg-9041

Step 1 Add to find the total space shuttle expenditures.
$$698.8 + 1,053.1 + 738.8 + 488.8 = 2,979.5$$

Step 2 For each central angle, set up a proportion to find the angle measure. Use a calculator to solve. Round to the nearest tenth.

$$\frac{698.8}{2,979.5} = \frac{a}{360} \quad a \approx 84.4° \qquad \frac{1,053.1}{2,979.5} = \frac{b}{360} \quad b \approx 127.2°$$

$$\frac{738.8}{2,979.5} = \frac{c}{360} \quad c \approx 89.3° \qquad \frac{488.8}{2,979.5} = \frac{d}{360} \quad d \approx 59.1°$$

Step 3 Draw a circle. Draw the central angles using the measures found in Step 2. Label each section. Include a title and a key.

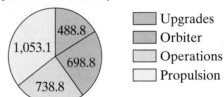

NASA Space Shuttle Expenditures (millions of dollars)

✓ Quick Check

Test Prep Tip

To find a percent of a number, change the percent to a decimal and then multiply.

2. **a.** Find the measure of the central angle that you would draw to represent summer.
   b. Use the information in the table at the right to make a circle graph.

Favorite Season

Season	Percent
Summer	40%
Spring	11%
Winter	4%
Fall	45%

1. **Vocabulary** In a circle graph, the sum of the sectors must equal ▪.

2. **Number Sense** A circle graph has five sectors. Two sectors are equal to 25% each. The third sector is equal to 35%. Which CANNOT be the value of either of the remaining two sectors?

    Ⓐ 22%   Ⓑ 11%   Ⓒ 10%   Ⓓ 1%

Find the measure of the central angle that you would draw to represent each percent in a circle graph.

3. 25%   4. 50%   5. 10%   6. 12.5%

Homework Exercises

For more exercises, see Extra Skills and Word Problems.

GO for Help

For Exercises	See Examples
7–9	1
10–11	2

Use the circle graph for Exercises 7–9.

7. What takes up the largest portion of Royston's day?

8. What percent of the day does Royston typically spend doing homework?

9. How many hours a day does Royston spend sleeping?

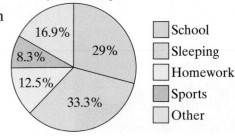

Royston's Day

16.9% · 29% · 8.3% · 12.5% · 33.3%

☐ School
☐ Sleeping
☐ Homework
☐ Sports
☐ Other

Use the information in each table to make a circle graph.

10. **Frozen Yogurt Sales**

Flavor	Scoops
Vanilla	84
Chocolate	107
Strawberry	43

11. **Movie Rentals**

Type	Number
Action	7
Comedy	9
Other	5

GPS 12. **Guided Problem Solving** Use the data to draw a circle graph.

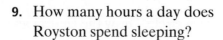

Transportation Mode	Walk	Bicycle	Bus	Car
Number of Students	252	135	432	81

- **Make a Plan** First find the total number of students. Then set up a proportion for each mode to find its central angle measure.
- **Carry Out the Plan** The total number of students is ▪. Use the proportions below.

$$\frac{252}{\blacksquare} = \frac{w}{360} \qquad \frac{135}{\blacksquare} = \frac{b}{360} \qquad \frac{432}{\blacksquare} = \frac{u}{\blacksquare} \qquad \frac{\blacksquare}{\blacksquare} = \frac{c}{\blacksquare}$$

Homework Video Tutor
Visit: PHSchool.com
Web Code: are-0707

Use the circle graph for Exercises 13–16.

13. Which country or region is most visited by United States travelers?

14. **Reasoning** Can you tell which country or region is least visited by United States travelers? Explain.

15. Approximately how many people travel to Europe from the United States each year?

16. **Writing in Math** Why use Europe rather than list every country individually?

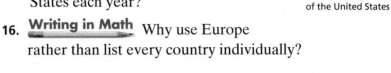

U.S. Foreign Travel (millions of people per year)

Source: Statistical Abstract of the United States

17. The table shows how many days each week students do volunteer work. Use the table to make a circle graph.

Days	1	2	3	4	5
Students	11	5	5	2	2

18. **Open-Ended** Describe a situation for which a circle graph is an appropriate display to represent the data. Describe a situation for which a circle graph is *not* an appropriate display to represent the data.

19. **Challenge** A circle graph shows a survey of the favorite ice cream flavors of all the students at Park School. Vanilla is the favorite flavor of 28 students. The central angle measure for vanilla is 72° in the circle graph. How many students are at Park School?

Test Prep and Mixed Review

Practice

Gridded Response

20. There are 150 animals in Sal's Pet Store. According to the circle graph, how many of the animals are dogs?

21. A carpenter renovating a house is sanding the dining room floor. She sands 300 ft² of wood floor in 1 hour and 40 minutes. What is the unit rate in square feet per minute?

22. The measure of $\angle ABC$ is 128°. What is the measure of its supplement in degrees?

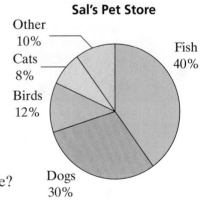

Sal's Pet Store

Find each sum or difference.

23. $\frac{2}{3} + \frac{3}{8}$ 24. $4\frac{1}{6} + 6\frac{2}{9}$ 25. $\frac{7}{8} - \frac{1}{4}$ 26. $14\frac{5}{8} - 6\frac{5}{12}$

GO for Help

For Exercises	See Lesson
23–26	3-3

Making a Circle Graph

You can use a spinner to generate data. You can use circle graphs to present the data.

ACTIVITY

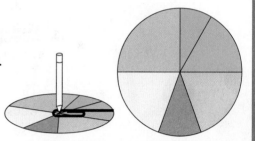

Step 1 Copy the spinner at the right. Use a protractor to measure and copy the central angles of the spinner.

Step 2 Straighten half a paper clip to use as the pointer. Use a pencil point to keep the loop of the paper clip at the center of the spinner.

Step 3 Make a table like the one at the right. Spin the paper clip. Use your frequency column to record the results of 100 spins.

Category	Tallies	Fraction	Angle
Red	■	■	■
Blue	■	■	■
Green	■	■	■
Yellow	■	■	■
Gray	■	■	■
Orange	■	■	■

1. Fill in the fraction of tallies for each color and the number of degrees in that fraction of a circle. What should be the sum of each column?

2. Make a circle graph for your data. Use a protractor to draw the central angles for your graph. Label each sector of your graph.

3. Compare your circle graph to the spinner that you used. Are they exactly the same? Explain.

✓ Checkpoint Quiz 2

Lessons 7-5 through 7-7

1. If two squares have the same area, are they congruent? Explain.

2. Use the information in the table to make a circle graph.

Town Middle School

Grade	6	7	8
Number of Students	75	100	125

Name each of the following for circle P.

3. two radii

4. a diameter

5. two central angles

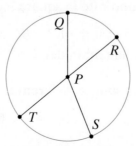

Percents and Circle Graphs

The circle graph shows people's milk preferences. If your school cafeteria ordered pints of milk for 450 milk-drinking students, how many pints of each type should the cafeteria order?

School Milk Preferences

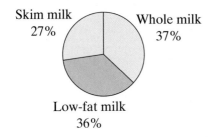

Skim milk 27%
Whole milk 37%
Low-fat milk 36%

What You Might Think

What do I know?
What do I want to find out?

How do I solve the problem?

What is the answer?

Is it reasonable?

What You Might Write

The graph shows whole, low-fat, and skim milk preferences. I want to find each percent for 450 students.

Whole milk: 37% · 450 = 166.5
Low-fat milk: 36% · 450 = 162
Skim milk: 27% · 450 = 121.5

Round: 166.5 rounds to 170.
       162 rounds to 160.
       121.5 rounds to 120.

Order 170 pints of whole milk, 160 pints of low-fat milk, and 120 pints of skim milk.

The numbers add to 450, with skim milk a smaller number than the other two. The answer is reasonable.

Think It Through

1. Do you think these data will change in ten years? In what way? Explain your reasoning.

Exercises

Solve the problems. For Exercises 2 and 3, answer the questions first.

2. The circle graph shows different age groups in the population of the United States as reported in the 2000 U.S. Census. If the population of the United States is about 281 million, approximately how many people are in your age group?

Age Groups

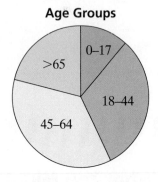

a. What do you know? What do you want to find out?

b. How can you estimate the percent of people in your age group?

3. A study collected percents of male and female teachers across the nation. The results are shown in the table below. If you have five classes each year, how many male teachers can you expect during your three middle school years? How many female teachers can you expect?

Teachers

Female	Male
72%	28%

a. What do you know? What do you want to find out?

b. Can a model help you find the answers?

4. Blood typing is important in transfusions and organ transplants. Use the data in the table to make a circle graph showing the percents of blood types in the United States. Use a calculator to find the number of U. S. citizens with each blood type. Use 281 million as the population of the United States.

U.S. Blood Type Percentages

Type	Positive	Negative
O	38%	7%
A	34%	6%
B	9%	2%
AB	3%	1%

5. Make a circle graph of how you spend time during a typical day in school. Limit your graph to five categories.

7-8 Constructions

Check Skills You'll Need

1. **Vocabulary Review** What do two *intersecting lines* share?

Use the points in each diagram to name the figure shown.

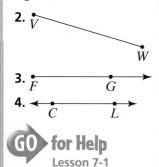

2.
V

W

3.
F   G

4.
C   L

GO for Help
Lesson 7-1

What You'll Learn

To construct congruent segments and perpendicular bisectors

🔊 **New Vocabulary** compass, midpoint, segment bisector, perpendicular lines, perpendicular bisector

Why Learn This?

Architects use congruent segments and perpendicular lines when they design buildings. Congruent segments and perpendicular lines can give a design a sense of balance.

You can use a geometric tool called a **compass** to draw a circle, or a part of a circle, called an arc.

You can use a compass and a straightedge (an unmarked ruler) to construct a congruent segment for a given segment.

EXAMPLE Constructing a Congruent Segment

1 Construct segment $\overline{CD}$ congruent to $\overline{AB}$.

A   B

Step 1 Draw a ray with endpoint *C*.

C

Step 2 Open the compass to the length of $\overline{AB}$.

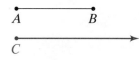

A   B

Step 3 Keep the compass open to the same width. Put the compass point on point *C*. Draw an arc that intersects the ray. Label the point of intersection *D*.

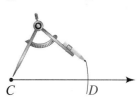

C   D

$\overline{CD}$ is congruent to $\overline{AB}$.

✓ Quick Check

● **1.** Draw a segment $\overline{TR}$ 25 mm long. Construct $\overline{SV}$ congruent to $\overline{TR}$.

The **midpoint** of a segment is the point that divides the segment into two segments of equal length.

A **segment bisector** is a line, segment, or ray that goes through the midpoint of a segment.

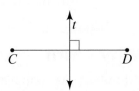

$\overline{AM}$ is congruent to $\overline{MB}$.

M is the midpoint of $\overline{AB}$.

Line ℓ is a segment bisector of $\overline{AB}$.

Perpendicular lines are lines that intersect to form right angles.

A segment bisector that is perpendicular to a segment is the **perpendicular bisector** of the segment. You can use a compass and a straightedge to construct the perpendicular bisector of a given segment.

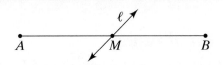 **Constructing a Perpendicular Bisector**

② Construct the perpendicular bisector of $\overline{AB}$.

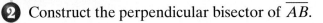

Step 1 Set the compass to more than half the length of $\overline{AB}$. Put the tip of the compass at A and draw an arc intersecting $\overline{AB}$.

Step 2 Keeping the compass set at the same width, put the tip at B and draw another arc intersecting $\overline{AB}$. Points C and D are where the arcs intersect.

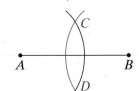

Step 3 Draw $\overleftrightarrow{CD}$. The intersection of $\overline{AB}$ and $\overleftrightarrow{CD}$ is point M. $\overleftrightarrow{CD}$ is the perpendicular bisector of $\overline{AB}$. Point M is the midpoint of $\overline{AB}$.

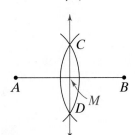

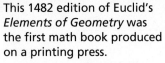

This 1482 edition of Euclid's *Elements of Geometry* was the first math book produced on a printing press.

Source: Wellesley College Library

✓ Quick Check

2. Draw a segment 3 in. long. Label the segment $\overline{XY}$. Construct the perpendicular bisector of $\overline{XY}$.

1. **Vocabulary** Q is the midpoint of $\overline{PR}$. Write a statement about two congruent segments having endpoint Q.

2. **Reasoning** Can you construct a different perpendicular bisector of $\overline{AB}$ in Example 2? Explain.

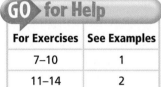
Point B is the midpoint of $\overline{AC}$. Complete each statement.

3. $AB = 4$ in., $AC = $ ■

4. $AC = 9$ m, $AB = $ ■

5. $AC = 7$ m, $BC = $ ■

6. $BC = 5$ ft, $AB = $ ■

Homework Exercises

For more exercises, see Extra Skills and Word Problems.

GO for Help

For Exercises	See Examples
7–10	1
11–14	2

Copy each segment. Then construct a congruent segment.

7. A •————————————• B

8. S •————————————• T

9. C •————————————• D

10. K •————————• L

Draw each segment. Then construct its perpendicular bisector.

11. a segment 4 in. long

12. a segment 10 cm long

13. a segment 5 in. long

14. a segment 13.5 cm long

15. **Guided Problem Solving** Draw $\overline{CD}$ at least 3 in. long. Construct and label a segment one fourth as long as $\overline{CD}$.
   - **Make a Plan** One half of one half is one fourth. So bisecting half of a line segment will give you one fourth of a line segment.
   - **Carry Out the Plan** Bisect $\overline{CD}$ and label the midpoint E. Then bisect $\overline{CE}$. That segment will be one fourth as long as $\overline{CD}$.

16. Draw $\overline{MN}$ about 4 in. long. Then construct $\overline{JK}$ two and one half times as long as $\overline{MN}$.

17. Draw $\overline{AB}$ about 5 in. long. Then construct $\overline{XY}$ so that the two line segments are perpendicular bisectors of each other.

18. **Patterns** Draw two large triangles, one acute and one obtuse. Construct the perpendicular bisector of each side. Make a conjecture about the perpendicular bisectors of the sides of any triangle.

19. **Writing in Math** How many midpoints does a segment have? How many segment bisectors does it have? How many perpendicular bisectors does it have? Explain.

Homework Video Tutor
Visit: PHSchool.com
Web Code: are-0708

Point *B* is the midpoint of *AC*. Complete each statement.

20. $AB = 2.25$ in., $AC = \blacksquare$ **21.** $AC = 8.4$ cm, $AB = \blacksquare$

22. $BC = 1.7$ ft, $AB = \blacksquare$ **23.** $AB = 17$ mm, $AC = \blacksquare$

24. $AC = 3$ in., $BC = \blacksquare$ **25.** $BC = 75$ cm, $AC = \blacksquare$

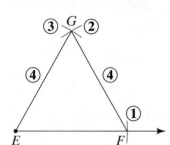

26. Follow the steps to construct $\triangle EFG$ with all sides congruent to $\overline{XY}$.

Step 1 Draw a segment $\overline{XY}$. Use a compass to construct $\overline{EF} \cong \overline{XY}$.

Step 2 Using the same compass width, place the compass tip on point F and draw an arc above $\overline{EF}$.

Step 3 Using the same compass width, place the compass tip on point E and make another arc above $\overline{EF}$, intersecting the first arc. Label the intersection G.

Step 4 Draw $\overline{EG}$ and $\overline{FG}$ to form $\triangle EFG$.

27. Use the construction techniques you learned in this lesson to draw a 90° angle without using a protractor.

28. **Challenge** A is the midpoint of $\overline{XY}$. Y is the midpoint of $\overline{XZ}$. Z is the midpoint of $\overline{AB}$. $\overline{XA}$ is 2 cm long. How long is $\overline{XB}$?

Test Prep and Mixed Review

Practice

Multiple Choice

29. Don bought items that cost $2.59, $3.48, $1.75, $0.63, and $0.98. He used a coupon worth $0.80. The tax totaled $0.73. If he gave the clerk a $10 bill, how much change did he receive?

Ⓐ $0.64   Ⓑ $0.96   Ⓒ $1.37   Ⓓ $9.36

30. Which problem situation matches the equation $0.80x = 400$?

Ⓕ In a recent election, 80% of the people voted for a new tax to repair streets. Four hundred people voted. What is x, the number who voted for the tax?

Ⓖ Eighty out of 400 of the items at one manufacturing plant were found to have flaws. What is x, the percent of items that contained flaws?

Ⓗ The Drake family has driven 80 miles. They need to travel 400 miles to reach their destination. What is x, the percent of their trip completed?

Ⓙ In a school survey, 400 students said they would like more variety in the cafeteria. This was 80% of those surveyed. What is x, the total number of students who were surveyed?

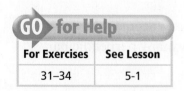

For Exercises	See Lesson
31–34	5-1

Write each ratio in two other ways.

31. 5 to 7   **32.** 6 : 13   **33.** $\dfrac{9}{4}$ **34.** $\dfrac{16}{25}$

Drawing a Picture

Sometimes a picture is not supplied with a problem. Then you can draw a picture to help you solve the problem. Make sure your picture is large enough to allow you to label all the parts.

EXAMPLE

$\triangle CRT \cong \triangle POV$. The measure of $\angle C$ is 41°, and the measure of $\angle T$ is 104°. What is the measure of $\angle O$?

Draw and label triangles CRT and POV. Label angles C and T. Label the corresponding angles in $\triangle POV$.

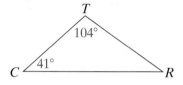 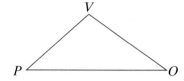

Write an equation to find the measure of $\angle O$.

Let $x = m\angle O = m\angle R$.

$$x + 41° + 104° = 180°$$
$$x + 145° = 180°$$
$$x + 145° - 145° = 180° - 145°$$
$$x = 35°$$

● The measure of $\angle O$ is 35°.

Exercises

Draw a picture to solve each problem.

1. $\overleftrightarrow{QR}$ intersects $\overleftrightarrow{ST}$ at point U. The measure of $\angle QUT$ is 123°, and the measure of $\angle TUR$ is 57°. What is the measure of $\angle SUR$?

    Ⓐ 57°   Ⓑ 90°   Ⓒ 123°   Ⓓ 133°

2. A right triangle has one angle that measures 16°. Which of the following could be the measures of the other two angles?

    Ⓕ 16°, 148°   Ⓖ 74°, 90°   Ⓗ 84°, 90°   Ⓙ 82°, 82°

3. Rectangle $ABCD$ shares $\overline{BC}$ with equilateral triangle BCE. The length of $\overline{CD}$ is 4 cm, and the perimeter of $ABCD$ is 14 cm. What is the perimeter of $\triangle BCE$?

    Ⓐ 3 cm   Ⓑ 6 cm   Ⓒ 9 cm   Ⓓ 14 cm

Vocabulary Review

🔊 acute angle (p. 330)
acute triangle (p. 337)
adjacent angles (p. 331)
angle (p. 330)
arc (p. 351)
central angle (p. 350)
chord (p. 350)
circle (p. 350)
circle graph (p. 354)
compass (p. 361)
complementary (p. 331)
congruent angles (p. 331)
congruent polygons (p. 346)
congruent sides (p. 336)
decagon (p. 340)
diameter (p. 350)
equilateral triangle (p. 336)
hexagon (p. 340)

intersecting lines (p. 325)
irregular polygon (p. 340)
isosceles triangle (p. 336)
line (p. 324)
midpoint (p. 362)
obtuse angle (p. 330)
obtuse triangle (p. 337)
octagon (p. 340)
parallel lines (p. 325)
parallelogram (p. 341)
pentagon (p. 340)
perpendicular bisector (p. 362)
perpendicular lines (p. 362)
plane (p. 325)
point (p. 324)
quadrilateral (p. 340)
radius (p. 350)
ray (p. 324)

rectangle (p. 341)
regular polygon (p. 340)
rhombus (p. 341)
right angle (p. 330)
right triangle (p. 337)
scalene triangle (p. 336)
segment (p. 324)
segment bisector (p. 362)
semicircle (p. 351)
skew lines (p. 325)
square (p. 341)
straight angle (p. 330)
supplementary (p. 331)
trapezoid (p. 341)
vertex (p. 330)
vertical angles (p. 331)

Go Online
PHSchool.com
For: Online vocabulary quiz
Web Code: arj-0751

Choose the correct term to complete each sentence.

1. (Parallel, Skew) lines lie in the same plane.

2. A (decagon, pentagon) is a polygon with five sides.

3. Angles whose sum is 180° are (complementary, supplementary).

4. A(n) (isosceles, scalene) triangle has no congruent sides.

5. An (acute, obtuse) angle measures less than 90°.

Skills and Concepts

Lessons 7-1, 7-2
- To identify segments, rays, and lines
- To classify angles and to work with pairs of angles

A **plane** is a flat surface that extends indefinitely in all directions and has no thickness. **Parallel lines** are lines that lie in the same plane and have no points in common. **Skew lines** do not lie in the same plane.

An **angle** is formed by two rays with a common endpoint. The sum of two **complementary** angles is 90°. The sum of two **supplementary** angles is 180°.

Find the complement and the supplement of each angle.

6. $m\angle A = 55°$ 7. $m\angle B = 27°$ 8. $m\angle C = 87°$ 9. $m\angle D = 12°$

Lessons 7-3, 7-4

- To classify triangles and to find the angle measures of triangles
- To classify polygons and special quadrilaterals

You can classify a triangle by the measure of its sides and angles. The sum of the measures of the angles of any triangle is 180°. A **polygon** is classified by the number of sides it has. A **regular polygon** has congruent sides and congruent angles.

Find the value of x. Then classify each triangle by its sides and angles.

10.

11.

12.

Identify each polygon and classify it as *regular* or *irregular*.

13.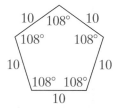

14.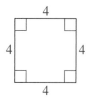

15.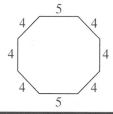

Lesson 7-5

- To identify congruent figures and to use them to find missing measures

Congruent polygons have the same size and shape. **Corresponding parts** of congruent polygons are congruent.

16. In the diagram, $\triangle ABC \cong \triangle MNP$. Find the missing side lengths and angle measures for the figures.

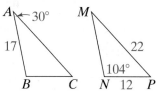

Lessons 7-6, 7-7

- To identify parts of a circle
- To analyze and construct circle graphs

A **circle** is the set of points in a plane that are all the same distance from the center. A circle can have **radii, diameters, central angles, chords,** and **arcs. Circle graphs** present data as percents or fractions of a total.

Name each of the following for circle *T*.

17. radii

18. diameters

19. center

20. chords

21. arcs longer than a semicircle

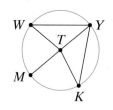

Lesson 7-8

- To construct congruent segments and perpendicular bisectors

You can use a **compass** to construct congruent segments and **perpendicular bisectors.**

22. Draw a segment. Construct a segment congruent to it.

23. Draw a segment. Construct its perpendicular bisector.

Go Online For: Online chapter test
PHSchool.com Web Code: ara-0752

Use the diagram for Exercises 1–3.

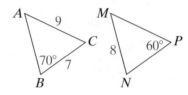

1. Name all the segments parallel to $\overline{AB}$.

2. Name all the segments intersecting $\overline{FG}$.

3. Name all the segments skew to $\overline{DH}$.

Use a protractor to measure each angle.

4.

5.

Find the measures of the complement and the supplement of each angle.

6. $m\angle H = 45°$

7. $m\angle R = 7°$

8. $m\angle K = 89°$

9. $m\angle P = 25°$

10. What is the supplement of a 102° angle?

11. Does a 98° angle have a complement? Explain.

12. Draw a segment. Construct its perpendicular bisector.

13. Draw a segment $\overline{AB}$. Construct a congruent segment $\overline{CD}$.

Find the value of x in each triangle. Classify each triangle by its side lengths and its angle measures.

14.

15.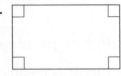

Identify each polygon.

16.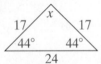

17.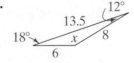

18. What is the name of a polygon with one pair of parallel sides?

In the diagram below, $\triangle ABC \cong \triangle MNP$. Complete each statement.

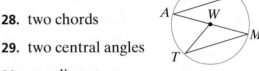

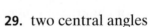

19. $\overline{AC} \cong$ ■

20. $\angle P \cong$ ■

21. ■ $\cong \overline{PN}$

22. $\angle B \cong$ ■

23. ■ $\cong \angle M$

24. $AB =$ ■

25. $m\angle N =$ ■

26. $MP =$ ■

Name each of the following for circle W.

27. three radii

28. two chords

29. two central angles

30. one diameter

31. three arcs shorter than half the circle

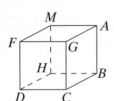

32. **Class Trip** Students earned the following amounts of money to pay the transportation costs of a class trip. Make a circle graph for the data.

Fundraiser	Money
Car wash	$150
Paper drive	$75
Book sale	$225
Food stand	$378

33. **Writing in Math** Briefly explain the differences and similarities among a rectangle, a rhombus, and a square.

Reading Comprehension

Read each passage and answer the questions that follow.

Energetic Math The amount of energy that Americans use each year varies greatly from state to state. People in Alaska use about 1,143.7 million BTU (British thermal units) per person. People in Hawaii use about 200.9 million BTU per person. People in Texas, Ohio, Vermont, and New York use about 587.8 million BTU, 370.2 million BTU, 283.8 million BTU, and 225.5 million BTU per person, respectively.

1. Energy consumption in Hawaii is, on average, about what percent of the energy consumption in Alaska?
   - Ⓐ 18% Ⓑ 21% Ⓒ 25% Ⓓ 550%

2. Energy consumption in Texas is, on average, about what percent of the consumption in Vermont?
   - Ⓕ 50%   Ⓗ 150%
   - Ⓖ 100%   Ⓙ 200%

3. People moving from New York to Ohio might expect their energy consumption to increase by about what percent?
   - Ⓐ 40%   Ⓒ 64%
   - Ⓑ 61%   Ⓓ 164%

4. For the states mentioned in the passage, what is the median energy consumption per person in millions of BTU?
   - Ⓕ 320 Ⓖ 327 Ⓗ 389 Ⓙ 469

The Value of Education People with more education generally earn more money. On average, college graduates make about $21 per hour. If you begin college, but donít finish, you can expect an average of about $13 per hour. High school graduates with no college earn about $11 per hour, and those who don't finish high school average about $8 per hour.

5. For the average earnings of high school dropouts compared to earnings of college graduates, which expression could you use to find the percent of increase?
   - Ⓐ $\dfrac{(21-8)}{8}$ Ⓒ $\dfrac{(21-11)}{11}$
   - Ⓑ $\dfrac{(13-11)}{11}$ Ⓓ $\dfrac{(21-11)}{21}$

6. Which is the best estimate of how much the average college graduate earns in a year? (Use 8 hours per day, 5 days per week.)
   - Ⓕ $8,400   Ⓗ $42,000
   - Ⓖ $21,000   Ⓙ $68,000

7. A person who drops out of high school will earn, on average, about what percent of the earnings of someone who completes high school but does not go to college?
   - Ⓐ 40%   Ⓒ 73%
   - Ⓑ 62%   Ⓓ 138%

8. A job pays $546 for 40 hours of work in one week. What percent is this of the average wage for a person who started college but didn't finish?
   - Ⓕ 95%   Ⓗ 155%
   - Ⓖ 105%   Ⓙ 215%

Applying Geometry

Golf Course Math A good miniature golf course should be challenging and creative. The best courses have some clever twist to delight even the most experienced players. For example, consider a course where you tee off right next to the hole and have to go all the way around, avoiding obstacles, to finish where you started.

Put It All Together

Materials ruler, protractor

1. Design a hole for a miniature golf course so that the tee (start) and the hole (finish) are right next to each other, and you end where you began. Shape the hole and arrange obstacles so it takes 5 strokes to play.

2. On your hole diagram, use a ruler to draw the path the ball might travel from the tee around the obstacles and back to the hole. Mark the starting (and ending) point A and label the others B, C, D, and E. What is the name of the polygon you drew?

3. Use a protractor to measure each of the internal angles of the course. Find the sum of the internal angles of your polygon.

4. Draw a different five-stroke path that the ball could follow. Find the sum of the internal angles. How does your answer compare with the first total? How does it compare with the totals that other students in your class are getting for their courses?

5. **a.** Draw two lines from one of the vertices to the two other non-adjacent vertices (for example, by connecting B to D and B to E). Make sure your lines stay inside the polygon. How many triangles did you make?

   b. Recall that the sum of the measures of the interior angles of one triangle is 180°. Calculate the sum of the measures of the interior angles of your polygon.

Miniature Golfing

There are about 150 professional miniature golfers in the United States.

Water hazard

Miniature Golf in America

Americans play about 11,550,000 rounds of miniature golf each year at an average cost of $4.25 per round.

Green

Putting green

Go Online
PHSchool.com
For: Information about miniature golf
Web Code: are-0753

What You've Learned

- In Chapter 5, you identified similar figures.
- In Chapter 7, you classified triangles, quadrilaterals, and other polygons.
- You identified the parts of a circle.

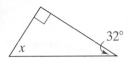 **Check Your Readiness**

GO for Help

For Exercises	See Lesson
1–2	1-3
3–5	2-1
6–9	3-6
10–12	7-3

Multiplying Decimals

Find each product.

1. $0.25 \cdot 3.14 \cdot 4$ **2.** $3 \cdot 20.5 \cdot 2$

Order of Operations

Simplify.

3. $3^3 \cdot (8 - 6)^2$ **4.** $(2^3 \cdot 5) - 6^2$ **5.** $6^2 \cdot 2 + 5^2$

Changing Units in the Customary System

Complete.

6. $3 \text{ c} = \blacksquare \text{ fl oz}$ **7.** $12 \text{ ft} = \blacksquare \text{ in.}$ **8.** $48 \text{ oz} = \blacksquare \text{ lb}$ **9.** $96 \text{ in.} = \blacksquare \text{ ft}$

Finding the Measures of Angles in Triangles

(**Algebra**) **Find the value of x in each triangle.**

10.

11.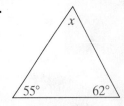

12.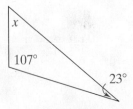

What You'll Learn Next

- In this chapter, you will find the areas of polygons, including triangles, parallelograms, and trapezoids.

- You will find the circumferences and areas of circles.

- You will classify three-dimensional figures and find their surface areas and volumes.

 Problem Solving Application On pages 432 and 433, you will work an extended activity on volume.

■))) Key Vocabulary

- area (p. 375)
- circumference (p. 394)
- cone (p. 411)
- cylinder (p. 410)
- hypotenuse (p. 405)
- irrational number (p. 401)
- net (p. 414)
- perimeter (p. 375)
- prism (p. 410)
- pyramid (p. 410)
- Pythagorean Theorem (p. 405)
- sphere (p. 411)
- square root (p. 400)
- surface area (p. 415)
- three-dimensional figure (p. 410)
- volume (p. 421)

Estimating Perimeter and Area

✓ Check Skills You'll Need

1. **Vocabulary Review** Name four units of length in the *customary system*.

Complete.

2. 6 ft = ■ in.

3. 48 in. = ■ ft

4. 17 ft = ■ in.

 **for Help**
Lesson 3-6

What You'll Learn

To estimate length, perimeter, and area

🔊 **New Vocabulary** area, perimeter

Why Learn This?

In some situations, an estimate of length or area will be enough to solve a problem. Painters estimate the area of a wall to make sure they buy enough paint.

A measurement must include a unit of measure to make sense. When you estimate, you can use familiar objects whose lengths you know.

⚬ length of a paper clip ≈ 1 inch

length of a textbook ≈ 1 foot

length of a baseball bat ≈ 1 yard

EXAMPLE Choosing Reasonable Estimates

1. Choose a reasonable estimate. Explain your choice.

   a. the length of a new pencil: 9 in. or 9 ft

   A new pencil is about 9 paper clips long. So 9 in. is reasonable.

   b. the height of a flagpole: 10 in. or 10 yd

   A flagpole is many baseball-bat lengths high. So 10 yd is reasonable.

✓ Quick Check

1. Which is a reasonable estimate for the distance between Boston, Massachusetts, and Washington, D.C., 400 ft or 400 mi? Explain.

The **perimeter** of a figure is the total distance around the figure.

The formula for perimeter *P* of a rectangle is
$P = 2\ell + 2w$ or
$P = 2(\ell + w)$.

For a list of formulas, go to p. 674.

EXAMPLE **Estimating Perimeter**

2 Estimate the perimeter of the rectangle.

Estimate length and width.

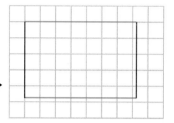

The length is about 7 units.
The width is about 5 units. →

Use the formula for perimeter of a rectangle.

$2(7 + 5) = 24$ ← Substitute for ℓ and *w*.

The perimeter is about 24 units long.

✓ Quick Check

2. Estimate the perimeter of the rectangle.

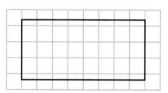

The **area** of a figure is the number of square units a figure encloses.

EXAMPLE **Estimating Area**

3 **Geography** Estimate the area of Lake Superior. Each square represents 900 mi².

Count the number of squares filled or almost filled. Then count the number of squares that are about half filled.

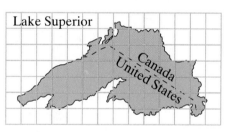

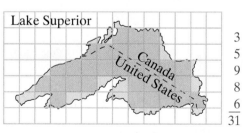

3	1
5	1
9	0
8	3
6	3
31	8

Add the filled squares and the half-filled squares. The total is $31 + \frac{1}{2}(8)$, or 35. Since each square represents 900 mi², multiply 35 by 900 mi².

The area is about 31,500 mi².

✓ Quick Check

3. Estimate the area of the shaded region. Each square represents 4 yd².

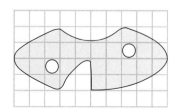

EXAMPLE Using Area and Perimeter

4 **Multiple Choice** Carl wants to paint a landscape. He will choose one of the four canvases shown below.

| | Canvas I | Canvas II | Canvas III | Canvas IV |

Each square on the grid represents 4 square feet. Which canvas has an area of about 48 ft^2 and a perimeter of about 28 ft?

  Ⓐ Canvas I   Ⓒ Canvas III
  Ⓑ Canvas II   Ⓓ Canvas IV

You can estimate each area by counting the number of filled squares. You can estimate each perimeter by finding the sum of the side lengths. Since each square represents 4 ft^2, the side length of each square is 2 ft.

Test Prep Tip

Making a table can help you decide which answer choices to eliminate.

Canvas	Area (ft^2)	Perimeter (ft)
I	32 ✗	
II	36 ✗	
III	48 ✔	32 ✗
IV	48 ✔	28 ✔

Since Canvases I and II do not have an area of about 48 ft^2, you can eliminate them.

Canvas III has an area of about 48 ft^2, but does not have a perimeter of about 28 ft.

Canvas IV has an area of about 48 ft^2 and has a perimeter of about 28 ft.

Canvas IV has the correct area and perimeter, so the answer is D.

✓ Quick Check

4. Each square represents 25 square feet. Estimate the area and perimeter of the figure.

✓ Check Your Understanding

1. **Vocabulary** Area is the number of ? units a figure encloses.

2. **Reasoning** Is it possible for the length of a rectangle to be greater than its perimeter? Explain.

Match each item with a reasonable estimate of its length.

3. length of a bowling lane   **A.** 16 ft

4. height of a coffee mug   **B.** 4 in.
                                   C. 20 yd
5. length of a car

For more exercises, see Extra Skills and Word Problems.

GO for Help

For Exercises	See Examples
6–9	1
10–11	2
12–13	3
14–15	4

Choose a reasonable estimate. Explain your choice.

6. length of a spoon: 4 in. or 4 ft

7. width of your hand: 6 in. or 6 ft

8. depth of an in-ground swimming pool: 10 in. or 10 ft

9. length of a mouse's tail: 2 in. or 2 yd

Estimate the perimeter of each figure. The length of one side of each square represents 1 ft.

10.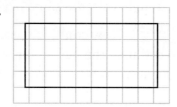

11.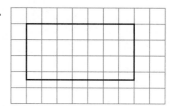

Estimate the area of each shaded region. Each square represents 25 mi².

12.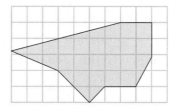

13.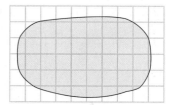

Estimate the area and perimeter. Each square represents 9 yd².

14.

15.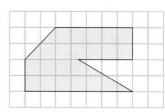

16. **Guided Problem Solving** In the diagram of the fish pond at the right, each square represents 1 ft². Estimate the area of the pond.
    - The number of full squares in the pond = ■.
    - The number of half squares in the pond = ■.
    - The area of the pond $\cong$ ■ $+ \frac{1}{2}$ ■.

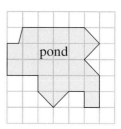

pond

17. Katy painted the window frame at the right. She did not paint the glass inside. If each square represents 1 ft², what is the area of the glass?

Glass

GO Online

Homework Video Tutor
Visit: PHSchool.com
Web Code: are-0801

Estimate each length in inches.  1 in.

18. |⊢————————————|

19. |⊢————|

20. |⊢————————|

21. |⊢————|

22. **Estimation** Measure the length of your shoe. Use your shoe length to estimate the length of your desk.

23. A diagram of a golf fairway is shown at the right. Each square represents 20 yd². Estimate the area.

hole #7

24. A rectangle has a perimeter of 14 ft. Write whole-number dimensions for another rectangle with the same perimeter.

25. **Writing in Math** How could you use a piece of string to estimate the perimeter of the puzzle piece at the right?

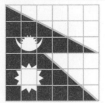

26. **Open Ended** Draw a rectangle on graph paper with a perimeter of 24 units and an area of 32 units².

27. An acre equals 43,560 ft². A theme park covers about 180 acres.
   a. Estimate the number of square feet in the theme park.
   b. The area of a football field is 57,600 ft². About how many football fields are equal to the area of the theme park?

Florida

28. **Challenge** In the map at the left, each square represents 5,575 mi². Use the map to estimate the area of Florida.

Test Prep and Mixed Review
Practice

Multiple Choice

29. The flag of Nepal at the right is not rectangular in shape. If each square on the grid represents 4 square inches, what is the approximate area of the flag shown?
   Ⓐ 18 in.²   Ⓒ 36 in.²
   Ⓑ 44 in.²   Ⓓ 84 in.²

30. Stewart Middle School has 243 seventh-grade students. About 32% of them attended the high school football game. About how many seventh-grade students attended the football game?
   Ⓕ Fewer than 75   Ⓗ Between 85 and 100
   Ⓖ Between 75 and 85   Ⓙ More than 100

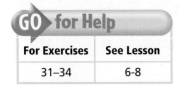

For Exercises	See Lesson
31–34	6-8

GO for Help

Find each percent of increase or decrease. Round to the nearest tenth.

31. 20 to 50   32. 32 to 8   33. 99 to 55   34. 75 to 110

Generating Formulas for Area

You can generate the area of a figure by separating or combining the areas of two figures you know.

ACTIVITY

1. Using graph paper, draw a parallelogram like the one at the right. When you draw the perpendicular segment, what two polygons are formed?

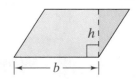

2. Cut out the parallelogram and then cut along the perpendicular segment.

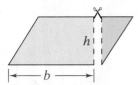

3. Rearrange the pieces to form a rectangle.
   a. What is the area of the rectangle?
   b. What was the area of the parallelogram?

4. How do b and h relate to the length and width of the rectangle? Write a formula for the area of a parallelogram.

ACTIVITY

5. Fold a piece of graph paper in half. On one side, draw a right triangle like the one at the right.

6. Cut out the triangle, cutting through both layers of the folded paper. You now have two congruent triangles.

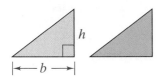

7. Arrange the pieces to form a rectangle.
   a. What is the area of the rectangle?
   b. What is the area of one triangle?

8. How do b and h relate to the length and width of the rectangle? Write a formula for the area of a triangle.

What You'll Learn

To find the area and perimeter of a parallelogram

🔊 **New Vocabulary** height of a parallelogram, base of a parallelogram

Why Learn This?

The floor plan of the building at the right is in the shape of a parallelogram. You can calculate the area of the parallelogram to determine how much office space is available on a given floor of the building.

The **height of a parallelogram** is the length of a perpendicular segment connecting one **base of a parallelogram** to the other.

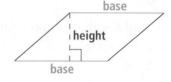

The diagram below relates the formula for the area of a rectangle to the formula for the area of a parallelogram.

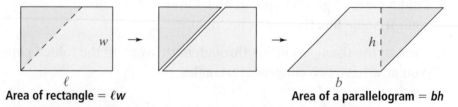

Area of rectangle = ℓw Area of a parallelogram = bh

KEY CONCEPTS **Area of a Parallelogram**

The area of a parallelogram is equal to the product of any base b and the corresponding height h.

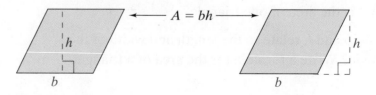

EXAMPLE **Finding the Area of a Parallelogram**

1 Find the area of the parallelogram.

$A = bh$ ← **Use the area formula.**

$= (9)(15)$ ← **Substitute.**

$= 135$ ← **Simplify.**

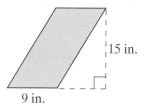
15 in.
9 in.

The area is 135 in.^{2}.

✓ Quick Check

1. Find the area of the parallelogram.

10 cm
9 cm

You can also use lengths of the sides of a rectangle to find perimeter.

EXAMPLE **Relating Perimeter and Area**

2 **Multiple Choice** Melinda wants to plant a rectangular garden and put a fence around it. She has 34 ft of fencing and she wants her garden to be as big as possible. Which dimensions should she use?

   Ⓐ Length of 9 ft and width of 8 ft

   Ⓑ Length of 10 ft and width of 7 ft

   Ⓒ Length of 12 ft and width of 6 ft

   Ⓓ Length of 14 ft and width of 5 ft

Since all answer choices give the length ℓ and width w, you can calculate both the perimeter $2\ell + 2w$ and the area $\ell \times w$.

Perimeter   **Area**

$2(9) + 2(8) = 34$ ✔ $9 \times 8 = 72$ ← **Perimeter is correct; find the area.**

$2(10) + 2(7) = 34$ ✔ $10 \times 7 = 70$ ← **Perimeter is correct; the area in choice A is greater.**

$2(12) + 2(6) = 36$ ✘   ← **Perimeter is greater than 34 ft.**

$2(14) + 2(5) = 38$ ✘   ← **Perimeter is greater than 34 ft.**

The rectangle with a length of 9 ft and a width of 8 ft will have the correct perimeter and the greatest area. The answer is A.

Test Prep Tip 🖊

If the first part in an answer choice is incorrect, do not bother to calculate the second part.

✓ Quick Check

2. What is the perimeter of the rectangle?

5 cm   area = 30 cm^2

1. **Vocabulary** What kind of angle is formed by perpendicular lines?

Two parallelograms have a base and a height that are equal. Tell whether each statement is true or false. Explain your answer.

2. The two parallelograms must be congruent.

3. The areas of the two parallelograms are equal.

Use the parallelogram at the right. Fill in the blank.

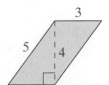

4. The formula for the area is $A = bh = (3)(\blacksquare)$.

5. The formula for the perimeter is $P = 2(\blacksquare) + 2(5)$.

For more exercises, see Extra Skills and Word Problems.

For Exercises	See Examples
6–15	1
16	2

Find the area of each parallelogram.

6.
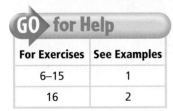

7.
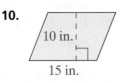

8.
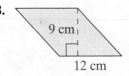

9.
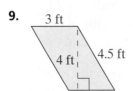

10.
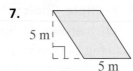

11.
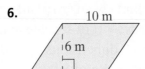

Find each area for base b and height h of a parallelogram.

12. $b = 14$ in.
$h = 6$ in.

13. $b = 25$ mi
$h = 25$ mi

14. $h = 40$ cm
$b = 0.5$ cm

15. $h = 1,000$ m
$b = 20$ m

16. A rectangular fish pond is 21 ft² in area. If the owner can surround the pond with a 20-foot fence, what are the dimensions of the pond?

17. **Guided Problem Solving** The diagram shows a park bounded by streets. The park is in the shape of a parallelogram. Each square is 10 yards on a side. What is the area of the park?
- What are the base and the height of the parallelogram?
- What formula should you use?

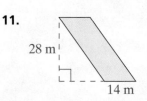

Find the missing measures for each rectangle.

18. $\ell = 14$ in.
    $w = \blacksquare$
    $A = \blacksquare$
    $P = 34$ in.

19. $\ell = \blacksquare$
    $w = 4.2$ m
    $A = 37.8$ m^2
    $P = \blacksquare$

20. $\ell = 7$ ft
    $w = \blacksquare$
    $A = 18.2$ ft^2
    $P = \blacksquare$

21. $\ell = \blacksquare$
    $w = 2$ cm
    $A = \blacksquare$
    $P = 25$ cm

22. **Geography** The shape of the state of Tennessee is similar to a parallelogram. Estimate the area of Tennessee.

23. **Reasoning** The rectangle and the parallelogram at the left have the same perimeter. How do you know that the area of the rectangle is greater than the area of the parallelogram?

24. **Writing in Math** A rectangular lot is 70.2 m long and 59.8 m wide. Is 42,000 m^2 a reasonable estimate for the area of the lot? Explain.

25. **Challenge** Find the area and perimeter of the figure at the right.

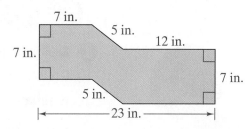

Test Prep and Mixed Review **Practice**

Multiple Choice

26. A playground has the shape of a parallelogram. If the base is 30 feet, and the corresponding height is 25 feet, what is its area?
    Ⓐ 55 ft^2 Ⓑ 187.5 ft^2 Ⓒ 375 ft^2 Ⓓ 750 ft^2

27. Which of the following expressions CANNOT be used to find the perimeter of a regular hexagon with sides of length h?
    Ⓕ $6h$ Ⓗ $3h \times 3h$
    Ⓖ $2h + 2h + 2h$ Ⓙ $6 \times h$

28. In Solomon's stamp collection, $\frac{4}{25}$ of the stamps are international. What percent of Solomon's stamps are international?
    Ⓐ 4%   Ⓑ 16%   Ⓒ 21%   Ⓓ 29%

GO for Help

For Exercises	See Lesson
29–33	6-3

Write each percent as a decimal and as a fraction in simplest form.

29. 200%   30. 135%   31. 152%   32. 0.03%   33. 0.45%

Perimeter and Area of a Triangle

What You'll Learn

To find the perimeter and area of a triangle

🔊 **New Vocabulary** base of a triangle, height of a triangle

Why Learn This?

You use perimeter when you solve problems involving borders. You can find perimeter to see if you have enough material to sew a border around the triangular quilt piece at the right.

To find the perimeter of a triangle, you can add the side lengths.

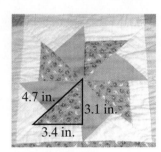

4.7 in.
3.1 in.
3.4 in.

EXAMPLE **Finding the Perimeter of a Triangle**

① **Quilting** How much material do you need to sew a border around the triangular piece on the quilt above?

Estimate $3.4 + 3.1 + 4.7 \approx 3 + 3 + 5 = 11$

$P = 3.4 + 3.1 + 4.7$ ← **Find the perimeter.**

$\quad = 11.2$ ← **Simplify.**

You need 11.2 in. of material to border the triangular piece.

Check for Reasonableness 11.2 is close to 11. The answer is reasonable.

✓ Quick Check

1. Mental Math How much fabric do you need to border a triangular quilt piece whose sides are 6 cm, 8 cm, and 10 cm long?

Any side of a triangle can be considered the **base of a triangle**. The **height of a triangle** is the length of the perpendicular segment from a vertex to the base opposite the vertex or to an extension of the base.

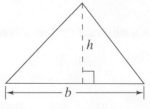
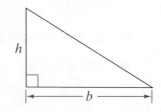
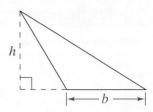

The formula for the area of a triangle follows from the formula for the area of a parallelogram.

The area of a parallelogram = *bh*.

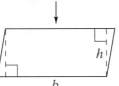

Draw one diagonal.

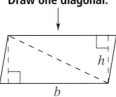

Break the parallelogram into two triangles.

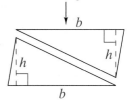

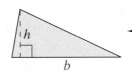 ← The area of a triangle is half the area of a parallelogram.

KEY CONCEPTS Area of a Triangle

The area of a triangle is equal to half the product of any base *b* and the corresponding height *h*.

$$A = \frac{1}{2}bh$$

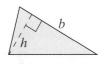

When you find the area of a triangle, remember that you only need the length of the base and the perpendicular height of the triangle.

EXAMPLE Finding the Area of a Triangle

2 Find the area of each triangle.

a.

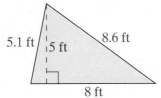

b.

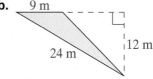

$$A = \frac{1}{2}bh$$ ← Use the area formula. → $$A = \frac{1}{2}bh$$

$$= \frac{1}{2}(8)(5)$$ ← Substitute. → $$= \frac{1}{2}(9)(12)$$

$$= 20$$ ← Simplify. → $$= 54$$

The area is 20 ft². The area is 54 m².

Vocabulary Tip

Areas are always measured in *square units*.

✓ **Quick Check**

2. Find the area of each triangle.

a.

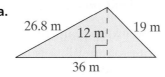

b.

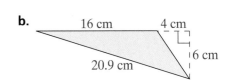

1. Vocabulary A triangle that has a 90° angle is a(n) __?__ triangle.

Each triangle's perimeter is 15 cm. Find the length of the missing side.

2. 4 cm, 5 cm, ■   **3.** 2 cm, 7 cm, ■   **4.** 1 cm, 7 cm, ■

Find the area of each triangle.

5. $b = 4$ cm, $h = 5$ cm   **6.** $b = 2$ in., $h = 7$ in.

7. A carpenter has blueprints for a wooden triangular patio. The base is 5 m and the height is 7 m. What is the area of the patio?

Homework Exercises

For more exercises, see Extra Skills and Word Problems.

GO for Help

For Exercises	See Examples
8–11	1
12–17	2

Find the perimeter of each triangle.

8.
4 ft, 3 ft, 4 ft 6 in.

9.
5 ft, 4 ft, 3.5 ft

10.
5.5 cm, 5 cm, 2 cm

11. You bend a drinking straw into the shape of an equilateral triangle. Each side is 4.5 cm long. How long is the straw?

Find the area of each triangle.

12.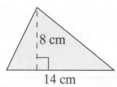
8 cm, 14 cm

13.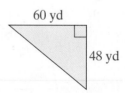
60 yd, 48 yd

14.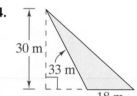
30 m, 33 m, 18 m

15.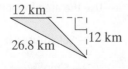
12 km, 26.8 km, 12 km

16.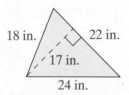
18 in., 22 in., 17 in., 24 in.

17.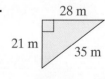
28 m, 21 m, 35 m

18. Guided Problem Solving An equilateral triangle's perimeter is 27 ft. The height of the triangle is 7.8 ft. What is the triangle's area?

• You can *Draw a Picture* to solve this problem. Sketch and label the triangle. Find the perimeter and then use the area formula.

19. A conservation group plans to buy a triangular plot of land. What is the area of the plot of land in the diagram?
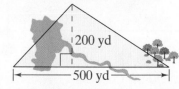
200 yd, 500 yd

Find the area for base *b* and height *h* of each triangle.

20. $b = 4.2$ in. **21.** $b = 12$ m **22.** $h = 6.2$ ft **23.** $h = 100$ km
$h = 6.3$ in. $h = 17$ m $b = 2.5$ ft $b = 200$ km

24. <u>Writing in Math</u> The base of a triangle is doubled and the height remains the same. Explain how the area changes. Use examples.

25. A rescue helicopter receives a distress call from a ship at sea. The diagram at the right displays the search pattern the helicopter will use. Each pass from a central point forms an equilateral triangle. What is the area of one of the triangular regions?

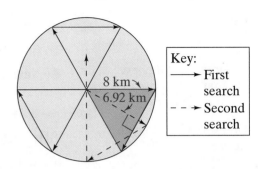

Careers Rescue swimmer is one of the jobs offered in the coast guard.

26. Two equilateral triangles with sides of length 6 inches are joined together to form a rhombus. What is the perimeter of the rhombus?

27. Reasoning One base of a triangle has a length of 6 ft and a corresponding height of 2 ft. This means that the area of the triangle is $\frac{1}{2}(6 \text{ ft} \cdot 2 \text{ ft}) = 6 \text{ ft}^2$. Another base of the same triangle has a length of 4 ft. What is its corresponding height? Explain.

28. Challenge The area of an isosceles right triangle is 121 ft². What is the approximate length of each of the two equal sides?

Test Prep and Mixed Review **Practice**

Multiple Choice

29. Which two of the figures shown have the same area?

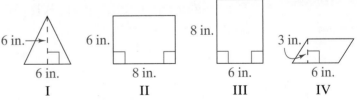

   Ⓐ Figures I and II   Ⓒ Figures I and IV
   Ⓑ Figures I and III   Ⓓ Figures II and IV

30. A square has a perimeter of *x* feet. What is its area in terms of *x*?

   Ⓕ $\dfrac{x^2}{16}$ Ⓖ $4x^2$ Ⓗ $\dfrac{x^2}{4}$ Ⓙ $\dfrac{x}{16}$

Algebra **Solve each proportion using mental math.**

31. $\dfrac{m}{35} = \dfrac{4}{5}$ **32.** $\dfrac{55}{99} = \dfrac{5}{x}$ **33.** $\dfrac{9}{p} = \dfrac{180}{200}$

GO **for Help**

For Exercises	See Lesson
31–33	5-4

Areas of Other Figures

Check Skills You'll Need

1. Vocabulary Review What is the *base of a parallelogram?*

Find the area of each figure.

2.
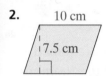
10 cm

7.5 cm

3.
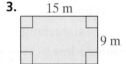
15 m

9 m

GO for Help
Lesson 8-2

What You'll Learn

To find the area of a trapezoid and the areas of irregular figures

🔊 **New Vocabulary** base of a trapezoid, height of a trapezoid

Why Learn This?

If you know how to find the area of simple figures, you can find the area of an irregular figure, such as the area of a backyard deck.

The formula for the area of a trapezoid follows from the formula for the area of a parallelogram.

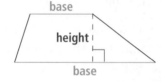

base

height

base

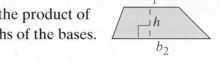

The two parallel sides of a trapezoid are the **bases of a trapezoid**, with lengths b_1 and b_2. The **height of a trapezoid** h is the length of a perpendicular segment connecting the bases.

If you put two identical trapezoids together, you get a parallelogram. The area of the parallelogram is $(b_1 + b_2)h$. The area of one trapezoid equals $\frac{1}{2}(b_1 + b_2)h$.

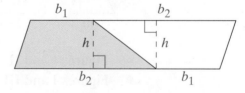

b_1 b_2

h h

b_2 b_1

KEY CONCEPTS Area of a Trapezoid

The area of a trapezoid is one half the product of the height and the sum of the lengths of the bases.

$$A = \frac{1}{2}h(b_1 + b_2)$$

b_1

h

b_2

EXAMPLE **Finding the Area of a Trapezoid**

1 Find the area of the trapezoid shown at the right.

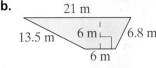

$A = \frac{1}{2}h(b_1 + b_2)$ ← **Use the area formula for a trapezoid.**

$= \frac{1}{2}(15)(8.5 + 13.5)$ ← **Substitute for *h*, *b₁*, and *b₂*.**

$= \frac{1}{2}(15)(22)$ ← **Add.**

$= 165$ ← **Multiply.**

The area of the trapezoid is 165 cm².

✓ Quick Check

1. Find the area of each trapezoid.

a.

b.

You can estimate the area of states shaped like trapezoids.

EXAMPLE **Application: Geography**

At Crater of Diamonds State Park in Arkansas, visitors can search for and keep diamonds and other gems.

2 Estimate the area of Arkansas by finding the area of the trapezoid shown.

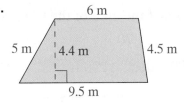

$A = \frac{1}{2}h(b_1 + b_2)$ ← **Use the area formula for a trapezoid.**

$= \frac{1}{2}(242)(250 + 190)$ ← **Substitute for *h*, *b₁*, and *b₂*.**

$= \frac{1}{2}(242)(440)$ ← **Add.**

$= 53,240$ ← **Multiply.**

The area of Arkansas is about 53,240 mi².

✓ Quick Check

2. Estimate the area of the figure at the right by finding the area of the trapezoid.

You can find the area of any figure by separating it into familiar figures.

● More Than One Way

Anna and Ryan are helping their friends build a large wooden deck. What is the area of the deck?

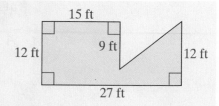

Anna's Method

I'll subtract the area of the triangle from the area of the rectangle.

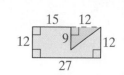

Area of the rectangle:	Area of the triangle:
$A = bh$	$A = \frac{1}{2}bh$
$= (27)(12) = 324$	$= \frac{1}{2}(12)(9) = 54$

Now I'll subtract the area of the triangle from the area of the rectangle.

$A = 324 - 54 = 270$

The area of the deck is 270 ft^2.

Ryan's Method

I'll add the areas of the rectangle and the trapezoid.

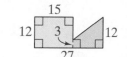

Area of the rectangle:	Area of the trapezoid:
$A = bh$	$A = \frac{1}{2}h(b_1 + b_2)$
$= (15)(12)$	$= \frac{1}{2}(12)(3 + 12)$
$= 180$	$= 90$

Now I'll add the two areas together.

$A = 180 + 90 = 270$

The area of the deck is 270 ft^2.

Choose a Method

Find the area of the figure.

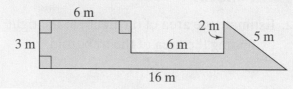

1. **Vocabulary** The perpendicular distance between the two parallel sides of a trapezoid is called the __?__ of the trapezoid.

Identify the bases b_1 and b_2 and height h of each trapezoid below.

2.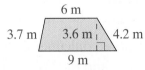

3.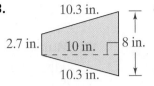

4.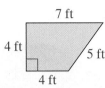

Homework Exercises

For more exercises, see **Extra Skills and Word Problems.**

GO for Help

For Exercises	See Examples
5–7	1–2

Find the area of each trapezoid.

5.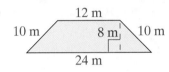

6.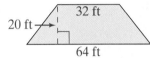

7. **Engineering** When the Erie Canal opened in 1825, it was hailed as an engineering marvel. Find the area of the trapezoidal cross section of the Erie Canal at the right.

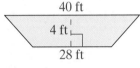

Not to scale

8. **Guided Problem Solving** Estimate the area of Nevada by finding the area of the trapezoid shown at the right.
   - Which measurements in the diagram will you use for the bases and the height?
   - How will you use the bases and height to calculate the area?

9. **Choose a Method** You plan to replace the carpeting in the room shown at the left. What is the area of the room?

Use familiar figures to find the area of each irregular figure.

10.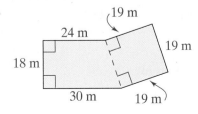

11.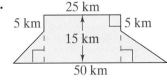

Find the area of each trapezoid, given the bases b_1 and b_2 and height h.

12. $b_1 = 3$ m
$b_2 = 7$ m
$h = 3$ m

13. $b_1 = 11$ in.
$b_2 = 16$ in.
$h = 9$ in.

14. $b_1 = 5.6$ cm
$b_2 = 8.5$ cm
$h = 6$ cm

15. $b_1 = 3\frac{1}{2}$ ft
$b_2 = 2\frac{1}{4}$ ft
$h = 2$ ft

16. **Writing in Math** Find the whole-number possibilities for the lengths of the bases of a trapezoid with a height of 1 m and an area of 3 m². Explain how you found your answer.

17. **Music** A hammered dulcimer is shaped like a trapezoid. The top edge is 17 in. long, and the bottom edge is 39 in. long. The distance from the top edge to the bottom edge is 16 in. What is the area of the dulcimer?

Use familiar figures to find the area and perimeter of each figure.

18.
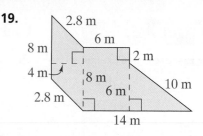

19.
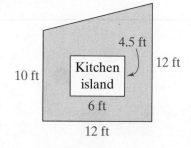

20. **Challenge** A trapezoid has an area of 184 in.². The height is 8 in. and the length of one base is 16 in. Write and solve an equation to find the length of the other base.

Test Prep and Mixed Review **Practice**

Multiple Choice

21. The Hernandez family is purchasing tile for the kitchen shown in the diagram. If tile is not needed for the island area, how many square feet of tile will be needed?

Ⓐ 27 ft²
Ⓒ 105 ft²
Ⓑ 93 ft²
Ⓓ 120 ft²

22. A carpenter finds that the measure of an angle formed between a vaulted ceiling and one wall is 67°. How many degrees is the supplement of this angle?

Ⓕ 23°   Ⓖ 103°   Ⓗ 113°   Ⓙ 157°

GO for Help

For Exercises	See Lesson
23–24	6-7

Find each payment.

23. $453 with a 6% sales tax

24. $49.95 with a 5.5% sales tax

Each square below represents 20 km². Estimate the area of each shaded region.

1.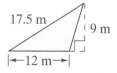

2.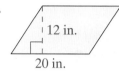

Find the area of each figure. Where necessary, use familiar figures.

3.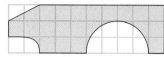

17.5 m   9 m

|←12 m→|

4.

12 in.

20 in.

5.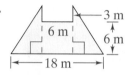

3 m

6 m

6 m

|← 18 m →|

8-5a   **Activity Lab**   **Hands On**

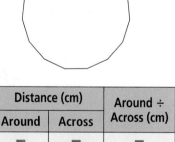

Modeling a Circle

When a regular polygon has many sides, it can be a model for a circle.

ACTIVITY

1. Form a chain of drinking straws by stapling them end to end.

2. Make a regular polygon using a chain of about 15 straws. Use another chain of straws to measure the widest distance across the polygon.

3. Record the number of straws you used in the table at the right. Measure the length of each straw to the nearest centimeter, and calculate the distance around and across each polygon.

Number of Straws		Distance (cm)		Around ÷ Across (cm)
Around	Across	Around	Across	
■	■	■	■	■
■	■	■	■	■

4. Repeat steps 2 and 3 using 20 straws and 30 straws.

5. Calculate and record the ratio of "distance around ÷ distance across" for each polygon. What pattern do you notice?

6. Suppose a regular polygon of 100 sides has a distance across of 100 cm. What is the distance around the polygon? Explain.

8-5 Circumference and Area of a Circle

Check Skills You'll Need

1. Vocabulary Review What is the name of the segment that connects a circle to its center?

Name each segment for circle *O*.

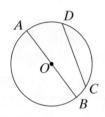

2. radius

3. chord

4. diameter

GO for Help
Lesson 7-6

What You'll Learn

To find the circumference and area of a circle

🔊 **New Vocabulary** circumference, pi

Why Learn This?

If you know how to find the circumference of a circle, you can find how far you must travel to move all the way around the circle.

In the picture below, a Sacagawea dollar rolls along a surface. The distance the dollar rolls is the same as the distance around the edge of the dollar. This distance is the coin's circumference. **Circumference** is the distance around a circle.

C

Pi is the ratio of a circle's circumference *C* to its diameter *d*. Use the symbol π for this ratio. So, $\pi = \frac{C}{d}$. The formula for the circumference comes from this ratio.

KEY CONCEPTS **Circumference of a Circle**

The circumference of a circle is π times the diameter *d*.

$$C = \pi d \text{ or } C = 2\pi r$$

Pi is a nonterminating and nonrepeating decimal. Both $\frac{22}{7}$ and 3.14 are good approximations for π. Many calculators have a key for π and display it to nine decimal places. Your results will vary slightly, depending on which value for π you use.

EXAMPLE Finding the Circumference of a Circle

1 **a.** Find the circumference of the circle using 3.14 for π.

b. Find the circumference of the circle using a calculator's π key.

13 m

5 ft

$C = \pi d$ ← **Use the formula for a circumference.** → $C = 2\pi r$

$= 3.14(13)$ ← **Substitute.** → $= 2\pi(5)$

$= 40.82$ **Use a calculator.** → ≈ 31.41592654

The circumference is about 40.8 m.

The circumference is about 31.4 ft.

✓ Quick Check

1. Find the circumference of the circle at the right. Round to the nearest tenth.

9 m

KEY CONCEPTS Area of a Circle

The area of a circle is the product of π and the square of the radius r.

$A = \pi r^2$

r

EXAMPLE Finding the Area of a Circle

2 A standard circus ring has a diameter of 13 m. What is the area of the ring? Round to the nearest tenth.

$r = \dfrac{13}{2} = 6.5$ ← **The radius is half of the diameter.**

$A = \pi r^2$ ← **Use the formula for the area of a circle.**

$= \pi(6.5)^2$ ← **Substitute 6.5 for the radius.**

$= 132.73328$ ← **Use a calculator.**

≈ 132.7 ← **Round to the nearest tenth.**

The area of a standard circus ring is about 132.7 m².

✓ Quick Check

2. Find the area of the circle. Round to the nearest square unit.

12 m

1. **Number Sense** Is it possible to write out the exact value of pi as a decimal? Explain.

Identify the radius, the diameter, and the circumference.

2. $1, 2\pi, 2$ 3. $4\pi, 4, 2$ 4. $7, 3.5, 22$ 5. $\dfrac{2}{\pi}, \dfrac{1}{\pi}, 2$

Homework Exercises

For more exercises, see Extra Skills and Word Problems.

GO for Help

For Exercises	See Examples
6–11	1
12–18	2

Find the circumference of each circle. Round to the nearest tenth.

6.
50 cm

7.
17 mm

8.
27 m

9.
40 in.

10.
7 cm

11.
8 mi

Find the area of each circle. Round to the nearest square unit.

12.
6 in.

13.
10 m

14.
25 cm

15.
30 ft

16.
22 cm

17.
15 km

18. **Social Studies** The circular bases of the traditional tepees of the Sioux and Cheyenne tribes have a diameter of about 15 ft. What is the area of the base? Round to the nearest square unit.

19. **Guided Problem Solving** A Ferris wheel has a diameter of 135 m. How far does a rider travel in one full revolution of the wheel? Round to the nearest unit.
    - What is the diameter of the circle?
    - What is the formula for circumference, using diameter?

20. In a circle with radius 5 cm, how long can the longest chord be?

Use $\pi \approx \frac{22}{7}$ to estimate the circumference and area for each circle. Where necessary, round to the nearest tenth.

21. $r = 14$ m   **22.** $r = \frac{7}{10}$ cm   **23.** $d = 22$ in.   **24.** $d = 12$ ft

25. Bicycles The front wheel of a high-wheel bicycle from the late 1800s was larger than the rear wheel to increase the bicycle's overall speed. The front wheel measured in height up to 60 in. Find the circumference and area of the front wheel of a high-wheel bicycle.

26. Archaeology The large stones of Stonehenge are arranged in a circle about 30 m in diameter. Find the area of the circle.

27. Writing in Math Use the π key to calculate the area of the circle at the right to the nearest hundredth. Which is the better estimate, 98 m^2 or 99 m^2? Explain.

5.6 m

28. Challenge The diagram shows a fountain at the center of a circular park. The radius of the circle is 30 ft. The circular region is divided into six equal parts. What is the length of the arc in the shaded region? Round to the nearest tenth.

Fountain

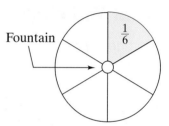

$\frac{1}{6}$

Test Prep and Mixed Review

Practice

Multiple Choice

29. Use a centimeter ruler to measure the radius of the button. What is the area of the button to the nearest square centimeter?
  Ⓐ 3 cm^2 Ⓒ 7 cm^2
  Ⓑ 22 cm^2 Ⓓ 89 cm^2

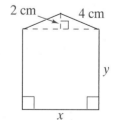

30. A homebuilder wants to use the logo shown on a sign. Which of the following expressions can be used to find the perimeter of the logo?
  Ⓕ $2 + 4 + x + y$
  Ⓖ $4 + 4 + x + 2y$
  Ⓗ $4 + 4 + 2x + 2y$
  Ⓙ $2 + 4 + 2x + 4y$

2 cm   4 cm

y

x

GO for Help

For Exercises	See Lesson
31–33	7-5

$\triangle CAT \cong \triangle DOG$. **Complete each congruence statement.**

31. $\angle A \cong$ ▨   **32.** $\angle G \cong$ ▨   **33.** $\overline{CT} \cong$ ▨

Areas of Irregular Figures

You can find the area of an irregular-shaped figure by combining basic shapes such as rectangles or triangles, or removing them from an existing figure.

Mosaic Erin is creating a mosaic and needs to buy tiles for her artwork. She wants to buy 10% more than the area to be covered. How many square inches of tile does she need to purchase?

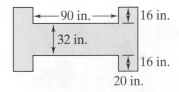

What You Might Think

What do I know?
What am I trying to find out?

How do I solve the problem?

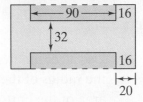

What do I need to calculate?

What is the answer?

What You Might Write

I know the dimensions of the art work. I need to find the area, plus 10%.

I'll subtract the area of the two smaller rectangles from the area of the whole rectangle. Then I'll add 10%.

The area of each smaller rectangle is 90 in. × 16 in., or 1,440 in.² The area of the larger rectangle is 130 in. × 64 in., or 8,320 in.².
The area of the artwork is 8,320 in.² − 2(1,440 in.²), or 5,440 in.².
Then I need to add 10%.
5,440 in.² × 1.10 = 5,984 in.²

Erin needs to buy 5,984 in.² of tile.

Think It Through

1. Why does multiplying by 1.1 add 10% to the area?

2. Is there a way to find the total area by adding instead of subtracting? Explain.

Exercises

Solve the problems. For Exercises 3 and 4, answer the questions first.

3. You plan to replace the carpeting in the room shown below. What is the area of the room?

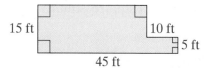

15 ft · 10 ft · 5 ft · 45 ft

a. What do you know? What do you need to find out?
b. Can you find the answer in two different ways? Explain.

4. Sam wants to paint the wall below. What is the area of the wall to the nearest tenth?

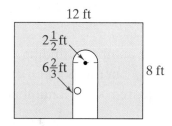

12 ft · $2\frac{1}{2}$ ft · $6\frac{2}{3}$ ft · 8 ft

a. What shapes make up the door?

5. Data from the 2000 U.S. Census for four states are in the table below. Order the states from smallest population per square mile, to greatest. Explain what this means.

State	Population	Area (mi²)
Alaska	626,932	663,267
Florida	15,982,378	65,755
New Jersey	8,414,350	8,721
Texas	20,851,820	268,581

6. Wilma agreed to cut the grass on the infield of the school track for $0.35 /yd² on her riding lawnmower. How much would she make each time she cut the grass?

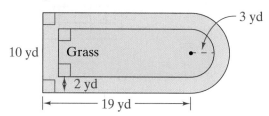

10 yd · Grass · 3 yd · 2 yd · 19 yd

Square Roots and Irrational Numbers

What You'll Learn

To find and estimate square roots and to classify numbers as rational or irrational

◀》 **New Vocabulary** perfect square, square root, irrational number

Why Learn This?

If you know the area of a square, you can find its square root to find the side lengths. You can use square roots when you install flooring.

A number that is the square of an integer is a **perfect square**. For example, the square of 2 is 4, so 4 is a perfect square.

The inverse of squaring a number is finding a **square root**. The symbol $\sqrt{\ }$ in this book indicates the positive square root of a number.

EXAMPLE Finding Square Roots of Perfect Squares

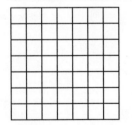
1 **Mental Math** Simplify $\sqrt{49}$.

Since $7^2 = 49$, $\sqrt{49} = 7$.

✓ Quick Check

1. Simplify.

   a. $\sqrt{64}$ **b.** $\sqrt{81}$ **c.** $\sqrt{225}$

If a number is not a perfect square, you can estimate its square root.

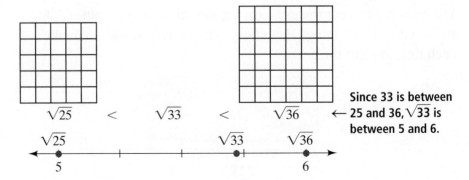

$\sqrt{25}$ < $\sqrt{33}$ < $\sqrt{36}$ ← Since 33 is between 25 and 36, $\sqrt{33}$ is between 5 and 6.

EXAMPLE **Estimating Square Roots**

② **Tiles** Juanita bought 40 tiles on sale. They measured 1 ft² each. What is the largest square bathroom floor she can tile?

$A = s^2$ ← Use the formula for the area of a square.

$40 = s^2$ ← Substitute 40 for the area.

$\sqrt{40} = \sqrt{s^2}$ ← Take the square root of each side.

$\sqrt{40} = s$ ← Simplify.

$\sqrt{36} < \sqrt{40} < \sqrt{49}$ ← Find the perfect squares close to 40.

$6 < \sqrt{40} < 7$ ← Simplify.

$\sqrt{40}$ is between 6 and 7. Since 40 is closer to 36 than to 49, $\sqrt{40}$ is about 6. So the largest floor she can tile is about 6 ft × 6 ft.

Vocabulary Tip

Read $\sqrt{40}$ as "the square root of 40."

✓ Quick Check

2. Suppose Juanita bought twice the number of tiles above. Estimate the dimensions of the largest square floor she can tile.

An **irrational number** is a number that cannot be written as a ratio of two integers. As decimals, irrational numbers neither terminate nor repeat. The diagram below summarizes these relationships.

For help with terminating decimals and repeating decimals, go to Lesson 2-6, Examples 1 and 2.

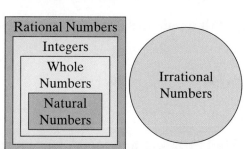

If a positive integer is not a perfect square, its square root is irrational.

Rational → $\sqrt{4}, \sqrt{9}, \sqrt{16}$

Irrational → $\sqrt{2}, \sqrt{3}, \sqrt{27}$

EXAMPLE **Classifying Numbers**

③ Identify each number as *rational* or *irrational*.

a. $\sqrt{14}$ irrational ← 14 is not a perfect square.

b. 0.323223222 . . . irrational ← The decimal neither terminates nor repeats.

c. -0.98 rational ← It is a terminating decimal.

✓ Quick Check

3. Identify each number as *rational* or *irrational*.

   a. $\sqrt{2}$ b. $\sqrt{81}$ c. $0.\overline{6}$ d. $1\frac{2}{7}$

1. **Vocabulary** The square root of the ? of a square is the same as the length of one side of the square.

2. **Number Sense** If you double the length of each side of a square, what happens to the area of the square?

Determine whether or not each decimal has a repeating pattern.

3. $2.3423423423\ldots$ 4. $0.1234567891011\ldots$ 5. $0.17893624775\ldots$

Homework Exercises

For more exercises, see Extra Skills and Word Problems.

GO for Help

For Exercises	See Examples
6–15	1
16–21	2
22–29	3

Simplify each square root.

6. $\sqrt{16}$ 7. $\sqrt{100}$ 8. $\sqrt{36}$ 9. $\sqrt{25}$ 10. $\sqrt{81}$

11. $\sqrt{169}$ 12. $\sqrt{144}$ 13. $\sqrt{121}$ 14. $\sqrt{1}$ 15. $\sqrt{9}$

Estimate the value of each square root.

16. $\sqrt{18}$ 17. $\sqrt{5}$ 18. $\sqrt{41}$ 19. $\sqrt{54}$ 20. $\sqrt{75}$

21. **Industrial Arts** A square carpet covers an area of 64 ft². What is the length of each side of the carpet?

Identify each number as *rational* or *irrational*.

22. $\sqrt{99}$ 23. $\sqrt{41}$ 24. $\sqrt{49}$

25. -0.4744 26. $-\dfrac{3}{2}$ 27. $-0.666666\ldots$

28. $0.12122122212222\ldots$ 29. $0.\overline{35}$

30. **Guided Problem Solving** A fence surrounds a square plot of land. The area of the land is 324 yd². Find the length of each side of the fence.

    Use the strategy *Systematic Guess and Check*.
    - $10 \times 10 = \blacksquare$ The initial guess is (correct, high, low).
    - $20 \times 20 = \blacksquare$ This guess is (correct, high, low).
    - $\blacksquare \times \blacksquare = 324$ This guess is correct.

31. The area of a square cover for a whirlpool bath is 144 ft². What is the length of each side of the cover?

32. **Open-Ended** Write three irrational numbers between 4 and 5.

33. **Writing in Math** What are the square roots of $\frac{1}{4}$ and $\frac{4}{9}$? Write a method of finding the square root of a fraction.

For each number, write all the sets to which it belongs. Choose from *irrational, rational, whole,* **or** *natural numbers,* **or** *integers.*

34. $\frac{3}{5}$ **35.** $0.\overline{23}$ **36.** $\sqrt{36}$ **37.** 4.5 **38.** $\frac{22}{7}$

Math in the Media Use the cartoon below for Exercises 39 and 40.

FOXTROT *by Bill Amend.*

39. Does the cartoon suggest that π is *rational* or *irrational*?

40. What rational numbers can you use to approximate π?

Draw and label a square to model each area.

41. 64 km^2 **42.** 81 m^2 **43.** 121 ft^2 **44.** 4 mi^2

Calculator Tip

Press **2nd** **x^2** 7 2 3
) **ENTER**.

45. Use a calculator to estimate $\sqrt{723}$ to the nearest tenth.

46. Challenge When an object falls, the distance that it falls is given by the formula $d = 16t^2$, where d is the distance in feet and t is the time in seconds. A stone falls from a bridge 1,600 ft above the water. How long does it take for the stone to reach the water?

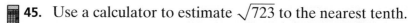
Test Prep and Mixed Review   **Practice**

Multiple Choice

47. The model represents $\sqrt{36} = 6$. Which arrangement can be used to represent $\sqrt{225}$?
  A. 2 rows of 15 small squares
  B. 2 rows of 25 small squares
  C. 15 rows of 15 small squares
  D. 25 rows of 25 small squares

48. A standard basketball rim has a circumference of about 56.6 inches. Which expression can be used to find the diameter of the rim?
  F. $\frac{56.6}{2\pi}$ H. $\frac{56.6}{\pi}$
  G. $56.6 \times \pi$ J. $56.6 \times 2\pi$

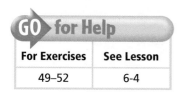
GO for Help

For Exercises	See Lesson
49–52	6-4

Find each answer.

49. 5% of 40   **50.** 60% of 90   **51.** 75% of 15   **52.** 30% of 120

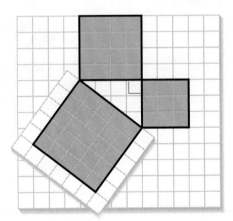

Exploring Right Triangles

Complete this activity to discover a special relationship among the side lengths of right triangles.

ACTIVITY

Step 1 Use centimeter graph paper to draw a right triangle with perpendicular sides that are 3 cm and 4 cm long.

Step 2 Draw squares that have the horizontal and vertical sides of the right triangle as sides.

Step 3 Use another piece of the graph paper to make a square on the side opposite the right angle, as shown at the right.

Exercises

1. What is the length of the side of the square opposite the right angle?

2. What is the area of each of the three squares?

3. Draw a right triangle on graph paper with perpendicular sides that are 8 cm and 15 cm long. Repeat Steps 2 and 3.
   a. What is the length of each side of the square made on the side opposite the right angle?
   b. What is the area of each of the three squares?

4. Construct three squares on the sides of the triangle at the right. What are the areas of the three squares?

5. a. **Patterns** What seems to be the relationship of the areas of the smaller two squares and the third square made on the sides of a right triangle?
   b. Write an equation for each triangle that compares the areas of its squares.

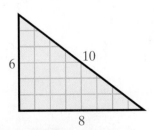

6. A rectangular park is shown at the right. The park is 630 yd long and 430 yd wide. How long is the path connecting opposite corners of the park? Round to the nearest tenth.

7. **Writing in Math** A triangle has side lengths 6 cm, 10 cm, and 12 cm. Explain why this triangle is not a right triangle.

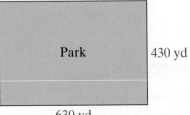

✓ Check Skills You'll Need

1. Vocabulary Review
A *perfect square* is the square of what kind of number?

Simplify each square root.

2. $\sqrt{4}$ **3.** $\sqrt{16}$

4. $\sqrt{36}$ **5.** $\sqrt{49}$

 **for Help**
Lesson 8-6

What You'll Learn

To use the Pythagorean Theorem to solve real-world problems

🔊 **New Vocabulary** legs, hypotenuse, Pythagorean Theorem

Why Learn This?

The lengths of the sides of a right triangle are related. When you understand the Pythagorean Theorem, you can use right triangles to find unknown distances.

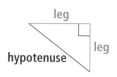

In a right triangle, the two shortest sides are the **legs**. The side opposite the right angle is the **hypotenuse**.

The **Pythagorean Theorem** states that in any right triangle, the sum of the squares of the lengths of the legs equals the square of the length of the hypotenuse.

$$a^2 + b^2 = c^2$$

You can find the length of a hypotenuse with the Pythagorean Theorem.

EXAMPLE   Finding the Length of a Hypotenuse

① The catcher throws a ball from home plate to second base. How far does the catcher throw?

$c^2 = a^2 + b^2$ ← **Pythagorean Theorem**

$c^2 = 90^2 + 90^2$ ← **Substitute.**

$c^2 = 8{,}100 + 8{,}100$ ← **Simplify.**

$c^2 = 16{,}200$

$\sqrt{c^2} = \sqrt{16{,}200} \approx 127.3$ ← **Take the square root of each side.**

To reach second base from home plate, the catcher throws about 127 ft.

✓ Quick Check

1. Find the length of the hypotenuse in the triangle at the right.

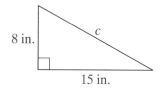

Online active math

For: Triangle Activity
Use: Interactive Textbook, 8-7

You can use the Pythagorean Theorem to find the length of a leg of a right triangle.

EXAMPLE **Finding the Length of a Leg**

② Find the length of the missing leg of the triangle.

$$a^2 + b^2 = c^2 \quad \leftarrow \textbf{Pythagorean Theorem}$$
$$a^2 + 8^2 = 10^2 \quad \leftarrow \textbf{Substitute.}$$
$$a^2 + 64 = 100 \quad \leftarrow \textbf{Simplify.}$$
$$a^2 + 64 - 64 = 100 - 64 \quad \leftarrow \textbf{Subtract 64 from each side.}$$
$$a^2 = 36 \quad \leftarrow \textbf{Simplify.}$$
$$\sqrt{a^2} = \sqrt{36} \quad \leftarrow \textbf{Take the square root of each side.}$$
$$a = 6$$

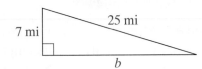

The length of the leg is 6 m.

✓ Quick Check

2. Find the missing length in the triangle below.

7 mi   25 mi

b

EXAMPLE **Application: Recreation**

③ A water slide starts 6 m above the water and extends 11 m horizontally. What is the length of the slide to the nearest tenth of a meter?

A sketch shows that the length of the slide is the length of the hypotenuse.

$$a^2 + b^2 = c^2 \quad \leftarrow \begin{array}{l}\textbf{Use the Pythagorean}\\ \textbf{Theorem.}\end{array}$$
$$6^2 + 11^2 = c^2 \quad \leftarrow \textbf{Substitute.}$$
$$157 = c^2 \quad \leftarrow \textbf{Simplify.}$$
$$\sqrt{157} = \sqrt{c^2} \quad \leftarrow \textbf{Take the square root of each side.}$$
$$c \approx 12.529964$$

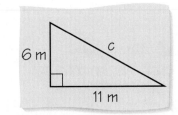

The slide is about 12.5 m.

✓ Quick Check

3. A support wire is attached to the top of a 60-m tower. It meets the ground 25 m from the base of the tower. How long is the wire?

Some water slides are straight, while others have curves.

1. **Vocabulary** The side opposite the right angle in a triangle is called the __?__ .

2. **Number Sense** If the longer leg of the triangle at the right is increased by 2, will the length of *t* increase by 2? Explain.

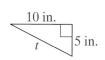

The lengths of two legs of a right triangle are given. Find the length of the hypotenuse to the nearest tenth.

3. 8 m and 11 m   4. 4 in. and 3 in.   5. 12 ft and 20 ft

For more exercises, see Extra Skills and Word Problems.

GO for Help

For Exercises	See Examples
6–8	1
9–15	2–3

Find the length of the hypotenuse of each triangle. Round to the nearest tenth of a unit, if necessary.

6.
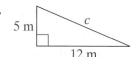

7.
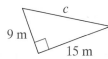

8.
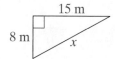

Find each missing length. Round to the nearest tenth, if necessary.

9.
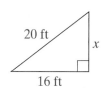

10.
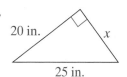

11.
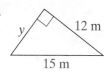

12.
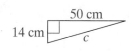

13.
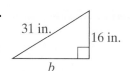

14.

15. A tennis court is 78 ft long and 27 ft wide. To the nearest foot, what is the length of the diagonal of a tennis court?

16. **Guided Problem Solving** A rectangular park is 600 m long and 300 m wide. You walk diagonally across the park from corner to corner. How far do you walk, to the nearest meter?
   • You can use the strategy *Draw a Diagram*. Label the diagram. Then use the Pythagorean Theorem.

17. A ladder is 6 m long. How much farther up a wall does the ladder reach when the base of the ladder is 2 m from the wall than when it is 3 m from the wall? Round to the nearest tenth of a meter.

The lengths of two sides of a right triangle are given. Find the length of the third side to the nearest tenth.

18. legs 8 yd and 11 yd

19. leg 18 m and hypotenuse 28 m

20. Find the perimeter and area of the triangle at the right. Round to the nearest tenth.

9 in.　14 in.

21. **Camping** A large tent has an adjustable center pole. A rope 26 ft long connects the top of the pole to a peg 24 ft from the bottom of the pole. What is the height of the pole? Round to the nearest hundredth if necessary.

22. The rectangular section of fencing at the right is reinforced with wood nailed across the diagonal of the rectangle. What is the length of the diagonal?

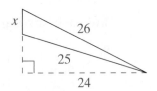

6 ft

8 ft

23. **Navigation** A dock is located 24 km directly east of a lighthouse. A sailboat is directly north of the lighthouse. The sailboat is 25 km from the dock. How far away from the lighthouse is the sailboat?

24. **Writing in Math** A triangle has side lengths measuring 10 m, 24 m, and 26 m. Explain how you use the Pythagorean Theorem to determine whether or not the triangle is a right triangle.

25. **Challenge** Find x.

x　26　25　24

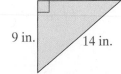
Test Prep and Mixed Review　　**Practice**

Multiple Choice

26. The hypotenuse of a right triangle is 12 cm long. Another side of the triangle is 8 cm long. Which equation can be used to find n, the length of the third side of the triangle?

Ⓐ $n = 12^2 + 8^2$

Ⓑ $n = \sqrt{12^2 + 8^2}$

Ⓒ $n = 12^2 - 8^2$

Ⓓ $n = \sqrt{12^2 - 8^2}$

27. Computers are used to design and improve spacesuits. An astronaut's arm is 32 inches long. What is the arm length in the computer image, if the computer image is $\frac{1}{8}$ of the actual length?

Ⓕ $\frac{1}{8}$ in.　　Ⓖ 4 in.　　Ⓗ 32 in.　　Ⓙ 256 in.

Algebra **Write and solve an equation to find the part of a whole.**

28. What number is 5% of 225?

29. What number is 60% of 40?

For Exercises	See Lesson
28–29	6-6

GO for Help

Three Views of an Object

Three-dimensional objects can be drawn to show length, width, and height. You can make drawings that show the *top view, front view,* and the *right side view.*

EXAMPLE **Drawing Three Views**

Draw the top, front, and right side views of the figure at the right.

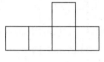 ← **Draw the top view as if you are looking down on the blocks.**

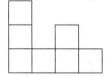 ← **Draw the front view as if you are in front of the blocks.**

 ← **Draw the right side view as if you are on the right side of the blocks.**

Exercises

Draw the top, front, and right side views of each figure.

1.

2.

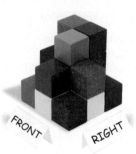

3.

Use the given views to draw a three-dimensional figure.

4.

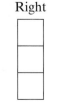

Top   Front   Right

5.

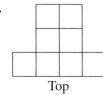

Top   Front   Right

Three-Dimensional Figures

Check Skills You'll Need

1. **Vocabulary Review**
   A __?__ is a polygon with all sides and angles congruent.

Use dot paper to draw each figure.

2. rhombus

3. trapezoid

4. rectangle

for Help
Lesson 7-4

What You'll Learn

To classify and draw three-dimensional figures

🔊 **New Vocabulary** three-dimensional figure, face, edge, bases, prism, height, cube, cylinder, pyramid, vertex, cone, sphere, center

Why Learn This?

You already know about some three-dimensional figures. You see them in many ordinary objects around you. If you know how to classify three-dimensional figures, you can describe the shapes of the objects you see.

A **three-dimensional figure,** or solid, is a figure that does not lie in a plane. A flat surface of a solid shaped like a polygon is called a **face.** Each segment formed by the intersection of two faces is an **edge.**

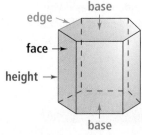

A **prism** is a three-dimensional figure with two parallel and congruent polygonal faces, called **bases.** The other faces are rectangles. The **height** of a prism is the length of a perpendicular segment that joins the bases. A prism is named for the shape of its bases.

A **cube** is a rectangular prism with faces that are all squares.

A **cylinder** has two congruent parallel **bases** that are circles. The **height** of a cylinder is the length of a perpendicular segment that joins the bases.

A **pyramid** has triangular faces that meet at one point, a **vertex**, and a **base** that is a polygon. A pyramid is named for the shape of its base.

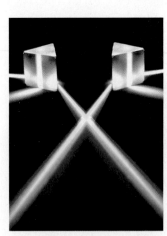

A glass prism can refract, or bend, light.

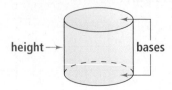

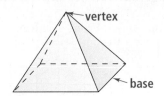

A **cone** has one circular **base** and one **vertex.**

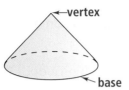

←vertex

←base

A **sphere** is the set of all points in space that are the same distance from a **center** point.

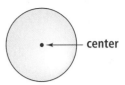

←center

EXAMPLE Naming Figures

① **Architecture** Look at the architectural blocks. Name Figure 3.

Figure 3 has two parallel, congruent bases that are circles.

Figure 3 is a cylinder.

✓ Quick Check

● **1.** Name Figures 1 and 2.

You can use graph paper to draw three-dimensional figures.

EXAMPLE Drawing Three-Dimensional Figures

Vocabulary Tip

Notice the word hexagon inside *hexagonal.* A hexagon has six sides, so a *hexagonal* prism is a prism with a six-sided base.

② Draw a hexagonal prism.

Step 1 Draw a hexagon.

Step 2 Draw a second hexagon congruent to the first.

Step 3 Connect the vertices. Use dashed lines for hidden edges.

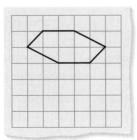

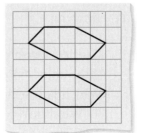

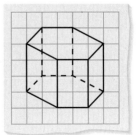

✓ Quick Check

● **2.** Use graph paper to draw a triangular prism.

1. **Vocabulary** A __?__ has two congruent parallel bases that are circles.

2. Which three-dimensional figure does NOT have a base?
   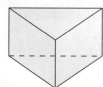
   Ⓐ cone   Ⓑ prism   Ⓒ pyramid   Ⓓ sphere

Describe each base and name each prism.

3.
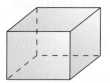

4.

5.
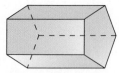

Homework Exercises

For more exercises, see **Extra Skills and Word Problems.**

Name each figure.

For Exercises	See Examples
6–11	1
12–14	2

6.

7.

8.

9.

10.
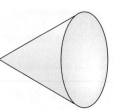

11.
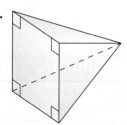

Use graph paper to draw each figure.

12. cylinder   13. pentagonal prism   14. square pyramid

15. **Guided Problem Solving** Refer to the three-dimensional figure shown at the right. Which two solids make up the figure?
    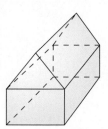
    • What polygon is the base of the lower portion?
    • What polygon is the base of the upper portion?

16. A solid has a rectangle for its base and four faces that are triangles. What is the solid?

GO Online
Homework Video Tutor
Visit: PHSchool.com
Web Code: are-0808

Name the three-dimensional figure in each photograph.

17.

18.

19.

Use the pentagonal pyramid at the right.

20. Name four edges that intersect $\overline{AB}$.

21. Name any edges that are parallel to $\overline{AB}$.

22. Name the five edges that are *not* parallel to $\overline{AB}$ and do *not* intersect $\overline{AB}$.

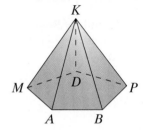

23. What are the areas of all the faces of the figure at the left?

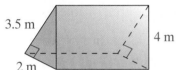

24. **Writing in Math** Are the edges of a cube congruent? Explain.

25. **Challenge** Identify the number of faces, edges, and vertices a hexagonal pyramid has.

 Test Prep and Mixed Review 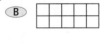 **Practice**

Multiple Choice

26. Which model represents 5^2?
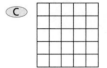

27. What is the measure of each angle of an equilateral triangle?
- F 180°, 90°, and 90°, because the sum of the angles in a triangle is 360° and two angles are congruent
- G 45°, 45°, and 90°, because the sum of the angles in a triangle is 180° and two angles are congruent
- H 60°, 60°, and 60°, because the sum of the angles in a triangle is 180° and all three angles are congruent
- J 45°, 45°, and 45°, because the sum of the angles in a triangle is 135° and all three angles are congruent

28. Which of the following has two bases that are regular polygons?
- A Pyramid   B Cylinder   C Cone   D Prism

29. The hypotenuse of a right triangle is 61 m long. One leg is 60 m long. What is the length of the third side?

GO for Help

For Exercise	See Lesson
29	8-7

<table>
<tr><td>

8-9

</td><td>

Surface Areas of Prisms and Cylinders

</td></tr>
</table>

Check Skills You'll Need

1. Vocabulary Review What is the *height of a triangle*?

Find the area of each triangle.

2.

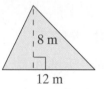

8 m

12 m

3.

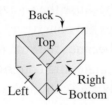

3 ft   6.7 ft

3.6 ft

2 ft   ← 4 ft →

GO for Help
Lesson 8-3

What You'll Learn

To find the surface areas of prisms and cylinders using nets

🔊 **New Vocabulary** net, surface area

Why Learn This?

When you wrap a birthday gift or cover a textbook, you are working with surface area. Surface area tells you how much material you need to cover something. You can use a net to solve surface area problems.

A **net** is a two-dimensional pattern that you can fold to form a three-dimensional figure. You can use nets to design boxes.

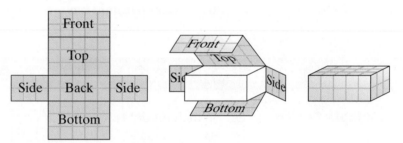

You can draw many different nets for a three-dimensional figure.

EXAMPLE **Drawing a Net**

1 Draw a net for the triangular prism at the right.

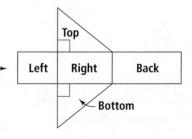

← Begin by labeling the bases and faces.

First draw one base. Then draw one face that connects both bases. Next, draw the other base. Draw the remaining faces.

Quick Check

● **1.** Draw a different net for the right triangular prism in Example 1.

The **surface area** of a prism is the sum of the areas of its faces. You measure surface area of a prism in square units. You can find the surface area by finding the area of its net.

GO for Help

For help with finding the area of a triangle, go to Lesson 8-3, Example 2.

EXAMPLE **Finding the Surface Area of a Prism**

② Find the surface area of the triangular prism.

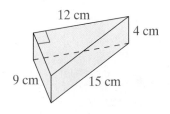

First draw a net for the prism.

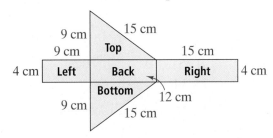

Then find the total area of the five faces.

left side	back	right side	top	bottom

$4(9)$ + $4(12)$ + $4(15)$ + $\frac{1}{2}(12)(9)$ + $\frac{1}{2}(12)(9) = 252$

The surface area of the triangular prism is 252 cm².

✓ Quick Check

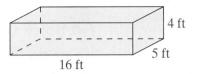

2. Find the surface area of the rectangular prism.

If you cut a label from a can, you will see that the label is a rectangle. The height of the rectangle is about the height of the can. The base length of the rectangle is the circumference of the can.

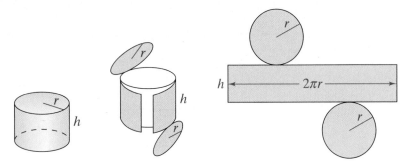

Similarly, if you cut up a cylinder, you get a rectangle and two circles.

You can use a net of a cylinder to find its surface area.

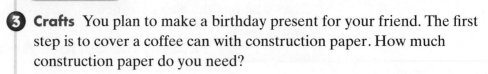

EXAMPLE Finding the Surface Area of a Cylinder

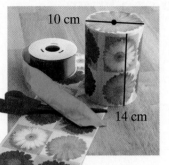

10 cm

14 cm

3 Crafts You plan to make a birthday present for your friend. The first step is to cover a coffee can with construction paper. How much construction paper do you need?

Step 1 Draw a net.

Step 2 Find the area of one circle.

$$A = \pi r^2$$
$$= \pi(5)^2$$
$$= \pi(25)$$
$$\approx 78.54$$

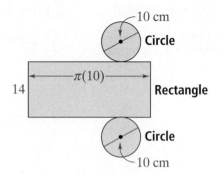

10 cm
Circle

$\pi(10)$

14   Rectangle

Circle
10 cm

Step 3 Find the area of the rectangle.

$$(\pi d)h = \pi(10)(14)$$
$$= 140\pi$$
$$\approx 439.82$$

Step 4 Add the areas of the two circles and the rectangle.

Surface area $= 78.54 + 78.54 + 439.82 = 596.9$

The amount of construction paper needed is about 597 cm^2.

✓ Quick Check

3. What is the surface area of the cylinder at the right? Round to the nearest tenth.

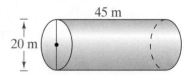

45 m

20 m

✓ Check Your Understanding

1. **Vocabulary** The __?__ of a prism is the sum of the areas of its faces.

2. **Reasoning** What kind of polygon is included in both a net of a triangular prism and a net of a rectangular prism?

Identify the figure formed by each net. Then find its surface area.

3.

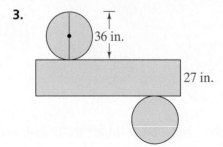

36 in.

27 in.

4.

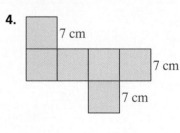

7 cm

7 cm

7 cm

416   **Chapter 8** Measurement

For more exercises, see Extra Skills and Word Problems.

GO for Help

For Exercises	See Examples
5–8	1
9–11	2
12–14	3

Draw a net for each three-dimensional figure.

5.

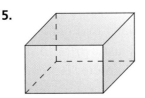

6.

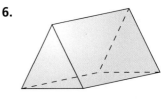

7.

8.

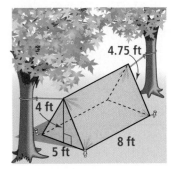

Find the surface area of each prism.

9.

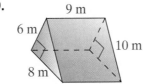

9 m
6 m
10 m
8 m

10.

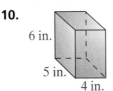

6 in.
5 in.
4 in.

11.

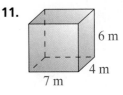

6 m
6 m
7 m
4 m

Vocabulary Tip

Cylindrical means "in the shape of a cylinder."

Find the surface area of each cylinder. Round to the nearest tenth.

12.

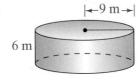

|←9 m→|
6 m

13.

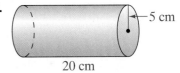

5 cm
20 cm

14. The diameter of the base of a cylindrical can is 4 in. The height of the can is 6.5 in. Find the can's surface area to the nearest tenth.

GPS **15.** **Guided Problem Solving** The tent at the right is similar to a triangular prism. Calculate the surface area of the tent to find the amount of fabric needed to make the tent.
- A triangular prism has ■ faces.
- Find and add the areas of the faces:
  surface area = ■ + ■ + ■ + ■ . . .

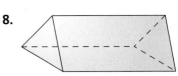

4.75 ft
4 ft
5 ft
8 ft

16. Some cans are cut from a large sheet of metal. Find the amount of metal needed to make a can similar to the one at the right. Round to the nearest tenth.

6 cm
12 cm

17. Calculate the surface area of a rectangular prism with a height of 4 in., a width of 16 in., and a length of 10 in.

Find the surface area of each cylinder given the base radius and height of the cylinder. Round to the nearest square unit.

18. $r = 3$ cm
$h = 10$ cm

19. $r = 7$ ft
$h = 25$ ft

20. $r = 12$ m
$h = 16$ m

21. $r = 10$ in.
$h = 3$ ft

22. A cosmetics company that makes small cylindrical bars of soap wraps the bars in plastic prior to shipping. Find the surface area of a bar of soap if the diameter is 5 cm and the height is 2 cm. Round to the nearest tenth.

23. Suppose you wish to make a cylindrical case that will exactly fit the bass drum at the left. What is the surface area of the case to the nearest tenth?

24. Error Analysis A student says the two cylinders at the right have the same surface area. Explain the student's error.

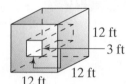

25. Writing in Math Which has a greater effect on the surface area of a cylinder—doubling the radius or doubling the height? Explain.

26. Open-Ended Draw a net for a prism that has a surface area of 72 cm².

27. Challenge Find the surface area of the figure at the right. Round to the nearest tenth.

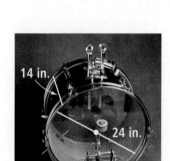
14 in.
24 in.

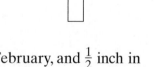
12 ft
3 ft
12 ft
12 ft

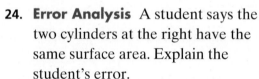

Test Prep and Mixed Review
Practice

Multiple Choice

28. Which solid can be formed from the net shown at the right?
- Ⓐ Triangular prism
- Ⓑ Rectangular prism
- Ⓒ Triangular pyramid
- Ⓓ Rectangular pyramid

29. Chip grows $\frac{3}{4}$ inch in January, $\frac{5}{8}$ inch in February, and $\frac{1}{2}$ inch in March. If the pattern continues, how much will he grow in May?
- Ⓕ $\frac{1}{8}$ in.
- Ⓗ $\frac{3}{8}$ in.
- Ⓖ $\frac{1}{4}$ in.
- Ⓙ $\frac{1}{2}$ in.

GO for Help

For Exercises	See Lesson
30–32	8-6

Identify each number as *rational* or *irrational*.

30. 2.22222 . . .

31. $\sqrt{625}$

32. $\sqrt{18}$

Patterns in 3-Dimensional Figures

You can explore number patterns using unit cubes.

Suppose you use unit cubes to make a larger cube with two unit cubes on an edge. You paint the outside of the larger cube. You need eight unit cubes to form the larger cube. Each cube has three sides painted.

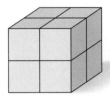

Exercises

Use the table for Exercises 1–3.

Number of Unit Cubes on an Edge	Total Number of Unit Cubes	Total Number Expressed as a Power	Number of Unit Cubes With Given Number of Sides Painted			
			0	1	2	3
2	8	2^3	0	0	0	8
3	■	■	■	■	■	■
4	■	■	■	■	■	■
5	■	■	■	■	■	■
6	■	■	■	■	■	■
7	■	■	■	■	■	■

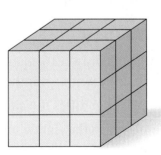

1. Copy and complete the table above. Use the figure at the right to help you fill in the row for 3 unit cubes on an edge.

2. a. **Patterns** Describe the number pattern you see in each of the last four columns of your table.
   b. Use the number patterns and extend the table for 8 number cubes on an edge.

3. a. **Number Sense** What is the total number of unit cubes in a cube with 10 unit cubes on an edge?
   b. If there are 15 unit cubes on an edge, how many unit cubes will have no side painted? One side painted? Two sides painted?
   c. **Reasoning** If 144 unit cubes have two sides painted, how many unit cubes are on one edge of the cube?

1. Find two consecutive whole numbers that $\sqrt{77}$ falls between.

2. Find the length of the sides of a square with an area of 324 cm².

Find each missing length.

3.
15 cm   x   36 cm

4.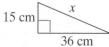
5 yd   3 yd   y

5.
15 m   z   17 m

Name each figure.

6.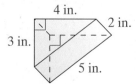

7.

8.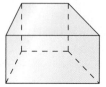

Find the surface area of each figure. Round to the nearest tenth.

9.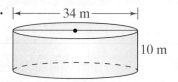
4 in.   2 in.   3 in.   5 in.

10.
34 m   10 m

MATH GAMES

Square Root Bingo

What You'll Need

● 20 index cards. On each card write one of the first 20 perfect squares (not including 0) under the square root symbol.

How To Play

● All players draw a 16-square playing board. In each square, they write a number from 1–20 without repeats.

● One player shuffles the cards and places them face down.

● The player to the right chooses the top card and places it face up. Players with the matching square root on their board make a mark on the appropriate square.

● The player to the right chooses the next card.

● The winner is the first player who has four marks diagonally, horizontally, or vertically.

 **Check Skills You'll Need**

1. **Vocabulary Review** How is π related to the circumference and the diameter of a circle?

Find the area of each circle. Round to the nearest square unit.

2.

12 m

3.

15 in.

 **for Help**
Lesson 8-5

 **nline**

Video Tutor Help
Visit: PHSchool.com
Web Code: are-0775

What You'll Learn

To find the volumes of prisms and cylinders

 New Vocabulary volume, cubic unit

Why Learn This?

Many storage silos are shaped like cylinders. You can use volume formulas to find the amount of storage space inside a figure like a silo.

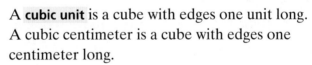

The **volume** of a three-dimensional figure is the number of cubic units needed to fill the space inside the figure.

A **cubic unit** is a cube with edges one unit long. A cubic centimeter is a cube with edges one centimeter long.

1 cm
1 cm
1 cm

Consider filling the rectangular prism below with cubic centimeters.

3 cm   4 cm
         10 cm

The bottom layer of the prism contains 10 · 4, or 40, cubes.

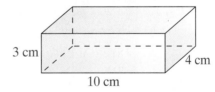
3 cm   4 cm
         10 cm

Three layers of 40 cubes fit in the prism. 3 · 40 = 120

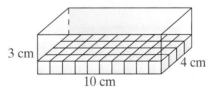
3 cm   4 cm
         10 cm

The volume of the prism is 120 cm³.

The previous calculation of volume suggests the following formula.

KEY CONCEPTS Volume of a Rectangular Prism

V = area of base · height
   = Bh
   = ℓwh

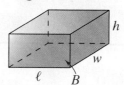

EXAMPLE Finding Volume of a Rectangular Prism

1 **Gridded Response** Mr. Cho is building a craft box like the one shown at the right. What is the volume of the craft box in cubic inches?

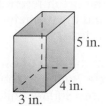

$V = \ell wh$ ← **Use the formula.**

$= (3)(4)(5)$ ← **Substitute.**

$= 60$ ← **Multiply.**

The volume of the craft box is 60 cubic inches.

☑ Quick Check

 1. If the height of the prism above is doubled, what is the volume?

The volume formulas for rectangular and triangular prisms are similar.

Test Prep Tip

When finding volume, remember to calculate the area of the base first.

KEY CONCEPTS Volume of a Triangular Prism

V = area of base · height
   = Bh

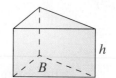

EXAMPLE Finding the Volume of a Triangular Prism

2 Find the volume of the triangular prism.

$V = Bh$ ← **Use the formula.**

$= (6)(6)$ ← **Substitute: $B = \frac{1}{2} \times 3 \times 4 = 6$.**

$= 36$ ← **Multiply.**

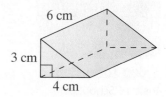

The volume of the triangular prism is 36 cm³.

☑ Quick Check

 2. If the height of the prism above is doubled, what is the volume?

The volume formula for a cylinder is also similar to the volume formula for a prism.

> **KEY CONCEPTS** **Volume of a Cylinder**
>
> V = area of base · height
> $\quad = Bh$
> $\quad = \pi r^2 h$
>
>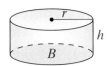

EXAMPLE **Finding the Volume of a Cylinder**

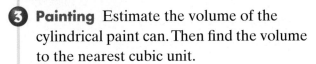
For: Volume Activity
Use: Interactive
Textbook, 8-10

3 **Painting** Estimate the volume of the cylindrical paint can. Then find the volume to the nearest cubic unit.

Estimate

$$V = \pi r^2 h \qquad \leftarrow \text{Use the formula.}$$
$$\approx (3)(4)^2(9) \qquad \leftarrow \text{Use 3 to estimate } \pi.$$
$$\approx (50)(9) \qquad \leftarrow \text{Use 50 to estimate 48 (3 · 16).}$$
$$\approx 450$$

The estimated volume is 450 in.^{3}.

Calculate

$$V = \pi r^2 h \qquad \leftarrow \text{Use the formula.}$$
$$\approx (\pi)(4)^2(9) \qquad \leftarrow \text{Substitute.}$$
$$\approx 452.38934 \qquad \leftarrow \text{Use a calculator.}$$
$$\approx 452 \qquad \leftarrow \text{Round to the nearest whole number.}$$

The calculated volume is about 452 in.^{3}.

Check for Reasonableness The calculated volume is close to the estimated volume, so the answer is reasonable.

✓ Quick Check

3. a. Estimate the volume of the cylinder. Then find the volume to the nearest cubic centimeter.

   b. Reasoning Suppose you estimate using 20 for 4^2 instead of 16 in Example 3. Will your estimate be reasonable?

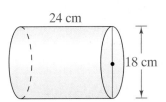

1. **Vocabulary** The number of cubic units needed to fill the space inside a three-dimensional figure is called the __?__.

2. How does the volume of a cylinder change if the height is doubled?

   Ⓐ It does not change. Ⓒ It quadruples.

   Ⓑ It doubles. Ⓓ It halves.

Find the volume of each figure, given the following dimensions.

3. triangular prism
   $B = 20$ in.^{2}; $h = 3$ in.

4. cylinder
   $r = 5$ cm; $h = 7$ cm

Homework Exercises

For more exercises, see Extra Skills and Word Problems.

GO for Help

For Exercises	See Examples
5–7	1
8–10	2
11–13	3

Find the volume of each rectangular prism.

5.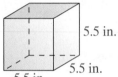
5.5 in.
5.5 in.
5.5 in.

6.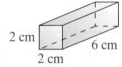
2 cm
2 cm
6 cm

7.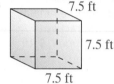
7.5 ft
7.5 ft
7.5 ft

Find the volume of each triangular prism.

8.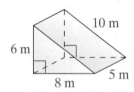
10 m
6 m
8 m
5 m

9.
4.5 in
2 in.
7 in.

10.
4 ft
4 ft
5 ft

Packaging Estimate the volume of each cylinder. Then find the volume to the nearest cubic unit.

11.
2 in.
7 in.

12.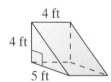
13 cm
33 cm

13.
7 in.
6.5 in.

14. **Guided Problem Solving** What is the volume of the object shown at the right?
    • Identify the two familiar solids that make up the object. What are they?
    • What is the volume of each familiar solid?

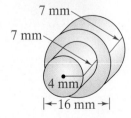
7 mm
7 mm
4 mm
16 mm

Find the height of each rectangular prism.

15. $V = 455$ cm^3
$\ell = 10$ cm
$w = 7$ cm

16. $V = 525$ m^3
$\ell = 7.5$ m
$w = 3.5$ m

17. $V = 5{,}832$ in.^{3}
$\ell = 18$ in.
$w = 18$ in.

18. Reasoning Compare the volumes of the figures. Why are their volumes different?

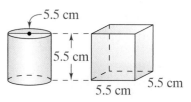

19. Writing in Math Explain how you can find the radius of a cylinder with a height of 10 in. and a volume of 385 in.^{3}. (Use $\pi = 3.14$.)

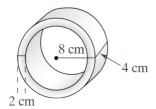

20. Find the volume of the figure at the left to the nearest cubic centimeter.

21. Aquariums A large aquarium is built in the shape of a cylinder. The diameter is 203 ft and the height is 25 ft. About how many million gallons of water does this tank hold? (1 gal $\approx$ 231 in.^{3})

22. A rectangular prism has a length of 3.1 m, a width of 2.2 m, and a height of 5.6 m. Find the volume to the nearest cubic meter.

23. Challenge A soft-drink can has a height of about 4.8 in. and a diameter of about 2.5 in. Suppose you need to put 12 cans in a rectangular case about 5 in. tall, 11 in. long, and 7.6 in. wide. Will the cans fit in the case? Explain.

Test Prep and Mixed Review
Practice

Gridded Response

24. Mrs. Panosian has a can of concentrated orange juice like the one at the right. What is the volume of the can in cubic centimeters?

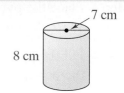

25. Nina created a project on water conservation. She found that you use 1.6 gallons of water each time you flush a toilet. At this rate, how many gallons of water would you use flushing 7 times?

26. Ethan collected five rocks that weighed a total of 43.4 kg. Two of the rocks were identical, and each weighed 13.3 kg. If two of the other rocks weighed 4.7 kg and 5.3 kg, what was the weight of the fifth rock in kilograms?

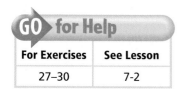
GO for Help

For Exercises	See Lesson
27–30	7-2

Find the measures of the complement and supplement of each angle.

27. $m\angle A = 40°$ **28.** $m\angle B = 65°$ **29.** $m\angle C = 37°$ **30.** $m\angle D = 5°$

Generating Formulas for Volume

In this activity, you will relate the volume of a pyramid to the volume of a prism.

ACTIVITY

Step 1 Using poster board, draw and cut out four congruent isosceles triangles like the one below.

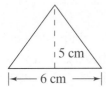

5 cm

|← 6 cm →|

Step 2 Tape the edges of the four triangles to form a pyramid without a base. What is the area of the missing base?

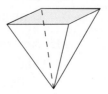

Step 3 Using poster board, draw and cut out four congruent rectangles and one square like the one below.

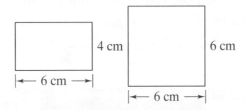

4 cm

|← 6 cm →|

6 cm

|← 6 cm →|

Step 4 Tape the edges of the polygons to form a prism without a base. Compare the areas of the missing base of the prism and the missing base of the pyramid.

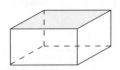

Step 5 Place the pyramid and the prism side by side. What do you notice about their heights?

Step 6 Fill the pyramid with rice. Pour the rice from the pyramid into the prism. Repeat until the prism is full.

Exercises

1. **a.** How many pyramids full of rice did you need to fill the prism?
   b. How does the volume of the pyramid compare to the volume of the prism?
   c. Make a conjecture about the formula for volume of a pyramid.

2. **Reasoning** To fill a cylinder with base area B and height h, you need 3 cones as shown at the right. Make a conjecture about the formula for volume of a cone.

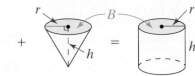

Measuring to Solve

Some test questions ask you to measure with a centimeter ruler before solving a problem.

EXAMPLE

The bottom of a bottle is circular, as shown at the right. Measure the radius of the bottle in centimeters.

Which of the following is closest to the circumference of the bottom of the bottle?

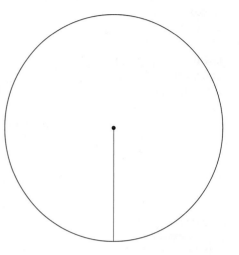

  Ⓐ 6 cm   Ⓒ 15 cm

  Ⓑ 9 cm   Ⓓ 19 cm

Use a centimeter ruler to measure the radius of the bottle. Label the radius. To find the circumference of the bottle, use the formula for the circumference of a circle.

$C = 2\pi r$, or πd

$C = 2\pi r = 2 \times \pi \times 3 \approx 18.84955 \ldots$

● The circumference of the bottle is about 19 cm. The answer is D.

Exercises

1. A vase has a circular base, as shown at the right. Measure the radius of the base in centimeters. Which of the following is the closest to the area of the circular base?

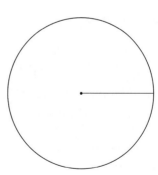

  Ⓐ 2 cm^2

  Ⓑ 6 cm^2

  Ⓒ 12 cm^2

  Ⓓ 24 cm^2

2. Celine bought earrings and made a gift box for them that is 4 cm high. The base of the box is shown at the right. Measure the dimensions of the base in centimeters. Which best represents the volume of the box?

  Ⓕ 6 cm^3 Ⓗ 12 cm^3

  Ⓖ 8 cm^3 Ⓙ 32 cm^3

Vocabulary Review

area (p. 375)
base(s) (pp. 380, 384, 388, 410, 411)
center of a sphere (p. 411)
circumference (p. 394)
cone (p. 411)
cube (p. 410)
cubic unit (p. 421)
cylinder (p. 410)
edge (p. 410)

face (p. 410)
height (pp. 380, 384, 388, 410)
hypotenuse (p. 405)
irrational number (p. 401)
legs (p. 405)
net (p. 414)
perfect square (p. 400)
perimeter (p. 375)
pi (p. 394)
prism (p. 410)

pyramid (p. 410)
Pythagorean Theorem (p. 405)
sphere (p. 411)
square root (p. 400)
surface area (p. 415)
three-dimensional figure (p. 410)
vertex (pp. 410, 411)
volume (p. 421)

Go Online
PHSchool.com
For: Online Vocabulary Quiz
Web Code: arj-0851

Choose the correct term to complete each sentence.

1. A(n) (edge, vertex) is the intersection of two faces.

2. The longest side of a right triangle is the (hypotenuse, leg).

3. A (prism, pyramid) has two parallel and congruent bases.

4. The perimeter of a circle is the (area, circumference) of the circle.

5. A (cone, cylinder) has one circular base and one vertex.

Skills and Concepts

Lesson 8-1
- To estimate length, perimeter, and area

The **area** of a figure is the number of square units it encloses.

6. Estimate the area of the shaded region. Each square represents 20 in.^{2}.

7. Choose a reasonable estimate for the width of a book—7 in. or 7 ft. Explain.

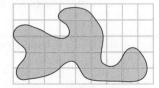

Lessons 8-2, 8-3, 8-4
- To find the area and perimeter of a parallelogram
- To find the perimeter and area of a triangle
- To find the area of a trapezoid and the areas of irregular figures

To find the area of an irregular figure, first separate it into familiar figures and find the area of each piece. Then add the areas.

parallelogram	triangle	trapezoid
$A = bh$	$A = \frac{1}{2}bh$	$A = \frac{1}{2}h(b_1 + b_2)$

Use familiar figures to find the area of each figure.

8.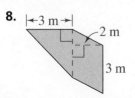

9.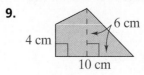

10.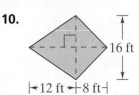

Lesson 8-5

- To find the circumference and area of a circle

To find the **circumference** of a circle, use the formula $C = \pi d = 2\pi r$. To find the area of a circle, use the formula $A = \pi r^2$.

Find the circumference and area of each circle.

11.
8 in.

12.
14 mi

13.
7 km

Lessons 8-6, 8-7

- To find and estimate square roots and to classify numbers as rational or irrational
- To use the Pythagorean Theorem to solve real-world problems

A **perfect square** is a square of an integer. The opposite of squaring a number is finding its **square root.** Many square roots are **irrational numbers,** or numbers that cannot be written as the ratio of two integers.

The **Pythagorean Theorem,** $a^2 + b^2 = c^2$, relates the lengths of the **legs** of a right triangle to the length of its **hypotenuse.**

14. **Art** A square piece of glass in a picture frame covers an area of 36 in.^{2}. What is the length of each side of the glass?

15. A pipeline is placed diagonally across a rectangular field that is 25 yd by 30 yd. How long is the pipeline, to the nearest yard?

Lesson 8-8

- To classify and draw three-dimensional figures

Some **three-dimensional figures** have only flat surfaces. **Prisms** and **pyramids** are named for the shape of their bases. **Cones** and pyramids have one **vertex.**

Name each figure.

16.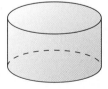

17.

18.

Lessons 8-9, 8-10

- To find the surface areas of prisms and cylinders using nets
- To find the volumes of prisms and cylinders

To find the **surface area** of a prism or cylinder, draw a **net** and find the area of the net. To find the **volume** of a prism, use the formula $V = Bh$. To find the volume of a cylinder, use the formula $V = \pi r^2 h$.

Find the surface area and volume for each figure.

19.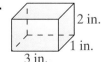
2 in.
1 in.
3 in.

20.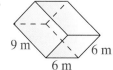
9 m
6 m
6 m

21.
14 yd
10 yd

Estimate the area of each shaded region. Each square represents 50 in.²

1.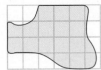

2.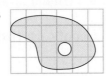

Find the area of each figure.

3.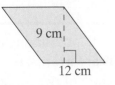
9 cm
12 cm

4.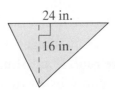
24 in.
16 in.

5.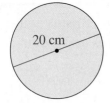
5 m
7.5 m
10 m

6.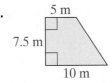
12 cm
12 cm
|← 20 cm →|

Find the circumference and area of each circle. Round to the nearest tenth.

7.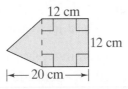
20 cm

8.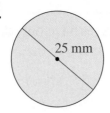
25 mm

Simplify each square root.

9. $\sqrt{9}$ **10.** $\sqrt{25}$ **11.** $\sqrt{49}$ **12.** $\sqrt{100}$

13. $\sqrt{121}$ **14.** $\sqrt{1}$ **15.** $\sqrt{64}$ **16.** $\sqrt{81}$

17. A square plot of land has an area of 100 m². What is the perimeter of the plot?

Find two consecutive whole numbers that each number falls between. Then estimate the number's value.

18. $\sqrt{55}$ **19.** $\sqrt{63}$ **20.** $\sqrt{8}$ **21.** $\sqrt{45}$

22. Construction The area of a window is 18 ft². The length of the window is two times the width of the window. What are the dimensions of the window?

Find each missing length to the nearest tenth.

23.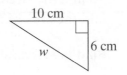
10 cm
6 cm
w

24.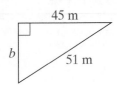
45 m
b
51 m

25. A ladder 26 ft long is placed 10 ft from the base of a house. How high up the side of the house does the ladder reach?

26. A support cable connects the top of a 30-m pole to an anchor 20 m from the base of the pole. How long is the support cable, to the nearest tenth of a meter?

Identify each number as *rational* or *irrational*.

27. $\sqrt{30}$ **28.** $3.\overline{7}$ **29.** $\frac{22}{7}$ **30.** π

Find the surface area to the nearest whole unit.

31.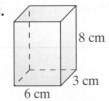
12 m
16 m
4 m
20 m

32.
28 in.
30 in.

Find the volume to the nearest whole unit.

33.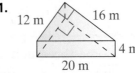
8 cm
3 cm
6 cm

34.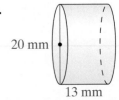
20 mm
13 mm

35. A triangular prism has a volume of 96 m³. The area of the base is 16 m². What is the height of the prism?

36. Writing in Math Explain how you would show that a triangle with side lengths 7 in., 24 in., and 25 in. is a right triangle.

37. Measurement The volume of a rectangular prism is 2,058 cm³. The length of the prism is three times the width. The height is 14 cm. Find the other dimensions.

Multiple Choice
Read each question. Then write the letter of the correct answer on your paper.

1. Which number has the greatest value?
   - Ⓐ 2
   - Ⓑ 3^3
   - Ⓒ 5^2
   - Ⓓ 20^1

2. Rectangle $ABCD$ has dimensions 3 in. $\times$ 4 in. What are the area and perimeter of $ABCD$?
   - Ⓕ $A = 12$ in.^{2}, $P = 12$ in.
   - Ⓖ $A = 12$ in.^{2}, $P = 14$ in.
   - Ⓗ $A = 6$ in.^{2}, $P = 12$ in.
   - Ⓙ $A = 12$ in.^{2}, $P = 7$ in.

3. The rectangles are similar. Which proportion could NOT be used to find the value of x?

   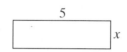

   - Ⓐ $\dfrac{7}{5} = \dfrac{2}{x}$
   - Ⓒ $\dfrac{x}{5} = \dfrac{2}{7}$
   - Ⓑ $\dfrac{x}{2} = \dfrac{7}{5}$
   - Ⓓ $\dfrac{2}{7} = \dfrac{x}{5}$

4. Which of the following could NOT be the length of the sides of a right triangle?
   - Ⓕ 8, 15, 17
   - Ⓗ 15, 35, 40
   - Ⓖ 10, 24, 26
   - Ⓙ 12, 16, 20

5. Which expression could you use to find the area of the cylinder's base?
   - Ⓐ $2 \cdot \pi \cdot 5$
   - Ⓑ $\pi \cdot 2.5 \cdot 2.5$
   - Ⓒ $\pi \cdot 5 \cdot 5$
   - Ⓓ $2 \cdot \pi \cdot 2.5 \cdot 6$

6. Which figure has the greastest volume?

   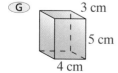
   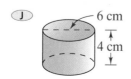

7. Which equation can you use to represent the following? Five more than half of the people (p) on the bus are students (s).
   - Ⓐ $\dfrac{p}{2} + 5 = s$
   - Ⓒ $\dfrac{p}{2} - 5 = s$
   - Ⓑ $(p - 5) \div 2 = s$
   - Ⓓ $(p + 5) \div 2 = s$

8. What is the value of x to the nearest tenth?
   - Ⓕ 17.0
   - Ⓗ 8.5
   - Ⓖ 12.7
   - Ⓙ 7

9. Which expression does NOT equal 12?
   - Ⓐ $\sqrt{144}$
   - Ⓒ $\sqrt{4} + \sqrt{64}$
   - Ⓑ $\sqrt{36} + \sqrt{36}$
   - Ⓓ $\sqrt{81} + \sqrt{9}$

10. What number is 75% of 150?
    - Ⓕ 11.25
    - Ⓗ 112.5
    - Ⓖ 20
    - Ⓙ 11,250

Gridded Response
Record your answer in a grid.

11. A triangle has a height of 8 ft and a base of 15 ft. Find the triangle's area in square feet.

12. **Sewing** You sew 34 squares for a quilt. This is 5% of the squares used in the quilt. How many squares are there to sew in all?

Short Response

13. Define a variable and write an inequality to model "To qualify for the long-jump finals, I need to jump at least 14 ft."

14. The area of a circular rug is 113.04 ft^2. What is the diameter of the rug? Use $\pi = 3.14$. Show your work.

Extended Response

15. The ratio of the corresponding sides of two similar triangles is 3 : 5. The sides of the smaller triangle are 9 m, 12 m, and 18 m. Find the perimeter of the larger triangle. Show your work.

Problem Solving Application

Applying Volume

Musical Shapes Today's music comes in many forms. You're probably most familiar with compact discs (CDs) and cassette tapes. Maybe you've also seen older vinyl records or the newer mini-discs. These forms of music look and play differently, but you may have noticed that the recorded areas all have the same geometric shape.

Put It All Together

Materials centimeter ruler, cassette tape, CDs

1. Wind the tape in a cassette completely around one of the spools, making a cylinder.
   a. Measure the diameter of the cylinder of tape and the height of the tape. Because the tape is inside a plastic cover, you may have to approximate these measurements.
   b. Find the volume of the cylinder.
   c. Notice that the center of the cylinder is a spool. Measure the diameter of the spool. Find its volume.
   d. Subtract the volume of the spool from the total volume. What is the volume of the magnetic tape?

2. **a.** Measure the radius of a CD.
   b. Find the height of the CD. (*Hint:* Stack several CDs, measure their combined height, and divide by the number of discs.)
   c. Find the volume of the CD.
   d. Measure the radius from the center of the CD to the beginning of the music area. (See the photo at the right.) This section contains no music. Find its volume.
   e. Subtract your answer to part (d) from your answer to part (c) to find the volume used for music.

Cassette tape

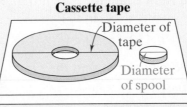

Diameter of tape

Diameter of spool

CD

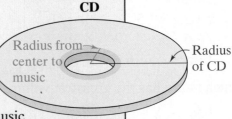

Radius from center to music

Radius of CD

3. **a.** How many minutes of music are on the tape? How many minutes are stored in each cubic centimeter of volume?
   b. How many minutes of music are on the CD? How many minutes are stored in each cubic centimeter of volume?
   c. **Writing in Math** Which format stores music more efficiently, a cassette or a CD? Explain.

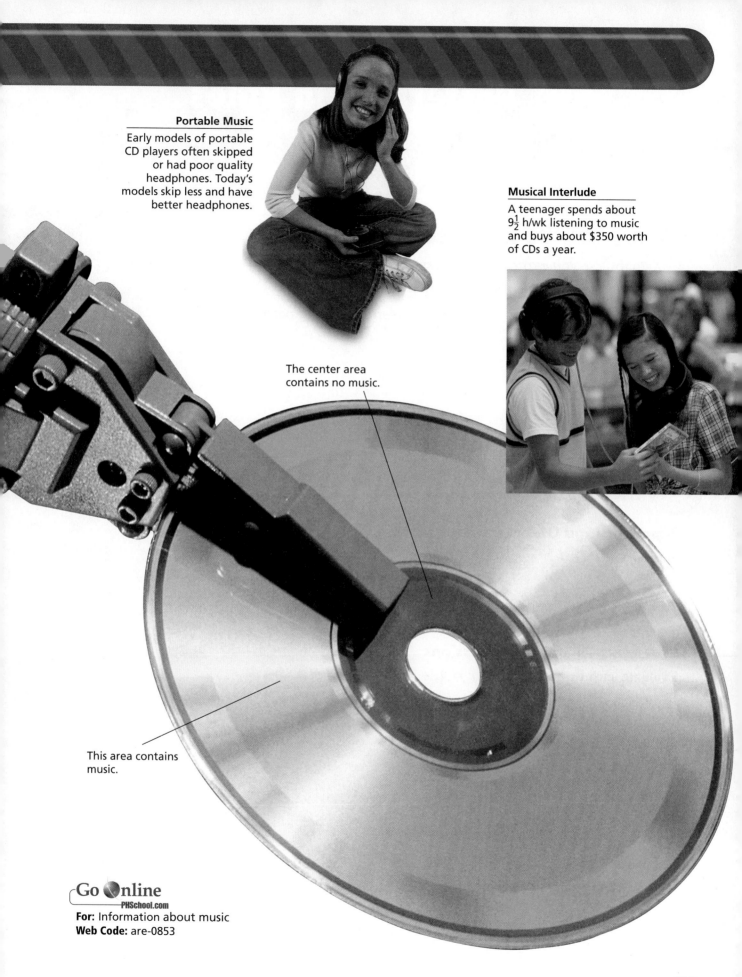

Portable Music
Early models of portable CD players often skipped or had poor quality headphones. Today's models skip less and have better headphones.

Musical Interlude
A teenager spends about $9\frac{1}{2}$ h/wk listening to music and buys about $350 worth of CDs a year.

The center area contains no music.

This area contains music.

Go Online
PHSchool.com
For: Information about music
Web Code: are-0853

CHAPTER 9 Patterns and Rules

What You've Learned

- In Chapter 4, you wrote algebraic expressions and equations to represent patterns and real-world situations.

- In Chapter 6, you solved application problems involving percents.

Check Your Readiness

GO for Help

For Exercises	See Lesson
1–4	2-1
5–8	4-1
9–14	4-6
15–19	6-2

Exponents and Order of Operations

Simplify.

1. $2^3 \cdot 2 - 4^2$

2. $2^3 \cdot (2 - 4)^2$

3. $(3 - 2)^2 - 2^2$

4. $4^3 + 4 \div 4$

Evaluating Algebraic Expressions

Evaluate each expression using $r = 4$, $s = -2$, and $t = 5.1$.

5. $3r - t$

6. rst

7. $8s^2 + rt$

8. $1.5(1 + s)^r$

Solving Two-Step Equations

Solve each equation.

9. $3x - 1 = 14$

10. $10 + 3n = 25$

11. $4(b - 3) = 7$

12. $\frac{2}{3}n - 10 = 14$

13. $\frac{x}{7} = 49$

14. $1.5 + \frac{4}{5}a = 21$

Percents, Fractions, and Decimals

Write each percent as a decimal.

15. 4%

16. 12%

17. 3.58%

18. 4.05%

19. 10.3%

What You'll Learn Next

- In this chapter, you will describe arithmetic and geometric sequences.

- You will represent patterns using tables, rules, and graphs.

- You will find simple and compound interest.

 Problem Solving Application On pages 482 and 483, you will work an extended activity on graphs.

Key Vocabulary

- arithmetic sequence (p. 442)
- balance (p. 469)
- compound interest (p. 469)
- conjecture (p. 443)
- formula (p. 472)
- function (p. 452)
- geometric sequence (p. 442)
- principal (p. 468)
- sequence (p. 442)
- simple interest (p. 468)

Choosing Scales and Intervals

To display data on a graph, you need to choose scales and intervals. A graph includes two *scales*, the horizontal axis and the vertical axis. An *interval* is the difference between the values on a scale.

EXAMPLE

Graph the data in the table at the right.

Step 1 Choose the scales and intervals.
Use the horizontal scale for the amount saved. Use the vertical scale for the interest earned. Start both scales at 0. Graphs that have from 6 to 10 intervals are easy to read. Since the greatest amount saved is $900, the horizontal scale needs to range from $0 to at least $900. Divide 900 by a factor from 6 to 10. Choose 9, since 900 is divisible by 9.

$900 \div 9 = 100$ ← Divide the greatest amount by a compatible number.

Use 9 intervals of $100 for the horizontal scale.
Since the greatest interest earned is $36, the vertical scale needs to range from $0 to at least $36. Divide 36 by a factor from 6 to 10.

$36 \div 9 = 4$ ← Divide the greatest amount by a compatible number.

Use 9 intervals of $4 for the vertical scale.

Step 2 Use points to represent the data.
The red dashes show how to plot the point representing interest earned of $14 for an amount saved of $350.

Interest on Savings

Amount Saved ($)	Interest Earned ($)
200	8
350	14
500	20
750	30
900	36

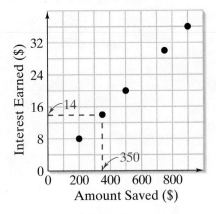

Interest on Savings

Exercises

1. a. **Number Sense** Use the table at the right. What interval can you use for time? For distance?
   b. Graph the data.

2. a. Graph the data in the Example using a vertical interval of $5.
   b. **Reasoning** Which interval is easier to use, $4 or $5? Explain.

Travel Speed

Time (min)	Distance (mi)
0	0
20	15
40	30
60	45
80	60

Check Skills You'll Need

1. **Vocabulary Review**
Is a *repeating decimal* a rational number? Explain.

Graph and label each point.

2. 7   3. $3\frac{1}{2}$

4. 2.3   5. 0.8

 **for Help**
Lesson 2-7

What You'll Learn

To graph data and to use graphs to make predictions

Why Learn This?

You may have heard that "a picture is worth a thousand words." Graphs can help you see patterns in data. The table at the right shows the conversion of yards to inches. A graph of the same data can be easier to understand.

Yards and Inches

Number of Yards	Number of Inches
1	36
2	72
3	108
4	144
5	180

EXAMPLE   Graphing Data

1 Graph the data in the table above.

The pattern in the first column of data suggests a horizontal interval of 1.

Graphs that have from 6 to 10 intervals are easy to read. The greatest value in the second column is 180. Divide 180 by a factor from 6 to 10. Choose 9, since 180 is divisible by 9.

$$180 \div 9 = 20 \quad \leftarrow \text{ Divide the greatest amount by a compatible number.}$$

Use 9 intervals of 20 for the vertical scale. Use points to represent the data.

Yards and Inches

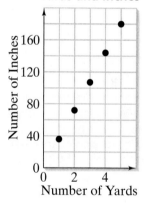

✓ Quick Check

1. Graph the data in the table below.

Yogurt Costs

Amount of Yogurt (c)	Price ($)
50	26
100	49
150	72
200	95

You can use a graph to make estimates between data points.

EXAMPLE **Estimating on a Graph**

2 **Multiple Choice** The graph shows the cost of renting a personal watercraft. Which is the best estimate for the cost of a $3\frac{1}{2}$-hour rental?

Ⓐ about $200

Ⓒ about $250

Ⓑ about $225

Ⓓ about $350

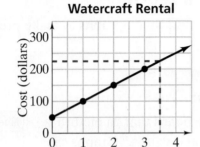

Watercraft Rental

Draw lines to locate the value on the vertical axis that corresponds to $3\frac{1}{2}$ on the horizontal axis.

The cost is greater than $200, but less than $250. Estimate the cost as $225.

The cost of a $3\frac{1}{2}$-hour rental is about $225. The correct answer is B.

✓ Quick Check

2. Use the graph in Example 2 to estimate the cost of a $1\frac{1}{2}$-hour rental.

You can use a graph to make a prediction. Extend the graph and find a corresponding value on the appropriate axis.

EXAMPLE **Making a Prediction**

Test Prep Tip

Make sure the lines you use to locate a point are parallel to the scales of the graph.

3 The graph shows the relationship between Celsius and Fahrenheit temperatures. Estimate the Celsius temperature for 160°F.

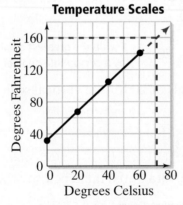

Temperature Scales

← Extend the graph beyond 160°F.

For 160°F, the Celsius temperature ← is slightly more than 70°. Estimate the answer.

A temperature of 160°F is about 71°C.

✓ Quick Check

3. Estimate the Fahrenheit temperature for 80°C.

Shoveling Snow

Hours Worked	Wages ($)
2	18
4	36
5	45
6	54

1. **Vocabulary** How can a graph help you make a prediction?

2. Use the data in the table at the left. If you were to graph wages on the vertical axis, what scale and interval would you use?

3. If you were to graph hours worked on the horizontal axis, what scale and interval would you use?

Choose a reasonable scale and interval to graph each set of data.

4. 70, 35, 55, 10, 43, 25, 80

5. 4,700; 2,000; 3,400; 1,650; 2,800

Homework Exercises

For more exercises, see Extra Skills and Word Problems.

GO for Help

For Exercises	See Examples
6–7	1
8–9	2
10–12	3

Graph the data in each table.

6. **Plant Growth**

Age (yr)	Height (cm)
5	90
7	95
9	102
11	110

7. **Used Dirt Bike Prices**

Age (yr)	Price ($)
2	43
4	37
6	30

Estimate using your graphs from Exercises 6 and 7.

8. the height of an 8-year-old plant

9. the age of a bike that is sold for $40

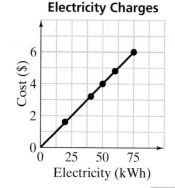

Electricity Charges

Estimate using the graph at the left.

10. the cost of 85 kilowatt-hours of electricity

11. the cost of 100 kilowatt-hours of electricity

12. the number of kilowatt-hours that cost $6.50

13. **Writing in Math** Describe what a graph looks like when both sets of values increase.

14. **Guided Problem Solving** Graph the data in the table. Then estimate the missing value.
   - **Make a Plan** Draw a graph. Extend the graph to locate the missing value.
   - **Carry Out the Plan** For a value of 6 on the horizontal scale, the value on the vertical scale is ▪.

Hours of Sleep	Math Test Score
9	93
8	85
7	74
6	n

Graph the data. Use the graph to estimate the missing value.

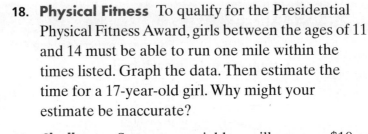

15.

Time (h)	Temp. (°C)
1	12
2	15
5	24
8	n

16.

Gallons	Quarts
2	8
3	n
5	20
6	24

17. a. **Geometry** Graph the perimeters of squares with side lengths of 1, 2, 3, 4, and 5 in. Use the graph for parts (b) and (c).
   b. Estimate the side length of a square with perimeter 9.6 in.
   c. Estimate the perimeter of a square with side length 3.5 in.
   d. **Calculator** Test your estimates with a calculator. Were your estimates correct?

18. **Physical Fitness** To qualify for the Presidential Physical Fitness Award, girls between the ages of 11 and 14 must be able to run one mile within the times listed. Graph the data. Then estimate the time for a 17-year-old girl. Why might your estimate be inaccurate?

Age (yr)	Time (min)
11	9.02
12	8.23
13	8.13
14	7.59

19. **Challenge** Suppose a neighbor will pay you $10 per week to wash windows. Another neighbor will give you $40 plus $7 per week.
   a. Make two tables, one for each neighbor, showing the amount you receive from each neighbor for 1, 2, 3, 4, and 5 weeks of work.
   b. Graph both sets of data on the same axes.
   c. How much will you receive from each neighbor after 10 weeks? Which job would you prefer?

The Presidential Fitness Challenge consists of five fitness tests, including pull-ups.

Test Prep and Mixed Review

Practice

Multiple Choice

20. Which of the following relationships is best represented by the data in the graph at the right?
   Ⓐ Conversion of quarts to pints
   Ⓑ Conversion of gallons to cups
   Ⓒ Conversion of cups to fluid ounces
   Ⓓ Conversion of gallons to fluid ounces

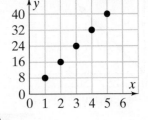

21. A small box measures 3 inches on each side. A larger box holds 125 of these small boxes. What is the volume of the larger box?
   Ⓕ 3,375 in.^{3} Ⓖ 1,125 in.^{3} Ⓗ 375 in.^{3} Ⓙ 26 in.^{3}

GO for Help

For Exercises	See Lesson
22–25	6-2

Write each percent as a decimal.

22. 38%   23. 5%   24. 150%   25. 6.2%

Finding Patterns

ACTIVITY

Use pattern blocks or draw diagrams.

1. Make the next two figures in the pattern below.

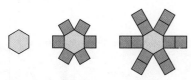

Figure 1   Figure 2   Figure 3

2. How many blocks do you add to each figure to make the next figure in the pattern?

3. Copy and complete the table.

4. Describe any patterns you notice in your table.

Figure	1	2	3	4	5	6	7	8
Number of Blocks	1	■	■	■	■	■	■	■

Exercises

Use the pattern of cubes pictured below for Exercises 1–4.

1. a. Number Sense How many cubes will be in the fourth prism?
   b. Build the fourth prism using colored cubes.

2. a. Number Sense How many cubes will be in the fifth prism?
   b. Build the fifth prism using colored cubes.

3. Copy and complete the table at the right.

4. (**Algebra**) Write a formula that relates the prism number p to the number of blocks n.

Prism	1	2	3	4	5
Number of Blocks	1	8	27	■	■

9-2 Number Sequences

✓ Check Skills You'll Need

1. **Vocabulary Review**
   The *additive inverse* of −8 is ■.

Add.

2. −3 + 3

3. −3 + 2

4. −3 + 1

5. −3 + 0

GO for Help
Lesson 1-7

What You'll Learn

To describe the patterns in arithmetic and geometric sequences and use the patterns to find terms

🔊 **New Vocabulary** sequence, arithmetic sequence, geometric sequence, conjecture

Why Learn This?

Some patterns are found in nature. If you can recognize a pattern in a list of numbers, you can make predictions about how the list will continue.

A **sequence** is a set of numbers that follow a pattern. Each number in a sequence is called a *term*. The set of numbers 1, 3, 5, 7, 9, ... has a pattern. If you add 2 to any number, you get the next number in the set.

In an **arithmetic sequence,** you find each term by adding a fixed number (called the common difference) to the previous term.

EXAMPLE Describing an Arithmetic Sequence

Vocabulary Tip

You pronounce *arithmetic sequence* as "ar ith MET ik SEE kwuns."

1 Describe the pattern in the sequence below. Then find the next three terms in the sequence.

Position	1	2	3	4
Value of Term	12	7	2	−3

　　　　　+(−5)　+(−5)　+(−5)　← **Find the common difference.**

Start with 12 and add −5 repeatedly.

The next three terms are −8, −13, and −18.

✓ Quick Check

1. Describe the pattern in the sequence. Find the next 3 terms.

Position	1	2	3	4	5
Value of Term	44	35	26	17	8

In a **geometric sequence,** you find each term by multiplying the previous term by a fixed number (called the common ratio). In the sequence 2, 7, 24.5, 85.75, ... you multiply each term by 3.5 to get the next term.

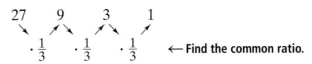

② Describe the pattern in $27, 9, 3, 1, \ldots$ Find the next three terms.

$$27 \quad 9 \quad 3 \quad 1$$
$$\cdot \frac{1}{3} \quad \cdot \frac{1}{3} \quad \cdot \frac{1}{3} \quad \leftarrow \text{Find the common ratio.}$$

Start with 27 and multiply by $\frac{1}{3}$ repeatedly.

Test Prep Tip

Dividing is the same as multiplying by a reciprocal.

$$1 \cdot \frac{1}{3} = \frac{1}{3} \quad \frac{1}{3} \cdot \frac{1}{3} = \frac{1}{9} \quad \frac{1}{9} \cdot \frac{1}{3} = \frac{1}{27} \quad \leftarrow \text{Find the next three terms.}$$

The next three terms are $\frac{1}{3}, \frac{1}{9},$ and $\frac{1}{27}$.

✓ Quick Check

2. Describe the pattern in $1,000; 100; 10; \ldots$ Find the next 3 terms.

A sequence is neither arithmetic nor geometric if there is no common difference or common ratio.

A **conjecture** is a prediction that suggests what you expect to happen. When you describe a pattern in a sequence, you are using *inductive reasoning*. Check your results whenever possible.

EXAMPLE Geometry

GO for Help

For help with ratios, go to Lesson 5-1, Example 1.

③ Describe the pattern to find the number of circles in each figure. Is the resulting sequence *arithmetic, geometric, both,* or *neither*?

$$3 \quad 6 \quad 10 \quad 15 \ldots \quad \leftarrow \text{number of circles in each figure}$$
$$+3 \quad +4 \quad +5 \quad \leftarrow \text{Look for a common difference or a common ratio.}$$

Start with 3. Add consecutive integers. First add 3, then add 4, and so on.

The sequence is neither arithmetic nor geometric. $\leftarrow$ conjecture

Check Is there a common ratio?

$$3 \quad 6 \quad 10 \quad 15$$
$$\cdot 2 \quad \cdot 1\frac{2}{3} \quad \cdot 1\frac{1}{2}$$

You cannot multiply by or add the same number to each $\leftarrow$ term to find the next term. The sequence is neither arithmetic nor geometric. The conjecture is correct.

✓ Quick Check

3. Identify each sequence as *arithmetic, geometric, both,* or *neither*.
   a. $1, 2, 6, 24, \ldots$ **b.** $2, 3, 6, 11, \ldots$ **c.** $10, 9, 8, 7, \ldots$

1. **Vocabulary** A pattern for a sequence is described as *start with 12 and divide by −4 repeatedly*. Is this a geometric sequence? Explain.

2. Can two different arithmetic sequences have the same common difference? Explain.

3. What is the common difference in the sequence 35, 29, 23, 17, . . . ?

Find the missing term in each sequence.

4. 6, 13, 20, ■, 34, 41

5. 100, 50, 25, ■, 6.125

Homework Exercises

For more exercises, see Extra Skills and Word Problems.

Describe the pattern for each sequence. Then find the next three terms.

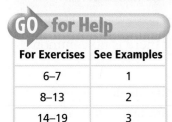

For Exercises	See Examples
6–7	1
8–13	2
14–19	3

6.

Position	1	2	3	4
Value of Term	−8	−1	6	13

7.

Position	1	2	3	4
Value of Term	25	21	17	13

8. 1, 2, 4, 8, . . .

9. 2, −6, 18, −54, . . .

10. 600, −300, 150, . . .

11. $\frac{1}{2}, \frac{1}{4}, \frac{1}{8}, \frac{1}{16}, \cdots$

12. −2, 4, −8, 16, . . .

13. $\frac{1}{4}, \frac{1}{12}, \frac{1}{36}, \frac{1}{108}, \cdots$

Identify each sequence as *arithmetic, geometric, both,* or *neither.*

14. 2, 5, 10, 17, 26, . . .

15. 1, 4, 9, 16, 25, . . .

16. 7, 14, 28, 56, . . .

17. −2, −2, −2, . . .

18. 300, 60, 12, 2.4, . . .

19. 84, 63, 42, 21, . . .

20. **Guided Problem Solving** A female bee has two biological parents—a female and a male. A male bee has only one biological parent, a female. The numbers of ancestors form a number sequence. Is the sequence *arithmetic, geometric, both,* or *neither?*

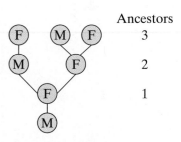

- **Make a Plan** Make a family tree of a male bee's ancestors. Show five generations. Find the number of ancestors in each generation.

21. **Running** Mario can run a mile in 9 min. After 4 months of training, he hopes to run a mile in 8 min. His time decreases by 15 s each month. What would you tell Mario about his conjecture?

22. A sequence starts with 7. The common difference is *D*. Write expressions for the next three terms in the sequence.

Calculator Make a conjecture about the next term in each sequence. Test your conjecture with a calculator.

23.
$2^4 = 16$
$2^3 = 8$
$2^2 = 4$
$2^1 = 2$
$2^0 = \blacksquare$

24.
$3^4 = 81$
$3^3 = 27$
$3^2 = 9$
$3^1 = 3$
$3^0 = \blacksquare$

25.
$4^4 = 256$
$4^3 = 64$
$4^2 = 16$
$4^1 = 4$
$4^0 = \blacksquare$

26. The Fibonacci sequence 1, 1, 2, 3, 5, 8, . . . occurs in nature. Find the ninth and tenth terms in the Fibonacci sequence. Is the Fibonacci sequence *arithmetic, geometric, both,* or *neither?*

27. a. How many blue tiles will be in the ninth figure of the pattern? How many yellow tiles will there be?
b. Describe the pattern.

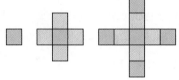

28. <u>**Writing in Math**</u> Every term in a sequence is 1. Is the sequence *arithmetic, geometric, both,* or *neither?* Explain.

29. Patterns Look at the pattern below. Make a conjecture about the next term in the sequence. Test your conjecture with a calculator.
$$123 \times 9 = 1{,}107 \quad 1{,}234 \times 9 = 11{,}106 \quad 12{,}345 \times 9 = 111{,}105$$

30. A sequence starts with 2. The common ratio is *R*. Write expressions for the next three terms in the sequence.

31. Challenge Make a conjecture about the next term in the sequence, and then find it.

Position	1	2	3	4	5	6
Value of Term	1	4	−1	6	−3	8

The spiral of a chambered nautilus shell follows the Fibonacci sequence.

Test Prep and Mixed Review **Practice**

Multiple Choice

32. Which sequence follows the rule $3n + 2$, where *n* is the position of a term in the sequence?

Ⓐ 3, 9, 27, 81, . . .   Ⓒ 3, 6, 9, 12, . . .
Ⓑ 5, 7, 9, 11, . . .   Ⓓ 5, 8, 11, 14, . . .

33. Which expression does the model at the right represent?
Ⓕ 9^2 Ⓗ 2^3
Ⓖ 9^3 Ⓙ 2^9

GO for Help

For Exercises	See Lesson
34–37	5-6

The scale on a map is 2 in. : 50 mi. Find the actual distance for each map distance. Round your answer to the nearest tenth of a mile.

34. 3 in.   **35.** $\frac{1}{2}$ in.   **36.** $1\frac{3}{4}$ in.   **37.** 5 in.

9-3 Patterns and Tables

Check Skills You'll Need

1. **Vocabulary Review** The *inverse operation* of subtraction is __?__ .

Solve each equation.

2. $x + 4 = -6$

3. $7 + t = 11$

4. $y - 5 = -13$

5. $a - (-3) = 17$

for Help
Lesson 4-3

What You'll Learn

To use tables to represent and describe patterns

Why Learn This?

At a market, it is common to display costs for different items. Sometimes making a table is the easiest way to organize data. Often you can make a table as your first step in solving a problem.

You can use a table to represent a pattern.

EXAMPLE Representing a Pattern

1 **Groceries** The table below shows the costs for different quantities of fish. Find the cost of 20 lb of fish.

Pounds of Fish	Price ($)	
1	6.50	$= 1 \times 6.5$
2	13.00	$= 2 \times 6.5$
3	19.50	$= 3 \times 6.5$
4	26.00	$= 4 \times 6.5$

← The values in the second column are 6.5 times the values in the first column.

To find the cost of 20 lb of fish, multiply 20 by 6.5.

$20 \cdot 6.5 = 130$

The cost of 20 lb of fish is $130.

Check for Reasonableness 20 lb is 10 times 2 lb. The cost for 2 lb is $13. $130 is 10 times $13, so the answer is reasonable.

Quick Check

Amount of Gas (gal)	Miles Driven
1	18.1
2	36.2
3	54.3
4	
5	

1. The table at the left shows the number of miles a car can travel using different amounts of gasoline. Copy and complete the table. Find the distance the car can travel using 15 gallons of gasoline.

Given a rule, you can find the value of a term using the position.

EXAMPLE Finding the Value of a Term

Test Prep Tip

You can eliminate choices as you find each value. Since the first term in the sequence is 2, you can eliminate choices C and D.

② **Multiple Choice** Which sequence follows the rule $-3n + 5$, where n represents the position of a term in a sequence?

Ⓐ 2, −1, −4, −7 . . .

Ⓒ −3, −6, −9, −12 . . .

Ⓑ 2, 1, 4, 7 . . .

Ⓓ 8, 11, 14, 17 . . .

Position	$-3n + 5$	Value of Term
1	$-3(1) + 5$	2
2	$-3(2) + 5$	−1
3	$-3(3) + 5$	−4
4	$-3(4) + 5$	−7

← Substitute 1, 2, 3, and 4 for n.

The correct answer is choice A.

✓ Quick Check

2. Use the rule $2n + 3$, where n represents the position of a term in a sequence. Find the first four terms in the sequence.

A table can help you write a variable expression to describe a sequence.

EXAMPLE Using a Table With a Sequence

Vocabulary Tip

Using a pattern to find any term in a sequence is often referred to as "finding the nth term."

③ Write an expression to describe the sequence 8, 16, 24, 32, . . . Then find the 10th term in the sequence.

8	16	24	32	. . .
Position 1	Position 2	Position 3	Position 4	and so on

Make a table that pairs the position of each term with its value.

Position	1	2	3	4	· · ·	10
	↓ · 8	↓ · 8	↓ · 8	↓ · 8	↓ · 8	↓ · 8
Value of Term Sequence	8	16	24	32	· · ·	■

The relationship is *Multiply the term number by 8.*

Let n = the term number. You can write the expression $n \cdot 8$, or $8n$.

$n \cdot 8 = 10 \cdot 8 = 80$ ← Substitute 10 for n to find the 10th term.

✓ Quick Check

3. Write an expression to describe the sequence −8, −7, −6, −5, . . . Find the 10th term in the sequence.

1. **Vocabulary** The expression $5n$ describes a sequence. When $n = 10$, the term position is ■ and the term value is ■.

2. **Mental Math** A sequence follows the rule $100n$, where n is the position of a term. Find the 10th term.

Find the next three numbers in each sequence.

3. 4, 12, 36, 108, ■, ■, ■

4. 4, 12, 20, 28, ■, ■, ■

Homework Exercises

For more exercises, see Extra Skills and Word Problems.

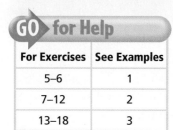

For Exercises	See Examples
5–6	1
7–12	2
13–18	3

Copy and complete each table.

5.

Cans of Soup	Number of Servings
3	9
4	12
5	15
6	■
7	■

6.

Dozens of Beads	Cost ($)
1	0.48
2	0.96
3	1.44
4	■
5	■

For Exercises 7–12, n represents the position of a term in a sequence. Find the first four terms in each sequence.

7. $n + 3$

8. $4n - 2$

9. $5n$

10. $6n + 1$

11. $n \div 4$

12. $n^2 - 3$

Write an expression to describe each sequence. Then find the 10th term.

13. 11, 22, 33, 44, ...

14. $-19, -18, -17, -16, \ldots$

15. $\frac{1}{2}, 1, 1\frac{1}{2}, 2, \ldots$

16. $-3, -6, -9, -12, \ldots$

17. $-18, -36, -54, -72, \ldots$

18. 100, 200, 300, 400, ...

19. **Guided Problem Solving** Suppose the average price for regular unleaded gasoline is $2.20 per gallon. Make a table that shows the price for 5, 10, 15, and 25 gallons of regular gasoline.
    - *Make a Table* that shows the price for 1, 2, and 3 gallons.
    - What is the pattern in the table?

20. **Music** The table shows costs for violin lessons. Copy and complete the table.

Time (h)	0.5	1	1.5	2
Cost ($)	12.50	■	■	■

Copy and complete each table.

21.

Miles	Time (h)
10	0.4
20	0.8
30	1.2
40	■
50	■

22.

Change in a Parking Meter ($)	Time Allowed to Park (h)
0.25	0.5
0.50	1
0.75	■
1.25	■

The freezing point of water is 0°C, or 273 K.

23. Temperature The relationship between Kelvin (K) and Celsius (C) temperatures is $K = 273 + C$. Make a table of Kelvin temperatures for Celsius temperatures of 0°, 20°, 40°, 80°, and 120°.

24. a. Copy and complete the table.
b. Writing in Math Explain how to find y when you know x.

x	0	1	2	3	4	■
y	−1	2	5	8	■	14

25. Geometry Use the relationship between side length and area to make a table for the areas of squares with side lengths of 2, 3, 5, 8, 10, and 12 in.

26. Make a table showing the number of blue and yellow squares in each group. How many blue squares will be in group 10?

27. Challenge Use the relationship $y = \frac{3}{2}x$.
a. Make a table that shows the values of y for $x = -2, -4, 2$, and 4.
b. Find the value of x when $y = 0$.

Test Prep and Mixed Review
Practice

Gridded Response

28. Isabel wants to cover her rectangular dining table with mosaic tiles that are 1 inch on each side. The table measures 3 feet by 4.5 feet. How many tiles does she need to cover the table?

29. Chencha has a part-time job after school. She earns $110.50 for 17 hours of work. How many dollars per hour does she earn?

30. Carlos plans to read every day for 6 days. He reads 9 pages on the first day, 18 pages on the second day, and 27 pages on the third day. If the pattern continues, how many pages will Carlos read on the sixth day?

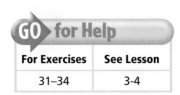
Go **for Help**

For Exercises	See Lesson
31–34	3-4

Find each product.

31. $\frac{1}{4}$ of 28   **32.** $\frac{3}{5} \cdot 25$ **33.** $\frac{2}{7} \cdot \frac{21}{50}$ **34.** $4\frac{2}{3} \cdot 4\frac{1}{2}$

Use the table below for Exercises 1–3.

Tablespoons	Teaspoons
1	3
3	9
4	12
6	18

1. Graph the data in the table.

2. Use the graph to estimate the number of teaspoons in 10 tablespoons.

3. Use the graph to estimate the number of tablespoons in 20 teaspoons.

Describe the pattern for each sequence. Then find the next three terms.

4. 7, 14, 21, 28, . . .

5. 250, 220, 190, 160, . . .

6. 2, 5, 11, 23, . . .

7. −4, 12, −36, 108, . . .

8. Identify each sequence in Exercises 4–7 as *arithmetic, geometric, both,* or *neither.*

9. Write an expression to describe the sequence 50, 100, 150, 200, . . . Then find the 10th term.

MATH AT WORK

Artists

Artists use a variety of materials to make images, such as oils, watercolors, plaster, or clay. Recently, many artists have begun to use computers. Graphic artists work for businesses. Fine artists display their works in galleries or museums.

Artists use mathematics when they mix different materials, sell their work, or estimate costs of their materials. Artists also create designs with patterns.

Go Online
PHSchool.com
For: more information about artists.
Web Code: arb-2031

Generating Formulas From a Table

You can write a formula for the area of a square that is missing its corners.

ACTIVITY

The corners of each square shown below are shaded.

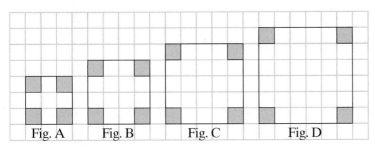

Fig. A   Fig. B   Fig. C   Fig. D

1. Copy and complete the table at the right to find the unshaded area of each square.

2. For each square, how is the area of the entire square related to the length of a side?

3. How many corners are shaded in each square?

4. What pattern do you notice about the unshaded area of each square?

Figure	A	B	C	D
Side Length	3			
Area of Square	9			
Unshaded Area	5			

Exercises

Find the area of a square that is missing its corners for each side length.

1. 7 units

2. 8 units

3. 10 units

4. Suppose a square has a side length of n units and all four corners are shaded. Write a formula for the unshaded area of the square.

Use your formula from Exercise 4 to find the unshaded area of each square with the given side length.

5. 100 units

6. 500 units

7. 1,000 units

9-4 Function Rules

✓ Check Skills You'll Need

1. Vocabulary Review
Why is 5 + 2 not an *algebraic expression*?

Evaluate $-4x + 1$ for each value of x.

2. -2 **3.** 0

4. $\frac{1}{4}$ **5.** $-\frac{1}{4}$

 **for Help**
Lesson 4-1

What You'll Learn

To write and evaluate functions

🔊 **New Vocabulary** function

Why Learn This?

The distance you travel in a car depends on the driving time. When one quantity depends on another, you say that one is a *function* of the other. So distance is a function of time. You can use functions to help you make predictions.

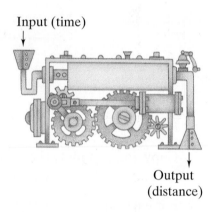

Input (time)

Output (distance)

In the diagram at the right, an input goes through the "function machine" to produce an output.

A **function** is a relationship that assigns exactly one output value for each input value.

EXAMPLE Writing a Function Rule

1 **Cars** You are traveling in a car at an average speed of 55 mi/h. Write a function rule that describes the relationship between the time and the distance you travel.

You can *make a table* to solve this problem.

Input: time (h)	1	2	3	4
Output: distance (mi)	55	110	165	220

distance in miles = 55 · time in hours   ← **Write the function rule in words.**

$d = 55t$ ← **Use variables *d* and *t* for distance and time.**

✓ Quick Check

1. Write a function rule for the relationship between the time and the distance you travel at an average speed of 62 mi/h.

The variables x and y are often used to represent input and output. You can describe the relationship between the values in the table in three ways.

Input x	Output y
1	4
2	5
3	6
4	7

Each output is 3 greater than the input.

$$\text{output} = \text{input} + 3$$
$$y = x + 3$$

EXAMPLE Using Tables to Analyze Functions

② Write a rule for the function represented by each table.

a.

x	y
0	0
1	−4
2	−8
3	−12

When $x = 0$, $y = 0$.
Each y equals
−4 times x.

The function rule is
$y = -4x + 0$, or $y = -4x$.

b.

x	y
0	−3
1	−1
2	1
3	3

When $x = 0$, $y = -3$.
Each y equals 2 times
x, plus −3.

The function rule is
$y = 2x + (-3)$, or $y = 2x - 3$.

✓ **Quick Check**

2. Write a rule for the function represented by the table below.

x	0	1	2	3
y	1	5	9	13

Given a function rule, you can evaluate the function for any input value.

EXAMPLE Evaluating Functions

③ Use the function $y = -3x + 5$. Find y for $x = 0, 1, 2,$ and 3. Then make a table for the function.

$y = -3(0) + 5 = 5$ ← Substitute 0, 1, 2, and 3 for x.

$y = -3(1) + 5 = 2$ List the values in a table. →

$y = -3(2) + 5 = -1$

$y = -3(3) + 5 = -4$

x	$y = -3x + 5$
0	5
1	2
2	−1
3	−4

✓ **Quick Check**

3. Use the function $y = 2x - 4$. Find y for $x = 0, 1, 2,$ and 3. Then make a table for the function.

1. **Vocabulary** Complete with *at least one* or *exactly one*: Every function pairs __?__ output value with each input value.

x	y
0	0
1	5
2	10
3	15

Use the function table at the left for Exercises 2–4.

2. What number does the function pair with 3?

3. Describe the pattern in the table using words.

4. Write a rule for the function represented by the table.

Homework Exercises

For more exercises, see **Extra Skills and Word Problems.**

GO for Help

For Exercises	See Examples
5–7	1
8–11	2
12–19	3

Write a function rule for each relationship.

5. the time *t* and distance *d* you travel at an average speed of 30 mi/h

6. the number *n* of words you type and the time *t* it takes, if you type at a rate of 32 words/min

7. the amount *c* of energy you burn and the time *t* you spend exercising, if you burn Calories at a rate of 12 Cal/min

Write a rule for the function represented by each table.

8.

x	y
0	4
1	5
2	6
3	7

9.

x	y
0	5
1	8
2	11
3	14

10.

x	y
0	1
1	−8
2	−17
3	−26

11.

x	y
0	0
1	−8
2	−16
3	−24

Use each function rule. Find y for x = 0, 1, 2, and 3. Then make a table for the function.

12. $y = x + 2$ 　 13. $y = 9 - x$ 　 14. $y = 4x$ 　 15. $y = x \div 2$

16. $y = -3x$ 　 17. $y = 2x + 1$ 　 18. $y = 4x - 2$ 　 19. $y = x^2 + 1$

20. **Guided Problem Solving** Write a function rule for the number *n* of inches in *f* feet. Then find the number of inches in 7 feet.
    - How many inches are in 1 foot?
    - How many inches are in *f* feet?

21. **Money** Suppose you put \$.50 in a piggy bank on July 1, \$1.00 on July 2, \$1.50 on July 3, and so on. Use *n* to represent the date. Write a function rule for the amount you put in for any date in July.

Write a rule for the function represented by each table.

22.

Laundry Loads	Cost ($)
1	2.75
2	5.50
3	8.25
4	11.00

23.

Time (h)	Kangaroo's Distance (km)
2	96
4	192
6	288

24. **Reading** A student can read 150 words in one minute.
   a. Write a function rule to represent the relationship between the number of words and the time in which they are read.
   b. How many words can the student read in 8 minutes?
   c. How long would it take the student to read 2,850 words?

25. **Writing in Math** Use the function table at the right. Describe the patterns you notice and explain how to find the function rule.

x	y
0	0
1	$\frac{1}{2}$
2	1
3	$1\frac{1}{2}$

26. One cm^3 is equal to 1 mL. Use this relationship to make a table showing the number of liters in 3 cm^3, 300 cm^3, and 3,000 cm^3. Then write a function rule.

27. Use the rule $y = 2x^2 - 4$. Evaluate the function for $x = -0.25$, $-\frac{1}{2}$, and $1\frac{1}{4}$.

28. **Challenge** Use the function machine at the right to make a table for integer inputs from -5 to 5. Which two input values result in an output of 22?

Input

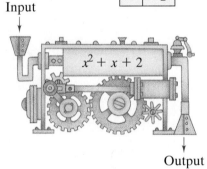

$x^2 + x + 2$

Output

Test Prep and Mixed Review   **Practice**

Multiple Choice

29. Which description shows the relationship between a term and n, its position in the sequence?

Position	1	2	3	4	n
Value of Term	6.50	13	19.50	26	■

   Ⓐ Add 6.50 to n.   Ⓒ Multiply n by 26.
   Ⓑ Add 26 to n.   Ⓓ Multiply n by 6.50.

30. Which of the following *never* names a quadrilateral with four congruent sides and four congruent angles?
   Ⓕ Trapezoid   Ⓖ Rectangle   Ⓗ Rhombus   Ⓙ Square

GO for Help

For Exercises	See Lesson
31–32	8-1

Choose a reasonable estimate. Explain your choice.

31. width of a nail: 1 mm or 1 m

32. length of a car: 4 m or 4 km

9-5 Using Tables, Rules, and Graphs

✓ Check Skills You'll Need

1. Vocabulary Review
What is a *sequence*?

Write an expression to describe each sequence.

2. 5, 10, 15, 20, . . .

3. −7, −5, −3, −1, . . .

4. 101, 202, 303, . . .

GO for Help
Lesson 9-3

What You'll Learn

To find solutions to application problems using tables, rules, and graphs

Why Learn This?

If you know your height in inches, you can find your height in feet. You can show the relationship between units such as inches and feet using a table, a rule, or a graph.

A graph can show the relationship between inputs and outputs.

EXAMPLE Graphing Using a Table

1 The table at the left shows the relationship between the number of inches (input) and the number of feet (output). The rule is $f = \frac{n}{12}$, where f represents the number of feet, and n represents the number of inches. Graph the relationship represented by the table.

Number of Inches	Number of Feet
12	1
24	2
36	3
48	4

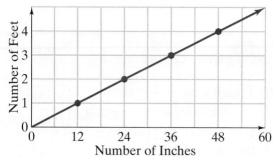

Graph inches on the horizontal axis and feet on the vertical axis.

Draw a line through the points.

✓ Quick Check

1. Graph the function represented by the table below.

Input x	Output y
0	3
1	5
2	7
3	9

Application: Plants

2 A plant grows 1.38 cm for each hour of sunlight it receives. Write and graph a rule to find the growth of the plant when it receives 4 h of sunlight.

Step 1 Write a rule.

Words | growth | equals | 1.38 | times | hours of sunlight

Let g = growth in centimeters.

Let s = hours of sunlight.

Equation g =   1.38 · s

Step 2 Make a table of values.

Hours of Sunlight (s)	1.38s	Centimeters of Growth (g)
1	1.38(1)	1.38
2	1.38(2)	2.76
3	1.38(3)	4.14
4	1.38(4)	5.52

Step 3 Make a graph.

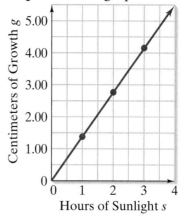

The plant grows 5.52 cm when it receives 4 h of sunlight.

Careers Botanists study the life and growth of plants.

✓ Quick Check

2. A bus travels 60 miles per hour. Write and graph a rule to find the number of miles the bus can travel in 4.5 hours.

✓ Check Your Understanding

1. **Vocabulary** What is a table of values?

2. **Reasoning** Does every relationship have an output of 0 for an input value of 0? Explain.

3. Graph the relationship represented by the table.

Input x	0	1	2	3
Output y	5	8	11	14

For more exercises, see Extra Skills and Word Problems.

GO for Help

For Exercises	See Examples
4–5	1
6–7	2

Graph the relationship represented by each table.

4.

Side Length of Square *s*	0	1	2	3	4
Perimeter of Square *P*	0	4	8	12	16

5.

Input *x*	Output *y*
0	1
1	4
2	7
3	10

For Exercises 6 and 7, write and graph a function to find the output for an input of 10 h.

6. **Employment** Total earnings *S* depends on the number *t* of hours worked. You earn $6/h.

7. **Air Travel** Total distance depends on the number *t* of hours traveled. Airplane speed averages 320 mi/h.

8. **Guided Problem Solving** It costs $120 per year to feed a cat. Write and evaluate a rule to find the cost of feeding a cat that lives to the maximum life span of 28 years.
   - **Make a Plan** Write a rule for the cost *c* of feeding a cat during its lifetime *y*.
   - **Carry Out the Plan** Substitute ■ for *y* to find the cost of feeding a cat that lives to the maximum life span.

9. The number of Calories *c* that are burned by walking depends on *t*, the number of hours spent walking. If you burn 300 Cal/h, how many Calories do you burn in 2.5 hours of walking?

GO Online

Homework Video Tutor
Visit: PHSchool.com
Web Code: are-0905

Match each graph with a rule.

10.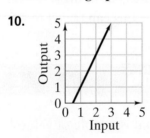

11.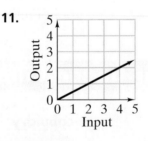

12.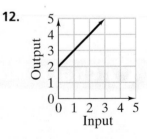

A. Output = $\frac{1}{2}$ · Input

B. Output = Input + 2

C. Output = 2 · Input − 1

13. **Writing in Math** For each situation, which would best represent the relationship—a table, a rule, or a graph? Explain your choice.
   a. You only have a few values or you do not know the rule.
   b. You have many input and output values.
   c. You want to see the relationship between the values.

14. a. Make a function table for the graph.
b. Write a rule for the function.

Graph each rule. Use input values of 1, 2, 3, 4, and 5.

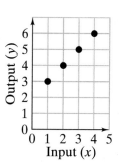

15. $y = 5x$ **16.** $y = 2x + 1$

17. $y = x \div 2$ **18.** $y = x - 3$

19. Open-Ended Choose one rule from Exercises 15–18. Describe a real-world situation that the rule could represent.

20. Flight Amelia Earhart set several flight speed records. The table at the right models the relationship between distance and time for a flight at Amelia Earhart's record speed.
a. Write a rule for the relationship represented by the table.
b. Find the average speed. Justify your answer.
c. Estimate the number of hours it would take to fly 1,890 mi.
d. Graph the rule.

Amelia Earhart's Flight

Time (h)	Distance (mi)
2	362
4	724
6	1,086
8	1,448

21. Challenge The area of an equilateral triangle depends on the side length s. The rule is $A = \frac{\sqrt{3}}{4}s^2$. Evaluate the rule for several values and make a table. Use 0.433 as an approximation of $\frac{\sqrt{3}}{4}$. Then graph the rule. Describe the shape of your graph.

In 1928, Amelia Earhart became the first woman to fly across the Atlantic Ocean.

 Test Prep and Mixed Review   **Practice**

Multiple Choice

22. Which of the following relationships is best represented by the data in the graph?
Ⓐ Conversion of feet to yards
Ⓑ Conversion of feet to inches
Ⓒ Conversion of miles to feet
Ⓓ Conversion of inches to yards

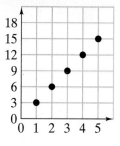

23. The circular base of a dome has a diameter of 60 ft. Which expression can be used to find the area of the base?
Ⓕ $2 \cdot 30 \cdot \pi$ Ⓗ $30 \cdot 30 \cdot \pi$
Ⓖ $2 \cdot 60 \cdot \pi$ Ⓙ $60 \cdot 60 \cdot \pi$

GO for Help

For Exercises	See Lesson
24–26	8-3

Find the area of a triangle with the given base and height.

24. 5 m, 2 m   **25.** 10 ft, 3 ft   **26.** 18 cm, 6 cm

Three Views of a Function

You can use a graphing calculator to graph a function.

EXAMPLE

Graph $y = 9 - x$ and make a table of values.

Step 1 Press WINDOW to set the range.

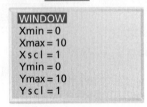

Step 2 Press Y= to enter the function.

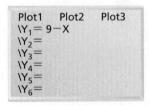

Step 3 Press GRAPH to view the graph.

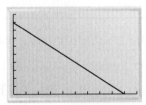

Step 4 Use the TblSet feature. Set TblStart = 0 and ΔTbl = 1.

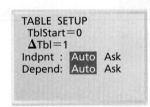

Step 5 Use the TABLE feature to make a table of values.

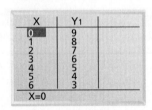

Step 6 Sketch the graph. Copy the table.

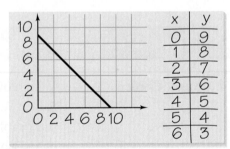

Exercises

Use a graphing calculator. Graph each function and make a table of values. Sketch the graph and copy the table of values.

1. $y = 2x$

2. $y = x - 3$

3. $y = 13 - 2x$

4. $y = x + 1$

5. $y = 3x - 4$

6. $y = 0.5x + 6$

7. **Reasoning** What values in the WINDOW feature would you use to view the graph of $y = 100x$? Explain.

9-6 Interpreting Graphs

Check Skills You'll Need

1. **Vocabulary Review** Give an example of an *input*.

Find the distance for each time. Use $d = rt$ with $r = 40$ mi/h.

2. 2.5 h   **3.** 3.5 h

4. $\frac{1}{4}$ h   **5.** $\frac{1}{2}$ h

GO for Help
Lesson 9-5

What You'll Learn

To describe and sketch graphs that represent real-world situations

Why Learn This?

You can see the history of an event by looking at a graph. You can use a graph like the one at the right to show your distance from home when you take a trip or run an errand.

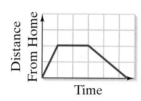

When you graph a relationship, you can see how one quantity changes compared to another.

EXAMPLE   Describing a Graph

1 Shopping The graph above relates time and your distance from home. What can you tell about the trip from the steepness of the lines?

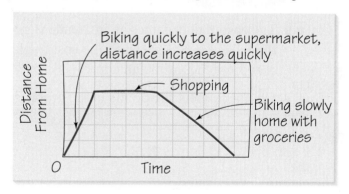

A steeper line on the graph shows faster speed. A horizontal line represents a period of no change in distance from home.

Quick Check

1. You live 6 blocks from school. The graph at the right shows your walk home on a sunny day. Describe what the graph shows.

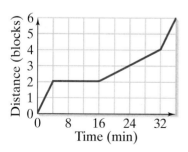

You can sketch a graph to describe a real-world situation.

EXAMPLE **Sketching a Graph**

② Transportation Ciara's mother drove her part of the way to school. Ciara waited for a friend and walked the rest of the way to school. She took a bus home. Sketch a graph to show the distance Ciara traveled compared to time.

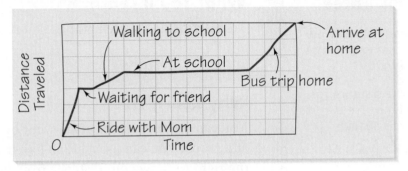

✔ Quick Check

2. Sketch a graph of the situation in Example 2 using *Distance from Home* instead of *Distance Traveled* for the vertical axis.

When you draw a graph, you may need to consider what is reasonable.

EXAMPLE **Graphing Data**

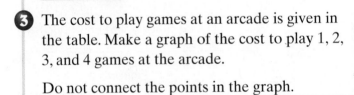

For: Graphing Activity
Use: Interactive
Textbook, 9-6

③ The cost to play games at an arcade is given in the table. Make a graph of the cost to play 1, 2, 3, and 4 games at the arcade.

Do not connect the points in the graph.

Number of Games	Cost ($)
1	2.00
2	3.50
3	5.00
4	6.50

Check for Reasonableness Each cost is for playing an entire game. Since you cannot pay for part of a game, connecting the points would not be meaningful.

✔ Quick Check

3. The table shows the number of cans in the cafeteria juice machine over time. Graph the data.

Time	Number of Cans
8 A.M.	30
9 A.M.	20
10 A.M.	19
11 A.M.	19

Match each situation with the appropriate graph.

1. height of a person from birth to age 20

2. air temperature in a 24-hour period starting at midnight

3. distance raced with a fall over a hurdle

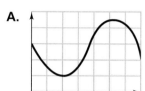

A.

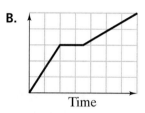

B.

C.

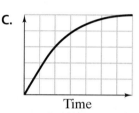

Homework Exercises

For more exercises, see Extra Skills and Word Problems.

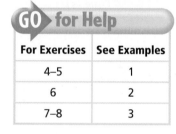

GO for Help

For Exercises	See Examples
4–5	1
6	2
7–8	3

Describe what each graph shows.

4. **Walking Home From School**

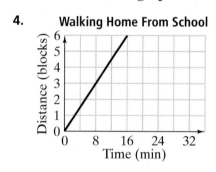

5. **Distance From Home**

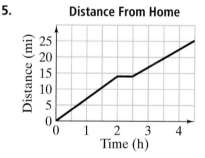

6. You ride your bike slowly up a steep hill and then quickly down the other side. Sketch a graph for the situation. Label each section and each axis. Show your speed on the bicycle on the vertical axis.

Graph the data. Should you connect the points on each graph? Explain.

7. **Lemonade Sales**

Cups Sold	Income ($)
1	0.75
2	1.50
3	2.25
4	3.00
5	3.75

8. **Miles From Home**

Time (h)	Miles
1	60
2	85
3	120
4	180

9. **Guided Problem Solving** You pay 5 cents a day for overdue library books. Make a graph of the fines for 1–5 days.
   - How can a table help you plot the points on the graph?
   - Should you connect the points on your graph?

10. Suppose you steadily pour sand into the bowl at the left. Which graph below better shows the relationship of the height of the sand over time? Explain.

A.
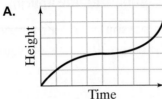

B.

(Height vs. Time — straight diagonal line)

11. The graph shows a 90-m race. One student starts 5 s after the other.
    a. Describe what the graph shows.
    b. Who wins the race?
    c. **Writing in Math** If the lines were parallel, what would the graph tell you about who wins the race?

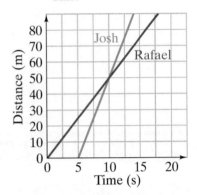

GO Online
Homework Video Tutor
Visit: PHSchool.com
Web Code: are-0906

Estimation The graph below shows what happens when a ball is thrown in the air.

12. When does the ball hit the ground?

13. Why are there two times when the ball's height is 20 ft? What are they?

14. When the time is 0, the height of the ball is *not* 0. Explain.

15. **Challenge** Describe what might have happened to make the data in the graph.

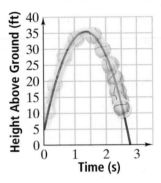

Test Prep and Mixed Review

Practice

Multiple Choice

16. Lee is starting his own business by selling personalized photo frames to his class for $19 each. It costs Lee $14 for materials to make one frame. Which equation can be used to find *p*, the amount of profit he makes by selling 25 frames?

    Ⓐ $p = (25 \times 19) - 14$ Ⓒ $p = 25 \times 19 \times 14$
    Ⓑ $p = 25(19 - 14)$ Ⓓ $p = 14(25 - 19)$

17. Which problem situation is NOT modeled by $y = 4x$?
    Ⓕ Cost of a call at $0.04/min   Ⓗ Perimeter of a trapezoid
    Ⓖ Janet's pay after working 4 h   Ⓙ Number of pens in 4 packs

For Exercises	See Lesson
18–21	2-4

Compare. Use <, =, or >.

18. $\frac{7}{9}$ ■ $\frac{3}{4}$ 19. $\frac{5}{14}$ ■ $\frac{2}{6}$ 20. $\frac{7}{30}$ ■ $\frac{1}{3}$ 21. $\frac{8}{24}$ ■ $\frac{2}{6}$

Write a rule for each table.

1.

x	0	1	2	3
y	0	5	10	15

2.

x	0	1	2	3
y	−3	0	3	6

3.

x	0	1	2	3
y	9	10	11	12

4. Graph $y = 2x - 4$.

For Exercises 5–7, use the graph at the right.

5. The graph shows a 50-m race. In this race Edwin had a 15-m head start over Carl. Who won the race?

6. By how many seconds did the winner win the race?

7. You walk for 3 h, eat lunch for 1 h, bike for 1 h, and then do homework for 2 h. Sketch a graph that describes your speed.

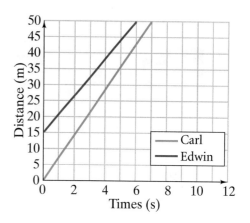

MATH GAMES

Lines in Space

What You'll Need

● 2 players and 2 coordinate grids similar to the one at the right

How To Play

● Without showing each other, Players A and B put three spaceships on their own grids. The lengths of the spaceships are four points, three points, and three points.

● Ships occupy adjacent grid points either left and right, up and down, or diagonally. Players choose whole-number points. They take turns trying to locate each other's ships by calling out function rules.

● If a function rule hits one or more sections of a spaceship, the player must announce a hit. See the table at the right.

● After 7 guesses each, the player who has hit the most sections of the other player's spaceships wins.

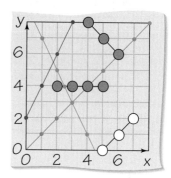

Rule	Result
$y = 2x + 2$?	Miss!
$y = -2x + 9$?	1 Hit!
$y = x$	2 Hits!

465

Solving Pattern Problems

Alondra lines up dominoes to see how many she can knock over by touching only one. She lines them up as shown below. If Alondra makes 20 rows, how many dominoes can she knock over?

What You Might Think

> What do I know? What do I want to find out?

> How can I show the main idea?

> How do I solve the problem?

> How can I check my answer?

What You Might Write

I can see one domino in the first row, two in the second, three in the third, and so on. I want to know how many are in 20 rows.

I see a pattern. I see these numbers of dominoes:

1, 2, 3, . . . 20. So, add 1 + 2 + 3 + . . . + 20.

One way to add the numbers is to make "pairs of 20s," such as 1 + 19 and 2 + 18. I get nine 20s, plus 10 and 20. Since $9 \cdot 20 + 10 + 20 = 210$, the answer is 210 dominoes.

I can add the numbers from 1 to 20 in order, using a calculator. I still get 210.

Think It Through

1. Write the numbers from 1 to 20. Show that you have nine pairs that add up to 20, plus 10 and 20.

2. If Alondra had made 30 rows, how many dominoes did she use?

3. **Number Sense** If Alondra had 300 dominoes, how many rows could she make? Explain.

Exercises

Solve each problem. For Exercises 4 and 5, answer the questions first.

4. William stacked cans of soup as shown below. What is the total number of cans would he need to make the stack 7 rows high?

  a. What do you know? What do you want to find out?
  b. Is there a pattern? If so, how can you find the sum?

5. One of the largest passenger jets, the Airbus A380, first flew in 2005. The dimensions of the A380 and the Wright Flyer are shown in the table below. Assume that Wright Flyers can be stacked on top of each other and that they always face the same direction inside a hangar. How many Wright Flyers could fit in a hangar built to house the A380?

Plane Dimensions

Plane	Length (ft)	Width (ft)	Height (ft)
Airbus A380	239	262	79
Wright Flyer	21	40	9

  a. A sketch of a box representing the dimensions of the Airbus A380 appears at the right. How can drawing a box that represents the Wright Flyer help you find the answer?

6. A lawnmower engine turns at about 2,500 rpm (revolutions per minute). How many times does the blade turn around every second? How many times does the blade turn around in half an hour?

7. A sheet of notebook paper is about 0.0025 inch thick. It is physically impossible to fold a piece of paper in half 13 times. If you could, how thick would the stack of folded paper be? If you could fold a piece of paper 25 times, how thick would the stack be?

Check Skills You'll Need

1. Vocabulary Review
What is a *percent*?

Change each percent to a decimal.

2. 4%   **3.** 9%

4. 2.0%   **5.** 6.5%

 **for Help**
Lesson 6-2

What You'll Learn

To find simple interest and compound interest

◀)) **New Vocabulary** principal, simple interest, compound interest, balance

Why Learn This?

Money may not grow on trees, but it can grow in a bank. When you deposit money, you earn money called interest. When you borrow money, you pay interest on your loan.

The original amount you deposit or borrow is the **principal**. Interest earned only on the principal is **simple interest**.

You can use a formula to calculate simple interest.

> **KEY CONCEPTS** **Simple Interest Formula**
>
> $$I = prt$$
>
> I is the interest earned, p is the principal, r is the interest rate per year, and t is the time in years.

Video Tutor Help
Visit: PHSchool.com
Web Code: are-0775

GO ● nline

EXAMPLE **Finding Simple Interest**

1 **Gridded Response** You borrow $300 for 5 years at an annual interest rate of 4%. What is the simple interest you pay in dollars?

$I = prt$ ← **Write the formula.**

$I = (300)(0.04)(5) = 60$ ← **Substitute. Use 0.04 for 4%.**

The interest is $60.

✓ Quick Check

1. Find the simple interest you pay on a $220 loan at a 5% annual interest rate for 4 years.

A graph can show the increase in interest earned over time.

EXAMPLE Graphing Simple Interest

For: Interest Activity
Use: Interactive
Textbook, 9-7

② You have $500 in an account that earns an annual rate of 5.1%. At the end of each year, you withdraw the interest you have earned. Graph the total interest you earn after 1, 2, 3, and 4 years.

Step 1 Make a table.

Time (yr)	Interest ($)
1	25.50
2	51.00
3	76.50
4	102.00

Step 2 Draw a graph.

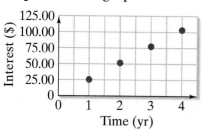

✓ Quick Check

2. Graph the simple interest earned on $950 at an annual rate of 4.2%.

Compound interest is interest that is paid on the original principal and on any interest that has been left in the account. The **balance** of an account is the principal plus the interest earned.

> **KEY CONCEPTS** Compound Interest Formula
>
> $$B = p(1 + r)^t$$
>
> B is the balance, p is the principal, r is the annual interest rate, and t is the time in years.

EXAMPLE Finding Compound Interest

GO for Help

For help using the order of operations with exponents, go to Lesson 2-1, Example 3.

③ **Banking** You deposit $5,000 in a bank account that pays 3.75% compound interest. What is your balance after 9 years?

$B = p(1 + r)^t$ ← Write the formula.

$= 5,000(1 + 0.0375)^9$ ← Substitute. Use 0.0375 for 3.75%.

$\approx 5,000(1.392813439)$ ← Use a calculator to simplify the power.

$= 6,964.07$ ← Round to the nearest cent.

The balance after 9 years is $6,964.07.

✓ Quick Check

3. You deposit $3,000 in a bank account that pays 4.25% compound interest. What is your balance after 12 years?

1. **Vocabulary** How do simple interest and compound interest differ?

2. Find the simple interest earned on $2000 at 10% for 6 years.

3. Find the compound interest earned on $2000 at 10% for 6 years.

4. True or False: Doubling the principal will double the balance.

Homework Exercises

For more exercises, see Extra Skills and Word Problems.

GO for Help

For Exercises	See Examples
5–8	1
9–14	2
15–19	3

Find the simple interest on a $340 loan at each rate.

5. 7% annual interest, 3 years

6. 12% annual interest, 5 years

7. 15% annual interest, 1 year

8. 4.6% annual interest, 6 years

Graph the total simple interest earned for each amount over 4 years.

9. $500 at 4.5%

10. $1,200 at 6.5%

11. $375 at 5.75%

12. $200 at 5.0%

13. $2,000 at 10%

14. $2,000 at 0.5%

Find the balance in each compound interest account.

15. $1,400 after 3 years at 5.5%

16. $1,800 after 11 years at 6.0%

17. $900 after 10 years at 4.62%

18. $2,500 after 50 years at 2.2%

19. You deposit $1,000 in a certificate of deposit that pays 5.9% compound interest. What is your balance after 3 years?

GPS 20. **Guided Problem Solving** You have $7,500 in a college savings account that earns 4.25% compound interest. What will the account balance be at the end of 12 years?
   - What is 4.25% expressed as a decimal?
   - What value do you substitute for each variable in the formula $B = p(1 + r)^t$?

21. You borrow $500 at 18% annual compound interest. You make no payments for 6 months. How much do you owe after 6 months?

22. Suppose you invest $2,000 for 5 years at 4% compounded annually. Which would increase your balance in 5 years the most?
   Ⓐ Doubling the starting amount from $2,000 to $4,000
   Ⓑ Doubling the interest rate to 8% annual interest
   Ⓒ Doubling the time from 5 years to 10 years

23. **Writing in Math** Would you prefer $2,000 at 6% compound interest for 5 years or $2,000 at 5% compound interest for 6 years? Explain.

The spreadsheet shows calculations using the compound interest formula. State which column corresponds to each variable.

	A	B	C	D	E
1	Year	Balance at Start of Year	Rate	Interest	Balance at End of Year
2	1st	$3,000.00	0.04	$120.00	$3,120.00
3	2nd	$3,120.00	0.04	$124.80	$3,244.80
4	3rd	$3,244.80	0.04	$129.79	$3,374.59

24. p **25.** r **26.** t **27.** B

28. Show how to calculate the amount in E4 in the spreadsheet above.

29. Calculator You invest $4,000 at 3% compound interest. What is the balance after 3 years?

30. Challenge You invest $2,000 in a simple interest account. The balance after 8 years is $2,720. What is the interest rate?

Test Prep and Mixed Review   Practice

Multiple Choice

31. When a principal p has a compound interest rate r for t years, the balance B is given by $B = p(1 + r)^t$. Which expression represents the balance for $200 invested for 6 years at a 5% compound interest rate?

   Ⓐ $200(1.06)^5$ Ⓒ $200(1.05)^6$

   Ⓑ $200(0.06)(5)$ Ⓓ $200(1.05)(6)$

32. Which situation is best represented by the graph of babies born in Texas?

   Ⓕ About 85 babies were born every hour.

   Ⓖ About 85 babies were born every 2 hours.

   Ⓗ About 85 babies were born every 3 hours.

   Ⓙ About 85 babies were born every 4 hours.

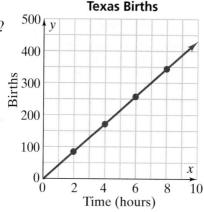

Texas Births

33. $\angle A$ and $\angle B$ are supplementary. The measure of $\angle A$ is 24°. What is the measure of $\angle B$?

   Ⓐ 24°   Ⓑ 66°   Ⓒ 156°   Ⓓ 336°

GO for Help

For Exercises	See Lesson
34–35	8-8

Use graph paper to draw each figure.

34. triangular prism   **35.** pentagonal pyramid

Transforming Formulas

Check Skills You'll Need

1. **Vocabulary Review**
   What is the *Division Property of Equality*?

Solve each equation.

2. $5a = 9$

3. $12 = 4.5t$

4. $\dfrac{p}{4} = -8$

 for Help
Lesson 4-4

What You'll Learn

To solve for a variable

◀)) **New Vocabulary** formula

Why Learn This?

Albert Einstein discovered the relationship between mass, energy, and the speed of light. The formula $E = mc^2$ shows this relationship.

A **formula** is a rule that shows the relationship between two or more quantities.

You can use the properties of equality to transform a formula and solve for a variable.

EXAMPLE   Transforming a Formula

1 The formula for the perimeter of a rectangle is $P = 2\ell + 2w$. Solve the formula for ℓ.

$$P = 2\ell + 2w \quad \leftarrow \text{Write the formula.}$$

$$P - 2w = 2\ell \quad \leftarrow \text{Use the Subtraction Property of Equality.}$$

$$\frac{P - 2w}{2} = \frac{2\ell}{2} \quad \leftarrow \text{Use the Division Property of Equality.}$$

$$\frac{P - 2w}{2} = \ell \quad \leftarrow \text{Simplify.}$$

Test Prep Tip

To solve a formula for a variable, you have to get the variable alone on one side of the equation.

✓ Quick Check

1. Solve each equation for x.
   a. $y = 2x - 4$
   b. $y = x + 3$
   c. $4y = 2x + 10$

You can transform formulas to solve real-world problems. First solve for the desired variable. Then substitute the values you know.

Video Tutor Help
Visit: PHSchool.com
Web Code: are-0775

EXAMPLE Application: Savings

2 Your bank account has an annual interest rate of 5.7%. How much should you invest in order to earn $100 in interest each year?

$$\frac{I}{rt} = p \quad \leftarrow \text{Use the simple interest formula } I = prt \text{ and solve for } p.$$

$$\frac{100}{(0.057)(1)} = p \quad \leftarrow \text{Substitute 100 for } I, 0.057 \text{ for } r, \text{ and 1 for } t.$$

$$1,754.39 \approx p \quad \leftarrow \text{Simplify.}$$

You should invest about $1,755.

✓ Quick Check

2. Find the interest rate that yields $120 interest each year on $2,000.

● More Than One Way

Your first four test scores were 85, 98, 79, and 92. To get an average score of at least 90, what minimum score do you need on the fifth test?

Will's Method

I'll use a variable for each score and let z be the missing score.

Formula for mean → $\quad 90 = \dfrac{v + w + x + y + z}{5}$

Mult. Prop. of Equality → $\quad 5(90) = v + w + x + y + z$

$5(90) - (v + w + x + y) = z \qquad \leftarrow$ Subtraction Prop. of Equality

$5(90) - (85 + 98 + 79 + 92) = z = 96 \quad \leftarrow$ Substitute and simplify.

I need a minimum score of 96 on the fifth test.

Sarah's Method

I'll work backward. The sum of the 5 scores divided by the number of scores is 90. Since $5 \cdot 90 = 450$, the sum is 450.

The sum of the first scores is $85 + 98 + 79 + 92$, or 354. So, for a total of 450, I need a score on the fifth test of $450 - 354$, or 96.

Choose a Method

Your scores on three tests are 95, 89, and 75. You can replace your lowest score with the mean of that score and a retest. For an average score of 90, what is the minimum you must score on the retest?

Reasoning Could the equation be a formula? Explain.

1. $3 + 4 = 7$

2. $3t + 4u = 7$

3. $3 + 4 = 7v$

Which operation must you use to solve each equation for x**?**

4. $1 + x = 13$

5. $x \div 4 = 52$

6. $7x = 35$

Homework Exercises

For more exercises, see Extra Skills and Word Problems.

GO for Help

For Exercises	See Examples
7–15	1
16–18	2

Solve each equation for the variable in red.

7. $x = yz$

8. $t = \dfrac{u + v}{2}$

9. $p = 3r - 5$

10. $P = 4s$

11. $q = \dfrac{p}{r}$

12. $p = s - c$

13. $A = \dfrac{1}{2}bh$

14. $h = \dfrac{k}{j}$

15. $I = prt$

16. How long would it take to earn $6,000 in interest on a principal of $9,000 at an annual simple interest rate of 4.1%?

17. You earn $1,400 simple interest on a principal of $12,500 in 4 years. What is the interest rate on your account?

18. Suppose you borrow money for a year at a simple interest rate of 7.2%. You pay $86.40 in interest. How much have you borrowed?

GPS **19.** **Guided Problem Solving** A real estate agent sells a house and earns 7% commission, or $8,400. Find the selling price of the house.
- What is a formula for the agent's commission? Let c represent the commission. Let s represent the selling price.
- For which variable should you solve?

20. **Geometry** Find the radius of the circle at the right.

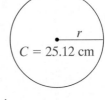

$C = 25.12$ cm

GO Online
Homework Video Tutor
Visit: PHSchool.com
Web Code: are-0908

21. The formula for converting F degrees Fahrenheit to C degrees Celsius is $C = \dfrac{5}{9}(F - 32)$. Solve the equation for F to generate the formula for converting C degrees Celsius into F degrees Fahrenheit.

22. **Choose a Method** During a 3-day premiere, a theater must sell an average of 200 tickets per night to make a profit. For the first two nights, 206 and 185 tickets were sold. How many tickets must be sold for the third night for the theater to make a profit?

23. **Writing in Math** Solve the formula $V = \ell wh$ for w. Then write and solve a problem involving the transformed version of the formula.

Solve each equation for the variable in red.

24. $x = 3y + 6$ **25.** $t = \frac{1}{2}r$ **26.** $w = 3n + 5m$

27. Construction Bricklayers use the formula $N = 7\ell h$ to estimate the number of bricks needed to cover a wall. N is the number of bricks, ℓ is the length of the wall in feet, and h is the height. If 980 bricks are used to build a wall 20 feet long, how high is the wall?

28. Weekly pay w is given by the formula $w = rh + 1.5rv$, where r is the regular hourly wage for a 40-h week, h is the number of regular hours you work, and v is the number of overtime hours you work beyond 40. Suppose your regular wage is \$9/h.
a. If you work 45 hours in one week, what do you earn?
b. For weekly pay of \$468, how many overtime hours do you work?

29. Challenge The surface area S of a cube with side e is $S = 6e^2$. Find the side length of a cube with a surface area of 150 cm^2.

Test Prep and Mixed Review
Practice

Multiple Choice

30. You want to paint a wall of the playhouse but not the door in the wall. How many square feet of wall do you need to paint?
Ⓐ 15 ft^2
Ⓑ 95 ft^2
Ⓒ 110 ft^2
Ⓓ 125 ft^2

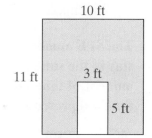

31. Ezra can swim 50 meters in 30 seconds. About how many seconds will it take him to swim a 200-meter race?
Ⓕ 60 sec   Ⓖ 80 sec   Ⓗ 120 sec   Ⓙ 150 sec

32. Which description shows the relationship between a term and n, its position in the sequence?

Term Number	1	2	3	4	5	n
Value of Term	12	24	36	48	60	■

Ⓐ Multiply n by 12.
Ⓑ Divide n by 12.
Ⓒ Add 12 to n.
Ⓓ Subtract 12 from n.

GO for Help

For Exercises	See Lesson
33–34	8-7

Find the missing side length. Round your answer to the nearest tenth.

33.

8 m c 12 m

34.

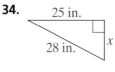

25 in.   28 in. x

More About Formulas

There are some formulas that are not just interesting mathematically, but are also part of your life. Consider the formulas below.

ACTIVITY

Use the graph at the right for Exercises 1–3.

1. Gold is measured in karats. The formula $P = \frac{25k}{6}$ gives you the percent of gold in k karats. Graph the percents of gold for 10, 12, 14, and 18 karats. Use the graph started at the right.

2. Extend the graph until you reach 100% gold. Which karat value corresponds to 100% gold?

3. Transform the formula $P = \frac{25k}{6}$ by solving for k. Which karat value corresponds to 100% gold?

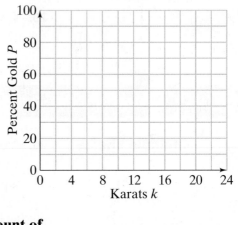
Gold

The SPF number of sunscreen s tells you how long you can stay in the sun safely. The formula $t = sn$ represents the amount of time t it takes skin to burn with sunscreen. The amount of time n represents how long it takes skin to burn without sunscreen.

4. Transform the formula above by solving for s.

5. A summer pool party might last 3 hours. Use the transformed formula to find what SPF number you should apply for $n = 15$ min.

Data Analysis Peter Brancazio developed the formula $v = 126 - \frac{5}{4}h$. This formula determines the vertical leap v needed for people of different heights h to slam-dunk a basketball. Both v and h are in inches.

6. Use the graph started at the right. Graph the results of this formula for heights of 5 ft, 5 ft 6 in., 6 ft, 6 ft 6 in., and 7 ft.

7. What do you think 126 represents in the formula? Most basketball hoops are about 10 ft high.

8. **Reasoning** Explain why the formula uses $\frac{5}{4}$ of height instead of exact height.

9. Transform the formula above to solve for h.

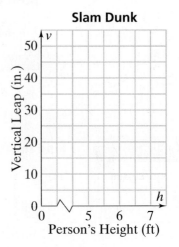
Slam Dunk

Test-Taking Strategies

Estimating the Answer

Using estimation can help you find an answer, check an answer, or eliminate one or more answer choices.

EXAMPLES

1 A store is having a 30%-off sale on all of its cross-training sneakers. What is the sale price on a pair of sneakers that regularly costs $84.99?

   Ⓐ $25.50   Ⓑ $51.99   Ⓒ $59.49   Ⓓ $79.99

You can estimate by changing $84.99 to a number that is easy to multiply in your head, such as $90. A 30% discount will result in a sale price that is 70% of the regular price.

$s = 0.7c$ ← Write a function rule for sale price. Let s = sale price. Let c = regular cost.

$\approx 0.7(90)$ ← Substitute the estimated value.

$= 63$ ← Use mental math.

The sale price will be a little less than $63. The answer is choice C.

2 The formula for converting Celsius temperatures to Fahrenheit temperatures is $F = \frac{9}{5}C + 32$. Sterling silver melts at approximately 893°C. What is the approximate Fahrenheit temperature?

   Ⓕ 998°F   Ⓖ 1,422°F   Ⓗ 1,639°F   Ⓙ 1,995°F

$F = \frac{9}{5}(893) + 32$ ← Substitute into the formula.

$\approx 2(900) + 32$ ← Estimate. $\frac{9}{5} \approx \frac{10}{5}$, or 2, and $893 \approx 900$.

$= 1{,}832$ ← This is an overestimate, since $900 > 893$ and $2 > \frac{9}{5}$.

According to your estimate, choices F and G are too low. Since 1,832 is an overestimate, you can eliminate choice J. The correct answer is choice H.

Exercises

1. A salon is offering a 20% discount on all haircuts. What is the discount price of a cut that regularly costs $23.50?

   Ⓐ $12.50   Ⓑ $14.75   Ⓒ $18.80   Ⓓ $22.00

2. The melting point of pure gold is 1,945°F. What is the approximate melting point in Celsius using the formula $C = \frac{5}{9}(F - 32)$?

   Ⓕ 1,063°C   Ⓖ 1,159°C   Ⓗ 1,205°C   Ⓙ 1,495°C

Chapter 9 Review

Vocabulary Review

🔊 arithmetic sequence (p. 442)
balance (p. 469)
compound interest (p. 469)
conjecture (p. 443)

formula (p. 472)
function (p. 452)
geometric sequence (p. 442)

principal (p. 468)
sequence (p. 442)
simple interest (p. 468)

Go Online
PHSchool.com
For: Vocabulary Quiz
Web Code: arj-0951

Choose the correct term to complete each sentence.

1. A sequence is (arithmetic, geometric) if each term is found by adding the same number to the previous term.

2. A (formula, function) has only 1 output value for each input value.

3. (Balance, Principal) is an amount deposited or borrowed.

4. Interest paid on an original deposit and on any interest that has been left in an account is (compound, simple) interest.

5. A (conjecture, formula) is a prediction.

Skills and Concepts

Lesson 9-1
• To graph data and to use graphs to make predictions

Graphs can help you visualize the relationship between data. Graphs have horizontal and vertical scales. Each scale is divided into intervals.

Graph the data in each table.

6.

Servings	1	2	3
Calories	280	560	840

7.

Time (days)	2	4	6
Pay ($)	15	30	45

8. Use your graph from Exercise 7 to estimate the pay for 11 days.

Lessons 9-2, 9-3
• To describe the patterns in arithmetic and geometric sequences and use the patterns to find terms
• To use tables to represent and describe patterns

A **sequence** is a set of numbers that follow a pattern. Find each term of an **arithmetic sequence** by adding a common difference to each term. Find each term of a **geometric sequence** by multiplying each term by a common ratio. Use a table to show patterns and find unknown quantities.

Identify each sequence as *arithmetic, geometric, both,* or *neither*.

9. 2, 10, 18, 26, . . .

10. 48, 4, $\frac{1}{3}$, . . .

11. 0, 1, 4, 13, 40, . . .

12. Write a variable expression to describe the sequence −6, −12, −18, −24, . . . Then find the 10th term.

Lessons 9-4, 9-5

- To write and evaluate functions
- To find solutions to application problems using tables, rules, and graphs

A **function** is a relationship that assigns one output value for each input value. Write a function rule by looking for patterns in a table. A graph can show the relationship between inputs and outputs.

Use the graph for Exercises 13–14 and the table for Exercises 15–16.

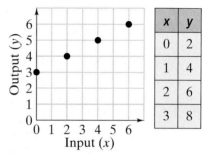

x	y
0	2
1	4
2	6
3	8

13. Make a table for the graph.

14. Write a rule for the graph.

15. Write a rule for the relationship represented by the table.

16. Graph the rule represented by the table.

17. Evaluate $y = -2x + 5$ for x-values -1, 0, 1, 2, and 3.

Lesson 9-6

- To describe and sketch graphs that represent real-world situations

A graph shows how one quantity changes relative to another. In a real-world context, you need to consider what is reasonable.

18. Describe a situation that the graph at the right might represent.

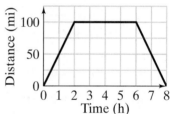

19. You walk at a rate of 3 mi/h for 3 h. You rest for 1 h and then walk 3 mi/h for an hour. Sketch a graph that shows the distance you travel over time.

Lesson 9-7

- To find simple interest and compound interest

Use the formula $I = prt$ to find **simple interest.** Use the formula $B = p(1 + r)^t$ to find the account **balance** with **compound interest.**

20. You deposit $1,500 in an account that earns 6% simple interest. How much interest do you earn in five years?

21. You deposit $2,500 in an account that pays 5.7% interest compounded annually. What is the balance after five years?

Lesson 9-8

- To solve for a variable

A **formula** is a rule that shows the relationship between quantities. Use properties of equality to solve for any variable in a formula.

Solve each formula for x.

22. $z = 3x + y$

23. $k = -4xyz$

24. $\frac{1}{9}x - 4 = \frac{z}{3}$

25. You borrow $200 at a 3% simple interest rate. About how much interest will you owe in 18 months?

Describe the pattern in each sequence. Find the next three terms.

1. $1, 3, 9, 27, \ldots$
2. $4, 9, 14, 19, \ldots$
3. $3, 4, 6, 9, \ldots$
4. $10, 8, 6, 4, \ldots$
5. $-23, -19, -15, \ldots$
6. $6, 3, 1.5, 0.75, \ldots$

7. Identify each sequence in Exercises 1–6 as *arithmetic, geometric, both,* or *neither*.

8. a. Graph the data.

Picture Framing

Photo Width (in.)	Framed Width (in.)
5	4.17
8	6.67
12	10

   b. Estimate the framed width for a photo that is 9.5 in. wide.
   c. Estimate the framed width for a photo 18 in. wide.

Make a function table for each function.

9. the cost of 1 to 5 books at $2.95 each

10. the perimeters of squares with sides of 5, 6, 7, 8, and 9 in.

Write a rule for each table.

11.

x	y
0	−2
1	−7
2	−12
3	−17

12.

x	y
0	1
1	3
2	5
3	7

13.

x	y
0	0
1	3
2	6
3	9

14. Graph the rules in Exercises 12 and 13.

Evaluate for $x = -2, 0,$ and 5.

15. $y = x - 5$
16. $y = 9 + x$
17. $y = 2x + 1$
18. $y = x^2 - 1$

19. Which is not an output for $y = 2x^2 - 5$?
    A. -3 B. 45   C. 27   D. -8

Use the graph at the right.

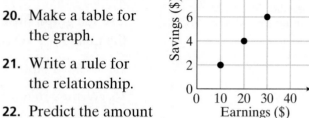

20. Make a table for the graph.

21. Write a rule for the relationship.

22. Predict the amount saved when $100 is earned.

23. **Sports** You dribble a basketball five times, pause briefly, and then shoot it into the basket. Sketch a graph that describes the ball's height as a function of time.

24. Describe what the graph below shows.

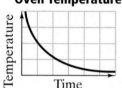

25. Suppose you borrow $500 from a bank that charges 14.5% compound interest. What do you owe after 4 years?

Solve each formula for *n*.

26. $3n - p = 6m$
27. $PV = nRT$
28. $s = (n - 2)180$
29. $(m + 1)n = b$

30. **Home Repairs** A plumber charges customers using the formula $C = 30t + 65$, where C is the amount he charges, and t is the number of hours he works. How many hours does he work when he charges $185?

31. **Science** Density is found using the formula $D = \frac{m}{V}$, where m is mass in grams (g), and V is volume in cubic centimeters (cm^3). What is the volume of a pearl with a density of 2.72 g/cm^3 and a mass of 1.768 g?

Reading Comprehension

Read each passage and answer the questions that follow.

Grade A To calculate grades for report cards, Ms. Sammler uses students' three test scores during the semester. She also gives credit for class participation. First, she finds the mean test score for each student, which she calls T. She then adds in the P factor—zero, three, or five points for class participation. She adds those items to get G, the grade.

1. Hari's test scores are 80, 85, and 90. He never contributes in class, so he gets zero for participation. What will his grade G be?
   - A 83
   - B 85
   - C 88
   - D 90

2. Ms. Sammler writes on the board and says, "Here is a mathematical equation that describes my system." What does she write?
   - F $G = \frac{1}{3}T + P$
   - H $3G = T + P$
   - G $G = T + P$
   - J $T = G + P$

3. Jennifer knows her test average is 88, so she is pleasantly surprised when she gets a 93 on her report card. What is her P factor?
   - A 0
   - B 3
   - C 5
   - D 6

4. Jaime gets five points for class participation and receives an 85 on his report card. Which set could NOT have been his test scores?
   - F 60, 80, 100
   - H 79, 80, 81
   - G 70, 70, 100
   - J 80, 81, 83

Archaeology Archaeologists find the age of materials like bone and wood using carbon-14 (C-14) dating. A tiny fraction (about one out of a trillion) of carbon atoms are radioactive C-14 that decays over time. Scientists measure the amount of C-14 left in an object to calculate its age. C-14 has a half-life of 5,700 years. This means that half of it remains after 5,700 years. In another 5,700 years, half of the remaining half will remain, and so on.

5. A 5,700-year-old bone has 10^{13} C-14 atoms. How much C-14 did it have originally?
   - A 10^{13} atoms
   - C 10^{14} atoms
   - B 2×10^{13} atoms
   - D 10^{26} atoms

6. A wood fragment is about 11,000 years old. About what part of its C-14 has decayed?
   - F 0.25
   - G 0.50
   - H 0.75
   - J 1.0

7. How old would an object be if only $\frac{1}{8}$ of its original carbon-14 atoms remained?
   - A $2 \times 5,700$ years
   - C $4 \times 5,700$ years
   - B $3 \times 5,700$ years
   - D $8 \times 5,700$ years

8. Radioactive potassium-40 (K-40) is found naturally in the human body. Its half-life is 1.3 billion years. After 1.3 billion years, how would the remaining percent of K-40 compare to the remaining percent of C-14?
   - F The percent of K-40 would be greater.
   - H The percent of C-14 would be greater.
   - G The same percent of each would remain.
   - J There would be more K-40 atoms than C-14 atoms.

Applying Graphs

Through the Ages Different animals have different life expectancies, which means they live different lengths of time. Reptiles, such as turtles, can live for more than a hundred years. Some insects, such as dragonflies, may live only a year or two.

You may know the saying that one dog year is like seven human years. That's because, on average, people live about seven times as long as dogs. But how do other animals compare? How old is a five-year-old cat or horse in human years? You can use graphs to make these comparisons.

The Long and the Short of It
Dragonflies can live as long as 6 or 7 years or as short as 6 or 7 months.

The front wings move independent of the back wings.

Ancient Insects
Archaeologists have found fossils of dragonflies over 200 million years old. Those dragonflies had wingspans up to 27 in. across. Today, the largest dragonflies have wingspans about 5 or 6 in. across.

Thorax

Head

Abdomen

Eyes

Six legs

Put It All Together

Data File Use the information on these two pages and on page 673 to make a graph comparing animal and human life expectancies.

1. **a.** Start your graph by labeling the *x*-axis "Animal Age" and labeling the *y*-axis "Human Age." Use a scale up to 40 on the *x*-axis and 100 on the *y*-axis.
    b. Graph the point (5, 35) to show that 5 dog years are equivalent to 35 human years. Draw a line through the origin and this point.
    c. Use the line you graphed to find the "human age" of an 8-year-old dog.
    d. Use the line you graphed to find your age in "dog years."

2. Use your graph from Question 1. Use 100 years as a human's maximum life span and choose at least three animals. Plot the points that compare each animal's maximum life span to a human's maximum life span. Use the points and the origin to draw lines for each animal.

3. Pick one of the animals from your graph. Compare the animal's life span to a human's life span. At what age would the animal be likely to start kindergarten? At what age would it graduate from high school? Mark those points on your graph.

4. Suppose you get a newborn kitten when you are 32 years old. How old will you be when you and the cat are the same age in human years?

5. **Reasoning** Many animals mature more quickly than people. They learn to walk a few hours after birth, and they are able to care for themselves in less than a year. Of the animals in your graph, which animal matures most rapidly compared to people? How can you tell by looking at the graph?

Go Online
PHSchool.com
For: Information about dragonflies
Web Code: are-0953

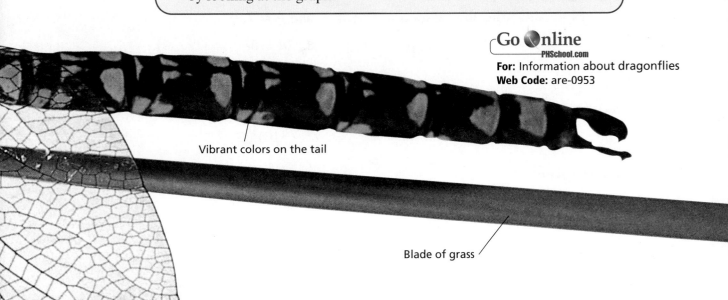

Vibrant colors on the tail

Blade of grass

CHAPTER 10

Graphing in the Coordinate Plane

What You've Learned

- In Chapter 4, you graphed inequalities on a number line.
- In Chapter 9, you represented patterns using tables, rules, and graphs.

 Check Your Readiness

GO for Help

For Exercises	See Lesson
1–4	1-6
5–8	4-1
9–12	2-1
13–18	7-2

Graphing Integers

(Algebra) **Graph each integer and its opposite.**

1. 7   **2.** -5

3. -3 **4.** 6

Evaluating Algebraic Expressions

Evaluate each expression using the values $a = 5$, $c = 2$, and $g = 7$.

5. $9g$ **6.** $-2a$ **7.** $8c - 10$ **8.** $2a - 5c$

Using Exponents

Simplify each expression.

9. 5^3 **10.** $(-2)^6$ **11.** 11^3 **12.** $(-10)^4$

Classifying Angles

Classify each angle as *acute*, *right*, *obtuse*, or *straight*.

13. $m\angle A = 43°$ **14.** $m\angle B = 90°$ **15.** $m\angle C = 148°$

16. $m\angle D = 180°$ **17.** $m\angle E = 167°$ **18.** $m\angle F = 79°$

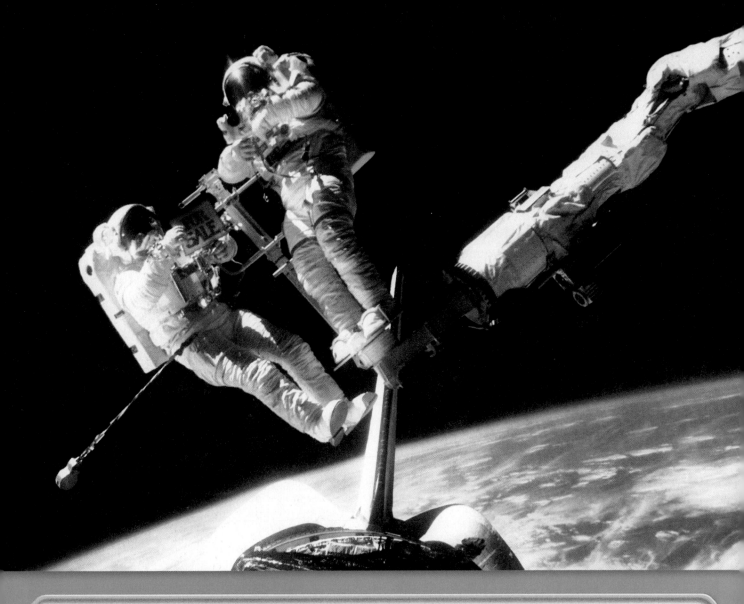

What You'll Learn Next

- In this chapter, you will graph and name points in the coordinate plane.

- You will graph linear and nonlinear relationships.

- You will graph transformations and identify symmetry.

Problem Solving Application On pages 528 and 529, you will work an extended activity on coordinates.

🔊 Key Vocabulary

- coordinate plane (p. 486)
- image (p. 510)
- linear equation (p. 492)
- line symmetry (p. 514)
- nonlinear equation (p. 504)
- ordered pair (p. 486)
- reflection (p. 515)
- rotation (p. 519)
- rotational symmetry (p. 519)
- transformation (p. 510)
- translation (p. 510)
- *x*-axis (p. 486)
- *x*-coordinate (p. 486)
- *y*-axis (p. 486)
- *y*-coordinate (p. 486)

10-1 Graphing Points in Four Quadrants

What You'll Learn

To name and graph points on a coordinate plane

 **New Vocabulary** coordinate plane, *x*-axis, *y*-axis, ordered pair, quadrants, origin, *x*-coordinate, *y*-coordinate

Why Learn This?

Maps use coordinates to help you locate streets and buildings. You can use coordinates to describe the location of a point on a grid.

A **coordinate plane** is a grid formed by a horizontal number line called the **x-axis** and a vertical number line called the **y-axis**.

An **ordered pair** (*x*, *y*) gives the location of a point.

O indicates the **origin**, where the axes intersect.

The axes divide the plane into four **quadrants**.

x-axis

y-axis

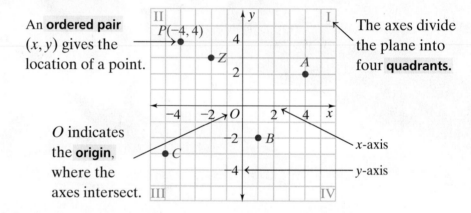

The first number of an ordered pair is the **x-coordinate**. It tells the number of horizontal units a point is from *O*. The second number is the **y-coordinate**. It tells the number of vertical units a point is from *O*.

EXAMPLE Naming Coordinates

1. **Multiple Choice** Name the coordinates of point *Z* in the graph above.

   Ⓐ (2, 3)   Ⓑ (−2, −3)   Ⓒ (−2, 3)   Ⓓ (2, −3)

Point *Z* is 2 units to the left of the *y*-axis, so the *x*-coordinate is −2. Point *Z* is 3 units up from the *x*-axis, so the *y*-coordinate is 3.

The coordinates of point *Z* are (−2, 3). The correct answer is C.

✓ **Quick Check**

1. Name the coordinates of *A, B,* and *C* in the graph above.

You can use an ordered pair to graph a point in a coordinate plane.

EXAMPLE Graphing Points

② Graph point $A(3, -5)$ in a coordinate plane. In which quadrant does the point lie?

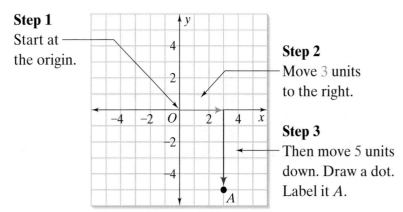

Step 1
Start at the origin.

Step 2
Move 3 units to the right.

Step 3
Then move 5 units down. Draw a dot. Label it A.

The point $A(3, -5)$ lies in quadrant IV.

✓ Quick Check

2. Graph point $R(-3, 5)$. In which quadrant does the point lie?

When you graph a polygon in a coordinate plane, first graph each vertex. Then draw line segments to connect adjacent vertices.

EXAMPLE Graphing Polygons

③ **Archaeology** Archaeologists record the location of objects they find by making a grid. Suppose you use graph paper to represent a rectangular dig that measures 9 ft by 6 ft. Draw a rectangle in a coordinate plane. Use $(0, 0)$ as one vertex and label all vertices.

Mark $(0, 0)$ as one vertex.

From the origin, count 9 units right and mark a vertex at $(9, 0)$.

From the origin, count 6 units up and mark a vertex at $(0, 6)$.

Mark the fourth vertex at $(9, 6)$.

Draw the sides of the rectangle.

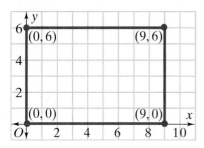

✓ Quick Check

3. In a coordinate plane, draw a different rectangle for the dig described above. Use $(0, 0)$ as one vertex and label all vertices.

Careers Archaeologists excavate artifacts to study how people lived in past cultures.

1. **Vocabulary** Name the coordinates of the origin.

Match each point with its coordinates.

2. *J*

3. *K*

4. *L*

5. *M*

A. $(3, 4)$

B. $(-3, 4)$

C. $(3, -4)$

D. $(-3, -4)$

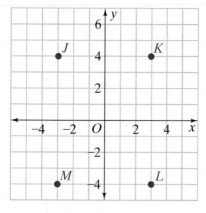

6. Which axis in a coordinate plane is vertical? Which axis is horizontal?

Homework Exercises

For more exercises, see Extra Skills and Word Problems.

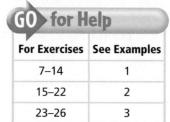

GO for Help

For Exercises	See Examples
7–14	1
15–22	2
23–26	3

Name the coordinates of each point.

7. *G*

8. *H*

9. *J*

10. *K*

11. *L*

12. *M*

13. *N*

14. *P*

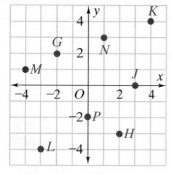

Graph each point on the same coordinate plane. Name the quadrant in which each point lies.

15. $Q(1, -4)$

16. $R(-5, 3)$

17. $S(-3, -2)$

18. $T(-6, 2)$

19. $U(5, -3)$

20. $V(2, 6)$

21. $W(6, 2)$

22. $Z(-4, -4)$

Graph each polygon. Use (0, 0) as one vertex. Label all vertices.

23. a square with side 3 units long

24. a square with side 6 units long

25. a rectangle with horizontal length 4 units and vertical length 2 units

26. a rectangle with horizontal length 2 units and vertical length 4 units

27. **Guided Problem Solving** Three vertices of a square are $(-2, -4)$, $(3, -4)$, and $(3, 1)$. What are the coordinates of the fourth vertex?
   - *Draw a Picture* by graphing the three vertices and drawing the two sides of the square.
   - Graph the fourth vertex of the square. What are its coordinates?

Without graphing, name the quadrant in which each point (x, y) lies.

28. $x < 0$ and $y < 0$ **29.** $x > 0$ and $y < 0$ **30.** $x < 0$ and $y > 0$

31. Geometry Graph a triangle with vertices $(2, 5), (8, 3),$ and $(2, 1)$. Classify the triangle by its angles and by its sides.

32. Science A bee's wings move at a rate of about 150 beats per second. The expression $150x$ gives the number of beats in x seconds. Graph the ordered pairs $(x, 150x)$ for $x = 1$, $x = 2$, and $x = 3$.

33. Reasoning List the coordinates of three points on the red line. If the x-coordinate of a point on the line is 37, what is the y-coordinate? Explain.

34. A scale drawing of a rectangular board shows three vertices at $(-3, -2), (-3, 2),$ and $(3, 2)$. Each unit represents 2 ft. Find the board's dimensions.

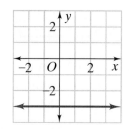

35. Writing in Math Explain how you can tell which quadrant an ordered pair is in by looking at the signs of its x- and y-coordinates.

36. Open-Ended Graph a parallelogram in a coordinate plane so that each vertex is in a different quadrant. Label all vertices.

37. Challenge A robot arm must move the black peg in the diagram at the right onto the white square. The peg must be moved around—not over—the red walls. List the coordinates of the vertices of a path the robot arm might follow to move the peg.

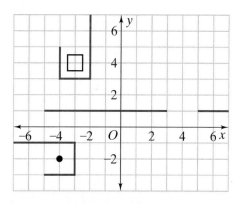

Test Prep and Mixed Review   **Practice**

Multiple Choice

38. Which point has the coordinates $(-3, 5)$ in the graph at the right?
   Ⓐ Point L Ⓒ Point N
   Ⓑ Point M Ⓓ Point P

39. Which three-dimensional figure has only squares as faces?
   Ⓕ Pyramid   Ⓗ Cube
   Ⓖ Cone   Ⓙ Cylinder

GO for Help

For Exercise	See Lesson
40	8-5

40. The radius of a circle is 11 cm long. Find the area of the circle to the nearest tenth.

Geometry in the Coordinate Plane

Graphing a figure in a coordinate plane can help you find the figure's perimeter or area.

EXAMPLES Finding Perimeter and Area

1 A map has a coordinate plane printed over it. Town Hall T is at the origin. Julio rides his bike from home H to school S. After school, Julio rides to the library L and then to his friend's house F. Finally, he rides back home. Each unit in the graph represents 1 kilometer. Use the graph to find the number of kilometers Julio rides.

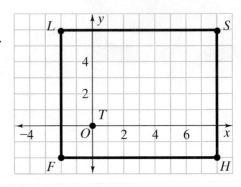

The perimeter of the rectangle represents the distance Julio rides. Since $8 + 10 + 8 + 10$ is 36, Julio rides 36 km.

2 Connect the points $L(-3, -2)$, $M(-1, 3)$, and $N(4, -2)$ to form $\triangle LMN$. Find the area of the triangle using the formula $A = \frac{1}{2}bh$.

The base of the triangle is 7 units. The distance from point M to the base is 5 units, so the height of the triangle is 5 units.

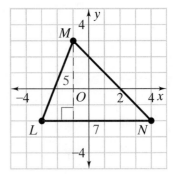

$$A = \frac{1}{2}bh$$

$$= \frac{1}{2} \cdot 7 \cdot 5 \quad \leftarrow \textbf{Substitute.}$$

$$= 17.5 \quad\quad \leftarrow \textbf{Simplify.}$$

● The area of the triangle is 17.5 units^2.

Exercises

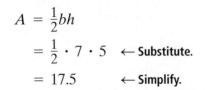

1. Yvonne walks from her house $(0, 0)$ to her aunt's house $(4, 0)$. She then walks to a park $(4, 2)$. From the park, she walks to the store $(0, 2)$ and then returns home. Graph and connect the points. If each unit in the graph represents 1 kilometer, how many kilometers does Yvonne walk in all?

2. Connect the points $A(4, -4)$, $B(4, 4)$, and $C(-2, 3)$ to form $\triangle ABC$. Find the area of the triangle.

3. Use graphing to find the area of a pentagon with vertices at $(-3, 4)$, $(-3, -9)$, $(6, -4)$, $(8, 0)$ and $(6, 9)$.

10-2 Graphing Linear Equations

What You'll Learn

To find solutions of linear equations and to graph linear equations

🔊 **New Vocabulary** graph of an equation, linear equation

Why Learn This?

Sometimes you can use an equation to describe a relationship between two quantities. Graphing the equation can make the relationship easier to see.

To make a swing, you need enough rope to reach the branch plus 5 feet to tie the rope. You can use $y = x + 5$ to describe the relationship between the number of feet x the tire hangs below the branch and the number of feet y of rope you need.

A solution of a linear equation is any ordered pair (x, y) that makes the equation true. To find a solution, choose a value of x and substitute it into the equation. Then find the corresponding value of y.

EXAMPLE Finding Solutions

1 Find three solutions of $y = x + 5$. Organize your solutions in a table.

x	x + 5	y	Solution (x, y)	Interpretation
6	6 + 5	11	(6, 11)	If the tire hangs 6 ft below the branch, you need 11 ft of rope.
7	7 + 5	12	(7, 12)	If the tire hangs 7 ft below the branch, you need 12 ft of rope.
10	10 + 5	15	(10, 15)	If the tire hangs 10 ft below the branch, you need 15 ft of rope.

✓ Quick Check

1. Find three solutions of each equation. Use $x = -2$, $x = 0$, and $x = 2$.

    a. $y = x + 8$ **b.** $y = x - 1$ **c.** $y = -2x$

Vocabulary Tip

Notice the word *line* in the word *linear*. A linear equation has a graph that is a line.

The **graph of an equation** is the graph of all the points with coordinates that are solutions of the equation. An equation is a **linear equation** when the graph of its solutions lies on a line.

EXAMPLE **Graphing to Test Solutions**

2 Use the solutions from Example 1 to graph the equation $y = x + 5$. Use the graph to test whether $(9, 13)$ is a solution to the equation.

Step 1 Plot the three ordered-pair solutions.

Step 2 Draw a line through the points.

Step 3 Test $(9, 13)$ by plotting the point in the same coordinate plane. Look to see if the point lies on the line of the graph of the equation.

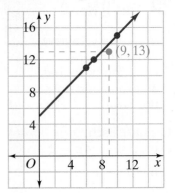

Since $(9, 13)$ is not on the line, $(9, 13)$ is not a solution of $y = x + 5$. For the tire to hang 9 ft below the branch, you need 14 ft of rope.

✓ Quick Check

2. Tell whether $(7, 12)$ is a solution of $y = 3x - 1$.

Linear equations may have negative values in their solutions. You can graph linear equations using positive values, negative values, and zero.

EXAMPLE **Graphing a Linear Equation**

3 Graph the linear equation $y = 2x + 1$.

Step 1 Make a table of solutions. Use zero as well as positive and negative values for x.

Step 2 Graph the points. Draw a line through the points.

x	y = 2x + 1	y	(x, y)
−1	y = 2(−1) + 1	−1	(−1, −1)
0	y = 2(0) + 1	1	(0, 1)
1	y = 2(1) + 1	3	(1, 3)
2	y = 2(2) + 1	5	(2, 5)

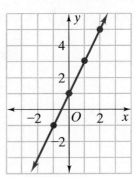

GO Online

Video Tutor Help

Visit: PHSchool.com
Web Code: are-0775

✓ Quick Check

3. Graph each linear equation.

    a. $y = x + 4$ **b.** $y = \frac{1}{2}x$ **c.** $y = -x$

1. **Vocabulary** What does the graph of the solution of a linear equation look like?

Use the equation $y = x - 7$ for Exercises 2–5.

x	x − 7	y	(x, y)
0	■	■	■
−3	■	■	■
10	■	■	■

2. Copy and complete the table at the left to find three solutions of the equation.

3. Graph the equation.

4. Is $(-1, -6)$ a solution of the equation?

5. How does a graph of the equation show that $(5, -2)$ is a solution?

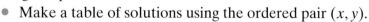

For more exercises, see Extra Skills and Word Problems.

GO for Help

For Exercises	See Examples
6–13	1
14–21	2
22–33	3

Find three solutions of each equation.

6. $y = x - 2$ 7. $y = x + 9$ 8. $y = x$ 9. $y = -x + 4$

10. $y = 5x$ 11. $y = -8x$ 12. $y = 3x + 1$ 13. $y = 4x - 5$

Tell whether each ordered pair is a solution of $y = x + 12$.

14. $(-12, 24)$ 15. $(12, 24)$ 16. $(0, -12)$ 17. $(-12, 0)$

18. $(7, 19)$ 19. $(24, 12)$ 20. $(6, 15)$ 21. $(9, 21)$

Graph each linear equation.

22. $y = x - 1$ 23. $y = x - 3$ 24. $y = 3x$ 25. $y = 5 + x$

26. $y = x + 4$ 27. $y = -5x$ 28. $y = 2 - x$ 29. $y = 4 - x$

30. $y = -x - 5$ 31. $y = \frac{1}{3}x$ 32. $y = 2x - 1$ 33. $y = \frac{1}{2}x + 4$

 34. **Guided Problem Solving** A shipping company charges $10 for delivery and $5 per pound shipped. The linear equation $y = 5x + 10$ models the cost of shipping an object that weighs x pounds. Graph the equation to find the cost to ship a vase that weighs 4 pounds.
   • Make a table of solutions using the ordered pair (x, y).
   • Graph the equation.
   • Which point on your graph shows the cost for a 4-lb vase?

35. **Pets** You are building a fence around a square pen for your pig. You want to use 46 ft of fencing, which accounts for a 2-ft opening. Graph the equation $P = 4s - 2$. Use your graph to find the length of each side of the pen.

On which of the following lines does each point lie? A point may lie on more than one line.

36. $(0, 0)$ **37.** $(3, 9)$ **38.** $(-2, -1)$

   I. $y = x + 6$ **II.** $y = x - 6$ **III.** $y = 2x + 3$

39. Error Analysis A student says that $(-1, -5)$ is a solution of $y = -3x - 2$. What error do you think the student made?

40. Honey bees produce about 50 lb of honey per hive each year. This situation can be represented by $y = 50x$, where x is the number of hives and y is the amount of honey in pounds. Make a table. Can 800 lb of honey be produced in one year with 16 hives?

41. Writing in Math Why is it a good idea to plot at least three points when you graph a linear equation?

42. Measurement Graph the equations $y = 12x$ and $y = \frac{1}{12}x$ on the same coordinate plane. Which of these equations models the conversion of x inches to y feet?

43. Challenge Tell whether the graph of $y = x - 5$ passes through the second quadrant. Explain how you know.

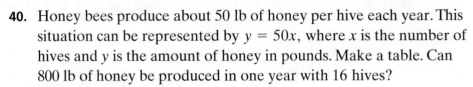

Multiple Choice

44. The data in the table at the left show the relationship between x, the diameter of a circle, and y, the radius of a circle. Which graph best represents the data?

Diameter, x (cm)	Radius, y (cm)
0	0
2	1
4	2
6	3

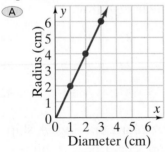

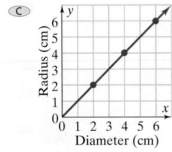

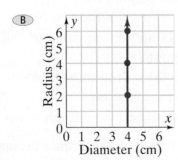

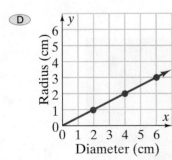

45. You have $480 in an account that pays 8% compound interest annually. What is your balance after 3 years?

Representing Data

A table is an organized way to represent data. Sometimes it is helpful to visualize the data by creating a graph.

EXAMPLE

The data in the table show the relationship between the diameter d and the circumference C of a circle.

Which graph best represents the data in the table at the right?

Diameter d (cm)	2	4	6	8
Circumference C (cm)	6.3	12.6	18.8	25.1

A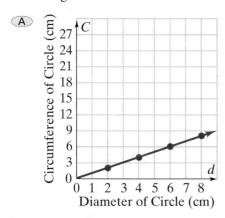

C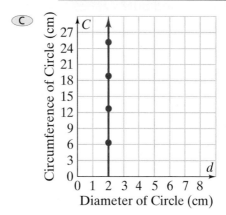

B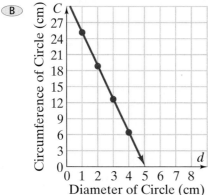

D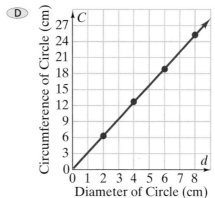

According to the data in the table and what you know to be true about circles, the circumference increases as the diameter increases.

Choice B shows the circumference *decreasing* as the diameter increases. Eliminate choice B.

Choice C shows a vertical line, which means the diameter is constant. A circle with one diameter cannot have several different circumferences. Eliminate choice C.

The first ordered pair is (2, 6.3). In the remaining graphs, this point appears only in choice D. The correct answer is choice D.

Practice Solving Problems

Jobs Mandy earns $6 per hour babysitting, plus $3 for transportation. How much will she earn for a 1-hour job and a 5-hour job this weekend?

What You Might Think

> What do I know?
> What am I trying to find out?

> How do I show the main idea?

> What does the graph look like?

> What is the answer?

What You Might Write

Mandy gets $3 to start and earns $6 per hour. I want to find out how much she will earn for a 1-hour job and for a 5-hour job.

I will graph $m = 6h + 3$ to show how much money m she earns after h hours of work.

Solve for $h = 1$ and $h = 5$.
If $h = 1$, then $m = 6(1) + 3$, or 9.
If $h = 5$, then $m = 6(5) + 3$, or 33.
Graph (1, 9) and (5, 33). I can connect the points with a solid line because Mandy can get paid for working part of an hour.

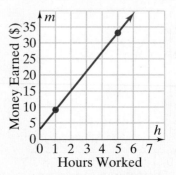

Mandy will earn $9 for the 1-hour job and $33 for the 5-hour job.

Think It Through

1. How does the equation $m = 6h + 3$ represent the amount of money m Mandy earns for h hours of work? Explain.

2. How much does Mandy earn for 2 hours, $3\frac{1}{2}$ hours, 4 hours, and $6\frac{1}{4}$ hours of work?

Exercises

Solve each problem. For Exercises 3 and 4, answer the questions first.

3. Fingernails grow an average of 1.5 in. per year. Suppose your nails are $\frac{1}{2}$ in. long on your tenth birthday. If you do not cut your nails, how long will they be on your sixteenth birthday?
   a. What do you know? What do you want to find out?
   b. What equation can you write to find the length of your fingernails at age 10 and age 16?
   c. How does graphing the equation give you additional information?

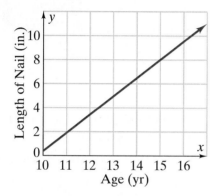

4. Romesh Sharma of India set a record for the longest fingernails. He had five fingernails on his left hand that had a total length of 33 ft. If his nails grew $\frac{1}{8}$ in. each month, about how long did it take to grow those nails? Assume that he started when he was born and never cut his fingernails.
   a. If the five nails were about the same length, about how long was each nail?
   b. How does the diagram below help you decide what to do?

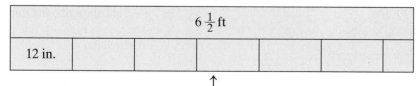

How many inches are in $6\frac{1}{2}$ feet?

5. In 1982, Larry Walters tied 42 helium balloons to an aluminum lawn chair. He floated above Los Angeles International Airport in his chair for 45 min. If Larry and all his equipment weighed 168 lb, how much did each balloon lift on average?

10-3 Finding the Slope of a Line

What You'll Learn

To find the slope of a line and use it to solve problems

◀)) **New Vocabulary** slope, rise, run

Why Learn This?

Elephants will not climb a ramp with more than a 33-degree slope. When ramps are constructed, they must meet safety standards that ensure they are not too steep. You can understand what factors affect steepness when you understand slope.

Slope is a ratio that describes the steepness of a line. Slope compares the vertical change in a line, called the **rise**, to the horizontal change, called the **run**. For any two points on a line, the ratio of rise to run is the same.

$$\text{slope} = \frac{\text{rise}}{\text{run}}$$

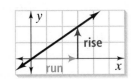

EXAMPLE Finding Slope

For: Slope Activity
Use: Interactive Textbook, 10-5

1. Find the slope of the line.

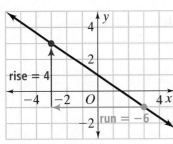

$$\text{slope} = \frac{\text{rise}}{\text{run}}$$

$$= \frac{4}{-6} \quad \leftarrow \text{ Substitute rise and run.}$$

$$= -\frac{2}{3} \quad \leftarrow \text{ Simplify.}$$

The slope of the line is $-\frac{2}{3}$.

✓ Quick Check

1. Find the slope of the line at the right.

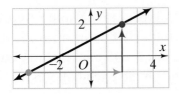

The slope of a line can be positive, negative, zero, or undefined. A line that goes upward from left to right has positive slope. A line that goes downward has negative slope. A horizontal line has a slope of 0. The slope of a vertical line is undefined because you cannot divide by 0.

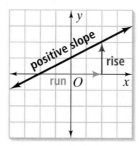
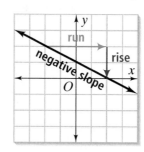
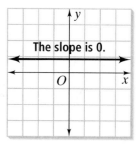

EXAMPLE   Application: Avalanches

2 Avalanches are likely to occur on trails where the absolute value of the slope is between 0.5 and 1. Find the slope of the trail and determine whether an avalanche is likely.

From point A to point B, the rise is 4 and the run is 7.

$$\text{slope} = \frac{\text{rise}}{\text{run}} = \frac{4}{7} \approx 0.57$$

The slope is about 0.57, so an avalanche is likely.

Vocabulary Tip

Snowboarders and skiers often use the word *slope* to refer to the side of a mountain.

✓ Quick Check

2. Slope is used to find the pitch, or steepness, of a roof. Roof A has a pitch of 3 to 12, which means it rises 3 in. for every 12 in. of run. What is the slope of Roof A?

You can use slope to graph a line if you know a point on the line.

EXAMPLE   Drawing Lines on a Graph

3 Draw a line through the origin with a slope of $-\frac{3}{2}$.

Step 1 Graph a point at $(0, 0)$.

Step 2 Move 3 units down and 2 units to the right. Graph a second point.

Step 3 Connect the points to draw a line.

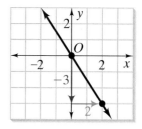

Test Prep Tip

You can also move 2 units to the left and 3 units up.

✓ Quick Check

3. Draw a line through $P(2, 1)$ with a slope of $\frac{4}{3}$.

1. **Vocabulary** The vertical change between two points on a line is called __?__, and the horizontal change is called __?__.

For Exercises 2–4, use the graph at the left.

2. Is the slope of the line positive or negative?

3. Use points A and D to find the slope of the line.

4. **Reasoning** Use points B and C to find the slope of the line. Does using different points affect the slope? Explain.

Homework Exercises

For more exercises, see Extra Skills and Word Problems.

GO for Help

For Exercises	See Examples
5–7	1
8–9	2
10–11	3

Find the slope of each line.

5.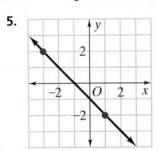

6.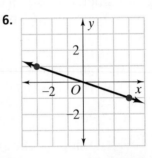

7.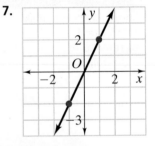

8.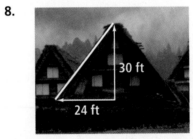

9.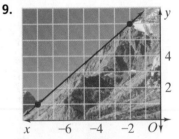

Draw a line with the given slope through the given point.

10. $P(0, 0)$, slope $= -3$

11. $R(6, 6)$, slope $= \dfrac{5}{2}$

GPS 12. **Guided Problem Solving** Some skiers prefer steep trails. Which trails would you recommend to those skiers? Explain.
- What is the slope of each trail?
- Which trails are the steepest?

Ski Trail	Total Rise	Total Run
Alpine	1,800 ft	7,200 ft
Diamond	1,840 ft	3,680 ft
Bear	1,900 ft	4,750 ft
Donner	750 ft	3,000 ft

13. **Reasoning** Draw a horizontal line through $(1, 3)$. Use two points on the line to explain why the slope of the line equals 0.

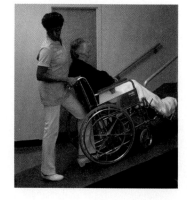

Graph the given points. Find the slope of the line through the points.

14. $(4, 8), (5, 10)$ **15.** $(4, -1), (-4, 1)$ **16.** $(2, 7), (3, -1)$

17. Roof A has a rise of 5 and a run of 3. Roof B has a rise of 3 and a run of 5. Which roof is steeper? Explain.

18. Ramps Guidelines for a wheelchair ramp allow a maximum of 1 in. of rise for every 12 in. of run. The ramp at the left runs 6 ft 8 in. and rises 2 ft 9 in. Does the ramp meet the guidelines? Explain.

19. Cars The graph shows the value of a car for the first seven years of ownership.
   a. What was the value of the car when it was new?
   b. What is the slope of the graph?
   c. What does the slope tell you about the relationship between the age of the car and its value?

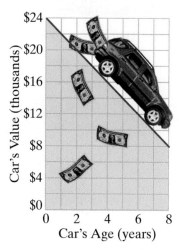

20. Error Analysis Your classmate graphs a line through $(4, 2)$ and $(5, -1)$ and finds that the slope equals 3. Explain why your classmate is incorrect.

21. Writing in Math Explain why it is more difficult to run up a hill with a slope of $\frac{1}{2}$ than a hill with a slope of $\frac{1}{6}$.

22. Challenge On the same coordinate plane, graph line r through points $(0, 4)$ and $(3, -3)$ and line s through points $(1, 7)$ and $(4, 0)$. Find the slopes of r and s. What are lines with equal slopes called?

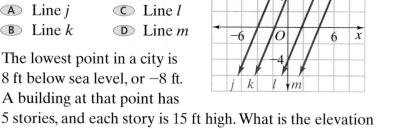
Test Prep and Mixed Review **Practice**

Multiple Choice

23. Which line in the graph at the right contains the ordered pair $(0, -4)$?
   Ⓐ Line j Ⓒ Line l
   Ⓑ Line k Ⓓ Line m

24. The lowest point in a city is 8 ft below sea level, or -8 ft. A building at that point has 5 stories, and each story is 15 ft high. What is the elevation of the top of the building?
   Ⓕ 12 ft   Ⓖ 20 ft   Ⓗ 67 ft   Ⓙ 75 ft

25. $\triangle ABC$ is an isosceles triangle. $\triangle XYZ$ has angle measures 45°, 70°, and 65°. Are the two triangles congruent? Explain.

GO for Help

For Exercise	See Lesson
25	7-5

Exploring Slope

You can use a graphing calculator to explore the relationship between an equation and the slope of its graph.

EXAMPLE

Use a graphing calculator to find the slope of $y = 2x + 1$.

Step 1 Use Y= to enter the equation.

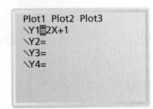

Step 2 Press ZOOM 0 ENTER for the integer mode.

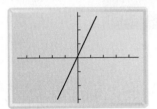

Step 3 Press TRACE. The x-coordinate is 0, and the y-coordinate is 1.

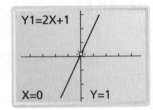

Step 4 Use ▶ to move the cursor to the right 1 unit.

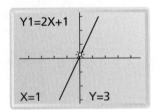

Step 5 Repeat step 4 and examine how the coordinates change. As the x-coordinate increases 1 unit, the y-coordinate increases 2 units. Another way to say this is that for every 1 unit of run, there are 2 units of rise.

$slope = \frac{rise}{run} = \frac{2}{1}$, or 2.

Exercises

Use a graphing calculator to find the slope of each equation.

1. $y = 2x - 3$
2. $y = x + 3$
3. $y = \frac{1}{3}x + 2$
4. $y = -3x$

5. Reasoning Look at each slope you found. How is the slope of a line represented in each equation?

Without graphing, find the slope of each line.

6. $y = 8x + 3$
7. $y = -x - 1$
8. $y = \frac{1}{2}x + 9$
9. $y = \frac{5}{2}x - 3$

Graph each point in the same coordinate plane. Identify the quadrant in which the point lies.

1. $K(-2, -5)$ **2.** $Q(-3, 4)$ **3.** $D(2, 1)$

Graph each linear equation.

4. $y = x + 7$ **5.** $y = -3x + 2$ **6.** $y = x - 3$

7. A dragonfly can reach a speed of 50 km/h. The dragonfly's speed can be represented using $d = 50t$, where d represents the distance in kilometers and t represents the time in hours. Graph this equation.

8. Find the slope of the line on the coordinate plane at the right.

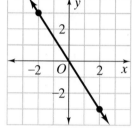

Draw a line with the given slope through the given point.

9. $P(-2, 0)$, slope $= 3$ **10.** $A(0, -3)$, slope $= \frac{1}{2}$

MATH GAMES

Hide and Seek

What You'll Need

- 2 players, two sheets of graph paper

How To Play

- Using graph paper, draw the first quadrant of the coordinate plane. Label the x- and y-axes from 0 to 10.
- Draw a triangle or rectangle on your graph. The ordered pairs for each vertex must be whole numbers.
- You and your opponent take turns trying to locate each vertex of the other's shape by calling out ordered pairs that are whole numbers.
- If your opponent's guess falls inside your figure, you say "inside." If it falls outside your figure, you say "outside." If it is on the border, you say "border." If the guess falls on a vertex, you must say "bingo."
- The first player to name all the vertices of the opponent's figure wins.

10-4 Graphing Nonlinear Relationships

What You'll Learn

To graph nonlinear relationships

◀)) **New Vocabulary** nonlinear equation

Why Learn This?

When you kick a ball in the air, the path the ball follows is a curve called a parabola. A parabola is a sign of a relationship that is not linear.

A **nonlinear equation** is an equation whose graph is not a line.

EXAMPLE Graphing a Nonlinear Equation

1 Graph $y = -x^2$ using integer values of x from -3 to 3.

Step 1 Make a table of solutions.

x	$-x^2$	y	(x, y)
-3	$-(-3)^2$	-9	$(-3, -9)$
-2	$-(-2)^2$	-4	$(-2, -4)$
-1	$-(-1)^2$	-1	$(-1, -1)$
0	$-(0)^2$	0	$(0, 0)$
1	$-(1)^2$	-1	$(1, -1)$
2	$-(2)^2$	-4	$(2, -4)$
3	$-(3)^2$	-9	$(3, -9)$

Step 2 Use each solution (x, y) to graph a point. Draw a curve through the points.

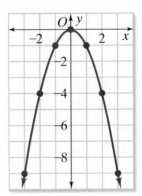

Quick Check

1. Graph $y = 2x^2$ using integer values of x from -3 to 3.

EXAMPLE **Graphing Absolute Value Equations**

② Graph $y = |x|$ using integer values of x from -2 to 2.

x	|x|	y	(x, y)
-2	$|-2|$	2	$(-2, 2)$
-1	$|-1|$	1	$(-1, 1)$
0	$|0|$	0	$(0, 0)$
1	$|1|$	1	$(1, 1)$
2	$|2|$	2	$(2, 2)$

← Make a table of values.

Graph the ordered pairs. Then connect the points. →

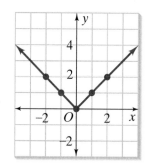

✓ Quick Check

● **2.** Graph $y = 2|x|$ using integer values of x from -2 to 2.

More Than One Way

The equation $y = x^3$ shows the nonlinear relationship between edge length x and volume y of a cube. Determine whether $(3, 12)$ is a solution of $y = x^3$.

Kayla's Method

I will use my graphing calculator. I press ☐Y= and enter $y = x^3$. Then I select the integer mode under ☐ZOOM. I can use the ☐TRACE feature to get the screen at the right.

At $x = 3$, $y = 27$, so $(3, 12)$ is not a solution.

Y1 = X³

X = 3   Y = 27

Carlos's Method

I will substitute 3 for x and 12 for y in the equation.

$y = x^3$

$12 \stackrel{?}{=} 3^3$ ← Substitute.

$12 \stackrel{?}{=} 27$ ← Simplify.

$12 \neq 27$

The equation is not true, so $(3, 12)$ is not a solution.

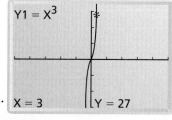

Choose a Method

Determine whether $(-3, 10)$ is a solution of $y = x^2 + 2$. Describe your method and explain why you chose it.

1. **Vocabulary** How can you tell whether an equation is linear or nonlinear?

Graph each equation using integer values of x from -3 to 3.

2. $y = x^2$ 3. $y = |x|$ 4. $y = -x^3$

5. **Number Sense** Why does the graph of the equation $y = x^2$ not fall in Quadrant III or Quadrant IV?

6. Describe the shape of the graph of the absolute value equation $y = |x|$.

7. **Mental Math** Is $P(1, -3)$ a solution of the equation $y = -x^3$?

Homework Exercises

For more exercises, see Extra Skills and Word Problems.

GO for Help

For Exercises	See Examples
8–16	1
17–22	2

Graph each equation using integer values of x from -3 to 3.

8. $y = 4x^2$ 9. $y = -3x^2$ 10. $y = \frac{1}{2}x^2$

11. $y = x^2 - 2$ 12. $y = x^2 + 2$ 13. $y = -x^2 + 3$

14. $y = -x^2 - 4$ 15. $y = (x + 1)^2$ 16. $y = (x - 1)^2$

Graph each equation using integer values of x from -3 to 3.

17. $y = 2|x|$ 18. $y = \frac{1}{3}|x|$ 19. $y = -|x|$

20. $y = -|x| + 2$ 21. $y = |x - 1|$ 22. $y = |x + 1|$

GPS 23. **Guided Problem Solving** According to legend, Galileo dropped two different objects from the Tower of Pisa to prove that they would fall at the same rate. The equation $d = 16t^2$ can be used to find the distance d, in feet, that the objects fall in t seconds. Graph the equation showing how far the objects fall between 0 and 5 seconds.
- Make a table of solutions. What values of t will you use?
- Graph the points. What is the greatest value of d in your graph?

24. Graph the equation $A = \pi r^2$ to show the relationship between radius r and area A of a circle. Use 3.14 as an approximation for π.

25. **Writing in Math** Explain why the graph of $y = -|x|$ has no points in Quadrant I or Quadrant II.

26. Use integer values of -3 to 3 to graph $y = 3|x| + 5$.

Match each graph with an equation.

27.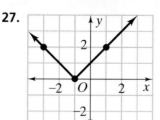

28.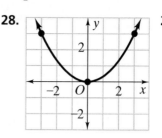

29.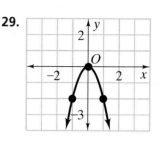

A. $y = |x + 1|$ **B.** $y = \frac{1}{3}x^2$ **C.** $y = \frac{1}{2}x^2$

D. $y = |x| - 1$ **E.** $y = 2x^2$ **F.** $y = -2x^2$

30. **Skydiving** Suppose a skydiver leaps from a plane at an altitude of 12,000 ft. The equation $h = -16t^2 + 12{,}000$ models the skydiver's height above the ground, in feet, at t seconds.
   a. Make a table to find the height at 0, 5, 10, and 20 seconds.
   b. Graph the equation. Use the graph to find the height at 12 s.

31. **Choose a Method** The equation $A = s^2$ shows the nonlinear relationship between side length s and area A of a square. Determine whether $(6.5, 42.25)$ is a solution of $A = s^2$.

32. **Challenge** The equation $S = 4\pi r^2$ gives the surface area S of a sphere with radius r. The equation $V = \frac{4}{3}\pi r^3$ gives the volume V of a sphere with radius r. For each equation, make a table of values using integer values of r from 0 to 5. Use 3 as an approximation for π. For what value of r will the graphs of the equations intersect?

Test Prep and Mixed Review   **Practice**

Multiple Choice

33. Which of the following relationships is represented in the graph?
   Ⓐ The relationship between the edge length and the volume of a cube
   Ⓑ The relationship between the side length and the surface area of a cube
   Ⓒ The relationship between the side length and the area of a square
   Ⓓ The relationship between the radius and the area of a circle

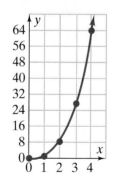

34. On Monday, $\frac{4}{7}$ of the students at school bought a hot lunch. About what percent of the students did NOT buy a hot lunch?
   Ⓕ 37%   Ⓖ 43%   Ⓗ 57%   Ⓙ 62%

GO for Help

For Exercise	See Lesson
35	8-10

35. Find the height of a rectangular prism with a volume of 357 cm³, a length of 6 cm, and a width of 8.5 cm.

Vocabulary Builder

High-Use Academic Words

High-use academic words are words that you will see often in textbooks and on tests. These words are not math vocabulary terms, but knowing them will help you to succeed in mathematics.

Direction Words

Some words tell what to do in a problem. I need to understand what these words are asking so that I give the correct answer.

Word	Meaning
Represent	To replace with other words or symbols
Predict	To say in advance the outcomes or effects
Compare	To say how two things are similar or different

Exercises

1. Draw a picture to represent the weather outside today.

2. Predict the weather tomorrow.

3. Compare the weather today with the weather six months ago.

4. A puppy weighed about 24 lb. She then gained about 12 lb per month, for x months. Which equation represents her growth?

    Ⓐ $y = 24x + 12$ Ⓑ $y = 12x + 24$ Ⓒ $y = 24x - 12$ Ⓓ $y = 12x - 24$

5. Use the graph at the right. Predict the value of y when x is 10.

6. Compare the slope of the line that goes through $(0, 0)$ and $(5, 2)$ with the slope of the line that goes through $(1, 1)$ and $(2, 5)$. Which slope is greater?

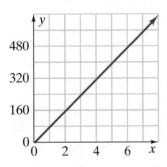

7. **Word Knowledge** Think about the word *conclude*.
    a. Choose the letter for how well you know the word.
        A. I know its meaning.
        B. I've seen it, but I don't know its meaning.
        C. I don't know it.
    b. **Research** Look up and write the definition of *conclude*.
    c. Use the word *conclude* in a sentence involving mathematics.

Slides, Flips, and Turns

To change the position of a geometric figure, you can use slides, flips, and turns.

A *slide* moves a figure so that every point moves the same direction and the same distance.

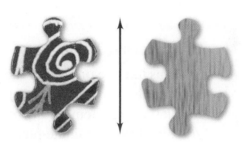

A *flip* reflects a figure over a line.

A *turn* rotates a figure around a point.

Exercises

Describe each transformation as a *slide, flip,* or *turn.*

1.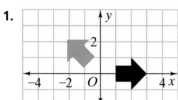

2.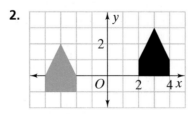

3.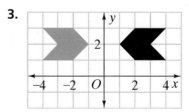

4. **Writing in Math** Describe how two flips can have the same effect as one slide. Include a drawing to illustrate your example.

5. **Open-Ended** Give an example that involves a slide, a flip, or a turn.

10-5 Translations

Check Skills You'll Need

1. **Vocabulary Review** Name the *x-coordinate* and the *y-coordinate* of point *A*(2, −5).

Graph each point on the same coordinate plane.

2. *E*(3, 1)

3. *R*(1, 0)

4. *G*(−3, −1)

5. *S*(2, −2)

for Help
Lesson 10-1

What You'll Learn

To graph and write rules for translations

🔊 **New Vocabulary** transformation, translation, image, prime notation

Why Learn This?

Patterns like the one at the right use translations. You can describe translations mathematically by graphing in a coordinate plane.

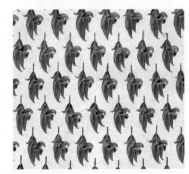

A **transformation** is a change in the position, shape, or size of a figure. Three types of transformations that change only the position are slides, flips, and turns. A slide is also known as a translation. A **translation** is a transformation that moves each point of a figure the same distance and in the same direction.

The result of a transformation is the **image** of the original. **Prime notation** is the way to name an image point. *A′* is read as "*A* prime."

EXAMPLE Translating a Point

1 **Multiple Choice** Translate point *F*(4, 1) left 3 units and up 2 units. What are the coordinates of the image *F″*?

ⓐ (1, −1)   ⓑ (1, 3)   ⓒ (7, −1)   ⓓ (7, 3)

Locate point *F* at (4, 1).

From point *F*, move 3 units left and 2 units up. Graph the image point *F′*.

The coordinates of *F′* are (1, 3). The answer is B.

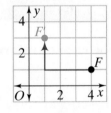

Test Prep Tip

Graphing helps you visualize a translation.

✓ Quick Check

1. Translate point *G*(−4, 1) right 1 unit and down 4 units. What are the coordinates of the image *G′*?

To show a translation, you can use arrow notation. For the translation of *F* to *F′* in Example 1, you write *F*(4, 1) → *F′*(1, 3).

Vocabulary Tip

A vertex is the point of intersection of two sides of a figure.

To translate a geometric figure, first translate each vertex of the figure. Then connect the image points. When a geometric figure is translated, the image is congruent to the original figure.

EXAMPLE Translating a Figure

2 The vertices of $\triangle ABC$ are $A(-4, 3)$, $B(-1, 4)$, and $C(-3, 1)$. Translate $\triangle ABC$ right 2 units and down 4 units. Use arrow notation to describe the translation.

Graph and label vertices A, B, and C. Draw $\triangle ABC$.

From each vertex, move right 2 units and down 4 units, and then draw an image point.

Label A', B', and C'. Draw $\triangle A'B'C'$.

Use arrow notation:
$A(-4, 3)$, $B(-1, 4)$, $C(-3, 1) \rightarrow A'(-2, -1)$, $B'(1, 0)$, $C'(-1, -3)$

✓ Quick Check

2. Graph $\triangle ABC$ from Example 2. Translate it left 3 units and up 1 unit. Use arrow notation to describe the translation.

You can also use arrow notation to write a rule for a translation.

EXAMPLE Writing a Rule for a Translation

3 **Animation** Computer animators use translations to move objects to new positions on the computer screen. Write a rule for the translation of spaceship A that a computer could apply to the other spaceships.

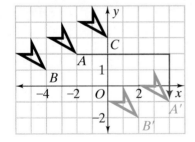

The horizontal change from A to A' is 6 units right, so $x \rightarrow x + 6$.

The vertical change from A to A' is 3 units down, so $y \rightarrow y - 3$.

The rule for the translation is $(x, y) \rightarrow (x + 6, y - 3)$.

Check Apply the rule to point B.
$(x, y) \rightarrow (x + 6, y - 3)$

$B(-4, 1) \rightarrow B'(-4 + 6, 1 - 3) = B'(2, -2)$ ✔ The answer checks.

✓ Quick Check

3. Write a rule for the translation of spaceship A to $(4, 3)$.

1. **Vocabulary** A translation is a type of __?__.

2. **Mental Math** Translate the origin $(0, 0)$ left 3 units and up 2 units. What are the coordinates of the image?

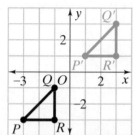

For Exercises 3–4, use the graph at the left.

3. Use arrow notation to show the translation.

$P(\blacksquare, \blacksquare), Q(\blacksquare, \blacksquare), R(\blacksquare, \blacksquare) \rightarrow P'(\blacksquare, \blacksquare), Q'(\blacksquare, \blacksquare), R'(\blacksquare, \blacksquare)$

4. Use words to describe the translation. Each point moves __?__ 4 units and __?__ 4 units.

Homework Exercises

For more exercises, see Extra Skills and Word Problems.

GO for Help

For Exercises	See Examples
5–9	1
10–14	2
15–16	3

Translate each point left 2 units and down 5 units. Write the coordinates of the image point.

5. $(3, 3)$ 6. $(0, 0)$ 7. $(-3, 2)$ 8. $(-6, -1)$ 9. $(6, -1)$

Graph each translation of $\triangle ABC$. Use arrow notation to show the translation.

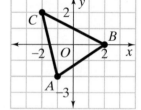

10. left 4 units

11. up 2 units

12. right 6 units, up 1 unit

13. down 2 units

14. left 3 units, up 3 units

Write a rule for the translation shown in each graph.

15.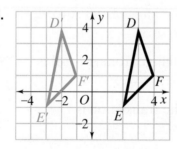

16.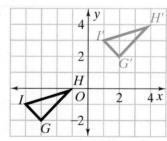

17. **Guided Problem Solving** Refer to the graph at the right. A graphics animator wants a plane to land on the runway and then move forward. Write two translations to complete the tasks.
   - What are the plane's coordinates?
   - What are the runway's coordinates?
   - What translation will move the plane horizontally?

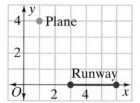

Graph each point and its image. Use words to describe the translation.

18. $M(3, 5) \rightarrow M'(6, 4)$

19. $G(-1, 6) \rightarrow G'(3, 7)$

20. $H(-2, -5) \rightarrow H'(-1, -3)$

21. $J(4, 0) \rightarrow J'(3, 4)$

22. **Aviation** Three airplanes are flying in a triangular formation. After 1 min, airplane P moves to P'. Give the new coordinates of each airplane and write a rule to describe the direction that the airplanes move.

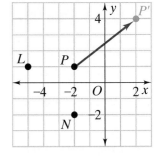

Write a rule for the translation described.

23. right 3 units and down 1 unit

24. right 4 units and up 1 unit

25. left 1 unit and up 4 units

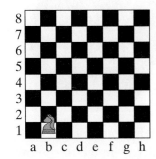

26. **Writing in Math** Why is it helpful to describe a translation by stating the horizontal change first?

27. **Challenge** Translations are used to move pieces on a chess board. A knight moves in an L shape: two vertical spaces and one horizontal space, or two horizontal spaces and one vertical space. What series of translations will move the knight from b1 to h7?

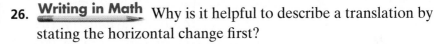
Test Prep and Mixed Review
Practice

Multiple Choice

28. If the quadrilateral shown at the right is translated 3 units to the left and 4 units down, what will be the new coordinates of point A?

    Ⓐ $(-2, 0)$ Ⓒ $(-8, 0)$

    Ⓑ $(-5, 4)$ Ⓓ $(-8, 8)$

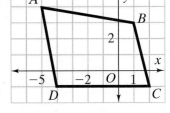

29. A container of juice holds 64 ounces. Which equation shows the remaining amount of juice j after you drink d ounces?

    Ⓕ $\dfrac{64}{d} = j$ Ⓖ $64 - d = j$ Ⓗ $64 + d = j$ Ⓙ $64d = j$

30. Jaleel spent $39.95 on a pair of shoes. The sales tax was 8.5%. About how much did Jaleel pay for the shoes, including tax?

    Ⓐ Less than $42   Ⓒ Between $45 and $48

    Ⓑ Between $42 and $45   Ⓓ More than $48

(Algebra) **Find three solutions of each equation.**

31. $y = 4x - 2$ **32.** $y = -3x - 6$ **33.** $y = 5x + 4$

GO for Help

For Exercises	See Lesson
31–33	10-2

Line Symmetry and Reflections

Check Skills You'll Need

1. **Vocabulary Review** When you translate a point, what do you call the new point?

Translate point $P(1, 3)$ as described. Write the coordinates of P'.

2. 4 units left

3. 2 units up

4. 4 units left and 2 units up

 for Help

Lesson 10-5

What You'll Learn

To identify lines of symmetry and to graph reflections

🔊 **New Vocabulary** line symmetry, line of symmetry, reflection, line of reflection

Why Learn This?

Symmetry is often seen in nature. A snowflake forms when water vapor freezes. Most snowflakes have line symmetry and rotational symmetry. The red line drawn on the snowflake divides it in half, and the two halves are mirror images of each other.

A figure has **line symmetry** if a line, called a **line of symmetry,** can be drawn through the figure so that one side is a mirror image of the other. If you fold along the red line of symmetry drawn on the snowflake, the right side of the snowflake fits exactly onto the left side.

EXAMPLE Identifying Lines of Symmetry

1. **Gridded Response** How many lines of symmetry does the flower have?

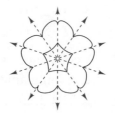

The flower has 5 lines of symmetry, so grid the answer 5 as shown.

✓ Quick Check

1. **Art** Sketch the mask and draw the line(s) of symmetry. Does the mask have line symmetry?

514 Chapter 10 Graphing in the Coordinate Plane

A **reflection** is a transformation that flips a figure over a line called a **line of reflection**.

EXAMPLE **Reflecting a Point**

2 Graph the point $A(3, -2)$ and its reflection over the indicated axis. Write the coordinates of the image.

a. y-axis

b. x-axis

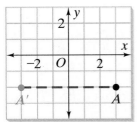

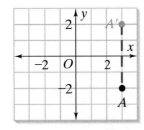

Test Prep Tip

When a point is reflected over the x-axis, the y-coordinate changes. When a point is reflected over the y-axis, the x-coordinate changes.

A is 3 units to the right of the y-axis, so A' is 3 units to the left of the y-axis.

A' has coordinates $(-3, -2)$.

A is 2 units below the x-axis, so A' is 2 units above the x-axis.

A' has coordinates $(3, 2)$.

✓ Quick Check

2. Graph the point $P(-4, 1)$ and its reflection over the indicated axis. Write the coordinates of the image.
   a. y-axis
   b. x-axis

When a figure is reflected, the image is congruent to the original figure.

EXAMPLE **Reflecting a Figure**

3 Draw the image of $\triangle ABC$ reflected over the y-axis. Use arrow notation to describe the original triangle and its image.

A is 1 unit to the left of the y-axis, so A' is 1 unit to the right of the y-axis.

B is 4 units to the left of the y-axis, so B' is 4 units to the right of the y-axis.

C is 2 units to the left of the y-axis, so C' is 2 units to the right of the y-axis.

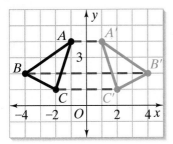

Draw $\triangle A'B'C'$ and use arrow notation:
$A(-1, 4)$, $B(-4, 2)$, $C(-2, 1) \rightarrow A'(1, 4)$, $B'(4, 2)$, $C'(2, 1)$

✓ Quick Check

3. Graph $\triangle ABC$ and its reflection over the x-axis. Use arrow notation to describe the original triangle and its image.

1. **Vocabulary** How is a line of reflection like a line of symmetry?

2. How many lines of symmetry does an equilateral triangle have?

Use the graph at the right.

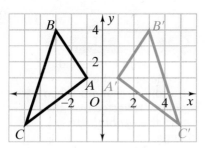

3. Use arrow notation to show the reflection.

   $A(\blacksquare, \blacksquare), B(\blacksquare, \blacksquare), C(\blacksquare, \blacksquare) \rightarrow$
   $A'(\blacksquare, \blacksquare), B'(\blacksquare, \blacksquare), C'(\blacksquare, \blacksquare)$

4. $\triangle ABC$ is reflected over the ___?___ -axis.

5. Compare the coordinate pair of each vertex of $\triangle ABC$ and its image.

Homework Exercises

For more exercises, see Extra Skills and Word Problems.

GO for Help

For Exercises	See Examples
6–9	1
10–15	2
16–18	3

Trace each figure and draw the line(s) of symmetry. If there are no lines of symmetry, write *none*.

6.
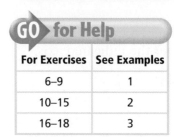

7.

8.

9.

Graph each point and its reflection over the indicated axis. Write the coordinates of the image.

10. $D(4, 2)$, x-axis   11. $F(-1, 5)$, y-axis   12. $G(-3, -2)$, y-axis

13. $H(2, -6)$, x-axis   14. $J(0, 3)$, x-axis   15. $K(-4, 0)$, y-axis

The vertices of a triangle are given. Graph the triangle, its reflection over the x-axis, and its reflection over the y-axis.

16. $P(1, 6), Q(6, 2), R(2, 0)$ 17. $S(-5, 1), T(-3, 5), V(-3, 1)$

18. The vertices of rectangle $ABCD$ are $A(-3, 3)$, $B(-1, 3)$, $C(-1, -1)$, and $D(-3, -1)$. Use arrow notation to describe the original rectangle and its reflection over the y-axis.

19. **Guided Problem Solving** A figure is a parallelogram but not a rectangle. It has two lines of symmetry. What type of figure is it?
   - *Act It Out* by drawing and cutting out several parallelograms.
   - Check for symmetry by folding.

Mental Math Without graphing, name the coordinates of the point's image after it is reflected over the *x*-axis and over the *y*-axis.

20. $(6, -1)$ **21.** $(-3, -4)$ **22.** $(-5, 8)$ **23.** $(7, 2)$

24. Geometry How many lines of symmetry does an isosceles right triangle have?

25. <u>Writing in Math</u> $\triangle WXY$ has vertices $W(-4, -2)$, $X(4, 2)$, and $Y(1, -4)$. Its image $\triangle W'X'Y'$ has vertices $W'(-4, 2)$, $X'(4, -2)$, and $Y'(1, 4)$. Over which axis is $\triangle WXY$ reflected? Explain.

26. Natural Science Give an example (other than a butterfly) of line symmetry seen in a plant or animal. Describe the line symmetry.

Use words and arrow notation to describe the transformation.

27.
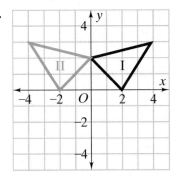

28.
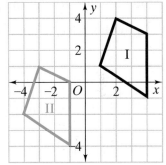

29. Challenge $L(0, 0)$, $M(0, 5)$, and $N(4, 0)$ are vertices of $\triangle LMN$. Graph $\triangle LMN$ in a coordinate plane. Reflect $\triangle LMN$ over the *x*-axis to form a larger triangle. Reflect the larger triangle over the *y*-axis to form a quadrilateral. What type of quadrilateral is formed?

Test Prep and Mixed Review   **Practice**

Gridded Response

30. $\triangle BCD$ has vertices $B(4, 3)$, $C(6, 3)$, and $D(1, 4)$. What is the *x*-coordinate of B' after $\triangle BCD$ is reflected over the *x*-axis?

31. A farmer has eight cows. Two are 3 years old, two are 5 years old, one is 6 years old, one is 7 years old, and one is 9 years old. The mean age of the farmer's eight cows is 5 years. What is the age in years of the remaining cow?

32. If $\angle B$ and $\angle C$ are complementary, and the measure of $\angle B$ is 27°, what is the measure of $\angle C$ in degrees?

Algebra Find the first four terms in each sequence.

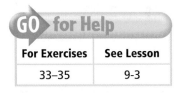

For Exercises	See Lesson
33–35	9-3

33. $3n + 2$ **34.** $-n + 4$ **35.** $-2n - 1$

Exploring Tessellations

A *tessellation* is a repeating pattern of figures that has no gaps or overlaps. Tessellations are made using transformations. An example of a tessellation is shown at the right.

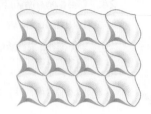

Use a square piece of cardboard.

1. Draw a curve from one vertex of the square to a neighboring vertex, as shown at the right.

2. Cut along the curve you drew. Translate the cutout piece to the opposite side of the square, and tape it down.

3. Draw the same curve on the bottom and repeat the process.

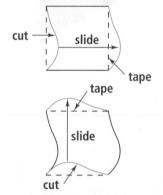

4. Trace around your figure on a piece of paper. Carefully translate the figure to the right so that the edges touch.

5. After you have covered a row, translate your figure downward to start a new row. Continue tracing until you have covered the paper.

6. **Reasoning** Can you make a tessellation with your figure using reflections? Explain.

✓ Checkpoint Quiz 2

Lessons 10-4 through 10-6

Graph each equation.

1. $y = 3x^2$
2. $y = |x| - 2$
3. $y = 2x^2 + 3$
4. $y = x - 1$

5. Is $(3, -5)$ a solution of $y = x^2 - 4$? Explain.

Translate each point right 3 units and up 7 units. Write the new coordinates.

6. $(-6, 2)$
7. $(9, -1)$
8. $(0, -7)$
9. $(-2, -3)$

10. Which of the following digits have lines of symmetry: 2, 3, 6, 8? Draw the lines of symmetry.

Rotational Symmetry and Rotations

What You'll Learn

To identify rotational symmetry and to rotate a figure about a point

🔊 **New Vocabulary** rotation, center of rotation, rotational symmetry, angle of rotation

Why Learn This?

Some objects rotate, which means to move in a circular manner. When you ride a unicycle, the wheel rotates, and you move!

A **rotation** is a transformation that turns a figure about a fixed point called the **center of rotation.** You describe a rotation by its angle measure and its direction.

The direction of every rotation in this book is counterclockwise unless noted as clockwise. If a figure can be rotated 180° or less and match the original figure, it has **rotational symmetry.**

EXAMPLE **Identifying Rotational Symmetry**

① **Windmills** Do the sails of the windmill have rotational symmetry? Use points O, A, A', A'', and A''' to explain.

Yes, the sails have rotational symmetry. The center of rotation is O.

If A is rotated 90°, the image is A'.
If A is rotated 180°, the image is A''.
If A is rotated 270°, the image is A'''.
If A is rotated 360°, it returns to its original position.

✓ Quick Check

1. Does the figure have rotational symmetry? Explain.

a.   b.   c.

The number of degrees a figure rotates is the **angle of rotation**. When a figure has rotational symmetry, the angle of rotation is the angle measure the figure must rotate to match the original figure.

EXAMPLE Finding an Angle of Rotation

2️⃣ The wheel below has rotational symmetry. Find the angle of rotation.

The wheel matches itself in 5 positions. The angle of rotation is 360° ÷ 5, or 72°.

✓ Quick Check

2. Find the angle of rotation of the flower at the left.

You can rotate a figure in a coordinate plane. Use the center of rotation and an angle.

EXAMPLE Rotating a Figure

3️⃣ Graph rectangle $ABCD$ with vertices $A(0, 0)$, $B(0, 2)$, $C(4, 2)$, and $D(4, 0)$. Rotate the rectangle as described. Write the coordinates of the vertices of the image.

a. 180° about point A

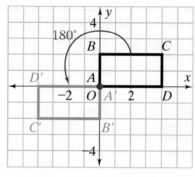

$A'(0, 0)$, $B'(0, -2)$, $C'(-4, -2)$, and $D'(-4, 0)$

b. 90° about its center, $(2, 1)$.

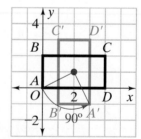

$A'(3, -1)$, $B'(1, -1)$, $C'(1, 3)$, and $D'(3, 3)$

🔴nline
active math

For: Transformations Activity
Use: Interactive Textbook, 10-7

✓ Quick Check

3. Graph $\triangle TRG$ with vertices $T(0, 0)$, $R(3, 3)$, and $G(5, 1)$. Rotate $\triangle TRG$ 180° about T. Write the coordinates of T', R', and G'.

1. **Vocabulary** Name two types of symmetry.

2. Name three types of transformations.

3. Does the figure at the right have rotational symmetry? If so, find the angle of rotation.

Estimation Estimate the angle measure of the rotation of △*RSO*.

4.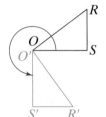

5.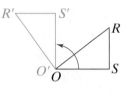

6.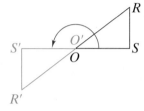

For more exercises, see **Extra Skills and Word Problems.**

GO for Help

For Exercises	See Examples
7–9	1
10–12	2
13–16	3

Does the figure have rotational symmetry? Explain.

7.

8.

9.

Each figure has rotational symmetry. Find the angle of rotation.

10.

11.

12.

Graph rectangle *PQRS* with vertices *P*(0, 0), *Q*(2, 0), *R*(2, 6), and *S*(0, 6). Rotate the rectangle as described. Write the new coordinates.

13. 180° about point *P*

14. 90° about its center, (1, 3)

15. 180° about its center, (1, 3)

16. 270° about its center, (1, 3)

GPS 17. **Guided Problem Solving** What is the clockwise angle of rotation of the hour hand on a clock as it moves from 4:00 to 5:00?
- To which number does the hour hand point at 4:00? At 5:00?
- How many degrees does the hour hand rotate in a full circle?

Mental Math A triangle lies entirely in Quadrant I. In which quadrant will the triangle lie after each rotation about $(0, 0)$?

18. $90°$ **19.** $180°$ **20.** $270°$ **21.** $360°$

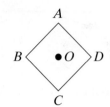

22. Open-Ended Draw a capital letter of the alphabet that has rotational symmetry. Mark a point at the center of rotation.

23. a. What rotation will move point A to point B? Point A to point C? Point A to point D?
   b. Does the square have rotational symmetry? Explain.

24. Clocks The second hand of a clock moves clockwise. It makes a full revolution once every minute. What is its clockwise angle of rotation after 20 seconds? After 45 seconds?

25. Writing in Math Describe an object in your classroom that has rotational symmetry. Explain how it shows rotational symmetry.

26. The arrow notation given shows how the vertices of a triangle are moved. Name the type of transformation and describe it with words. $A(2, 4) \rightarrow A'(4, -4)$, $B(4, 4) \rightarrow B'(2, -4)$, and $C(3, 0) \rightarrow C'(3, 0)$

27. Challenge Graph the point $E(-6, -2)$ and its three images after $90°$, $180°$, and $270°$ rotations about the origin. Connect the four points. What type of quadrilateral is formed?

Test Prep and Mixed Review   **Practice**

Multiple Choice

28. If $\overline{MN}$ is translated 5 units to the right and 2 units up, what will be the coordinates of point M?

   Ⓐ $(1, 1)$ Ⓒ $(-11, 1)$
   Ⓑ $(7, 7)$ Ⓓ $(11, -1)$

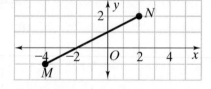

29. Which expression does the model best represent?

   Ⓕ $1\frac{3}{4} \div \frac{1}{2}$ Ⓗ $1.5 \div \frac{1}{2}$
   Ⓖ $1\frac{3}{4} \times \frac{1}{2}$ Ⓙ $7 \times 3\frac{1}{2}$

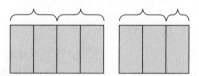

30. What is the value of the expression $(4 + 2)^2 \times 2 + 9 \div 3$?
   Ⓐ 7   Ⓑ 27   Ⓒ 42   Ⓓ 75

GO for Help

For Exercises	See Lesson
31–33	7-3

Algebra Suppose the sides of a triangle have the given measures. Classify each triangle by its sides.

31. $4s, 4s, 4s$ **32.** $2.2y, 1.5y, 2.2y$ **33.** $3k, 4k, 5k$

Answering the Question Asked

When answering a question, be sure to answer the question that is asked. Read the question carefully and identify the information you need to find. Eliminate answer choices that are not related to the question that is asked.

EXAMPLE

Point M is translated 3 units to the right and 2 units down.

What are the coordinates of M'?

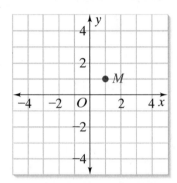

A (4, 3)	**C** (4, −1)
B (−2, −1)	**D** (3, −2)

Choice A translates point M 3 units to the right and 2 units *up*. Choice B translates M 3 units to the *left* and 2 units down. Choice C translates M 3 units to the right and 2 units down. Choice D translates M *2 units* to the right and *3 units* down. The correct answer is C.

Exercises

1. Which line contains the ordered pair (−1, −3)?
   A Line *a*
   B Line *b*
   C Line *c*
   D Line *d*

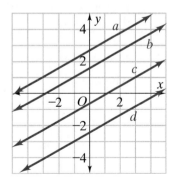

Vocabulary Review

angle of rotation (p. 520)
center of rotation (p. 519)
coordinate plane (p. 486)
graph of an equation (p. 492)
image (p. 510)
linear equation (p. 492)
line of reflection (p. 515)
line of symmetry (p. 514)
line symmetry (p. 514)

nonlinear equation (p. 504)
ordered pair (p. 486)
origin (p. 486)
prime notation (p. 510)
quadrants (p. 486)
reflection (p. 515)
rise (p. 498)
rotation (p. 519)
rotational symmetry (p. 519)

run (p. 498)
slope (p. 498)
transformation (p. 510)
translation (p. 510)
x-axis (p. 486)
x-coordinate (p. 486)
y-axis (p. 486)
y-coordinate (p. 486)

Choose the correct term to complete each sentence.

1. A flip over a line is a (translation, reflection).

2. A rotation turns a figure about a fixed point called the (center of rotation, angle of rotation).

3. (Rotation, Slope) compares the vertical change, called the rise, to the horizontal change, called the run.

4. The second number in a(n) (coordinate plane, ordered pair) is the *y*-coordinate.

5. If a graph of the solutions of an equation is a line, then the equation is a (linear equation, nonlinear equation).

Go Online
PHSchool.com
For: Vocabulary Quiz
Web Code: arj-1051

Skills and Concepts

Lessons 10-1, 10-2
• To name and graph points on a coordinate plane
• To find solutions of linear equations and to graph linear equations

An **ordered pair** (x, y) gives the coordinates of a point. Any ordered pair that makes an equation true is a solution of the equation. The **graph of an equation** is the graph of coordinates that are solutions of the equation.

Graph each point on the same coordinate plane. Name the quadrant in which each point lies.

6. $A(1, -5)$ 7. $B(-3, -4)$ 8. $C(-2, 3)$

Find three solutions of each equation.

9. $y = x + 3$ 10. $y = x - 5$

11. $y = 2x + 1$ 12. $y = -x - 2$

Lessons 10-3, 10-4

- To find the slope of a line and use it to solve problems
- To graph nonlinear relationships

Slope is a ratio that describes the steepness of a line.

$$\text{slope} = \frac{\text{rise}}{\text{run}}$$

A **nonlinear equation** is an equation with a graph that is not a straight line.

Draw a line with the given slope through the given point.

13. $B(2, 4)$, slope = 2

14. $R(-1, 2)$, slope = $\frac{1}{3}$

Make a table of values for each equation. Use integer values of x from −3 to 3. Then graph the equation.

15. $y = x^2 - 1$ **16.** $y = |x| + 1$ **17.** $y = 2x^2 - 2$ **18.** $y = 4|x|$

Lessons 10-5, 10-6

- To graph and write rules for translations
- To identify lines of symmetry and to graph reflections

A **transformation** is the change of the position, shape, or size of a figure. A **translation** is a transformation that moves every point of a figure the same distance and in the same direction.

A figure has **line symmetry** when one side of the figure is a mirror image of the other side. A **reflection** is a transformation that flips a figure over a line.

Graph each transformation of $\triangle ABC$. Use arrow notation to show the translation.

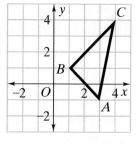

19. down 2 units **20.** left 3 units

21. right 3 units and down 5 units

22. Graph $\triangle ABC$ from Exercises 19–21. Then graph its reflection over the x-axis. Use arrow notation to describe the transformation.

Lesson 10-7

- To identify rotational symmetry and to rotate a figure about a point

A **rotation** is a transformation that turns a figure about a fixed point.

Does each figure have rotational symmetry? If it does, find the angle of rotation.

23.

24.

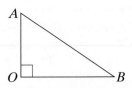
Graph each point on the same coordinate plane.

1. $A(1, 4)$

2. $B(-2, -1)$

3. $C(3, -2)$

4. $D(-3, 2)$

Graph each polygon. Use $(0, 0)$ as one vertex and label all vertices.

5. a square with side 4 units long

6. a rectangle with horizontal length 3 units and vertical length 5 units.

Determine whether each ordered pair is a solution of $y = -2x + 5$.

7. $(3, -5)$

8. $(2.5, 0)$

9. $(4, -3)$

10. $(0, 5)$

Graph each linear equation.

11. $y = x - 3$

12. $y = 3x + 1$

13. $y = -x + 2$

14. $y = 2x - 4$

Graph each pair of points. Determine the slope of the line through the points.

15. $E(7, 1)$, $F(-3, 3)$

16. $G(-2, 6)$, $H(0, 0)$

17. $L(-4, 0)$, $M(0, 2)$

18. $S(8, 5)$, $T(1, -1)$

Draw a line with the given slope through the given point.

19. $P(-2, -1)$, slope $\frac{1}{4}$

20. $R(2, 4)$, slope $-\frac{2}{3}$

Graph each equation for integer values of x from -3 to 3.

21. $y = x^2 - 2$

22. $y = 2|x| + 1$

23. **Advertising** To advertise in the classified section of a local paper costs $2 plus $.25 for each word. Make a table to graph the equation $y = 0.25x + 2$, where x is the number of words and y is the total cost.

24. Draw the images of the triangle after rotations of 90°, 180°, and 270° about O.

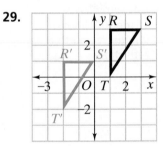

The graph of $\triangle ABC$ has vertices at $A(1, 3)$, $B(5, 8)$, and $C(7, 1)$. Graph each image of $\triangle ABC$ for each transformation described. Use arrow notation to show the transformation.

25. translated right 1 unit and down 3 units

26. translated left 3 units and up 2 units

27. reflected over the y-axis

Write a rule for the translation shown in each graph.

28.

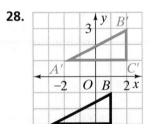

29.

Use the two figures below for Exercises 30 and 31.

30. Trace each figure and draw the line(s) of symmetry. If there are no lines of symmetry, write *none*.

31. Does each figure have rotational symmetry? If so, what is the angle of rotation?

32. **Writing in Math** Give an example of a rotation, a reflection, and a translation you might see in the real world.

Multiple Choice
Read each question. Then write the letter of the correct answer on your paper.

1. Which rule best describes the function in the table?

x	y
0	0
1	1
2	4
3	9

   Ⓐ $y = x + 2$

   Ⓑ $y = x$

   Ⓒ $y = 2x$

   Ⓓ $y = x^2$

2. A bus company charges $10.50 per ticket for a trip between two cities. Each trip costs the company $200. Which equation describes the profit the company makes on each trip?

   Ⓕ $P = 10.5x + 200$

   Ⓖ $P = 10.5x - 200$

   Ⓗ $P = 200x + 10.5$

   Ⓙ $P = 10.5 + x - 200$

3. A muffin recipe calls for $2\frac{1}{4}$ c of flour and makes 12 muffins. How many muffins can you make with 6 c of flour?

   Ⓐ 24   Ⓑ 30   Ⓒ 32   Ⓓ 45

4. What is the ones digit of 7^{23}?

   Ⓕ 3   Ⓖ 5   Ⓗ 7   Ⓙ 9

5. For which linear equation is $(-3, 0.5)$ NOT a solution?

   Ⓐ $x - 2y = 4$ Ⓒ $x = -6y$

   Ⓑ $4y = 3x + 11$ Ⓓ $x + 6y = 0$

6. A bag of 15 lemons costs $2.30. What is the approximate unit price of a lemon?

   Ⓕ $.075   Ⓗ $.15

   Ⓖ $.13   Ⓙ $.30

7. Which translation moves $\triangle ABC$ to $\triangle A'B'C'$?

   Ⓐ $(x, y) \rightarrow (x - 3, y)$

   Ⓑ $(x, y) \rightarrow (x + 3, y)$

   Ⓒ $(x, y) \rightarrow (x, y - 3)$

   Ⓓ $(x, y) \rightarrow (x, y + 3)$

   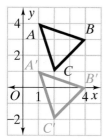

8. Order the numbers 0.361×10^7, 4.22×10^7, and 13.5×10^6 from least to greatest.

   Ⓕ 13.5×10^6, 0.361×10^7, 4.22×10^7

   Ⓖ 4.22×10^7, 13.5×10^6, 0.361×10^7

   Ⓗ 0.361×10^7, 13.5×10^6, 4.22×10^7

   Ⓙ 13.5×10^6, 4.22×10^7, 0.361×10^7

9. Of 26 letters in the alphabet, 5 are vowels. What percent are vowels?

   Ⓐ about 19%   Ⓒ about 30%

   Ⓑ about 21%   Ⓓ about 33%

10. Which expression has the greatest value?

    Ⓕ $\frac{3}{4}(8)$ Ⓖ $2 \cdot 3.1$ Ⓗ 23   Ⓙ $\frac{2}{3} \cdot \frac{6}{5}$

11. A map has a scale of 2 in. : $\frac{1}{2}$ mi. Find the actual distance for a map distance of $5\frac{1}{2}$ in.

    Ⓐ $13\frac{3}{4}$ mi   Ⓒ $5\frac{1}{2}$ mi

    Ⓑ 11 mi   Ⓓ $1\frac{3}{8}$ mi

Gridded Response
Record your answer in a grid.

12. What is the next term in this pattern?
    $500, 250, 125, \ldots$

13. Find the circumference in centimeters of a circle with a radius of 5 cm. Use 3.14 for π.

Short Response

14. A right triangle has legs of 12 ft and 16 ft. Find the longest side of the triangle.

15. A rectangular yard has a perimeter of 96 ft. To support a fence, 12 posts will be placed at equal intervals. How far apart are the posts?

Extended Response

16. You paid $385 for car repairs. The garage charged $125 for parts and $65 per hour for labor. Write and solve an equation to find the number of hours the mechanic worked on your car. Show your work.

Problem Solving Application

Applying Coordinates

On Your Mark! Do you remember the great pod-racing scene in *Star Wars Episode I*? The racers built their own Pod racers, so each one looked and flew differently. Some Pod racers got off to a fast start, but couldn't maintain their speed. Others started out slowly, then sped up. To build a winning Pod racer, you'd want to know the length of the race, so you could choose the best engine.

Anakin Skywalker's control pod with cockpit computer

The ring rotates for stability, keeping the pod upright.

Put It All Together

Suppose you are designing a pod for the big race. You have four engines to choose from. Each performs differently. The table shows test results for each engine recorded at ten checkpoints around the track.

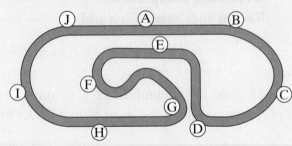

1. Make a graph, labeling the *x*-axis from 0 to 900 s, and the *y*-axis from 0 to 4,000 m. Plot the time–distance points for each of the four engines. (*Hint:* Use a different color for each engine.)
2. **a.** Connect the points for each engine.
   b. How are the graphs for the engines similar? How are they different?
3. **a.** Which engine starts a pod at the fastest speed?
   b. Which engine starts a pod at the slowest speed?
   c. Which two engines move the pod at a constant speed?
   d. Which engines speed up or slow down during the race?
   e. Which engine makes the pod go fastest at the end of 4,000 m?
4. **Reasoning** Suppose the big race is 2,000 m long. Which engine would you choose to complete the course the fastest? Would your answer change if the race were 3,000 m? Explain.

Anakin's fuel atomizer and distribution system make his engines perform better than some larger engines.

Anakin's Podracer

Each of the two Radon-Ulzer 620C racing engines, modified by Anakin Skywalker, is 7 m long. The estimated top speed of the Pod racer is 947 km/h.

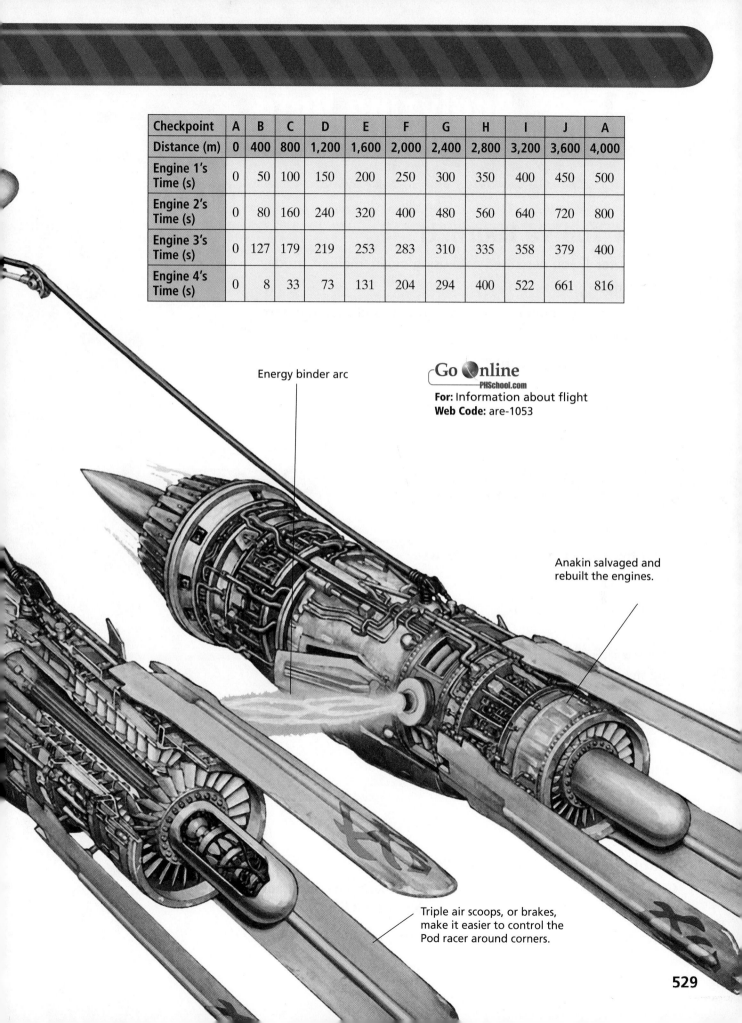

Checkpoint	A	B	C	D	E	F	G	H	I	J	A
Distance (m)	0	400	800	1,200	1,600	2,000	2,400	2,800	3,200	3,600	4,000
Engine 1's Time (s)	0	50	100	150	200	250	300	350	400	450	500
Engine 2's Time (s)	0	80	160	240	320	400	480	560	640	720	800
Engine 3's Time (s)	0	127	179	219	253	283	310	335	358	379	400
Engine 4's Time (s)	0	8	33	73	131	204	294	400	522	661	816

Energy binder arc

Go Online
PHSchool.com

For: Information about flight
Web Code: are-1053

Anakin salvaged and rebuilt the engines.

Triple air scoops, or brakes, make it easier to control the Pod racer around corners.

What You've Learned

- In Chapter 1, you described data using mean, median, mode, and range.
- In Chapter 7, you interpreted circle graphs and used them to represent data.
- In Chapter 10, you graphed points in the coordinate plane.

Check Your Readiness

GO for Help

For Exercises	See Lesson
1–2	1-6
3–6	1-10
7–10	5-4
11–14	10-1

Comparing Numbers

Order the numbers from least to greatest.

1. $32, -31, 34, -30, 13, 33$

2. $11.1, 10.9, 11.3, 11.5, 10.2$

Finding the Median

Find the median of each set of data.

3. $15, 9, 16, 12, 8, 10, 13$ 4. $27, 35, 24, 56, 29, 37$

5. $55, 69, 112, 67, 32, 123, 45$ 6. $8.9, 8.5, 7.6, 8.4, 9.1, 8.5$

Solving Proportions

(Algebra) **Solve each proportion.**

7. $\frac{3}{4} = \frac{a}{24}$ 8. $\frac{2}{b} = \frac{3}{21}$ 9. $\frac{n}{52} = \frac{17}{13}$ 10. $\frac{12}{5} = \frac{a}{45}$

Graphing on the Coordinate Plane

Graph each point on the same coordinate plane. Name the quadrant in which each point lies or the axis on which the point lies.

11. $(-4, 7)$ 12. $(0, -5)$ 13. $(6, 3)$ 14. $(2, 0)$

What You'll Learn Next

- In this chapter, you will represent data using line plots, line graphs, bar graphs, stem-and-leaf plots, scatter plots, and Venn diagrams.

- You will interpret double bar graphs and double line graphs.

- You will identify misleading graphs and statistics.

 Problem Solving Application On pages 576 and 577, you will work an extended activity on data analysis.

🔊 Key Vocabulary

- biased question (p. 551)
- cell (p. 538)
- double bar graph (p. 539)
- double line graph (p. 539)
- frequency table (p. 532)
- histogram (p. 533)
- legend (p. 539)
- line plot (p. 533)
- negative trend (p. 568)
- no trend (p. 568)
- population (p. 550)
- positive trend (p. 568)
- random sample (p. 550)
- sample (p. 550)
- scatter plot (p. 567)
- spreadsheet (p. 538)
- stem-and-leaf plot (p. 544)

Reporting Frequency

Check Skills You'll Need

1. Vocabulary Review
What is an *integer*?

Order the numbers from least to greatest.

2. 23, 45, 61, 87, 91, 16, 22, 52

3. −41, 42, −43, 45, 43, −47

 **for Help**
Lesson 1-6

What You'll Learn

To represent data using frequency tables, line plots, and histograms

🔊 **New Vocabulary** frequency table, line plot, histogram

Why Learn This?

When you count the number of times a particular event or item occurs, you measure frequency. You can use frequency to analyze events such as extreme weather events.

A **frequency table** is a table that lists each item in a data set and the number of times each item occurs.

EXAMPLE Making a Frequency Table

① **Hurricanes** The data below show the number of hurricanes in the Atlantic Ocean each year for a period of 30 years. Make a frequency table of the data.

7 4 9 8 8 10 3 9 11 3 4 4 4 8 7
5 3 4 7 5 2 2 7 9 5 5 5 6 6 4

Atlantic Ocean Hurricanes

Number	2	3	4	5	6	7	8	9	10	11
Tally	//	///	ᵗᑋᏼᏼ /	ᵗᑋᏼᏼ	//	////	///	///	/	/
Frequency	2	3	6	5	2	4	3	3	1	1

✓ Quick Check

1. The data below show the number of U.S. Representatives for 22 states. Make a frequency table of the data.

4 3 1 2 1 5 4 1 7 2 8 1 3 8 5 9 3 5 7 3 1 9

A **line plot** is a graph that shows the shape of a data set by stacking **✗**'s above each data value on a number line.

EXAMPLE Making a Line Plot

② Make a line plot of the data in Example 1.

Step 1 Draw a number line from the least to the greatest value (from 2 to 11).

Step 2 Write an ✗ above each value for each time the value occurs in the data.

Atlantic Ocean Hurricanes

```
          ✗
          ✗   ✗
          ✗   ✗       ✗
      ✗   ✗   ✗       ✗   ✗   ✗
  ✗   ✗   ✗   ✗   ✗   ✗   ✗   ✗
  ✗   ✗   ✗   ✗   ✗   ✗   ✗   ✗   ✗   ✗
  2   3   4   5   6   7   8   9   10  11
```

✓ Quick Check

2. Make a line plot of the number of students in math classes: 24 27 21 25 25 28 22 23 25 25 28 22 23 25 22 24 25 28 27 22.

Vocabulary Tip

The *histo* in histogram is short for *history*.

A **histogram** is a bar graph with no spaces between the bars. The height of each bar shows the frequency of data within that interval. The intervals of a histogram are of equal size and do not overlap.

EXAMPLE Making a Histogram

③ Make a histogram of the data in Example 1.

Make a frequency table. Use the equal-sized intervals 2–3, 4–5, 6–7, 8–9, and 10–11. Then make a histogram.

Atlantic Ocean Hurricanes

Number	Frequency
2–3	ℍℓℓ
4–5	ℍℓℓ ℍℓℓ I
6–7	ℍℓℓ I
8–9	ℍℓℓ I
10–11	II

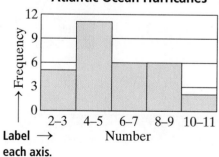

Atlantic Ocean Hurricanes

Label → each axis.

✓ Quick Check

3. Make a histogram of the ages of employees at a retail store: 28 20 44 72 65 40 59 29 22 36 28 61 30 27 33 55 48 24 28 32.

Voting-Age Population Registered to Vote (percent)

State	Percent
Calif.	54
Fla.	63
Ga.	62
Ind.	67
N.C.	69
Ore.	75
Tex.	61
Va.	64

● More Than One Way

Use the table at the left to make a data display.

Anna's Method

I can make a line plot. I'll use six intervals of 4.

Voting-Age Population Registered to Vote (percent)

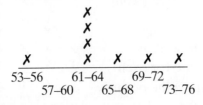

```
                X
                X
                X
   X            X     X     X     X
  53–56      61–64      69–72
      57–60      65–68      73–76
```

Ryan's Method

I can make a histogram. I'll use five intervals of 5.

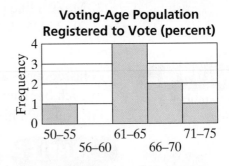

Voting-Age Population Registered to Vote (percent)

Choose a Method

Display the data in the table. Explain your choice of data display.

Number of Hours Worked per Week

Number	35	36	37	38	39	40	41	42	43	44
Tally	ЖL	///	ЖL //	ЖL //	ЖL /	ЖL ЖL	///	ЖL		/

✓ Check Your Understanding

Use the data in the frequency table below.

Number	15	16	17	18	19	20	21	22	23	24
Tally	ЖL /	/	///		//	///	/	////	ЖL	//

1. Make a line plot of the data. **2.** Make a histogram of the data.

For more exercises, see Extra Skills and Word Problems.

GO for Help

For Exercises	See Examples
3–5	1
6–8	2
9–10	3

Make a frequency table of the data.

3. tickets sold: 45 48 51 53 50 46 46 50 51 48 46 45 50 49 46

4. number of TVs: 1 3 2 2 1 4 1 2 2 1 3 1 3 3 2 2 3 1

5. student ages:
   13 12 14 12 11 12 13 14 13 13 14 11 12 12 13 11 11

Make a line plot of the data.

6. number of plants sold per person:
   5 10 11 8 7 11 9 8 6 7 12 10 10 9 8 7 6

7. miles from home to shopping center:
   2 4 10 5 4 6 7 9 5 5 3 1 10 8 6 4 3

8. blocks walked from home to school:
   2 8 10 1 2 9 8 7 6 8 4 3 8 9 1 3 10 12 6 4 8

Make a histogram of the data.

9.
How Many Amusement Parks Did You Visit Last Year?

Number of Parks	0–2	3–5	6–8	9–11
Frequency	10	4	3	1

10.
How Many Hours Do You Sleep Each Night?

Number of Hours	5–6	7–8	9–10	11–12
Frequency	4	12	9	1

11. **Guided Problem Solving** At the right are the times at which 16 people get up each morning. Display the data to show the most common half-hour interval.

5:30	6:45	5:45	6:15
6:25	6:20	7:15	7:45
8:00	7:00	8:00	7:30
6:00	7:10	7:50	6:10

   • What type of display will you use?
   • Use the interval 5:30–5:59 first. What are the other intervals?

Use the graph at the right.

12. **Books** The line plot shows the number of books each bookstore customer bought. How many customers bought more than three books?

13. How many customers bought an even number of books?

Number of Books Purchased

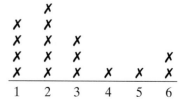

Use the histogram for Exercises 14–16.

14. **Movies** About how many people saw fewer than two movies?

15. **Writing in Math** How can you find the number of people who answered the survey? Explain.

16. **Reasoning** Can you tell how many people saw exactly 7 movies? Explain.

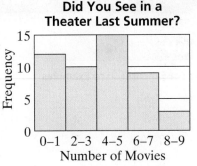

17. **Choose a Method** Display the data below, which give 26 responses to the question, "How many siblings do you have?"

1 3 4 2 2 1 3 1 0 2 0 1 3 4 2 1 0 1 2 0 3 4 2 5 2 6.

18. **Challenge** The table shows home prices. Draw two histograms for the data, one with 4 intervals and one with 8.

$129,000	$132,000	$121,000	$115,000
$138,000	$152,000	$147,000	$136,000
$137,000	$148,000	$175,000	$127,000
$192,000	$133,000	$167,000	$154,000

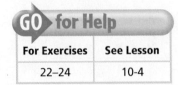

Test Prep and Mixed Review   **Practice**

Multiple Choice

19. The line plot shows the number of children of each of 12 recent U.S. presidents. Which set of data does the line plot show?

Ⓐ 1 6 2 2 4 4 2 2 3 2 2 6

Ⓑ 1 6 2 2 6 4 2 3 1 2 4 4

Ⓒ 1 6 2 2 2 4 2 3 3 2 4 4

Ⓓ 1 5 6 2 2 4 2 3 2 2 4 4

Number of Children of U.S. Presidents

```
         X
         X        X
 X       X        X              X
 X       X   X    X              X
 1   2   3   4    5    6
```

20. A square park measures 45 m on each side. The sidewalk around the park's edge encloses a square area of grass that is 42 m on each side. What is the area of the sidewalk?

Ⓕ 261 m²   Ⓖ 1,764 m²   Ⓗ 1,890 m²   Ⓙ 2,025 m²

21. Which expression can be used to find the perimeter of a rectangular trampoline with a length of 16 feet and width w?

Ⓐ $16 + 2w$ Ⓑ $32 + 2w$ Ⓒ $16w$ Ⓓ $32 + w$

GO for Help

For Exercises	See Lesson
22–24	10-4

(**Algebra**) **Make a table of values for each equation. Use integer values of x from -3 to 3. Then graph each parabola.**

22. $y = x^2 - 1$ 23. $y = 3x^2$ 24. $y = -3x^2$

Venn Diagrams

A Venn diagram shows relationships between sets of items. Each set is represented separately. Items that belong to both sets are represented by the intersection.

EXAMPLE Using a Venn Diagram

Geography There are 22 states that are all or partly in the eastern time zone, and 15 states that are all or partly in the central time zone. This includes the 5 states that are in both the eastern and central time zones. How many states are in at least one of the two time zones?

Draw a Venn diagram.

There are 17 + 5 + 10, or 32 states in either or both the eastern and central time zones.

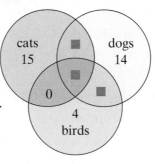

Eastern Time Zone States 22 − 5 = 17   5   Central Time Zone States 15 − 5 = 10

Exercises

Forty students have pets. Thirty-two students have cats or dogs or both, but no birds. Eight students have birds. One student has all three kinds of pets.

cats 15   dogs 14   0   4 birds

1. Copy and complete the Venn diagram.

2. How many students have only dogs and birds? Only dogs and cats?

3. **Reasoning** A new student who has only fish joins the class. How many of the existing sets would this new set overlap?

4. **Geography** There are 10 states that are completely in the central time zone, and 6 states that are completely in the mountain time zone. There are 21 states that are completely in one of the time zones, or in both. Use a Venn diagram to find how many states are in both time zones.

5. **Data Collection** Conduct a survey of your class. Ask students whether they have brothers, sisters, both, or neither. Use a Venn diagram to display the results.

Spreadsheets and Data Displays

Check Skills You'll Need

1. Vocabulary Review
A(n) __?__ is the difference between values on a scale.

Graph the data.

2.

Age (yr)	Height (in.)
1	29
2	33
3	36
4	39

 **for Help**
Lesson 9-1

What You'll Learn

To interpret spreadsheets, double bar graphs, and double line graphs

🔊 **New Vocabulary** spreadsheet, cell, double bar graph, legend, double line graph

Why Learn This?

You can use spreadsheets to draw graphs and compare data, such as the number of households with VCRs or DVD players.

A **spreadsheet** is a tool for organizing and analyzing data. Spreadsheets are arranged in lettered columns and numbered rows.

A **cell** is a box where a column and a row of a spreadsheet meet. You use a letter and a number to identify each cell.

EXAMPLE   Using a Spreadsheet

① **Electronics** The spreadsheet below shows the number of U.S. households with VCRs and the number with DVD players.

a. What value is in cell C3? What does the value represent?

Column C and row 3 meet at cell C3. The value is 6. The value represents the number of U.S. households, in millions, with DVD players in 2000.

b. How many U.S. households had VCRs in 2004?

Cell B7 shows that 97 million U.S. households had VCRs in 2004.

U.S. Households (millions)

	A	B	C
1	Year	VCRs	DVDs
2	1999	89	2
3	2000	92	6
4	2001	95	15
5	2002	96	28
6	2003	96	42
7	2004	97	62

✓ Quick Check

1. a. What value is in cell B4? What does the value represent?
   b. Which cell shows the number of DVD players in 2003?

A **double bar graph** is a graph that uses bars to compare two sets of data. The **legend,** or key, identifies the data that are compared.

EXAMPLE **Using a Double Bar Graph**

2 In which year did the number of households with DVD players first exceed 50 million?

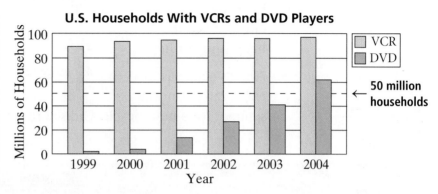

U.S. Households With VCRs and DVD Players

U.S. households with DVD players first exceeded 50 million in 2004.

✓ Quick Check

2. In which year did the number of U.S. households with DVD players first exceed 10 million?

A **double line graph** is a graph that compares changes in two sets of data over time.

EXAMPLE **Predicting With a Double Line Graph**

3 **Estimation** Use the graph to estimate the year in which the number of households with DVD players equals the number of households with VCRs.

U.S. Households With VCRs and DVD Players

The two lines appear to intersect in 2005.

You can estimate that the number of households with DVD players equals the number with VCRs in 2005.

✓ Quick Check

3. Copy and extend the graph. Estimate the number of DVD players in U.S. households in 2006.

Use the data in the spreadsheet.

1. How did Abby earn $50 in June?

2. How much money did Abby earn babysitting in July?

3. Abby's goal was to earn $250 during the summer for a new bicycle. Did she reach her goal?

Abby's Summer Earnings ($)

	A	B	C	
1	Month	Babysitting	Lawn Mowing	
2	June	36	50	
3	July	62	40	
4	August	55	40	

Homework Exercises

For more exercises, see Extra Skills and Word Problems.

GO for Help

For Exercises	See Examples
4–12	1
13–17	2
18–21	3

Give the content or value of each cell.

4. A2   5. D2

6. B3   7. C2

Which cell contains the given word or value?

8. Protein   9. Animal   10. 28   11. 46   12. Cat

Nutrition in One Brand's Dog and Cat Foods (Calories per 100 Calories)

	A	B	C	D	
1	Animal	Fat	Carbohydrates	Protein	
2	Dog	37	37	26	
3	Cat	46	26	28	

Libraries Use the double bar graph below for Exercises 13–17.

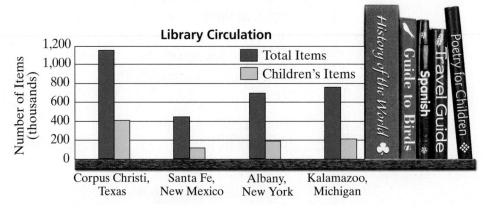

13. Which library circulated the most children's items?

14. Which library had the greatest total circulation?

15. Which libraries circulated fewer than 600,000 children's items?

16. Which libraries circulated more than 500,000 total items?

17. **Estimation** Which two libraries had about the same circulation?

Industry Use the double line graph below for Exercises 18–21.

18. About how many bikes were produced in 1960?

19. In which years did automobile production exceed 23 million?

20. **Reasoning** The two lines begin to separate widely after 1967. Why might this be?

21. **Estimation** About what year was bicycle production closest to automobile production?

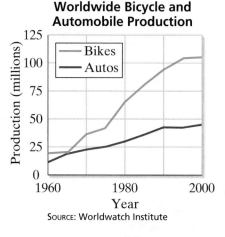

Worldwide Bicycle and Automobile Production

SOURCE: Worldwatch Institute

22. **Guided Problem Solving** Use the graph. Estimate the total population increase of the four states from 1990 to 2000.
  - The 1990 total population of the four states was ▪.
  - The 2000 total population of the four states was ▪.
  - Find the population increase.

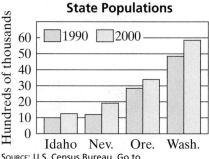

State Populations

SOURCE: U.S. Census Bureau. Go to **PHSchool.com** for a data update.
Web Code: arg-9041

23. **Writing in Math** Describe how you would display measurements of a pet's growth over several years. What measurements would you use? How would you display them?

Sacajawea Middle School Enrollment

Grade	Girls	Boys
Grade 6	37	48
Grade 7	50	44
Grade 8	45	40

24. **Multiple Choice** Which graph best represents the data at the left?

Ⓐ **Sacajawea Middle School Enrollment**

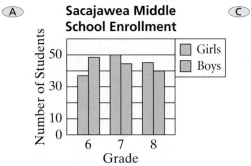

Ⓒ **Sacajawea Middle School Enrollment**

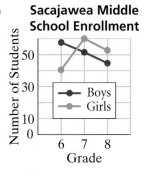

Ⓑ **Sacajawea Middle School Enrollment**

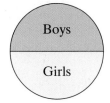

Ⓓ **Sacajawea Middle School Enrollment**

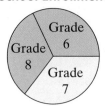

25. Reasoning You want to show grade averages in English and math every month throughout the year. Should you use a double bar or a double line graph? Explain.

26. Data Collection Find the number of students in several grades of your school last year. Find the number of students in those same grades this year. Record your data in a spreadsheet.

27. Challenge Make a double line graph of the data in the spreadsheet. Data points are (x_1, y_1) and (x_2, y_2).

   a. From the graph, find the missing y-values in the spreadsheet.

   b. Estimation Estimate the coordinates of the point of intersection of the lines.

	A	B	C	D
1	x_1	y_1	x_2	y_2
2	0	1	0	4
3	1	?	1	5
4	2	?	2	?
5	3	10	3	?
6	4	13	4	8
7	5	16	5	9
8	6	19	6	10

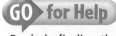

For help finding the intersection of two lines, go to Lesson 7-1, Example 2.

Test Prep and Mixed Review

Practice

Multiple Choice

28. Which statement is NOT supported by the graph?

  Ⓐ Computer use increased in Japan from 2001 to 2004.

  Ⓑ The United States had about 6 times as many computer users as the United Kingdom in 2001.

  Ⓒ There were more U.S. computer users in 2004 than in all the other listed countries combined.

  Ⓓ Germany had twice as many computer users as Japan in 2001.

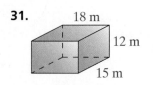

29. In quadrilateral $FGHJ$, the measures of $\angle F$, $\angle G$, and $\angle H$ are 95°, 105°, and 45°. What is the measure of $\angle J$? Justify your reasoning.

  Ⓕ 115°; the sum of the angle measures of a quadrilateral is 360°.

  Ⓖ 125°; the sum of the angle measures of a quadrilateral is 360°.

  Ⓗ 135°; $\angle J$ is supplementary to $\angle H$.

  Ⓙ 175°; the sum of the angle measures of a quadrilateral is 420°.

GO for Help

For Exercises	See Lesson
30–32	8-9

Find the surface area of each prism.

30.
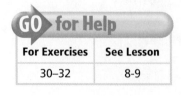
10 in.
8 in.
7 in.
6 in.

31.
18 m
12 m
15 m

32.
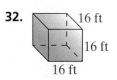
16 ft
16 ft
16 ft

11-2b Activity Lab

Technology

Graphing Using Spreadsheets

You can use spreadsheet software to graph data.

ACTIVITY

1. Enter the data in the table below into a spreadsheet. Use three column headings: Year, Men's Winning Time, and Women's Winning Time.

Olympic Winning Times in 400 Meters Freestyle (min)

Year	1980	1984	1988	1992	1996	2000	2004
Men	3.51	3.51	3.47	3.45	3.48	3.41	3.43
Women	4.09	4.07	4.04	4.07	4.07	4.06	4.05

2. Use the graphing capability of the software. Show the data as a double bar graph. Label the horizontal scale "Year" and label the vertical scale "Men's and Women's Winning Times." Title the graph "Olympic Winning Times in 400 Meters Freestyle."

3. **Data Analysis** Use the graph to compare the winning times for men and women.

4. Make a double line graph. Label the scales as you did in Exercise 2.

5. **Data Analysis** How is the double line graph similar to the double bar graph in Exercise 2?

6. Which display, a double bar graph or a double line graph, do you prefer to use for this set of data? Explain.

Use the bar graph displayed at the right.

7. Use spreadsheet software to make the graph.

8. Use the software to convert the graph to a double line graph.

9. Which display, a double bar graph or a double line graph, do you prefer for this set of data? Explain.

10. (**Algebra**) Suppose 380 boys were surveyed. About how many boys chose tomatoes as their favorite burger topping?

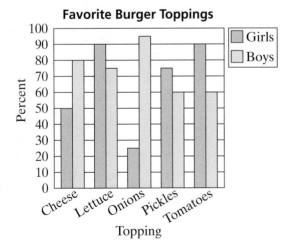

What You'll Learn

To represent and interpret data using stem-and-leaf plots

◀ﻪ) **New Vocabulary** stem-and-leaf plot

Why Learn This?

You can use a stem-and-leaf plot to compare measurements such as the different heights of teammates.

A **stem-and-leaf plot** is a graph that uses the digits of each number to show the data distribution. Each data value is broken into a "stem" (digit or digits on the left) and a "leaf" (digit or digits on the right).

EXAMPLE **Making a Stem-and-Leaf Plot**

1 **Sports** The list gives the height in inches of each player on the San Antonio Spurs basketball team during a season. Make a stem-and-leaf plot of the data: 77 74 81 83 78 84 79 82 75 82 79 79.

Step 1 Write the stems. All the data values are in the 70s and 80s, so use 7 to represent 70 and 8 to represent 80. Draw a vertical line to the right of the stems.

stems →
```
7 |
8 |
```

Step 2 Write the leaves. For these data, the leaves are the values in the ones place.

```
7 | 7 4 8 9 5 9 9    ← leaves
8 | 1 3 4 2 2
```

Step 3 Make the stem-and-leaf plot with the leaves in order from least to greatest. Add a key to explain the leaves. Add a title.

San Antonio Spurs Heights of Players
```
7 | 4 5 7 8 9 9 9
8 | 1 2 2 3 4
```
Key → **Key:** 7 | 4 means 74 in.

Quick Check

1. Make a stem-and-leaf plot of the wind speeds (in miles per hour) recorded during a storm: 9, 14, 30, 16, 18, 25, 29, 25, 38, 34, 33.

You can use a stem-and-leaf plot to compare two sets of data. From a stem, the leaves increase in value outward in each direction.

EXAMPLE Analyzing a Stem-and-Leaf Plot

2 **Weather** Use the stem-and-leaf plot below. How many times did each city receive 3.5 in. of precipitation in a month?

Monthly Precipitation (in.)

Charlotte, N.C.		Portland, Me.
7	2	9
9 8 8 7 7 5 5 4 4 2	3	1 1 3 4 5 6 7 9
4	4	1 5
	5	2

← Find the values with a stem of 3 and leaves of 5.

Key: $4.3 \leftarrow 3 \mid 4 \mid 1 \rightarrow 4.1$

Charlotte twice received 3.5 in. of precipitation in a month. Portland received 3.5 in. of precipitation in a month only once.

✓ **Quick Check**

● **2.** Which city had a higher median monthly precipitation? Explain.

EXAMPLE Application: U.S. Presidential Elections

3 **Multiple Choice** The plot below shows the number of electoral votes for president each state (plus the District of Columbia) has.

Number of Electoral Votes by State

0	3 3 3 3 3 3 3 3 4 4 4 4 4 5 5 5 5 5 6 6 6 7 7 7 7 8 8 9 9 9
1	0 0 0 0 1 1 1 1 2 3 5 5 5 5 7
2	0 1 1 7
3	1 4
4	
5	5

Key: 0 | 3 means 3 votes

Which statement is best supported by the stem-and-leaf plot?
Which statement is best supported by the stem-and-leaf plot?
- Ⓐ The mean is 2.5 votes.
- Ⓒ The mode is 8 votes.
- Ⓑ The median is 8 votes.
- Ⓓ The range is 55 votes.

The middle value is 8, so the median is 8. The correct answer is choice B.

✓ **Quick Check**

● **3.** Find the correct values for mean, mode, and range in Example 3.

Test Prep Tip ⒶⒷⒸⒹ

List the data from the least to the greatest value. Then find the mean, median, mode, or range.

11-3 Stem-and-Leaf Plots **545**

1. **Vocabulary** In a stem-and-leaf plot, what is the difference between a stem and a leaf?

Use the stem-and-leaf plot at the left.

```
4 | 3 6 7
5 | 1 2
6 | 1 7
7 | 1 8
8 | 2 6 8
```
Key: 8 | 2 means 82

2. **Number Sense** What does the number 6 represent when it is a stem? A leaf?

3. How many data values are in the set?

4. What is the least value? The greatest value?

5. Copy and complete the graph with new data items 60 and 72.

Homework Exercises

For more exercises, see Extra Skills and Word Problems.

Draw a stem-and-leaf plot for each set of data.

6. sales of twelve companies (millions of dollars):
   1.3 1.4 2.3 1.4 2.4 2.5 3.9 1.4 1.3 2.5 3.6 1.4

7. high temperatures (°F) in a desert:
   99 113 112 98 100 103 101 111 104 108 109 112 113 118

GO for Help

For Exercises	See Examples
6–7	1
8–10	2
11–13	3

Height Use the stem-and-leaf plot at the right to answer each question.

8. How many males are 65 in. tall?

9. What is the height of the shortest male? The shortest female?

10. What is the tallest female's height?

Student Height (in.)

Female		Male
7 4 3 1 0 0	5	6 7
8 5 4 1 0	6	2 3 5 5 6 7 9
0	7	1 2 3 4 6

Key: 61 ← 1 | 6 | 3 → 63

Is the statement supported by the graph above? Explain.

11. The median height for females is 57 in.

12. The mode of all heights is 65 in.

13. The range of heights for males is 20 in.

14. **Guided Problem Solving** Find the mean, median, and range of the data in the graph.
    - What is the place value of the leaves?
    - What is the order of the data from least to greatest?
    - How many data items are there?

Distances Walked by Fundraisers (km)

```
16 | 1 1 2 3 5 5
17 | 0 2 2
18 | 4 5 8 9
19 | 3 6 7 9 9 9
```
Key: 19 | 3 means 19.3

Number of Counties in Western States

SOURCE: National Association of Counties

15. Multiple Choice Which graph best represents the data?

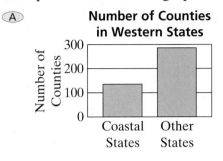

A

Number of Counties in Western States

(Bar graph: Coastal States ~130, Other States ~285; y-axis Number of Counties 0–300)

C

Number of Counties in Western States

1	5 7
2	3 9
3	3 6 9
4	4
5	6 8
6	4

Key: 1 | 5 means 15 counties

B

Number of Counties in Western States

(Pie chart: Other States 73%, Coastal States 27%)

D

Number of Counties in Western States

(Histogram: Number of States 0–6; 10–29, 30–49, 50–69 Number of Counties)

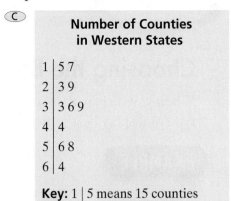

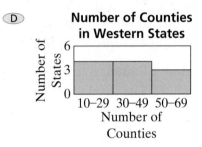

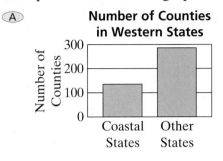

GO nline

Homework Video Tutor
Visit: PHSchool.com
Web Code: are-1103

16. a. Data Collection Measure the width of the hands of at least 10 people. Use metric units. Make a stem-and-leaf plot of the data.

b. Writing in Math Write two true statements about the data.

17. Challenge The median of a data set is 48. Find the value of the missing data item: 23 34 42 ■ 62 67.

Test Prep and Mixed Review

Practice

Multiple Choice

18. The amount of iron in high-protein foods is shown. Which statement is NOT supported by the data?

Ⓐ There are three foods with 2.1 mg of iron or more.

Ⓑ The modes are both 0.7 and 2.6 mg.

Ⓒ The mean and median are the same.

Ⓓ The median is 1.45 mg.

Iron in Three Ounces of High-Protein Foods (mg)

0	7 7 9
1	1 4 5 6
2	1 6 6

Key: 0 | 7 means 0.7

19. A store is having a 30%-off sale. Hunter opens a store charge card and gets an additional 20% off his first purchase. What is the final cost of an item that was priced originally at $25?

Ⓕ $10.00   Ⓖ $12.50   Ⓗ $14.00   Ⓙ $17.50

20. A figure lies entirely in Quadrant I of a coordinate plane. In which quadrant will the figure lie after a 270° rotation about (0, 0)?

GO for Help

For Exercise	See Lesson
20	10-7

Choosing the Best Display

When you display data, you should consider which type of display best represents the data.

EXAMPLE

A city council conducts a survey to decide how to develop a new public park. The council asks people to choose one of four park uses, as shown in the table. Choose the best display to represent the data. Explain your choice.

Step 1 Summarize the purpose of the data display.
The display must compare data for two age groups.

Step 2 Narrow down your options.
There are too many responses to use a line plot. Each person chose one use for the park. Since there is no overlap, you can eliminate a Venn diagram. You are not showing the distribution of data over a range, so you can eliminate a stem-and-leaf plot. There is no change over time, so you can eliminate a line graph.

Step 3 Choose one of the remaining displays.
Both a circle graph and a double bar graph can compare parts to wholes. In this situation, the table compares two sets of data across the same four categories, so the best option is a double bar graph.

City Park Use Survey Results

Use	18 and Under	Over 18
Tennis	72	86
Basketball	114	95
Skate Park	173	57
Garden	48	139

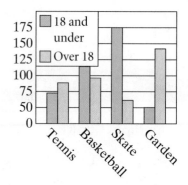

Exercises

Reasoning Match each data set at the left with the best type of data display at the right. Explain your choices.

1. the number of students who hold part-time jobs, tutor, play sports, or do a combination of all three activities

2. favorite pizza topping, by percent of students in a class

3. the popularity of different bikes among boys and among girls

4. changes in desktop and laptop computer prices over time

5. the height in centimeters of each student in a class

6. the number of letters in the first names of students in your class

A. line plot
B. double line graph
C. double bar graph
D. stem-and-leaf plot
E. circle graph
F. Venn diagram

Checkpoint Quiz 1

1. Make a frequency table and a line plot of the data below.
   5 7 8 3 5 4 6 7 8 9 1 2 5 4 2 1 3

2. Graph the data below. Explain why you chose the graph you drew.

Art Show Attendance

Day	Sun.	Mon.	Tue.	Wed.	Thur.	Fri.	Sat.
Number of Adults	54	29	22	28	12	15	49
Number of Children	32	21	16	20	8	10	36

Give the content or value (millions of dollars) of each cell in the spreadsheet.

3. B3   4. A1   5. A3   6. B1

Tell which cell has the given word or value in the spreadsheet.

7. 6,527   8. Health   9. 983

10. Make a stem-and-leaf plot of these 18-hole golf scores.
    93 120 112 89 87 124 117 95 117 121 113 95

U.S. Service Industries Revenue 1998–2003

	A	B
1	Industry	Revenue (millions)
2	Trucking	$983
3	Health	$6,527
4	Broadcasting	$2,734

11-4a Activity Lab

Data Collection

Writing Survey Questions

1. Choose a topic about which you would like people's opinions. Write five survey questions that do not influence the answer.

2. You want to survey people who will give you all kinds of responses. What group of people should you survey?

3. How many people should you survey?

4. **Data Collection** Conduct the survey. Display the results of your survey in a graph.

5. Consider the results of your survey. Do you think your questions influenced the answers? If so, how would you change the questions?

What You'll Learn

To identify a random sample and to write a survey question

◀)) **New Vocabulary** population, sample, random sample, biased question

Why Learn This?

You can use a survey to gather information from a group of people. Pollsters use surveys to understand group preferences.

A **population** is a group of objects or people. The population of an election is all the people who vote in that election. It is not practical to ask all the voters how they expect to vote. Pollsters select a **sample,** or a part of the population. A sample is called a **random sample** when each member of a population has the same chance of being selected.

EXAMPLE **Identifying a Random Sample**

❶ You survey customers at a mall. You want to know which stores they shop at the most. Which sample is more likely to be random? Explain.

a. You survey shoppers in a computer store.

Customers that shop in a particular store may not represent all the shoppers in the entire mall. This sample is not random.

b. You walk around the mall and survey shoppers.

By walking around, you give everyone in the mall the same chance to be surveyed. This sample is more likely to be random.

✓ Quick Check

1. You survey a store's customers. You ask why they chose the store. Which sample is more likely to be random? Explain.
  a. You survey 20 people at the entrance from 5:00 P.M. to 8:00 P.M.
  b. You survey 20 people at the entrance throughout the day.

Vocabulary Tip

Bias means "slant." A biased question slants the answers in one direction.

When you conduct a survey, ask questions that do not influence the answer. A **biased question** is a question that makes an unjustified assumption or makes some answers appear better than others.

EXAMPLE Identifying Biased Questions

2 **Music** Is each question *biased* or *fair?* Explain.

a. "Do you think that soothing classical music is more pleasing than the loud, obnoxious pop music that teenagers listen to?"

This question is biased against pop music. It implies that all pop music is loud and that only teenagers listen to it. The adjectives "soothing" and "obnoxious" may also influence responses.

b. "Which do you think is the most common age group of people who like pop music?"

This question is fair. It does not assume that listeners of pop music fall into only one age group.

c. "Do you prefer classical music or pop music?"

This question is fair. It does not make any assumptions about classical music, pop music, or people.

✓ Quick Check

2. Is each question *biased* or *fair?* Explain.
   a. Do you prefer greasy meat or healthy vegetables on your pizza?
   b. Which pizza topping do you like best?

✓ Check Your Understanding

Vocabulary Match each statement with the appropriate term.

1. a group of objects or people
2. makes some answers appear better
3. gives members of a group the same chance to be selected

A. biased question
B. random sample
C. population

You want to determine the favorite spectator sport of seventh-graders at your school. You ask the first 20 seventh-graders who arrive at a soccer game, "Is soccer your favorite sport to watch?"

4. What was the population of your survey? What was the sample?

5. The survey (was, was not) random.

6. You used a (biased, fair) question.

For more exercises, see Extra Skills and Word Problems.

GO for Help

For Exercises	See Examples
7–10	1
11–15	2

Which sample is more likely to be random? Explain.

7. You want to survey teens about their snacking habits.
   a. You ask people at a party to name their favorite snack.
   b. You ask several teens entering a grocery store.

8. You want to know the most popular book among all the students at your school.
   a. You ask students from different grades at your school.
   b. You ask a group of your friends.

9. You want to know which baseball team is regarded as the best.
   a. You ask everyone seated in your section of the ballpark.
   b. You ask several visitors at a tourist attraction.

10. You want to survey seventh-grade students about computer use.
   a. You ask seventh-graders leaving the cafeteria after lunch.
   b. You ask seventh-graders entering a library on Friday night.

Is each question *biased* or *fair*? Explain.

11. Do you prefer to exercise or to watch television?

12. Do you prefer rock music or jazz?

13. Do you prefer harsh rock music or inspiring jazz?

14. Do you prefer unhealthy snacks or nutritious snacks?

15. What type of snack do you prefer?

GPS **16.** **Guided Problem Solving** You are creating a survey to find out which weekend activity students prefer: shopping at the mall or watching a movie. Describe how you would find a random sample. Then write a question you could use for your survey.
   • What is the population you will need to survey?
   • Is your question fair or biased?

17. 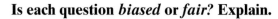 **Writing in Math** Which of the two surveys below would you use to determine attitudes about carnivals? Explain.

Survey	Question	Yes	No	Don't Know
A	Do you like going to noisy, overpriced carnivals?	53%	46%	1%
B	Do you like going to carnivals?	72%	27%	1%

18. Suppose you study the eating habits of college students. What question would you ask someone to determine whether he or she is a member of the population you want to study?

GO Online
Homework Video Tutor
Visit: PHSchool.com
Web Code: are-1104

Careers A park ranger needs a college degree related to park management, natural history, forestry, or outdoor recreation.

19. **Parks** Suppose you are gathering information about visitors to Yosemite National Park. You survey every tenth person entering the park. Would you get a random sample of visitors? Explain.

Clothes A clothing company surveys women ages 18 to 35 to decide the price of a suit. Is each method a random sample? Explain.

20. Select names at random from a national telephone directory. Call these people and survey the person that answers.

21. Select names from a national telephone directory. Call these people and survey any woman 18 to 35 who answers.

22. **Challenge** A newspaper surveys 3 out of every 100 people of voting age in a community. The community has 38,592 people of voting age. How many people are surveyed?

Test Prep and Mixed Review

Practice

Multiple Choice

23. A class is surveyed about computers and services. Which of the following gives the most detailed information about the results?

Ⓐ **Home Computer Use**

Activity	Number of Students
Internet	6
Printer	4
Both	4

Ⓒ **Home Computer Use**

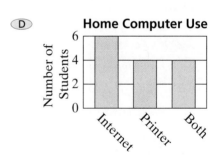

Ⓑ **Home Computer Use**

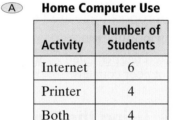

Printer 28% Internet 44% Both 28%

Ⓓ **Home Computer Use**

(bar graph: Number of Students vs Internet, Printer, Both)

24. Ann, Betty, Cat, and Diane are married to Liem, Martin, Nate, and Pedro, but not in that order. Martin is Cat's brother. Cat is not married to Pedro. Ann and Nate are married. Diane's husband is an only child. Who is married to Betty?

Ⓕ Liem   Ⓖ Martin   Ⓗ Nate   Ⓙ Pedro

Write a rule for each sequence. Then find the next three terms.

25. 3, 8, 13, 18, . . .   26. −2, 1, 4, 7, . . .   27. 27, 16, 5, −6, . . .

11-5 Estimating Population Size

✓ Check Skills You'll Need

1. Vocabulary Review
A *proportion* is an equation stating that two __?__ are equal.

Solve each proportion.

2. $\frac{2}{3} = \frac{a}{15}$

3. $\frac{n}{36} = \frac{11}{9}$

4. $\frac{42}{63} = \frac{6}{k}$

GO for Help
Lesson 5-4

What You'll Learn

To estimate population size using proportions

Why Learn This?

Researchers use the *capture/recapture method* to estimate animal population size. They collect, mark, and release animals. Then they capture another group of animals. The number of marked animals in the second group indicates the population size.

The following proportion is used to estimate a deer population.

$$\frac{\text{number of marked deer counted}}{\text{total number of deer counted}} = \frac{\text{total number of marked deer}}{\text{estimate of deer population}}$$

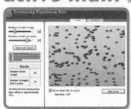

Online active math

For: Population Activity
Use: Interactive Textbook, 11-5

EXAMPLE   Using the Capture/Recapture Method

1 **Gridded Response** Researchers count 48 marked deer and a total of 638 deer on a flight over an area. They know there are 105 marked deer. Write a proportion to estimate the deer population in the area.

$$\frac{\text{number of marked deer counted}}{\text{total number of deer counted}} = \frac{\text{total number of marked deer}}{\text{estimate of deer population}}$$

$\dfrac{48}{638} = \dfrac{105}{x}$ ← Write a proportion.

$48x = 105 \cdot 638$ ← Write the cross products.

$48x = 66{,}990$ ← Multiply.

$\dfrac{48x}{48} = \dfrac{66{,}990}{48}$ ← Divide each side by 48.

$x \approx 1{,}396$ ← Round to the nearest integer.

There are about 1,396 deer.

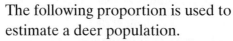

✓ Quick Check

1. Suppose the researchers in Example 1 count 638 deer, but only 35 marked deer. Estimate the total deer population in the area.

1. **Vocabulary** What is the capture/recapture method of estimating an animal population?

Use a proportion to estimate each animal population. Exercises 2 and 3 have been started for you.

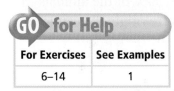

Test Prep Tip

You can check your answer to a proportion by verifying that the cross products are equal.

2. total trout counted: 2,985

   tagged trout counted: 452

   total tagged trout: 1,956

   $$\frac{\text{tagged trout counted}}{\text{total trout counted}} = \frac{\text{total tagged trout}}{x}$$

3. total bass counted: 3,102

   tagged bass counted: 198

   total tagged bass: 872

   $$\frac{\text{tagged bass counted}}{\text{total bass counted}} = \frac{\text{total tagged bass}}{x}$$

4. total rabbits counted: 5,804

   marked rabbits counted: 3,214

   total marked rabbits: 5,398

5. total black bears counted: 218

   marked black bears counted: 25

   total marked black bears: 35

Homework Exercises

For more exercises, see **Extra Skills and Word Problems.**

GO for Help

For Exercises	See Examples
6–14	1

Estimate the total deer population for each year in the table.

6. Year 1
7. Year 2
8. Year 3
9. Year 4
10. Year 5
11. Year 6
12. Year 7
13. Year 8
14. Year 9

Year	Total Deer Counted	Marked Deer Counted	Total Marked Deer
1	1,173	65	101
2	1,017	42	83
3	1,212	32	60
4	1,707	30	36
5	1,612	68	89
6	1,590	37	59
7	1,417	42	54
8	1,608	85	110
9	1,469	52	83

GPS 15. **Guided Problem Solving** In a study, a fish and game department worker catches, tags, and frees 124 catfish in a lake. A few weeks later, he catches and frees 140 catfish. Thirty-five have tags. Estimate the number of catfish in the lake.
   - number of marked catfish counted = ■
   - total number of catfish counted = ■
   - total number of marked catfish = ■

16. **Data Analysis** Use your answers to Exercises 6–14 above. Describe how the deer population changed over time.

Use the report for Exercises 17 and 18.

17. A biologist spilled juice on the report. Find the number of alligators that were caught, tagged, and set free.

18. <u>Writing in Math</u> Explain how counting a high percent of the marked alligators affects your alligator estimate.

Alligator Population	
Number caught, tagged, and set free	
Number recaptured	105
Number recaptured with tags	50
Estimated total population	132

19. **Sharks** A biologist is studying the shark population off the Florida coast. He captures, tags, and sets free 38 sharks. A week later, 8 out of 25 sharks captured have tags. He uses the proportion $\frac{25}{8} = \frac{38}{x}$ to estimate that the population is about 12.
   a. **Error Analysis** Find the error in the biologist's proportion.
   b. Estimate the shark population.

20. **Reasoning** A class helps determine the squirrel population in a park. Students capture, tag, and free squirrels. A few squirrels lose their tags. How will this affect the population estimate? Explain.

21. **Challenge** In a capture/recapture program, 30% of the animals recaptured have tags. Suppose 70 animals were originally captured, tagged, and released. Estimate the population.

Test Prep and Mixed Review

Practice

Gridded Response

22. The table at the right shows the results of a biologist who captures, tags, and sets free lake trout. About what is the trout population in the lake?

Trout Population	
Number Tagged	150
Number Recaptured	100
Number Recaptured with Tags	60

23. Alexandro needs 300 cubic inches of clay to make a sculpture. The clay comes in blocks that are 5 inches wide, 3 inches tall, and 4 inches deep. How many blocks does Alexandro need?

24. Partners A and B split their profits in a ratio of 2 : 3. If Partner A makes a profit of $2,700, how much profit, in dollars, does Partner B make? Assume Partner B makes more than Partner A.

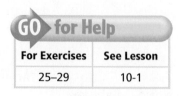

For Exercises	See Lesson
25–29	10-1

Algebra **Graph each point on the same coordinate plane.**

25. (3, 4) 26. (0, 0) 27. (−5, −2) 28. (−1, −2) 29. (4, −3)

Graphing Population Data

You can represent population data in different ways.
The table below shows data about U.S. households.

U.S. Households

Year	Number of Households (millions)	People per Household
1950	42.9	3.38
1960	53.0	3.29
1970	63.4	3.11
1980	80.3	2.75
1990	91.9	2.63
2000	105.5	2.59

You can also represent the data above using a double line graph.

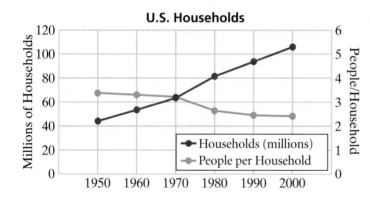

ACTIVITY

Use the data in the table above for Exercises 1–3.

1. Make a line graph. Label the horizontal axis "Millions of Households." Label the vertical axis "People per Household."

2. Describe the relationship that the line graph in Exercise 1 shows between the number of people per household and the number of households.

3. Use unit rates. Estimate the U. S. population for each year listed.

4. Extend your graph in Exercise 1 to 2010. Estimate the number of households and the number of people per household in 2010.

5. Use unit rates to estimate the U.S. population in 2010.

Describing Data

Poll A middle-school class was polled on whether the school should change its mascot. A 0 rating meant the student was strongly against the change. A 10 rating meant the student was strongly in favor of the change. The line plot below shows the data. Whitney computed the mean. Was the mean a good descriptor of how the students felt?

Mascot Survey Result

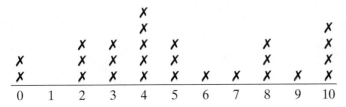

What You Might Think

What do I know? What do I want to find out?

What is the mean?

Does the mean represent the students' feelings?

What You Might Write

I know the students' ratings. I need to find the mean, which is the sum of the ratings divided by 26. I need to find out whether the mean represents how the students felt.

total = 3 × 2 + 3 × 3 + 5 × 4 + 3 × 5 +
6 + 7 + 3 × 8 + 9 + 4 × 10
= 136

mean = 136 ÷ 26, or about 5.2

I do not think so. Thirteen students were against the change. Ten students were for the change. The median of 4.5 or mode of 4 would better show how students felt.

Think It Through

1. **Reasoning** How did Whitney know to divide by 26 to find the mean? Explain.

2. Explain how to find the median of 4.5 and the mode of 4.

Exercises

Solve each problem. For Exercises 3 and 4, answer the questions first.

3. Jax has a weekly test in math. His scores on the last five tests were 78, 92, 86, 94, and 95. What score does he need on his next exam to have an average of 90?
   a. What do you know? What do you want to find out?
   b. How does a diagram like the one below help you understand what to do?

$600 \times 90\% = 540$					
78	92	86	94	95	■

4. Suppose a fox and a lizard compete in a 300-ft race. The fox runs at a rate of 30 ft/s. The lizard runs at a rate of 10 ft/s and starts 15 seconds before the fox. Who wins the race? Explain.
   a. What do you know? What do you want to find out?
   b. How does a table like the one below help you understand what to do?

Animal	Distance (ft)	Rate (ft/s)	Time (s)
Fox	300	30	■
Lizard	300	10	■

5. A tsunami is a big wave. A tsunami that struck land in 1883 was 120 ft high. An office building is about 12 ft high per floor. How many floors high was this wave?

6. Parents were asked in a survey, "Should the school require uniforms?" A 0 rating meant the parent was strongly against uniforms. A 5 rating meant the parent was strongly for uniforms. The frequency table below shows the survey results. Which measure—the mean, the median, or the mode—would best describe the data? Explain.

Parent Survey Results

Rating	0	1	2	3	4	5
Tally	𝍷𝍷𝍷 𝍷𝍷𝍷 ///	/	///	///	//	𝍷𝍷𝍷 //

Using Data to Persuade

Check Skills You'll Need

1. **Vocabulary Review**
   An *outlier* mostly affects the __?__ of a data set.

2. Find the mean, median, and mode. 122, 106, 113, 116, 120, 123, 119, 117, 123, 111

 **for Help**
Lesson 1-10

What You'll Learn

To identify misleading graphs and statistics

Why Learn This?

A graph can be a powerful way to present data. How you draw a graph can affect the impression you give about the data.

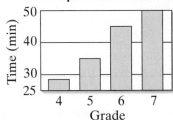

The graph above is misleading. It leads you to think that fourth-grade students spend almost no time on homework.

EXAMPLE Redrawing Misleading Graphs

1 Redraw the graph above so it is not misleading.

Method 1 Start the vertical scale at 0.

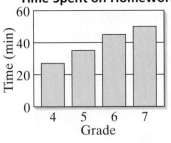

Method 2 Use a break in the vertical scale.

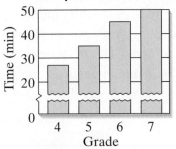

Quick Check

1. When is a break in a vertical scale especially useful?

Graphs can also mislead if the vertical or horizontal axes have unequal or very large intervals.

EXAMPLE Misleading Intervals

2 Profit Marketers use the graph below to show investors that annual profits increase steadily. Explain why the graph is misleading.

Annual Profit

The intervals of the horizontal axis are not equal. Annual profits increase $100,000 over the first 5 years. Profits then increase only $100,000 in 10 years. Annual profits increase at a slower rate.

✓ Quick Check

2. **a.** Redraw the graph in Example 2. Use equal intervals on both axes.
   b. Redraw the graph at the right so it does not mislead.

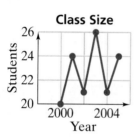

Class Size

Use of the mean, median, or mode of a data set can inform or mislead.

EXAMPLE Misleading Use of Data Measures

3 Multiple Choice You survey students in your class to find the number of pets per student. The results are shown. You want to convince your parents to let you have four pets. Which measure of the data should you use?

How Many Pets Do You Have?

0, 0, 0, 1, 1, 1, 1, 1, 1, 2, 2, 2, 3, 4, 7, 15, 27

Ⓐ Mean Ⓒ Mode
Ⓑ Median Ⓓ Range

Test Prep Tip ⊙⊙⊙⊙

Calculate each data measure. Then think about what kind of information or impression each measure provides.

The median and the mode are both 1 pet. Although these measures represent the typical number of pets, they are too low to convince your parents to let you have 4 pets. The range, 27 pets, is too large and only shows how much the number of pets varies. The mean is 4 pets. You can use this measure to influence your parents. The correct answer is A.

✓ Quick Check

3. Which two values in the data above would you consider outliers?

You can mislead by showing part of the data or by leaving out facts.

"Home of the Under-500-Calorie Burger"

EXAMPLE Application: Advertising

4 Below are data about Harry's hamburgers. Is the advertisement at the left for Harry's Hamburger Land misleading?

Item	Calories	Fat (g)	Average Number Sold Daily
Kiddie Burger	480	35	80
Hamburger Plus	575	42	68
Health Burger	580	40	65
Golden Fries Hamburger	660	57	43
Burger Deluxe	700	55	75

Only one hamburger has less than 500 Calories. The ad is misleading.

✓ Quick Check

4. How could you change the poster to better reflect the data?

✓ Check Your Understanding

Use the graph at the right.

1. Does the vertical scale start at 0?

2. Are equal intervals used on both the horizontal and vertical axes?

3. **Number Sense** The graph makes the price change seem (greater, less) than it really is.

4. Redraw the graph so that it does not mislead.

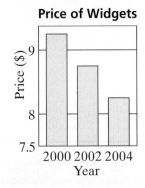

Price of Widgets

Homework Exercises

For more exercises, see Extra Skills and Word Problems.

GO for Help

For Exercises	See Examples
5–7	1–2
8–11	3–4

5. **Nutrition** Farnaz asks students at her school, "What's your favorite fruit?" She draws the graph below. Why is it misleading?

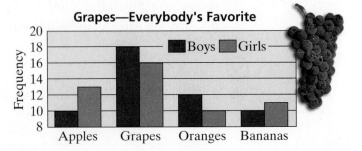

Grapes—Everybody's Favorite

For Exercises 6 and 7, tell what impression the graph gives and tell how the graph makes this impression. Then use the data to draw a graph that does not mislead.

6.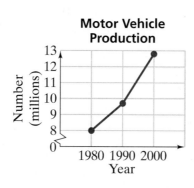

Motor Vehicle Production

7.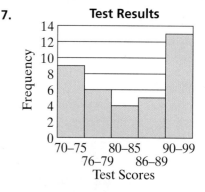

Test Results

 **GO for Help**

For help with calculating the mean, median, or mode of a data set, go to Lesson 1-10, Examples 1–3.

8. You score 93, 83, 76, 92, and 76 on five science exams.
   a. You want to show your parents how well you are doing in class. Should you use the mean, median, or mode? Explain.
   b. Your teacher wants to encourage you to work harder. Which measure should your teacher use? Explain.

9. **Bowling** The table shows the scores of two students in a bowling match.
   a. Bill says he won the match because he has a higher average. Is he correct?
   b. Kisha says she won the match. How can she justify this statement?

Bowling Scores

Game	1	2	3
Kisha	81	60	93
Bill	78	95	91

10. **Reasoning** You shop for bikes and find 7 types priced at $119, $139, $149, $179, $189, $199, and $209. You want to buy the $189 bike. Should you use the mean, median, or mode to convince your parents that this is a reasonable price for a bike? Explain.

11. **Number Sense** To raise money for charity, your class holds a car wash. You pay $15 for washing materials and collect $128 in donations. Can you say you raised $128 for charity? Explain.

 GPS 12. **Guided Problem Solving** Use the data at the right to make two line graphs. The first graph should show great change in the winning times and the second graph should show little change.

   - **Make a Plan** Use a break for the vertical scale of the first graph. Use increments of 0.01 to 0.05 s. Start the vertical scale of the next graph at 0. Use increments of 0.5 to 2 s.
   - **Check the Answer** The first graph should suggest a greater variation in winning times than the second graph shows.

Men's 100-Meter Winning Times

Year	Time (s)
1988	9.92
1992	9.96
1996	9.84
2000	9.87
2004	9.85

SOURCE: *Sports Almanac*

13. **Open-Ended** Find a graph in a newspaper or magazine. Is the graph trying to mislead you? Explain.

Homework Video Tutor
Visit: PHSchool.com
Web Code: are-1106

Business Use the graph below for Exercises 14–18.

14. What does the graph suggest?

15. Why does the graph give the impression described in Exercise 14?

16. Use the data to draw a graph that does not mislead.

17. **Reasoning** Why would a company draw the misleading graph? Explain.

18. You want to show that the company is successful. Should you use the mean, median, or mode to suggest the greatest profit? Explain.

19. **Writing in Math** Spotless Cleaners sends out 200 customer surveys. The company gets 100 replies with 97 customers saying they are satisfied. In an ad, Spotless Cleaners says that 97% of its customers are satisfied. Is this statement misleading? Explain.

20. **Challenge** Research the cost of U.S. postage stamps for the past six years. Use your data to draw a graph that gives the impression of a large increase in stamp cost over time.

Profits for 2001–2005

Test Prep and Mixed Review   **Practice**

Multiple Choice

21. A town's population is shown. If the trend continues, which is the best prediction of the population in 2010?
    Ⓐ Fewer than 22,000 people
    Ⓑ Between 22,000 and 29,000 people
    Ⓒ Between 29,000 and 36,000 people
    Ⓓ More than 36,000 people

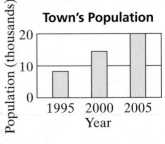

Town's Population

22. Which of the following can have a single base that is a hexagon?
    Ⓕ Prism   Ⓖ Cone   Ⓗ Cylinder   Ⓙ Pyramid

23. What is the value of the expression $18 \div (9 - 6)^2 + 2 \times 6$?
    Ⓐ 14   Ⓑ 24   Ⓒ 30   Ⓓ 108

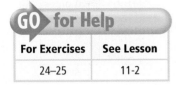

GO for Help

For Exercises	See Lesson
24–25	11-2

Estimation Use the graph.

24. Estimate the total amount spent on theater and opera from 1999 to 2003.

25. Estimate the total amount spent on movie tickets from 1999 to 2003.

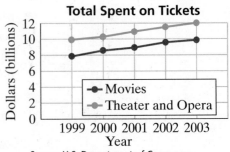

Total Spent on Tickets

SOURCE: U.S. Department of Commerce

1. Use the data at the right. Make a graph that would persuade filmmakers to make more movies in Georgia.

2. The data below show the class sizes at a school. Would you use the mean, the median, or the mode to convince the principal that there is a high number of students per class? Explain.
27 29 34 24 29 19 30 19 25 22 27 19

3. **Open-Ended** Choose a survey topic and write a biased survey question and a fair survey question.

4. Which is the best way to survey a random sample of students from your school about their favorite radio station? Explain.
   Ⓐ Survey 5 students in each first-period class.
   Ⓑ Survey 12 students in the band.
   Ⓒ Call 25 friends.
   Ⓓ Survey each student in your math class.

Movies Filmed in Georgia

Year	Number
1997	10
1998	5
1999	4
2000	8
2001	4
2002	4
2003	6
2004	8

SOURCE: 2005 Georgia Film Sourcebook

Use a proportion to estimate each animal population.

5. total wild horses counted: 1,583
   marked wild horses counted: 496
   total marked wild horses: 1,213

6. total turtles counted: 51
   marked turtles counted: 32
   total marked turtles: 108

MATH AT WORK

Pollsters

Pollsters interview people to find out their opinions and their preferences about specific topics. They must understand the topic of interest well in order to ask the right questions. If pollsters ask poor-quality questions, they will not get accurate responses.

Pollsters use math to analyze the data they collect. They find the mean, median, mode, and range of the data. Their analysis gives us an overall view of the data. They often graph data to display their findings.

Go Online
PHSchool.com **For:** more information about pollsters
Web Code: arb-2031

Two-Variable Data Collection

Isle Royale, the largest island in Lake Superior, is a favorable location for studying wolf and moose populations. The table shows wolf and moose population estimates during a 20-year period.

Moose and Wolf Populations on Isle Royale, Michigan

Year	Wolf	Moose	Year	Wolf	Moose
1985	22	1,115	1995	16	2,422
1986	20	1,192	1996	22	1,163
1987	16	1,268	1997	24	500
1988	12	1,335	1998	14	699
1989	12	1,397	1999	25	750
1990	15	1,216	2000	29	850
1991	12	1,313	2001	19	900
1992	12	1,590	2002	17	1,100
1993	13	1,879	2003	19	900
1994	17	1,770	2004	29	750

SOURCE: National Park Service

ACTIVITY

1. Describe the changes in the wolf population over the years.

2. Describe the changes in the moose population over the years.

3. Make a graph that shows the wolf population on the horizontal scale and the moose population on the vertical scale. Graph the ordered pairs (wolf, moose) for each year.

4. **Data Analysis** Do you see a relationship between the two populations? Explain.

Exercises

5. **Data Collection** Collect data on the length of your classmates' feet and the length of their forearms. Record the data in a table.

6. Display the data in an appropriate graph.

7. Do you see a relationship between the two lengths? Explain.

Exploring Scatter Plots

What You'll Learn

To draw and interpret scatter plots

◀)) **New Vocabulary** scatter plot, positive trend, negative trend, no trend

Why Learn This?

You can graph data, such as the data shown below, as points in a coordinate plane. The graph may show an important pattern.

Book Bag Weights

Number of Books	3	3	4	4	5	6	6	7	7	8
Weight (lb)	6	8	6.5	9	10	7.5	12	9.5	11	12

A **scatter plot** is a graph that relates two sets of data. To make a scatter plot, graph the two sets of data as ordered pairs.

EXAMPLE Making Scatter Plots

1 **Weights** Graph the data in the table above in a scatter plot.

Each column in the table represents a point on the scatter plot.

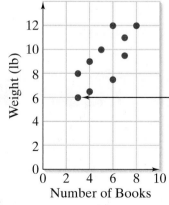

Book Bag Weights

This point is for the book bag that holds 3 books and weighs 6 lb.

Quick Check

1. Graph the data in the table below in a scatter plot.

Height (in.)	58	64.5	67.5	65.5	63.5	64	71	62.5	69
Arm Span (in.)	57.5	64	68.5	66	62.5	66	72	63	70

The scatter plot in Example 1 shows a relationship, or *trend*. As the number of books increases, the weight of the bag generally increases.

You can examine a scatter plot to see what kind of trend is shown.

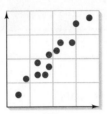

Positive trend

As one set of values increases, the other set tends to increase.

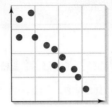

Negative trend

As one set of values increases, the other set tends to decrease.

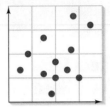

No trend

There is no apparent relationship among the data.

EXAMPLE **Describing Trends in Scatter Plots**

2 **Trees** Describe the trend in the scatter plot.

As the age of a tree increases, the diameter of the tree tends to increase.

The scatter plot shows a positive trend.

✓**Quick Check**

2. Suppose you draw a line that follows the trend shown in the scatter plot. Is the slope of the line positive or negative?

Age and Diameter of Trees

SOURCE: USDA Forest Service

Check Your Understanding

1. **Vocabulary** How does a scatter plot relate two sets of data?

Use the scatter plot in Example 2 for Exercises 2–5.

2. What does the point at (25, 8) represent?

3. A tree that is 40 years old has a diameter of about 9 in. Is this data point shown on the scatter plot?

4. **Estimation** A tree is 28 years old. Estimate its diameter.

5. **Estimation** A tree has a diameter of 10 in. Estimate its age.

For more exercises, see Extra Skills and Word Problems.

GO for Help

For Exercises	See Examples
6–8	1
9–14	2

Graph each set of data in a scatter plot.

6.

Temperature (°F)	Weight of Clothing (lb)
60	5.5
58	5.2
50	6.2
42	6.8
36	7.8
32	7.4
30	8.4
26	9.9
22	10.9
20	12

7.

Hours Studying	Test Grade
0.5	68
0.75	70
1	82
1	78
1.25	78
1.25	86
1.25	94
1.5	82
1.75	90
2	88

8.

Price of CD ($)	14	13	7	10	18	12	23	17	12	19	15
Number of Songs	15	10	11	12	14	19	20	9	7	10	11

Describe the trend in each scatter plot.

9.
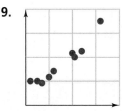

10.
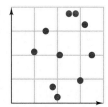

11.
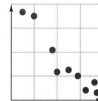

12.
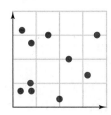

13.
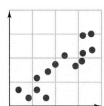

14.
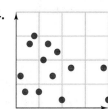

GPS 15. **Guided Problem Solving** Use the data below. Predict the electrical use in a month that has an average temperature of 60°F.

Monthly Electrical Use

Average Temperature (°F)	77	72	68	45	39	50	35	30	47
Electricity Use (kWh)	170	143	168	236	260	196	244	309	266

- **Make a Plan** Make a scatter plot with °F on the horizontal axis. Draw a line that is close to most of the data points. Use the line to estimate the electricity use at 60°F.
- **Carry Out the Plan** The scatter plot shows a ___?___ trend. The ordered pair (60, ▦) represents the electricity use at 60°F.

16. Carmella made a scatter plot comparing the daily temperature and the number of people at a beach. Which of the three scatter plots below most likely represents the data? Explain your choice.

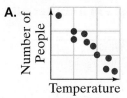

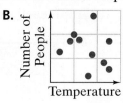

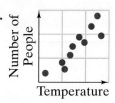

Make a scatter plot using the data in the table. Use the average ticket cost and the number of admissions.

17. Data Analysis What kind of trend do you see? Explain.

18. Writing in Math How would the scatter plot change if you switched the two axes? Would the trend change? Explain.

19. Challenge Make a scatter plot with "Year" as the horizontal scale and "Admissions" as the vertical scale. Predict the number of admissions in 2010.

Movie Attendance

Year	Average Ticket Cost (dollars)	Admissions (millions)
1997	4.59	1,388
1998	4.69	1,481
1999	5.08	1,465
2000	5.39	1,421
2001	5.66	1,487
2002	5.81	1,689
2003	6.03	1,574
2004	6.21	1,536

SOURCE: Motion Picture Association of America

Test Prep and Mixed Review   **Practice**

Multiple Choice

20. The survey results of 23 students are shown. Which statement is supported by the graph?

Ⓐ Most students read 6–11 books.
Ⓑ Most students read 0–5 books.
Ⓒ The median was about 7 books.
Ⓓ The mean was about 6 books.

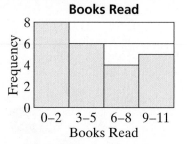

21. Which sequence follows the rule $3n + 1$, where n represents the position of a term in the sequence?

Ⓕ 4, 7, 10, 13, 16, . . .
Ⓖ 4, 8, 13, 16, 20, . . .
Ⓗ 1, 7, 10, 13, 19, . . .
Ⓙ 4, 6, 7, 8, 9, . . .

22. Which statement is always true about a right isosceles triangle?

Ⓐ It has 3 congruent sides.
Ⓑ It has no congruent sides.
Ⓒ It has three 60° angles.
Ⓓ It has two acute angles.

23. There are 35 marked seals in a region. Biologists count 36 seals, of which 8 are marked. About how many seals are in the region?

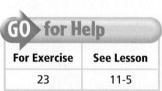

For Exercise	See Lesson
23	11-5

Interpreting Data

Before you answer a question that involves data, make sure you understand the information displayed in the graph. Then try to relate each of the answer choices to the data.

EXAMPLE

The stem-and-leaf plot at the right shows the different costs of hair dryers. What is the mode hair dryer price?

Ⓐ $4   Ⓑ $20   Ⓒ $24   Ⓓ $25

The stems are tens digits. So the hair dryer prices range from $15 to $35. Choice A is the mode of the leaves, not of the data. Choice B is the range of the data. Choice D is the median. The correct answer is C.

Hair Dryer Prices

1	5 7
2	0 4 4 6
3	0 1 3 5

Key: 1 | 7 means $17.

Exercises

Use the double bar graph.

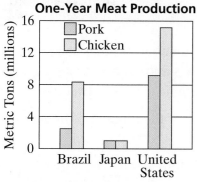

One-Year Meat Production

SOURCE: U.S. Department of Agriculture

1. What is the approximate range of chicken production?
   Ⓐ 14,000,000 metric tons   Ⓒ 7,000,000 metric tons
   Ⓑ 11,000,000 metric tons   Ⓓ 4,000,000 metric tons

2. Which statement is NOT supported by the graph?
   Ⓕ The mean of pork produced is about 4,000,000 metric tons.
   Ⓖ The mean of chicken produced is about 8,000,000 metric tons.
   Ⓗ All countries produced more chicken than pork.
   Ⓙ Brazil produced more pork than Japan.

3. What is the approximate median of pork production?
   Ⓐ 1,200,000 metric tons   Ⓒ 6,700,000 metric tons
   Ⓑ 2,600,000 metric tons   Ⓓ 9,300,000 metric tons

Chapter 11 Review

Vocabulary Review

For: Online vocabulary quiz
Web Code: arj-1151

- ◀)) biased question (p. 551)
- cell (p. 538)
- double bar graph (p. 539)
- double line graph (p. 539)
- frequency table (p. 532)
- histogram (p. 533)
- legend (p. 539)
- line plot (p. 533)
- negative trend (p. 568)
- no trend (p. 568)
- population (p. 550)
- positive trend (p. 568)
- random sample (p. 550)
- sample (p. 550)
- scatter plot (p. 567)
- spreadsheet (p. 538)
- stem-and-leaf plot (p. 544)

Choose the correct term to complete each sentence.

1. A (line, stem-and-leaf) plot separates the digits of the data.

2. A (negative, positive) trend involves a set of values that increases as another set of values decreases.

3. A (cell, legend) identifies the data being compared.

4. A (line plot, scatter plot) shows data by stacking ✗s above values.

5. A (population, random sample) is a whole group.

Go Online
PHSchool.com

Skills and Concepts

Lesson 11-1
- To represent data using frequency tables, line plots, and histograms

A **frequency table** lists data items with the number of times each item occurs. A **line plot** shows data by stacking ✗'s above data values on a number line. A **histogram** is a bar graph with no spaces between bars.

6. Make a frequency table and a line plot for the number of hours of TV watched per person per week:
   5 7 9 5 3 6 8 6 5 7 6 8 7 7 6 5 4 4 5 6.

7. Use the table below to make a histogram.

How Many Pencils or Pens Are in Your Backpack?

Number of Pencils or Pens	0–4	5–9	10–14	15–19
Frequency	6	13	7	4

Airplanes The line plot at the right shows responses to a survey.

8. What do the numbers in the line plot represent?

9. How many people answered the survey?

How Many Times Have You Flown in an Airplane?

```
 X         X
 X    X    X
 X    X    X    X
 X    X    X    X              X
─────────────────────────────────
 1    2    3    4    5    6
```

Lessons 11-2, 11-3

- To interpret spreadsheets, double bar graphs, and double line graphs
- To represent and interpret data using stem-and-leaf plots

A **double bar graph** compares two sets of data. A **double line graph** compares changes over time of two sets of data. A **stem-and-leaf plot** uses the digits of each number to show the shape of the data.

Education Use the double bar graph for Exercises 10–12.

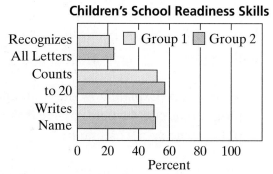

Children's School Readiness Skills

10. In which skill did Group 2 excel the most?

11. In which skill did the two groups differ the most?

12. In which skill did the two groups differ the least?

13. Draw a stem-and-leaf plot for the temperatures below.

    48 54 45 60 50 70 66 69 40 61 50 60 58
    47 40 27 23 60 47 40 29 16 55 36 19 27

Lessons 11-4, 11-5

- To identify a random sample and to write a survey question
- To estimate population size using proportions

A **biased question** makes some answers appear better than others. You can use the capture/recapture method to estimate **population** size.

Tell whether each question is *biased* **or** *fair.* **Explain.**

14. What is your favorite activity after school?

15. Do you like the calm, soothing ocean?

16. **Biology** Researchers know that there are 53 marked wolves in an area. On a flight over the area, they count 18 marked wolves and a total of 125 wolves. Estimate the total wolf population.

Lessons 11-6, 11-7

- To identify misleading graphs and statistics
- To draw and interpret scatter plots

Graphs can mislead if they use unequal intervals or improper breaks on an axis. A **scatter plot** relates two sets of data, showing whether the data have a **positive trend,** a **negative trend,** or **no trend.**

17. How is the graph at the right misleading?

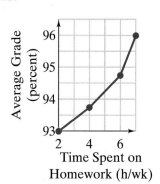

Describe the trend in each scatter plot.

18.

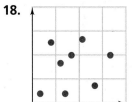

19.

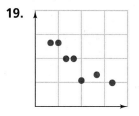

Chapter 11 Test

Go Online For: Online chapter test
PHSchool.com **Web Code:** ara-1152

A pollster asks 20 people how many hours they sleep each night. Use the data below to draw each data display in Exercises 1–5.

8 7.5 9 7 8 7.5 6 6.5 9.5 7.5
8 7.5 8 7 8 6.5 8 8.5 8.5 7.5

1. frequency table   2. line plot

3. histogram   4. stem-and-leaf plot

5. **Reasoning** Explain how the stem-and-leaf plot in Exercise 4 would change if the person who said 9 had said 12.

Use the spreadsheet below for Exercises 6–10.

	A	B	C	D
1	Student	Test 1	Test 2	Quiz
2	Alice	86	85	8
3	Xavier	91	89	9
4	Timotheo	79	84	8

6. What is the content of cell A3?

7. What is the content of cell C2?

8. In which cell is the word *Quiz?*

9. In which cell is the value 79?

10. In which cell is the word *Student?*

Is each question *biased* or *fair?* Explain.

11. Do you prefer watching comedies or dramas?

12. Do you like watching violent sports or informative documentaries on TV?

13. Do you like sunny summers or dark winters?

14. Which season do you like best?

15. **Writing in Math** Explain how you can get a random sample of the people who use a town library.

Sales Use the double line graph below.

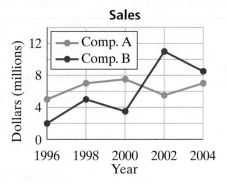

16. Estimate the year in which the sales were equal.

17. In which year were sales lowest for each company?

18. Redraw the graph to emphasize the highest sales for each company.

19. **Wages** Five students work at a store. Their hourly earnings are $8, $7.50, $12, $8.50, and $8. One student who earns $8 wants a raise. Should he use the mean, the median, or the mode to convince the boss?

Use a proportion to estimate each population.

20. total counted: 102
    tagged counted: 38
    total tagged: 56

21. total counted: 958
    tagged counted: 210
    total tagged: 305

22. a. Make a scatter plot of the data below.

Students' Ages and Heights

Age	12	13	12	14	14	13
Height (in.)	57	60	56	63	65	61

b. Describe the trend in the scatter plot.

Reading Comprehension

Read each passage and answer the questions that follow.

Baker Coordinates Mr. Baker, a math teacher, experimented with points on a coordinate plane. He invented an operation that he named after himself. To "bake" the point (x, y), make a new point with an x-coordinate that is the square of the original x-coordinate and with a y-coordinate that is the original y-coordinate.

1. If you bake the point (x, y), what ordered pair describes the coordinates of the new point?
   - (A) (x, y)
   - (B) (x^2, y)
   - (C) (x, y^2)
   - (D) (x^2, y^2)

2. If you bake a point in the second quadrant, in which quadrant is the new point located?
   - (F) I
   - (G) II
   - (H) III
   - (J) IV

3. If you bake a point in the third quadrant, in which quadrant is the new point located?
   - (A) I
   - (B) II
   - (C) III
   - (D) IV

4. If a point not on an axis has been baked, in which quadrants could the new point be located?
   - (F) either the first or second
   - (G) either the first or third
   - (H) either the first or fourth
   - (J) either the second or third

Capital Geometry In 1790, George Washington hired Pierre L'Enfant to design a capital city. L'Enfant created an orderly grid for Washington, D.C. Streets that run north and south are numbered, and streets running east and west have letter names. Numbers and letters begin at the Capitol and run in both directions, so there are two 10th Streets and two K Streets. When you give an address, you also have to state its quadrant. The quadrants correspond to the four quadrants on a coordinate plane, but people call them by their compass directions: NE, SE, NW, and SW.

5. Ford's Theatre is located at 511 10th St. NW. In what quadrant is this?
   - (A) I
   - (B) II
   - (C) III
   - (D) IV

6. Which word describes the location of the Capitol on the street grid of Washington, D.C.?
   - (F) intercept
   - (G) origin
   - (H) perimeter
   - (J) vertex

7. How many points are there where a 4th Street intersects an I Street?
   - (A) one
   - (B) two
   - (C) four
   - (D) eight

8. A race is run along K Street. It starts at the intersection of 6th Street in NW, and goes to the point where K Street meets 6th Street in NE. What distance does the race cover?
   - (F) 4 blocks
   - (G) 8 blocks
   - (H) 12 blocks
   - (J) 24 blocks

Applying Data Analysis

Bicycle Business Line graphs can communicate information more quickly than data tables because plots show how the data points are related. But line graphs can also be misleading. They can make a downward slide seem slight or an upward spike seem like a significant trend. You have to look critically at line graphs to see whether you're being informed . . . or misinformed.

Put It All Together

Materials graph paper

1. The table shows sales data for three bicycle companies. Pick one of the bicycle companies and activities on page 577. In each case, put the year on the horizontal axis and the sales on the vertical axis.

2. **Writing in Math** Compare your two line graphs. Which gives the more accurate view of the company's actual performance? Explain.

3. **Research** Find a graph in a newspaper. Is the graph a fair representation of the data? How could you change the graph to give a different impression?

Annual Sales for Three Bicycle Manufacturers (thousands of dollars)

Year	BETTER BIKES	Deals on Wheels	Super Cycles
1996	$2,520	$2,920	$3,210
1997	$2,369	$3,008	$3,082
1998	$2,298	$2,978	$2,958
1999	$2,160	$2,978	$3,106
2000	$2,073	$3,007	$2,920
2001	$1,991	$3,158	$2,832
2002	$1,871	$3,316	$2,889
2003	$1,778	$3,448	$3,062

BETTER BIKES

Sales have gone down since 1996.

A. Draw an optimistic line graph for the next stockholders' meeting.

B. Draw another line graph for the president of the company. Make the drop in sales look very serious.

Deals on Wheels

Sales have generally gone up over the last eight years.

A. Draw a line graph that will help convince the bank to give the company a big loan.

B. Draw a line graph showing employees why they can't have big raises this year.

Super Cycles

Although sales have gone up and down over the last eight years, sales rose from 2001 to 2003.

A. Draw a line graph that makes Super Cycles look incredibly successful by the year 2010. Use a dashed line to extend the graph.

B. Draw a line graph that a possible buyer of the company might use.

Go Online
PHSchool.com
For: Information about bicycles
Web Code: are-1153

Using Probability

What You've Learned

- In Chapter 3, you simplified fractions.
- In Chapter 6, you converted between fractions, decimals, and percents.
- In Chapter 11, you made line plots, line graphs, bar graphs, stem-and-leaf plots, and scatter plots to represent data.

 Check Your Readiness

GO for Help

For Exercises	See Lesson
1–6	5-1
7–12	5-4
13–22	6-2

Writing Ratios

Write each ratio in simplest form.

1. $\frac{9}{24}$ **2.** $\frac{20}{54}$ **3.** $\frac{15}{65}$

4. $\frac{16}{22}$ **5.** $\frac{21}{84}$ **6.** $\frac{18}{42}$

Using Proportional Reasoning

(**Algebra**) **Solve each proportion.**

7. $\frac{3}{10} = \frac{x}{30}$ **8.** $\frac{n}{14} = \frac{25}{8}$ **9.** $\frac{22}{c} = \frac{66}{15}$

10. $\frac{16}{35} = \frac{20}{y}$ **11.** $\frac{a}{24} = \frac{24}{9}$ **12.** $\frac{19}{38} = \frac{f}{21}$

Percents, Fractions, and Decimals

Write each decimal as a percent.

13. 0.46   **14.** 0.265   **15.** 0.07   **16.** 0.256   **17.** 0.82

Write each fraction as a percent. When necessary, round to the nearest tenth of a percent.

18. $\frac{4}{5}$ **19.** $\frac{5}{11}$ **20.** $\frac{8}{14}$ **21.** $\frac{12}{30}$ **22.** $\frac{15}{32}$

What You'll Learn Next

- In this chapter, you will find the probabilities of independent and dependent events.
- You will make sample spaces to represent all the possible outcomes in a probability experiment.
- You will find permutations and combinations.

Problem Solving Application On pages 622 and 623, you will work an extended activity on probability.

12-1 Probability

Check Skills You'll Need

1. **Vocabulary Review**
   In what three forms can you write a *rational number*?

Write each fraction as a decimal and as a percent.

2. $\frac{31}{50}$ 3. $\frac{19}{20}$

4. $\frac{11}{40}$ 5. $\frac{11}{10}$

 **for Help**
Lesson 6-2

What You'll Learn

To find the probability and the complement of an event

◀» **New Vocabulary** outcome, event, theoretical probability, complement

Why Learn This?

In sports, a coin toss often determines which team gets the ball first.

An **outcome** is the result of an action. For example, getting tails is a possible outcome of flipping a coin. An **event** is a collection of possible outcomes. If all the outcomes are equally likely, you can use a formula to find the theoretical probability.

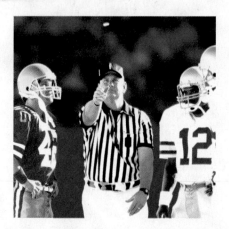

KEY CONCEPTS **Theoretical Probability**

theoretical probability $= P(\text{event}) = \dfrac{\text{number of favorable outcomes}}{\text{total number of possible outcomes}}$

You can express probability as a fraction, a decimal, or a percent.

EXAMPLE **Finding Probability**

① You select a letter at random from the letters shown. Find the probability of selecting a vowel. Express the probability as a fraction, a decimal, and a percent.

The event *vowel* has 2 outcomes, A and E, out of 5 possible outcomes.

$P(\text{vowel}) = \dfrac{2}{5}$ ← number of favorable outcomes
     ← total number of possible outcomes

$= \dfrac{2}{5}$, 0.4, or 40%   ← Write as a fraction, decimal, and percent.

Vocabulary Tip

You read *P*(vowel) as "the probability of a vowel."

✓ Quick Check

● **1.** Find *P*(consonant) as a fraction for the letters in Example 1.

All probabilities range from 0 to 1. The probability of rolling a 7 on a number cube is 0, so that is an *impossible* event. The probability of rolling a positive integer less than 7 is 1, so that is a *certain* event.

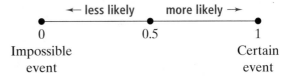

The **complement** of an event is the collection of outcomes not contained in the event. The sum of the probabilities of an event and its complement is 1. So $P(\text{event}) + P(\text{not event}) = 1$.

EXAMPLES Finding Probabilities From 0 to 1

2 **Clothes** The picture shows the jeans in Juanita's closet. She selects a pair of jeans with her eyes shut. Find $P(\text{dark color})$.

There are 8 possible outcomes. Since there are 3 black pairs and 2 blue pairs, the event *dark color* has 5 favorable outcomes.

$$P(\text{dark color}) = \frac{5}{8} \quad \begin{array}{l} \leftarrow \textbf{number of favorable outcomes} \\ \leftarrow \textbf{total number of possible outcomes} \end{array}$$

3 Refer to Juanita's closet. Find $P(\text{red})$.

The event *red* has no favorable outcome.

$$P(\text{red}) = \frac{0}{8}, \text{ or } 0 \quad \begin{array}{l} \leftarrow \textbf{number of favorable outcomes} \\ \leftarrow \textbf{total number of possible outcomes} \end{array}$$

4 Refer to Juanita's closet. Find $P(\text{not dark color})$.

$$P(\text{dark color}) + P(\text{not dark color}) = 1 \quad \leftarrow \begin{array}{l} \textbf{The sum of probabilities of an} \\ \textbf{event and its complement is 1.} \end{array}$$

$$\frac{5}{8} + P(\text{not dark color}) = 1 \quad \leftarrow \textbf{Substitute } \tfrac{5}{8} \textbf{ for } P(\text{dark color}).$$

$$\frac{5}{8} - \frac{5}{8} + P(\text{not dark color}) = 1 - \frac{5}{8} \quad \leftarrow \begin{array}{l}\textbf{Subtract } \tfrac{5}{8} \textbf{ from} \\ \textbf{each side.}\end{array}$$

$$P(\text{not dark color}) = \frac{3}{8} \quad \leftarrow \textbf{Simplify.}$$

GO for Help

For help with subtracting fractions, go to Lesson 3-2, Example 3.

✓ Quick Check

You roll a number cube once. Find each probability.

2. $P(\text{multiple of 3})$ **3.** $P(\text{not multiple of 2})$ **4.** $P(9)$

1. **Vocabulary** Define *event* without using the word *outcome*.

2. $P(A) = \frac{1}{3}$. Write an expression for $P(\text{not } A)$.

You select a marble from those shown. Match each event with its probability.

3. $P(\text{red})$ A. $\frac{5}{7}$

4. $P(\text{yellow})$ B. $\frac{2}{7}$

5. $P(\text{blue})$ C. 0

6. $P(\text{red or blue})$ D. 1

Homework Exercises

For more exercises, see Extra Skills and Word Problems.

GO for Help

For Exercises	See Examples
7–12	1
13–21	2

You mix the letters A, C, Q, U, A, I, N, T, A, N, C, and E thoroughly. Without looking, you select one letter. Find the probability of each event as a fraction, a decimal, and a percent.

7. $P(T)$ 8. $P(A)$ 9. $P(\text{vowel})$

10. $P(\text{consonant})$ 11. $P(N)$ 12. $P(Q \text{ or } C)$

You spin the spinner once. Find each probability.

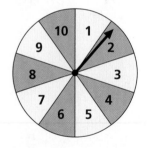

13. $P(12)$ 14. $P(2 \text{ or } 4)$

15. $P(\text{multiple of } 3)$ 16. $P(\text{even})$

17. $P(\text{not } 1)$ 18. $P(\text{not a factor of } 10)$

19. $P(\text{less than } 11)$ 20. $P(\text{not divisible by } 3)$

21. **Science** Six out of the 111 elements are noble gases. You write the names of all the elements on cards and select a card at random. What is the probability of *not* picking a noble gas?

GPS 22. **Guided Problem Solving** The table shows data about a group of people's hair colors. You select a person at random from the group. What is $P(\text{not black hair})$?
   • How many people are in the group?
   • How many people do *not* have black hair?

Hair Color

Color	Number
Blond	58
Brown	64
Black	97

GO Online
Homework Video Tutor
Visit: PHSchool.com
Web Code: are-1201

23. **Writing in Math** Describe a real-life situation where the probability of an event is 1. Then describe the complement of that situation.

You spin the spinner once. Find each probability.

24. P(not green) 25. P(purple or blue)

26. P(white) 27. P(not purple)

Government The U.S. House of Representatives has 435 members. Each member's name is put into a hat and one name is chosen at random. Find each probability as a decimal to the nearest hundredth.

28. P(Florida)

29. P(Texas)

30. P(not Illinois)

31. P(Pennsylvania)

U.S. House of Representatives

State	Number	State	Number
Florida	25	Illinois	19
Pennsylvania	19	Texas	32

SOURCE: U.S. Census Bureau. Go to **PHSchool.com** for a data update. Web Code arg-9041

32. **a.** Suppose $P(E) = 0.3$. Find P(not E).
   b. Suppose P(not E) = 65%. Find $P(E)$.

33. **Challenge** A bag contains an unknown number of marbles. You know that $P(\text{red}) = \frac{1}{4}$ and $P(\text{green}) = \frac{1}{4}$. What can you conclude about how many marbles are in the bag?

Test Prep and Mixed Review

Practice

Multiple Choice

34. The model represents the equation $3x + 5 = 14$. What is the value of x?

   Ⓐ $x = \frac{11}{5}$ Ⓒ $x = 3$

   Ⓑ $x = 6$ Ⓓ $x = \frac{19}{3}$

35. Suppose 2 out of every 25 people in your state are 10 to 14 years old. Which equation can be used to find x, the percent of people in your state who are 10 to 14 years old?

   Ⓕ $\frac{x}{100} = \frac{25}{2}$ Ⓖ $\frac{100}{x} = \frac{10}{14}$ Ⓗ $\frac{100}{25} = \frac{2}{x}$ Ⓙ $\frac{x}{100} = \frac{2}{25}$

36. Karl buys a pair of jeans that regularly costs $38. They are on sale for 25% off. Karl also buys a shirt that costs $23. The sales tax is 4.5%. What other information is necessary to find Karl's correct change?

   Ⓐ The sale price of the jeans
   Ⓑ The total cost of the purchase
   Ⓒ The amount he paid for the sales tax
   Ⓓ The amount he gave the cashier

GO for Help

For Exercises	See Lesson
37–39	9-8

Algebra Solve each equation for the variable in red.

37. $a = bc$ 38. $n = \frac{g + w}{4}$ 39. $q = 2t + 8$

Odds

The probability ratio compares favorable outcomes to all possible outcomes. When outcomes are equally likely, you can write ratios, called *odds*, that compare favorable outcomes to unfavorable outcomes.

Odds in favor of an event = the ratio of the number of favorable outcomes to the number of unfavorable outcomes

Odds against an event = the ratio of the number of unfavorable outcomes to the number of favorable outcomes

EXAMPLE **Finding Odds**

Coins Five quarters are shown below. Find the odds that a quarter you select at random shows at least one musical instrument.

odds in favor = 2 to 3 or 2 : 3   ← Two have an instrument. Three do not.

The odds that a quarter shows at least one musical instrument are 2 to 3 in favor.

Exercises

1. Refer to the example above. Find the odds that a quarter selected at random shows a race car.

You roll a number cube once. Find the odds in favor of each outcome.

2. rolling a 5

3. rolling a multiple of 3

4. rolling an odd number

5. You spin a spinner with equal sections lettered A–Z once. The spinner lands on the first letter of your name. Calculate the odds for and against this event.

Exploring Probability

If you toss one coin 100 times, you might expect to get heads and tails about the same number of times. What happens when you toss *two* coins 100 times?

EXAMPLE

Toss two coins 10 times. Record the results. Use the results to determine which event is most likely: two heads (HH), two tails (TT), or one head and one tail (HT).

The table below shows one set of results.

Toss	1	2	3	4	5	6	7	8	9	10
Result	HH	HT	HT	TT	HH	HT	TT	HT	HH	HT

In all, there are three outcomes of HH, two outcomes of TT, and five outcomes of HT. One head and one tail is the most likely event.

Exercises

1. Conduct an experiment in which you use two coins, such as a penny and a nickel. Place them in a small paper cup. Cover the top, and shake the cup before each coin toss. Toss both coins 100 times. Make a table to record each result.

2. Are your results similar to other students' results? Explain.

3. **Reasoning** Are the three outcomes all equally likely? Or is one outcome more likely to occur than the others? Explain.

Three students play the game at the right.

4. Is a game with these rules fair? Explain why or why not.

5. **Open-Ended** How might you change the rules to make the game fair?

6. Conduct an experiment to test your new game. Do you still think your game is fair? Explain.

GAME RULES

1. Player A receives 1 point if two heads (HH) are tossed.

2. Player B receives 1 point if two tails (TT) are tossed.

3. Player C receives 1 point if one head and one tail (HT) are tossed.

Check Skills You'll Need

1. **Vocabulary Review** Explain the difference between an *event* and an *outcome*.

You roll a number cube once. Find each probability.

2. *P*(4)

3. *P*(multiple of 2)

4. *P*(8)

for Help

Lesson 12-1

What You'll Learn

To find experimental probability and to use simulations

🔊 **New Vocabulary** experimental probability

Why Learn This?

Manufacturers collect data on the quality of their products. They use experimental probability to determine how many defective items they can expect to produce.

Probability based on experimental data or observations is called **experimental probability**.

KEY CONCEPTS **Experimental Probability**

$$P(\text{event}) = \frac{\text{number of times an event occurs}}{\text{total number of trials}}$$

GO Online

Video Tutor Help

Visit: PHSchool.com
Web Code: are-0775

EXAMPLE **Finding Experimental Probability**

1 You attempt 16 free throws in a basketball game. Your results are shown. What is the experimental probability of making a free throw?

Results of Free Throw Attempts

0 = miss			1 = make				
0	0	1	1	1	0	1	0
0	1	0	1	1	0	0	1

$P(\text{free throw}) = \dfrac{8}{16}$ ← number of throws made
← total number of attempted free throws

$= \dfrac{1}{2}$ ← Simplify.

The experimental probability of making a free throw is $\dfrac{1}{2}$.

✓ Quick Check

1. In 60 coin tosses, 25 are tails. Find the experimental probability.

EXAMPLE Application: Manufacturing

Test Prep Tip

You can write and solve a proportion using a probability ratio to make a prediction.

2 Multiple Choice A bicycle company checks a random sample of bikes. The results are shown. If the trend continues, which is the best prediction of the number of defective bikes in a batch of 1,300?

Quality Control Results	
Defective Bikes	Bikes Checked
12	400

Ⓐ 430 bikes   Ⓑ 390 bikes   Ⓒ 43 bikes   Ⓓ 39 bikes

The experimental probability that a bike is defective is $\frac{12}{400}$, or $\frac{3}{100}$.

Let x represent the predicted number of defective bikes.

defective bikes → $\dfrac{3}{100} = \dfrac{x}{1,300}$ ← defective bikes   ← **Write a proportion.**
bikes checked →   ← bikes checked

$3(1,300) = 100x$ ← **Write the cross products.**

$3,900 = 100x$ ← **Simplify.**

$\dfrac{3,900}{100} = \dfrac{100x}{100}$ ← **Divide each side by 100.**

$39 = x$ ← **Simplify.**

You can predict that 39 bikes are defective. The correct answer is D.

✓ Quick Check

2. Predict the number of defective bikes in a batch of 3,500.

You can simulate, or model, events to find experimental probabilities.

EXAMPLE Simulating an Event

3 Find the experimental probability that 2 of 3 children in a family are girls. Assume that girls and boys are equally likely.

Simulate the problem by tossing three coins. Let "heads" represent a girl and "tails" represent a boy. A sample of 20 coin tosses is shown.

T T H	T T T	(H T H)	H T T	(H T H)
T T H	(H H T)	H T T	T H T	H H H
(H H T)	T T H	(T H H)	(H T H)	T H T
T H T	T H T	T H T	H H H	H H H

$P(\text{two girls}) = \dfrac{6}{20}$, or $\dfrac{3}{10}$ ← number of times *two heads* occur
                        ← total number of tosses

The experimental probability that 2 of 3 children are girls is $\dfrac{3}{10}$.

✓ Quick Check

3. What is the experimental probability that 3 children are all boys?

1. **Vocabulary** What is the difference between theoretical probability and experimental probability? Explain.

You toss a coin 40 times and get 18 tails. Find each experimental probability.

2. $P(\text{heads}) = \dfrac{22}{\blacksquare}$

3. $P(\text{tails}) = \dfrac{\blacksquare}{40}$

4. **Mental Math** In a bird sanctuary, the experimental probability that any bird you see is a robin is about $\frac{1}{8}$. Suppose this trend continues. There are 48 birds. Predict the number of robins you see.

5. You want to find the probability that three out of five babies are boys. You decide to toss coins to simulate the problem. How many coins would you use? Explain.

Homework Exercises

For more exercises, see Extra Skills and Word Problems.

GO for Help

For Exercises	See Examples
6–8	1–2
9–12	3

Find each experimental probability.

6. tosses: 80; tails: 40; $P(\text{tails}) = $ ___?___

7. tosses: 250; heads: 180; $P(\text{heads}) = $ ___?___

8. **Manufacturing** The quality-control engineer of Top Notch Tool Company finds flaws in 8 of 60 wrenches examined. Predict the number of flawed wrenches in a batch of 2,400.

Baseball A baseball team averages one win to every one loss. Use a simulation to find each experimental probability for three games.

9. $P(\text{three wins})$

10. $P(\text{1 win and 2 losses})$

11. $P(\text{2 wins and 1 loss})$

12. $P(\text{three losses})$

13. **Guided Problem Solving** During hockey practice, Yuri blocked 19 out of 30 shots and Gene blocked 17 out of 24 shots. For the first game, the coach wants to choose the goalie with the greater probability of blocking a shot. Which player should he choose?
    • **Make a Plan** Find the experimental probability that each player will block the shot.

14. **a. Science** The probability that a male human is colorblind is 8%. Suppose you interview 1,000 males. About how many would you expect to be colorblind?
    b. Reasoning Will you always get the same number? Explain.

15. A company checks washers at four plants and records the number of defective washers. Find each experimental probability.

Plant	Number of Washers	Number Defective	P(Defective)
1	2,940	588	▨
2	1,860	93	▨
3	640	26	▨
4	3,048	54	▨

Data Analysis Use the data shown. Find each experimental probability.

16. P(Sunday)   **17.** P(Monday)

18. P(Tuesday)   **19.** P(Friday)

20. P(weekday)   **21.** P(weekend)

Students' Birthdays

```
X
X   X
X   X                       X
X   X   X       X           X
X   X   X   X   X   X   X
X   X   X   X   X   X   X
─────────────────────────
Su  M  Tu  W  Th  F  Sa
```

22. **Writing in Math** Describe a possible simulation to solve the following problem. You guess on six true-or-false questions. What is the probability that you guess exactly two answers correctly?

23. **Challenge** On any day, a company has x torn posters in stock. On Monday, the total number of torn posters is 252. Express $P(\text{torn})$ on Monday in terms of x. If $P(\text{torn}) = \frac{1}{42}$, what is x?

Test Prep and Mixed Review   **Practice**

Multiple Choice

24. The picture shows the number of colored shirts sold this week at Joan's Clothing Shop. If the trend continues, which is the best prediction of the number of orange shirts sold in one year?

Ⓐ 20   Ⓑ 130   Ⓒ 260   Ⓓ 1,362

25. The scale on a map of Texas is 1 in. : 31 mi. Which distance on the map should represent the 420 mi from Amarillo to El Paso?
Ⓕ 1.25 in.   Ⓖ 13.5 in.   Ⓗ 135 in.   Ⓙ 13,824 in.

GO for Help

For Exercises	See Lesson
26–29	12-1

You spin the spinner once. Find each probability.

26. P(purple)   **27.** P(blue)

28. P(blue or yellow)   **29.** P(not yellow)

Random Numbers

You can use a random number table to simulate some problems. To generate a random number table in a spreadsheet, follow these steps.

Step 1 Highlight the group of cells to use for your table.

Step 2 Select the Format Cells menu.

Step 3 Choose the category Custom and enter 0000. Click OK.

Step 4 Use the formula RAND()*10,000. This will make a group of 4 digits in each cell of a spreadsheet. (*Note:* Each time you generate a random number table, you will get a different group of digits.)

	A	B	C	D
1	2260	1927	7807	0912
2	8879	6235	5897	8068
3	8121	4646	8368	1613
4	0821	8911	3022	0307
5	9393	5403	4930	4898

EXAMPLE

A rare lily bulb has a 50% chance of growing. You plant four bulbs. What is the experimental probability that all four will grow?

Use the random number table. Let even digits represent *grows*, and let odd digits represent *does not grow*. Then a 4-digit number of all even digits represents the event *all four grow*. Of 20 groups, 3 consist entirely of even digits. So the experimental probability of four bulbs growing is $\frac{3}{20}$, or 15%.

2260 1927 7807 0912
8879 6235 5897 8068
8121 4646 8368 1613
0821 8911 3022 0307
9393 5403 4930 4898

← Any group of 4 even digits represents *all four grow.*

Exercises

Use the random number table above or generate your own.

1. Suppose there is a 30% probability of being stopped by a red light at each of four stoplights. What is the experimental probability of being stopped by at least two red lights? Let 0, 1, and 2 represent red lights.

2. **Reasoning** Suppose there is a 60% chance of a red light at each stoplight. How many digits would you use to represent getting a red light? Explain.

3. **Writing in Math** Write a probability problem you can solve using a random number table. Solve your problem.

Sample Spaces

What You'll Learn

To make and use sample spaces and to use the counting principle

🔊 **New Vocabulary** sample space, counting principle

Why Learn This?

When you are at a salad bar, you can choose from different vegetables, fruits, and dressings. You may want to know all the possible combinations of ingredients you can use.

The collection of all possible outcomes in an experiment is the **sample space.** You can use the sample space to find the probability of an event.

EXAMPLE **Finding a Sample Space**

1 **a.** Make a table to find the sample space for rolling two number cubes colored red and blue. Write the outcomes as ordered pairs.

	1	2	3	4	5	6
1	(1, 1)	(2, 1)	(3, 1)	(4, 1)	(5, 1)	(6, 1)
2	(1, 2)	(2, 2)	(3, 2)	(4, 2)	(5, 2)	(6, 2)
3	(1, 3)	(2, 3)	(3, 3)	(4, 3)	(5, 3)	(6, 3)
4	(1, 4)	(2, 4)	(3, 4)	(4, 4)	(5, 4)	(6, 4)
5	(1, 5)	(2, 5)	(3, 5)	(4, 5)	(5, 5)	(6, 5)
6	(1, 6)	(2, 6)	(3, 6)	(4, 6)	(5, 6)	(6, 6)

← There are 36 possible outcomes.

b. Find the probability of rolling at least one 3.

There are 11 outcomes with at least one 3. There are 36 possible outcomes. So the probability of rolling at least one 3 is $\frac{11}{36}$.

✓ Quick Check

1. Give the sample space for tossing two coins. Find the probability of getting two heads.

You can also show a sample space by using a tree diagram. Each branch of the tree represents one choice.

 **Using a Tree Diagram**

2 **River Travel** Suppose you are going to travel on a river. You have two choices of boats—a kayak or a rowboat. You can go upstream on three smaller streams, to the north, northwest, and northeast.

a. What is the sample space for your journey?

Make a tree diagram for the possible outcomes.

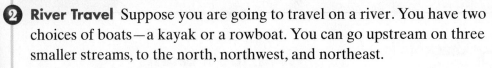

Boat	Stream	Outcome
	North	Kayak, North
Kayak	Northwest	Kayak, Northwest
	Northeast	Kayak, Northeast
	North	Rowboat, North
Rowboat	Northwest	Rowboat, Northwest
	Northeast	Rowboat, Northeast

← There are six possible outcomes.

b. Suppose you select a trip at random. What is the probability of selecting a kayak and going directly north?

There is one favorable outcome (kayak, north) out of six possible outcomes. The probability is $\frac{1}{6}$.

Quick Check

2. a. Suppose a canoe is added as another choice of boats in Example 2. Draw a tree diagram to show the sample space.

b. Find the probability of selecting a canoe at random for the trip.

In Example 2 above, there are 2 choices of boats and 3 choices of direction. There are 2×3, or 6, total possible choices. This suggests a simple way to find the number of outcomes—using the **counting principle.**

KEY CONCEPTS **The Counting Principle**

Suppose there are m ways of making one choice and n ways of making a second choice. Then there are $m \times n$ ways to make the first choice followed by the second choice.

Example

If you can choose a shirt in 5 sizes and 7 colors, then you can choose among 5×7, or 35, shirts.

EXAMPLE **Using the Counting Principle**

3 **Gridded Response** How many different sandwiches can you order when you choose one bread and one meat from the menu?

Use the counting principle.

Bread		Meat
number of choices	×	number of choices
5	×	6	=	30

There are 30 different sandwiches available.

✓ **Quick Check**

3. A manager at the Deli Counter decides to add chicken to the list of meat choices. How many different sandwiches are now available?

✓ Check Your Understanding

1. **Vocabulary** What is a sample space?

2. Complete the tree diagram for tossing a coin three times.

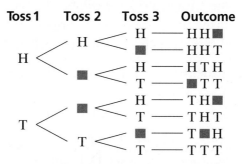

Use your completed diagram from Exercise 2 to find each probability.

3. $P(\text{HHH}) = \dfrac{\blacksquare}{8}$

4. $P(\text{TTT}) = \dfrac{1}{\blacksquare}$

5. $P(\text{at least one H}) = \dfrac{\blacksquare}{8}$

6. $P(\text{exactly 2 T's}) = \dfrac{\blacksquare}{8}$

7. If you toss 4 coins, how many possible outcomes are there?

8. Find the number of different couches that you can make using 16 different fabrics and 8 patterns.

9. **Multiple Choice** An architect has 3 different widths he can use for a rectangular building design. He also has 4 different lengths to use for the design. How many different designs are possible?

Ⓐ 3 　　　Ⓑ 4 　　　Ⓒ 7 　　　Ⓓ 12

For more exercises, see Extra Skills and Word Problems.

GO for Help

For Exercises	See Examples
10–12	1
13–14	2
15–16	3

Make a table to show the sample space for each situation and find the number of outcomes. Then find the probability.

10. You toss two coins. What is the probability of getting one tail and one head?

11. You roll a number cube once. What is the probability of rolling a number less than 4?

12. You toss a coin and spin a spinner. The spinner has four equal sections that are numbered from 1 to 4. Find the probability of getting tails and spinning a 4.

Make a tree diagram. Then find the probability of each event.

13. A spinner is half red and half blue. If you spin the spinner twice, what is the probability that you will get red both times?

14. You choose at random from the letters A, B, C, and D, and you roll a number cube once. What are the chances you get A and 5?

Use the counting principle.

15. Cooking You make a recipe with herbs and spices for a party. You have four herbs—basil, bay leaves, chives, and dill. You also have three spices—paprika, pepper, and garlic powder. How many different recipes with one herb and one spice can you make?

16. Education A school has four art teachers, three music teachers, and eight history teachers. In how many ways can a student be assigned an art teacher, a music teacher, and a history teacher?

17. Guided Problem Solving A traveler chooses one city tour at random from buses D, E, and F. He then chooses one harbor tour at random from boats 1, 2, and 3. What is the probability that he takes tours with bus D and boat 2?
- Draw a diagram of all the possible outcomes.
- How many outcomes include tours with bus D and boat 2?

A spinner has four equal sections numbered 1 through 4. You spin it twice. Use the sample space below to find each probability.

18. $P(1, 2)$

19. $P(1, \text{odd})$

20. $P(\text{even}, \text{odd})$

GO Online

Homework Video Tutor
Visit: PHSchool.com
Web Code: are-1203

		Second Spin			
		1	**2**	**3**	**4**
First Spin	**1**	(1, 1)	(1, 2)	(1, 3)	(1, 4)
	2	(2, 1)	(2, 2)	(2, 3)	(2, 4)
	3	(3, 1)	(3, 2)	(3, 3)	(3, 4)
	4	(4, 1)	(4, 2)	(4, 3)	(4, 4)

Find the number of outcomes for each situation.

21. Pick one of 7 boys and one of 12 girls.

22. Toss five coins once each.

23. a. **Clothes** Ardell has four suit jackets (white, blue, green, and tan) and four dress shirts in the same colors. How many different jacket-and-shirt outfits does Ardell have?
    b. Suppose he grabs a suit jacket and a dress shirt without looking. What is the probability that they will *not* be the same color?

24. <u>**Writing in Math**</u> Explain how to use the counting principle to find the number of outcomes in a sample space.

Use the menu for Exercises 25–28.

25. List all the possible drink orders.

26. You order lemonade and popcorn. Draw a tree diagram to show the sample space.

27. **Reasoning** A manager uses the counting principle to find P(small popcorn, medium lemonade) $= \frac{1}{24}$. Do you agree? Explain.

28. **Challenge** Find the probability that you randomly select the same size popcorn and drink.

CITY CINEMA

POPCORN
small $3.00
medium . .$4.00
large $5.00

FRUIT PUNCH or LEMONADE
small $2.75
medium . .$3.00
large $3.25
jumbo . . . $3.75

Careers Tailors fit designer clothes for important events.

Test Prep and Mixed Review   **Practice**

Gridded Response

29. The data in the stem-and-leaf plot at the right show the lengths of principal rivers in Africa. What is the median length, in miles, of the rivers?

30. Suppose $\frac{21}{25}$ of your classmates can attend your birthday party. What is this fraction expressed as a decimal?

African River Lengths (hundreds of miles)
0 | 6 7 7
1 | 0 0 0 1 2 3 7
2 | 6 7
4 | 1
Key: 2 | 6 means 2,600 miles

31. Trista has purple, yellow, and red wrapping paper. She can use blue or white ribbon. She has four shapes of gift tags. In how many different ways can she choose one wrapping paper, one ribbon, and one gift tag?

32. A hockey player makes 3 goals out of 9 shots in a game. What is the experimental probability that he does not make a goal?

For Exercise	See Lesson
32	12-2

12-3b Activity Lab

Data Analysis

Using Data to Predict

Katie and Tim play the following game to decide who should mow the lawn each week.

• Katie or Tim places three black marbles and three white marbles into a bag.

• Tim pulls out two marbles.

• If the marbles match, Katie mows the lawn. Otherwise, Tim mows the lawn.

The table below shows the results of the first 15 trials.

Marble Selection Results

Event	Number of Times
Marbles matched	6
No match	9

ACTIVITY

1. **Estimation** Use the data from the table above. Assume the data trend continues. For Katie and Tim, estimate the number of times that each one mows the lawn in 45 trials.

2. **Data Collection** Simulate the game with three red cubes and three yellow cubes. Put the cubes in a bag. Select two cubes at random. Record whether or not they match. Return the cubes to the bag, and repeat until you have recorded 45 trials.

3. **Reasoning** Describe how the results of your experiment compare to your predictions. Is the game fair? Explain.

4. Tim thinks the probability that the marbles match equals the probability that they do not match. Use diagrams and what you have learned to show why the probabilities are not equal. Find the probability that the two marbles match and the probability that they do not match.

5. Add a fourth cube of each color into the bag. Find the probability of selecting two cubes that match. Predict the number of matches in 49 trials.

6. **Data Analysis** Test your prediction. Record the results of 49 trials. Compare your results to your prediction. Is this game more fair or less fair than the original game? Explain.

You spin the spinner at the right once. Write each probability as a fraction, a decimal, and a percent.

1. $P(2 \text{ or } 3)$ **2.** $P(\text{even})$ **3.** $P(\text{not } 4)$ **4.** $P(\text{not even})$

You spin the spinner twice.

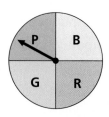

5. Give the sample space.

6. Find $P(\text{green, then green})$

7. Find $P(\text{purple, then blue})$

8. Forestry The table shows a sample of the number of spruce trees counted in a forest area. Find the experimental probability of selecting a Serbian spruce.

9. A true-or-false quiz has five questions. Use a simulation or a sample space to find the probability of guessing at random and getting exactly three correct answers.

Spruce Trees

Tree Type	Number
Norway spruce	32
Serbian spruce	20
Colorado spruce	67

12-4a   Activity Lab

Exploring Multiple Events

You want to make a necklace using two colors of beads. You decide which colors to use by selecting from the beads at the right. You select the first bead at random. You put the bead back and make another selection at random.

1. Give the sample space for the colors of the two beads. Write the outcomes as ordered pairs.

2. What is the probability of selecting a red bead first?

3. What is the probability of selecting red beads twice?

4. Suppose you now select a red bead and do not replace it. How many beads of each color are left?

5. Reasoning Does the probability of selecting a red bead second depend on whether you replace the first red bead? Explain.

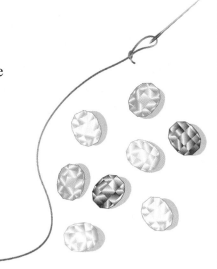

Compound Events

✓ Check Skills You'll Need

1. **Vocabulary Review** Describe multiplying fractions using the terms *denominator* and *numerator*.

Find each product.

2. $\frac{3}{4} \cdot \frac{3}{4}$ 3. $\frac{3}{5} \cdot \frac{2}{5}$

4. $\frac{1}{5} \cdot \frac{1}{4}$ 5. $\frac{3}{7} \cdot \frac{2}{7}$

GO for Help
Lesson 3-4

What You'll Learn

To find the probability of independent and dependent events

🔊 **New Vocabulary** compound event, independent events, dependent events

Why Learn This?

You can find the probability of more than one event, such as winning a game twice.

A **compound event** consists of two or more events. Two events are **independent events** if the occurrence of one event does not affect the probability of the occurrence of the other.

KEY CONCEPTS   **Probability of Independent Events**

If A and B are independent events, then $P(A, \text{then } B) = P(A) \times P(B)$.

EXAMPLE   **Probability of Independent Events**

1 **Multiple Choice** You and a friend play a game twice. What is the probability that you win both games? Assume $P(\text{win})$ is $\frac{1}{2}$.

  Ⓐ $\frac{1}{2}$ Ⓑ $\frac{4}{9}$ Ⓒ $\frac{1}{4}$ Ⓓ $\frac{1}{8}$

$$
\begin{aligned}
P(\text{win, then win}) &= P(\text{win}) \times P(\text{win}) &&\leftarrow \text{Winning is the first and second event.} \\
&= \frac{1}{2} \times \frac{1}{2} &&\leftarrow \text{Substitute } \tfrac{1}{2} \text{ for } P(\text{win}). \\
&= \frac{1}{4} &&\leftarrow \text{Multiply.}
\end{aligned}
$$

The probability of winning both games is $\frac{1}{4}$. The correct answer is C.

✓ Quick Check

● **1.** Find $P(\text{win, then lose})$.

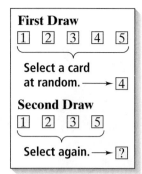

First Draw

⌈1⌉ ⌈2⌉ ⌈3⌉ ⌈4⌉ ⌈5⌉

Select a card
at random. ⟶ ⌈4⌉

Second Draw

⌈1⌉ ⌈2⌉ ⌈3⌉ ⌈5⌉

Select again. ⟶ ⌈?⌉

Suppose you play a game with cards numbered 1–5. You draw two cards at random. You draw the first card and do not replace it. The probability in the second draw depends on the result of the first draw.

Two events are **dependent events** if the occurrence of one event affects the probability of the occurrence of the other event.

> **KEY CONCEPTS** **Probability of Dependent Events**
>
> If event B depends on event A, then
> $P(A, \text{then } B) = P(A) \times P(B \text{ after } A)$.

EXAMPLES **Probability of Dependent Events**

2 You select a card at random from those below. The card has the letter M. Without replacing the M card, you select a second card. Find the probability that you select a card with the letter A after you select M.

⌈M⌉⌈A⌉⌈T⌉⌈H⌉⌈E⌉⌈M⌉⌈A⌉⌈T⌉⌈I⌉⌈C⌉⌈S⌉

There are 10 cards remaining after you select an M card.

$P(A) = \dfrac{2}{10}$ ← **number of cards with the letter A**
  ← **number of cards remaining**

$= \dfrac{1}{5}$ ← **Simplify.**

The probability of selecting an A for the second card is $\frac{1}{5}$.

3 You select a card from a bucket that contains 26 cards lettered A–Z without looking. Without replacing the first card, you select a second one. Find the probability of choosing C and then M.

The events are dependent. After the first selection, 25 letters remain.

$P(C, \text{then } M) = P(C) \times P(M \text{ after } C)$ ← **Use the formula for dependent events.**

$= \dfrac{1}{26} \times \dfrac{1}{25}$ ← **Substitute.**

$= \dfrac{1}{650}$ ← **Multiply.**

The probability of choosing C and then M is $\frac{1}{650}$.

Online
active math

For: Probability Activity
Use: Interactive
  Textbook, 12-4

✓ Quick Check

2. Use the cards in Example 2. You select a T card at random. Without replacing the T card, you select a second card. Find $P(S)$.

3. Suppose another 26 cards lettered A–Z are put in the bucket in Example 3. Find $P(J, \text{then } J)$.

● More Than One Way

You toss a coin three times. What is the probability of getting three heads?

Brianna's Method

Each toss of a coin is an independent event. The probability of getting heads for one coin toss is $\frac{1}{2}$. I can multiply the probabilities of the three coin tosses.

$P(\text{three heads}) = \frac{1}{2} \times \frac{1}{2} \times \frac{1}{2} = \frac{1}{8}$

The probability of three heads is $\frac{1}{8}$.

Chris's Method

I can make a tree diagram for the coin tosses. A favorable outcome is one with 3 heads.

The tree diagram shows 1 favorable outcome out of 8 possible outcomes. The probability of three heads is $\frac{1}{8}$.

Toss 1	Toss 2	Toss 3	Outcome
H	H	H	H H H
		T	H H T
	T	H	H T H
		T	H T T
T	H	H	T H H
		T	T H T
	T	H	T T H
		T	T T T

Choose a Method

You toss a coin four times. What is the probability of getting tails all four times? Describe your method and explain why you chose it.

✓ Check Your Understanding

1. **Vocabulary** How do independent and dependent events differ?

2. **Multiple Choice** Two independent events A and B both have a probability of $\frac{1}{3}$. Which expression represents $P(A, \text{then } B)$?

   Ⓐ $\frac{1}{3} + \frac{1}{3}$ Ⓑ $\frac{1}{3} \times \frac{1}{3}$ Ⓒ $\frac{1}{3} + \frac{1}{2}$ Ⓓ $\frac{1}{3} \times \frac{1}{2}$

Are the two events *independent* or *dependent*?

3. You toss a nickel. Then you toss a dime.

4. You select a card. Then you select again without replacement.

For more exercises, see Extra Skills and Word Problems.

GO for Help

For Exercises	See Examples
5–10	1
11–19	2
20–22	3

You roll a number cube twice. Find each probability.

5. $P(1, \text{then } 2)$

6. $P(3, \text{then even})$

7. $P(\text{less than } 4, \text{then } 1)$

8. $P(\text{odd, then even})$

9. $P(\text{divisible by } 2, \text{then } 5)$

10. $P(\text{greater than } 2, \text{then odd})$

An arrangement of 8 students is shown below. The numbers of all the students are in a basket. The teacher selects a number and replaces it. Then the teacher selects a second number. Find each probability.

11. $P(\text{student 1, then student 8})$

12. $P(\text{student in row A, then student in row B})$

13. $P(\text{student in row A, then student 6, 7, or 8})$

Row	Student			
A	1	2	3	4
B	5	6	7	8

You select the letter A from the group. Without replacing the A, you select a second letter. Find each probability.

14. $P(Z)$

15. $P(\text{vowel})$

16. $P(\text{red})$

17. $P(\text{blue})$

18. $P(\text{consonant})$

19. $P(\text{not } K)$

A box contains 20 cards numbered 1–20. You select a card. Without replacing the first card, you select a second card. Find each probability.

20. $P(1, \text{then } 20)$ **21.** $P(3, \text{then even})$ **22.** $P(\text{even, then } 7)$

23. Guided Problem Solving Five girls and seven boys want to be the two broadcasters for a school show. To be fair, a teacher puts their names in a hat and selects two. Find $P(\text{girl, then boy})$.

- **Make a Plan** The selections of the two names are (dependent, independent) events. Find the probability of selecting a girl first. Then find the probability of selecting a boy after selecting a girl.
- **Carry Out the Plan** $P(\text{girl first}) = \frac{5}{\square}$; $P(\text{boy after girl}) = \frac{7}{\square}$

Two coins are dropped at random into the boxes in the diagram below.

24. What is the theoretical probability that both coins fall into a shaded box?

25. In 50 trials, both coins land in a shaded box twice. What is the experimental probability that both coins fall into a shaded box?

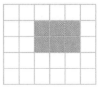

26. Events with no outcomes in common are called *disjoint events* or *mutually exclusive events*. To find the probability of mutually exclusive events, add the probabilities of the individual events. Suppose you select a number from 21 to 30 at random. What is the probability of selecting a number that is even or prime?

Choose a Method A bag contains 3 blue marbles, 4 red marbles, and 2 white marbles. Three times you draw a marble and return it. Find each probability.

27. P(red, then white, then blue)   28. P(all white)

29. **Reasoning** Events are complementary if they cover all possibilities with no overlap. Are the following sets of events *complementary, mutually exclusive,* or *neither?* Explain.
   a. A traffic light shows red, yellow, or green or is broken.
   b. A student receives an A, B, or C on a test.

30. **Writing in Math** When you select marbles without replacing them, are the events *independent* or *dependent?* Explain.

31. **Challenge** You have two spinners with colors on them. The probability of spinning green on both spinners is $\frac{5}{21}$. The probability of spinning green on the first one alone is $\frac{1}{3}$. What is the probability of spinning green on the second spinner alone?

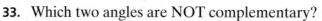
Test Prep and Mixed Review   **Practice**

Multiple Choice

32. Dominica rolls a number cube once and spins the spinner at the right once. Which choice shows all the possible outcomes when she rolls an odd number and spins an odd number?
   Ⓐ $(1, 1), (1, 3), (3, 1), (3, 3), (5, 1)$
   Ⓑ $(1, 1), (2, 2), (3, 3), (4, 3), (5, 3), (6, 3)$
   Ⓒ $(1, 1), (1, 3), (3, 1), (3, 3), (5, 1), (5, 3)$
   Ⓓ $(1, 1), (3, 3), (5, 5)$

33. Which two angles are NOT complementary?
   Ⓕ 1°, 89°   Ⓖ 33°, 57°   Ⓗ 22°, 68°   Ⓙ 42°, 56°

34. William worked $2\frac{3}{4}$ hours on Saturday and $3\frac{3}{4}$ hours on Sunday. On Monday, he worked half as many hours as he did on Saturday and Sunday combined. How many hours did he work Monday?
   Ⓐ $1\frac{3}{8}$ hours   Ⓑ $1\frac{7}{8}$ hours   Ⓒ $3\frac{1}{4}$ hours   Ⓓ $6\frac{1}{2}$ hours

35. Make a table to show the sample space for one spin of a spinner with equal sections numbered from 1 to 3 and one toss of a coin.

GO for Help

For Exercise	See Lesson
35	12-3

Vocabulary Builder

High-Use Academic Words

High-use academic words are words that you will see often in textbooks and on tests. These words are not math vocabulary terms, but knowing them will help you succeed in mathematics.

Direction Words

Some words tell what to do in a problem. I need to understand what these words are asking so that I give the correct answer.

Word	Meaning
Analyze	To examine in detail to determine relationships
List	To present information in some order or to give examples
Persuade	To cause someone to do or believe something, especially by reasoning

Exercises

Match each situation with the correct word.

1. You do a survey in which you write the types of cereal people prefer and the number of times people choose each type of cereal.

2. You convince the manager of a diner to serve a certain type of cereal based on a survey.

3. You determine the cereal preferences of people based on a survey.

A. analyze
B. list
C. persuade

4. List all the possible outcomes of flipping a coin and rolling a number cube. Then find the probability that an outcome is heads and even.

5. Analyze the data at the right. How would you use the data to persuade a disc jockey to play hip-hop music? Explain.

6. **Word Knowledge** Think about the word *outcome*.
   a. Choose the letter for how well you know the word.
      A. I know its meaning.
      B. I've seen it, but I don't know its meaning.
      C. I don't know it.
   b. **Research** Look up and write the definition of *outcome*.
   c. Use the word in a sentence involving mathematics.

Music Preference Survey

Type of Music	Frequency
Hip-hop	~~IIII~~ ~~IIII~~ ~~IIII~~
House	III
Country	IIII
Rock	~~IIII~~ IIII

Practice With Probability

Members of a math club solve problems worth 1 to 4 points. Then the club has a drawing for three prizes based on the number of points members have earned.

Each student's name is put in a hat once for every point he or she earns. A student can win only one prize. Based on the table below, what are the chances that Anna wins first prize, Cole wins second prize, and Dillon wins third prize?

Points Earned

Name	Frequency	Name	Frequency
Anna	𝍸𝍸 𝍸𝍸 𝍸𝍸 𝍸𝍸 𝍸𝍸 𝍸𝍸 𝍸𝍸 𝍸𝍸 𝍸𝍸 𝍸𝍸 𝍸𝍸 𝍸𝍸	Cole	𝍸𝍸 𝍸𝍸 𝍸𝍸 𝍸𝍸 𝍸𝍸 𝍸𝍸 𝍸𝍸 𝍸𝍸 𝍸𝍸 𝍸𝍸 I
Dillon	𝍸𝍸 𝍸𝍸 𝍸𝍸 𝍸𝍸 𝍸𝍸 𝍸𝍸 𝍸𝍸 𝍸𝍸 𝍸𝍸 𝍸𝍸 III	Raja	𝍸𝍸 𝍸𝍸 𝍸𝍸 𝍸𝍸 𝍸𝍸 𝍸𝍸 𝍸𝍸 𝍸𝍸 𝍸𝍸 II
Bailcy	𝍸𝍸 𝍸𝍸 𝍸𝍸 𝍸𝍸 𝍸𝍸 𝍸𝍸 𝍸𝍸 I	Rosa	𝍸𝍸 𝍸𝍸 𝍸𝍸 𝍸𝍸 𝍸𝍸 𝍸𝍸 𝍸𝍸 𝍸𝍸 𝍸𝍸 𝍸𝍸 III

What You Might Think

What do I know? What do I want to find out?

How can I solve the problem?

What is the answer?

What You Might Write

I know each person's number of points. I want to know the chances that Anna wins first, Cole wins second, and Dillon wins third.

Anna's chances are $\frac{60}{300}$. After Anna wins first prize, she cannot win again. So Cole's chances are $\frac{51}{240}$. Then Dillon's chances are $\frac{53}{189}$.

The chances of the three winning in that order are $\frac{60}{300} \times \frac{51}{240} \times \frac{53}{189}$. This is about 0.01, or 1%.

Think It Through

1. Why are Anna's chances $\frac{60}{300}$? Why are Cole's chances $\frac{51}{240}$ if Anna wins first? Why are Dillon's chances $\frac{53}{189}$ if Cole wins second?

2. How can you use a calculator to verify $\frac{60}{300} \times \frac{51}{240} \times \frac{53}{189} \approx 0.01$?

Exercises

Solve each problem. For Exercise 3, answer the questions first.

3. Fran's chances of making free throws in basketball are 80% based on her performance this season. If the trend continues, what are the chances she will make both of her next two free throws?
   a. What do you know? What do you want to find out?
   b. How can you solve the problem? Explain.

4. You play the card game In Between with the following rules.
   • Use 30 cards numbered 1–30.
   • You turn over two cards at random.
   • You win if the next card turned over is between the two cards.

   For the cards displayed at the right, what is the probability you will win?

5. Janice agrees to work for her neighbor for a year. In return, her neighbor will pay her $480 and give her a car. Janice has to stop working after 9 months. Since she does not work the full year, she gets only $60 and the car. How much is the car worth?

6. George participates in a 3-mile walk for hunger. He averages 6 miles per hour for the first mile, 5 miles per hour for the next mile, and 4 miles per hour for the last mile. How long does it take him to walk the 3 miles?

7. Students study the advantages and disadvantages of year-round schools (YRS). They then express their opinions in a poll. A "0" means the student is strongly against YRS. A "10" means the student is strongly for YRS.

   YRS Survey Results

   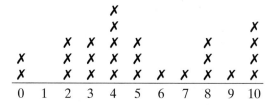

   The line plot shows the data collected. Find the mean, median, and mode of the data. Which measure best represents how the students feel about YRS? Explain.

✓ Check Skills You'll Need

1. Vocabulary Review
What is a *product*?

Find each product.

2. $10 \cdot 9$

3. $20 \cdot 19$

4. $8 \cdot 7 \cdot 6$

5. $10 \cdot 9 \cdot 8$

6. $5 \cdot 4 \cdot 3$

GO for Help
Lesson 1-8

What You'll Learn

To find permutations

◀)) **New Vocabulary** permutation, factorial

Why Learn This?

Sometimes the order of the outcomes is important, such as the order of letters in words.

A **permutation** is an arrangement of items in a particular order. Suppose you arrange the four letters O, P, S, and T in two ways. The permutation STOP is different from the permutation POTS because the order of the letters is different.

EXAMPLE   Finding Permutations

① Find the number of permutations of the letters L, I, K, and E. The first letter can be any of the four letters. You have three choices for the second, two for the third, and one for the fourth letter.

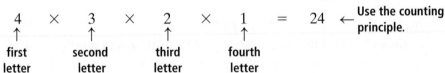

$$4 \quad \times \quad 3 \quad \times \quad 2 \quad \times \quad 1 \quad = \quad 24 \quad \leftarrow \begin{array}{l}\textbf{Use the counting} \\ \textbf{principle.}\end{array}$$

first letter   second letter   third letter   fourth letter

There are 24 different permutations.

✓ Quick Check

1. Find the number of permutations of the letters H, A, N, D, L, and E.

There are $4 \times 3 \times 2 \times 1$ permutations of the letters C, A, R, and E. The product of all positive integers less than or equal to a number is the **factorial** for that number. You write 4 factorial as 4!.

$$4! = 4 \times 3 \times 2 \times 1$$

⬤nline active math

For: Permutations Activity
Use: Interactive Textbook, 12-5

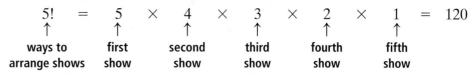 **EXAMPLE** Finding Permutations Using Factorials

② **Television** A TV station has five shows to broadcast on a weeknight. How many different arrangements of the shows can they make?

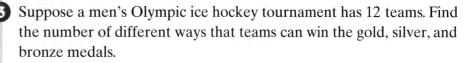

5!	=	5	×	4	×	3	×	2	×	1	=	120
↑		↑		↑		↑		↑		↑		
ways to arrange shows		first show		second show		third show		fourth show		fifth show		

Calculator Tip

To evaluate 5!, press 5 **MATH**. Scroll right to option PRB. Select option 5—"!". Press **ENTER**.

The station can make 120 different arrangements of the shows.

✓ Quick Check

2. Write the number of permutations for the letters G, R, A, V, I, E, and S in factorial form. Then multiply.

The sample space below shows the two-letter permutations of the 4 letters in STOP. There are 4 possible choices for the first letter and 3 possible choices for the second letter. The number of permutations is 4 × 3 = 12.

ST	OP	TP	TS	PO	PT
TO	PS	OS	OT	SP	SO

EXAMPLE Application: Olympics

③ Suppose a men's Olympic ice hockey tournament has 12 teams. Find the number of different ways that teams can win the gold, silver, and bronze medals.

There are 12 possible teams that can win the gold medal. After that, there are 11 teams that can win the silver medal. Finally, there are 10 teams that can win the bronze medal.

12	×	11	×	10	=	1,320	← Use the counting principle.
↑		↑		↑			
gold medal		silver medal		bronze medal			

There are 1,320 different ways that teams can win the three medals.

✓ Quick Check

3. a. Women's Olympic ice hockey tournaments have eight teams. Find the number of different ways that teams can win the gold, silver, and bronze medals.

  b. Reasoning In Example 3, the number is not found by finding 12!. Explain why.

1. **Vocabulary** What is a permutation?

2. **Multiple Choice** How many permutations are there of the words *star*, *square*, and *triangle?*

   Ⓐ 1   Ⓑ 3   Ⓒ 6   Ⓓ 9

Match each set of digits to the correct number of permutations.

3. even digits 2 through 8   **A.** 120

4. odd digits 1 through 9   **B.** 24
   C. 362,880
5. all digits 1 through 9

6. **Reasoning** Does 3! + 2! = 5!? Justify your answer.

For more exercises, see Extra Skills and Word Problems.

GO for Help

For Exercises	See Examples
7–12	1
13–19	2
20–25	3

Find the number of permutations of each group of letters.

7. W, O, R, L, D   8. H, U, M, A, N   9. T, O, Y

10. P, I, C, K, L, E   11. L, U, N, C, H, E, S   12. M, A, R, S

Write the number of permutations in factorial form. Then simplify.

13. C, A, T   14. R, A, T, E, S   15. P, A, C, K

16. D, E, P, A, R, T   17. I, N, C, L, U, D, E   18. L, U, C, K, Y

19. **Planning** You plan to shop, call a friend, study, and exercise, all in one day. How many arrangements of activities can you plan?

Find the number of two-letter permutations of the letters.

20. R, E, P, S   21. Q, I, E, R, T, Y, U   22. G, D, X, Z, C

23. A, E, I, O, U, Y   24. M, A, P, L, E   25. L, A, P

26. **Guided Problem Solving** Two sisters and a brother line up for movie tickets. Find the probability that they line up boy-girl-girl.
    - **Make a Plan** Make a sample space. Remember, each sister counts separately, so use B, G, and g for the three siblings. Use the sample space to find the probability.
    - **Carry Out the Plan** Write a ratio to find probability.

Find the value of each factorial expression.

27. 4!   28. 6!   29. 7!   30. 8!   31. 10!

32. The password to access a computer consists of 3 lower-case letters. You do not have the password. What is the greatest number of passwords you can try before you have access?

33. **Writing in Math** Describe two different ways you can use a calculator to find the value of 6!.

34. **Tourism** The owner of a tour boat business has 15 employees. There are three different jobs—driving the boat, checking the boat for safety, and managing the money. In how many different ways can the jobs be assigned to three different people?

Find the value of each expression.

35. $5! \div 2!$ **36.** $4! \div 3!$ **37.** $6! \div 4!$ **38.** $7! \div 3!$

39. **Soccer** The team names and uniform colors for a soccer league are shown.
  a. Show the sample space of the different name-color possibilities.
  b. Use the counting principle to support your answer to part (a).

Team Name	Uniform Color
Scorers	Blue
Defenders	Green
Passers	Red

40. **Challenge** Write an algebraic expression to show how many two-letter permutations are possible with $(n - 2)$ different letters.

Test Prep and Mixed Review

Practice

Multiple Choice

41. You can play one sport and join one music group. The sports are football, soccer, and tennis. The groups play rock or hip-hop. Which list shows all possible arrangements of a sport and a music group?
  Ⓐ (football, rock), (football, hip-hop), (soccer, rock), (soccer, hip-hop), (tennis, rock), (tennis, hip-hop)
  Ⓑ (football, rock), (football, soccer), (football, tennis), (soccer, rock), (tennis, hip-hop)
  Ⓒ (football, rock), (soccer, rock), (tennis, rock)
  Ⓓ (football, rock), (football, hip-hop), (soccer, tennis), (tennis, rock), (tennis, hip-hop)

42. A Fahrenheit temperature is 32° more than $\frac{9}{5}$ of a Celsius temperature C. Which algebraic expression represents the Fahrenheit temperature for a given Celsius temperature?
  Ⓕ $32 + \frac{9}{5}$ Ⓖ $\frac{9}{5}C + 32$ Ⓗ $(32)\frac{9}{5} + C$ Ⓙ $\frac{9}{5}C - 32$

GO for Help

For Exercises	See Lesson
43–45	12-4

You have a set of 16 cards numbered 1–16. You select a card and put it back into the set. Then you select another card. Find each probability.

43. $P(2, \text{ then } 6)$ **44.** $P(\text{even, then odd})$ **45.** $P(16, \text{ then odd})$

Check Skills You'll Need

1. **Vocabulary Review** Explain why CAT and ACT are not the same *permutations*.

Find the number of permutations of each group of letters.

2. G, I, R, L

3. H, I, K, E, R, S

for Help
Lesson 12-5

What You'll Learn

To find combinations

◀)) **New Vocabulary** combination

Why Learn This?

Sometimes the order of objects does not matter. You may only care about the combination of objects.

Whether you pack your hat before your scarf, or your scarf before your hat, you have still packed the two items. A **combination** is a grouping of objects in which the order of the objects does not matter.

Vocabulary Tip

Combination comes from a Latin word that means "together."

EXAMPLE **Application: Clothing**

1 The colors of four scarves are listed. You decide to pack two scarves. How many different combinations of two scarves are possible?

Color	Letter
Blue	b
Yellow	y
Green	g
Red	r

Step 1 Let letters represent the scarves. Make a list of all the possible permutations.

(b, y) (y, b) (g, b) (r, b) (b, g) (y, g)

(g, y) (r, y) (b, r) (y, r) (g, r) (r, g)

Step 2 Cross out any group containing the same letters as another group.

(b, y) (y, b) (g, b) (r, b) (b, g) (y, g)

(g, y) (r, y) (b, r) (y, r) (g, r) (r, g)

Six different combinations of two colors are possible.

Quick Check

1. How many different combinations of two seashells can you make from three seashells?

For help with permutations, go to Lesson 12-5, Example 1.

In Example 1, the total number of permutations for four scarves taken two at a time is 4 × 3. The number of permutations of the smaller group, two scarves, is 2 × 1. You can find the number of combinations by dividing the total number of permutations by the number of permutations for the smaller group.

$$\text{combinations} = \frac{\text{total number of permutations}}{\text{number of permutations of smaller group}} = \frac{4 \times 3}{2 \times 1} = 6$$

EXAMPLE Application: Careers

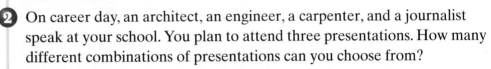

2 On career day, an architect, an engineer, a carpenter, and a journalist speak at your school. You plan to attend three presentations. How many different combinations of presentations can you choose from?

Step 1 Find the total number of permutations.

$$4 \quad \times \quad 3 \quad \times \quad 2 \quad = \quad 24 \text{ permutations} \quad \leftarrow \text{ Use the counting principle.}$$

first choice   second choice   third choice

Step 2 Find the number of permutations of the smaller group.

$$3 \quad \times \quad 2 \quad \times \quad 1 \quad = \quad 6 \text{ permutations} \quad \leftarrow \text{ Use the counting principle.}$$

Step 3 Find the number of combinations.

$$\frac{\text{total number of permutations}}{\text{number of permutations of smaller group}} = \frac{24}{6} \quad \leftarrow \text{ Divide.}$$
$$= 4 \quad \leftarrow \text{ Simplify.}$$

You can attend 4 combinations of presentations.

✓ Quick Check

2. If you go to two presentations, how many different combinations of presentations can you choose from?

✓ Check Your Understanding

1. **Vocabulary** Why is order not important in finding combinations?

Would you solve Exercises 2–4 using a *combination* or a *permutation*?

2. choosing three pieces of fruit from seven pieces

3. giving first and second place awards

4. choosing five books from a list of ten books

5. Write an expression for each combination in Exercises 2–4.

For more exercises, see Extra Skills and Word Problems.

GO for Help

For Exercises	See Examples
6–8	1
9–16	2

For Exercises 6 and 7, use the table to make an organized list.

6. **Swimming** The four swimmers listed at the right are trying out for the swim team. Two will make the team. How many different combinations of two swimmers are possible?

Swimmer	Letter
Noah	N
Olivia	O
Kevin	K
Chloe	C

7. If 3 swimmers will make the team, how many combinations of 3 swimmers are possible?

8. Five campers want to go on a hiking trip. A camp counselor will choose three of them. How many different combinations are possible?

Find the number of combinations.

9. Choose two people from three.　　10. Choose three people from five.

11. Choose two people from six.　　12. Choose four people from six.

Sports Use the poster for Exercises 13–16. Find the number of combinations for each situation.

13. Participate in 2 track events.

14. Participate in 2 games.

15. Participate in 2 field events.

16. Participate in 3 track events.

 17. **Guided Problem Solving**
You have six pizza toppings. How many different 3-topping pizzas can you make?
   - total permutations:
     $6 \times \blacksquare \times \blacksquare$
   - permutations of smaller group: $\blacksquare \times 2 \times 1$

TRACK AND FIELD DAY

Track Events
▸ 50-m run
▸ 100-m relay
▸ 100-m hurdles
▸ 200-m run

Field Events
▸ high jump
▸ long jump
▸ disc throw

Games
▸ baseball throw
▸ run the bases relay

GO Online
Homework Video Tutor
Visit: PHSchool.com
Web Code: are-1206

Evaluate each expression.

18. $\dfrac{4!}{3!}$　　19. $\dfrac{5!}{2!}$　　20. $\dfrac{6!}{4!}$　　21. $\dfrac{7!}{3!}$

22. **Music** You have 5 different CDs to play. Your CD player can hold 3 CDs. How many different combinations of 3 CDs can you select?

23. Twelve students organize a trip. Two of them are assigned to collect money. In how many ways can these two students be chosen?

24. Reasoning To open a combination lock, you must dial the numbers in the right order. Explain why "permutation lock" might be more appropriate than "combination lock" as a name for the lock shown at the left.

Determine whether each situation involves a combination or a permutation. Then answer the question.

25. You select three books from a bookshelf that holds eight books. How many different sets of books can you choose?

26. Four students stand beside one another for a photograph. How many different orders are possible?

27. Writing in Math Use your own words and an example to explain the difference between a permutation and a combination.

Calculator Tip

To find $_4C_2$, press 4 [MATH].
Scroll right to option PRB.
Select option 4—*nCr*. Press 2 [ENTER].

You can use a graphing calculator to find the number of combinations. Use $_nC_r$ where *n* is the total number of items, C is combinations, and *r* is the number of items in a grouping. Evaluate each combination.

28. $_7C_3$ **29.** $_6C_3$ **30.** $_8C_5$

31. Challenge You want to mix two of the paint colors below. Use the number of possible combinations to find *P*(blue and green).

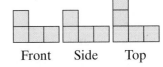
Test Prep and Mixed Review   **Practice**

Multiple Choice

32. Julia sold magazine subscriptions for a fundraiser. The numbers of subscriptions she sold in the last seven days were 5, 2, 3, 2, 7, 1, and 4. Which measure of data is represented by 2 subscriptions?
   Ⓐ Mean   Ⓑ Mode   Ⓒ Median   Ⓓ Range

33. The top, side, and front views of an object are shown at the right. Which solid matches the views?

Front   Side   Top

Ⓕ 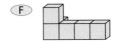   Ⓖ   Ⓗ   Ⓙ

GO for Help

For Exercises	See Lesson
34–36	12-5

Write the number of permutations in factorial form. Then simplify.

34. D, O, G   **35.** S, H, O, E   **36.** D, R, U, M, S

You select a letter at random from the group at the right. You replace the letter and make another selection. Find each probability.

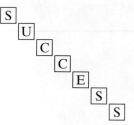

1. P(vowel, then S)
2. P(vowel, then C)
3. P(C, then E)
4. P(T, then S)
5. P(U, then consonant)

You have 4 blue cards, 1 red card, and 3 green cards. You select a card at random, do not replace it, and select a second card. Find each probability.

6. P(green, then red)
7. P(blue, then green)
8. P(red, then blue)

9. You decide to put the pictures of six friends in a row on a bulletin board. In how many different ways can you arrange the pictures?

10. How many different combinations of four flowers can you make from six different flowers?

Teams A, B, C, and D enter a cheerleading competition.

11. Give the sample space of the different orders in which the teams can perform.

12. The two best teams will advance to the next round. How many different combinations of two best teams are possible?

Products of Winners

What You'll Need

● two number cubes

How To Play

● Take turns rolling two number cubes. Find the product of the two numbers. If the product is even, Player A scores a point. If the product is odd, Player B scores a point.

● After 15 rolls each, the player with more points wins. Who would you rather be, Player A or Player B?

Product Chart

	1	2	3	4	5	6
1	1	2	3	■	■	■
2	2	4	■	■	■	■
3	■	■	■	■	■	■
4	■	■	■	■	■	■
5	■	■	■	■	■	■
6	■	■	■	■	■	■

Eliminating Answers

Before you try to answer a multiple-choice question, you may be able to save time by eliminating some answer choices. Then you can choose your answer carefully from the remaining options.

EXAMPLE

A bag contains ten blue, six red, and four green pens. You select a pen at random. What is the probability of not choosing a green pen?

(A) $\frac{1}{5}$ (B) $\frac{4}{5}$ (C) $\frac{5}{6}$ (D) $\frac{9}{11}$

Look at the denominator of each choice. The number of possible outcomes is $10 + 6 + 4$, or 20. The denominator of the answer must be 20 or a factor of 20. Eliminate choices C and D because they have denominators of 6 and 11.

Estimate the magnitude of the answer. Since most of the pens are not green, the probability of *not* choosing a green pen is a fraction greater than $\frac{1}{2}$. Since choice A is less than $\frac{1}{2}$, you can eliminate choice A.

The correct answer is choice B.

Exercises

1. A school has 1,060 students. The results of a survey are shown.

Students Surveyed	Students Who Produced Computer Art
40	24

   If the trend in the table continues, which is the best prediction of the total number of students who produced computer art?
   (A) 260 students   (C) 640 students
   (B) 480 students   (D) 790 students

2. A wheel is divided evenly into three sections labeled A, B, and C. You spin it twice. Which list shows all the possible outcomes?
   (F) (A, B), (B, A), (A, C), (C, A), (B, C), (C, B)
   (G) (A, A), (A, B), (B, A), (A, C), (C, A), (B, C), (C, C)
   (H) (A, A), (A, B), (B, A), (A, C), (C, A), (B, B), (B, C), (C, B), (C, C)
   (J) (A, B), (B, A), (A, C), (C, A), (B, C), (C, B), (A, A), (B, B)

Chapter 12 Review

Vocabulary Review

) combination (p. 610)
complement (p. 581)
compound event (p. 598)
counting principle (p. 592)
dependent events (p. 599)

event (p. 580)
experimental probability
  (p. 586)
factorial (p. 606)
independent events (p. 598)

outcome (p. 580)
permutation (p. 606)
sample space (p. 591)
theoretical probability (p. 580)

Choose the correct term to complete each sentence.

1. A (combination, permutation) is a grouping of objects in which the order of the objects does not matter.

2. An outcome or a group of outcomes is called a(n) (event, factorial).

3. Two events are (dependent, independent) if the occurrence of one event does not affect the probability of the occurrence of the other.

4. The (odds in favor of, odds against) an event is the ratio of the number of favorable outcomes to the number of unfavorable outcomes.

5. (Theoretical, Experimental) probability is based on observations.

Go Online
PHSchool.com
For: Online vocabulary quiz
Web Code: arj-1251

Skills and Concepts

Lesson 12-1
• To find the probability and the complement of an event

You can find the **theoretical probability** of an event using this formula.

$$P(\text{event}) = \frac{\text{number of favorable outcomes}}{\text{total number of possible outcomes}}$$

You select a card at random from the cards shown at the right. Find each probability.

T R U M P E T

6. $P(P)$ 7. $P(\text{vowel})$ 8. $P(\text{not P})$

Lesson 12-2
• To find experimental probability and to use simulations

You find the **experimental probability** of an event using this formula.

$$P(\text{event}) = \frac{\text{number of times an event occurs}}{\text{total number of trials}}$$

Games A computer game company makes random checks of its games. Of 200 games, 4 are found to be defective.

9. Find the experimental probability that a game is defective.

10. If the trend continues, predict the number of defective games in a batch of 1,600.

616 Chapter 12 Chapter Review

Lesson 12-3
- To make and use sample spaces and to use the counting principle

The collection of all possible outcomes in a probability experiment is called a **sample space.** You can use the **counting principle** to find the number of outcomes of an event.

Use the menu below for Exercises 11–13.

Appetizers	Soups
Egg Rolls	Won-ton
Fried Won-tons	Sizzling Rice

Main Dishes
Almond Chicken
Sweet & Sour Pork
Beef with Broccoli

11. At the China Panda, if you order the family dinner, you choose one appetizer, one soup, and one main dish from the menu. Draw a tree diagram to show the sample space.

12. You ask the restaurant to choose the meal for you at random. What is the probability of getting the egg roll, won-ton soup, and almond chicken for your meal?

13. Use the counting principle to find the number of possible dinners.

Lesson 12-4
- To find the probability of independent and dependent events

A **compound event** consists of two or more events. Two events are **independent events** if the occurrence of one event does not affect the probabilty of the occurrence of the other. Two events are **dependent events** if the occurrence of one event affects the probability of the occurrence of the other.

A hat contains the names of eight girls and six boys. You select two names without replacing the first name. Find each probability.

14. P(boy, then boy)   15. P(girl, then boy)   16. (girl, then girl)

17. Two independent events A and B both have a probability of $\frac{1}{4}$. Find $P(A$, then $B)$.

Lessons 12-5, 12-6
- To find permutations
- To find combinations

A **permutation** is an arrangement of objects in a particular order. A **combination** is a grouping of objects in which order does not matter.

18. Five students compete on a relay team. Only four of them can race at a time. How many different teams are possible?

19. Four students are selected for a relay team. In how many ways can they line up for the race?

Use the data. Find the experimental probability of each event as a fraction, a decimal, and a percent.

Marker Color	Frequency
Purple	6
Green	2
White	3
Black	5

1. P(purple)

2. P(green)

3. P(orange)

4. a. Quality Control Factory workers test 80 batteries. Four batteries are defective. What is the experimental probability that a battery is defective?

b. Assume this trend continues. Predict the number of defective batteries in a batch of 1,600.

There are six open containers arranged as shown. You toss a ball and it falls into one of the containers. Find each probability.

5. P(number greater than 4)

6. P(even number)

7. P(4)

8. P(7)

You have a bag that contains 6 blue, 2 green, 3 red, and 1 white marble. You select a marble at random. Find each probability.

9. P(blue)

10. P(white)

11. P(not green)

12. P(red)

13. P(green, then red when green is replaced)

14. P(red, then blue when red is not replaced)

15. a. Find the number of two-letter permutations of the letters M, A, T, H.

b. Find the number of two-letter combinations of the letters M, A, T, H.

16. Each of the letters D E T E R M I N E D is written on a card. You mix the cards thoroughly. What is the probability of selecting an E and then an M, if the first card is replaced before selecting the second card?

17. Writing in Math Suppose you toss a coin several times and record the results. Out of 20 trials, you get tails 9 times. What is the experimental probability of getting heads? Explain why this may differ from the theoretical probability.

A car comes in the colors and models listed in the table below. Assume there is the same chance of selecting any color or model.

Colors	Models
Silver	Hatchback
Gray	Coupe
Black	Sedan

18. Give the sample space.

19. Find the probability that a car selected at random is a silver hatchback.

20. Find the probability that a car selected at random is a yellow coupe.

21. You have the same chance of getting any one of four prizes when you buy Good Morning Cereal. You want to use a simulation to find the probability of getting all four prizes when you buy four boxes of cereal. Which statement is *not* true?

Ⓐ You can simulate the problem by using a spinner divided into four equal sections.

Ⓑ A possible answer is four boxes.

Ⓒ The more trials you perform, the better your results should be.

Ⓓ The result of your simulation is an experimental probability.

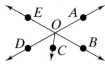
Multiple Choice

Read each question. Then write the letter of the correct answer on your paper.

Go **Online** For: Online end-of-course test
PHSchool.com Web Code: ara-1254

1. Use rounding to estimate. Which sum is between 14 and 15?
   (A) $13.71 + 1.5$
   (B) $9.02 + 5.738$
   (C) $2.69 + 12.49$
   (D) $3.772 + 12.04$

2. Which expression CANNOT be rewritten using the Distributive Property?
   (F) $3(2 + 8)$
   (G) $5(2 \cdot 3)$
   (H) $(18 - 9)7$
   (J) $9(14 - 6)$

3. What is the solution of $-15 = m - 9$?
   (A) -24 (B) -6 (C) 6 (D) 24

4. Which jar of peanut butter is the best buy?
   (F) an 18-oz jar for $1.69
   (G) a 30-oz jar for $2.59
   (H) a 32-oz jar for $2.89
   (J) a 24-oz jar for $2.09

5. Sarah bought a remnant of fabric $5\frac{1}{8}$ yd long to make pennants for the school contest. How many pennants can she make if $\frac{3}{4}$ yd is needed for each pennant?
   (A) 5   (B) 6   (C) 7   (D) 8

6. Which choice does NOT equal the others?
   (F) 4% of 3,000
   (G) 40% of 30
   (H) 40% of 300
   (J) 30% of 400

7. Suppose you spin the spinners once. What is the probability that the sum of the numbers is 10?

   (A) 0   (B) $\frac{1}{4}$ (C) $\frac{1}{2}$ (D) $\frac{3}{4}$

8. What is the volume of a rectangular prism that has dimensions 1 in., 2 in., and 3 in.?
   (F) 6 in.^3
   (G) 18 in.^3
   (H) 22 in.^3
   (J) 27 in.^3

9. How can 64 be written using exponents?
   (A) 2^6 (B) 4^3 (C) 8^2
   (D) All of the above are correct.

10. In the diagram at the right, which two angles are adjacent angles?

    (F) $\angle EOD, \angle DOC$
    (G) $\angle BOC, \angle BOD$
    (H) $\angle AOE, \angle BOC$
    (J) $\angle AOB, \angle EOD$

11. A circle has circumference 56.52 ft. What is its area? Use 3.14 for π.
    (A) 28.26 ft^2
    (B) 56.52 ft^2
    (C) 254.34 ft^2
    (D) $1,017.36 \text{ ft}^2$

12. What is the solution of the inequality $-4p < 36$?
    (F) $p > 9$
    (G) $p < -9$
    (H) $p > -9$
    (J) $p < 9$

13. If the area of the shaded region is 4 in.^2, what is the best estimate for the area of the unshaded region?
    (A) 4 in.^2
    (B) 8 in.^2
    (C) 12 in.^2
    (D) 16 in.^2

14. What percent of the letters of the alphabet are the vowels a, e, i, o, and u?
    (F) about 15%
    (G) about 19%
    (H) about 30%
    (J) about 33%

15. What is the order of the numbers from least to greatest? $\frac{1}{8}, -0.18, 0.2, -\frac{2}{13}$
    (A) $-\frac{2}{13}, -0.18, \frac{1}{8}, 0.2$
    (B) $-0.18, -\frac{2}{13}, 0.2, \frac{1}{8}$
    (C) $-0.18, -\frac{2}{13}, \frac{1}{8}, 0.2$
    (D) $-\frac{2}{13}, 0.2, \frac{1}{8}, -0.18$

16. What is the solution of $\frac{x}{6} = \frac{20}{32}$?
    (F) 3   (G) 3.75   (H) 4.8   (J) 5

17. Which equation has the solution 4?

ⓐ $k + 3 = -7$ ⓒ $y - 8 = 12$

ⓑ $5 + x = 9$ ⓓ $1 + a = 3$

18. What is the slope of the line?

ⓕ $-\frac{3}{2}$

ⓖ $\frac{1}{3}$

ⓗ $\frac{1}{2}$

ⓙ 2

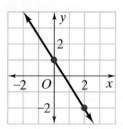

19. You plan to build a set of steps. The steps must reach a height of $8\frac{1}{2}$ ft. Each step can be no more than $7\frac{3}{4}$ in. high. What is the least number of steps you need to build?

ⓐ 11   ⓑ 12   ⓒ 13   ⓓ 14

20. Rectangle $ABCD$ and rectangle $AXYZ$ are similar. How long is $\overline{XY}$?

ⓕ 2.5 cm   ⓗ 1.6 cm

ⓖ 2 cm   ⓙ 1.5 cm

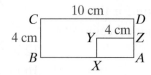

21. How many two-letter permutations of the letters C, A, R contain the letter R?

ⓐ 2   ⓑ 3   ⓒ 4   ⓓ 6

22. Use the function $y = 4x - 5$. What is the value of y for $x = 0, 1, 2,$ and 3?

ⓕ $-5, 1, 3, 2$ ⓗ $-5, 9, 13, 7$

ⓖ $5, 0, 1, 2$ ⓙ $-5, -1, 3, 7$

23. Which expression shows the prime factorization of 120?

ⓐ $2 \cdot 3 \cdot 4 \cdot 5$ ⓒ $2^3 \cdot 3 \cdot 5$

ⓑ $2 \cdot 3 \cdot 20$ ⓓ $3^2 \cdot 13$

24. What is the value of x in the triangle?

ⓕ 23°

ⓖ 27°

ⓗ 33°

ⓙ 53°

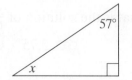

Gridded Response

Use the bar graph below for Exercises 25–27.

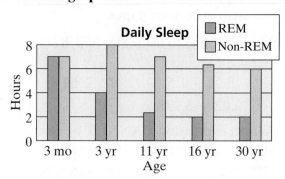

25. About how many hours per day does an 11-year-old spend in non-REM sleep?

26. About how many more hours does a 3-month-old spend in REM sleep than a 30-year-old?

27. About how many fewer hours does an 11-year-old spend in non-REM sleep than a 3-year-old?

For Exercises 28–30, use the graph below. The graph shows the height of an object over time.

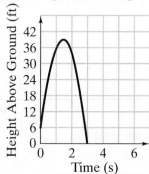

28. How many feet is the greatest height the object reaches?

29. How many seconds does it take the object to hit the ground?

30. How many feet is the initial height of the object?

31. Write 7.8×10^2 in standard form.

Short Response

32. Write a problem that $\frac{x}{3} + 11 = 16$ will solve.

33. Cards A through G are in a hat. You select a card at random. You select a second card without replacement. Find the probability that both cards are vowels. Show your work.

34. The triangles at the right are congruent. Write six congruencies involving corresponding parts of the triangles.

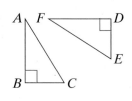

35. **a.** Write 0.9% as a decimal.
b. Write 0.9% as a fraction.

36. Find the number of pounds in 72 ounces.

Tell whether each graph shows a reflection or a translation. Name the line of symmetry or write a rule for the translation.

37.

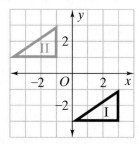

38.

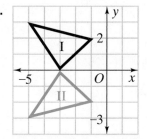

39. A map with the scale 2 in. : 250 mi shows two ponds to be 4 in. apart. How many miles apart are the ponds? Show your work.

40. Find the product 8(89) using the Distributive Property. Show your work.

41. Find the area of each triangle below.

a.

b.

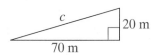

42. Find c to the nearest tenth.

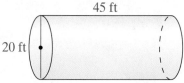

Extended Response

43. Find the mean, median, and mode of the data in the stem-and-leaf plot. Show your work.

7	0 0 5 8
8	1 5 6 9 9
9	4

Key: 7 | 0 means 70

44. You have $50 saved at the beginning of the month. You plan to save $25 each month. The equation $y = 25x + 50$ models your savings plan.
a. Graph this equation in the first quadrant of the coordinate plane.
b. How much will you have saved in 6 months?
c. In how many months will you have saved $150?

45. St. Francis, Torrey Pines, and Marina schools all compete for the championship in field hockey.
a. Make a table to find the sample space of possible outcomes of first, second, and third place.
b. In how many outcomes does St. Francis win with Marina in second place?
c. In how many outcomes does Torrey Pines or Marina win the championship?

46. **a.** Draw a net of the cylinder shown.

b. Find the surface area of the cylinder to the nearest tenth. Show your work.

47. You treat a friend to dinner. The cost of the food items from the menu totals $20.46. The sales tax on the food is 5%. You give a tip of 25% (before tax) for excellent service.
a. How much is the sales tax?
b. How much is the tip?
c. What is the total cost of the dinner?

Problem Solving Application

Applying Probability

Against All Odds? Your friend claims to be a great coin flipper who gets heads 50% of the time. Without doing any math, you know this is not a special skill—the results are pure chance. Suppose another friend claims to be a great free-throw shooter because of a 30% free-throw success rate. This claim is harder to evaluate. How can you tell if it's luck or skill?

Put It All Together

Materials compass, ruler, calculator

1. Suppose that your friend can hit the rim of the basket every time. Figure 1 shows the basket from above. Shots A, B and C just barely touch the rim.

   a. Copy Figure 1. Draw a circle centered on point P that connects the centers of balls A, B, and C. This is the *landing zone*. The center of the ball is within this circle for each shot.

   b. Research Find the radius of a men's basketball and of a basketball hoop. Calculate the area of the landing zone.

2. A "swish" shot passes through the net without touching the rim. Figure 2 shows ball D swishing through the net, falling just within the rim.

   a. Copy Figure 2. Draw two more balls (E and F) that also fall just within the rim.

   b. Draw a circle centered on point P that connects the centers of balls D, E, and F. This is the target zone. The center of the ball will be within this circle every time the ball "swishes" the net.

   c. Calculate the area of the target zone.

3. Suppose you are shooting baskets at random. Find the probability that a ball hitting the landing zone will also be in the target zone as follows:

$$\text{Probability of "swish"} = \frac{\text{area of target zone}}{\text{area of landing zone}}$$

   Calculate this probability. Convert it to a percent.

4. **Writing in Math** A shot doesn't have to be a swish to count as a basket. Explain how else a basket can be made, and what factors affect the probability of making a basket.

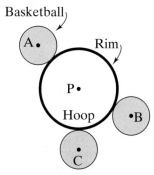

Figure 1

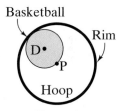

Figure 2

Basketball in the United States
In 2002, high school basketball teams included 540,597 boys and 456,169 girls.

Go Online
PHSchool.com
For: Information about basketball
Web Code: are-1253

Chapter Projects

B o a r d W a l k

What makes a board game so much fun? You have challenges like road blocks or false paths that make you backtrack. Then you land on a lucky square that lets you leap forward past your opponent. Best of all, you are with your friends as you play!

Create a Board Game For this chapter project, you will use integers to create a game. Then you will play your game with friends or family for a trial run. Finally you will decorate your game and bring it to class to play.

Go Online
PHSchool.com
For: Information to help you complete your project
Web Code: ard-0161

making THE measure

In the high jump, as in most sports, a consistent system of measurement allows athletes to make comparisons. It took the decree of a king to create one such system!

Back in the 12th century, King Henry I of England decided that a yard was the distance from the tip of his nose to the end of his thumb. How far is it from the tip of your nose to the end of your thumb? Is it more than a yard or less? Is it the same distance for everyone?

Invent Your Own Ruler For the chapter project, you will design a new system for measuring distance. Your final project will be a new ruler, together with a report on its usefulness.

Go Online
PHSchool.com
For: Information to help you complete your project
Web Code: ard-0261

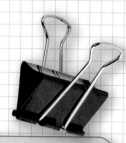

Toss and Turn

Did you ever make pancakes? The recipe can be pretty simple—an egg, some pancake mix, milk, and maybe some oil. Or forget the mix and start from scratch! Either way, you can vary the ingredients to suit your tastes. Do you want to include some wheat germ? How about some pecans, or maybe some fruit? Bananas are always in season!

Chapter 3 *Operations With Fractions*

Write Your Own Recipe For the chapter project, you will write your own recipe for pancakes. Your final project will be a recipe that will feed everyone in your class.

Go Online
PHSchool.com
For: Information to help you complete your project
Web Code: ard-0361

READ ALL ABOUT IT!

Flexible hours! Great pay! Work before or after school! Newspaper deliverers needed! Suppose to earn extra money you get a job delivering newspapers in your neighborhood. You plan to save the money you make so that you can buy yourself brand new snow skiing gear.

Chapter 4 *Equations and Inequalities*

Make a Savings Plan In this chapter, you will figure out how much time you can commit to your job, how much money you can earn per week, and how much money you need to make per week in order to reach your savings goal. As part of your final project, you will write a letter to your boss at the newspaper office describing your level of commitment as a newspaper deliverer.

Go Online
PHSchool.com
For: Information to help you complete your project
Web Code: ard-0461

Weighty Matters

Have you ever loved a pet so much that you wanted a statue made of it? Imagine a statue of your pet on the front steps of your home. "Gee, what a wise way to spend hard-earned money," your admiring neighbors would say. Or maybe not. In addition to being expensive, these statues would also be heavy. For instance, a 35-lb dog cast in gold would weigh about 670 lb.

Using Specific Gravity For the chapter project, you will find the weight of different animals and the weight of different metals. Your final project will be a table of animals with their weights, the weight of their statues in different materials, and the cost of the statues.

Go Online
PHSchool.com
For: Information to help you complete your project
Web Code: ard-0561

chills and thrills

Your world is spinning. You are screaming. And you are loving every minute of it! Even though you are scared, you know that you will come to a safe stop at the end of the ride.

A successful amusement park attraction must be both fun and safe. Planners of amusement parks use a lot of math to create thrills but avoid any spills.

Take a Survey For the chapter project, you will decide which rides are most likely to be most popular. Your final product will be a recommendation about which rides to include in a proposed amusement park for your town.

Go Online
PHSchool.com
For: Information to help you complete your project
Web Code: ard-0661

Raisin' the Roof

Look around you. Triangles are everywhere in construction! You see them in bridges, in buildings, in scaffolding: even in bicycle frames! This project will give you a greater appreciation of the importance of triangles in construction. You might also develop a taste for raisins!

Chapter 7 Geometry

Build a Tower For the chapter project, you will use toothpicks and raisins to build geometric shapes. Your final product will be a tower strong enough to support a baseball.

Go Online
PHSchool.com
For: Information to help you complete your project
Web Code: ard-0761

SHAPE UP AND SHIP OUT

Space is money! So before cargo is prepared for shipment in large containers, it is packaged in smaller containers based on its size and shape.

Cans of tuna are examples of items you buy in cylindrical containers. Would you pack two cylinders side-by-side or one above the other? One arrangement wastes cardboard! But which one?

Chapter 8 Measurement

Design Boxes for Shipping Cylinders For the chapter project, you will design boxes to hold cylindrical items. Your final product will be a model of a box that holds six cylinders.

Go Online
PHSchool.com
For: Information to help you complete your project
Web Code: ard-0861

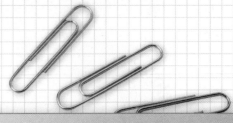

happy *landings*

Imagine this—you have just opened your parachute and you are floating through the air. Exciting, huh? How long it takes you to come to the ground can be predicted because the change in height versus time occurs in a predictable pattern. Many other things change in a predictable pattern, for instance, the height of a burning candle and the growth of money in a bank account.

Graphing Data For the chapter project, you will find how fast a container of water will empty if there is a hole in it. Your final project will be a graph of the data you collect.

Go Online
PHSchool.com
For: Information to help you
 complete your project
Web Code: ard-0961

People's *choice*

You're an advertising executive, and you want to know which of three television shows is the most popular. So you plan to conduct a poll of viewers.

But how many viewers do you survey? Polling is expensive, so you don't want to poll too many. Polling too few viewers might give you the wrong information. Here's your chance to explore the process!

Finding a Sample Size Fill a container with three different kinds of beans. Use the beans to find the sample size that best predicts the percent of each kind of bean in the container.

Go Online
PHSchool.com
For: Information to help you
 complete your project
Web Code: ard-1061

Chances are there's at least one person in a large crowd who has the same birthday as you! How many people do you think have the same favorite food? How many like the same television show? What kinds of cars do the people in the crowd have? Pollsters face questions like these all the time, and they take surveys to help answer them.

Estimate the Size of a Crowd and Take a Survey For the chapter project, you will use averages to estimate the size of a crowd. You will also take a survey and present your results in a graph.

Go Online
PHSchool.com

For: Information to help you complete your project
Web Code: ard-1161

Everybody Wins

Remember the game "Rock, Paper, Scissors"? It is an unusual game because paper wins over rock, rock wins over scissors, and scissors win over paper. You can use mathematics to create and investigate a situation with similar characteristics.

Make Three Number Cubes For this chapter project, you will design three number cubes A, B, and C, which have a surprising property: A usually beats B, B usually beats C, and C usually beats A. Your final step will be to construct your cubes.

Go Online
PHSchool.com

For: Information to help you complete your project
Web Code: ard-1261

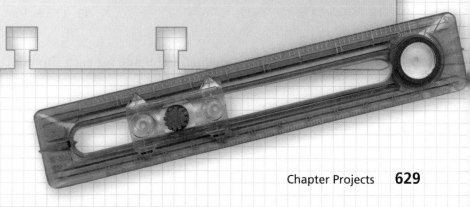

Extra Practice

Skills

● **Lesson 1-1**   Use any estimation strategy to estimate.

1. $2.7236 - 0.6512$ **2.** $2.4 + 0.86$ **3.** $106.3 \div 7.92$ **4.** 7.06×9.23

● **Lesson 1-2**   Find each sum or difference.

5. $5.87 + 2.41$ **6.** $9.31 - 4.08$ **7.** $7.2 + 1.907$ **8.** $4.86 - 2.161$

● **Lessons 1-3 and 1-4**   Find each product or quotient.

9. 2.9×1.7 **10.** $6.09 \cdot 1.3$ **11.** $7.68 \cdot 0.4$ **12.** $(5.2 \cdot 1.5) \cdot 6$

13. $30.6 \div 3.6$ **14.** $44.856 \div 7.12$ **15.** $17.172 \div 3.24$ **16.** $62.37 \div 2.7$

● **Lesson 1-5**   Write the number that makes each statement true.

17. ■ L $= 90$ mL   **18.** 0.6 mL $=$ ■ L   **19.** ■ mg $= 2.7$ kg   **20.** ■ km $= 620{,}000$ m

● **Lesson 1-6**   Compare using <, =, or >.

21. $|-3|$ ■ $|-2|$ **22.** $|10|$ ■ $|-10|$ **23.** $|-19|$ ■ $|9|$ **24.** $|-11|$ ■ $|-12|$

● **Lesson 1-7**   Find the value of each expression.

25. $-110 + 5 - (-5)$ **26.** $3 - 6 + 3$ **27.** $(-3) + (-2) + (-1)$ **28.** $2 - 2 - 4$

29. $(-9) + 8 - (-1)$ **30.** $-7 + (12 - 8)$ **31.** $4 + 11 - (-13)$ **32.** $-14 + (-7)$

● **Lesson 1-8**   Find each product or quotient.

33. $-5 \cdot (-9)$ **34.** $11 \cdot (-3)$ **35.** $-45 \div (-9)$ **36.** $\frac{-121}{11}$

● **Lesson 1-9**   Find the value of each expression.

37. $2(8 - 45)$ **38.** $24 - (3 + 19)$ **39.** $3(21 + 7)$ **40.** $3(61 + 9)$

41. $(18 - 24)(7)$ **42.** $8 \cdot 6 - 47$ **43.** $(53 - 9) \div 11$ **44.** $27 \cdot (31 - 7)$

● **Lesson 1-10**   Find the mean, median, and mode for each situation.

45. prices of different brands of cameras:
$150, $100, $240, $220, $195, $225

46. number of seconds to run the 100-meter dash:
9, 13, 14, 11, 12, 12, 15, 14, 10, 13, 9, 12

Word Problems

● **Lesson 1-1**

47. **Weather** In Chicago, Illinois, the average wind speed is 10.3 mi/h. In Great Falls, Montana, the average wind speed is 12.5 mi/h. What is the difference in wind speeds?

● **Lessons 1-2 and 1-3**

48. The weight of your kitten is 4.5 kg. The weight of your friend's kitten is 2.7 kg. How much more does your kitten weigh?

49. **Estimation** Your new job pays $8.20 per hour. Estimate how much you will earn if you work for 4 hours.

● **Lesson 1-4**

50. You buy four packages of shoe laces. You pay with a $10 bill and receive $3.24 in change. What is the price of each package?

● **Lesson 1-5**

51. You are making a banner. You have a sheet of paper that is 2 m wide and want to leave a 35-cm blank margin on either side. How many centimeters can you use for text?

● **Lessons 1-6 through 1-8**

52. Scores for a local golf tournament vary from 6 under par (-6) to 51 over par. Find the range of the scores.

53. **Fitness** Your pulse rate tells how fast your heart beats. Suppose your pulse after running is 160 beats per minute (bpm). After 4 min of rest, your pulse is 84 bpm. At what rate did your pulse decrease?

● **Lesson 1-9**

54. You go with 5 friends to an art museum. The admission fee is $5.25 per person. A special exhibition costs an additional $4.75 per person. Use mental math to find the total cost.

● **Lesson 1-10**

55. Find the mean of 2.4, 3.4, 6.1, 4.7, 2.9, 2.6, 3.3, 3.6, 2.7, and 3.2. Identify the outlier. Then find the mean without the outlier.

Skills

● **Lesson 2-1** Simplify. Use paper and pencil, a model, or a calculator.

1. 100^1
2. 5^3
3. $(-5)^4$
4. -6^2
5. $(12-5)^3$

● **Lesson 2-2** Find the GCF of each pair of numbers.

6. $35, 49$
7. $11, 12$
8. $28, 40$
9. $17, 34$
10. $16, 26$
11. $16, 86$

● **Lesson 2-3** Write each fraction in simplest form.

12. $\frac{21}{24}$
13. $\frac{65}{100}$
14. $\frac{15}{75}$
15. $\frac{40}{80}$
16. $\frac{72}{108}$
17. $\frac{110}{225}$

● **Lesson 2-4** Compare each pair of fractions. Use <, =, or >.

18. $\frac{1}{4} \blacksquare \frac{2}{9}$
19. $\frac{3}{7} \blacksquare \frac{1}{2}$
20. $\frac{2}{5} \blacksquare \frac{4}{10}$
21. $\frac{5}{6} \blacksquare \frac{7}{8}$
22. $\frac{3}{5} \blacksquare \frac{2}{3}$

● **Lessons 2-5 and 2-6** Write each mixed number as an improper fraction.

23. $7\frac{7}{8}$
24. $3\frac{5}{7}$
25. $3\frac{1}{4}$
26. $4\frac{2}{5}$
27. $10\frac{1}{6}$
28. $2\frac{2}{5}$

Write each fraction as a decimal.

29. $\frac{4}{5}$
30. $\frac{1}{9}$
31. $\frac{7}{8}$
32. $\frac{13}{4}$
33. $\frac{28}{8}$
34. $\frac{100}{6}$

● **Lesson 2-7** Order from least to greatest.

35. $\frac{9}{12}, 0.35, \frac{3}{6}, -1.0$
36. $-1.8, \frac{1}{4}, \frac{1}{3}, 3.5$
37. $\frac{10}{11}, 0.\overline{6}, \frac{1}{2}, 0.375$

● **Lesson 2-8** Write in scientific notation.

38. $5,000$
39. $160,000$
40. $4,700,000$
41. $7,900,000,000$

Word Problems

● **Lesson 2-1**

42. Your class is collecting pennies to give to a charity. You donate 2¢ on the first day. Each day, you double the amount you donate. How many pennies will you donate on the tenth day?

43. Geometry Let m represent the side length of one square. Let n represent the side length of another square. Find the total area of $m^2 + n^2$ for $m = 3$ and $n = 2$.

● Lessons 2-2 and 2-3

44. Suppose you just fed your cat and bird. You feed your cat every 5 hours and your bird every 12 hours. In how many hours will you feed them at the same time again?

45. The shutter of a camera opens and closes quickly. For each exposure time of $\frac{1}{4}$ s, $\frac{1}{125}$ s, and $\frac{1}{250}$ s, write an equivalent fraction with a denominator of 1,000.

● Lesson 2-4

46. The same number of oranges, apples, and pears are in a fruit basket. After one week, $\frac{3}{8}$ of the oranges, $\frac{1}{5}$ of the apples, and $\frac{1}{2}$ of the pears have not been eaten. Which fruit is most popular? Explain.

● Lesson 2-5

47. Baking You can make a loaf of challah bread by braiding 6 strands of dough together. What is the number of loaves of bread you can make with 40 strands of dough? Write your answer as a mixed number.

48. The distance from your house to the mall is $18\frac{1}{2}$ miles. Write the distance as an improper fraction in fourths of a mile.

● Lessons 2-6 and 2-7

49. Surveys When students are asked which enrichment class they prefer, 0.25 choose sign language, $\frac{10}{48}$ choose starting a business, $\frac{5}{12}$ choose robotics, and 0.125 choose origami. List their choices in decreasing order of preference.

50. A plant measures $6\frac{1}{12}$ in. Write this value as a decimal.

51. The amount of water in three different barrels is $3.\overline{6}$ gal, $\frac{16}{5}$ gal, and $3\frac{5}{6}$ gal. Which barrel contains the most water?

52. A baseball player has a batting average of .305. Write this decimal as a fraction in simplest form.

53. A stock price changes each day. The following list shows the daily price change for 7 days: 0.09, −0.70, −0.11, 0.3, 0.67, −0.28, 0.54. Order the price changes from least to greatest.

Skills

● **Lesson 3-1** Use benchmarks to estimate each sum or difference.

1. $\frac{2}{5} + \frac{7}{9}$

2. $\frac{3}{4} + \frac{5}{6}$

3. $\frac{3}{4} - \frac{1}{5}$

4. $\frac{8}{9} + \frac{7}{15}$

5. $9\frac{8}{10} + 8\frac{2}{10}$

6. $15\frac{2}{5} - 5\frac{4}{7}$

7. $71\frac{1}{5} - 5\frac{2}{3}$

8. $99\frac{9}{19} + \frac{1}{5}$

● **Lessons 3-2 and 3-3** Find each sum or difference.

9. $\frac{2}{3} + \frac{2}{3}$

10. $\frac{7}{10} - \frac{3}{10}$

11. $\frac{7}{12} - \frac{1}{4}$

12. $\frac{1}{6} + \frac{3}{4}$

13. $4\frac{3}{8} + 2\frac{5}{8}$

14. $5\frac{2}{5} - 1\frac{4}{5}$

15. $11 - 3\frac{1}{8}$

16. $7\frac{2}{5} + 3\frac{1}{4}$

● **Lessons 3-4 and 3-5** Find each product or quotient.

17. $\frac{3}{8} \cdot \frac{2}{5}$

18. $\frac{1}{4}$ of $\frac{4}{5}$

19. $\frac{5}{6}$ of 30

20. $2\frac{7}{8} \cdot \frac{4}{5}$

21. $\frac{3}{5} \div \frac{1}{5}$

22. $9 \div \frac{3}{4}$

23. $\frac{5}{6} \div \frac{3}{8}$

24. $3\frac{2}{3} \div 2\frac{1}{2}$

● **Lesson 3-6** Complete.

25. $\frac{3}{4}$ gal = ■ c

26. 4,500 lb = ■ t

27. $\frac{3}{8}$ mi = ■ yd

28. $12\frac{2}{3}$ lb = ■ oz

29. $6\frac{1}{2}$ t = ■ lb

30. 2 yd, 1 ft = ■ yd

● **Lesson 3-7** Choose the more precise measurement.

31. 25 g, 2.55 kg

32. 2 t, $5\frac{1}{4}$ lb

33. 28 pt, 15 qt

34. 7 L, 35.95 mL

35. 0.75 g, 1,000 mg

36. 120 min, 2 h

Word Problems

● **Lesson 3-1**

37. Estimation Use benchmarks to estimate the total weight of two bags of cheese that weigh $\frac{1}{8}$ lb and $\frac{2}{5}$ lb.

38. Estimation From the following daily mileages, estimate the median number of miles a runner jogged: $9\frac{3}{5}$, $5\frac{1}{4}$, $7\frac{5}{10}$, $1\frac{7}{8}$, $6\frac{3}{4}$, $3\frac{2}{8}$.

● **Lessons 3-2 and 3-3**

39. Write a number sentence for the model at the right.

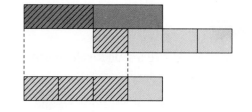

40. **Geometry** A side of a square is $\frac{4}{5}$ cm long. What is the perimeter of the square?

41. The Grand Canyon in Arizona has a maximum depth of $1\frac{1}{8}$ mi. The Black Canyon in Colorado has a maximum depth of $\frac{1}{2}$ mi. Find the difference between the depths.

42. You want to build a fence that has twice the perimeter of a triangular plot of land. The land plot has dimensions $1\frac{1}{2}$ yd, 2 yd, and $3\frac{1}{4}$ yd. What is the perimeter of the fence?

● **Lessons 3-4 and 3-5**

43. At an apple orchard, you pick $10\frac{2}{5}$ lb of apples. You give $\frac{3}{8}$ of the apples to your friend. How many pounds of apples do you give your friend?

For each serving size in the table below, find the number of ounces and the number of Calories.

Nonfat Yogurt

	Servings	$\frac{1}{4}$	$\frac{1}{2}$	$\frac{3}{4}$	1	$1\frac{1}{2}$	2
44.	Ounces	a. ■	b. ■	c. ■	8	d. ■	e. ■
45.	Calories	a. ■	b. ■	c. ■	160	d. ■	e. ■

46. During a $2\frac{3}{4}$-hour assembly, each speaker spoke for $\frac{1}{4}$ of an hour. How many speakers were there?

47. Suppose you have $6\frac{4}{5}$ cantaloupes. How many fifths of a cantaloupe can you cut?

● **Lesson 3-6**

48. A woman is 66 in. tall. What is her height in feet?

49. A marathon runner needs to run 137,280 feet to complete the race. How many miles is the race?

● **Lesson 3-7**

50. **Measurement** You measure the length of a book to be 12 in. Your friend measures the same book to be 1 ft long. You know that 12 in. equals 1 ft. Does this mean that the two measurements are equally precise? Explain.

CHAPTER 4

Extra Practice

Skills

● **Lesson 4-1** Write an algebraic expression and draw a diagram for each word phrase.

1. The difference of a number n and 3

2. 17 more than s students

3. 5 fewer than d days

4. 6 more than the quotient of n and 2

5. Copy and complete the table at the right. Substitute the value on the left for the variable in the expression at the top of each column. Then evaluate.

x	$3(x-1)$	$3x-1$	$3x+1$
5	■	■	■
2	■	■	■

● **Lesson 4-2** Use mental math to solve each equation.

6. $5b = 30$

7. $n + 5 = 17$

8. $m - 8 = 15$

9. $\frac{z}{3} = 9$

● **Lesson 4-3** Solve each equation. Check your answer.

10. $t - 13 = -29$

11. $17 + d = -7$

12. $d + 112 = 159$

13. $y - 68 = 94$

● **Lesson 4-4** Solve each equation. Check your answer.

14. $\frac{m}{5} = -15$

15. $-7y = -42$

16. $0.4t = 16$

17. $\frac{x}{12} = -8$

● **Lesson 4-5** Solve each equation using number sense.

18. $7t + 5 = 40$

19. $2d - 12 = 18$

20. $5w - 18 = 7$

21. $\frac{z}{4} + 5 = 15$

● **Lesson 4-6** Solve each equation. Check your answer.

22. $\frac{r}{-6} + 4 = 3$

23. $12m + 24 = 0$

24. $-6g - 9 = 15$

25. $\frac{k}{-3} - 2 = -20$

● **Lessons 4-7 through 4-9** Solve each inequality. Graph the solution.

26. $y + 5 \geq 11$

27. $p + 7 < -3$

28. $a - 9 \leq 1$

29. $d - 3 > -13$

30. $3y \geq 33$

31. $\frac{p}{7} < -2$

32. $\frac{a}{-8} \leq -7$

33. $4d > -36$

Word Problems

● **Lesson 4-1**

34. A dance club spends $20 on advertising to promote its fall show. Write an algebraic expression for the amount of money left in the budget if the club starts with d dollars.

● **Lesson 4-2**

35. Kobayashi set a world record for hot dog eating when he ate 50 hot dogs in 720 seconds. Write an equation and estimate the number of seconds it took him to eat one hot dog.

36. You mail a package at the post office. The postage costs $12.18. You pay with a $20 bill. Write an equation and estimate the amount of change you receive.

● **Lessons 4-3 through 4-6**   **Write and solve an equation for each situation.**

37. A peregrine falcon can fly as fast as 220 mi/h. This speed is 150 mi/h faster than the maximum running speed of a cheetah. What is the speed of a cheetah?

38. A snorkeler looks at coral 4.5 feet below sea level, or at −4.5 ft. A scuba diver looks at coral located at 10 times that depth. How far below sea level does the scuba diver descend?

39. An auto rental agency offers a rate of $38 per day plus $.30/mile. After a one-day rental, Misha's bill was $74. How many miles did Misha drive?

40. A pair of running shoes costs $37 less than twice the cost of a pair of basketball sneakers. The sneakers cost $48.50. How much do the running shoes cost?

● **Lesson 4-7**   **Write an inequality for each statement.**

41. The space shuttle can carry more than 38,000 pounds.

42. Today your break will be shorter than 15 minutes.

43. A song is less than 5 minutes long.

44. A shelf can hold at most 250 pounds.

● **Lessons 4-8 and 4-9**   **Write and solve an inequality for each problem.**

45. A ride at an amusement park requires a rider to be at least 48 in. tall. Your little brother is 37 in. tall. How many inches must he grow in order to ride?

46. For your party, you plan a game where each player needs three spoons. You buy a box of 50 spoons. At most, how many people can play the game?

Skills

● **Lesson 5-1** Write each ratio in two other ways.

1. $\frac{2}{3}$ **2.** 3 : 5   **3.** 4 to 7   **4.** 15 : 5   **5.** $\frac{25}{50}$

● **Lesson 5-2** Find each unit price. Then determine the better buy.

6. soap: 32 fl oz for $2.29   **7.** cereal: 12 oz for $3.95   **8.** cider: 2 pt for $2.49
           48 fl oz for $3.19   16 oz for $4.80   6 pt for $7.14

9. milk: 1 gal for $1.99   **10.** pasta: 8 oz for $1.29   **11.** fish: 2 lb for $13.98
          3 gal for $5.69   32 oz for $4.99   3 lb for $17.97

12. fabric: 3 yd for $12.48   **13.** rice: 2 lb for $1.89   **14.** juice: 2 L for $5.99
            5 yd for $20.30   8 lb for $6.79   0.5 L for $1.25

● **Lesson 5-3** By using cross products, tell whether the ratios can form a proportion.

15. $\frac{4}{3}, \frac{12}{9}$ **16.** $\frac{8}{5}, \frac{11}{7}$ **17.** $\frac{21}{6}, \frac{7}{2}$ **18.** $\frac{6}{24}, \frac{2}{4}$ **19.** $\frac{50}{6}, \frac{3}{2}$

● **Lesson 5-4** Solve each proportion using cross products.

20. $\frac{12}{a} = \frac{3}{5}$ **21.** $\frac{n}{12} = \frac{4}{16}$ **22.** $\frac{7}{8} = \frac{n}{4}$ **23.** $\frac{7}{10} = \frac{14}{a}$ **24.** $\frac{7}{n} = \frac{17.5}{5}$

● **Lesson 5-5** Each pair of figures is similar. Find the value of each variable.

25. 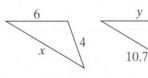   **26.**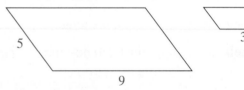

● **Lesson 5-6** The scale on a drawing is 0.5 in. : 15 ft. Find the actual length for each drawing length. Round to the nearest tenth, if necessary.

27. 15 in.   **28.** 20 in.   **29.** 10 in.   **30.** 40 in.   **31.** 15.5 in.   **32.** 1.25 in.

Word Problems

● **Lesson 5-1**

33. Nutrition The U.S. Department of Agriculture (USDA) recommends that no more than $\frac{3}{10}$ of your Calories come from fat. In a bowl of Tasty Crunch cereal, 15 out of 120 Calories are from fat. Is this within the USDA recommendation? Explain.

Lesson 5-2

34. Suppose you swim 500 yd in 3 min 20 s. What is your unit rate in seconds?

35. A bottle of 250 multivitamins costs $14.99. A bottle of 500 multivitamins costs $32.99. Which bottle is the better buy?

Lesson 5-3

36. For a game, you need 3 yellow marbles for every 8 red marbles. If you have 42 yellow marbles and 112 red marbles, do you have the appropriate numbers of marbles for the game? Explain.

Lesson 5-4

37. **Business** You sell packs of 12 pens for $3.48. At this rate, how much should you charge for a pack of 20 pens?

38. There are 385 mosquitoes in 11 ft^3 of a room. Predict the number in 15 ft^3.

39. There are 144 tulips in 8 m^2 of a garden. Predict the number in 25 m^2.

40. A recipe for fruit salad serves 4 people. It calls for 2 oranges and 16 grapes. You want to serve 10 people. How many oranges and grapes will you need?

Lesson 5-5

41. **Geometry** The ratio of the corresponding sides of two similar rectangles is 5 : 7. The smaller rectangle has a length of 3 cm and a width of 5 cm. Find the perimeter of the larger rectangle.

42. **Indirect Measurement** A student is 4 ft tall and his shadow is 3 ft long. A nearby building has a shadow 51 ft long. How tall is the building?

43. A woman stands near a telephone pole. She is 150 cm tall and her shadow is 3 m long. The shadow of the telephone pole is 30 m long. How tall is the telephone pole?

Lesson 5-6

44. The scale of a map is $\frac{1 \text{ cm}}{3.75 \text{ km}}$. Find the actual distance for a map distance of 8 cm.

45. The scale of a drawing is $\frac{1}{2}$ in. : 12 ft. Find the length of a drawing for an actual length of 84 ft.

Skills

● **Lesson 6-1   Write each ratio as a percent.**

1. $\dfrac{4}{5}$ 2. $\dfrac{11}{5}$ 3. $\dfrac{3}{25}$ 4. $\dfrac{19}{20}$ 5. $\dfrac{1}{10}$ 6. $\dfrac{3}{2}$

● **Lesson 6-2   Write each percent as a decimal.**

7. 37.5%   8. 11.375%   9. 2.55%   10. 9%   11. 1.111%   12. 97.05%

● **Lesson 6-3   Write each percent as a fraction in simplest form.**

13. 225%   14. 0.1%   15. 0.07%   16. 398%   17. 156%   18. 0.2%

● **Lesson 6-4   Find each answer using mental math.**

19. 30% of 285   20. 51% of 326   21. 9% of 1,250   22. 49% of 88   23. 101% of 150

● **Lesson 6-5   Write a proportion and solve.**

24. 54 is what percent of 135?   25. What percent of 48 is 2.4?   26. What percent of 200 is 120?

27. 8 is what percent of 20?   28. 32.5 is what percent of 130?   29. What percent of 150 is 27?

● **Lesson 6-6   Write and solve an equation to find the part of a whole.**

30. 30% of 250 is what number?   31. What number is 90% of 70?   32. 45% of 200 is what number?

33. What number is 7% of 88?   34. 4% of 200 is what number?   35. What number is 22% of 1?

● **Lesson 6-7   Find each payment.**

36. $75 with a 5% sales tax   37. $219 with a 3.5% sales tax   38. $85.65 with a 3% sales tax

● **Lesson 6-8   Find each percent of change. Round to the nearest tenth. State whether the change is an increase or a decrease.**

39. 25 to 40   40. 95 to 45   41. 108 to 110   42. 50 to 95   43. 125 to 75

44. 8.5 to 10   45. 100 to 15   46. 63.5 to 20   47. 111 to 150   48. 25.9 to 30.2

Word Problems

● **Lesson 6-1**

49. **Art** Draw and shade the first letter of your name on a 10-by-10 grid. Determine what percent of the grid is shaded.

● **Lesson 6-2** **The table shows the percent of the Recommended Daily Allowance for some of the nutrients in a 6-oz baked potato.**

Potato Facts

Nutrient	RDA
Magnesium	14%
Iron	34%
Vitamin B6	35%

Source: National Institutes of Health

50. Write each percent as a fraction and as a decimal.

51. **Nutrition** Suppose you eat a 6-oz baked potato. What percent of each nutrient do you still need to meet the Recommended Daily Allowance?

● **Lessons 6-3 through 6-6**

52. **Environment** A study has suggested that desert areas throughout the world could increase as much as 185% in the next 100 years due to global warming. Write the percent as a decimal and a fraction.

53. Four hundred students attended a school dance. If 35% of the students were boys, how many boys attended the dance?

54. The regular price of a backpack is $34. A store sells the backpack at 30% off. What is the sale price?

55. An awards banquet is attended by 120 people. Ribbons are awarded for first, second, and third place in each of 25 categories. No one gets more than one ribbon. What percent of the people attending the banquet receive a ribbon?

56. A frozen yogurt shop sold 45 strawberry cones on Friday. This is 30% of the number of strawberry cones they sold that week. How many strawberry cones did they sell that week?

● **Lesson 6-7**

57. You go to a stylist for a haircut. The cost of the haircut is $12.50. Find the amount of a 15% tip for the stylist.

58. A salesperson earns a salary of $2,500, plus 4% commission on sales of $1,500. What are the salesperson's total earnings?

● **Lesson 6-8**

59. If the cost of a dozen eggs rises from $.99 to $1.34, what is the percent of the increase?

60. A television is on sale for $449.95. This is $30 off the original price. Find the percent of the discount.

61. A bookstore pays $4.25 for paperback books and charges $9.95. What is the maximum percent of discount the store can offer, while making a profit of $2 on each book? Check your answer.

Skills

● **Lesson 7-1** Name each segment, ray, or line.

1.

2.
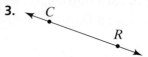

3.

● **Lesson 7-2** Find the measures of the complement and the supplement of each angle.

4. $m\angle A = 25°$ **5.** $m\angle U = 15°$ **6.** $m\angle T = 85°$ **7.** $m\angle C = 46°$

● **Lesson 7-3** Find x in each triangle.

8.
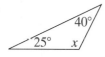

9.

10.
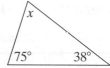

● **Lesson 7-4** Classify each polygon. Then name the congruent sides and angles.

11.
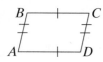

12.
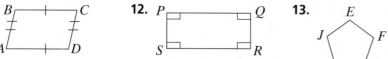

13.

14.
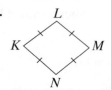

● **Lesson 7-5** △*ABD* ≅ △*CED*. Complete each congruence statement.

15. ∠*A* ≅ ▪   **16.** ∠*D* ≅ ▪   **17.** $\overline{AD}$ ≅ ▪   **18.** $\overline{AB}$ ≅ ▪

● **Lessons 7-6 and 7-7**

19. Surveys In a survey of 500 people, 86 preferred Brand A. Find the measure of the central angle that you would draw to represent Brand A in a circle graph.

● **Lesson 7-8** Copy each segment. Then construct its perpendicular bisector.

20.
A •————————————• *D*

21.

Word Problems

● **Lesson 7-1**

22. Draw $\overline{AB}$, with $\overline{AC}$ on $\overline{AB}$.

23. Why are two lines drawn on a chalkboard *not* skew?

● **Lessons 7-2 and 7-3**

24. Geography On a map, the measure of one of the angles formed by two intersecting roads is 79°. Find the measures of the complement and the supplement of the angle.

25. A triangular window has two angles that measure 32° and 116°. Find the measure of the third angle. Then classify the triangle.

● **Lesson 7-4**

26. A frame for a house has two pairs of opposite sides that are parallel. What shapes can the frame be?

● **Lesson 7-5**

27. Manufacturing Workers make sure that the same parts for a product manufactured on an assembly line are all congruent. To do this, they compare each part to a sample part. Are the triangles congruent?

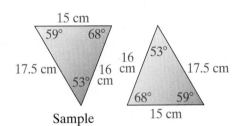

Sample

● **Lesson 7-6**

28. Suppose your watch says 12:15 P.M. What kind of angle is the central angle formed by the two hands of your watch?

● **Lesson 7-7**

29. Survey The data show the results of a survey on the preferred day for grocery shopping. Use the data to draw a circle graph.

Day	Percent	Day	Percent
Monday	4	Friday	17
Tuesday	5	Saturday	29
Wednesday	12	Sunday	7
Thursday	13	No preference	13

● **Lesson 7-8**

30. Draw $\overline{CD}$ at least 3 in. long. Construct and label a segment that is one half as long as $\overline{CD}$.

Skills

● **Lesson 8-1** Estimate the area of each shaded region. Each square represents 100 ft².

1.
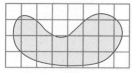

2.
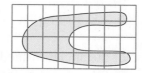

3.
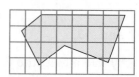

● **Lesson 8-2** Find each area for a triangle with base *b* and height *h*.

4. $b = 7$ cm
$h = 12$ cm

5. $b = 10$ km
$h = 25$ km

6. $b = 100$ m
$h = 3.6$ m

7. $b = 60$ in.
$h = 40$ in.

● **Lessons 8-3 and 8-4** Find the area of each parallelogram or trapezoid.

8.
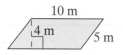

9.
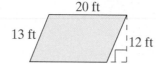

10.
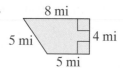

● **Lesson 8-5** Use $\pi \approx 3.14$ to estimate the circumference and area for each circle.

11. $d = 1.5$ km

12. $r = 6$ cm

13. $r = 9$ m

14. $d = 20$ in.

● **Lesson 8-6** Simplify each square root.

15. $\sqrt{1}$

16. $\sqrt{4}$

17. $\sqrt{49}$

18. $\sqrt{81}$

19. $\sqrt{900}$

20. $\sqrt{3,600}$

● **Lesson 8-7** Find each missing length.

21.
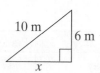

22.
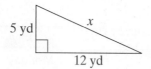

23.
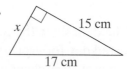

● **Lessons 8-8 and 8-9** Name each figure and find its surface area.

24.
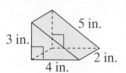

25.
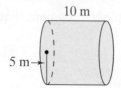

26.
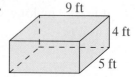

- **Lesson 8-10**

   27. Find the volume of the figures in Exercises 25 and 26.

   Word Problems

- **Lessons 8-1 and 8–2**

   28. Which is a reasonable estimate for the perimeter of a school building—600 ft or 600 yd? Explain your choice.

   29. Patterns Copy and complete the table by finding the perimeter and area of each rectangle. What happens to the perimeter and area of a rectangle when you double, triple, or quadruple the dimensions?

ℓ	w	P	A
3 in.	1 in.	■	■
6 in.	2 in.	■	■
9 in.	3 in.	■	■
12 in.	4 in.	■	■

- **Lessons 8-3 and 8-4**

   30. A triangular mirror is 12 in. wide and 37 in. tall. Find its area.

   31. A park wall is designed to have the irregular shape shown. Use familiar figures to find the area of the park.

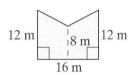
12 m   8 m   12 m   16 m

- **Lesson 8-5**

   32. A circular pool has a diameter of 20 ft. What area needs to be covered? Round to the nearest square foot.

- **Lessons 8-6 and 8-7**

   33. Science The distance that an object falls is given by the formula $d = 16t^2$, where d is the distance in feet and t is the time in seconds. A stone falls 1,600 ft into water. How long does it take for the stone to reach the water?

   34. A ladder leans against a building. The bottom of the ladder is 5 ft from the building. The ladder reaches a window that is 17 ft from the ground. How long is the ladder? Round your answer to the nearest tenth.

- **Lesson 8-8**

   35. Use graph paper to draw a trapezoidal prism.

- **Lessons 8-9 and 8-10**   **A jewelry box is 12 in. long, 7 in. wide, and 3 in. tall.**

   36. Find the surface area of the jewelry box.

   37. Find the volume of the jewelry box.

CHAPTER 9 Extra Practice

Skills

● **Lessons 9-1 and 9-3** Graph the data in each table. In Exercise 3, first find the values of the variables.

1.

Hours of Study	Science Test Score
1	72
2	77
3	89
4	92

2.

Time (mo)	Savings (dollars)
2	125
4	295
6	420
8	625

3.

A	B
15	45
17	51
19	57
23	q
p	81

● **Lesson 9-2** Identify each sequence as *arithmetic, geometric,* or *neither.*

4. 7, 10, 13, 16, . . .

5. 800, 400, 200, 100, . . .

6. 50, 25, 48, 24, . . .

● **Lesson 9-4** Write a rule for the function represented by each table.

7.

x	y
0	0
1	6
2	12
3	18

8.

x	y
0	−2
1	−1
2	0
3	1

9.

x	y
0	1
1	4
2	7
3	10

10.

x	y
0	10
1	8
2	6
3	4

● **Lesson 9-5** Graph each function. Use input values of 1, 2, 3, 4, and 5.

11. $y = x + 5$

12. $y = 8 - x$

13. $y = 2x^2$

● **Lesson 9-6**

14. On her trip to the library, Arlene walked two blocks to the bus stop in five minutes. She rode the bus for 15 min. The bus stopped three times for one minute each time. Sketch a graph to represent Arlene's trip.

● **Lesson 9-7** Find the balance in each compound interest account.

15. $1,000 principal
5% annual interest rate
4 years

16. $700 principal
4% annual interest rate
12 years

17. $1,500 principal
5.5% annual interest rate
7 years

● **Lesson 9-8** Solve each equation for the variable in red.

18. $V = \ell wh$

19. $y = mx + b$

20. $P = 2\ell + 2w$

Word Problems

● **Lesson 9-1**

21. **Publishing** The table shows costs of printing books. Estimate the cost of printing 2,500 books and the cost of printing 7,500 books.

Number of Books	Cost ($)
5,000	175,000
10,000	290,000

● **Lesson 9-2**

22. A boss pays new employees $8/h the first year, $9/h the second year, $10/h the third year, and $15/h the fourth year. Is the pattern *arithmetic, geometric, both,* or *neither*?

● **Lesson 9-3**

23. There are 12 eggs in a dozen. Use this relationship to make a table that shows the number of eggs you have in 10, 20, 30, and 50 dozen eggs.

● **Lesson 9-4**

24. Write a function rule that relates the number of miles m you travel in h hours if you drive at an average speed of 50 mi/h.

● **Lesson 9-5**

25. **Geometry** The area of a square is a function of its side length. Write and graph a function rule to represent this concept. Describe the shape of your graph.

● **Lesson 9-6**

26. Sketch a graph for the following situation. You run 3 blocks from the library and then walk 5 more blocks to your home. Show the distance on the vertical axis and time on the horizontal axis.

● **Lesson 9-7**

27. **Finance** You invest $1,000 at 5% for 9 months. How much simple interest do you earn?

● **Lesson 9-8**

28. **Sports** The formula for a batting average a is $a = \frac{h}{n}$, where h is the number of hits and n is the number of times at bat. The highest major-league lifetime batting average was .366 by Ty Cobb, who had 4,189 hits. About how many times at bat did he have?

Skills

● **Lessons 10-1 and 10-3**   Use the graph for Exercises 1–6.

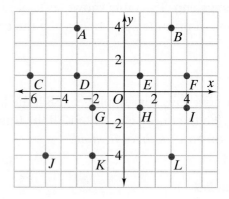

Name the point with the given coordinates.

1. $(-2, -1)$ **2.** $(1, 1)$ **3.** $(3, 4)$

Find the slope of the line through the points.

4. A and E **5.** G and E **6.** B and F

● **Lesson 10-2**   Tell whether each ordered pair is a solution of $y = x + 18$.

7. $(2, 20)$ **8.** $(22, 4)$ **9.** $(36, -18)$

● **Lesson 10-4**   Make a table of solutions for each equation. Use integer values of x from -3 to 3. Then graph each equation.

10. $y = x^2$ **11.** $y = x^2 - 4$ **12.** $y = 3x^2$ **13.** $y = 4|x|$

● **Lesson 10-5**   Write a rule for the translation shown in each graph.

14.
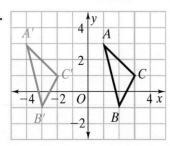

15.
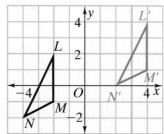

16.
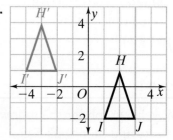

● **Lesson 10-6**   Use the graph from Exercises 1–6 to answer Exercise 17.

17. Is the triangle formed by points E, B, and F a reflection, a rotation, or a translation of the image formed by points H, L, and I? Explain.

● **Lesson 10-7**   Graph the square $ABCD$ with vertices $A(2, -3)$, $B(4, -5)$, $C(6, -3)$, and $D(4, -1)$. Then connect the vertices in order.

18. Draw the image of $ABCD$ after a rotation of $180°$ about point A.

19. Write the coordinates of the image of $ABCD$.

Word Problems

● **Lessons 10-1 and 10–2**

20. **Geometry** Graph the points $G(1, 4)$, $H(-2, 4)$, $J(-2, -5)$, and $K(1, -5)$. Connect the points to form a polygon. Classify the polygon by its angles and its sides.

21. **Finance** You have $35 saved. You plan to save $5 each week from now on. The plan is modeled by $y = 5x + 35$. Graph the equation to find the amount of money you will have saved after 8 weeks.

22. **Aviation** A Learjet aircraft can travel at a speed of 400 mi/h. The equation $y = 400x$ represents the distance y traveled during x hours in flight. Graph the equation to find the distance traveled in 5 hours.

● **Lessons 10-3 and 10-4**

23. Find the slopes of j and k in the graph at the right. Which line has a negative slope?

24. The slope of a piece of land is its grade. If the grade of a piece of land is 12%, what is its slope?

25. **Physics** An object falls from an initial height of 6,000 ft. The equation $h = -16t^2 + 6,000$ represents the height of the object, in feet, after t seconds. Make a table of values to find the height of the object after 0, 2, 4, and 10 seconds. Then graph the equation.

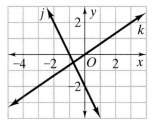

● **Lessons 10-5 through 10-7**

26. You show a friend that the path you take to school can be seen as a translation on a coordinate plane. The point $M(3, 5)$ represents your house. The point $M'(2, -3)$ represents your school. Write a rule to describe your path to school.

27. Trace the figure at the right and draw the line(s) of symmetry. If there are no lines of symmetry, write *none*.

Figure II is the image of Figure I. Identify each transformation as a *translation*, a *reflection*, or a *rotation*.

28.

29.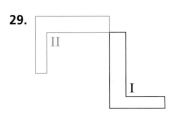

Skills

● **Lesson 11-1** **Use the data below for Exercises 1 and 2.**
high temperatures (°F): 85, 88, 91, 84, 90, 85, 84, 90, 88, 86, 85, 92, 85, 86, 88

  1. Make a frequency table.

  2. Make a line plot.

● **Lesson 11-2** **Use the graph for Exercises 3–5.**

  3. Which team has won the most matches?

  4. Which team has won the fewest matches?

  5. About how many more matches has Team A won than Team D?

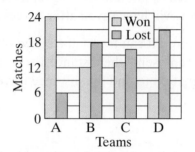

● **Lesson 11-3** **The table shows the number of stories of some tall buildings in the United States. Use the table to answer Exercises 6 and 7.**

  6. Draw a stem-and-leaf plot for the data.

  7. What is the range of the data?

Number of Stories				
73	44	57	64	48
60	55	51	77	40
80	72	60	82	57

● **Lesson 11-4**

  8. Write a fair survey question and a biased survey question.

● **Lesson 11-5**

  9. Suppose 25 sea gulls were marked in a nesting area. Later, 500 sea gulls were counted, 19 of which were marked. Estimate the population.

● **Lesson 11-6** **The graph shows the growth of a company's DVD sales.**

  10. Decide whether the graph appears misleading. If so, explain how the graph makes the misleading impression.

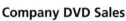
Company DVD Sales
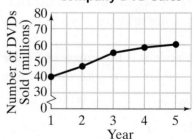

● **Lesson 11-7** **The data show the heights and weights of some 7-year-olds.**

Height	40 in.	39 in.	42 in.	45 in.	48 in.	43 in.	41 in.
Weight	56 lb	52 lb	62 lb	75 lb	72 lb	67 lb	62 lb

  11. Make a scatter plot of the data. Describe any trend you see in the data.

Word Problems

● **Lesson 11-1**

12. You survey students about how many times they ate at a restaurant last month. The results are shown. Make a histogram of the data.

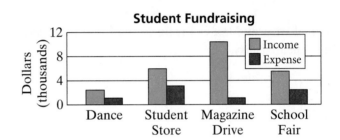

How Many Meals Did You Eat Out Last Month?

Number of Meals	0–3	4–7	8–11	12–15
Frequency	8	12	3	7

13. You record the daily temperature (°F) for the month of June, Make a frequency table of the temperatures below.
    82 81 88 88 87 92 91 85 92 83 82 84 86 89 90
    87 86 84 83 84 87 86 90 91 87 86 80 84 91 90

● **Lesson 11-2   Use the double bar graph.**

14. Which fundraisers had incomes of more than $4,000?

15. Which fundraiser made the most profit? The least profit?

Student Fundraising

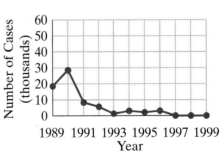

● **Lessons 11-3 through 11-5**

16. **Science** A botanist measures the heights of giant sunflowers in inches. Draw a stem-and-leaf plot for the height data below.
    98 99 94 87 83 74 69 88 78 99 100 87 77.

17. An urban planner wants to know how road construction affects bus drivers. How can the planner survey a random sample of bus drivers?

18. **Ecology** Marine biologists are studying the otter population in a coastal region. There are 20 marked sea otters in the region. In a survey, the biologists count 42 sea otters, of which 12 are marked. About how many sea otters are in the area?

● **Lessons 11-6 and 11-7   For Exercises 19 and 20, use the graph at right showing measles cases in the United States.**

19. What does the graph suggest about the occurrence of measles in 1990?

20. Use the data to draw a graph that does not mislead.

21. What trend do you expect to see in a scatter plot in which the horizontal axis represents hours spent watching television and the vertical axis represents hours spent studying? Explain.

Skills

● **Lesson 12-1** **You roll a number cube. Find each probability.**

1. rolling a 2

2. rolling a 3 or 5

3. rolling a 2, 4, or 6

● **Lesson 12-2**

4. A quality control engineer at a factory inspected 300 glow sticks for quality. The engineer found 15 defective glow sticks. What is the experimental probability that a glow stick is defective?

The number of wins and losses for basketball teams are shown. Find each experimental probability.

5. Kingwood, Humble, Texas
Wins: 37, Losses: 4
Find P(Win).

6. Westchester, Los Angeles, Calif
Wins: 25 Losses: 3
Find P(Loss).

● **Lesson 12-3** **Make a table to show the sample space for each situation. Then find the number of outcomes.**

7. You toss three coins.

8. You spin a number 1 to 6 and toss a coin.

9. You choose one letter from each of the two sets of letters E, F, G, H and A, B, C.

10. You toss two coins and spin a spinner with three congruent sections colored red, white, and blue. Draw a tree diagram to find the sample space. Then find P(2 heads, then blue).

● **Lesson 12-4** **A bag contains 6 green marbles, 8 blue marbles, and 3 red marbles. Find $P(B)$ after A has happened.**

11. A: Draw a green marble. Keep it.
B: Draw a red marble.

12. A: Draw a blue marble. Replace it.
B: Draw a red marble.

● **Lessons 12-5 and 12-6** **State whether the situation is a *permutation* or a *combination*. Then answer the question.**

13. In how many ways can a committee of 2 be chosen from 5 members?

14. In how many ways can a president and a treasurer be selected from a club of 5 members?

Word Problems

● **Lessons 12-1 and 12-2**

15. You write the letters M, I, S, S, I, S, S, I, P, P, and I on cards and mix them in a hat. You select one card without looking. Find the probability of selecting an I.

16. Suppose you have 3 red, 3 black, and 3 blue marbles in your pocket. Does the probability of randomly selecting a black marble equal the probability of randomly selecting a blue one? Explain.

17. A quality-control inspector finds flaws in 6 of 45 tools examined. If the trend continues, what is the best prediction of the number of defective tools in a batch of 540?

18. Crispy Cereal offers one free prize in every box: a baseball card, a keychain, or a bracelet. You buy 3 boxes. Find the experimental probability of *not* getting a baseball card. Simulate the problem.

● **Lessons 12-3 and 12-4**

19. Make a tree diagram for choosing one letter at random from each of two sets of letters: A, B, and C and W, X, Y, and Z. Then find the probability of choosing an A and a W.

20. A spinner has equal sections numbered 1 to 3. You spin the spinner 4 times. How many different outcomes are possible?

21. You drop a coin twice inside the rectangle. Estimate the probability that the coin lands in one of the circles both times. Use 3 for π.

22. A volleyball team won 31 games and lost 4 games in one season. The coach has a summary sheet for each game. The coach selects two sheets at random to compare. Find P(win, then loss) without replacement.

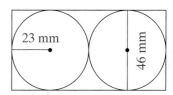

23 mm   46 mm

● **Lessons 12-5 and 12-6**

23. There are 20 teams that compete in a tournament. Find the number of different ways that two teams can finish in first and second place.

24. You scramble the letters P, A, and N. Make an organized list of the sample space. Then find the number of the groups that form real words. What are they?

25. You have six toppings to use for a pizza. How many different three-topping pizzas can you make?

26. A club of 50 people wants to select 4 members as representatives. How many different combinations of 4 people are possible?

Comparing and Ordering Whole Numbers

The numbers on a number line are in order from least to greatest.

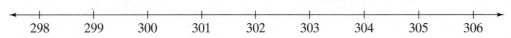

You can use a number line to compare whole numbers. Use the symbols > (is greater than) and < (is less than).

EXAMPLE

1 Use > or < to compare the whole numbers.

a. 303 ■ 299

303 is to the right of 299.

303 > 299

b. 301 ■ 305

301 is to the left of 305.

301 < 305

The value of a digit depends on its place in a number. Compare digits starting from the left.

EXAMPLE

2 Use > or < to compare the whole numbers.

a. 12,060,012,875 ■ 12,060,012,675

8 hundreds > 6 hundreds, so
12,060,012,875 > 12,060,012,675

b. 465,320 ■ 4,653,208

0 millions < 4 millions, so
465,320 < 4,653,208

Exercises

Use > or < to compare the whole numbers.

1. 3,660 ■ 360

2. 74,328 ■ 74,238

3. 88,010 ■ 8,101

4. 87,524 ■ 9,879

5. 295,286 ■ 295,826

6. 829,631 ■ 842,832

7. 932,401 ■ 932,701

8. 60,000 ■ 500,000

9. 1,609,372,002 ■ 609,172,002

10. 45,248,315,150 ■ 45,283,718,150

Order the numbers from least to greatest.

11. 3,747; 3,474; 3,774; 3,347; 3,734

12. 70,903; 70,309; 73,909; 73,090

13. 32,056,403; 302,056,403; 30,265,403; 30,256,403

14. 884,172; 881,472; 887,142; 881,872

Rounding Whole Numbers

You can use number lines to help you round numbers.

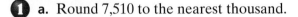

EXAMPLE

1 **a.** Round 7,510 to the nearest thousand.

b. Round 237 to the nearest ten.

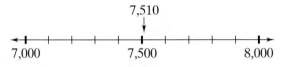 

7,510 is between 7,000 and 8,000.

7,510 rounds to 8,000.

237 is between 230 and 240.

237 rounds to 240.

To round a number to a particular place, look at the digit to the right of that place. If the digit is less than 5, round down. If the digit is 5 or more, round up.

EXAMPLE

2 Round to the place of the underlined digit.

a. 3,4<u>6</u>3,280

The digit to the right of the 6 is 3, so 3,463,280 rounds down to 3,460,000.

b. 28<u>9</u>,543

The digit to the right of the 9 is 5, so 289,543 rounds up to 290,000.

Exercises

Round to the nearest ten.

1. 42 **2.** 89 **3.** 671 **4.** 3,482 **5.** 7,029 **6.** 661,423

Round to the nearest thousand.

7. 5,800 **8.** 3,100 **9.** 44,500 **10.** 9,936 **11.** 987 **12.** 313,591

13. 5,641 **14.** 37,896 **15.** 82,019 **16.** 808,155 **17.** 34,501 **18.** 650,828

Round to the place of the underlined digit.

19. 68,<u>8</u>52 **20.** <u>4</u>51,006 **21.** 3,40<u>6</u>,781 **22.** 2<u>8</u>,512,030 **23.** 71,2<u>2</u>5,003

24. 96,<u>3</u>59 **25.** 4<u>0</u>1,223 **26.** <u>8</u>,902 **27.** 3,6<u>7</u>7 **28.** 2,551,<u>7</u>50

29. 6<u>8</u>,663 **30.** 70<u>1</u>,803,229 **31.** 56<u>5</u>,598 **32.** 32,<u>8</u>10 **33.** 1,0<u>4</u>6,300

Multiplying Whole Numbers

When you multiply by a two-digit number, first multiply by the ones and then multiply by the tens. Add the products.

EXAMPLE

1 Multiply 62×704.

Step 1	Step 2	Step 3
704	704	704
× 62	× 62	× 62
1408	1408	1408
	42240	+ 42240
		43,648

EXAMPLE

2 Find each product.

a. 93×6

$$
\begin{array}{r}
93 \\
\times\ 6 \\
\hline
558
\end{array}
$$

b. 25×48

$$
\begin{array}{r}
48 \\
\times\ 25 \\
\hline
240 \\
+\ 960 \\
\hline
1,200
\end{array}
$$

c. 80×921

$$
\begin{array}{r}
921 \\
\times\ 80 \\
\hline
73,680
\end{array}
$$

Exercises

Find each product.

1. 74 ×6	**2.** 35 ×9	**3.** 53 ×7	**4.** 80 ×8	**5.** 98 ×4	**6.** 65 ×8
7. 512 ×3	**8.** 407 ×9	**9.** 225 ×6	**10.** 340 ×5	**11.** 816 ×7	**12.** 603 ×3
13. 70 ×36	**14.** 41 ×55	**15.** 38 ×49	**16.** 601 ×87	**17.** 271 ×34	**18.** 450 ×67

19. 6×82 **20.** 405×5 **21.** 81×9 **22.** 3×274 **23.** 553×4

24. 60×84 **25.** 52×17 **26.** 31×90 **27.** 78×52 **28.** 43×66

29. 826×3 **30.** 702×4 **31.** 5×128 **32.** 6×339 **33.** 781×7

Dividing Whole Numbers

First estimate the quotient by rounding the divisor, the dividend, or both. When you divide, after you bring down a digit, you must write a digit in the quotient.

EXAMPLE

Find each quotient.

a. $741 \div 8$

Estimate:
$720 \div 8 \approx 90$

$$
\begin{array}{r}
92 \text{ R5} \\
8\overline{)741} \\
-72 \\
\hline
21 \\
-16 \\
\hline
5
\end{array}
$$

b. $838 \div 43$

Estimate:
$800 \div 40 \approx 20$

$$
\begin{array}{r}
19 \text{ R21} \\
43\overline{)838} \\
-43 \\
\hline
408 \\
-387 \\
\hline
21
\end{array}
$$

c. $367 \div 9$

Estimate:
$360 \div 9 \approx 40$

$$
\begin{array}{r}
40 \text{ R7} \\
9\overline{)367} \\
-360 \\
\hline
7
\end{array}
$$

Exercises

Divide.

1. $4\overline{)61}$
2. $8\overline{)53}$
3. $7\overline{)90}$
4. $3\overline{)84}$
5. $6\overline{)81}$

6. $6\overline{)469}$
7. $3\overline{)653}$
8. $8\overline{)645}$
9. $9\overline{)231}$
10. $4\overline{)415}$

11. $60\overline{)461}$
12. $40\overline{)213}$
13. $70\overline{)517}$
14. $30\overline{)432}$
15. $80\overline{)276}$

16. $43\overline{)273}$
17. $52\overline{)281}$
18. $69\overline{)207}$
19. $38\overline{)121}$
20. $81\overline{)433}$

21. $94\overline{)1,368}$
22. $62\overline{)1,147}$
23. $55\overline{)2,047}$
24. $85\overline{)1,450}$
25. $46\overline{)996}$

26. $94 \div 4$
27. $66 \div 9$
28. $90 \div 5$
29. $69 \div 6$
30. $58 \div 8$

31. $323 \div 5$
32. $849 \div 7$
33. $404 \div 8$
34. $934 \div 3$
35. $619 \div 6$

36. $777 \div 50$
37. $528 \div 20$
38. $443 \div 40$
39. $312 \div 40$
40. $335 \div 60$

41. $382 \div 72$
42. $580 \div 68$
43. $279 \div 43$
44. $232 \div 27$
45. $331 \div 93$

46. $614 \div 35$
47. $423 \div 28$
48. $489 \div 15$
49. $1,134 \div 51$
50. $1,103 \div 26$

Place Value and Decimals

Each digit in a decimal has both a place and a value. The value of any place is one tenth the value of the place to its left. In the chart below, the digit 5 is in the hundredths place. So its value is 5 hundredths.

thousands	hundreds	tens	ones	.	tenths	hundredths	thousandths	ten-thousandths	hundred-thousandths
2	8	3	6	.	7	5	0	1	4

EXAMPLE

a. In what place is the digit 8?

hundreds

b. What is the value of the digit 8?

8 hundreds

Exercises

Use the chart above. Write the place of each digit.

1. 3   **2.** 4   **3.** 6   **4.** 7   **5.** 1   **6.** 0

Use the chart above. Write the value of each digit.

7. 3   **8.** 4   **9.** 6   **10.** 7   **11.** 1   **12.** 0

Write the value of the digit 6 in each number.

13. 0.162   **14.** 0.016   **15.** 13.672   **16.** 1,640.8   **17.** 62.135

18. 26.34   **19.** 6,025.9   **20.** 0.6003   **21.** 2,450.65   **22.** 615.28

23. 3.16125   **24.** 1.20641   **25.** 0.15361   **26.** 1.55736   **27.** 10.0563

Write the value of the underlined digit.

28. 2_4_.0026   **29.** 14.9_3_1   **30.** 5.78_9_4   **31.** 0._8_7   **32.** 10.056_3_

Reading and Writing Decimals

A place value chart can help you read and write decimals. When there are no ones, write a zero before the decimal point.

billions	hundred millions	ten millions	millions	hundred thousands	ten thousands	thousands	hundreds	tens	ones	.	tenths	hundredths	thousandths	ten-thousandths	hundred-thousandths	millionths	Read
									0	.	0	7					7 hundredths
								2	3	.	0	1	4				23 and 14 thousandths
3	0	0	0	0	0	0	0	0	0	.	8						3 billion and 8 tenths
									5	.	0	0	0	1	0	2	5 and 102 millionths

EXAMPLE

a. Write thirteen ten-thousandths in numerals.

Ten-thousandths is 4 places after the decimal point. So the decimal will have 4 places after the decimal point. The number is 0.0013.

b. Write 1.025 in words.

The digit 5 is in the thousandths place. So 1.025 is one and twenty-five thousandths.

Exercises

Write a number for the given words.

1. three hundredths
2. twenty-one millions
3. six and two hundredths
4. two billion and six tenths
5. two and five hundredths
6. five thousand twelve
7. seven millionths
8. forty-one ten-thousandths
9. eleven thousandths
10. one and twenty-five millionths
11. three hundred four thousandths

Write each number in words.

12. 5,700.4
13. 3,000,000.09
14. 12.000069
15. 900.02
16. 25.00007
17. 0.00015

Rounding Decimals

You can use number lines to help you round decimals.

EXAMPLE

1 **a.** Round 1.627 to the nearest tenth.

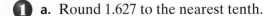

1.627 is between 1.6 and 1.7.

1.627 rounds to 1.6.

b. Round 0.248 to the nearest hundredth.

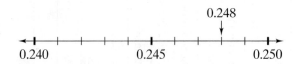

0.248 is between 0.24 and 0.25.

0.248 rounds to 0.25.

To round a number to a particular place, look at the digit to the right of that place. If the digit is less than 5, round down. If the digit is 5 or more, round up.

EXAMPLE

2 **a.** Round 2.4301 to the nearest whole number.

The digit to the right of 2 is 4, so 2.4301 rounds down to 2.

b. Round 0.0515 to the nearest thousandth.

The digit to the right of 1 is 5, so 0.0515 rounds up to 0.052.

Exercises

Round to the nearest tenth.

1. 2.75	**2.** 3.816	**3.** 19.72	**4.** 401.1603	**5.** 499.491	**6.** 3.949
7. 4.67522	**8.** 20.397	**9.** 399.956	**10.** 129.98	**11.** 96.4045	**12.** 125.66047

Round to the nearest hundredth.

13. 31.723	**14.** 14.869	**15.** 1.78826	**16.** 0.1119	**17.** 736.941	**18.** 9.6057
19. 0.699	**20.** 4.231	**21.** 12.09531	**22.** 5.77125	**23.** 0.9195	**24.** 4.0033

Round to the nearest thousandth.

25. 0.4387	**26.** 0.0649	**27.** 3.4953	**28.** 8.07092	**29.** 0.6008	**30.** 6.0074

Round to the nearest whole number.

31. 3.942	**32.** 10.4	**33.** 79.52	**34.** 105.3002	**35.** 431.23	**36.** 0.4962

Multiplying Decimals

When you multiply decimals, first multiply as if the factors were whole numbers. Then, count the decimal places in both factors to find how many places are needed in the product.

EXAMPLE

1 Multiply 2.5×1.8.

$$
\begin{array}{r}
1.8 \quad \leftarrow \textbf{one decimal place} \\
\times\ 2.5 \quad \leftarrow \textbf{one decimal place} \\
\hline
90 \\
+\ 360 \\
\hline
4.50 \quad \leftarrow \textbf{two decimal places}
\end{array}
$$

EXAMPLE

2 Find each product.

a. 0.7×1.02

$$
\begin{array}{r}
1.02 \\
\times\ 0.7 \\
\hline
0.714
\end{array}
$$

b. 0.03×407

$$
\begin{array}{r}
407 \\
\times\ 0.03 \\
\hline
12.21
\end{array}
$$

c. 0.62×2.45

$$
\begin{array}{r}
2.45 \\
\times\ 0.62 \\
\hline
490 \\
+\ 14700 \\
\hline
1.5190
\end{array}
$$

d. 75×3.06

$$
\begin{array}{r}
3.06 \\
\times\ 75 \\
\hline
1530 \\
+\ 21420 \\
\hline
229.50
\end{array}
$$

Exercises

Multiply.

1. $\begin{array}{r} 0.3 \\ \times\ 8 \end{array}$

2. $\begin{array}{r} 5 \\ \times\ 0.06 \end{array}$

3. $\begin{array}{r} 0.04 \\ \times\ 7 \end{array}$

4. $\begin{array}{r} 6 \\ \times\ 0.8 \end{array}$

5. $\begin{array}{r} 3.1 \\ \times\ 0.05 \end{array}$

6. $\begin{array}{r} 14 \\ \times\ 0.2 \end{array}$

7. $\begin{array}{r} 3.1 \\ \times\ 6 \end{array}$

8. $\begin{array}{r} 0.05 \\ \times\ 43 \end{array}$

9. $\begin{array}{r} 0.27 \\ \times\ 5 \end{array}$

10. $\begin{array}{r} 72 \\ \times\ 0.6 \end{array}$

11. $\begin{array}{r} 0.8 \\ \times\ 312 \end{array}$

12. $\begin{array}{r} 4.56 \\ \times\ 7 \end{array}$

13. 5×2.41

14. 704×0.3

15. 9×1.35

16. 1.2×0.3

17. 0.04×2.5

18. 6.6×0.3

19. 15.1×0.02

20. 0.8×31.3

21. 0.07×25.1

22. 42.2×0.9

23. 0.6×30.02

24. 0.05×11.8

25. 71.13×0.4

26. 48×2.1

27. 6.3×85

28. 0.42×98

29. 76×3.3

30. 0.77×51

31. 5.2×4.8

32. 0.12×6.1

Zeros in the Product

When you multiply with decimals, start at the right of the product to count the number of decimal places. Sometimes you need to write extra zeros to the left of a product before you can place the decimal point.

EXAMPLE

1 Multiply 0.03×0.51.

Step 1

$$
\begin{array}{r}
0.51 \quad \leftarrow \text{two decimal places} \\
\times\ 0.03 \quad \leftarrow \text{two decimal places} \\
\hline
153 \quad \leftarrow \text{four decimal places}
\end{array}
$$

Step 2

$$
\begin{array}{r}
0.51 \\
\times\ 0.03 \\
\hline
0.0153
\end{array}
$$

$\leftarrow$ Put extra zeros to the left. Then place the decimal point.

EXAMPLE

2 Find each product.

a. 0.2×0.3

$$
\begin{array}{r}
0.3 \\
\times\ 0.2 \\
\hline
0.06
\end{array}
$$

b. 0.5×0.04

$$
\begin{array}{r}
0.04 \\
\times\ 0.5 \\
\hline
0.020
\end{array}
$$

c. 4×0.02

$$
\begin{array}{r}
0.02 \\
\times\ 4 \\
\hline
0.08
\end{array}
$$

d. 0.02×0.45

$$
\begin{array}{r}
0.45 \\
\times\ 0.02 \\
\hline
0.0090
\end{array}
$$

Exercises

Multiply.

1. $\begin{array}{r} 0.1 \\ \times\ 0.6 \end{array}$

2. $\begin{array}{r} 0.4 \\ \times\ 0.2 \end{array}$

3. $\begin{array}{r} 0.05 \\ \times\ 0.06 \end{array}$

4. $\begin{array}{r} 0.01 \\ \times\ 8 \end{array}$

5. $\begin{array}{r} 0.7 \\ \times\ 0.02 \end{array}$

6. $\begin{array}{r} 0.03 \\ \times\ 0.4 \end{array}$

7. $\begin{array}{r} 0.03 \\ \times\ 0.9 \end{array}$

8. $\begin{array}{r} 0.06 \\ \times\ 0.5 \end{array}$

9. $\begin{array}{r} 0.2 \\ \times\ 0.02 \end{array}$

10. $\begin{array}{r} 7 \\ \times\ 0.01 \end{array}$

11. $\begin{array}{r} 0.05 \\ \times\ 0.05 \end{array}$

12. $\begin{array}{r} 0.6 \\ \times\ 0.06 \end{array}$

13. 0.4×0.08

14. 0.07×0.05

15. 0.03×0.03

16. 0.09×0.05

17. 0.5×0.08

18. 0.06×0.7

19. 0.07×0.01

20. 0.16×0.2

21. 0.01×0.74

22. 0.47×0.08

23. 0.76×0.1

24. 0.19×0.3

25. 0.5×0.17

26. 0.31×0.08

27. 0.14×0.05

28. 0.07×0.85

29. 0.45×0.06

30. 0.4×0.23

31. 0.17×0.06

32. 0.3×0.24

Dividing a Decimal by a Whole Number

When you divide a decimal by a whole number, first divide as if the numbers were whole numbers. Then put a decimal point in the quotient directly above the decimal point in the dividend.

1 Divide $0.256 \div 8$.

Step 1

$$
\begin{array}{r}
32 \\
8\overline{)0.256} \\
-24 \\
\overline{16} \\
-16 \\
\overline{0}
\end{array}
$$

Step 2

$$
\begin{array}{r}
0.032 \\
8\overline{)0.256} \\
-24 \\
\overline{16} \\
-16 \\
\overline{0}
\end{array}
$$

← **Put extra zeros to the left. Then place the decimal point.**

2 Find each quotient.

a. $12.6 \div 6$

$$
\begin{array}{r}
2.1 \\
6\overline{)12.6} \\
-12 \\
\overline{06} \\
-6 \\
\overline{0}
\end{array}
$$

b. $37.26 \div 81$

$$
\begin{array}{r}
0.46 \\
81\overline{)37.26} \\
-324 \\
\overline{486} \\
-486 \\
\overline{0}
\end{array}
$$

c. $0.666 \div 9$

$$
\begin{array}{r}
0.074 \\
9\overline{)0.666} \\
-63 \\
\overline{36} \\
-36 \\
\overline{0}
\end{array}
$$

Exercises

Divide.

1. $4\overline{)28.56}$ **2.** $5\overline{)16.5}$ **3.** $9\overline{)6.984}$ **4.** $6\overline{)91.44}$ **5.** $4\overline{)35.16}$

6. $81\overline{)33.291}$ **7.** $22\overline{)2.42}$ **8.** $26\overline{)1,723.8}$ **9.** $83\overline{)15.272}$ **10.** $39\overline{)26.91}$

11. $17.52 \div 2$ **12.** $10.53 \div 9$ **13.** $14.49 \div 7$ **14.** $37.14 \div 6$

15. $0.0324 \div 9$ **16.** $0.1352 \div 8$ **17.** $0.0882 \div 6$ **18.** $0.8682 \div 6$

19. $79.599 \div 13$ **20.** $45.918 \div 18$ **21.** $59.7 \div 15$ **22.** $74.664 \div 12$

23. $12.342 \div 22$ **24.** $29.792 \div 32$ **25.** $22.568 \div 26$ **26.** $11.340 \div 36$

Powers of Ten

You can use shortcuts when multiplying and dividing by powers of ten.

When you multiply by...	move the decimal point...	When you divide by...	move the decimal point...
1,000	3 places to the right.	1,000	3 places to the left.
100	2 places to the right.	100	2 places to the left.
10	1 place to the right.	10	1 place to the left.
0.1	1 place to the left.	0.1	1 place to the right.
0.01	2 places to the left.	0.01	2 places to the right.

EXAMPLE

Multiply or divide.

a. 0.3×0.01

$0.00.3$ ← Move the decimal point 2 places to the left.

$0.3 \times 0.01 = 0.003$

b. $0.18 \div 1,000$

$0.000.18$ ← Move the decimal point 3 places to the left.

$0.18 \div 1,000 = 0.00018$

Exercises

Multiply.

1. 3.2×0.01

2. $1,000 \times 0.12$

3. 0.7×0.1

4. 0.01×6.2

5. 0.09×100

6. 23.6×0.01

7. 5.2×10

8. $0.08 \times 1,000$

9. 100×0.05

10. 0.1×0.24

11. 18.03×0.1

12. 6.1×100

Divide.

13. $82.3 \div 0.1$

14. $0.4 \div 1,000$

15. $5.02 \div 0.01$

16. $16.5 \div 100$

17. $236.7 \div 0.1$

18. $45.28 \div 10$

19. $0.9 \div 1,000$

20. $1.03 \div 0.01$

21. $42.6 \div 0.1$

22. $203.05 \div 0.01$

23. $4.7 \div 10$

24. $0.07 \div 100$

Multiply or divide.

25. 0.32×0.1

26. $0.03 \div 100$

27. $2.6 \div 0.1$

28. $12.6 \times 1,000$

29. $0.8 \div 1,000$

30. 0.01×6.7

31. 100×0.15

32. $23.5 \div 10$

Zeros in Decimal Division

When you are dividing by a decimal, sometimes you need to use extra zeros in the dividend, the quotient, or both.

EXAMPLE

Find each quotient.

a. $0.14 \div 0.04$

Multiply by 100.

$$
\begin{array}{r}
3.5 \\
0.04\overline{)0.14.0} \\
-12 \\
\hline
20 \\
-20 \\
\hline
0
\end{array}
$$

b. $0.00434 \div 0.07$

Multiply by 100.

$$
\begin{array}{r}
0.062 \\
0.07\overline{)0.00.434} \\
-42 \\
\hline
14 \\
-14 \\
\hline
0
\end{array}
$$

c. $0.045 \div 3.6$

Multiply by 10.

$$
\begin{array}{r}
0.0125 \\
3.6\overline{)0.0.4500} \\
-36 \\
\hline
90 \\
-72 \\
\hline
180 \\
-180 \\
\hline
0
\end{array}
$$

Exercises

Divide.

1. $0.4\overline{)0.001}$

2. $0.05\overline{)0.0023}$

3. $0.02\overline{)0.000162}$

4. $0.6\overline{)0.0015}$

5. $1.2\overline{)0.078}$

6. $0.34\overline{)0.00119}$

7. $0.12\overline{)0.009}$

8. $2.5\overline{)0.021}$

9. $0.0017 \div 0.02$

10. $0.003 \div 0.6$

11. $0.01099 \div 0.7$

12. $0.104 \div 0.05$

13. $0.0945 \div 0.09$

14. $0.00045 \div 0.3$

15. $0.052 \div 0.8$

16. $0.142 \div 0.04$

17. $0.034 \div 0.05$

18. $0.0019 \div 0.2$

19. $0.9 \div 0.2$

20. $0.000175 \div 0.07$

21. $0.0084 \div 1.4$

22. $0.259 \div 3.5$

23. $0.00468 \div 0.52$

24. $0.00056 \div 0.16$

25. $0.0612 \div 7.2$

26. $0.17701 \div 3.1$

27. $0.00063 \div 0.18$

28. $0.011 \div 0.25$

29. $0.3069 \div 9.3$

30. $0.000924 \div 0.44$

31. $0.03234 \div 0.35$

32. $0.00123 \div 8.2$

33. $0.03225 \div 0.75$

34. $0.006 \div 0.75$

35. $0.73 \div 0.25$

36. $0.68 \div 0.002$

37. $0.398 \div 0.05$

38. $0.0004 \div 0.002$

39. $0.125 \div 0.005$

Adding and Subtracting Fractions With Like Denominators

When you add or subtract fractions with the same denominator, first add or subtract the numerators. Write the answer over the denominator.

EXAMPLE

1 Add or subtract. Write the answer in simplest form.

a. $\frac{5}{16} + \frac{3}{16}$

$$\begin{array}{r} \frac{5}{16} \\ + \frac{3}{16} \\ \hline \frac{8}{16} = \frac{1}{2} \end{array}$$

b. $\frac{7}{8} - \frac{1}{8}$

$$\begin{array}{r} \frac{7}{8} \\ - \frac{1}{8} \\ \hline \frac{6}{8} = \frac{3}{4} \end{array}$$

c. $\frac{3}{5} + \frac{2}{5}$

$$\frac{3}{5} + \frac{2}{5} = \frac{5}{5} = 1$$

To add or subtract mixed numbers, add or subtract the fractions first. Then add or subtract the whole numbers.

EXAMPLE

2 Add or subtract. Write the answer in simplest form.

a. $2\frac{5}{8} + 3\frac{1}{8}$

$$\begin{array}{r} 2\frac{5}{8} \\ + 3\frac{1}{8} \\ \hline 5\frac{6}{8} = 5\frac{3}{4} \end{array}$$

b. $4\frac{3}{4} - 1\frac{1}{4}$

$$\begin{array}{r} 4\frac{3}{4} \\ - 1\frac{1}{4} \\ \hline 3\frac{2}{4} = 3\frac{1}{2} \end{array}$$

c. $5\frac{5}{6} + 2\frac{5}{6}$

$$5\frac{5}{6} + 2\frac{5}{6} = 7\frac{10}{6}$$
$$= 7 + 1 + \frac{4}{6}$$
$$= 8\frac{2}{3}$$

Exercises

Add or subtract. Write the answers in simplest form.

1. $\begin{array}{r} \frac{2}{5} \\ + \frac{2}{5} \\ \hline \end{array}$

2. $\begin{array}{r} \frac{2}{6} \\ - \frac{1}{6} \\ \hline \end{array}$

3. $\begin{array}{r} \frac{2}{7} \\ + \frac{2}{7} \\ \hline \end{array}$

4. $\begin{array}{r} 9\frac{1}{3} \\ - 8\frac{1}{3} \\ \hline \end{array}$

5. $\begin{array}{r} 8\frac{6}{7} \\ - 4\frac{2}{7} \\ \hline \end{array}$

6. $\begin{array}{r} 3\frac{1}{10} \\ + 1\frac{3}{10} \\ \hline \end{array}$

7. $\frac{3}{8} + \frac{2}{8}$

8. $\frac{3}{6} - \frac{1}{6}$

9. $\frac{6}{8} - \frac{3}{8}$

10. $\frac{2}{9} + \frac{1}{9}$

11. $\frac{4}{5} - \frac{1}{5}$

12. $\frac{3}{4} + \frac{1}{4}$

13. $8\frac{7}{10} + 2\frac{3}{10}$

14. $1\frac{4}{5} + 3\frac{3}{5}$

15. $2\frac{2}{9} + 3\frac{4}{9}$

16. $8\frac{5}{8} - 3\frac{3}{8}$

17. $9\frac{7}{10} - 2\frac{3}{10}$

18. $9\frac{3}{4} + 1\frac{3}{4}$

Metric Units of Length

The basic unit of length in the metric system is the meter. All the other units are based on the meter. In the chart below, each unit is 10 times the value of the unit to its left.

Unit	Millimeter	Centimeter	Decimeter	Meter	Decameter	Hectometer	Kilometer
Symbol	mm	cm	dm	m	dam	hm	km
Value	0.001 m	0.01 m	0.1 m	1 m	10 m	100 m	1,000 m

To change a measure from one unit to another, start by using the chart to find the relationship between the two units.

EXAMPLE

Complete each equation.

a. $0.8 \text{ km} = \blacksquare \text{ m}$

$1 \text{ km} = 1{,}000 \text{ m}$

$0.8 \times 1{,}000 = 800$ ← To change km to m, multiply by 1,000.

$0.8 \text{ km} = 800 \text{ m}$

c. $\blacksquare \text{ cm} = 2.1 \text{ km}$

$1 \text{ km} = 100{,}000 \text{ cm}$

$2.1 \times 100{,}000 = 210{,}000$ ← To change km to cm, multiply by 100,000.

$210{,}000 \text{ cm} = 2.1 \text{ km}$

b. $17.2 \text{ mm} = \blacksquare \text{ cm}$

$1 \text{ mm} = 0.1 \text{ cm}$

$17.2 \times 0.1 = 1.72$ ← To change mm to cm, multiply by 0.1.

$17.2 \text{ mm} = 1.72 \text{ cm}$

d. $\blacksquare \text{ m} = 5{,}200 \text{ cm}$

$1 \text{ cm} = 0.01 \text{ m}$

$5{,}200 \times 0.01 = 52$ ← To change cm to m, multiply by 0.01.

$52 \text{ m} = 5{,}200 \text{ cm}$

Exercises

Complete each equation.

1. $1 \text{ mm} = \blacksquare \text{ cm}$

2. $1 \text{ m} = \blacksquare \text{ km}$

3. $1 \text{ mm} = \blacksquare \text{ m}$

4. $1 \text{ cm} = \blacksquare \text{ m}$

5. $1.2 \text{ cm} = \blacksquare \text{ km}$

6. $\blacksquare \text{ km} = 45{,}000 \text{ mm}$

7. $\blacksquare \text{ m} = 30 \text{ km}$

8. $6.2 \text{ cm} = \blacksquare \text{ mm}$

9. $3.3 \text{ km} = \blacksquare \text{ m}$

10. $0.6 \text{ mm} = \blacksquare \text{ cm}$

11. $72 \text{ cm} = \blacksquare \text{ m}$

12. $180 \text{ m} = \blacksquare \text{ mm}$

13. $\blacksquare \text{ cm} = 13 \text{ km}$

14. $\blacksquare \text{ m} = 530 \text{ cm}$

15. $4{,}900 \text{ mm} = \blacksquare \text{ m}$

16. $\blacksquare \text{ cm} = 24 \text{ m}$

17. $\blacksquare \text{ km} = 106{,}000 \text{ cm}$

18. $259{,}000 \text{ mm} = \blacksquare \text{ m}$

19. $1{,}200{,}000 \text{ mm} = \blacksquare \text{ km}$

Metric Units of Capacity

The basic unit of capacity in the metric system is the liter. All the other units are based on the liter. In the chart below, each unit is 10 times the value of the unit on the left. Note that we use a capital L as the abbreviation for *liter* to avoid confusion with the number 1.

Unit	Milliliter	Centiliter	Deciliter	Liter	Decaliter	Hectoliter	Kiloliter
Symbol	mL	cL	dL	L	daL	hL	kL
Value	0.001 L	0.01 L	0.1 L	1 L	10 L	100 L	1,000 L

To change a measure from one unit to another, start by using the chart to find the relationship between the two units.

EXAMPLE

Complete each equation.

a. $245 \text{ mL} = \blacksquare \text{ L}$

$1 \text{ mL} = 0.001 \text{ L}$

$245 \times 0.001 = 0.245$ ← To change mL to L, multiply by 0.001.

$245 \text{ mL} = 0.245 \text{ L}$

b. $\blacksquare \text{ mL} = 4.5 \text{ kL}$

$1 \text{ kL} = 1,000,000 \text{ mL}$

$4.5 \times 1,000,000 = 4,500,000$ ← To change kL to mL, multiply by 1,000,000.

$4,500,000 \text{ mL} = 4.5 \text{ kL}$

Exercises

Complete each equation.

1. $1 \text{ L} = \blacksquare \text{ mL}$

2. $1 \text{ mL} = \blacksquare \text{ kL}$

3. $1 \text{ kL} = \blacksquare \text{ L}$

4. $1 \text{ kL} = \blacksquare \text{ mL}$

5. $200 \text{ L} = \blacksquare \text{ kL}$

6. $1.3 \text{ kL} = \blacksquare \text{ mL}$

7. $\blacksquare \text{ kL} = 240 \text{ L}$

8. $0.6 \text{ mL} = \blacksquare \text{ L}$

9. $\blacksquare \text{ kL} = 106,000 \text{ L}$

10. $72 \text{ kL} = \blacksquare \text{ mL}$

11. $\blacksquare \text{ mL} = 1.5 \text{ kL}$

12. $\blacksquare \text{ kL} = 450,000 \text{ mL}$

13. $4,900 \text{ L} = \blacksquare \text{ kL}$

14. $\blacksquare \text{ kL} = 200,000 \text{ mL}$

15. $\blacksquare \text{ L} = 8 \text{ mL}$

16. $4.2 \text{ L} = \blacksquare \text{ mL}$

17. $57,000,000 \text{ mL} = \blacksquare \text{ L}$

18. $28,000 \text{ kL} = \blacksquare \text{ L}$

19. $\blacksquare \text{ mL} = 9,000 \text{ L}$

20. $4,000 \text{ L} = \blacksquare \text{ mL}$

21. $870 \text{ L} = \blacksquare \text{ kL}$

Metric Units of Mass

The basic unit of mass in the metric system is the gram. All the other units are based on the gram. In the chart below, each unit is 10 times the value of the unit to its left.

Unit	Milligram	Centigram	Decigram	Gram	Decagram	Hectogram	Kilogram
Symbol	mg	cg	dg	g	dag	hg	kg
Value	0.001 g	0.01 g	0.1 g	1 g	10 g	100 g	1,000 g

To change a measure from one unit to another, start by using the chart to find the relationship between the two units.

EXAMPLE

Complete each equation.

a. $2.3 \text{ kg} = \blacksquare \text{ g}$

$1 \text{ kg} = 1,000 \text{ g}$

$2.3 \times 1,000 = 2,300$ ← To change kg to g, multiply by 1,000.

$2.3 \text{ kg} = 2,300 \text{ g}$

b.

$\blacksquare \text{ g} = 250 \text{ mg}$

$1 \text{ mg} = 0.001 \text{ g}$

$250 \times 0.001 = 0.25$ ←To change mg to g, multiply by 0.001.

$0.25 \text{ g} = 250 \text{ mg}$

Exercises

Complete each equation.

1. $1 \text{ mg} = \blacksquare \text{ g}$

2. $1 \text{ g} = \blacksquare \text{ kg}$

3. $1 \text{ mg} = \blacksquare \text{ kg}$

4. $1 \text{ g} = \blacksquare \text{ mg}$

5. $1 \text{ kg} = \blacksquare \text{ g}$

6. $1 \text{ kg} = \blacksquare \text{ mg}$

7. $\blacksquare \text{ g} = 8 \text{ mg}$

8. $1,500 \text{ mg} = \blacksquare \text{ kg}$

9. $\blacksquare \text{ kg} = 200,000 \text{ g}$

10. $\blacksquare \text{ mg} = 3.7 \text{ g}$

11. $0.6 \text{ mg} = \blacksquare \text{ g}$

12. $370 \text{ g} = \blacksquare \text{ kg}$

13. $\blacksquare \text{ kg} = 300,000 \text{ mg}$

14. $900 \text{ g} = \blacksquare \text{ mg}$

15. $\blacksquare \text{ kg} = 5.7 \text{ mg}$

16. $120 \text{ g} = \blacksquare \text{ kg}$

17. $\blacksquare \text{ kg} = 440 \text{ g}$

18. $\blacksquare \text{ kg} = 1,006,000 \text{ mg}$

19. $0.009 \text{ kg} = \blacksquare \text{ mg}$

20. $0.2 \text{ mg} = \blacksquare \text{ g}$

21. $8.6 \text{ kg} = \blacksquare \text{ g}$

Table 1 Measures

Metric	Customary
Length	**Length**
10 millimeters (mm) = 1 centimeter (cm) 100 cm = 1 meter (m) 1,000 mm = 1 m 1,000 m = 1 kilometer (km)	12 inches (in.) = 1 foot (ft) 36 in. = 1 yard (yd) 3 ft = 1 yd 5,280 ft = 1 mile (mi) 1,760 yd = 1 mi
Area	**Area**

100 square millimeters (mm^2) =
  1 square centimeter (cm^2)
10,000 cm^2 = 1 square meter (m^2)
	144 square inches (in.^{2}) =
	  1 square foot (ft^2)
	9 ft^2 = 1 square yard (yd^2)
	4,840 yd^2 = 1 acre

Volume	**Volume**

1,000 cubic millimeters (mm^3) =
  1 cubic centimeter (cm^3)
1,000,000 cm^3 = 1 cubic meter (m^3)
	1,728 cubic inches (in.^{3}) =
	  1 cubic foot (ft^3)
	27 ft^3 = 1 cubic yard (yd^3)

Mass	**Mass**
1,000 milligrams (mg) = 1 gram (g) 1,000 g = 1 kilogram (kg)	16 ounces (oz) = 1 pound (lb) 2,000 lb = 1 ton (t)
Liquid Capacity	**Liquid Capacity**
1,000 milliliters (mL) = 1 liter (L)	8 fluid ounces (fl oz) = 1 cup (c) 2 c = 1 pint (pt) 2 pt = 1 quart (qt) 4 qt = 1 gallon (gal)

Time

1 minute (min) = 60 seconds (s)
1 hour (h) = 60 min
1 day (d) = 24 h
1 year (yr) = 365 d

Table 2 Reading Math Symbols

$\approx$	is approximately equal to	p. 4
$-$	minus (subtraction)	p. 4
$=$	is equal to	p. 4
$+$	plus (addition)	p. 5
$\div$	divide (division)	p. 5
$(\ )$	parentheses for grouping	p. 9
$\times, \cdot$	times (multiplication)	p. 13
$|a|$	absolute value of a	p. 31
$-a$	opposite of a	p. 31
$>$	is greater than	p. 32
$<$	is less than	p. 32
$\circ$	degrees	p. 34
$[\ ]$	brackets for grouping	p. 48
a^n	nth power of a	p. 68
$\wedge$	raise to a power (calculator key)	p. 69
$\ldots$	and so on	p. 97
$\neq$	is not equal to	p. 136
$\frac{1}{a}$	reciprocal of a	p. 141
$\overset{?}{=}$	Is the statement true?	p. 174
$\geq$	is greater than or equal to	p. 205
$\leq$	is less than or equal to	p. 205
$a : b$	ratio of a to b	p. 228
$\angle A$	angle with vertex A	p. 251
AB	length of segment $\overline{AB}$	p. 251
$\sim$	is similar to	p. 252
$\triangle ABC$	triangle with vertices ABC	p. 252
$\%$	percent	p. 274
$\overleftrightarrow{AB}$	line AB	p. 324
$\overrightarrow{AB}$	ray AB	p. 324

$\overline{AB}$	segment AB	p. 324
$\parallel$	is parallel to	p. 325
$\angle ABC$	angle with sides BA and BC	p. 330
$m\angle ABC$	measure of angle ABC	p. 330
$\cong$	is congruent to	p. 346
$\overset{\frown}{AB}$	arc AB	p. 351
d	diameter	p. 353
r	radius	p. 353
$\perp$	is perpendicular to	p. 362
P	perimeter	p. 375
ℓ	length	p. 375
w	width	p. 375
A	area	p. 380
b	base length	p. 380
h	height	p. 380
b_1, b_2	base lengths of a trapezoid	p. 388
C	circumference	p. 394
π	pi, an irrational number approximately equal to 3.14	p. 394
$\sqrt{x}$	nonnegative square root of x	p. 400
V	volume	p. 421
B	area of base	p. 422
(a, b)	ordered pair with x-coordinate a and y-coordinate b	p. 486
$F \rightarrow F'$	F maps onto F'	p. 510
A'	image of A, A prime	p. 510
$P(\text{event})$	probability of the event	p. 580
$n!$	n factorial	p. 606

Table 3 Squares and Square Roots

Number	Square	Positive Square Root	Number	Square	Positive Square Root
n	n^2	$\sqrt{n}$	n	n^2	$\sqrt{n}$
1	1	1.000	51	2,601	7.141
2	4	1.414	52	2,704	7.211
3	9	1.732	53	2,809	7.280
4	16	2.000	54	2,916	7.348
5	25	2.236	55	3,025	7.416
6	36	2.449	56	3,136	7.483
7	49	2.646	57	3,249	7.550
8	64	2.828	58	3,364	7.616
9	81	3.000	59	3,481	7.681
10	100	3.162	60	3,600	7.746
11	121	3.317	61	3,721	7.810
12	144	3.464	62	3,844	7.874
13	169	3.606	63	3,969	7.937
14	196	3.742	64	4,096	8.000
15	225	3.873	65	4,225	8.062
16	256	4.000	66	4,356	8.124
17	289	4.123	67	4,489	8.185
18	324	4.243	68	4,624	8.246
19	361	4.359	69	4,761	8.307
20	400	4.472	70	4,900	8.367
21	441	4.583	71	5,041	8.426
22	484	4.690	72	5,184	8.485
23	529	4.796	73	5,329	8.544
24	576	4.899	74	5,476	8.602
25	625	5.000	75	5,625	8.660
26	676	5.099	76	5,776	8.718
27	729	5.196	77	5,929	8.775
28	784	5.292	78	6,084	8.832
29	841	5.385	79	6,241	8.888
30	900	5.477	80	6,400	8.944
31	961	5.568	81	6,561	9.000
32	1,024	5.657	82	6,724	9.055
33	1,089	5.745	83	6,889	9.110
34	1,156	5.831	84	7,056	9.165
35	1,225	5.916	85	7,225	9.220
36	1,296	6.000	86	7,396	9.274
37	1,369	6.083	87	7,569	9.327
38	1,444	6.164	88	7,744	9.381
39	1,521	6.245	89	7,921	9.434
40	1,600	6.325	90	8,100	9.487
41	1,681	6.403	91	8,281	9.539
42	1,764	6.481	92	8,464	9.592
43	1,849	6.557	93	8,649	9.644
44	1,936	6.633	94	8,836	9.695
45	2,025	6.708	95	9,025	9.747
46	2,116	6.782	96	9,216	9.798
47	2,209	6.856	97	9,409	9.849
48	2,304	6.928	98	9,604	9.899
49	2,401	7.000	99	9,801	9.950
50	2,500	7.071	100	10,000	10.000

Table 4 For Use With Problem Solving Applications

Chapter 1

Temperature Extremes and Annual Precipitation

Location	High Temperature (°F)	Low Temperature (°F)	Annual Precipitation (in.)
Anchorage, Alaska	86	−38	14.7
El Paso, Tex.	109	−8	8.0
Indianapolis, Ind.	107	−25	39.2
Miami, Fla.	100	28	59.9
Pago Pago, Amer. Samoa	98	67	193.6
San José, Costa Rica	92	49	70.8
South Pole Station	6	−107	0.1

SOURCE: *The Weather Almanac*

Chapter 9

Animal Longevity

Animal	Birth Weight (Male) (g)	Maximum Life Span (yr)
Dragonfly	1	0.1
Rat	6	3.3
Salmon	15	13
Spoonbill	45	10
Rabbit	65	13
Cat	98	28
Dog (cocker spaniel)	240	20

Formulas and Properties

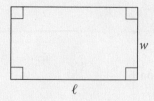

$P = 2\ell + 2w$

$A = \ell w$

Rectangle

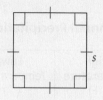

$P = 4s$

$A = s^2$

Square

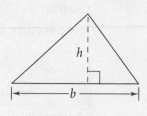

$A = \frac{1}{2}bh$

Triangle

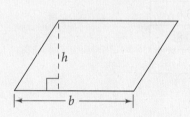

$A = bh$

Parallelogram

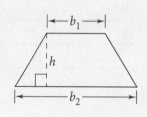

$A = \frac{1}{2}(b_1 + b_2)h$

Trapezoid

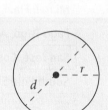

$C = 2\pi r$ or $C = \pi d$

$A = \pi r^2$

Circle

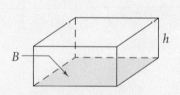

$V = Bh$

Rectangular Prism

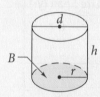

$V = Bh$

Cylinder

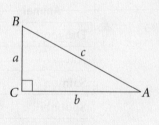

$a^2 + b^2 = c^2$

Pythagorean Theorem

Properties of Real Numbers

Unless otherwise stated, the variables $a, b, c,$ and d used in these properties can be replaced with any number represented on a number line.

Identity Properties

Addition	$a + 0 = a$ and $0 + a = a$
Multiplication	$a \cdot 1 = a$ and $1 \cdot a = a$

Commutative Properties

Addition	$a + b = b + a$
Multiplication	$a \cdot b = b \cdot a$

Associative Properties

Addition	$(a + b) + c = a + (b + c)$
Multiplication	$(a \cdot b) \cdot c = a \cdot (b \cdot c)$

Inverse Properties

Addition

$a + (-a) = 0$ and $-a + a = 0$

Multiplication

$a \cdot \frac{1}{a} = 1$ and $\frac{1}{a} \cdot a = 1 \ (a \neq 0)$

Distributive Properties

$a(b + c) = ab + ac \quad (b + c)a = ba + ca$

$a(b - c) = ab - ac \quad (b - c)a = ba - ca$

Properties of Equality

Addition	If $a = b$, then $a + c = b + c$.
Subtraction	If $a = b$, then $a - c = b - c$.
Multiplication	If $a = b$, then $a \cdot c = b \cdot c$.
Division	If $a = b$, and $c \neq 0$, then $\frac{a}{c} = \frac{b}{c}$.
Substitution	If $a = b$, then b can replace a in any expression.
Reflexive	$a = a$
Symmetric	If $a = b$, then $b = a$.
Transitive	If $a = b$ and $b = c$, then $a = c$.

Cross Products Property

$\frac{a}{c} = \frac{b}{d}$ is equivalent to $ad = bc$.

Zero Product Property

If $ab = 0$, then $a = 0$ or $b = 0$.

Closure Property

$a + b$ is a unique real number.

ab is a unique real number.

Density Property

Between any two rational numbers, there is at least one other rational number.

Properties of Inequality

Addition	If $a > b$, then $a + c > b + c$.
	If $a < b$, then $a + c < b + c$.
Subtraction	If $a > b$, then $a - c > b - c$.
	If $a < b$, then $a - c < b - c$.

Multiplication

If $a > b$ and $c > 0$, then $ac > bc$.

If $a < b$ and $c > 0$, then $ac < bc$.

If $a > b$ and $c < 0$, then $ac < bc$.

If $a < b$ and $c < 0$, then $ac > bc$.

Division

If $a > b$ and $c > 0$, then $\frac{a}{c} > \frac{b}{c}$.

If $a < b$ and $c > 0$, then $\frac{a}{c} < \frac{b}{c}$.

If $a > b$ and $c < 0$, then $\frac{a}{c} < \frac{b}{c}$.

If $a < b$ and $c < 0$, then $\frac{a}{c} > \frac{b}{c}$.

Transitive   If $a > b$ and $b > c$, then $a > c$.

English/Spanish Illustrated Glossary

A

Absolute value (p. 31) The absolute value of a number is its distance from 0 on a number line.

Valor absoluto (p. 31) El valor absoluto de un número es su distancia del 0 en una recta numérica.

-7 is 7 units from 0, so $|-7| = 7$.

Acute angle (p. 330) An acute angle is an angle with a measure between 0° and 90°.

Ángulo agudo (p. 330) Un ángulo agudo es un ángulo que mide entre 0° y 90°.

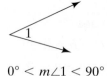

$0° < m\angle 1 < 90°$

Acute triangle (p. 337) An acute triangle has three acute angles.

Triángulo acutángulo (p. 337) Un triángulo acutángulo tiene tres ángulos agudos.

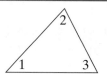

$\angle 1$, $\angle 2$, and $\angle 3$ are acute.

Addition Property of Equality (p. 180) The Addition Property of Equality states that if the same value is added to each side of an equation, the results are equal.

Propiedad aditiva de la igualdad (p. 180) La propiedad aditiva de la igualdad establece que si se suma el mismo valor a cada lado de una ecuación, los resultados son iguales.

Since $\frac{20}{2} = 10$, $\frac{20}{2} + 3 = 10 + 3$.
If $a = b$, then $a + c = b + c$.

Addition Property of Inequality (p. 210) The Addition Property of Inequality states that if you add the same value to each side of an inequality, the relationship between the two sides does not change.

Propiedad aditiva de la desigualdad (p. 210) La propiedad aditiva de la desigualdad establece que si sumas el mismo valor a cada lado de una desigualdad, la relación entre los dos lados no cambia.

If $a > b$, then $a + c > b + c$.
Since $4 > 2$, $4 + 11 > 2 + 11$.
If $a < b$, then $a + c < b + c$.
Since $4 < 9$, $4 + 11 < 9 + 11$.

Additive inverse (p. 38) Two numbers whose sum is 0 are additive inverses.

Inverso aditivo (p. 38) Dos números cuya suma es 0 son inversos aditivos.

$(-5) + 5 = 0$

Adjacent angles (p. 331) Adjacent angles share a vertex and a side but have no interior points in common.

Ángulos adyacentes (p. 331) Los ángulos adyacentes comparten un vértice y un lado, pero no tienen puntos interiores en común.

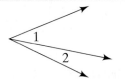

$\angle 1$ and $\angle 2$ are adjacent angles.

Algebraic expression (p. 169) An algebraic expression is a mathematical phrase that uses variables, numbers, and operation symbols.

Expresión algebraica (p. 169) Una expresión algebraica es un enunciado matemático que usa variables, números y símbolos de operaciones.

$2x - 5$ is an algebraic expression.

Angle (p. 330) An angle is formed by two rays with a common endpoint called a vertex.

Ángulo (p. 330) Un ángulo está formado por dos rayos que tienen un punto final común llamado vértice.

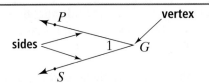

$\angle 1$ is made up of $\overrightarrow{GP}$ and $\overrightarrow{GS}$ with common endpoint G.

Angle of rotation (p. 520) The angle of rotation is the number of degrees that a figure rotates.

Ángulo de rotación (p. 520) El ángulo de rotación es el número de grados que se rota una figura.

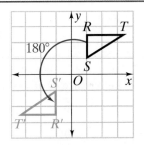

$\triangle RST$ has been rotated $180°$ to $\triangle R'S'T'$.

Arc (p. 351) An arc is part of a circle.

Arco (p. 351) Un arco es parte de un círculo.

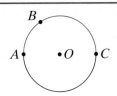

$\overset{\frown}{AB}$ is an arc of circle O. $\overset{\frown}{ABC}$ is a semicircle of circle O.

Area (p. 375) The area of a figure is the number of square units it encloses.

Área (p. 375) El área de una figura es el número de unidades cuadradas que contiene.

The area of each square is 1 ft^2. $\ell = 6$ ft and $w = 4$ ft, so the area is 24 ft^2.

English/Spanish Glossary

Arithmetic sequence (p. 442)   In an arithmetic sequence, each term is the result of adding a fixed number (called the common difference) to the previous term.

The sequence 4, 10, 16, 22, 28, . . . is an arithmetic sequence. You add 6 to each term to find the next term.

Progresión aritmética (p. 442)   En una progresión aritmética, cada término es el resultado de sumar un número fijo al término anterior.

Associative Property of Addition (p. 9)   The Associative Property of Addition states that changing the grouping of the addends does not change the sum.

$(2 + 3) + 7 = 2 + (3 + 7)$
$(a + b) + c = a + (b + c)$

Propiedad asociativa de la suma (p. 9)   La propiedad asociativa de la suma establece que cambiar la agrupación de los sumandos no cambia la suma.

Associative Property of Multiplication (p. 15)   The Associative Property of Multiplication states that changing the grouping of factors does not change the product.

$(3 \cdot 4) \cdot 5 = 3 \cdot (4 \cdot 5)$
$(a \cdot b) \cdot c = a \cdot (b \cdot c)$

Propiedad asociativa de la multiplicación (p. 15)   La propiedad asociativa de la multiplicación establece que cambiar la agrupación de los factores no altera el producto.

Balance (p. 469)   The balance of an account is the principal plus the interest earned.

You deposit $100 and earn $5 interest. Your balance is $105.

Saldo (p. 469)   El saldo de una cuenta es el capital más los intereses ganados.

Base (p. 68)   When a number is written in exponential form, the number that is used as a factor is the base.

$5^4 = 5 \times 5 \times 5 \times 5$
⌐ base

Base (p. 68)   Cuando un número se escribe en forma exponencial, el número que se usa como factor es la base.

Bases of three-dimensional figures (pp. 410, 411)   See *Cone, Cylinder, Prism,* and *Pyramid.*

Bases de figuras tridimensionales (pp. 410, 411)   Ver *Cone, Cylinder, Prism* y *Pyramid.*

Bases of two-dimensional figures (pp. 380, 384, 388)   See *Parallelogram, Triangle,* and *Trapezoid.*

Bases de figuras bidimensionales (pp. 380, 384, 388)   Ver *Parallelogram, Triangle* y *Trapezoid.*

Benchmark (p. 120) A benchmark is a convenient number used to replace fractions that are less than 1.

Using benchmarks, you would estimate $\frac{5}{6} + \frac{4}{9}$ as $1 + \frac{1}{2}$.

Punto de referencia (p. 120) Un punto de referencia es un número conveniente que se usa para reemplazar fracciones menores que 1.

Biased question (p. 551) A biased question is a question that makes one answer appear better than another.

"Do you prefer good food or junk food?"

Pregunta tendenciosa (p. 551) Una pregunta tendenciosa es una pregunta que hace que una respuesta parezca mejor que otra.

Box-and-whisker plot (p. 58) A box-and-whisker plot is a graph that summarizes a data set along a number line. There is a box in the middle and whiskers at either side.

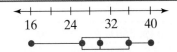

Gráfica de caja y brazos (p. 58) Una gráfica de caja y brazos es un diagrama que resume un conjunto de datos usando una recta línea. Hay una caja en el centro y extensiones a cada lado.

The box-and-whisker plot uses these data: 16 19 26 26 27 29 30 31 34 34 38 39 40.
The lower quartile is 26. The median is 30. The upper quartile is 36.

Capture/recapture (p. 554) Capture/recapture is a sampling technique that uses proportions to estimate animal populations.

Captura/recaptura (p. 554) Captura/recaptura es una técnica de muestreo que usa las proporciones para estimar poblaciones animales.

Cell (p. 538) A cell is a box where a row and a column meet.

Celda (p. 538) Una celda es una caja donde se unen una fila y una columna.

	A	B	C	D	E
1	0.50	0.70	0.60	0.50	2.30
2	1.50	0.50	2.75	2.50	7.25

Column C and row 2 meet at the shaded box, cell C2.

Center of a circle (p. 350) A circle is named by its center.

Centro de un círculo (p. 350) Un círculo es denominado por su centro.

Circle O

Center of a sphere (p. 411)   See *Sphere.*

Centro de una esfera (p. 411)   Ver *Sphere.*

Center of rotation (p. 519)   The center of rotation is a fixed point about which a figure is rotated.

Centro de rotación (p. 519)   El centro de rotación es un punto fijo alrededor del cual rota una figura.

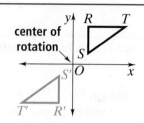

O is the center of rotation.

Central angle (p. 350)   A central angle is an angle with its vertex at the center of a circle.

Ángulo central (p. 350)   Un ángulo central es un ángulo que tiene el vértice en el centro de un círculo.

∠*AOB* is a central angle of circle *O*.

Chord (p. 350)   A chord is a segment that has both endpoints on the circle.

Cuerda (p. 350)   Una cuerda es un segmento que tiene ambos extremos sobre el círculo.

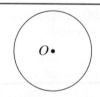

$\overline{CB}$ is a chord of circle *O*.

Circle (p. 350)   A circle is the set of points in a plane that are all the same distance from a given point called the center.

Círculo (p. 350)   Un círculo es el conjunto de puntos de un plano que están a la misma distancia de un punto dado llamado centro.

Circle graph (p. 354)   A circle graph is a graph of data where a circle represents the whole.

Gráfica circular (p. 354)   Una gráfica circular es una gráfica de datos donde un círculo representa el todo.

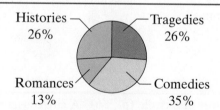

The circle graph represents the types of plays William Shakespeare wrote.

Circumference (p. 394) Circumference is the distance around a circle. You calculate the circumference of a circle by multiplying the diameter by π.

Circunferencia (p. 394) La circunferencia es la distancia alrededor de un círculo. La circunferencia de un círculo se calcula multiplicando el diámetro por π.

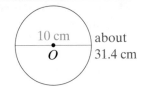

The circumference of a circle with a diameter of 10 cm is 10π, or approximately 31.4 cm.

Combination (p. 610) A combination is a grouping of objects in which the order of the objects does not matter.

Combinación (p. 610) Una combinación es una agrupación de objetos en que el orden de los objetos no tiene importancia.

You choose two vegetables from carrots, peas, and spinach. The possible combinations are carrots and peas, carrots and spinach, and peas and spinach.

Commission (p. 305) A commission is pay that is equal to a percent of sales.

Comisión (p. 305) Una comisión es un pago que es igual a un porcentaje de las ventas.

A salesperson receives a 6% commission on sales of $200. Her commission is $12.

Commutative Property of Addition (p. 9) The Commutative Property of Addition states that changing the order of the addends does not change the sum.

Propiedad conmutativa de la suma (p. 9) La propiedad conmutativa de la suma establece que al cambiar el orden de los sumandos no se altera la suma.

$3 + 1 = 1 + 3$
$a + b = b + a$

Commutative Property of Multiplication (p. 15) The Commutative Property of Multiplication states that changing the order of the factors does not change the product.

Propiedad conmutativa de la multiplicación (p. 15) La propiedad conmutativa de la multiplicación establece que al cambiar el orden de los factores no se altera el producto.

$6 \cdot 3 = 3 \cdot 6$
$a \cdot b = b \cdot a$

Compass (p. 361) A compass is a geometric tool used to draw circles or arcs.

Compás (p. 361) Un compás es una herramienta que se usa en geometría para dibujar círculos o arcos.

Compatible numbers (p. 5) Compatible numbers are numbers that are easy to compute mentally.

Números compatibles (p. 5) Los números compatibles son números con los que se puede calcular mentalmente con facilidad.

Estimate $151 \div 14.6$.

$151 \approx 150, \; 14.6 \approx 15$
$150 \div 15 = 10$
$151 \div 14.6 \approx 10$

Complement (p. 581) The complement of an event is the collection of outcomes not contained in the event.

The event *no rain* is the complement of the event *rain*.

Complemento (p. 581) El complemento de un suceso es la colección de resultados que el suceso no incluye.

Complementary (p. 331) Two angles are complementary if the sum of their measures is 90°.

Complementario (p. 331) Dos ángulos son complementarios si la suma de sus medidas es 90°.

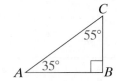

$\angle BCA$ and $\angle CAB$ are complementary angles.

Composite number (p. 75) A composite number is a whole number greater than 1 that has more than two factors.

24 is a composite number. Its factors are 1, 2, 3, 4, 6, 8, 12, and 24.

Número compuesto (p. 75) Un número compuesto es un número entero mayor que 1, que tiene más de dos factores.

Compound event (p. 598) A compound event is an event that consists of two or more events. The probability of a compound event can be found by multiplying the probability of one event by the probability of a second event.

If $P(A) = \frac{1}{3}$ and $P(B) = \frac{1}{2}$, then $P(A, \text{then } B) = \frac{1}{6}$.

Suceso compuesto (p. 598) Un suceso compuesto es un suceso que está formado por dos o más sucesos. La probabilidad de un suceso compuesto se puede hallar al multiplicar la probabilidad de un suceso por la probabilidad de un segundo suceso.

Compound interest (p. 469) Compound interest is interest paid on the original principal and on any interest that has been left in the account. You can use the formula $B = p(1 + r)^t$ where B is the balance in the account, p is the principal, r is the annual interest rate, and t is the time in years that the account earns interest.

You deposit $500 in an account earning 5% annual interest.
The balance after six years is $500(1 + 0.05)^6$, or $670.05.

Interés compuesto (p. 469) El interés compuesto es el interés que se paga sobre el principal original y sobre cualquier interés que ha quedado en la cuenta. Se puede usar la fórmula $B = p(1 + r)^t$ donde B es el saldo en la cuenta, p es el principal, r es la tasa de interés anual y t es el tiempo en años en que la cuenta gana interés.

Cone (p. 411) A cone is a three-dimensional figure with one circular base and one vertex.

Cono (p. 411) Un cono es una figura tridimensional con una base circular y un vértice.

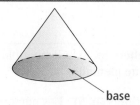

base

Congruent angles (p. 331) Congruent angles are angles that have the same measure.

Ángulos congruentes (p. 331) Los ángulos congruentes son ángulos que tienen la misma medida.

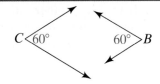

$$\angle B \cong \angle C$$

Congruent polygons (p. 346) Congruent polygons are polygons with the same size and shape.

Polígonos congruentes (p. 346) Los polígonos congruentes son polígonos que tienen el mismo tamaño y forma.

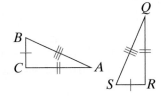

$$\triangle ABC \cong \triangle QSR$$

Congruent sides (p. 336) Congruent sides have the same length.

Lados congruentes (p. 336) Los lados congruentes tienen la misma longitud.

$\triangle EFG$ is an equilateral triangle.
$$\overline{EF} \cong \overline{FG} \cong \overline{GE}$$

Conjecture (p. 443) A conjecture is a prediction that suggests what can be expected to happen.

Conjetura (p. 443) Una conjetura es una predicción que sugiere lo que se puede esperar que ocurra.

Every clover has three leaves.

Coordinate plane (p. 486) A coordinate plane is formed by a horizontal number line called the x-axis and a vertical number line called the y-axis.

Plano de coordenadas (p. 486) Un plano de coordenadas está formado por una recta numérica horizontal llamada eje de x y por una recta numérica vertical llamada eje de y.

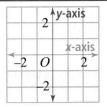

Corresponding parts (p. 346) Corresponding parts of congruent polygons are congruent.

Partes correspondientes (p. 346) Las partes correspondientes de los polígonos congruentes son congruentes.

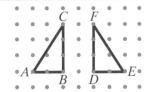

$$\overline{AB} \cong \overline{ED}, \overline{BC} \cong \overline{DF}, \overline{CA} \cong \overline{FE}$$
$$\angle A \cong \angle E, \angle B \cong \angle D, \angle C \cong \angle F$$
$$\triangle ABC \cong \triangle EDF$$

Counting principle (p. 592)   If there are *m* ways of making one choice from a first situation and *n* ways of making a choice from a second situation, then there are *m* × *n* ways to make the first choice followed by the second.

Toss a coin and roll a standard number cube. The total number of possible outcomes is 2 × 6 = 12.

Principio de conteo (p. 592)   Si hay *m* maneras de hacer una elección para una primera situación y *n* maneras de hacer una elección para una segunda situación, entonces hay *m* × *n* maneras de hacer la primera elección seguida de la segunda.

Cross products (p. 239)   For two ratios, the cross products are found by multiplying the denominator of one ratio by the numerator of the other ratio.

In the proportion $\frac{2}{5} = \frac{10}{25}$, the cross products are 2 · 25 and 5 · 10.

Productos cruzados (p. 239)   En dos razones, los productos cruzados se hallan al multiplicar el denominador de una razón por el numerador de la otra razón.

Cube (p. 410)   A cube is a rectangular prism whose faces are all squares.

Cubo (p. 410)   Un cubo es un prisma rectangular cuyas caras son todas cuadrados.

Cubic unit (p. 421)   A cubic unit is a cube whose edges are one unit long.

1 cm

Unidad cúbica (p. 421)   Una unidad cúbica es un cubo cuyos lados tienen una unidad de longitud.

Cylinder (p. 410)   A cylinder is a three-dimensional figure with two congruent parallel bases that are circles.

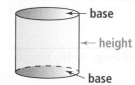

base

height

base

Cilindro (p. 410)   Un cilindro es una figura tridimensional con dos bases congruentes paralelas que son círculos.

D

Decagon (p. 340)   A decagon is a polygon with 10 sides.

Decágono (p. 340)   Un decágono es un polígono que tiene 10 lados.

Dependent events (p. 599) Two events are dependent events if the occurrence of one event affects the probability of the occurrence of the other event.

Suppose you draw two marbles, one after the other, from a bag. If you do *not* replace the first marble before drawing the second marble, the events are dependent.

Sucesos dependientes (p. 599) Dos sucesos son dependientes si el acontecimiento de uno afecta la probabilidad de que el otro ocurra.

Diameter (p. 350) A diameter is a segment that passes through the center of a circle and has both endpoints on the circle.

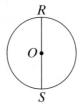

Diámetro (p. 350) Un diámetro es un segmento que pasa por el centro de un círculo y que tiene ambos extremos sobre el círculo.

$\overline{RS}$ is a diameter of circle O.

Discount (p. 311) The difference between the original price and the sale price of an item is called the discount.

A $20 book is discounted by $2.50 to sell for $17.50.

Descuento (p. 311) Se llama descuento a la diferencia entre el precio de un artículo y su precio de venta.

Distributive Property (p. 49) The Distributive Property shows how multiplication affects an addition or subtraction: $a(b + c) = ab + ac$.

$$2\left(3 + \tfrac{1}{2}\right) = 2 \cdot 3 + 2 \cdot \tfrac{1}{2}$$
$$8(5 - 3) = 8 \cdot 5 - 8 \cdot 3$$

Propiedad distributiva (p. 49) La propiedad distributiva muestra cómo la multiplicación afecta a una suma o a una resta: $a(b + c) = ab + ac$.

Divisible (p. 73) A whole number is divisible by a second whole number if the first number can be divided by the second number with a remainder of 0.

16 is divisible by 1, 2, 4, 8, and 16.

Divisible (p. 73) Un número entero es divisible por un segundo número entero si el primer número se puede dividir por el segundo número y el residuo es 0.

Division Property of Equality (p. 186) The Division Property of Equality states that if both sides of an equation are divided by the same nonzero number, the sides remain equal.

Since $3(2) = 6$, $3(2) \div 2 = 6 \div 2$. If $a = b$ and $c \neq 0$, then $\frac{a}{c} = \frac{b}{c}$.

Propiedad de división de la igualdad (p. 186) La propiedad de división de la igualdad establece que si ambos lados de una ecuación se dividen por el mismo número distinto de cero, los dos lados se mantienen iguales.

Division Property of Inequality (p. 214) The Division Property of Inequality states that if you divide an inequality by a positive number, the direction of the inequality is unchanged. If you divide an inequality by a negative number, *reverse* the direction of the inequality sign.

Propiedad de división de la desigualdad (p. 214) La propiedad de división de la desigualdad establece que si se divide una desigualdad por un número positivo, la dirección de la desigualdad no cambia. Si se divide una desigualdad por un número negativo, se *invierte* la dirección del signo de desigualdad.

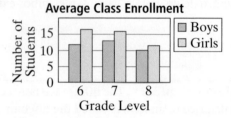

If $a > b$ and $c > 0$, then $\frac{a}{c} > \frac{b}{c}$.
Since $2 > 1$ and $3 > 0$, $\frac{2}{3} > \frac{1}{3}$.
If $a < b$ and $c > 0$, then $\frac{a}{c} < \frac{b}{c}$.
Since $2 < 4$ and $3 > 0$, $\frac{2}{3} < \frac{4}{3}$.
If $a > b$ and $c < 0$, then $\frac{a}{c} < \frac{b}{c}$.
Since $2 > 1$ and $-4 < 0$, $\frac{2}{-4} < \frac{1}{-4}$.
If $a < b$ and $c < 0$, then $\frac{a}{c} > \frac{b}{c}$.
Since $2 < 4$ and $-4 < 0$, $\frac{2}{-4} > \frac{4}{-4}$.

Double bar graph (p. 539) A double bar graph is a graph that uses bars to compare two sets of data.

Gráfica de doble barra (p. 539) Una gráfica de doble barra es una gráfica que usa barras para comparar dos conjuntos de datos.

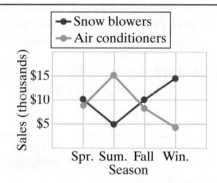

This double bar graph shows class size for grades 6, 7, and 8 for boys and girls.

Double line graph (p. 539) A double line graph is a graph that compares changes over time for two sets of data.

Gráfica de doble línea (p. 539) Una gráfica de doble línea es una gráfica que compara los cambios de dos conjuntos de datos a través del tiempo.

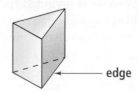

This double line graph represents seasonal air conditioner and snow blower sales (in thousands of dollars) for a large department-store chain.

Edge (p. 410) An edge is a segment formed by the intersection of two faces of a three-dimensional figure.

Arista (p. 410) Una arista es un segmento formado por la intersección de dos caras de una figura tridimensional.

edge

Equation (p. 174)   An equation is a mathematical sentence with an equal sign.

$27 \div 9 = 3$ and $x + 10 = 8$ are examples of equations.

Ecuación (p. 174)   Una ecuación es una oración matemática con un signo igual.

Equilateral triangle (p. 336)   An equilateral triangle is a triangle with three congruent sides.

Triángulo equilátero (p. 336)   Un triángulo equilátero es un triángulo que tiene tres lados congruentes.

$\overline{SL} \cong \overline{LW} \cong \overline{WS}$

Equivalent fractions (p. 82)   Equivalent fractions are fractions that name the same amount.

$\frac{1}{2}$ and $\frac{25}{50}$ are equivalent fractions.

Fracciones equivalentes (p. 82)   Las fracciones equivalentes son fracciones que indican la misma cantidad.

Equivalent ratios (p. 229)   Equivalent ratios name the same number. Equivalent ratios written as fractions are equivalent fractions.

The ratios $\frac{4}{7}$ and $\frac{8}{14}$ are equivalent.

Razones equivalentes (p. 229)   Las razones equivalentes indican el mismo número. Las razones equivalentes escritas como fracciones son fracciones equivalentes.

Evaluating expressions (p. 170)   To evaluate an expression, replace each variable with a number. Then follow the Order of Operations.

To evaluate the expression $3x + 2$ for $x = 4$, substitute 4 for x.
$3x + 2 = 3(4) + 2 = 14$

Evaluación de una expresión (p. 170)   Para evaluar una expresión, se reemplaza cada variable con un número. Luego se sigue el orden de las operaciones.

Event (p. 580)   A collection of possible outcomes is an event.

When you toss a coin, "heads" and "tails" are possible events.

Suceso (p. 580)   Un suceso es un grupo de resultados posibles.

Experimental probability (p. 586)   For a series of trials, the experimental probability of an event is the ratio of the number of times an event occurs to the total number of trials.
$P(\text{event}) = \frac{\text{number of times an event occurs}}{\text{total number of trials}}$

A basketball player makes 19 baskets in 28 attempts. The experimental probability that the player makes a basket is $\frac{19}{28} \approx 68\%$.

Probabilidad experimental (p. 586)   En una serie de pruebas, la probabilidad experimental de un suceso es la razón del número de veces que ocurre un suceso al número total de pruebas.
$P(\text{suceso}) = \frac{\text{número de veces que ocurre un suceso}}{\text{número total de pruebas}}$

Exponent (p. 68)   An exponent tells how many times a number, or base, is used as a factor.

Exponente (p. 68)   Un exponente dice cuántas veces se usa como factor un número, o base.

exponent
$$3^4 = 3 \times 3 \times 3 \times 3$$
Read 3^4 as *three to the fourth power*.

Face (p. 410)   A face is a flat surface of a three-dimensional figure that is shaped like a polygon.

Cara (p. 410)   Una cara es una superficie plana de una figura tridimensional que tiene la forma de un polígono.

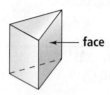

face

Factor (p. 75)   A factor is a whole number that divides another whole number with a remainder of 0.

Divisor (p. 75)   Un divisor es un número entero que divide a otro número entero y el residuo es 0.

1, 2, 3, 4, 6, 12, 18, and 36 are factors of 36.

Factorial (p. 606)   A factorial is the product of all positive integers less than or equal to a number. The symbol for factorial is an exclamation point.

Factorial (p. 606)   Una factorial es el producto de todos los enteros positivos menores o iguales que un número. El símbolo de factorial es un signo de cierre de exclamación.

$$5! = 5 \times 4 \times 3 \times 2 \times 1 = 120$$

Formula (p. 472)   A formula is a rule that shows the relationship between two or more quantities.

Fórmula (p. 472)   Una fórmula es una regla que muestra la relación entre dos o más cantidades.

The formula $P = 2\ell + 2w$ gives the perimeter of a rectangle in terms of its length and width.

Frequency table (p. 532)   A frequency table is a table that lists each item in a data set with the number of times the item occurs.

Tabla de frecuencia (p. 532)   Una tabla de frecuencia es una tabla que registra todos los elementos de un conjunto de datos y el número de veces que ocurre cada uno.

Household Telephones

Phones	Tally	Frequency
1	卌 |||	8
2	卌		6
3						4

This frequency table shows the number of household telephones for a class of students.

Function (p. 452) A function is a relationship that assigns exactly one output value for each input value.

Función (p. 452) Una función es una relación que asigna exactamente un valor resultante a cada valor inicial.

Wages *s* are a function of the number of hours worked *w*. If you earn $6/h, then your wages can be expressed by the function $s = 6w$.

Geometric sequence (p. 442) In a geometric sequence, each term is the result of multiplying the previous term by a fixed number (called the common ratio).

Progresión geométrica (p. 442) En una progresión geométrica, cada término es el resultado de la multiplicación del término anterior por un número fijo llamado rayón común.

The sequence $1, 3, 9, 27, 81, \ldots$ is a geometric sequence. You multiply each term by 3 to find the next term.

Graph of an equation (p. 492) The graph of an equation is the graph of all the points with coordinates that are solutions of the equation.

Gráfica de una ecuación (p. 492) La gráfica de una ecuación es la gráfica de todos los puntos cuyas coordenadas son soluciones a la ecuación.

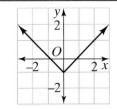

The coordinates of all the points on the graph satisfy the equation $y = |x| - 1$.

Greatest common factor (GCF) (p. 75) The greatest common factor of two or more numbers is the greatest number that is a factor of all of the numbers.

Máximo común divisor (MCD) (p. 75) El máximo común divisor de dos o más números es el mayor número que es divisor de todos los números.

The GCF of 12 and 30 is 6.

Height of three-dimensional figures (p. 410) See *Cylinder* and *Prism*.

Altura de figuras tridimensionales (p. 410) Ver *Cylinder* y *Prism*.

Height of two-dimensional figures (pp. 380, 384, 388) See *Parallelogram*, *Triangle*, and *Trapezoid*.

Altura de figuras bidimensionales (pp. 380, 384, 388) Ver *Parallelogram*, *Triangle* y *Trapezoid*.

Hexagon (p. 340) A hexagon is a polygon with six sides.

Hexágono (p. 340) Un hexágono es un polígono que tiene seis lados.

Histogram (p. 533) A histogram is a bar graph with no spaces between the bars. The height of each bar shows the frequency of data within that interval.

Histograma (p. 533) Un histograma es una gráfica de barras sin espacio entre las barras. La altura de cada barra muestra la frecuencia de los datos dentro del intervalo.

The histogram gives the frequency of board game purchases at a local toy store.

Horizontal (p. 499) Horizontal lines are parallel to the *x*-axis.

Horizontal (p. 499) Las rectas horizontales son paralelas al eje de *x*.

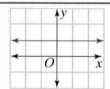

Hypotenuse (p. 405) In a right triangle, the hypotenuse is the longest side, which is opposite the right angle.

Hipotenusa (p. 405) En un triángulo rectángulo, la hipotenusa es el lado más largo, que es el lado opuesto al ángulo recto.

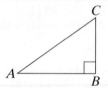

$\overline{AC}$ is the hypotenuse of $\triangle ABC$.

Identity Property of Addition (p. 9) The Identity Property of Addition states that the sum of 0 and *a* is *a*.

$7 + 0 = 7$
$a + 0 = a$

Propiedad de identidad de la suma (p. 9) La propiedad de identidad de la suma establece que la suma de cero y *a* es *a*.

Identity Property of Multiplication (p. 15) The Identity Property of Multiplication states that the product of 1 and *a* is *a*.

$7 \cdot 1 = 7$
$a \cdot 1 = a$

Propiedad de identidad de la multiplicación (p. 15) La propiedad de identidad de la multiplicación establece que el producto de 1 y *a* es *a*.

Image (p. 510) An image is the result of a transformation of a point, line, or figure.

Imagen (p. 510) Una imagen es el resultado de una transformación de un punto, una recta o una figura.

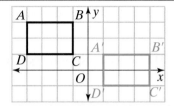

$A'B'C'D'$ is the image of $ABCD$.

Improper fraction (p. 91) An improper fraction has a numerator that is greater than or equal to its denominator.

$\frac{24}{15}$ and $\frac{16}{16}$ are improper fractions.

Fracción impropia (p. 91) Una fracción impropia tiene un numerador mayor o igual que su denominador.

Independent events (p. 598) Two events are independent events if the occurrence of one event does not affect the probability of the occurrence of the other.

Suppose you draw two marbles, one after the other, from a bag. If you replace the first marble before drawing the second marble, the events are independent.

Sucesos independientes (p. 598) Dos sucesos son independientes si el acontecimiento de uno no afecta la probabilidad de que el otro suceso ocurra.

Indirect measurement (p. 253) Indirect measurement uses proportions and similar triangles to measure distances that would be difficult to measure directly.

Medición indirecta (p. 253) La medición indirecta usa proporciones y triángulos semejantes para medir las distancias que serían difíciles de medir directamente.

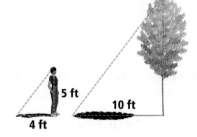

A 5-ft-tall person standing near a tree has a shadow 4 ft long. The tree has a shadow 10 ft long. The height of the tree is 12.5 ft.

Inductive reasoning (p. 443) Inductive reasoning involves looking for a pattern and writing a rule to describe the pattern in a sequence.

By inductive reasoning, the next number in the pattern 2, 4, 6, 8, . . . is 10.

Razonamiento inductivo (p. 443) El razonamiento inductivo implica buscar un patrón y escribir una regla para describir el patrón en una secuencia.

English/Spanish Glossary

Inequality (p. 205)   An inequality is a mathematical sentence that contains one of the signs $<$, $>$, $\leq$, $\geq$, or $\neq$.

$x < -5$, $x > 8$, $x \leq 1$, $x \geq -11$, $x \neq 7$

Desigualdad (p. 205)   Una desigualdad es una oración matemática que contiene uno de los signos $<$, $>$, $\leq$, $\geq$ o $\neq$.

Integers (p. 31)   Integers are the set of positive whole numbers, their opposites, and 0.

$\ldots -3, -2, -1, 0, 1, 2, 3, \ldots$

Enteros (p. 31)   Los enteros son el conjunto de números enteros positivos, sus opuestos y el 0.

Intersecting lines (p. 325)   Intersecting lines have exactly one point in common.

Rectas que se intersecan (p. 325)   Las rectas que se intersecan tienen exactamente un punto en común.

Inverse operations (p. 181)   Inverse operations are operations that undo each other.

Addition and subtraction are inverse operations.

Operaciones inversas (p. 181)   Las operaciones inversas son las operaciones que se anulan entre ellas.

Irrational number (p. 401)   An irrational number is a number that cannot be written as the ratio of two integers. In decimal form, an irrational number cannot be written as a terminating or repeating decimal.

The numbers π and $2.41592653\ldots$ are irrational numbers.

Número irracional (p. 401)   Un número irracional es un número que no se puede escribir como una razón de dos enteros. Como decimal, un número irracional no se puede escribir como decimal finito o periódico.

Irregular polygon (p. 340)   An irregular polygon is a polygon with sides that are not all congruent and/or angles that are not all congruent.

Polígono irregular (p. 340)   Un polígono irregular es un polígono que tiene lados que no son todos congruentes y/o ángulos que no son todos congruentes.

$KLMN$ is an irregular polygon.

Isosceles triangle (p. 336)   An isosceles triangle is a triangle with at least two congruent sides.

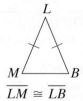

Triángulo isósceles (p. 336)   Un triángulo isósceles es un triángulo que tiene al menos dos lados congruentes.

$\overline{LM} \cong \overline{LB}$

Least common denominator (LCD) (p. 87) The least common denominator of two or more fractions is the least common multiple (LCM) of their denominators.

The LCD of the fractions $\frac{3}{8}$ and $\frac{7}{10}$ is 40.

Mínimo común denominador (MCD) (p. 87) El mínimo común denominador de dos o más fracciones es el mínimo común múltiplo (MCD) de sus denominadores.

Least common multiple (LCM) (p. 74) The least common multiple of two or more numbers is the least multiple that is common to all of the numbers.

The LCM of 15 and 6 is 30.

Mínimo común múltiplo (MCM) (p. 74) El mínimo común múltiplo de dos o más números es el menor múltiplo que es común con todos los números.

Legend (p. 539) A legend, or key, identifies data that are compared.

Leyenda (p. 539) Una leyenda, o clave, identifica categorías en una gráfica.

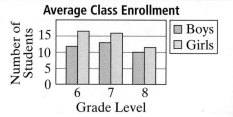

Legs of a right triangle (p. 405) The legs of a right triangle are the two shorter sides of the triangle.

Catetos de un triángulo rectángulo (p. 405) Los catetos de un triángulo rectángulo son los dos lados más cortos del triángulo.

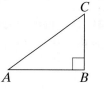

$\overline{AB}$ and $\overline{BC}$ are the legs of $\triangle ABC$.

Line (p. 324) A line is a series of points that extends in two opposite directions without end.

Recta (p. 324) Una recta es una serie de puntos que se extiende indefinidamente en dos direcciones opuestas.

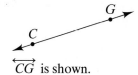

$\overleftrightarrow{CG}$ is shown.

Linear equation (p. 492) An equation is a linear equation when the graph of its solutions lies on a line.

Ecuación lineal (p. 492) Una ecuación es lineal cuando la gráfica de sus soluciones es una línea.

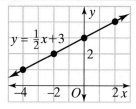

$y = \frac{1}{2}x + 3$ is a linear equation because the graph of its solutions is a line.

English/Spanish Glossary

Line of reflection (p. 515)   A line of reflection is a line over which a figure is reflected.

Eje de reflexión (p. 515)   Un eje de reflexión es una recta sobre la cual se refleja una figura.

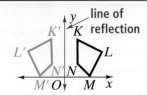

KLMN is reflected over the *y*-axis.

Line of symmetry (p. 514)   A line of symmetry divides a figure into mirror images.

Eje de simetría (p. 514)   Un eje de simetría divide una figura en imágenes reflejas.

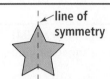

Line plot (p. 533)   A line plot is a graph that shows the shape of a data set by stacking ✗'s above each data value on a number line.

Diagrama de puntos (p. 533)   Un diagrama de puntos es una gráfica que muestra la forma de un conjunto de datos agrupando ✗ sobre cada valor de una recta numérica.

Pets Owned by Students

```
     X
     X           X
 X   X   X   X
 X   X   X   X   X
 0   1   2   3   4
```

The line plot shows the number of pets owned by each of 12 students.

Line symmetry (p. 514)   A figure has line symmetry when one side is the mirror image of the other side.

Simetría lineal (p. 514)   Una figura tiene simetría lineal cuando un lado es la imagen refleja del otro lado.

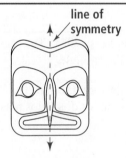

The left and right sides of the mask are mirror images of each other.

M

Markup (p. 311)   The markup is the difference between the selling price and the original cost.

Sobrecosto (p. 311)   El sobrecosto es la diferencia entre el precio de venta y el costo original.

A store buys a shirt for $15 and sells it for $25. The markup is $10.

Mean (p. 53) The mean of a set of data values is the sum of the data divided by the number of data items.

Media (p. 53) La media de un conjunto de valores de datos es la suma de los datos dividida por el número de datos.

The mean temperature (°F) for the set of temperatures 44, 52, 48, 55, 61, and 67 is $\frac{44 + 52 + 48 + 55 + 61 + 67}{6} = 54.5$.

Median (p. 54) The median of a data set is the middle value when the data are arranged in numerical order. When there is an even number of data values, the median is the mean of the two middle values.

Mediana (p. 54) La mediana de un conjunto de datos es el valor del medio cuando los datos están organizados en orden numérico. Cuando hay un número par de valores de datos, la mediana es la media de los dos valores del medio.

Temperatures (°F) for five days arranged in order are 44, 48, 52, 55, and 58. The median temperature is 52°F because it is the middle number in the set of data.

Midpoint (p. 362) The midpoint of a segment is the point that divides the segment into two segments of equal length.

Punto medio (p. 362) El punto medio de un segmento es el punto que divide el segmento en dos segmentos de igual longitud.

$X \quad M \quad Y$

$XM = YM$. M is the midpoint of $\overline{XY}$.

Mixed number (p. 91) A mixed number is the sum of a whole number and a fraction.

Número mixto (p. 91) Un número mixto es la suma de un número entero y una fracción.

$3\frac{11}{16}$ is a mixed number.

$3\frac{11}{16} = 3 + \frac{11}{16}$

Mode (p. 54) The mode of a data set is the item that occurs with the greatest frequency.

Moda (p. 54) La moda de un conjunto de datos es el dato que sucede con mayor frecuencia.

The mode of the set of prices $2.50, $2.75, $3.60, $2.75, and $3.70 is $2.75.

Multiple (p. 74) A multiple of a number is the product of that number and any nonzero whole number.

Múltiplo (p. 74) Un múltiplo de un número es el producto de ese número y cualquier número entero diferente de cero.

The number 39 is a multiple of 13.

Multiplication Property of Equality (p. 188) The Multiplication Property of Equality states that if each side of an equation is multiplied by the same number, the results are equal.

Propiedad multiplicativa de la igualdad (p. 188) La propiedad multiplicativa de la igualdad establece que si cada lado de una ecuación se multiplica por el mismo número, los resultados son iguales.

Since $\frac{12}{2} = 6$, $\frac{12}{2} \cdot 2 = 6 \cdot 2$.
If $a = b$, then $a \cdot c = b \cdot c$.

Multiplication Property of Inequality (p. 216) The Multiplication Property of Inequality states that if you multiply an inequality by a positive number, the direction of the inequality is unchanged. If you multiply an inequality by a negative number, *reverse* the direction of the inequality sign.

Propiedad multiplicativa de la desigualdad (p. 216) La propiedad multiplicativa de la desigualdad establece que cuando se multiplica una desigualdad por un número positivo, la dirección de la desigualdad no cambia. Si se multiplica una desigualdad por un número negativo, se *invierte* la dirección del signo de la desigualdad.

If $a > b$ and $c > 0$, then $ac > bc$.
Since $3 > 2$ and $7 > 0$, $3 \cdot 7 > 2 \cdot 7$.
If $a < b$ and $c > 0$, then $ac < bc$.
Since $3 < 5$ and $7 > 0$, $3 \cdot 7 < 5 \cdot 7$.
If $a > b$ and $c < 0$, then $ac < bc$.
Since $3 > 2$ and $-6 < 0$,
$3 \cdot (-6) < 2 \cdot (-6)$.
If $a < b$ and $c < 0$, then $ac > bc$.
Since $3 < 5$ and $-6 < 0$,
$3 \cdot (-6) > 5 \cdot (-6)$.

Negative trend (p. 568) There is a negative trend between two sets of data if one set of values tends to increase while the other set tends to decrease.

Tendencia negativa (p. 568) Hay una tendencia negativa entre dos conjuntos de datos si un conjunto de valores tiende a aumentar, mientras el otro conjunto tiende a disminuir.

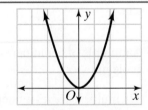

Net (p. 414) A net is a two-dimensional pattern that can be folded to form a three-dimensional figure.

Plantilla (p. 414) Una plantilla es un patrón bidimensional que se puede doblar para formar una figura tridimensional.

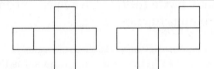

These are nets for a cube.

Nonlinear equation (p. 504) The graph of a nonlinear equation is not a straight line.

Ecuación no lineal (p. 504) La gráfica de una ecuación no lineal no es una recta.

$y = x^2$ is an example of a nonlinear equation.

No trend (p. 568) There is no trend between two sets of data if the points show no relationship to each other.

Sin tendencia (p. 568) Sin tendencia entre dos conjuntos de datos significa que no hay relación alguna entre los puntos.

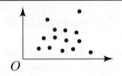

O

Obtuse angle (p. 330) An obtuse angle is an angle with a measure greater than 90° and less than 180°.

Ángulo obtuso (p. 330) Un ángulo obtuso es un ángulo que mide más de 90° y menos de 180°.

Obtuse triangle (p. 337) An obtuse triangle is a triangle with one obtuse angle.

Triángulo obtusángulo (p. 337) Un triángulo obtusángulo es un triángulo que tiene un ángulo obtuso.

Octagon (p. 340) An octagon is a polygon with eight sides.

Octágono (p. 340) Un octágono es un polígono que tiene ocho lados.

Odds (p. 584) When outcomes are equally likely, odds are expressed as the following ratios:

odds *in favor* of an event = the ratio of the number of favorable outcomes to the number of unfavorable outcomes
odds *against* an event = the ratio of the number of unfavorable outcomes to the number of favorable outcomes

You roll a standard number cube. The odds in favor of getting a 4 are 1 : 5.

Posibilidades (p. 584) Cuando los resultados son igualmente posibles, las posibilidades se expresan como las siguientes razones:

posibilidades *en favor* de un suceso = la razón del número de resultados favorables al número de resultados desfavorables
posibilidades *en contra* de un suceso = la razón del número de resultados desfavorables al número de resultados favorables

---

Open sentence (p. 174) An open sentence is an equation with one or more variables.

$b - 7 = 12$

Proposición abierta (p. 174) Una proposición abierta es una ecuación con una o más variables.

Opposites (p. 31) Opposites are two numbers that are the same distance from 0 on a number line, but in opposite directions.

17 and −17 are opposites.

Opuestos (p. 31) Opuestos son dos números que están a la misma distancia del 0 en una recta numérica, pero en direcciones opuestas.

Ordered pair (p. 486)   An ordered pair identifies the location of a point. The *x*-coordinate shows a point's position left or right of the *y*-axis. The *y*-coordinate shows a point's position up or down from the *x*-axis.

Par ordenado (p. 486)   Un par ordenado identifica la ubicación de un punto. La coordenada *x* muestra la posición de un punto a la izquierda o derecha del eje de *y*. La coordenada *y* muestra la posición de un punto arriba o abajo del eje de *x*.

The *x*-coordinate of the point $(-2, 1)$ is -2, and the *y*-coordinate is 1.

Order of operations (pp. 48, 69)
1. Work inside grouping symbols.
2. Do all work with exponents.
3. Multiply and divide in order from left to right.
4. Add and subtract in order from left to right.

Orden de las operaciones (pp. 48, 69)
1. Trabaja dentro de los signos de agrupación.
2. Trabaja con los exponentes.
3. Multiplica y divide en orden de izquierda a derecha.
4. Suma y resta en orden de izquierda a derecha.

$2^3(7 - 4) = 2^3 \cdot 3 = 8 \cdot 3 = 24$

Origin (p. 486)   The origin is the point of intersection of the *x*- and *y*-axes on a coordinate plane.

Origen (p. 486)   El origen es el punto de intersección de los ejes de *x* y de *y* en un plano de coordenadas.

The ordered pair that describes the origin is $(0, 0)$.

Outcome (p. 580)   An outcome is any of the possible results that can occur in an experiment.

Resultado (p. 580)   Un resultado es cualquiera de los posibles desenlaces que pueden ocurrir en un experimento.

The outcomes of rolling a standard number cube are 1, 2, 3, 4, 5, and 6.

Outlier (p. 53)   An outlier is a data item that is much higher or much lower than the other items in a data set.

Valor extremo (p. 53)   Un valor extremo es un dato que es mucho más alto o más bajo que los demás datos en un conjunto de datos.

An outlier in the data set 6, 7, 9, 10, 11, 12, 14, and 52 is 52.

P

Parallel lines (p. 325)   Parallel lines are lines in the same plane that never intersect.

Rectas paralelas (p. 325)   Las rectas paralelas son rectas en el mismo plano que nunca se intersecan.

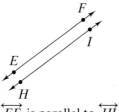

$\overleftrightarrow{EF}$ is parallel to $\overleftrightarrow{HI}$.

Parallelogram (p. 341)   A parallelogram is a quadrilateral with both pairs of opposite sides parallel.

Paralelogramo (p. 341)   Un paralelogramo es un cuadrilátero cuyos pares de lados opuestos son paralelos.

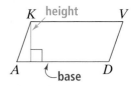

$\overline{KV}$ is parallel to $\overline{AD}$ and $\overline{AK}$ is parallel to $\overline{DV}$, so $KVDA$ is a parallelogram.

Pentagon (p. 340)   A pentagon is a polygon with five sides.

Pentágono (p. 340)   Un pentágono es un polígono que tiene cinco lados.

Percent (p. 274)   A percent is a ratio that compares a number to 100.

Porcentaje (p. 274)   Un porcentaje es una razón que compara un número con 100.

$\frac{25}{100} = 25\%$

Percent of change (p. 310)   The percent of change is the percent a quantity increases or decreases from its original amount.

Porcentaje de cambio (p. 310)   El porcentaje de cambio es el porcentaje que aumenta o disminuye una cantidad a partir de su cantidad original.

The number of employees increases from 14 to 21. The percent of change is $\frac{21 - 14}{14} = 50\%$.

Perfect square (p. 400)   A perfect square is a number that is the square of an integer.

Cuadrado perfecto (p. 400)   Un cuadrado perfecto es un número que es el cuadrado de un entero.

Since $25 = 5^2$, 25 is a perfect square.

Perimeter (p. 375)   The perimeter of a figure is the distance around the figure.

Perímetro (p. 375)   El perímetro de una figura es la distancia alrededor de la figura.

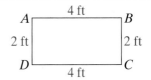

The perimeter of rectangle $ABCD$ is 12 ft.

Permutation (p. 606)   A permutation is an arrangement of objects in a particular order.

Permutación (p. 606)   Una permutación es un arreglo de objetos en un orden particular.

The permutations of the letters W, A, and X are WAX, WXA, AXW, AWX, XWA, and XAW.

Perpendicular bisector (p. 362)   A perpendicular bisector is a segment bisector that is perpendicular to the segment.

Mediatriz (p. 362)   Una mediatriz es una bisectriz de un segmento que es perpendicular a ese segmento.

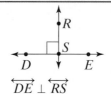

$\overleftrightarrow{MK} \perp \overline{AB}$, $AM = MB$. $\overleftrightarrow{MK}$ is the perpendicular bisector of $\overline{AB}$.

Perpendicular lines (p. 362)   Perpendicular lines intersect to form right angles.

Rectas perpendiculars (p. 362)   Las rectas perpendiculares se intersecan para formar ángulos rectos.

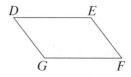

$\overleftrightarrow{DE} \perp \overleftrightarrow{RS}$

Pi (p. 394)   Pi (π) is the ratio of the circumference C of any circle to its diameter d.

Pi (p. 394)   Pi (π) es la razón de la circunferencia C de cualquier círculo a su diámetro d.

$\pi = \dfrac{C}{d}$

Plane (p. 325)   A plane is a flat surface that extends indefinitely in all directions.

Plano (p. 325)   Un plano es una superficie plana que se extiende indefinidamente en todas las direcciones.

$DEFG$ is a plane.

Point (p. 324)   A point is a location that has no size.

Punto (p. 324)   Un punto es una ubicación que no tiene tamaño.

• A

A is a point.

Polygon (p. 252)   A polygon is a closed figure formed by three or more line segments that do not cross.

Polígono (p. 252)   Un polígono es una figura cerrada que está formada por tres o más segmentos de recta que no se cruzan.

Population (p. 550)   A population is a group of objects or people about which information is wanted.

Población (p. 550)   Una población es un grupo de objetos o personas sobre el que se busca información.

A class of 25 students is a sample of the population of a school.

Positive trend (p. 568) There is a positive trend between two sets of data if one set of values tends to increase while the other set tends to increase.

Tendencia positive (p. 568) Existe una tendencia positiva entre dos conjuntos de datos si un conjunto de valores tiende a aumentar mientras el otro conjunto también tiende a aumentar.

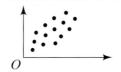

Power (p. 68) A power is a number that can be expressed using an exponent.

Potencia (p. 68) Una potencia es un número que se puede expresar usando un exponente.

$3^4, 5^2,$ and 2^{10} are powers.

Precision (p. 154) Precision refers to the exactness of a measurement, determined by the unit of measure.

Precisión (p. 154) La precisión se refiere a la exactitud de una medida, determinada por la unidad de medida.

$\frac{1}{16}$ in. is a smaller unit than $\frac{1}{4}$ in., so $\frac{1}{16}$ in. is more precise than $\frac{1}{4}$ in.

Prime factorization (p. 75) Writing a composite number as the product of its prime factors is the prime factorization of the number.

Descomposición en factores primos (p. 75) Escribir un número compuesto como el producto de sus factores primos es la descomposición en factores primos del número.

The prime factorization of 12 is $2 \cdot 2 \cdot 3$, or $2^2 \cdot 3$.

Prime notation (p. 510) Prime notation is used to identify an image point.

Notación prima (p. 510) La notación prima se usa para identificar un punto de imagen.

Point $F'(4, 1)$ is the image of point $F(4, 3)$ after a translation.

Prime number (p. 75) A prime number is a whole number with exactly two factors, 1 and the number itself.

Número primo (p. 75) Un número primo es un entero que tiene exactamente dos factores, 1 y el mismo número.

13 is a prime number because its only factors are 1 and 13.

Principal (p. 468) Principal is the original amount deposited or borrowed.

Capital (p. 468) El capital es el monto original que se deposita o se toma prestado.

You deposit $500 in a savings account. Your principal is $500.

Prism (p. 410) A prism is a three-dimensional figure with two parallel and congruent polygonal faces, called bases. A prism is named for the shape of its base.

Prisma (p. 410) Un prisma es una figura tridimensional que tiene dos caras poligonales paralelas y congruentes llamadas bases. Un prisma recibe su nombre por la forma de su base.

Rectangular Prism   Triangular Prism

Probability (pp. 580, 586)   Probability is used to describe the likeliness that an event will happen. See *Experimental probability* and *Theoretical probability.*

Probabilidad (pp. 580, 586)   La probabilidad se usa para describir la posibilidad de que ocurra un suceso. Ver *Experimental probability* y *Theoretical probability.*

Proportion (p. 238)   A proportion is an equation stating that two ratios are equal.

$\frac{3}{12} = \frac{9}{36}$ is a proportion.

Proporción (p. 238)   Una proporción es una ecuación que establece que dos razones son iguales.

Pyramid (p. 410)   A pyramid is a three-dimensional figure with triangular faces that meet at a vertex and a base that is a polygon. A pyramid is named for the shape of its base.

Pirámide (p. 410)   Una pirámide es una figura tridimensional que tiene caras triangulares que coinciden en un vértice y una base que es un polígono. Una pirámide recibe su nombre por la forma de su base.

Triangular Pyramid   Rectangular Pyramid

Pythagorean Theorem (p. 405)   In any right triangle, the sum of the squares of the lengths of the legs (a and b) is equal to the square of the length of the hypotenuse (c): $a^2 + b^2 = c^2$.

Teorema de Pitágoras (p. 405)   En cualquier triángulo rectángulo, la suma del cuadrado de la longitud de los catetos (a y b) es igual al cuadrado de la longitud de la hipotenusa (c): $a^2 + b^2 = c^2$.

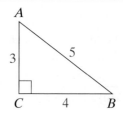

The right triangle has leg lengths 3 and 4 and hypotenuse length 5. $3^2 + 4^2 = 5^2$

Q

Quadrants (p. 486)   The x- and y-axes divide the coordinate plane into four regions called quadrants.

Cuadrantes (p. 486)   Los ejes de x y de y dividen el plano de coordenadas en cuatro regiones llmadas cuadrantes.

The quadrants are labeled I, II, III, and IV.

Quadrilateral (p. 340)   A quadrilateral is a polygon with four sides.

Cuadrilátero (p. 340)   Un cuadrilátero es un polígono que tiene cuatro lados.

R

Radius (p. 350) A radius of a circle is a segment that connects the center of a circle to the circle.

Radio (p. 350) Un radio de un círculo es un segmento que conecta el centro del círculo con el círculo.

$\overline{OA}$ is a radius of circle O.

Random sample (p. 550) In a random sample, each member of the population has an equal chance of being selected.

Muestra aleatoria (p. 550) En una muestra aleatoria, cada miembro de la población tiene la misma posibilidad de ser elegido.

For the population *customers at a mall*, a random sample would be every 20th customer entering in a 2-hour period.

Range (p. 55) The range of a data set is the difference between the greatest and the least values.

Rango (p. 55) El rango de un conjunto de datos es la diferencia entre los valores mayor y menor.

Data set: 62, 109, 234, 35, 96, 49, 201
Range: $234 - 35 = 199$

Rate (p. 232) A rate is a ratio that compares two quantities measured in different units.

Tasa (p. 232) Una tasa es una razón que compara dos cantidades medidas en diferentes unidades.

You read 116 words in 1 min.
Your reading rate is $\frac{116 \text{ words}}{1 \text{ min}}$.

Ratio (p. 228) A ratio is a comparison of two quantities by division.

Razón (p. 228) Una razón es una comparación de dos cantidades mediante la división.

There are three ways to write a ratio: 9 to 10, 9 : 10, and $\frac{9}{10}$.

Rational number (p. 102) A rational number is a number that can be written as a quotient of two integers, where the divisor is not 0.

Número racional (p. 102) Un número racional es un número que se puede escribir como cociente de dos enteros, donde el divisor es diferente de cero.

$\frac{1}{3}$, -5, 6.4, 0.666 . . . , $-2\frac{4}{5}$, 0, and $\frac{7}{3}$ are rational numbers.

Ray (p. 324) A ray is part of a line, with one endpoint and all the points of the line on one side of the endpoint.

Rayo (p. 324) Un rayo es una parte de una recta que tiene un extremo y todos los puntos de la recta a un lado del extremo.

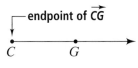

$\overrightarrow{CG}$ represents a ray.

Reciprocal (p. 141)   Two numbers are reciprocals if their product is 1.

The numbers $\frac{4}{9}$ and $\frac{9}{4}$ are reciprocals.

Recíproco (p. 141)   Dos números son recíprocos si su producto es 1.

Rectangle (p. 341)   A rectangle is a parallelogram with four right angles.

Rectángulo (p. 341)   Un rectángulo es un paralelogramo que tiene cuatro ángulos rectos.

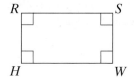

Reflection (p. 515)   A reflection, or flip, is a transformation that flips a figure over a line of reflection.

Reflexión (p. 515)   Una reflexión es una transformación que voltea una figura sobre un eje de reflexión.

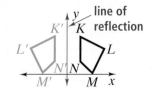

$K'L'M'N'$ is a reflection of $KLMN$ over the y-axis.

Regular polygon (p. 340)   A regular polygon is a polygon with all sides congruent and all angles congruent.

Polígono regular (p. 340)   Un polígono regular es un polígono que tiene todos los lados y todos los ángulos congruentes.

$ABDFEC$ is a regular hexagon.

Repeating decimal (p. 97)   A repeating decimal is a decimal that repeats without end. The repeating block can be one or more digits.

Decimal periódico (p. 97)   Un decimal periódico es un decimal que repite los mismos dígitos interminablemente. El bloque que se repite puede ser un dígito o más de un dígito.

$0.888 \ldots = 0.\overline{8}$
$0.272727 \ldots = 0.\overline{27}$

Rhombus (p. 341)   A rhombus is a parallelogram with four congruent sides.

Rombo (p. 341)   Un rombo es un paralelogramo que tiene cuatro lados congruentes.

Right angle (p. 330)   A right angle is an angle with a measure of 90°.

Ángulo recto (p. 330)   Un ángulo recto es un ángulo que mide 90°.

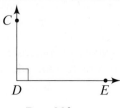

$m\angle D = 90°$

Right triangle (p. 337)   A right triangle is a triangle with one right angle.

Triángulo rectángulo (p. 337)   Un triángulo rectángulo es un triángulo que tiene un ángulo recto.

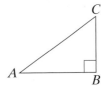

Since $\angle B$ is a right angle, $\triangle ABC$ is a right triangle.

Rise (p. 498)   The rise of a line is a vertical change in a line. See *Slope*.

Distancia vertical (p. 498)   La distancia vertical de una recta es el cambio vertical de la recta. Ver *Pendiente de una recta*.

Rotation (p. 519)   A rotation is a transformation that turns a figure about a fixed point O, called the center of rotation.

Rotación (p. 519)   Una rotación es una transformación que gira una figura sobre un punto fijo O, llamado centro de rotación.

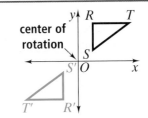

$\triangle RST$ has been rotated about the origin O to $\triangle R'S'T'$.

Rotational symmetry (p. 519)   A figure has rotational symmetry if it can be rotated 180° or less and match the original figure.

Simetría rotacional (p. 519)   Una figura tiene simetría rotacional si se puede rotar 180° o menos y calzar sobre la figura original.

This figure has 60° rotational symmetry.

Run (p. 498)   The run of a line is a horizontal change in a line. See *Slope*.

Distancia horizontal (p. 498)   La distancia horizontal de una recta es el cambio horizontal de la recta. Ver *Pendiente de una recta*.

Sample (p. 550)   A sample is a part of the population.

Muestra (p. 550)   Una muestra es una parte de la población.

A class of 25 students is a sample of a school population. The sample size is 25.

Sample space (p. 591)   Sample space is the collection of all possible outcomes in a probability experiment.

Espacio muestral (p. 591)   El espacio muestral es el total de todos los resultados posibles en un experimento de probabilidad.

The sample space for tossing two coins is HH, HT, TH, TT.

English/Spanish Glossary

Scale (p. 259) A scale is the ratio that compares a length in a drawing to the corresponding length in the actual object.

Escala (p. 259) Una escala es la razón que compara la longitud en un dibujo con la longitud correspondiente en el objeto real.

A 25-mi road is 1 in. long on a map. The scale can be written three ways:
1 in. : 25 mi, $\frac{1 \text{ in.}}{25 \text{ mi}}$, 1 in. = 25 mi.

Scale drawing (p. 259) A scale drawing is an enlarged or reduced drawing of an object that is similar to the actual object.

Dibujo a escala (p. 259) Un dibujo a escala es un dibujo aumentado o reducido de un objeto que es semejante al objeto real.

Maps and floor plans are scale drawings.

Scalene triangle (p. 336) A scalene triangle is a triangle with no congruent sides.

Triángulo escaleno (p. 336) Un triángulo escaleno es un triángulo cuyos lados no son congruentes.

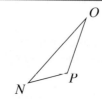

Scatter plot (p. 567) A scatter plot is a graph that relates two sets of data.

Diagrama de dispersión (p. 567) Un diagrama de dispersión es una gráfica que relaciona dos conjuntos de datos.

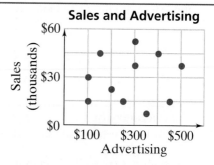

The scatter plot shows amounts spent by several companies on advertising (in dollars) versus product sales (in thousands of dollars).

Scientific notation (p. 107) A number in scientific notation is written as the product of two factors. The first factor is a number greater than or equal to 1 and less than 10; the second factor is a power of 10.

Notación científica (p. 107) Un número en notación científica se escribe como el producto de dos factores. El primer factor es un número mayor o igual a 1 y menor que 10; el segundo factor es una potencia de 10.

37,000,000 is written as 3.7×10^7 in scientific notation.

Segment (p. 324) A segment has two endpoints and all the points of the line between the points.

Segmento (p. 324) Un segmento tiene dos extremos y todos los puntos de la recta entre los puntos extremos.

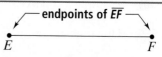

$\overline{EF}$ represents the segment shown.

Segment bisector (p. 362) A segment bisector is a line, segment, or ray that goes through the midpoint of a segment.

Mediatriz de un segmento (p. 362) Una mediatriz de un segmento es una recta, segmento o rayo que pasa por el punto medio de un segmento.

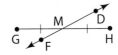

$GM = MH. \overleftrightarrow{FD}$ is a bisector of $\overline{GH}$.

Semicircle (p. 351) A semicircle is half a circle. See *Arc*.

Semicírculo (p. 351) Un semicírculo es la mitad de un círculo. Ver *Arco*.

Sequence (p. 442) A sequence is a set of numbers that follow a pattern.

Secuencia (p. 442) Una secuencia es un conjunto de números que sigue un patrón.

$3, 6, 9, 12, 15, \ldots$ is a sequence.

Similar polygons (p. 252) Two polygons are similar if their corresponding angles have the same measure and the lengths of their corresponding sides are proportional.

Polígonos semejantes (p. 252) Dos polígonos son semejantes si sus ángulos correspondientes tienen la misma medida y las longitudes de sus lados correspondientes son proporcionales.

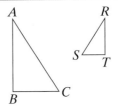

$\triangle ABC \sim \triangle RTS$

Simple interest (p. 468) Simple interest is interest calculated only on the principal. Use the formula $I = prt$ where I is the interest, p is the principal, r is the annual interest rate, and t is time in years.

Interés simple (p. 468) El interés simple se calcula sólo en relación al principal. Se usa la fórmula $I = prt$ donde I es el interés, p es el principal, r es la tasa de interés anual y t es el tiempo en años.

The simple interest earned on $200 invested at 5% annual interest for three years is $200 · 0.05 · 3, or $30.

Simplest form (p. 82) A fraction is in simplest form when the numerator and denominator have no common factors other than 1.

Mínima expresión (p. 82) Una fracción está en su mínima expresión cuando el numerador y el denominador no tienen otro factor común más que el uno.

The simplest form of $\frac{3}{9}$ is $\frac{1}{3}$.

Skew lines (p. 325) Skew lines lie in different planes. They are neither parallel nor intersecting.

Rectas cruzadas (p. 325) Las rectas cruzadas están en planos diferentes. No son paralelas ni se intersecan.

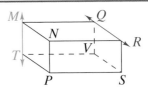

$\overleftrightarrow{MT}$ and $\overleftrightarrow{QR}$ are skew lines.

Slope of a line (p. 498) Slope is a ratio that describes the steepness of a line.

$$\text{slope} = \frac{\text{rise}}{\text{run}}$$

Pendiente de una recta (p. 498) La pendiente es la razón que describe la inclinación de una recta.

$$\text{pendiente} = \frac{\text{cambio vertical}}{\text{cambio horizontal}}$$

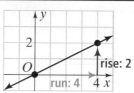

The slope of the given line is $\frac{2}{4} = \frac{1}{2}$.

Solution (pp. 174, 205) A solution is any value or values that make an equation or inequality true.

4 is the solution of $x + 5 = 9$.
7 is a solution of $x < 15$.

Solución (pp. 174, 205) Una solución es cualquier valor o valores que hacen que una ecuación o una desigualdad sea verdadera.

Sphere (p. 411) A sphere is the set of all points in space that are the same distance from a center point.

Esfera (p. 411) Una esfera es el conjunto de todos los puntos en el espacio que están a la misma distancia de un punto central.

Spreadsheet (p. 538) A spreadsheet is a tool used for organizing and analyzing data. Spreadsheets are arranged in numbered rows and lettered columns.

Hoja de cálculo (p. 538) Una hoja de cálculo es una herramienta que se usa para organizar y analizar datos. Las hojas de cálculo se organizan en filas numeradas y columnas en orden alfabético.

	A	B	C	D	E
1	0.50	0.70	0.60	0.50	2.30
2	1.50	0.50	2.75	2.50	7.25

In the spreadsheet, column C and row 2 meet at the shaded box, cell C2.

Square (p. 341) A square is a parallelogram with four right angles and four congruent sides.

Cuadrado (p. 341) Una cuadrado es un paralelogramo que tiene cuatro ángulos rectos y cuatro lados congruentes.

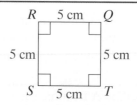

$QRST$ is a square. $\angle Q$, $\angle R$, $\angle S$, and $\angle T$ are right angles, and $\overline{QR} \cong \overline{RS} \cong \overline{ST} \cong \overline{TQ}$.

Square root (p. 400) Finding the square root of a number is the inverse of squaring a number.

$\sqrt{9} = 3$ because $3^2 = 9$.

Raíz cuadrada (p. 400) Hallar la raíz cuadrada de un número es el inverso de elevar un número al cuadrado.

Stem-and-leaf plot (p. 544) A stem-and-leaf plot is a graph that uses the digits of each number to show the shape of the data. Each data value is broken into a "stem" (digit or digits on the left) and a "leaf" (digit or digits on the right).

Diagrama de tallo y hojas (p. 544) Un diagrama de tallo y hojas es una gráfica en la que se usan los dígitos de cada número para mostrar la forma de los datos. Cada valor de los datos se divide en "tallo" (dígito o dígitos a la izquierda) y "hojas" (dígito o dígitos a la derecha).

stem	leaves
27	7
28	5 6 8
29	6 9
30	8

Key: 27 | 7 means 27.7

This stem-and-leaf plot displays recorded times in a race. The stem represents the whole number of seconds. The leaves represent tenths of a second.

Straight angle (p. 330) A straight angle is an angle with a measure of 180°.

Ángulo llano (p. 330) Un ángulo llano es un ángulo que mide 180°.

$m\angle TPL = 180°$

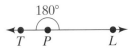

Subtraction Property of Equality (p. 180) The Subtraction Property of Equality states that if the same number is subtracted from each side of an equation, the results are equal.

Propiedad sustractiva de la igualdad (p. 180) La propiedad sustractiva de la igualdad establece que si se resta el mismo número a cada lado de una ecuación, los resultados son iguales.

Since $\frac{20}{2} = 10$, $\frac{20}{2} - 3 = 10 - 3$.
If $a = b$, then $a - c = b - c$.

Subtraction Property of Inequality (p. 211) When you subtract the same number from each side of an inequality, the relationship between the two sides does not change.

Propiedad sustractiva de la desigualdad (p. 211) Cuando se resta el mismo número a cada lado de una desigualdad, la relación entre los dos lados no cambia.

If $a > b$, then $a - c > b - c$.
Since $9 > 6$, $9 - 2 > 6 - 2$.
If $a < b$, then $a - c < b - c$.
Since $9 < 13$, $9 - 2 < 13 - 2$.

Supplementary (p. 331) Supplementary angles are two angles whose measures add to 180°.

Suplementario (p. 331) Los ángulos suplementarios son dos ángulos cuyas medidas suman 180°.

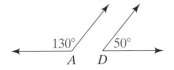

$\angle A$ and $\angle D$ are supplementary angles.

Surface area of a prism (p. 415) The surface area of a prism is the sum of the areas of its faces.

Área total de un prisma (p. 415) El área total de un prisma es la suma de las áreas de sus caras.

Each square = 1 in.^{2}

$4 \cdot 12$ in.$^2 + 2 \cdot 9$ in.$^2 = 66$ in.^{2}

Terminating decimal (p. 96) A terminating decimal is a decimal that stops, or terminates.

Both 0.6 and 0.7265 are terminating decimals.

Decimal finito (p. 96) Un decimal finito es un decimal que termina.

Theoretical probability (p. 580) The formula used to compute the theoretical probability of an event is
$$P(\text{event}) = \frac{\text{number of favorable outcomes}}{\text{total number of possible outcomes}}.$$

Suppose you select a letter from the letters H, A, P, P, and Y. The theoretical probability of selecting a P is $\frac{2}{5}$.

Probabilidad teórica (p. 580) La fórmula que se usa para calcular la probabilidad teórica de un suceso es
$$P(\text{suceso}) = \frac{\text{número favorable de resultados}}{\text{número total de resultados posibles}}.$$

Three-dimensional figure (p. 410) Three-dimensional figures are figures that do not lie in a plane.

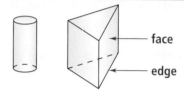

Figura tridimensional (p. 410) Las figuras tridimensionales son figuras que no están en un solo plano.

Tip (p. 304) A tip is a percent of a bill given to a person providing a service.

A lunch bill is $18. You leave a 20% tip of $3.60.

Propina (p. 304) Una propina es un porcentaje de una cuenta que se le da a una persona por el servicio prestado.

Transformation (p. 510) A transformation is a change of the position, shape, or size of a figure. Three types of transformations that change position only are translations, reflections, and rotations.

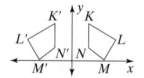

$K'L'M'N'$ is a reflection, or flip, of $KLMN$ across the y-axis.

Transformacion (p. 510) Una transformación es un cambio de posición, forma o tamaño de una figura. Tres tipos de transformaciones que cambian la posición son las traslaciones, las reflexiones y las rotaciones.

Translation (p. 510) A translation is a transformation that moves every point of a figure the same distance and in the same direction.

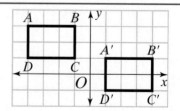

$A'B'C'D'$ is a translation image of $ABCD$.

Traslación (p. 510) Una traslación es una transformación que mueve cada punto de una figura la misma distancia y en la misma dirección.

Trapezoid (p. 341) A trapezoid is a quadrilateral with exactly one pair of parallel sides.

Trapecio (p. 341) Un trapecio es un cuadrilátero que tiene exactamente un par de lados paralelos.

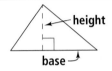

$\overline{UV}$ is parallel to $\overline{WY}$.

Trend (p. 568) A trend is a relationship between two sets of data. See *Positive trend*, *Negative trend*, and *No trend*.

Tendencia (p. 568) Una tendencia es una relación entre dos conjuntos de datos. Ver *Positive trend*, *Negative trend* y *No trend*.

Triangle (p. 340) A triangle is a polygon with three sides.

Triángulo (p. 340) Un triángulo es un polígono que tiene tres lados.

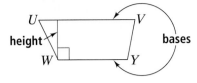

 U

Unit cost (p. 233) A unit rate that gives the cost per unit is a unit cost.

Costo unitario (p. 233) Un costo unitario es una tasa unitaria que da el costo por unidad.

$$\frac{\$5.98}{10.2 \text{ fl oz}} = \$.59/\text{fl oz}$$

Unit rate (p. 232) The rate for one unit of a given quantity is called the unit rate.

Tasa unitaria (p. 232) La tasa para una unidad de una cantidad dada se llama tasa unitaria.

If you drive 130 mi in 2 h, your unit rate is $\frac{65 \text{ mi}}{1 \text{ h}}$, or 65 mi/h.

 V

Variable (p. 169) A variable is a letter that stands for a number. The value of an algebraic expression varies, or changes, depending upon the value given to the variable.

x is a variable in the equation $9 + x = 7$.

Variable (p. 169) Una variable es una letra que representa un número. El valor de una expresión algebraica varía, o cambia, dependiendo del valor que se le dé a la variable.

Vertex of an angle (p. 330) The vertex of an angle is the point of intersection of two sides of an angle.

Vértice de un ángulo (p. 330) El vértice de un ángulo es el punto de intersección de dos lados de un ángulo.

Vertex of a polygon (p. 330) The vertex of a polygon is any point where two sides of a polygon meet.

Vértice de un polígono (p. 330) El vértice de un polígono es cualquier punto donde se encuentran dos lados de un polígono.

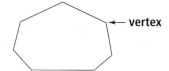

Vertical (p. 499) Vertical lines are parallel to the *y*-axis.

Vertical (p. 499) Las rectas verticales son paralelas al eje de *y*.

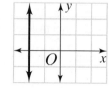

Vertical angles (p. 331) Vertical angles are formed by two intersecting lines. Vertical angles are opposite each other.

Ángulos verticales (p. 331) Los ángulos verticales están formados por dos rectas que se intersecan. Los ángulos verticales son opuestos entre sí.

∠1 and ∠2 are vertical angles, as are ∠3 and ∠4.

Volume (p. 421) The volume of a three-dimensional figure is the number of cubic units needed to fill the space inside the figure.

Volumen (p. 421) El volumen de una figura tridimensional es el número de unidades cúbicas que se necesitan para llenar el espacio dentro de la figura.

The volume of the rectangular prism is 36 cubic units.

X

x-axis (p. 486) The *x*-axis is the horizontal number line that, together with the *y*-axis, forms the coordinate plane.

Eje de *x* (p. 486) El eje de *x* es la recta numérica horizontal que, junto con el eje de *y*, forma el plano de coordenadas.

x-coordinate (p. 486) The x-coordinate is the first number in an ordered pair. It tells the number of horizontal units a point is from the origin, O.

Coordenada x (p. 486) La coordenada *x* es el primer número en un par ordenado. Indica el número de unidades horizontales a las que un punto está del orígen, *O*.

The *x*-coordinate is −2 for the ordered pair (−2, 1).
The point is 2 units to the left of the origin.

y-axis (p. 486) The y-axis is the vertical number line that, together with the x-axis, forms the coordinate plane.

Eje de y (p. 486) El eje de *y* es la recta numérica vertical que, junto con el eje de *x*, forma el plano de coordenadas.

y-coordinate (p. 486) The y-coordinate is the second number in an ordered pair. It tells the number of vertical units a point is from the origin, O.

Coordenada y (p. 486) La coordenada *y* es el segundo número en un par ordenado. Indica el número de unidades verticales a las que un punto está del orígen, *O*.

The *y*-coordinate is 1 for the ordered pair (−2, 1). The point is 1 unit up from the *x*-axis.

Zero pair (p. 36) The pairing of one "+" chip with one "−" chip is called a zero pair.

Par cero (p. 36) El emparejamiento de una ficha "+" con una ficha "−" se llama par cero.

⊕ ⊖ ⟵ a zero pair

Zero Property (p. 15) The Zero Property states that the product of 0 and any number is 0.

Propiedad del cero (p. 15) La propiedad del cero establece que el producto de cero y cualquier número es cero.

$6 \cdot 0 = 0$
$a \cdot 0 = 0$

English/Spanish Glossary

Chapter 1

Check Your Readiness | p. 2

1. < **2.** > **3.** 37 **4.** 76 **5.** 216 **6.** 214 **7.** 3 tenths
8. 6 thousandths **9.** 9 ones **10.** 3 hundredths
11. 7 ten-thousandths **12.** four hundred
twenty-one and five tenths **13.** five thousand six
and twenty-five hundredths **14.** fifteen and four
thousandths **15.** three hundred twenty-nine
thousandths **16.** seven hundred ten and four
hundred thirteen thousandths **17.** 34.12
18. 278.79 **19.** 3.60 **20.** 81.80 **21.** 17.00

Lesson 1-1 | pp. 4–5

Check Skills You'll Need 1. An estimate is an answer
with a calculation; a guess is an answer without a
calculation. **2.** 83,000 **3.** 400 **4.** 24,110 **5.** 3,500

Quick Check 1 a. 3 **b.** 6 **c.** 30 **2.** about $14 **3.** Yes;
you can buy about 48 ÷ 16, or 3, DVDs from
category B. This is half the number of DVDs you
can buy from category D.

Lesson 1-2 | pp. 8–9

Check Skills You'll Need 1. Place value is the position
and value of a digit in a decimal. **2.** 8 hundredths
3. 8 tenths **4.** 8 hundreds **5.** 8 thousandths

Quick Check 1. 8.02 min **2.** 11.89 **3.** 10.3

Lesson 1-3 | pp. 14–18

Check Skills You'll Need 1. Estimating gives an
approximate answer. **2.** 15 **3.** 28 **4.** 10

Quick Check 1. 11.583 **2.** 63

Checkpoint Quiz 1 1. $10 **2.** $11 **3.** Answers may
vary. Sample: about 6 **4.** Answers may vary.
Sample: about 13 **5.** 24.57 **6.** 14.321 **7.** 2.92
8. 21.86 **9.** 12.1584 **10.** 0.096 **11.** 51.072
12. 11.118 **13.** = **14.** 487.5 words **15.** 6.45 lb

Lesson 1-4 | pp. 20–21

Check Skills You'll Need 1. Numbers that are easy to
compute mentally. **2–4.** Answers may vary.
Samples are given.
2. 8 **3.** 13 **4.** 7

Quick Check 1 a. 2.3 **b.** 106 **c.** 14.7
2. 5.2 smoothies

Lesson 1-5 | pp. 26–27

Check Skills You'll Need 1. Commutative **2.** 2.5
3. 4,567 **4.** 3 **5.** 70

Quick Check 1 a. 180 mL **b.** 500 mg **2.** 34,000 mL
3. 4.690 kg

Lesson 1-6 | pp. 31–32

Check Skills You'll Need 1. Associative **2.** 4,244.8
3. 0.5397 **4.** 6,425.1

Quick Check 1 a. 8 **b.** −13 **c.** 22 **2.** 8 **3.** −8 < −2
4. −4, −1, 2, 3

Checkpoint Quiz 2 1. 1.2 **2.** 3.15 **3.** 1.7 **4.** 500
5. 4.1 **6.** 1,700 **7.** > **8.** < **9.** = **10.** 240 mL

Lesson 1-7 | pp. 38–40

Check Skills You'll Need 1. the same distance from
zero as the number **2.** −73 **3.** 49 **4.** −22
5. −13 **6.** 424 **7.** 13

Quick Check 1 a. −7 **b.** −8 **c.** 0 **2 a.** −162 **b.** −18
c. 0 **3.** −7 **4.** 21 **5 a.** −137 − (−155) **b.** 18 ft

Lesson 1-8 | pp. 44–45

Check Skills You'll Need 1. zero **2.** 4 **3.** 5 **4.** −35 **5.** 0

Quick Check 1. 28 **2.** −524 ft/h

Lesson 1-9 | pp. 48–49

Check Skills You'll Need 1. Comm. Prop. of Add.
2. 12.1 **3.** 18.2 **4.** 20

Quick Check 1 a. −15 **b.** 0 **c.** −9 **2.** $23.93 **3.** 126

Lesson 1-10 | pp. 53–55

Check Skills You'll Need 1. division **2.** 13 **3.** −4 **4.** −2

Quick Check 1. 224 **2.** −1.5 **3 a.** 17 **b.** no mode
c. pen **4.** 143°F

Chapter 2

Check Your Readiness | p. 66

1. 5.5 **2.** 1.423 **3.** 3.89 **4.** 677.447 **5.** < **6.** <
7. = **8.** < **9.** < **10.** > **11.** −27 **12.** 9 **13.** −9
14. 4 **15.** 28 **16.** 2 **17.** 1

Lesson 2-1 — pp. 68–69

Check Skills You'll Need 1. before **2.** 2 **3.** 12 **4.** −10 **5.** 1

Quick Check 1 a. 44^4 **b.** $(-2)^2$ **2 a.** 243 **b.** 1,000,000,000 **c.** 9.61 **3 a.** −27 **b.** −27 **c.** 62

Lesson 2-2 — pp. 74–79

Check Skills You'll Need 1. 0 **2.** 24 **3.** 21 **4.** 12

Quick Check 1 a. 20 **b.** 35 **c.** 60 **2.** Composite; the factors of 15 are 1, 3, 5, and 15. Since 15 has more than two factors, 15 is composite. **3.** $72 = 2^3 \cdot 3^2$ **4.** 8

Checkpoint Quiz 1 1. 75 **2.** 1 **3.** 54 **4.** 12 **5.** 70 **6.** 60 **7.** 1, 3, 13, 39 **8.** 1, 2, 4, 13, 26, 52 **9.** 1, 2, 5, 10, 11, 22, 55, 110 **10.** 1, 2, 4, 5, 8, 10, 20, 25, 40, 50, 100, 200 **11.** $2^5 \cdot 3$ **12.** $2 \cdot 3 \cdot 5^2$ **13.** $3^2 \cdot 5^2$ **14.** $3^2 \cdot 37$ **15.** 24 ft

Lesson 2-3 — pp. 82–83

Check Skills You'll Need 1. It is the greatest factor that divides both numbers. **2.** 2 **3.** 12 **4.** 5 **5.** 1

Quick Check 1. Answers may vary. Sample: $\frac{8}{10}$, $\frac{12}{15}$

2. Answers may vary. Sample: $\frac{9}{15}$, $\frac{3}{5}$ **3.** $\frac{2}{3}$ **4.** $\frac{2}{5}$

Lesson 2-4 — pp. 87–88

Check Skills You'll Need 1. least common multiple **2.** 12 **3.** 20 **4.** 8 **5.** 45

Quick Check 1 a. < **b.** < **c.** > **2.** $\frac{5}{32}$ in., $\frac{1}{4}$ in., $\frac{5}{16}$ in., $\frac{3}{8}$ in.

Lesson 2-5 — pp. 91–92

Check Skills You'll Need 1. The numerator and denominator have no common factors other than 1. **2.** $\frac{3}{5}$ **3.** $\frac{5}{6}$ **4.** $\frac{3}{4}$ **5.** $\frac{5}{12}$

Quick Check 1. $\frac{21}{8}$ **2.** 3

Lesson 2-6 — pp. 96–101

Check Skills You'll Need 1. In simplest form, they are the same. **2–5.** Answers may vary. Samples are given.

2. $\frac{4}{5}$, $\frac{8}{10}$ **3.** $\frac{3}{4}$, $\frac{6}{8}$ **4.** $\frac{2}{3}$, $\frac{8}{12}$ **5.** $\frac{1}{5}$, $\frac{2}{10}$

Quick Check 1. 0.625 **2.** $0.\overline{5}$ **3 a.** $1\frac{91}{250}$ **b.** $2\frac{12}{25}$ **c.** $3\frac{3}{5}$ **4.** 1.862, $1\frac{7}{15}$, $1\frac{3}{8}$ **5.** cats, dogs, fish, birds

Checkpoint Quiz 2 1. $\frac{1}{2}$ **2.** $\frac{7}{10}$ **3.** $\frac{5}{8}$ **4.** > **5.** < **6.** = **7.** $4\frac{5}{6}$ **8.** $\frac{37}{9}$ **9.** $16\frac{2}{5}$ **10.** 0.00015, 0.004, 0.0112

Lesson 2-7 — pp. 102–103

Check Skills You'll Need 1. Terminating decimal; the decimal stops **2.** 0.75 **3.** $-0.\overline{7}$ **4.** $1.\overline{3}$ **5.** 0.25

Quick Check 1. $-\frac{2}{3} < -\frac{1}{6}$ **2.** $-4.2 > -4.9$

3. $-6\frac{1}{4}$, -4, 6.55, $12\frac{1}{2}$

Lesson 2-8 — pp. 106–107

Check Skills You'll Need 1. factor **2.** 27 **3.** 16 **4.** 100,000 **5.** 16

Quick Check 1. 1.69×10^5 **2.** 640,000

Chapter 3

Check Your Readiness — p. 118

1. −40 **2.** −24 **3.** 100 **4.** 18 **5.** −45 **6.** 60 **7.** −3 **8.** 20 **9.** 9 **10.** 21 **11.** 12 **12.** 9 **13.** $\frac{3}{4}$ **14.** $\frac{1}{2}$ **15.** $\frac{7}{8}$ **16.** $\frac{3}{8}$ **17.** $\frac{1}{3}$ **18.** $\frac{5}{9}$ **19.** $\frac{2}{3}$ **20.** $\frac{2}{7}$

Lesson 3-1 — pp. 120–121

Check Skills You'll Need 1. When you estimate by rounding, you round a number to the nearest unit. When you use compatible numbers, you look for numbers that are easy to compute mentally. **2.** 7 **3.** 4 **4.** 8 **5.** 6 **6.** 2

Quick Check 1. about $\frac{1}{2}$ **2.** about 6 in. **3 a.** about 20 **b.** about 48 **c.** about 14 **4 a.** about 6 **b.** about 6 **c.** about 9

Lesson 3-2 — pp. 126–127

Check Skills You'll Need 1. equivalent **2.** 4 **3.** 8 **4.** 24

Quick Check 1 a. $\frac{4}{5}$ **b.** $\frac{1}{4}$ **c.** 1 **2 a.** $\frac{7}{12}$ **b.** $\frac{11}{14}$ **3.** $\frac{7}{8}$ mi

Lesson 3-3 — pp. 130–134

Check Skills You'll Need 1. When two fractions have the same denominator, you can compare them by looking at the numerators. **2.** < **3.** <

Quick Check 1 a. $4\frac{1}{3}$ **b.** $4\frac{4}{5}$ **c.** 1 **2 a.** 1 **b.** $12\frac{1}{24}$ **c.** $4\frac{3}{10}$ **3.** $1\frac{1}{2}$ ft

Checkpoint Quiz 1 1. about $5\frac{1}{2}$ in. **2.** about $13\frac{1}{2}$ in. **3.** about 5 in. **4.** $\frac{1}{6}$ **5.** 2 **6.** $5\frac{9}{10}$ **7.** $8\frac{19}{20}$ **8.** $\frac{2}{9}$ **9.** $11\frac{5}{8}$ **10.** $21\frac{5}{8}$ in.

Lesson 3-4 — pp. 136–137

Check Skills You'll Need 1. The numerator is greater than the denominator. **2.** $\frac{13}{5}$ **3.** $\frac{13}{2}$ **4.** $\frac{5}{3}$ **5.** $\frac{19}{4}$

Quick Check **1 a.** $\frac{3}{20}$ **b.** $\frac{2}{3}$ **c.** $\frac{8}{15}$ **2.** 63 members **3 a.** $10\frac{19}{24}$ **b.** $4\frac{17}{25}$ **c.** $15\frac{3}{32}$

Lesson 3-5 — pp. 141–142

Check Skills You'll Need **1.** multiplication **2.** $\frac{2}{7}$ **3.** $\frac{5}{18}$ **4.** 45 **5.** 4

Quick Check **1 a.** $3\frac{1}{2}$ **b.** $\frac{5}{6}$ **c.** 20 **2 a.** $1\frac{25}{44}$ **b.** $\frac{3}{4}$ **c.** $1\frac{3}{16}$ **3.** $5\frac{19}{30}$cans

Lesson 3-6 — pp. 148–153

Check Skills You'll Need **1.** It consists of a whole number and a fraction. **2.** $1\frac{1}{12}$ **3.** $\frac{5}{8}$ **4.** $12\frac{1}{4}$ **5.** $4\frac{1}{4}$

Quick Check **1.** $1\frac{7}{12}$ ft **2.** $6\frac{1}{4}$ c **3.** 74 oz

Checkpoint Quiz 2 **1.** $\frac{2}{7}$ **2.** $3\frac{1}{4}$ **3.** $\frac{1}{5}$ **4.** $9\frac{11}{32}$ **5.** $\frac{11}{15}$ **6.** $11\frac{1}{9}$ yd^2 **7.** $\frac{2}{3}$ **8.** $6\frac{2}{3}$ **9.** 2 **10.** $\frac{4}{5}$ **11.** 13 **12.** $45\frac{3}{4}$ min **13.** $3\frac{1}{3}$ **14.** $2\frac{1}{4}$ **15.** $8\frac{1}{2}$

Lesson 3-7 — pp. 154–155

Check Skills You'll Need **1.** meter; liter; gram **2.** 100 **3.** 0.001 **4.** 10 **5.** 1,000 **6.** 0.001

Quick Check **1.** 13 in. **2.** 12.5 g **3.** $10\frac{1}{5}$ mi **4 a.** $\frac{1}{8}$ in. **b.** $\frac{1}{16}$ in. **5.** 14.1 g **6.** 44 m

Chapter 4

Check Your Readiness — p. 166

1. 4.414 **2.** 8.6 **3.** 0.79 **4.** 15.21 **5.** −36 **6.** 1 **7.** 42 **8.** −6 **9.** 20 **10.** 1 **11.** 1 **12.** 6 **13.** 7 **14.** 38 **15.** > **16.** = **17.** > **18.** <

Lesson 4-1 — pp. 169–170

Check Skills You'll Need **1.** order of operations **2.** 11 **3.** 10 **4.** −10 **5.** 3

Quick Check **1.** $p - 16$ **2.** $9t$ **3.** Answers may vary. Sample: a number decreased by 50, 50 less than a number, 50 subtracted from a number **4.** 56

Lesson 4-2 — pp. 174–175

Check Skills You'll Need **1.** variable **2.** $y + 4$ **3.** $v - 6$ **4.** $\frac{k}{9}$

Quick Check **1 a.** 5 **b.** 8 **2 a.** 10 **b.** −16.1 **c.** 8.8 **d.** −9 **3.** about 26 boxes

Lesson 4-3 — pp. 180–182

Check Skills You'll Need **1.** equation **2.** about 9 **3.** about 18 **4.** about 25

Quick Check **1.** 168 **2.** $7.95 **3 a.** Check students' work. **b.** 116

Lesson 4-4 — pp. 186–191

Check Skills You'll Need **1.** simplest form **2.** $\frac{1}{4}$ **3.** 4 **4.** 1 **5.** a

Quick Check **1 a.** −7.2 **b.** 9 **c.** 3 **2.** $5c = 110$; $22 **3.** −390

Checkpoint Quiz 1 **1.** $x - 4$ **2.** $3x$ **3.** $\frac{4}{x}$ **4.** $x + 9$ **5.** −4.4 **6.** 1.8 **7.** −9.1 **8.** 48 **9.** $y + 18 = 1825$; $y = 1807$ **10.** 24 years 8 months

Lesson 4-5 — pp. 194–196

Check Skills You'll Need **1.** algebraic expression **2.** 1 **3.** 13 **4.** 24 **5.** −2

Quick Check **1.** Let s = son's age; $3s - 2$ **2.** 37 **3 a.** 4 **b.** 5 **c.** 11 **4.** Let b = number of 3-point baskets; $8 + 3b = 23$; 5 baskets.

Lesson 4-6 — pp. 200–201

Check Skills You'll Need **1.** Multiplication Property of Equality **2.** 6 **3.** −5 **4.** −64 **5.** −18

Quick Check **1.** 1 **2.** 200 **3.** Let m = number of markers; $0.79m + 1.25 = 7.57$; 8 markers

Lesson 4-7 — pp. 205–209

Check Skills You'll Need **1.** opposites **2.** > **3.** > **4.** < **5.** >

Quick Check **1.** −2, 1.4 **2.** **3.** $x < 4$ **4.** $t \leq 62$

Checkpoint Quiz 2 **1.** 5 **2.** 40 **3.** 2 **4.** −9 **5.** −2 **6.** −5 **7.** Let c = the cost of a skirt; $12 + 2c = 38$; $13. **8.**

9.

10.

Lesson 4-8 — pp. 210–211

Check Skills You'll Need **1.** because they "undo" each other **2.** −6 **3.** 1 **4.** 9 **5.** 7

Quick Check **1.** $y < 7$;

2 a. $x > -4$;

b. $y < 1$;

c. $w \leq -9$;

3. Let p = number of points; $p + 109 > 200$; $p > 91$; you need more than 91 points.

Lesson 4-9 — pp. 214–216

Check Skills You'll Need 1. You can add to each side of an equation or inequality without changing the relationship. **2.** $x \le 2$ **3.** $p > 7$ **4.** $3 \ge d$ **5.** $r < -6$

Quick Check 1 a. $p > -9$;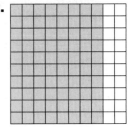

b. $m \le 3$;

c. $n > -3$;   **2.** 416 min

3. $k > 20$;

Chapter 5

Check Your Readiness — p. 226

1. 14.4 **2.** 114.66 **3.** 47.7 **4.** 1.12 **5.** 2.6 **6.** 10.52 **7.** −8 **8.** 60 **9.** −2 **10.** 75 **11.** > **12.** < **13.** = **14.** > **15.** $\frac{3}{4}$ **16.** $\frac{1}{2}$ **17.** $\frac{3}{8}$ **18.** $\frac{1}{3}$ **19.** $\frac{2}{7}$

Lesson 5-1 — pp. 228–229

Check Skills You'll Need 1. Equivalent fractions are fractions that name the same amount. **2.** $\frac{1}{2}$ **3.** $\frac{7}{9}$ **4.** $\frac{4}{7}$ **5.** $\frac{1}{3}$

Quick Check 1 a. 7 to 12, 7 : 12, $\frac{7}{12}$ **b.** 7 to 5; 7 : 5; $\frac{7}{5}$ **2.** Answers may vary. Samples: $\frac{14}{18}, \frac{35}{45}$ **3.** $\frac{6}{5}$ **4 a.** not equivalent **b.** not equivalent **c.** equivalent

Lesson 5-2 — pp. 232–237

Check Skills You'll Need 1. division **2.** $\frac{3}{5}$ **3.** $\frac{3}{1}$ **4.** $\frac{11}{8}$ **5.** $\frac{1}{9}$

Quick Check 1. 70 heartbeats per min **2.** $7.00 **3.** $.064/fl oz, $.056/fl oz; the 64-fl-oz bottle is the better buy.

Checkpoint Quiz 1 1. 7 to 52, $\frac{7}{52}$ **2.** $\frac{2}{3}$ **3.** $\frac{1}{3}$ **4.** 12 to 7 **5.** 2 : 3 **6.** 42 words/min **7.** 9 points/game **8.** $.2633, $.2475; the second item is the better buy. **9.** $7.80, $6.57; the second item is the better buy. **10.** 15 pizzas

Lesson 5-3 — pp. 238–239

Check Skills You'll Need 1. LCM **2.** > **3.** = **4.** < **5.** >

Quick Check 1. no; $\frac{5}{6} \ne \frac{5}{7}$ **2 a.** yes; 48 = 48 **b.** yes; 36 = 36 **c.** no; 36 ≠ 40

Lesson 5-4 — pp. 244–245

Check Skills You'll Need 1. A ratio is a unit rate when you are finding the rate for one unit of something. **2.** 8 km/d **3.** 62 mi/h **4.** 25 push-ups/min **5.** 60 words/min

Quick Check 1 a. $6.37 **b.** $119.51 **2 a.** 9 **b.** 2 **c.** 10 **3 a.** 16.8 **b.** 27.2 **c.** 192.5

Lesson 5-5 — pp. 250–257

Check Skills You'll Need 1. proportion **2.** 6 **3.** 12 **4.** 42 **5.** 9.5

Quick Check 1. 20 **2.** 36 ft

Checkpoint Quiz 2 1. no **2.** yes **3.** no **4.** yes **5.** $8.40 **6.** $16.50 **7.** 120° **8.** 26° **9.** 9 **10.** 12

Lesson 5-6 — pp. 259–261

Check Skills You'll Need 1. For two ratios, the cross products are found by multiplying the denominator of each ratio by the numerator of the other ratio. **2.** 8 **3.** 15 **4.** 1 **5.** 7

Quick Check 1. 10 m **2.** about 206 km **3.** 1 in. : 16 in. **4.** 5 in.

Chapter 6

Check Your Readiness — p. 272

1. 5 **2.** 14 **3.** 5 **4.** 10 **5.** $\frac{17}{20}$ **6.** $\frac{2}{5}$ **7.** $\frac{17}{25}$ **8.** $\frac{5}{4}$ **9.** $\frac{1}{100}$ **10.** 30 **11.** 800 **12.** 8.4 **13.** 3 **14.** 80 **15.** 2.16 **16.** 200

Lesson 6-1 — pp. 274–275

Check Skills You'll Need 1. Equivalent ratios have the same value. **2–5.** Answers may vary. Samples are given.

2. $\frac{4}{10}, \frac{6}{15}$ **3.** $\frac{26}{100}, \frac{39}{150}$ **4.** $\frac{6}{50}, \frac{9}{75}$ **5.** $\frac{2}{20}, \frac{3}{30}$

Quick Check 1. $\frac{54}{100}$; 54% **2.**

3 a. $\frac{3}{4}$; 75% **b.** $\frac{1}{2}$; 50% **c.** $\frac{7}{10}$; 70% **4.** 80%

Lesson 6-2   pp. 279–281

Check Skills You'll Need 1. A repeating decimal is a decimal that repeats without end. **2.** 0.3125 **3.** 0.275 **4.** $0.\overline{4}$ **5.** $0.1\overline{3}$

Quick Check 1. 60.7% **2 a.** 0.35 **b.** 0.125 **c.** 0.078 **3.** 52.5% **4.** $\frac{3}{50}$ **5 a.** 29%, $\frac{3}{10}$, $\frac{11}{25}$, 0.74 **b.** 0.08, 15%, $\frac{7}{20}$, 50%

Lesson 6-3   pp. 284–285

Check Skills You'll Need 1. 100 **2.** 1% **3.** 98% **4.** 95% **5.** 8%

Quick Check 1. 1.25; $\frac{5}{4}$ or $1\frac{1}{4}$ **2.** 0.0035; $\frac{7}{2,000}$ **3.** 280% **4.** 0.46%

Checkpoint Quiz 1 1. 0.45; $\frac{9}{20}$ **2.** 1.35; $1\frac{7}{20}$ **3.** 0.0098; $\frac{49}{5,000}$ **4.** 56% **5.** $\frac{1}{6}$, 20%, 0.245, $\frac{1}{4}$ **6.** $\frac{16}{25}$; 64% **7.**

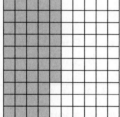

8. about 0.6% **9.** 35% **10.** 75%

Lesson 6-4   pp. 290–291

Check Skills You'll Need 1. multiplication **2.** 1,200 **3.** 1,350 **4.** 70.2 **5.** 29.7

Quick Check 1. 105 **2.** 960 **3 a.** about 60 **b.** about 100 **c.** about 600

Lesson 6-5   pp. 294–295

Check Skills You'll Need 1. ratios **2.** 8 **3.** 15 **4.** 87.5

Quick Check 1. 25% **2.** 17 **3.** 15 problems

Lesson 6-6   pp. 298–299

Check Skills You'll Need 1. If both sides of an equation are divided by the same nonzero number, the results are equal. **2.** 17 **3.** 48

Quick Check 1. 150 seats **2.** 16.2 **3.** about 20.5%

Lesson 6-7   pp. 304–305

Check Skills You'll Need 1. left **2.** 0.065 **3.** 0.0425 **4.** 0.15 **5.** 0.2

Quick Check 1. $195.18 **2 a.** about $8.70 **b.** about $9.30 **c.** about $7.50 **3.** $192 **4.** $849

Checkpoint Quiz 2 1. $58.\overline{3}$% **2.** 16 **3.** 84% **4.** 45% **5.** 68.4 **6.** 222 **7.** $313.95 **8.** $82.45 **9.** $35.50 **10.** $77

Lesson 6-8   pp. 310–311

Check Skills You'll Need 1. 500 and $16n$ **2.** 10 **3.** 12.5 **4.** 50

Quick Check 1. 1.9% **2.** 99.4% **3.** 40%

Chapter 7

Check Your Readiness   p. 322

1. < **2.** > **3.** > **4.** < **5.** 2 **6.** 15 **7.** 12 **8.** 105 **9.** 5 **10.** 94 **11.** 80 **12.** 16 **13.** 111 **14.** 46 **15.** 108 **16.** 86.4 **17.** 16.2 **18.** 64.8

Lesson 7-1   pp. 324–325

Check Skills You'll Need 1. <, >, ≤, ≥, ≠

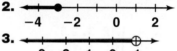

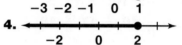

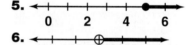

Quick Check 1 a. $\overrightarrow{PD}$ **b.** $\overline{RS}$ **c.** $\overleftrightarrow{AV}$ **2 a.** $\overline{EF}, \overline{HD}$ **b.** $\overline{EB}, \overline{CB}, \overline{AB}, \overline{GH}, \overline{DH}$ **c.** $\overline{FC}, \overline{EF}, \overline{BC}, \overline{HD}$

Lesson 7-2   pp. 330–332

Check Skills You'll Need 1. equation **2.** 70 **3.** 140 **4.** 74 **5.** 158

Quick Check 1. obtuse **2.** 53° **3.** 108°; 72°; 108°

Lesson 7-3   pp. 336–337

Check Skills You'll Need 1. an angle with a measure greater than 0° and less than 90° **2.** right **3.** obtuse

Quick Check 1. isosceles **2 a.** right **b.** acute **3.** 22°

Lesson 7-4   pp. 340–342

Check Skills You'll Need 1. an equilateral triangle **2.** equilateral **3.** isosceles **4.** scalene

Quick Check 1 a. The octagon is irregular because the sides are not all congruent. **b.** The triangle is regular because all sides and all angles are congruent. **c.** Multiply the side length by the number of sides the polygon has. **2 a.** hexagons, triangles **b.** squares, triangles, rhombuses **3.** Answers may vary. An example is given.

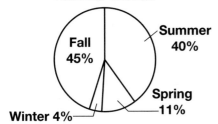

Checkpoint Quiz 1 1. $\overline{XZ}$ **2.** $\overleftrightarrow{NM}$ **3.** $\overline{KV}$ **4.** 78°; 168° **5.** 43°; 133° **6.** 25°; 115° **7.** 70° **8.** equilateral **9.** obtuse isosceles **10.** right scalene **11.** Equilateral $\triangle PQT$ is regular, square $QRST$ is regular, and pentagon $PQRST$ is irregular.

Lesson 7-5	pp. 346–347

Check Skills You'll Need 1. Two polygons are similar if corresponding angles are congruent and corresponding side lengths have the same proportion. **2.** 3.15 m **3.** 56° **4.** 52°

Quick Check 1. Congruent; the sides and angles all have the same measure. **2.** No; the sides are different lengths. **3 a.** $\overline{AB} \cong \overline{FG}$; $\overline{BC} \cong \overline{GH}$; $\overline{CD} \cong \overline{HI}$; $\overline{DA} \cong \overline{IF}$; $\angle A \cong \angle F$; $\angle B \cong \angle G$; $\angle C \cong \angle H$; $\angle D \cong \angle I$ **b.** 15.5; 139°

Lesson 7-6	pp. 350–351

Check Skills You'll Need 1. 2 **2.** $\overline{FR}$ **3.** $\overleftrightarrow{ZJ}$ **4.** $\overrightarrow{NK}$

Quick Check 1. $\angle AOB$, $\angle AOC$, $\angle AOD$, $\angle BOC$, $\angle BOD$, $\angle COD$ **2.** $\overline{ZY}$, $\angle ZYX$, $\widehat{YZX}$ **3.** $\widehat{CDE}$, $\widehat{CE}$

Lesson 7-7	pp. 354–358

Check Skills You'll Need 1. Every percent can be written as a decimal by moving the decimal point two places to the left. Thus 25% becomes 0.25. So taking the percent of a number is the same as multiplying by a decimal. **2.** 90 **3.** 216 **4.** 259.2

Quick Check 1. about 470 million **2 a.** 144° **b.**

Favorite Season

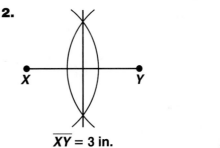

Checkpoint Quiz 2 1. Yes. The square root of the area is the side length. Since both squares have the same area, they have the same side length.

Being squares, they both have four right angles. Congruent sides and congruent angles means the squares are congruent. **2.**

Town Middle School

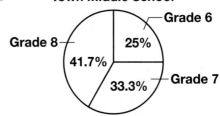

25% (90°) for 6th grade 33.3% (120°) for 7th grade, and 41.7% (150°) for 8th grade. **3.** $\overline{QP}$, $\overline{RP}$, $\overline{SP}$, $\overline{TP}$ **4.** $\overline{TR}$ **5.** $\angle RPS$, $\angle SPT$, $\angle TPQ$, and $\angle QPR$

Lesson 7-8	pp. 361–362

Check Skills You'll Need 1. a common point **2.** $\overline{VW}$ **3.** $\overrightarrow{FG}$ **4.** $\overleftrightarrow{CL}$

Quick Check 1.

T   25 mm   R

S   V

2.

X   Y

$\overline{XY} = 3$ in.

Chapter 8

Check Your Readiness	p. 372

1. 3.14 **2.** 123 **3.** 108 **4.** 4 **5.** 97 **6.** 24 **7.** 144 **8.** 3 **9.** 8 **10.** 58° **11.** 63° **12.** 50°

Lesson 8-1	pp. 374–376

Check Skills You'll Need 1. inch, foot, yard, mile **2.** 72 **3.** 4 **4.** 204

Quick Check 1. 400 mi; driving distances are usually measured in miles. **2–4.** Answers may vary. Samples are given. **2.** about 24 units **3.** about 92 yd^2 **4.** area: about 300 ft^2; perimeter: about 100 ft

Lesson 8-2	pp. 380–381

Check Skills You'll Need 1. Changing the order of the factors does not change the product. **2.** 450 **3.** 28.08 **4.** 57.12 **5.** 2.04

Quick Check **1.** 90 cm^2 **2.** 22 cm

Lesson 8-3   pp. 384–385

Check Skills You'll Need **1.** $\frac{1}{2}$ **2.** 3 **3.** 2 **4.** 5 **5.** 4.5

Quick Check **1.** 24 cm **2 a.** 216 m^2 **b.** 48 cm^2

Lesson 8-4   pp. 388–389

Check Skills You'll Need **1.** It is one of a pair of opposite sides. **2.** 75 cm^2 **3.** 135 m^2

Quick Check **1 a.** 34.1 m^2 **b.** 81 m^2 **2.** 8.75 in.^{2}

Checkpoint Quiz 1 **1.** 420 km^2 **2.** 360 km^2 **3.** 54 m^2 **4.** 240 in.^{2} **5.** 90 m^2

Lesson 8-5   pp. 394–395

Check Skills You'll Need **1.** radius **2.** $\overline{OA}$ or $\overline{OB}$ **3.** $\overline{DC}$ or $\overline{AB}$ **4.** $\overline{AB}$

Quick Check **1.** 28.3 m **2.** 452 m^2

Lesson 8-6   pp. 400–401

Check Skills You'll Need **1.** Multiply the number by itself. **2.** 64 **3.** 144 **4.** 4 **5.** 49

Quick Check **1 a.** 8 **b.** 9 **c.** 15 **2.** about 9 ft × 9 ft **3 a.** irrational **b.** rational **c.** rational **d.** rational

Lesson 8-7   pp. 405–406

Check Skills You'll Need **1.** an integer **2.** 2 **3.** 4 **4.** 6 **5.** 7

Quick Check **1.** 17 in. **2.** 24 mi **3.** 65 m

Lesson 8-8   pp. 410–411

Check Skills You'll Need **1.** regular polygon

2. **3.**

4.

Quick Check **1.** triangular prism; cone

2.

Lesson 8-9   pp. 414–416

Check Skills You'll Need **1.** The height of a triangle is the length of the perpendicular segment from a vertex to the base opposite the vertex or to an extension of the base. **2.** 48 m^2 **3.** 6 ft^2

Quick Check **1.** Answers may vary. Sample:

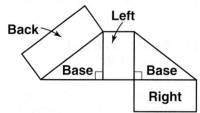

2. 328 ft^2
3. 3,455.8 m^2

Checkpoint Quiz 2 **1.** $8 < \sqrt{77} < 9$ **2.** 18 cm
3. 39 cm **4.** 4 yd **5.** 8 m **6.** sphere **7.** cone
8. rectangular prism **9.** 36 in.^{2} **10.** 2,884 m^2

Lesson 8-10   pp. 421–423

Check Skills You'll Need **1.** $\pi = \frac{C}{d}$ **2.** 113 m^2
3. 177 in.^{2}

Quick Check **1.** 120 in.^{3} **2.** 72 cm^3 **3 a.** about
6,000 cm^3; 6,107 cm^3 **b.** The estimate will be a
little large.

Chapter 9

Check Your Readiness   p. 434

1. 0 **2.** 32 **3.** −3 **4.** 65 **5.** 6.9 **6.** −40.8 **7.** 52.4
8. 1.5 **9.** 5 **10.** 5 **11.** $4\frac{3}{4}$ **12.** 36 **13.** 343
14. $24\frac{3}{8}$ **15.** 0.04 **16.** 0.12 **17.** 0.0358
18. 0.0405 **19.** 0.103

Lesson 9-1   pp. 437–438

Check Skills You'll Need **1.** Yes; it can be written as a fraction. **2-5.**

Quick Check **1.**

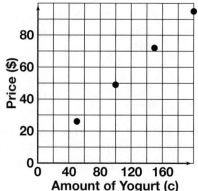

2. about $125 **3.** about 175°

Lesson 9-2
pp. 442–443

Check Skills You'll Need 1. 8 **2.** 0 **3.** −1 **4.** −2 **5.** −3

Quick Check 1. Start with 44 and add −9 repeatedly; −1, −10, −19. **2.** Start with 1,000 and multiply by $\frac{1}{10}$ repeatedly; 1, $\frac{1}{10}$, $\frac{1}{100}$. **3 a.** neither **b.** neither **c.** arithmetic

Lesson 9-3
pp. 446–450

Check Skills You'll Need 1. addition **2.** −10 **3.** 4 **4.** −8 **5.** 14

Quick Check 1.

Amount of Gas (gal)	Miles Driven
1	18.1
2	36.2
3	54.3
4	72.4
5	90.5

271.5 miles **2.** 5, 7, 9, 11 **3.** $n − 9$; 1

Checkpoint Quiz 1 1.

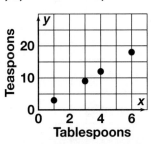

2. 30 teaspoons **3.** 7 tablespoons **4.** Start with 7 and add 7 repeatedly; 35, 42, 49. **5.** Start with 250 and add −30 repeatedly; 130, 100, 70. **6.** Start with 2, then add 3, 6, 12, 24 and so on; 47, 95, 191. **7.** Start with −4 and multiply by −3 repeatedly; −324, 972, −2,916. **8.** arithmetic; arithmetic; neither; geometric **9.** 50n; 500

Lesson 9-4
pp. 452–453

Check Skills You'll Need 1. The expression has no variable. **2.** 9 **3.** 1 **4.** 0 **5.** 2

Quick Check 1. $d = 62t$ **2.** $y = 4x + 1$ **3.**

x	y
0	−4
1	−2
2	0
3	2

Lesson 9-5
pp. 456–457

Check Skills You'll Need 1. a set of numbers that follow a pattern **2.** 5n **3.** 2n − 9 **4.** 101n

Quick Check 1.

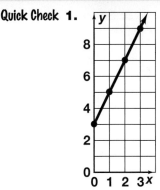

2. $d = 60t$; 270 mi

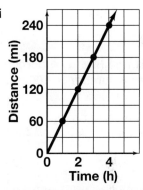

Lesson 9-6
pp. 461–465

Check Skills You'll Need 1. Answers will vary. **2.** 100 mi **3.** 140 mi **4.** 10 mi **5.** 20 mi

Quick Check 1. You walk two blocks at a fast pace and then stop for 12 min. Then you walk 2 blocks at a slower pace and 2 blocks at the faster pace.
2.

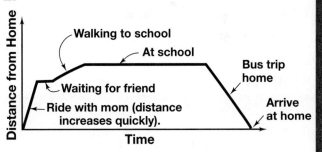

3.

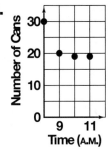

Checkpoint Quiz 2 1. $y = 5x$ **2.** $y = 3x − 3$

3. $y = x + 9$ **4.**   **5.** Edwin **6.** 1 s

7.
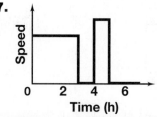

Lesson 9-7 pp. 468–469

Check Skills You'll Need 1. A percent is a ratio that compares a number to 100. **2.** 0.04 **3.** 0.09 **4.** 0.020 **5.** 0.065

Quick Check 1. $44.00 **2.**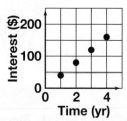
3. $4,943.49

Lesson 9-8 pp. 472–473

Check Skills You'll Need 1. If you divide each side of an equation by the same nonzero number, the two sides remain equal. **2.** $\frac{9}{5}$ **3.** $2\frac{2}{3}$ **4.** −32

Quick Check 1 a. $x = \frac{y + 4}{2}$ **b.** $x = y - 3$
c. $x = 2y - 5$ **2.** 6%

Chapter 10

Check Your Readiness p. 484

1.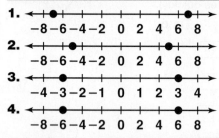

2.

3.

4.

5. 63 **6.** −10 **7.** 6 **8.** 0 **9.** 125 **10.** 64 **11.** 1,331 **12.** 10,000 **13.** acute **14.** right **15.** obtuse **16.** straight **17.** obtuse **18.** acute

---

Lesson 10-1 pp. 486–487

Check Skills You'll Need 1. They are the same distance from zero, but in opposite directions.

2.
3.
4.
5.
6.
7.
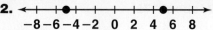

Quick Check 1. (4, 2), (1, −2), (−5, −3)
2. 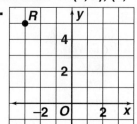 Quadrant II

3. Answers may vary. Sample:

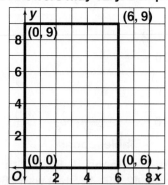

Lesson 10-2 pp. 491–492

Check Skills You'll Need 1. an equal sign **2.** 9 **3.** 6 **4.** 1 **5.** 10

Quick Check 1 a. (−2, 6), (0, 8), (2, 10)
b. (−2, −3), (0, −1), (2, 1)
c. (−2, 4), (0, 0), (2, −4) **2.** no

3 a. 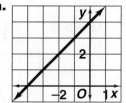 **b.**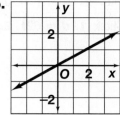

c.

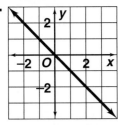

Lesson 10-3   pp. 498–499

Check Skills You'll Need 1. The numerator and denominator have no common factors other than 1.

2. $\frac{3}{4}$ **3.** $-\frac{2}{3}$ **4.** $\frac{1}{3}$ **5.** -5

Quick Check 1. $\frac{1}{2}$ **2.** $\frac{1}{4}$ **3.**

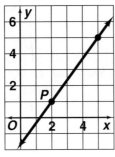

Checkpoint Quiz 1 1–3.

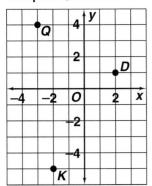

1. III **2.** II **3.** I **4.**

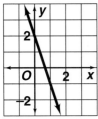

5.   **6.**

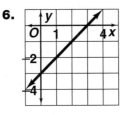

7.

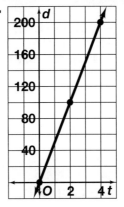

8. $-\frac{3}{2}$ **9.**

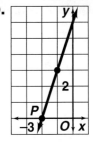

10.

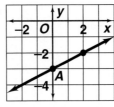

Lesson 10-4   pp. 504–505

Check Skills You'll Need 1. An equation is linear when the graph of its solutions is a line. **2–4. Answers may vary. Samples are given.**

2. (0, 12), (−2, 10), (3, 15)

3. (0, −20), (5, −15), (−10, −30)

4. (0, 0), (1, 15), (−2, −30)

Quick Check 1.

x	−3	−2	−1	0	1	2	3
y	18	8	2	0	2	8	18

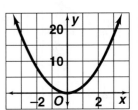

2.

x	−2	−1	0	1	2
y	4	2	0	2	4

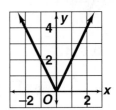

Lesson 10-5   pp. 510–511

Check Skills You'll Need 1. The x-coordinate is 2, and the y-coordinate is −5.

2-5.

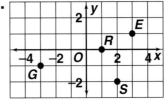

Quick Check 1. (−3, −3)

2.

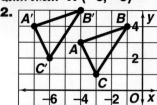

A(−4, 3), B(−1, 4),
C(−3, 1) → A′(−7, 4),
B′(−4, 5), C′(−6, 2)

3. $(x, y) \rightarrow (x + 6, y + 1)$

4.

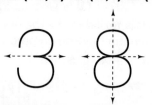

5. No; $3^2 - 4 \neq -5$. **6.** (−3, 9) **7.** (12, 6) **8.** (3, 0)
9. (1, 4) **10.** 3 and 8

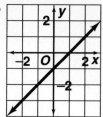

Lesson 10-6   pp. 514–518

Check Skills You'll Need 1. image **2.** (−3, 3) **3.** (1, 5)
4. (−3, 5)

Quick Check 1.   yes

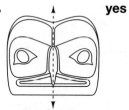

2 a–b.

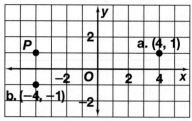

a. (4, 1)

b. (−4, −1)

3.

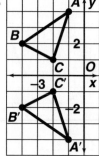

A(−1, 4), B(−4, 2),
C(−2, 1) → A′(−1, −4),
B′(−4, −2), C′(−2, −1)

Checkpoint Quiz 2 1.

2.

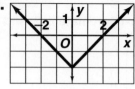

3.

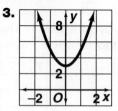

Lesson 10-7   pp. 519–520

Check Skills You'll Need 1. 90°

2.   acute

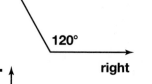

60°

3.   obtuse

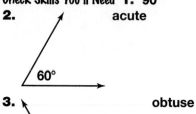

120°

4.   right

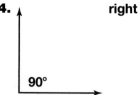

90°

5.   straight

180°

Quick Check 1 a. Yes; it looks the same as you move
each point to another point. **b.** No; it does not
match the original figure after any rotation of 180°
or less. **c.** Yes; it looks the same as the original
when it is rotated 180°. **2.** 60°

3.

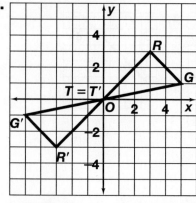

T′(0, 0), R′(−3, −3), G′(−5, −1)

Chapter 11

1. −31, −30, 13, 32, 33, 34 **2.** 10.2, 10.9, 11.1,
11.3, 11.5 **3.** 12 **4.** 32 **5.** 67 **6.** 8.5 **7.** 18 **8.** 14
9. 68 **10.** 108 11–14.
11. II **12.** *y*-axis
13. I **14.** *x*-axis

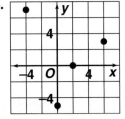

Check Skills You'll Need 1. An integer is a positive or
negative whole number, or 0. **2.** 16, 22, 23, 45, 52,
61, 87, 91 **3.** −47, −43, −41, 42, 43, 45

Quick Check 1.

U.S. Representatives for 22 States

Number of Represen- tatives	Tally	Frequency
1	ЖI	5
2	II	2
3	IIII	4
4	II	2
5	III	3
6		0
7	II	2
8	II	2
9	II	2

2. Number of Students
in Math Classes

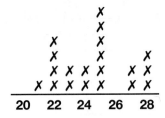

3.

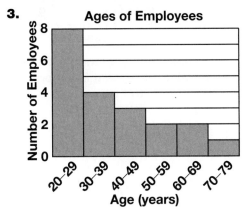

Ages of Employees

Check Skills You'll Need 1. interval
2.

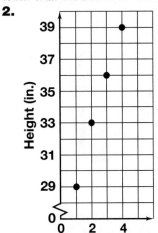

Quick Check 1 a. 95; 95 million households with
VCRs in 2001 **b.** C6 **2.** 2001 **3.** Answers may
vary. Sample: about 130 million

Check Skills You'll Need 1. the middle value of a set of
data **2.** 42 **3.** 6.4 **4.** 122.5

Quick Check 1. Wind Speeds Recorded
During Storm (mph)

```
0 | 9
1 | 4 6 8
2 | 5 5 9
3 | 0 3 4 8
```

Key: 0 | 9 means 9

2. Charlotte, N.C.; Charlotte had a median of
3.6 in., while Portland had a median of 3.55 in.
3. 10.5; 3; 52

Checkpoint Quiz 1 1.

Number	Tally	Frequency
1	II	2
2	II	2
3	II	2
4	II	2
5	III	3
6	I	1
7	II	2
8	II	2
9	I	1

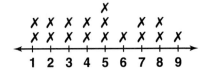

2. Graphs and explanations may vary. Sample graph:

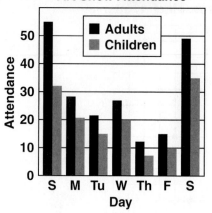

Art Show Attendance

3. $6,527 million **4.** Industry **5.** Health
6. Revenue (millions) **7.** B3 **8.** A3 **9.** B2
10.

8	7 9
9	3 5 5
10	
11	2 3 7 7
12	0 1 4

Key: 8 | 7 means 87

Lesson 11-4   pp. 550–551

Check Skills You'll Need 1. percent **2.** 80% **3.** 25%
4. 7%

Quick Check 1 a. Answers may vary. Sample: Less likely to be random; you may get only people shopping after work. **b.** More likely to be random; you won't just get people shopping after work. **2 a.** Biased; the question implies that meat is greasy and vegetables are healthy. **b.** Fair; the question makes no assumptions about pizza toppings.

Lesson 11-5   p. 554

Check Skills You'll Need 1. ratios **2.** 10 **3.** 44 **4.** 9

Quick Check 1. about 1,914 deer

Lesson 11-6   pp. 560–562

Check Skills You'll Need 1. mean **2.** 117; 118; 123

Quick Check 1. when space is limited or when you want to focus on a narrow range of data

---

2 a.

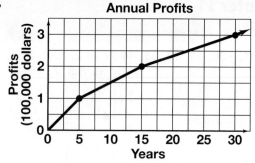

Annual Profits

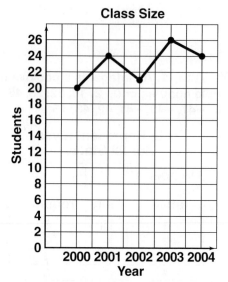

Class Size

3. 15 and 27 **4.** Answers may vary. Sample: "Home of the under-500-Cal Kiddie Burger."

Checkpoint Quiz 2 1.

Movies Filmed in Georgia

2. Median; it is a higher value than mean or mode. **3.** Answers will vary. **4.** A; it is a more diverse sample. **5.** about 3,871 horses **6.** about 172 turtles

Lesson 11-7   pp. 567–568

Check Skills You'll Need 1. horizontal

2-7.

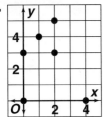

Quick Check 1.

2. positive

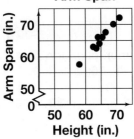

Height and Arm Span

Chapter 12

Check Your Readiness	p. 578

1. $\frac{3}{8}$ **2.** $\frac{10}{27}$ **3.** $\frac{3}{13}$ **4.** $\frac{8}{11}$ **5.** $\frac{1}{4}$ **6.** $\frac{3}{7}$ **7.** 9 **8.** 43.75
9. 5 **10.** 43.75 **11.** 64 **12.** 10.5 **13.** 46%
14. 26.5% **15.** 7% **16.** 25.6% **17.** 82%
18. 80% **19.** 45.5% **20.** 57.1% **21.** 40%
22. 46.9%

Lesson 12-1	pp. 580–581

Check Skills You'll Need 1. fraction, decimal, percent
2. 0.62; 62% **3.** 0.95; 95% **4.** 0.275; 27.5%
5. 1.1; 110%

Quick Check 1. $\frac{3}{5}$ **2.** $\frac{1}{3}$ **3.** $\frac{1}{2}$ **4.** 0

Lesson 12-2	pp. 586–587

Check Skills You'll Need 1. Answers may vary. Sample:
An outcome is a single result, but an event can be
a group of results. **2.** $\frac{1}{6}$ **3.** $\frac{1}{2}$ **4.** 0

Quick Check 1. $\frac{5}{12}$ **2.** 105 bikes **3.** $\frac{1}{20}$

Lesson 12-3	pp. 591–593

Check Skills You'll Need 1. factor tree **2.** 3 · 5
3. 2 · 7 **4.** 2 · 13 **5.** 5 · 11

Quick Check 1.

H	T	; $\frac{1}{4}$
H	HH	HT
T	TH	TT

2 a.

Vessel	Stream	Outcome	**b.** $\frac{1}{3}$
Kayak	N	K, N	
	NW	K, NW	
	NE	K, NE	
Canoe	N	C, N	
	NW	C, NW	
	NE	C, NE	
Rowboat	N	R, N	
	NW	R, NW	
	NE	R, NE	

3. 35 sandwiches

Checkpoint Quiz 1 1. $\frac{2}{5}$; 0.4; 40% **2.** $\frac{2}{5}$; 0.4; 40%
3. $\frac{4}{5}$; 0.8; 80% **4.** $\frac{3}{5}$; 0.6; 60% **5.** PP, PB, PR, PG,
BB, BR, BG, BP GG, GP, GB, GR, RR, RB, RP, RG
6. $\frac{1}{16}$ **7.** $\frac{1}{16}$ **8.** $\frac{20}{119}$ **9.** $\frac{5}{16}$

Lesson 12-4	pp. 598–599

Check Skills You'll Need 1. To multiply fractions, multiply
the numerators and multiply the denominators.
2. $\frac{9}{16}$ **3.** $\frac{6}{25}$ **4.** $\frac{1}{20}$ **5.** $\frac{6}{49}$

Quick Check 1. $\frac{1}{4}$ **2.** $\frac{1}{10}$ **3.** $\frac{1}{1,326}$

Lesson 12-5	pp. 606–607

Check Skills You'll Need 1. the result of multiplication
2. 90 **3.** 380 **4.** 336 **5.** 720 **6.** 60

Quick Check 1. 720 **2.** 7! = 5,040 **3 a.** 336 **b.** The
example selects only 3 teams from the 12
choices, so the answer is $12 \times 11 \times 10$, not 12!

Lesson 12-6	pp. 610–611

Check Skills You'll Need 1. The letters are not in the
same order. **2.** 24 **3.** 720

Quick Check 1. 3 **2.** 12

Checkpoint Quiz 2 1. $\frac{6}{49}$ **2.** $\frac{4}{49}$ **3.** $\frac{2}{49}$ **4.** 0 **5.** $\frac{5}{49}$
6. $\frac{3}{56}$ **7.** $\frac{12}{56}$ or $\frac{3}{14}$ **8.** $\frac{4}{56}$ or $\frac{1}{14}$ **9.** 720 ways
10. 15 combinations **11.** ABCD, ABDC, ACBD,
ACDB, ADBC, ADCB, BACD, BADC, BCAD, BCDA,
BDAC, BDCA, CABD, CADB, CBAD, CBDA, CDAB,
CDBA, DABC, DACB, DBAC, DBCA, DCAB, DCBA
12. 6 combinations

Selected Answers

Chapter 1

Lesson 1-1
pp. 6–7

EXERCISES 1. Rounded numbers are numbers rounded to the nearest whole number, whereas compatible numbers are chosen because they are easy to compute mentally. **3.** C **5.** B **7.** 11 **9.** 90 **13.** 19 **15.** 14 **19.** 4 **21.** 10 **29.** about $2 **33.** about $26; (390 ÷ 30) × $2 **37.** 706.8, 761.8, 768.0, 768.1

Lesson 1-2
pp. 10–11

EXERCISES 1. Assoc. Prop. of Add. **3.** 40 **5.** 19 **7.** 0 **9.** 105.8 **11.** 7.582 **19.** 5.26 **21.** 0.0645 **27.** 43.5 **29.** 39.5 **35.** > **37.** 122.4 m **39.** 4.67 in. **41.** sailfish; 0.008 mi/h **45.** 136

Lesson 1-3
pp. 16–17

EXERCISES 1. Comm. Prop. of Mult. **3.** The product is divided by 10. **5.** 2 **7.** 0; zero property **9.** 3; commutative property **13.** 0.15 **15.** 3.915 **21.** 0 **23.** 21.5 **33.** 0.432 **39.** 13.52 million **41.** $11.04 **45.** 1.643

Lesson 1-4
pp. 22–23

EXERCISES 1. dividend **3.** 4 **5.** 400 **7.** 6 **9.** 12 **17.** 0.75 **19.** 740 **27.** 4,490 **29.** 3.02 **33.** 14 yd **35.** The quotient is greater than the divisor; dividing by a number less than one is the same as multiplying by a whole number. **37.** 1.45 in. **41.** 6.7

Lesson 1-5
pp. 28–30

EXERCISES 1. 1,000 **3.** 0.01 **5.** 0.064 **7.** 0.00849 **9.** 22 m **11.** 900 **13.** 58,000 **23.** C **25.** D **29.** millimeters **33.** 1,250 g **35.** 5 mugs **37.** No; a double batch needs 2.02 L. **41.** 6.35

Lesson 1-6
pp. 33–34

EXERCISES 1. Whole numbers do not include negative numbers. **3 a.** sometimes true **b.** sometimes true **c.** sometimes true **d.** sometimes true **5.** −4 **7.** 2 **9.** 5 **11.** −12 **13.** 8 **15.** −11 **23.** 11 **25.** 1 **33.** < **35.** < **41.** −5, −2, −1, 0, 7 **45 a.** Omaha, Nebr. Bismarck, N. Dak. **47.** −3551, −3515, −3155, −3151 **49.** No; there are no integers between the integers −3 and −4. **53.** 453

Lesson 1-7
pp. 41–42

EXERCISES 1. A; always **3.** C; never **5.** 8 **7.** −1 **9.** 1 **13.** 38 **15.** 0 **19.** 13 **21.** 25 **29.** −1 + 4 = 3 **31.** −2 **33.** 8:00 A.M. **41.** >

Lesson 1-8
pp. 46–47

EXERCISES 1. B **3.** 4 **5.** 80 **7.** −2 **9.** −5 **11.** 36 **13.** 21 **19.** 3 **21.** −14 **31.** −1 **35.** 6 min **37 a.** 278 − 5(15) **b.** $203 **41.** 1.42

Lesson 1-9
pp. 50–51

EXERCISES 1. multiplication **3.** 11(2) should be 11(0.2). **5.** 20; 4 **7.** 30; 2; 160 **9.** 7 **11.** 3 **17.** 145 **19.** 19.8 **27.** (4 + 4) ÷ 4 − 4 = −2 **29.** 1,840 ft^2 **31.** 3,351 ft **39.** −60

Lesson 1-10
pp. 55–57

EXERCISES 1. outlier **3.** 5 **5.** Median; the outlier 45 greatly affects the mean. **7.** 3.5; 3.5; no mode; 1 **9.** 8 **13.** 8 **17.** 51 and 58 **21.** 10 **29.** Answers may vary. Samples are given. 1, 2, 3, 5, 5 **33.** 87 cartons **37.** 123, 213, 231, 312, 321

Chapter Review
pp. 60–61

1. Distr. Prop. **2.** Assoc. Prop. of Add. **3.** absolute value **4.** mode **5.** order of operations

Exercises 6–9. Answers may vary. Samples are given.

6. 7; compatible numbers **7.** 52, rounding **8.** 63, rounding **9.** 6; front-end estimation **10.** 3.7 **11.** 0.567 **12.** 0.73 **13.** 16.875 **14.** 7.31 lb **15.** 0.456 **16.** 14,200 **17.** 340 **18.** 71.47 m **19.** < **20.** = **21.** > **22.** > **23.** 6 **24.** 29 **25.** −30 **26.** −25 **27.** 3.425 **28.** 13.13 **29.** 19 **30.** 162.4 **31.** 2; 2; 2; 3

Chapter 2

Lesson 2-1
pp. 70–71

EXERCISES 1. The exponent tells you how many times the base is used as a factor. **3.** −625 **7.** B **9.** 2^6 **11.** 6^3 **15.** 81 **17.** 0.000064 **25.** 39

27. 39 **31.** $60 \cdot 60 \cdot 60$; 60^3
33.

Power of 10	Value	Number of Zeros
10^1	10	1
10^2	100	2
10^3	1,000	3
10^4	10,000	4
10^5	100,000	5

35. 12 **37.** Positive; $(-672)^2$ is positive and larger than 192. **45.** 40

Lesson 2-2   pp. 77–78

EXERCISES 1. A factor is a whole number that divides another whole number with a remainder of 0. A multiple of a number is the product of the number and another whole number. **3.** 2
5. Composite; the factors are 1, 2, 4, 7, 14 and 28.
7. Composite; the factors are 1, 2, 13 and 26.
9. 36 **11.** 10 **17.** 1, 2, 4, 5, 10, 20 **21.** prime
25. $3^2 \cdot 5$ **27.** $2^2 \cdot 3 \cdot 7$ **33.** 2 **35.** 16 **43.** 1
45. 50 **47.** 6 boxes **49.** Yes; both can be written as $2^3 \cdot 3$. **55.** $-5, -4, 3, 6$

Lesson 2-3   pp. 84–85

EXERCISES 1. No; the GCF of the numerator and denominator of a fraction in simplest form is 1.
3. No; the student added 4 instead of multiplying by 4 **7.** $\frac{10}{12}, \frac{15}{18}$ **9.** $\frac{4}{18}, \frac{6}{27}$ **15.** $\frac{4}{12}, \frac{1}{3}$ **17.** $\frac{9}{27}, \frac{1}{3}$
23. $\frac{3}{4}$ **31.** Answers may vary. Sample: $\frac{5}{8}, \frac{10}{16}$
33. D **37.** Answers may vary. Sample: $\frac{2a}{2b}, \frac{3a}{3b}$
41. 17.09

Lesson 2-4   pp. 89–90

EXERCISES 1. The LCM of the denominators of two or more fractions is the LCD. **3.** 63 **5.** 24
7. > **9.** < **11.** < **19.** $\frac{1}{9}, \frac{1}{8}, \frac{1}{6}$ **21.** $\frac{5}{8}, \frac{7}{9}, \frac{2}{1}$
29. $\frac{3}{4}$ in.; the $\frac{3}{8}$-in. nail is not long enough to go all the way through the board. **31.** = **33.** >
35. what they say **37.** $\frac{3}{4} > \frac{7}{10}$ **45.** 72

Lesson 2-5   pp. 93–94

EXERCISES 1. Both are larger than 1. **3.** proper fraction **5.** improper fraction **7.** 8 **9.** It is a whole number because 72 is divisible by 12.
11. $\frac{23}{4}$ **13.** $\frac{23}{5}$ **21.** $8\frac{1}{3}$ **23.** $2\frac{7}{12}$ **33.** $\frac{1}{12}$ **35.** 1
37. $1\frac{5}{8}$ in., $\frac{13}{8}$ in. **39.** $4\frac{3}{8}$ mi **41.** $3\frac{2}{8}, 3\frac{1}{4}, \frac{26}{8}$
45. -12

Lesson 2-6   pp. 99–100

EXERCISES 1. A terminating decimal stops, whereas a repeating decimal has a block of digits that repeat without end. **3.** $1\frac{3}{8}$ **5.** $3\frac{99}{100}$
7. $0.5, 1\frac{1}{3}, 1.\overline{9}, 2$ **9.** 0.8 **11.** $0.\overline{6}$ **17.** $\frac{33}{50}$ **19.** $3\frac{3}{4}$
25. $3.84, 3\frac{41}{50}, 3.789, 3$ **31.** < **33.** > **35.** when the numerator is not a multiple of 3
37. N.Y.: $\frac{4,572}{19,227}$ Tex.: $\frac{6,267}{22,490}$ Calif.: $\frac{9,596}{33,893}$ Fla.: $\frac{4,003}{17,397}$
Ohio: $\frac{2,779}{11,459}$ **39.** Fla., N.Y., Ohio, Tex., Calif.
41. The quotients are 0.5, 5, 50, 500, 5,000, and 50,000. As the divisor gets smaller, the quotient gets larger because divisor $\times$ quotient = dividend.
45. 0.36

Lesson 2-7   pp. 104–105

EXERCISES 1. Answers may vary. Sample: A rational number is a number that can be written as a quotient of two integers. **3.** >
5. $-236, -7\frac{1}{7}, -3.\overline{3}, 0, \frac{41}{99}$ **7.** > **9.** <
19. $-1.0, -\frac{3}{4}, 0.25, \frac{3}{2}$ **25.** > **27.** > **29.** frog
31. $\frac{3}{4}$ **35.** $\frac{1}{2}$

Lesson 2-8   pp. 108–109

EXERCISES 1. It is written as the product of two factors, one greater than or equal to 1 and less than 10, and the other a power of 10. **3.** 3 **5.** B
7. A **9.** 7.5×10^7 **11.** 4.4×10^4 **17.** 3,400
27. 1,600 lb **31.** 3.5×10^5
33. about 3.3×10^2 h **37.** 60

Chapter Review   pp. 112–113

1. exponent **2.** prime **3.** factors **4.** equivalent fraction **5.** GCF **6.** -16 **7.** -64 **8.** 125 **9.** 60
10. $2^2 \cdot 3 \cdot 7$ **11.** $2 \cdot 3 \cdot 13$ **12.** $2 \cdot 3^2 \cdot 5$
13. $2^2 \cdot 23$ **14.** 5^3 **15.** 210 days from now
16. $\frac{1}{6}, \frac{1}{4}, \frac{1}{3}$ **17.** $\frac{1}{4}, \frac{3}{8}, \frac{2}{5}$ **18.** $\frac{3}{8}, \frac{1}{2}, \frac{5}{6}$ **19.** $\frac{5}{9}, \frac{7}{12}, \frac{2}{3}$
20. store B **21.** $5\frac{3}{4}$ h **22.** 6 **23.** $2\frac{1}{4}$ **24.** $6\frac{2}{3}$
25. 25 **26.** 7 **27.** $0.\overline{3}$ **28.** $0.\overline{5}$ **29.** 2.5 **30.** 0.8
31. 0.08 **32.** $-\frac{7}{8}, 0.\overline{3}, \frac{3}{4}$ **33.** $-\frac{4}{11}, -0.3, 2.7$
34. $-\frac{5}{6}, -0.5, 2.2$ **35.** 7.123×10^6 **36.** 906,000
37. 8.19×10^4 **38.** 601,500,000

Chapter 3

Lesson 3-1   pp. 122–123

EXERCISES 1. Answers may vary. Sample: A benchmark is a convenient number used to replace a fraction. Examples are 0, $\frac{1}{2}$, and 1 for fractions between 0 and 1. **3.** 1 **5.** $\frac{1}{2}$ **7.** 1 **9.** 7 **11.** about $\frac{1}{2}$ **13.** about $\frac{1}{2}$ **21.** about 10 **23.** about 5 **29.** about 4 **35.** about 29 **37.** 2 h **39.** about $\frac{1}{2}$ t **41.** about $4\frac{1}{2}$ t **49.** $11\frac{1}{8}$

Lesson 3-2   pp. 128–129

EXERCISES 1. Answers may vary. Sample: It doesn't make sense to add fractions with different denominators. For example, $\frac{1}{2} + \frac{1}{3} \neq \frac{2}{5}$. **3.** 16 **5.** 6 **7.** 1 **9.** $\frac{2}{3}$ **11.** $\frac{23}{40}$ **13.** $\frac{1}{18}$ **15.** $1\frac{1}{2}$ **17.** $\frac{2}{5}$ **27.** $1\frac{5}{8}$ **29.** $1\frac{3}{10}$ **37.** positive **41.** $\frac{1}{2}$ **43.** $\frac{7}{10}$ **45.** $\frac{17}{20}$ **51.** -2.4, 1.34, $\frac{7}{3}$, $\frac{25}{6}$

Lesson 3-3   pp. 132–133

EXERCISES 1. $3\frac{3}{4}$ **3.** $2\frac{2}{5}$ **5.** $3\frac{3}{2}$ **7.** $\frac{19}{10}$ **9.** $8\frac{1}{5}$ **15.** $18\frac{5}{6}$ **19.** $11\frac{1}{3}$ **25.** $29\frac{3}{20}$ **29.** $7\frac{7}{8}$ mi **31.** $4\frac{1}{2}$ in.² **33.** $10\frac{5}{8}$ c.i. **37.** 115

Lesson 3-4   pp. 138–139

EXERCISES 3. $2\frac{1}{4} \cdot 1\frac{2}{3} = \frac{9}{4} \cdot \frac{5}{3}$ **5.** No; you do not need to find a common denominator, since you reduce the product anyway. **7.** $\frac{1}{3}$ **9.** $\frac{5}{18}$ **15.** 12 **17.** 26 **25.** 12 **27.** $3\frac{2}{3}$ **33.** $8\frac{1}{2}$ c **35.** 0 **39.** $\frac{7}{8}$ mi **41.** 28 games **43.** 2 mi²; $6\frac{3}{5}$ mi **47.** 76

Lesson 3-5   pp. 143–145

EXERCISES 1. $1\frac{1}{2} \div \frac{1}{2}$ **3.** 4 **5.** $\frac{2}{7}$ **7.** A **9.** 8 **11.** $\frac{5}{8}$ **21.** $\frac{6}{13}$ **23.** $1\frac{1}{2}$ **35.** Your friend found the reciprocal of $\frac{3}{8}$ without changing $5\frac{3}{8}$ to an improper fraction; $\frac{8}{43}$. **37.** 800 nails **39.** 6 costumes **41.** 1 **47.** 12 ft **53.** 2,564

Lesson 3-6   pp. 150–151

EXERCISES 1. multiply **3.** multiply **5.** divide **7.** It takes more smaller units to equal the larger units. **9.** $4\frac{1}{2}$ **11.** $6\frac{1}{6}$ **17.** 3 **19.** $\frac{1}{2}$ **23.** 12 **25.** 5,000 **31.** 9,560 ft **33.** 2,400 **35.** $3\frac{1}{2}$ **39.** 4 ft **41.** no; quarter pound = 4 oz **47.** 3

Lesson 3-7   pp. 156–157

EXERCISES 1. 4 in., 4 in., $3\frac{6}{8}$ in. **3.** $3\frac{12}{16}$ in. **5.** $4\frac{1}{2}$ ft **7.** $11\frac{15}{16}$ in. **9.** 56 lb **17.** 2 lb **19.** 4 ft **21.** 8.9 oz **25.** 2 cm **27.** about $4\frac{2}{8}$ in. **29.** ft **31.** cm **35.** 541 ft **41.** about 6

Chapter Review   pp. 160–161

1. reciprocal **2.** benchmark **3.** precision **4.** benchmark; precision **5.** about 1 **6.** about $\frac{1}{2}$ **7.** about 1 **8.** about $\frac{1}{2}$ **9.** about 3 **10.** about 25 **11.** about 14 **12.** about 10 **13.** about 8 mi **14.** $1\frac{7}{12}$ **15.** $6\frac{13}{15}$ **16.** $15\frac{5}{12}$ **17.** $5\frac{13}{24}$ **18.** $11\frac{1}{20}$ min **19.** $\frac{1}{4}$ **20.** $\frac{9}{10}$ **21.** 9 **22.** $94\frac{23}{24}$ **23.** $39\frac{7}{12}$ m² **24.** $\frac{1}{2}$ **25.** 6 **26.** $3\frac{3}{5}$ **27.** $\frac{5}{18}$ **28.** $3\frac{2}{11}$ ft **29.** $3\frac{1}{2}$ **30.** $1\frac{1}{2}$ **31.** 5 **32.** 2 **33.** 4,000 **34.** 7 **35.** about $9\frac{1}{2}$ ft **36.** 12 c **37.** 5.5 L **38.** 8.75 m **39.** 23 h **40.** 25 g **41.** $11\frac{3}{16}$ in. **42.** 7 g **43.** 13 yd **44.** 11.6 cm **45.** 21.00 lb **46.** 5 L **47.** 5.13 m

Chapter 4

Lesson 4-1   pp. 171–172

EXERCISES 1. An algebraic expression differs from a numerical expression because it contains at least one variable, and the value changes. **3.** addition

5–7. Answers may vary. Samples are given:

5. the product of 5 and w **7.** the quotient of w and 4 **9.** 6 **11.** 6 **13.** $\frac{p}{5}$ **17–19.** Answers may vary. Samples are given. **17.** two more than a number **19.** nine and one tenth less than a number **25.** 42 **27.** 3 **33.** $10n$ **35.** Answers may vary. Sample: Multiply 24(60) to find the number of minutes in 24 h. Then multiply the answer by 1,260, the number of beats per minute. The heart beats 1,814,400 times in 24 h. **39.** Answers may vary. Sample: The second student charges $15 to start and $3/h. **43.** 45

Lesson 4-2   pp. 176–177

EXERCISES 1. solution **3.** yes **5.** no **7.** -3 **9.** -4 **11.** 288 **15.** -8 **17.** -4 **21.** about 19 **27.** 54 **29.** 20 **33.** $4d = 360$ **35.** 31.89 in. **37.** $4c = 67.80$; about $17; no; the total should be about 4($12.95), or $51.80. **41.** 1

Lesson 4-3 pp. 182–184

EXERCISES 1. Inverse **3.** 12 **5.** −49 **7.** 205.4
19. 9 **25.** B **31.** 119 **33.** −0.9
37. $p − 8.45 = 21.50$; $29.95
39. Let r = the number of runs needed;
$3 + 4 + 2 + 6 +$
$8 + r = 30$;
43. 33

Lesson 4-4 pp. 188–190

EXERCISES 1. Multiplication Property of
Equality **3.** Division Property of Equality
5. Division Property of Equality **7.** C **9.** 12
11. −5 **23.** −24 **25.** 100.8 **39.** 50 **41.** 85 **45.**
15 yr **47.** b is the reciprocal of a, and $b \neq 0$.
55. $\frac{23}{28}$

Lesson 4-5 pp. 196–198

EXERCISES 1. A one-step expression uses only
one operation, while a two-step expression uses
two. **3.** B **5.** C **7.** 70 **9.** Let h = your height;
$6h + 1$. **13.** 1.5 **15.** −0.9 **21.** 15.2 **23.** 7
33. 11.5 **35.** 45 **39.** 9 min **41.** Answers may
vary. Sample: You need to keep the equation
"balanced." **47.** =

Lesson 4-6 pp. 202–204

EXERCISES 1. Let m = number of miles;
$2.00 + 0.50m = 5.00$; 6 mi **3.** 12 **5.** −3
7. 8 **31.** Let h = number of additional hours;
$3.95 + 1.25h = 7.70$; 3 h. **35.** 11 **39.** 15 credits

Lesson 4-7 pp. 207–208

EXERCISES 1. inequality **3.** C **5.** −1 **7.** −2
11.

13.

19. $x \leq 6$
25. $a \geq 17$;

31. $w \leq 3$

33. −3, −2, or −1 **39.** −4, −2, −1, 2, 4, 7

Lesson 4-8 pp. 212–213

EXERCISES 1. Addition Property of Inequality
3. C **5.** B **7.** $g \leq −6$;

9. $y \geq 16$;

17. $n \geq 1$;

19. $p \leq −4$;

29. $w > -\frac{1}{2}$

31. $j \geq −5$ **35.** No; the solution of $x + 5 \leq −2$ is
$x \leq −7$, and the solution of $−2 \leq x + 5$ is
$x \geq −7$. **39.** no more than 1,220 Cal **43.** $\frac{16}{5}$

Lesson 4-9 pp. 216–218

EXERCISES 1. The inequality symbol is
reversed. **3.** > **5.** >

7. $p > 12$;

9. $x < −8$;

19. $p < −15$;

21. $w \leq −21$;

35. $4x \leq −44$; $x \leq −11$ **41.** $50.2 < t$ **43.** at
most 3 hot dogs **45.** 4 bags of peanuts; $.50
47. The student should not have reversed the
inequality symbol.
49. $−3.x + 10 > 19$; $x < −3$;

53. $−3.8\overline{3}$; 3.6; 2.2

Chapter Review pp. 220–221

1. variable **2.** inequality **3.** equation
4. algebraic expression **5.** solution of an
inequality **6.** 5 **7.** 6 **8.** 13 **9.** 4 **10.** −7 **11.** 20
12. 4 **13.** 72 **14.** 24 **15.** 84 **16.** 99 **17.** −12
18. 52 **19.** 5 **20.** 43 **21.** −54 **22.** 114 tickets
23. 1 **24.** 12 **25.** −3
26. $140 + 35w = 1,050$; 26 wk
27. $t \leq 10$;

28. $r < 5$;

29. $h < −22$;

30. $p \geq −15$;

31. $g > 17$;

32. $m \geq −7$;

33. $x \geq 20$;

CHAPTER 5

Lesson 5-1   pp. 230–231

EXERCISES 1. Equivalent ratios name the same amount, as do equivalent fractions.

3–5. Answers may vary. Samples are given.

3. 2 to 16 **5.** 20 to 18 **7.** $\frac{17}{24}$ **9.** equivalent
11. equivalent **13.** 21 to 25, 21 : 25, $\frac{21}{25}$

14–16. Answers may vary. Samples are given.

15. 12 to 14 **17.** $\frac{1}{2}$ **19.** $\frac{3}{200}$ **23.** equivalent
31 a. 8 : 4, 7.5 : 3, 3.5 : 1 **b.** 10 qt antifreeze, 5 qt water **37.** 45

Lesson 5-2   pp. 234–235

EXERCISES 1. Answers may vary. Sample: It gives the cost of one item. **3.** 147; 7 **5.** 8 g
7. 16 points/game **11.** $30 **15.** $.93/oz
17. $.06/fl oz, $.05/fl oz; the 50-fl-oz detergent is the better buy. **23.** $.75/pt **25.** $.60/lb
27 a. 1 person/mi² **b.** No; answers may vary. Sample: Some regions of the state are more densely populated than others. **29.** about 39,421,000 times; about 108,000 times; about 75 times **33.** 29

Lesson 5-3   pp. 240–241

EXERCISES 1. ratios **3.** 8 **5.** 9 **7.** 12 **9.** No; you need to multiply the numerator of one by the denominator of the other. They do form a proportion.

$$\frac{3}{4} \overset{?}{=} \frac{12}{16}$$
$$3 \cdot 16 \overset{?}{=} 4 \cdot 12$$
$$48 = 48$$

11. no **13.** yes **31.** no **33.** no **35.** Yes; the weight ratios $\frac{174}{29}$ and $\frac{102}{17}$ are proportional because 174 · 17 = 102 · 29. **37.** yes; $\frac{26}{1} = \frac{104}{4}$

39. $\frac{4n}{3}$ and $\frac{12n}{9}$ will always form a proportion because $36n = 36n$ for all values of n. **43.** 105

Lesson 5-4   pp. 246–248

EXERCISES 1. Answers may vary. Sample: Finding a unit rate gives you a denominator of 1, so you only need to multiply to solve the proportion. $\frac{5}{1} = \frac{x}{8}$, $x = 40$ **3.** 4 **5.** 12 **7.** $7.90
9. $59.00 **11.** 6 **13.** 6 **17.** 20 **19.** 85.75 **31.** 5
33. 6.9
35. 240 should be the numerator. $\frac{2}{3} = \frac{240}{n}$
43. −6, −3, −2, 1, 8

Lesson 5-5   pp. 254–255

EXERCISES 1. Two polygons are similar if corresponding angles have the same measure and the lengths of the corresponding sides form equivalent ratios. **3.** $\overline{AB}$ **7.** 11.2 ft **15.** 6
17. 2.88 km **19.** 99 cm **23.** 5

Lesson 5-6   pp. 261–263

EXERCISES 1. ratio; length **3.** No; the scale should be written as **model : actual**, or 8 ft : 6 ft.
5. 7 in. **7.** 165 ft **9.** 495 ft **13.** about 38 mi
23. Answers may vary. Sample: 1 cm : 1.9 m
25a. 1 in. : 4 ft **b.** 0.5 in.

Chapter Review   pp. 266–267

1. a scale drawing **2.** unit cost **3.** rate **4.** scale
5. similar **6.** $\frac{3}{10}$ **7.** $\frac{16}{5}$ **8.** 3 : 1 **9.** 15 : 4 **10.** $\frac{1}{4}$
11. $\frac{39}{97}$, 39 to 97, 39 : 97 **12.** 6 passengers/car
13. 75 Cal/serving **14.** 23 students/classroom
15. $4/kg **16.** $0.28/oz, $0.31/oz; the 10-oz size is the better buy. **17.** 3 ft² per minute **18.** 12
19. 25 **20.** 3 **21.** 136 **22.** $\frac{5}{3} = \frac{x}{250,000}$; 417,000
board feet **23.** 7.5 ft **24.** 15 ft **25.** 45
26. $x = 45$, $y = 36$ **27.** 6,300 mi **28.** 0.75 in.

Chapter 6

Lesson 6-1   pp. 276–277

EXERCISES 1. $\frac{32}{100}$; 32% **3.** 67% **5.** 90%
7. $\frac{64}{100}$; 64% **11.** 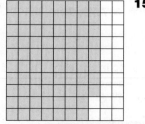 **15.** $\frac{4}{5}$, 80%

21. 60% **23.** 84% **25.** 55% **27.** 70% **29.** 52%
31. about 19% **33.** about 28% **39.** −2, −3

Lesson 6-2   pp. 282–283

EXERCISES 1. 62%, $\frac{62}{100}$, 0.62 **3.** $\frac{1}{2}$, 0.54, 55%
5. 57% **7.** 9% **11.** 0.88 **15.** 90% **17.** 8.3%
21. $\frac{3}{20}$ **23.** $\frac{1}{5}$ **27.** 12%, 0.25, $\frac{1}{2}$
33.

Topping	With Olives	Plain	With Onions and Green Peppers
Percent of the Pizza	37.5%	12.5%	50%
Number of Slices	3	1	4

35 a. 79%, $\frac{16}{20}$, $\frac{21}{25}$, 85%, $\frac{9}{10}$, 92% **b.** 85%
39. $-0.9 \leq x$

Lesson 6-3   pp. 286–287

EXERCISES 1. 1.5; $\frac{3}{2}$ or $1\frac{1}{2}$ **3.** 825% **5.** 4
7. Answers may vary. Sample: A decimal that is less than 1% has zeros in the tenths and hundredths place, such as 0.009. A decimal that is greater than 100% has a number other than zero before the decimal point, such as 1.01.
9. 1.3; $1\frac{3}{10}$ **11.** 3.45; $3\frac{9}{20}$ **21.** 160% **23.** 258%
35. 270% **37.** 1,001% **39.** 1.66; $1\frac{33}{50}$

41. 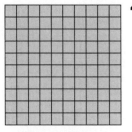 **43.**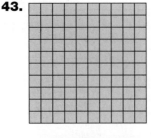

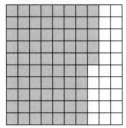 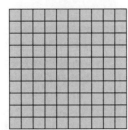

45. 0.26% **47.** No; it cannot be more than 100% fat. **49.** Yes; it is reasonable that $\frac{1}{2}$ of 1% of the seeds will not grow. **53.** $\frac{7}{25}$

Lesson 6-4   pp. 292–293

EXERCISES 1. 29 **3.** 58.08 **5.** $\frac{1}{5} \cdot 60 = 12$
7. $\frac{3}{20} \cdot 40 = 6$ **9.** Answers may vary. Sample: You would probably use a fraction when the percent can be written as a fraction that is compatible with the other number. You would use a decimal for all other cases. **11.** 16 **13.** 27.6 **19.** 57.2
21. 474 **29.** about 30 **31.** about 80 **37.** 160.38
39. 42.38 **41.** 6,800 forest fires **45.** 26 students
49. 60

Lesson 6-5   pp. 296–297

EXERCISES 1. percent; 25% **3.** whole; 16 **5.** C
7. B **9.** 10% **11.** 2% **15.** 5 **17.** 2.25 **21.** 18.75
23. 80 **27.** $\frac{90}{n} = \frac{40}{100}$; 225 **29.** $\frac{54}{144} = \frac{n}{100}$; 37.5
31. 37.5% **35.** The number 100 always appears as the denominator of one of the ratios, since percent means "out of 100." **41.** $\frac{1}{3}$

Lesson 6-6   pp. 300–301

EXERCISES 1. No; "20% of 40" asks for a part, "20 is what percent of 40" asks for a percent, and "20 is 40% of what number" asks for a whole.
3. C **5.** $625p = 500$; 80% **7.** $0.96x = 24$; 25
13. $x = 0.41 \cdot 800$; 328 **17.** $18 = 48x$; 37.5%
23. 69% **27.** 49% **29.** about 190 people
31. 45 members **37.** yes

Lesson 6-7   pp. 306–307

EXERCISES 1. You earn 8% of the amount you sell. **3.** $3.60 **5.** $27 **7.** $.71 **9.** $77.12
11. about $10.35 **15.** $96 **21.** $23 **23.** 5%
25. $6,800 **33.** $2.35/lb

Lesson 6-8   pp. 312–314

EXERCISES 1. Answers may vary. Sample: They both involve the difference between the original price and the selling price. Percent of markup is a percent of increase and percent of discount is a percent of decrease. **3.** $\frac{15}{35}$, 43% increase
5. $\frac{374}{748}$, 50% decrease **7.** A **9.** 13% **11.** 50%
17. 50% **23.** 56% **29.** 25% decrease
33. $53.30

35.

	A	B	C	D
1	Yr	Sales	Change ($)	Change (%)
2	1	200,000	—	—
3	2	240,000	40,000	20%
4	3	300,000	60,000	25%
5	4	330,000	30,000	10%

41. $471.30

Chapter Review   pp. 316–317

1. C **2.** E **3.** D **4.** B **5.** A **6.** 0.65; $\frac{13}{20}$
7. 0.02; $\frac{1}{50}$ **8.** 0.018; $\frac{9}{500}$ **9.** 0.625; $\frac{5}{8}$ **10.** 37.5%
11. 16% **12.** 44.82 **13.** 0.64 **14.** 97.2 **15.** 70%
16. 47.5 **17.** 252 **18.** 12 **19.** 72 **20.** 20%
21. $57.60 **22.** about $10.52 **23.** $268 **24.** $63
25. $216 **26.** $275 **27.** $225 **28.** 16.7% decrease **29.** 20% increase **30.** 15% increase
31. 40% increase **32.** 72% decrease **33.** 16.7% decrease **34.** 31% decrease

Chapter 7

EXERCISES 1. Skew lines **3.** $\overline{LC}$ **5.** $\overleftrightarrow{KE}$
7. $\overline{BC}$, $\overline{FE}$ **9.** $\overline{LC}$ **11.** $\overleftrightarrow{ZV}$ **15.** $\overline{AE}$, $\overline{EF}$, $\overline{DH}$, $\overline{GH}$
21. yes **25.**

29. $\overleftrightarrow{EF}$ and $\overleftrightarrow{GH}$ do not lie in the same plane.
31. $\overrightarrow{UV}$, $\overline{UV}$, $\overleftrightarrow{UV}$, $\overrightarrow{VU}$, $\overleftrightarrow{VW}$, $\overleftrightarrow{VY}$,
$\overleftrightarrow{WY}$, $\overleftrightarrow{WX}$, $\overline{WX}$, $\overrightarrow{XW}$, $\overline{WX}$,
$\overrightarrow{YZ}$, $\overline{YZ}$

35. about 9% increase

EXERCISES 1. Vertical angles lie opposite each other, while adjacent angles lie next to each other. **3.** acute, 45°, 135° **5.** acute, 15°, 105° **7.** obtuse **9.** 11°; 101° **11.** 78°; 168° **19.** 57° **23.** 159.8° and 69.8° **25.** The student used the wrong scale on the protractor. **27.** about 65° **29.** Answers may vary. Sample: ∠JHK and ∠BHC, ∠HCD and ∠BCL **31.** ∠HCB

EXERCISES 1. no **3.** obtuse scalene **5.** acute isosceles **7.** scalene **9.** obtuse **13.** 64° **17.** isosceles **21.** 44° **23.** An equilateral triangle is always isosceles because it has 3 congruent sides. An isosceles triangle is not always equilateral because it has at least 2 congruent sides. **27.** 1.16; $\frac{29}{25}$

EXERCISES 1. A trapezoid is a quadrilateral with only one pair of parallel sides. A parallelogram is a quadrilateral with two pairs of parallel sides. **3.** quadrilateral, parallelogram **5.** quadrilateral, parallelogram, rhombus, rectangle, square **7.** The parallelogram is irregular because the sides are not all congruent. **9.** rectangles, trapezoids **11.**

15. Trapezoid; $\overline{PQ}$ is parallel to $\overline{RS}$.
17. JN = 5 in.; $m\angle J$ = $m\angle K = m\angle L = m\angle N$ = 90°
19.

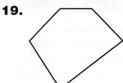

23. No; it would be a rectangle.

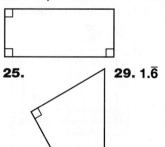

25.   **29.** $1.\overline{6}$

EXERCISES 1. Yes. Similar polygons have congruent angles and sides in proportion. If the proportion is 1 to 1, then the polygons are not just similar, but congruent. **3.** Congruent; all corresponding sides and angles are congruent. **5.** Not congruent; not all corresponding sides and angles are congruent.
7. $\overline{CV} \cong \overline{JP}$; $\overline{VR} \cong \overline{PX}$;   **11.** △SRT **15.** $\overline{BD}$
   $\overline{RC} \cong \overline{XJ}$; ∠C ≅ ∠J;
   ∠V ≅ ∠P; ∠R ≅ ∠X
   VR = 9; $m\angle V$ = 83°;
   $m\angle X$ = 41°; $m\angle J$ = 56°

17. ∠C **21.** $\overline{XY} \cong \overline{BA}$; $\overline{YZ} \cong \overline{AD}$;
25. 25% $\overline{ZW} \cong \overline{DC}$; $\overline{WX} \cong \overline{CB}$;
           ∠Y ≅ ∠A; ∠Z ≅ ∠D;
           ∠W ≅ ∠C; ∠X ≅ ∠B
           YZ = 11; ZW = 18;
           $m\angle Y$ = 127°; $m\angle D$ = 83°;
           $m\angle B$ = 83°

EXERCISES 1. A radius is a line from the center of a circle to a point on the circle. A diameter is a line between two points on a circle that passes through the center of the circle. **3.** M **5.** $\overline{JL}$

7. ∠JMK, ∠KML, ∠JML **9.** $\overline{OC}$, $\overline{OK}$, $\overline{OD}$

13. $\overset{\frown}{TR}$, $\overset{\frown}{RS}$, $\overset{\frown}{ST}$ **15.** $\overset{\frown}{CD}$, $\overset{\frown}{DB}$, $\overset{\frown}{CB}$

19–21. Answers may vary. Samples are given.

19. ∠FDG, ∠GDH **21.** △FDG **27.** 22.6 cm
31. 400 m **35.** acute

Lesson 7-7   pp. 356–357

EXERCISES 1. the whole circle, 360°, 100%
3. 90° **5.** 36° **7.** sleeping
11.

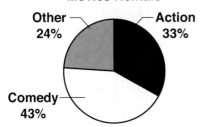

Movies Rentals

- Other 24%
- Action 33%
- Comedy 43%

13. Mexico **15.** 11.7 million people
17.

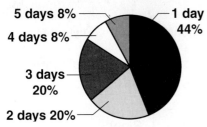

Students Volunteering

- 5 days 8%
- 4 days 8%
- 3 days 20%
- 2 days 20%
- 1 day 44%

19. 140 students **23.** $1\frac{1}{24}$

Lesson 7-8   pp. 363–364

EXERCISES 1. Answers may vary. Since Q is the midpoint of $\overline{PR}$, $\overline{PQ}$ and $\overline{QR}$ are congruent.
3. 8 in. **5.** $3\frac{1}{2}$ m **17.**

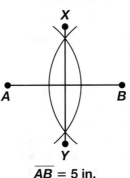

$\overline{AB} = 5$ in.

21. 4.2 cm **23.** 34 mm **27.**
31. $\frac{5}{7}$, 5 : 7

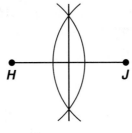

Chapter Review   pp. 366–367

1. parallel **2.** pentagon **3.** supplementary
4. scalene **5.** acute **6.** 35°, 125° **7.** 63°, 153°
8. 3°, 93° **9.** 78°, 168°
10. 120°; isosceles; obtuse

11. 60°; equilateral; acute
12. 31°; scalene; right **13.** pentagon; regular
14. square, regular **15.** octagon, irregular
16. $m\angle M = 30°$,
$m\angle C = m\angle P = 46°$,
$m\angle B = 104°$, $AC = 22$,
$BC = 12$, $MN = 17$

17. $\overline{TW}, \overline{TY}, \overline{TK}, \overline{TM}$
18. $\overline{MY}$ **19.** T **20.** $\overline{WY}$; $\overline{KY}$

21. $\overparen{WYM}, \overparen{YKW}, \overparen{KMY}, \overparen{MWK}, \overparen{WYK}$
22.

23.

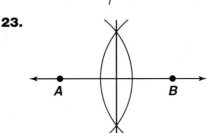

Chapter 8

Lesson 8-1   pp. 376–378

EXERCISES 1. square **3.** C **5.** A **7.** 6 in.; it is less than a foot. **11.** about 20 ft **13.** about 875 mi² **15.** area: about 198 yd²; perimeter: about 81 yd **19.** about $\frac{1}{2}$ in. **23.** Answers may vary. Sample: about 500 yd² **27 a.** about 7,840,000 ft²
b. about 136 **31.** 150% increase

Lesson 8-2   pp. 382–383

EXERCISES 1. right **3.** True; $A = bh$, so if the bases are equal and the heights are equal, the areas will be equal. **5.** 3 **7.** 25 m² **9.** 12 ft² **13.** 625 mi² **19.** 9 m; 26.4 m **21.** 10.5 cm; 21 cm²
23. They have the same bases, but the height of the parallelogram must be less than the height of the rectangle because a leg is shorter than the hypotenuse.
25. area = 161 in.²;
perimeter = 62 in.

29. 2; 2 **31.** 1.52; $1\frac{13}{25}$

Lesson 8-3 pp. 386–387

EXERCISES 1. right **3.** 6 cm **5.** 10 cm^2
7. 17.5 m^2 **9.** 12.5 ft **13.** 1,440 yd^2 **15.** 72 km^2
19. 50,000 yd^2 **21.** 102 m^2 **23.** 10,000 km^2
25. 27.68 km^2 **27.** 3 ft; if b = 4 and h= the
corresponding height, then the area of the
triangle is $\frac{1}{2}$(4)h; or 2h. Since the area is 6 ft^2,
2h = 6. So h = 3. **31.** 28

Lesson 8-4 pp. 391–392

EXERCISES 1. height

3. b_1 = 2.7 in., b_2 = 8 in.,
  h = 10 in.

5. 144 m^2 **11.** 500 km^2 **13.** 121.5 in.^{2} **15.** $5\frac{3}{4}$ ft^2
17. 448 in.^{2} **19.** 104 m^2; 45.6 m **23.** $480.18

Lesson 8-5 pp. 396–397

EXERCISES 1. No; π is nonrepeating

and nonterminating. **3.** 2; 4; 4π **5.** $\frac{1}{\pi}$; $\frac{2}{\pi}$; 2

7. 53.4 mm **9.** 251.3 in. **13.** 314 m^2 **15.** 707 ft^2
21. 88 m; 616 m^2 **23.** 69.1 in.; 380.3 in.^{2}
25. about 188 in.; about 2,827 in.^{2} **31.** $\angle O$

Lesson 8-6 pp. 402–403

EXERCISES 1. area **3.** yes **5.** no **7.** 10 **9.** 5
17. about 2 **19.** about 7 **23.** irrational
25. rational **31.** 12 ft **35.** rational **37.** rational
39. irrational
41.

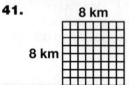

8 km

8 km

1 square = 1 km^2

43.

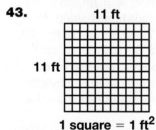

11 ft

11 ft

1 square = 1 ft^2

45. about 26.9 **49.** 2

Lesson 8-7 pp. 407–408

EXERCISES 1. hypotenuse **3.** 13.6 m **5.** 23.3 ft
7. 17.5 m **9.** 12 ft **11.** 9 m **17.** 0.5 m
19. 21.4 m **21.** 10 ft **23.** 7 km **25.** 3
29. n = 0.60 · 40; 24

Lesson 8-8 pp. 412–413

EXERCISES 1. cylinder **3.** rectangle; rectangular
prism **5.** pentagon; pentagonal prism **7.** cone
9. hexagonal pyramid **13.**

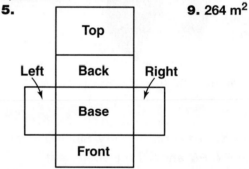

17. rectangular prism **19.** cone **21.** none
23. 64 m^2 **25.** 7 faces; 12 edges; 7 vertices
29. 11 m

Lesson 8-9 pp. 416–418

EXERCISES 1. surface area **3.** cylinder about
5,089.4 in.^{2}
5.

	Top	
Left	Back	Right
	Base	
	Front	

9. 264 m^2

13. 785.4 cm^2 **17.** 528 in.^{2} **19.** 1,407 ft^2
21. 2,890 in.^{2} **23.** 1960.4 in.^{2} **27.** 990 ft^2
31. rational

Lesson 8-10 pp. 424–425

EXERCISES 1. volume **3.** 60 in.^{3} **5.** 166.375 in.^{3}
9. 31.5 in.^{3} **11.** about 84 in.^{3}; 88 in.^{3} **15.** 6.5 cm
17. 18 in. **21.** about 6 million gal **23.** Yes; the
height of the can is less than the height of the
case. Since 3(2.5) < 7.6, 3 cans will fit along the
width of the case. Since 4(2, 5) < 11, 4 cans will
fit along the length of the case. Then the case can
hold 3 × 4, or 12 cans. **27.** 50°; 140°

Chapter Review pp. 428–429

1. edge **2.** hypotenuse **3.** prism
4. circumference **5.** cone **6.** about 400 in.^{2}
7. 7 in.; the width is less than a foot. **8.** 10.5 m^2
9. 38 cm^2 **10.** 160 ft^2 **11.** 25.1 in.; 50.3 in.^{2}
12. 44 mi; 153.9 mi^2 **13.** 22 km; 38.5 km^2
14. 6 in. **15.** 39 yd **16.** cylinder **17.** rectangular
pyramid **18.** pentagonal pyramid **19.** 22 in.^{2};
6 in.^{3} **20.** 288 m^2; 324 m^3 **21.** 747.7 yd^2;
1,539.4 yd^3

Chapter 9

EXERCISES 1. A graph shows how the data are changing. **3.** Answers may vary. Sample: 0–8; 4 intervals of 2 **5.** 0–5,000; 10 intervals of 500

7.

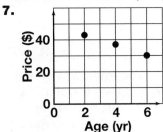

9. about 3 yr

11. about $8 **15.**

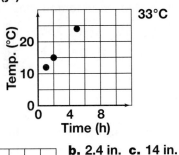

33°C

17 a.

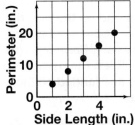

b. 2.4 in. **c.** 14 in.

d. Check students' work.

19 a.

Number of Weeks	Pay ($)
1	10
2	20
3	30
4	40
5	50

Number of Weeks	Pay ($)
1	47
2	54
3	61
4	68
5	75

b.

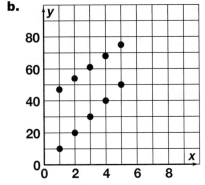

c. first neighbor: $100; second neighbor: $110; working for the second neighbor **23.** 0.05

EXERCISES 1. Yes; dividing by −4 is the same as multiplying by $-\frac{1}{4}$. **3.** −6 **5.** 12.5 **7.** Start with 25 and add −4 repeatedly; 9, 5, 1. **9.** Start with 2 and multiply by −3 repeatedly; 162, −486, 1,458. **15.** neither **17.** both **21.** Answers may vary. Sample: He may be correct, but he cannot keep decreasing his time by 15 s indefinitely. **23.** 1 **25.** 1 **27 a.** 17; 16 **b.** Blue tiles: start with 1, add 0, 4, 0, 4 and so on; yellow tiles: start with 0, add 4, 0, 4, 0 and so on. **29.** 123,456 × 9 = 1,111,104 **35.** 12.5 mi

EXERCISES 1. 10; 50 **3.** 324; 972; 2,916

5.

Cans of Soup	Number of Servings
3	9
4	12
5	15
6	18
7	21

7. 4, 5, 6, 7 **9.** 5, 10, 15, 20 **13.** 11n; 110 **15.** $\frac{n}{2}$; 5 **21.**

Miles	Time (h)
10	0.4
20	0.8
30	1.2
40	1.6
50	2.0

23.

Celsius	Kelvin
0	273
10	283
20	293
40	313
80	353
120	393

25.

Side Length (in.)	Area (in.^{2})
2	4
3	9
5	25
8	64
10	100
12	144

Selected Answers

27 a.

x	y
−4	−6
−2	−3
2	3
4	6

b. 0 **31.** 7

15.

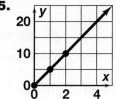

17.

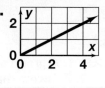

25. 15 ft²

Lesson 9-4   **pp. 454–455**

EXERCISES 1. exactly one **3.** Each output is 5 times the input. **5.** $d = 30t$ **9.** $y = 3x + 5$

13.

x	y
0	9
1	8
2	7
3	6

15.

x	y
0	0
1	$\frac{1}{2}$
2	1
3	$\frac{3}{2}$

21. $y = (0.50)n$ **23.** $d = 48h$ **25.** Answers may vary. Sample: The y-values increase by $\frac{1}{2}$ when the x-values increase by 1.
27. −3.875, −3.5, −0.875 **31.** 1 mm; it is less than 1 m.

Lesson 9-5   **pp. 457–459**

EXERCISES 1. a table showing the relationship between the input and output of a function

3.

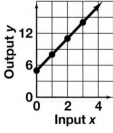

5.

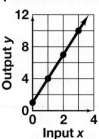

7. $d = 320t$; 3,200 mi

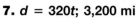

9. 750 Calories **11.** A

Lesson 9-6   **pp. 463–464**

EXERCISES 1. C **3.** B **5.** You travel at a steady pace for 2 h, stop for $\frac{1}{2}$ h, and then travel at the same steady pace for 2 h. **7.** You should not connect the points because you sell only whole-number glasses of lemonade.

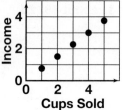

11 a. The graph shows that Josh caught up to Rafael after about 10 s. **b.** Josh **13.** The ball is 20 ft high on the way up and on the way down. It reaches that height after about 0.4 s and about 2.4 s. **15.** Answers may vary. Sample: A person threw a ball into the air. It left the person's hand 5 feet above the ground and landed on the ground about 2.75 seconds later. **19.** >

Lesson 9-7   **pp. 470–471**

EXERCISES 1. Simple interest is calculated only on the principal. Compound interest is calculated on the principal and any interest left in the account. **3.** $1,543.12 **5.** $71.40

9.

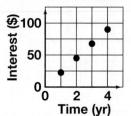

11.

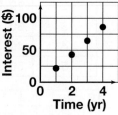

15. $1,643.94 **21.** $543.14 **25.** C **27.** E **29.** $4,370.91 **35.**

Lesson 9-8
pp. 474–475

EXERCISES 1. No; it cannot be used to show the relationship between two quantities. **3.** No; it cannot be used to show the relationship between two quantities. **5.** multiplication **7.** $y = \frac{x}{z}$
9. $r = \frac{p+5}{3}$ **21.** $F = \frac{9}{5}C + 32$
23. $w = \frac{V}{\ell \cdot h}$ **25.** $r = 2t$ **27.** 7 ft **29.** 5 cm **33.** 14.4 m

Chapter Review
pp. 478–479

1. arithmetic **2.** function **3.** principal
4. compound **5.** conjecture
6.

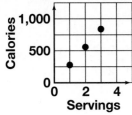

7.

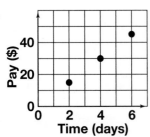

8. $82.50 **9.** arithmetic **10.** geometric
11. neither **12.** $-6n$; -60 **13.**

x	y
0	3
2	4
4	5
6	6

14. $y = \frac{1}{2}x + 3$ **15.** $y = 2x + 2$
16.

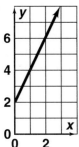

17. 7, 5, 3, 1, −1

18. Answers may vary. Sample: You travel for 2 h at a constant rate of 50 mi/h. You stop for 4 h, and then return to your starting place at a constant rate of 50 mi/h.

19.

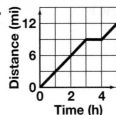

20. $450.00

21. $3,298.49 **22.** $x = \frac{z-y}{3}$ **23.** $x = -\frac{k}{4yz}$
24. $x = 9\left(\frac{z}{3} + 4\right)$, or
$x = 3z + 36$
25. $9.00

Chapter 10

Lesson 10-1
pp. 488–489

EXERCISES 1. (0, 0) **3.** A **5.** D **7.** (−2, 2)
9. (3, 0) **15.** IV **17.** III

23–26. Answers may vary. Samples are given.

23.

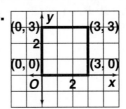

29. IV

31.

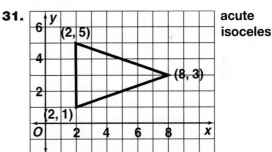

acute isoceles

33. Answers may vary. Sample: (−3, −3), (0, −3), (4, −3); if the x-coordinate is 37, the y-coordinate would be −3 because it is a straight horizontal line.

Lesson 10-2
pp. 493–494

EXERCISES 1. a line **3.**

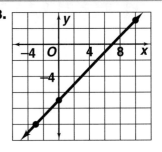

5. The point (5, −2) lies on the line.
7. (0, 9), (2, 11), (−3, 6) **9.** (0, 4), (2, 2), (−1, 5)
15. yes **17.** yes **23.**

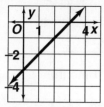

25.

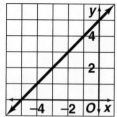

37. I, III

39. The student thought the product of −3 and −1 was −3; it is 3. **43.** No; for $x < 0$, the y-values are negative. **45.** $604.66

Lesson 10-3 pp. 500–501

EXERCISES 1. rise; run **3.** −2 **5.** –1 **7.** 2
11.

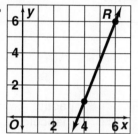

15. $-\frac{1}{4}$

17. Roof A; the slope of roof A is $\frac{5}{3}$, and the slope of roof B is $\frac{3}{5}$. Since $\frac{5}{3} > \frac{3}{5}$, roof A is steeper.
19 a. $24,000 **b.** −2 **c.** Every year, the value of the car decreases $2,000. **25.** No; an isosceles triangle has two equal angles, but $\triangle XYZ$ does not.

Lesson 10-4 pp. 506–507

EXERCISES 1. If the solutions of an equation form a line, it is linear. If the graph of the solutions is not a line, it is nonlinear.
3.

x	−3	−2	−1	0	1	2	3
y	3	2	1	0	1	2	3

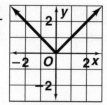

5. Answers may vary. Sample: Squaring a positive or a negative number always results in a positive

number. So for all values of x, x^2 is positive, and y is always positive. **7.** no
9.

x	−3	−2	−1	0	1	2	3
y	−27	−12	−3	0	−3	−12	−27

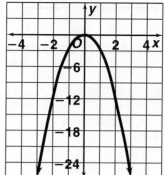

11.

x	−3	−2	−1	0	1	2	3
y	7	2	−1	−2	−1	2	7

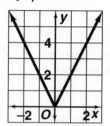

17.

x	−3	−2	−1	0	1	2	3
y	6	4	2	0	2	4	6

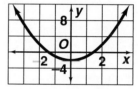

19.

x	−3	−2	−1	0	1	2	3
y	−3	−2	−1	0	−1	−2	−3

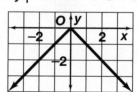

27. A 29. F 31. yes; $6.5^2 = 42.25$ 35. 7 cm

EXERCISES 1. transformation
3. $P(-3, -3) \rightarrow P'(1, 1)$
　$Q(-1, -1) \rightarrow Q'(3, 3)$
　$R(-1, -3) \rightarrow R'(3, 1)$

5. $(1, -2)$ **7.** $(-5, -3)$

11.
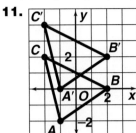

$A(-1, -2)$, $B(2, 0)$,
$C(-2, 2) \rightarrow A'(-1, 0)$,
$B'(2, 2)$, $C'(-2, 4)$

13.
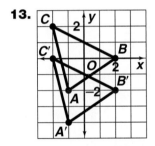

$A(-1, -2)$, $B(2, 0)$,
$C(-2, 2) \rightarrow A'(-1, -4)$,
$B'(2, -2)$, $C'(-2, 0)$

15. $(x, y) \rightarrow (x - 5, y)$

19.
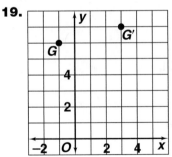
right 4 units, up 1 unit

21.
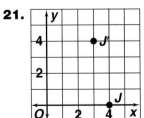
left 1 unit, up 4 units

23. $(x, y) \rightarrow (x + 3, y - 1)$
25. $(x, y) \rightarrow (x - 1, y + 4)$
27. Answers may vary. Sample: up 2, right 1; right 2, up 1; up 2, right 1; right 2, up 1
31. $(-1, -6)$; $(0, -2)$; $(1, 2)$

EXERCISES 1. A line of reflection produces a mirror image of the figure, and a line of symmetry divides a figure into mirror images.
3. $A(-1, 1)$, $B(-3, 4)$,
　$C(-5, -2) \rightarrow A'(1, 1)$,
　$B'(3, 4)$, $C'(5, -2)$

5. The x-coordinates are opposites; the y-coordinates are the same. **7.** none **11.** $(1, 5)$
13. $(2, 6)$ **17.**
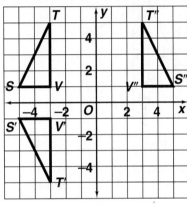

21. $(-3, 4)$, $(3, -4)$ **23.** $(7, -2)$, $(-7, 2)$
27. reflection; y-axis; $(x, y) \rightarrow (-x, y)$
29.
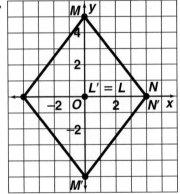
rhombus

33. $(0, 2)$, $(1, 5)$, $(2, 8)$, $(3, 11)$

EXERCISES 1. line symmetry and rotational symmetry **3.** yes; 120° **5.** 90° **7.** No; it does not match the original figure after any rotation of 180° or less. **11.** 180°

13.

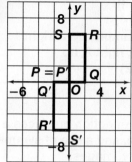

$P'(0, 0), Q'(-2, 0), R'(-2, -6), S'(0, -6)$

19. III **21.** I **23 a.** 90°; 180°; 270° **b.** Yes; the image stays the same after rotation.

27.

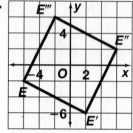

square **31.** equilateral

Chapter Review pp. 524–525

1. reflection **2.** center of rotation **3.** slope
4. ordered pair **5.** linear equation

6–8.

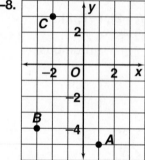

6. IV **7.** III **8.** II

9–11. Answers may vary. Samples are given.

9. (0, 3), (−2, 1), (5, 8)
10. (0, −5), (5, 0), (−1, −6)
11. (0, 1), (2, 5), (−3, −5)
12. (0, −2), (4, −6), (−3, 1)
13.

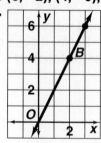

14.

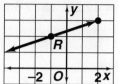

15.

x	−3	−2	−1	0	1	2	3
y	8	3	0	−1	0	3	8

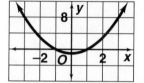

16.

x	−3	−2	−1	0	1	2	3
y	4	3	2	1	2	3	4

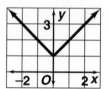

17.

x	−3	−2	−1	0	1	2	3
y	16	6	0	−2	0	6	16

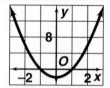

18.

x	−3	−2	−1	0	1	2	3
y	12	8	4	0	4	8	12

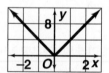

19. $A(3, -1), B(1, 1),$ $C(4, 4) \rightarrow A'(3, -3),$ $B'(1, -1), C'(4, 2)$

20. $A(3, -1), B(1, 1),$ $C(4, 4) \rightarrow A'(0, -1),$ $B'(-2, 1), C'(1, 4)$

21. $A(3, -1), B(1, 1),$ $C(4, 4) \rightarrow A'(6, -6),$ $B'(4, -4), C'(7, -1)$

22.

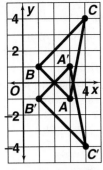

$A(3, -1), B(1, 1),$
$C(4, 4) \rightarrow A'(3, 1),$
$B'(1, -1), C'(4, -4)$

23. yes; 90°
24. yes; 180°

Chapter 11

Lesson 11-1   pp. 534–536

EXERCISES 1.

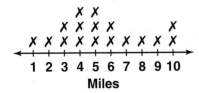

14   16   18   20   22   24

3.

Tickets Sold	Tally	Frequency
45	II	2
46	IIII	4
47		0
48	II	2
49	I	1
50	III	3
51	II	2
52		0
53	I	1

7.   **Miles From Home to Shopping Center**

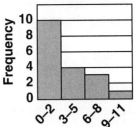

9.   **How Many Amusement Parks Did You Visit Last Year?**

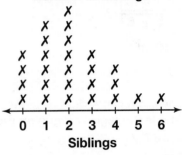

13. 8 customers
17. Answers may vary. Sample:

Number of Siblings

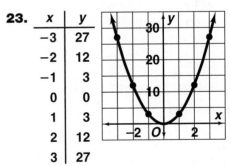

23.

x	y
−3	27
−2	12
−1	3
0	0
1	3
2	12
3	27

Selected Answers

Lesson 11-2
pp. 540–542

EXERCISES 1. lawn mowing **3.** yes **5.** 26
9. A1 **11.** B3 **13.** Corpus Christi, Texas **15.** all of them **19.** 1975–2000 **25.** Double line graph; line graphs are best for showing change over time.
27 a.

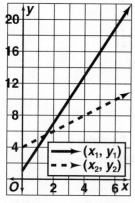

B3 = 4, B4 = 7, D4 = 6, D5 = 7

b. (1.5, 5.5) **31.** 1,332 m²

Lesson 11-3
pp. 546–547

EXERCISES 1. The stem is the digit or digits on the left, and the leaf is the digit or digits on the right. **3.** 12 **5.**

4	3 6 7
5	1 2
6	0 1 7
7	1 2 8
8	2 6 8

Key: 8 | 2 means 82

7.
High Temperatures
in the Desert (°F)

9	8 9
10	0 1 3 4 8 9
11	1 2 2 3 3 8

Key: 9 | 8 means 98

9. 56 in.; 50 in. **11.** No; the median height for females is 58.5 in. **13.** Yes; 76 − 56 = 20.
15. C **17.** 54

Lesson 11-4
pp. 551–553

EXERCISES 1. C **3.** B **5.** was not **7.** Part (b); the sample is more diverse. **11.** Fair; the question makes no assumptions. **13.** Biased; the question uses the terms *harsh* and *inspiring*.
19. Yes; surveying every 10th person is random, and you should get a mix of ages and genders.
21. Yes; you will survey people in your population without any bias. **25.** Start with 3 and add 5 repeatedly; 23, 28, 33

Lesson 11-5
pp. 555–556

EXERCISES 1. Researchers capture, mark, and release animals, and then capture another group of animals. The number of marked animals in the second group indicates population size. **3.** about 13,661 bass **5.** about 305 bears **7.** about 2,010 deer **9.** about 2,048 deer **17.** 63 alligators
19 a. The proportion should be $\frac{8}{25} = \frac{38}{x}$.
b. 119 sharks **21.** about 233 animals

Lesson 11-6
pp. 562–564

EXERCISES 1. no **3.** greater **5.** The vertical axis starts with 8 instead of 0. The title is also misleading since grapes are not everyone's favorite. **7.** The graph gives the impression that the largest group of students received the highest scores. There are uneven intervals on the x-axis.

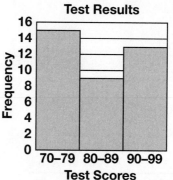

15. It reverses the scale on the x-axis. **17.** The company wants to give the impression that it is profitable even though it's not. **25.** about 45 billion

Lesson 11-7
pp. 568–570

EXERCISES 1. It illustrates what happens to one set of data when the other increases. **3.** yes
5. about 47 years

7.

Does Studying Affect Grades?

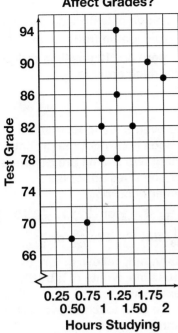

Hours Studying

9. positive **11.** negative **17.** Positive; the values are both increasing.
19. Answers may vary. Sample: 1,750 million

Movie Attendance

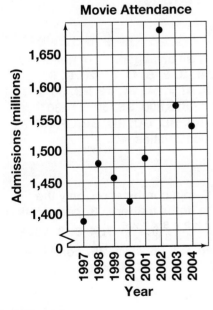

Year

23. 158 seals

Chapter Review pp. 572–573

1. stem-and-leaf **2.** negative **3.** legend **4.** line plot **5.** population

---

6.

Hours	Tally	Frequency
3			1
4				2
5							5
6							5
7						4
8				2
9			1

Number of Hours of TV (weekly)

Number of Hours of TV People Watch per Week

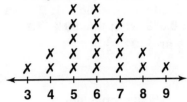

7. **How Many Pencils or Pens Are in Your Backpack?**

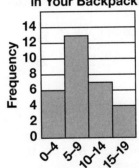

Pencils or Pens

8. the number of times a person has flown
9. 14 people **10.** counts to 20 **11.** counts to 20
12. writes name **13.**

```
7 | 0
6 | 0 0 0 1 6 9
5 | 0 0 4 5 8
4 | 0 0 0 5 7 7 8
3 | 6
2 | 3 7 7 9
1 | 6 9
```

Key: 1 | 6 means 16

14. Fair; the question makes no assumptions about the activity. **15.** Biased; the question assumes the ocean is calm and soothing.
16. about 368 wolves **17.** The *y*-axis interval starts at 93, so it appears that the student who studied 6 h did twice as well as the student who studied 4 h. **18.** no trend **19.** negative

Chapter 12

EXERCISES 1. Answers may vary. Sample: the result or group of results of an action **3.** B **5.** A
7. $\frac{1}{12}$; $0.08\overline{3}$; about 8.3% **9.** $\frac{1}{2}$; 0.5; 50% **13.** 0
15. $\frac{3}{10}$ **25.** $\frac{3}{4}$ **27.** $\frac{2}{4}$ or $\frac{1}{2}$ **37.** $\frac{a}{b}$

EXERCISES 1. Theoretical probability is computed by the formula
$P(\text{event}) = \frac{\text{number of favorable outcomes}}{\text{total number of possible outcomes}}$.
Experimental probability is based on experimental data or observation.
3. 18 **5.** 5 coins; one for each baby **7.** $\frac{18}{25}$
15. $\frac{1}{5}$; $\frac{1}{20}$; $\frac{13}{320}$; $\frac{9}{508}$ **17.** $\frac{6}{25}$ **19.** $\frac{2}{25}$ **21.** $\frac{7}{25}$
23. $\frac{x}{252}$; 6 **27.** $\frac{3}{9}$ or $\frac{1}{3}$

EXERCISES 1. the collection of all possible outcomes in an experiment **3.** 1 **5.** 7 **7.** 16
9. D **11.** 1 2 3 4 5 6; $\frac{3}{6}$ or $\frac{1}{2}$
13. 1st Spin   2nd Spin; $\frac{1}{4}$

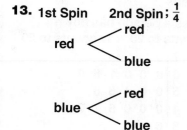

15. 12 recipes **19.** $\frac{2}{16}$ or $\frac{1}{8}$ **23 a.** 16 outfits
b. $\frac{12}{16}$ or $\frac{3}{4}$ **25.** small fruit punch, small lemonade, medium fruit punch, medium lemonade, large fruit punch, large lemonade, jumbo fruit punch, jumbo lemonade **27.** No; there are 12 possible orders, so the probability for each order is $\frac{1}{12}$.

EXERCISES 1. Two events are independent if the occurrence of one does not affect the probability of the other occurring; two events are dependent if the occurrence of one does affect the probability of the other occurring.
3. independent **5.** $\frac{1}{36}$ **7.** $\frac{3}{36}$ or $\frac{1}{12}$ **11.** $\frac{1}{64}$ **15.** $\frac{2}{7}$
17. $\frac{5}{7}$ **21.** $\frac{10}{380}$ or $\frac{1}{38}$ **25.** $\frac{1}{25}$ **27.** $\frac{24}{729}$ or $\frac{8}{243}$
29 a. Complementary; red, yellow, green, or broken are all the possible events of a traffic light. **b.** Mutually exclusive; since a student can only receive one grade on a test, the events have no outcomes in common.
31. $\frac{5}{7}$ **35.**

	1	2	3
H	H1	H2	H3
T	T1	T2	T3

EXERCISES 1. an arrangement of items in a particular order **3.** B **5.** C **7.** 120 **9.** 6
13. 3! = 6 **15.** 4! = 24 **21.** 42 **23.** 30 **27.** 24
29. 5,040 **31.** 3,628,800 **35.** 60 **37.** 30
39 a. BS, GS, RS, BD, GD, RD, BP, GP, RP
b. 3 × 3 = 9 possibilities **43.** $\frac{1}{256}$

EXERCISES 1. In a combination, only the grouping of the items matters. **3.** permutation
5. $\frac{7 \times 6 \times 5}{3 \times 2 \times 1}$, $\frac{10 \times 9 \times 8 \times 7 \times 6}{5 \times 4 \times 3 \times 2 \times 1}$ **7.** 4 **9.** 3 **13.** 6
19. 60 **21.** 840 **23.** 66 ways **25.** combination; 56 sets **29.** 20 **31.** $\frac{1}{6}$ **35.** 4! = 24

1. combination **2.** event **3.** independent

4. odds in favor of **5.** Experimental **6.** $\frac{1}{7}$ **7.** $\frac{2}{7}$

8. $\frac{6}{7}$ **9.** $\frac{1}{50}$ **10.** 32

11. Appetizer   Soup   Main Dish

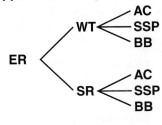

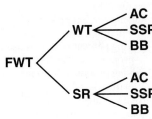

12. $\frac{1}{12}$ **13.** 12 dinners **14.** $\frac{30}{182}$ or $\frac{15}{91}$

15. $\frac{48}{182}$ or $\frac{24}{91}$ **16.** $\frac{56}{182}$ or $\frac{4}{13}$ **17.** $\frac{1}{16}$ **18.** 5 teams

19. 24 ways

Index

A

Absolute value, 31–32, 33, 61

Absolute value equation, 505, 506, 507, 525

***Act It Out* Problem Solving Strategy,** xl, xli, 516, 596

Activity Lab
Box-and-Whisker Plots, 58
Choosing Appropriate Units, 153
Choosing Scales and Intervals, 436
Choosing the Best Display, 548
Comparing Fractions, 86
Comparing Fractions and Decimals, 95
Describing Patterns, 168
Divisibility Tests, 73
Drawing Similar Figures, 256
Estimating in Different Systems, 158
Exploring Multiple Events, 597
Exploring Percent of Change, 309
Exploring Probability, 585
Exploring Right Triangles, 404
Exploring Similar Figures, 251
Exploring Slope, 502
Finding Patterns, 441
Generating Formulas for Area, 379
Generating Formulas for Volume, 426
Generating Formulas From a Table, 451
Geometry in the Coordinate Plane, 490
Graphing Population Data, 557
Graphing Using Spreadsheets, 543
Inequalities in Bar Graphs, 209
Interpreting Rates Visually, 242
Keeping the Balance, 178
Making a Circle Graph, 358
Measuring Angles, 329
Modeling a Circle, 393
Modeling Decimal Division, 19
Modeling Decimal Multiplication, 13
Modeling Equations, 179
Modeling Fraction Division, 140
Modeling Fraction Multiplication, 135
Modeling Integer Addition and Subtraction, 36–37
Modeling Integer Multiplication, 43
Modeling Two-Step Equations, 199
More About Formulas, 476
Percent Equations, 308
Plan a Trip, 264
Properties and Equality, 52
Random Numbers, 590
Rational Number Cubes, 278
Representing Data, 495
Scale Drawings and Models, 258
Sides and Angles of a Triangle, 335
Slides, Flips, and Turns, 509
Solving Puzzles, 152
Three Views of a Function, 460
Three Views of an Object, 409
Two-Variable Data Collection, 566

Using a Scientific Calculator, 72
Using Data to Predict, 596
Using Fraction Models, 125
Using Percent Data in a Graph, 289
Using Proportions With Data, 243
Using Spreadsheets, 173
Using Tables to Compare Data, 101
Venn Diagrams, 537
Writing Survey Questions, 549
See also Algebra Thinking Activity Lab; Data Analysis Activity Lab; Data Collection Activity Lab; Hands On Activity Lab; Technology Activity Lab

Acute angle, 330, 333

Acute triangle, 337, 338, 367

Addition
Associative Property of, 9, 60
Commutative Property of, 9, 60
compensation and mental math, 12
of decimals, 8–11, 17, 62, 66, 166
estimating by front-end estimation, 5
estimating by rounding, 4
of fractions, 125–129, 160, 162, 666
of fractions, using models, 125
Identity Property of, 9
of integers, 36–42, 44, 118, 177
of mixed numbers, 130–134, 160, 162
on number lines, 12, 38–39
order of operations, 48–51, 61, 166
solving equations by, 180–184, 190, 199–204, 210, 322
solving inequalities by, 210–213, 221

Addition Property
of Equality, 52, 180
of Inequality, 210, 214

Additive inverses, 38, 44

Adjacent angles, 331

Algebra
applications of percent, 304–307, 317
Cross-Products Property, 239
Distributive Property, 49–51, 61, 62, 66, 133
dividing by fractions, 141
estimating population size, 554–556, 573
exercises that use, 42, 47, 71, 94, 100, 145, 226, 231, 241, 254, 262, 272, 293, 314, 338, 339, 372, 387, 408, 441, 484, 513, 517, 522, 530, 536, 543, 556, 578, 583
finding angle measures, 332–334, 337–339
finding missing measure in similar figures, 253
finding percent of change, 309–314, 317
finding slope of a line, 498–502, 525
function rules, 452–455, 479
graphing linear equations, 491–494
graphing points in four quadrants, 486–489, 524, 530

graphing using a table, 456–459, 479
interpreting graphs, 461–464, 479
multiplication, symbols indicating, 15
multiplying fractions, 136, 139
nonlinear relationships, 504–507, 525
number sequences, 442–445, 478
patterns and graphs, 436–440, 478
patterns and tables, 168, 446–449, 478
Properties of Addition, 9
Properties of Equality, 52, 180, 186, 188
Properties of Inequality, 210, 211, 214, 216
Properties of Multiplication, 15
ratios, 228
solving percent problems using equations, 298–301, 317
solving percent problems using proportions, 294–297, 317
solving proportions using mental math, 245
transforming formulas, 472–475, 479
using scale drawings, 259

Algebra Thinking Activity Lab
Interpreting Rates Visually, 242
Keeping the Balance, 178
More About Formulas, 476
Percent Equations, 308
Properties and Equality, 52
Solving Puzzles, 152

Algebraic expressions
defined, 169, 220
evaluating, 170–172, 191, 194–197, 220, 434, 484
modeling, 49, 169, 170, 185
writing, 168–172, 194–197

Analysis
of circle graph, 354
error analysis, 6, 50, 55, 78, 84, 129, 133, 139, 144, 151, 182, 190, 218, 231, 240, 248, 261, 313, 327, 334, 418, 494, 501, 556

Angle(s)
acute, 330, 333
adjacent, 331
central, 350, 351, 352, 355, 367
classifying, 330–331, 333, 484
complementary, 331–334, 366
congruent, 331
corresponding, 252
defined, 329, 330
identifying, 331, 333
at intersecting lines, 331–334
measuring, 329, 331, 372, 484
obtuse, 330, 333
right, 330, 333
of rotation, 520, 521, 525
straight, 330, 333
sum, in triangles, 335, 337, 338
supplementary, 331–334, 366
of triangles, 335, 337, 338
vertex of, 330
vertical, 331

Annual interest rate, 468–471, 479

Applications
advertising, 562
of arcs, 351
avalanches, 499
careers, 611
changing fractions to decimals, 98
clothing, 610
of congruent figures, 347
dividing mixed numbers, 142
finding percent, 285, 299
geography, 69
indirect measurement, 253
manufacturing, 587
Olympics, 607
order of operations for expressions, 49
ordering fractions, 88
plants, 457
savings, 473
solving equations, 187, 196
solving inequalities, 211, 215
subtracting fractions, 127
subtracting integers, 40
using Pythagorean Theorem, 406
writing expressions, 170
writing inequalities, 206
See also Real-world applications

Approximation. *See* Estimation

Arc
in constructions, 361, 362
defined, 351
naming, 351, 352, 367

Area, 375–392, 428
of circles, 395, 396, 397, 416, 429
defined, 375, 428
estimating, 375–376, 377, 428
exercises that use, 50, 51
finding, in coordinate plane, 490
of irregular figures, 390–392, 398–399, 428, 451
modeling, 69, 451
of parallelograms, 379–383, 385, 428
of rectangles, 416
relating perimeter and, 376, 377, 381, 382–383
of squares, 400, 451
of trapezoids, 388–389, 391–392, 428
of triangles, 379, 385–387, 428

Arithmetic
Cross-Products Property, 239
Distributive Property, 49–51, 61, 62, 66, 133
dividing by fractions, 141
multiplying fractions, 136
order of operations, 48–51, 61, 166
Properties of Addition, 9
Properties of Equality, 52, 180, 186, 188
Properties of Inequality, 210, 211, 214, 216
ratios, 228
sequence, 442, 444–445, 478

Arrow notation, 511, 512, 525

Assessment
Chapter Reviews, 60–61, 112–113, 160–161, 220–221, 266–267,
316–317, 366–367, 428–429, 478–479, 524–525, 572–573, 616–617
Chapter Tests, 62, 114, 162, 222, 268, 318, 368, 430, 480, 526, 574, 618
Checkpoint Quizzes, 18, 35, 79, 101, 134, 153, 191, 209, 237, 257, 288, 309, 345, 358, 393, 420, 450, 465, 503, 518, 549, 565, 597, 614
open-ended, 47, 190, 197, 204, 222, 254, 256, 297, 307, 338, 349, 352, 357, 378, 402, 418, 459, 489, 509, 522, 563, 585
Test Prep, 7, 11, 17, 23, 30, 34, 42, 47, 51, 57, 71, 78, 85, 90, 94, 100, 105, 109, 123, 129, 133, 139, 145, 151, 157, 172, 177, 184, 190, 198, 204, 208, 213, 218, 231, 235, 241, 248, 255, 263, 277, 283, 287, 293, 297, 301, 307, 314, 327, 334, 339, 344, 349, 353, 357, 364, 378, 383, 387, 392, 397, 403, 408, 413, 418, 425, 440, 445, 449, 455, 459, 464, 471, 475, 489, 494, 501, 507, 513, 517, 522, 536, 542, 547, 553, 556, 564, 570, 583, 589, 595, 602, 609, 613
Test Prep Cumulative Review, 163, 223, 319, 431, 527, 619–621
Test Prep Reading Comprehension, 63, 115, 269, 369, 481, 575
See also Tests, preparing for

Associative Property
of Addition, 9, 60
of Multiplication, 15, 60
validating conclusions using, 9, 15

Axes, of graph, 486

B

Balance, 469, 479

Balance scales, 52, 178

Bar graph
double, 539–542, 543, 573
floating, 209
inequalities in, 209

Base
of cone, 411
of cylinder, 410
of an exponent, 68
of parallelogram, 379, 380–383
of prism, 410, 412
of pyramid, 410
of three-dimensional figures, 410–411, 412, 429
of trapezoid, 388–392
of triangle, 379, 384–387
of two-dimensional figures, 379, 380, 384, 388

Benchmarks, 120, 122–123, 160, 308

Biased question, 551, 552, 573

Bisector
perpendicular, 362, 363, 367
segment, 362

Board game project, 624

Box-and-whisker plots, 58

C

Calculator
with decimals, 97, 98
exercises that use, 95, 100, 133, 139, 184, 397, 403, 440, 445, 466, 471
with exponents, 68
for finding angle measures, 355
for finding area of circle, 395
for finding circumference, 395
for finding factorials, 607
for finding percent of a number, 354
for finding percents, 280, 285
for finding volume, 423
with fractions and mixed numbers, 98
graphing. *See* Graphing calculator
Math feature, 607, 613
with Pythagorean Theorem, 406
using scientific, 72

Calculator Tip, 68, 97, 403, 607, 613

Capacity
conversion factors, 236
customary units of, 148, 149–151
metric units of, 26, 28–30, 61, 668

Capture/Recapture Method, 554–556, 573

Careers
archaeologist, 487
astronaut, 241
botanist, 457
fabric designer, 353
journalist, 98
landscape architect, 23
marine biologist, 145
park ranger, 553
rescue swimmer, 387
scientist, 313
tailor, 595
veterinarian, 175
See also Math at Work

Carry Out the Plan, xxxii–xlix, 22, 70, 128, 138, 189, 240, 300, 348, 356, 363, 439, 458, 569, 601, 608

Cartesian plane, 486

Cell, spreadsheet, 538, 572

Celsius temperatures, 158, 168, 449, 477

Center
of circle, 350, 352, 367
of dilation, 256
of rotation, 519, 520
of sphere, 411

Centimeter (cm), 26, 27

Central angle, 350, 351, 352, 355, 367

Central tendency
mean. *See* Mean
median. *See* Median
mode. *See* Mode
range. *See* Range

Certain events, 581

Challenge, 7, 11, 17, 23, 30, 34, 42, 47, 51, 57, 71, 78, 85, 90, 94, 100, 105, 109, 123, 129, 133, 139, 145, 151, 157, 172, 184, 190, 198, 204, 208, 213, 218, 231, 235, 241, 248, 255, 263, 277, 283, 287,

Cooperative Learning. *See* Chapter
   Projects
Coordinate, 486–490, 524
   naming, 486
   x-coordinate, 486, 488
   y-coordinate, 486, 488
Coordinate plane, 486–489, 524
   defined, 486
   geometry in, 490
   graphing points on, 487
   graphing polygons, 487, 488, 490
   quadrants in, 486–489, 524, 530
Corresponding parts
   of congruent figures, 346, 347, 348
   of similar figures, 252–253
Cost, unit, 233, 234, 266
Counting principle, 592–593, 594, 606,
   607, 611, 617
Cross product
   solving proportions using, 245, 247,
     267, 322
   using, 239–240, 267
Cross-Products Property, 239
Cube, 410
Cubes, rational number, 278
Cubic unit, 421
Cumulative Review. *See* Test Prep
   Cumulative Review
Customary system of measurement,
   148–151, 161, 670
   for capacity, 148, 149–151
   choosing appropriate units, 153
   choosing reasonable estimates, 26, 29,
     374, 375, 428
   conversions in, 148–151, 161, 162, 236,
     372
   for length, 148, 150–151, 374, 375, 428
   for weight (mass), 148, 149–151
Cylinder
   bases of, 410
   defined, 410
   height of, 410
   surface area of, 416, 417, 418, 429
   volume of, 423, 424, 425, 429

D

Data
   collecting, 243, 532–537, 549–553, 566,
     572, 573
   displaying. *See* Displaying data
   graphing, 437, 439, 462, 463, 478
   interpreting, 571
   using to persuade, 560–564
   using to predict results, 596
Data analysis, 129
   box-and-whisker plots, 58
   circle graphs, 354–357, 367
   describing data, 558
   double bar graph, 539–542, 543, 573
   double line graph, 539, 541, 542, 557,
     573
   exercises that use, 56–57, 177, 293, 476,
     543, 555, 557, 566, 570, 589, 596

frequency table, 532–536, 572, 603, 604
histogram, 533–536, 572
interpreting data, 571
line plot, 533–535, 558, 572
mean. *See* Mean
median. *See* Median
misleading graphs, 560–564, 573
misleading statistics, 558, 561, 563
mode. *See* Mode
outlier, 53
population size, 554–557, 573
quartiles, 58
random samples, 550, 552
range. *See* Range
scatter plots, 567–570, 573
stem-and-leaf plot, 544–547, 573
survey, 54, 98, 238, 289, 293, 294,
   549–553, 573, 626, 629
trends, 568, 569, 573
using data to persuade, 560–564, 573
using spreadsheets, 173, 314, 538, 539,
   540, 543, 590
Venn diagrams, 537, 575
Data Analysis Activity Lab
   Box-and-Whisker Plots, 58
   Choosing Scales and Intervals, 436
   Choosing the Best Display, 548
   Exploring Percent of Change, 309
   Graphing Population Data, 557
   Inequalities in Bar Graphs, 209
   Representing Data, 495
   Using Data to Predict, 596
   Using Percent Data in a Graph, 289
   Using Tables to Compare Data, 101
Data Collection
   exercises that use, 537, 542, 547, 549,
    596
Data Collection Activity Lab
   Making a Circle Graph, 358
   Two-Variable Data Collection, 566
   Using Proportions With Data, 243
   Writing Survey Questions, 549
Decagons, 340, 343
Decameter (dam), 27
Decimal(s)
   adding, 8–11, 17, 62, 66, 166
   annexing zeros to divide, 21, 22
   changing to fractions, 97, 99
   changing to, from fractions, 95–97, 99,
    113
   comparing, 11, 103, 104, 113, 530
   dividing, 6, 19–23, 30, 120, 226, 663,
    665
   dividing decimal by decimal, 20, 62
   estimating with, 4–5, 8, 14, 60
   modeling, 13, 19, 20, 103, 278, 279
   multiplying, 13–17, 26, 31, 226, 372,
    661
   ordering, 98, 99, 113
   place value and, 2, 658
   reading and writing, 659
   repeating, 97, 98, 99, 113, 401
   rounding, 660
   Skills Handbook, 658–665
   subtracting, 9, 10–11, 17, 62, 66, 166

terminating, 96, 99, 113, 401
   writing as percents, 279, 282, 578
   writing percents as, 280, 282, 316, 434
Decimal points, aligning, 8, 9
Decimeter (dm), 27
Decrease, percent of, 310, 311, 313, 378
Deductive reasoning. *See* Reasoning
Defects, 587, 588, 589, 616
Denominator
   common, 126, 128, 130, 666
   different, 127, 131
   simplifying fractions, 82, 83, 113
   See also Least Common Denominator
    (LCD)
Dependent event, 599, 600–601, 617
Diagnostic Test, xxx–xxxi
Diagonal, 344
Diagram
   drawing, 404
   for ratios, 228, 232, 233
   for solving equations, 185, 186, 192,
    196
   tree, 592, 593, 594, 600, 617
   Venn, 537, 575
   for writing algebraic expressions, 169,
    170
Diameter
   of circle, 351, 352, 367
   defined, 350
   finding circumference and area of
    circle, 394–397
Difference. *See* Subtraction
Dilation, 256
Direction Words, 124, 185
Discounts
   finding discounted price, 312
   percent of, 311, 313, 317
Discrete Mathematics
   combination, 610–613, 617
   counting principle, 592–593, 594, 606,
    607, 611, 617
   factorial, 606–607, 609
   permutation, 606–609, 611, 617
   tree diagram, 592, 593, 594, 617
Disjoint events, 602
Displaying data
   choosing best display, 548
   circle graph, 354–359
   double bar graph, 539–542, 543, 573
   double line graph, 539, 541, 542, 557,
    573
   graphing population data, 557
   line plot, 533–535, 558, 572
   reporting frequency, 532–536, 572,
    603, 604
   in spreadsheet. *See* Spreadsheet
   stem-and-leaf plot, 544–547, 573
   using data to persuade, 560–564, 573
   Venn diagram, 537, 575
Distributive Property, 49–51, 61, 62, 66,
   133
Dividend, 20

Index

M

Make a Plan, xxxii–xlix, 22, 70, 128, 138, 189, 230, 240, 300, 348, 356, 363, 439, 444, 458, 563, 569, 588, 601, 608

Make a Table **Problem Solving Strategy,** xlii, xliii, 377, 448, 506, 559

Manipulatives
 algebra tiles, 43, 179, 199
 beads, 597
 blocks, 409, 441
 cardboard, 518
 cards, 599, 600, 601, 605, 609, 614, 616
 centimeter graph paper, 404
 chips, 36–37
 coins, 584, 585, 587, 588, 593, 594, 595, 600, 601
 compass, 361, 362, 367
 construction paper, 288
 cubes, 441, 596
 dictionary, 257
 dot paper, 342, 343
 graph (grid) paper, 13, 258, 342, 343, 379, 404, 411, 412, 465, 503
 index cards, 79, 191, 420
 marbles, 596, 602, 618
 number cubes, 278, 584, 594, 601, 614, 629
 paper models, 19, 86, 125, 135, 140
 poster board, 426
 protractor, 251, 329, 335, 358
 ruler, 155, 156, 157, 260, 262, 263, 397, 427, 624
 spinner, 358, 582, 583, 589, 594, 597
 straightedge, 361, 362
 straws, 335, 393
 unit cubes, 419

Maps, 259–263
 exercises that use, 42, 163, 262, 267, 268
 finding distance on, 260
 scale of, 259, 260, 264
 trip planning with, 264

Markup, percent of, 311, 313, 317

Mass
 conversion factors, 236
 customary units of weight, 148, 150–151
 metric units of, 26, 27, 28–30, 61, 669

Math at Work
 architect, 345
 artist, 450
 automotive engineer, 237
 detective, 18
 pollster, 565
 songwriter, 134

Math Games
 Evaluating Expressions, 191
 Factor Cards, 79
 Hide and Seek, 503
 Lines in Space, 465
 Order, Please!, 288
 Products of Winners, 614
 Square Root Bingo, 420

Math in the Media, 109, 283, 344, 403

Mathematical Techniques. *See* Estimation; Guided Problem Solving; Mental Math; Number Sense

Mean
 defined, 53
 describing data, 558
 finding, 53, 56, 57, 61, 218, 473
 misleading use of, 561, 563
 from stem-and-leaf plots, 545, 546, 571

Measurement, 670
 of angles, 329–334, 337–339, 372, 484
 customary system of. *See* Customary system of measurement
 estimating in different systems, 158
 exercises that use, 28–30, 61, 134, 142, 150–151, 162, 254, 255, 267, 430, 494
 indirect, 253, 254, 255, 267
 measuring to solve problems, 427
 metric system of. *See* Metric system of measurement
 precision of, 154–157, 161, 162
 units of. *See* Unit of measurement

Measures of central tendency
 mean. *See* Mean
 median. *See* Median
 mode. *See* Mode
 range. *See* Range

Median
 defined, 54
 describing data, 558
 finding, 54, 56, 57, 58, 61, 115, 218, 530
 misleading use of, 561, 563
 from stem-and-leaf plots, 545, 546, 571

Mental Math, 9, 10, 12, 15, 16, 23, 48, 49, 50, 55, 62, 78, 93, 129, 133, 139, 143, 184, 202, 246, 268, 282, 286, 306, 448, 506, 512, 517, 522, 588
 estimating answers, 477
 finding percent of a number, 291, 292
 finding perimeter, 384
 finding square roots of perfect squares, 400
 solving equations using, 175, 176, 177, 195
 solving proportions using, 245

Meter, 26, 27

Metric system of measurement, 26–30, 667–670
 for capacity, 26, 28–30, 61, 668
 choosing appropriate units, 153
 choosing reasonable estimates, 26, 29
 converting, 27–28, 34, 47, 61, 62
 estimating in, 26
 for length, 26, 28–30, 61, 667
 for mass, 26, 27, 28–30, 61, 669
 multiplying to change units, 27
 prefixes for metric units, 27

Midpoint, 362

Milligram (mg), 26

Milliliter (mL), 26

Millimeter (mm), 26, 27

Misleading graph, 560–564, 573

Misleading statistics, 561, 563

Missing measure in similar figures, 253, 254, 267

Mixed numbers
 adding and subtracting, 130–134, 160, 162
 defined, 91, 113
 described, 148
 dividing, 142–145, 161, 162
 estimating with, 92, 121–123
 improper fractions and, 136, 213
 modeling, 91, 140, 146
 multiplying, 137–139, 161, 162
 multiplying by whole numbers, 137
 writing as improper fractions, 92, 93
 writing as percents, 285, 286
 writing improper fractions as, 92, 93, 113

Mixed Review, 7, 11, 17, 23, 30, 34, 42, 47, 51, 57, 71, 78, 85, 90, 94, 100, 105, 109, 123, 129, 133, 139, 145, 151, 157, 172, 177, 184, 190, 198, 204, 208, 213, 218, 231, 235, 241, 248, 255, 263, 277, 283, 287, 293, 297, 301, 307, 314, 327, 334, 339, 344, 349, 353, 357, 364, 378, 383, 387, 392, 397, 403, 408, 413, 418, 425, 440, 445, 449, 455, 459, 464, 471, 475, 489, 494, 501, 507, 513, 517, 522, 536, 542, 547, 553, 556, 564, 570, 583, 589, 595, 602, 609, 613

Mode
 defined, 54
 describing data, 558
 finding, 54, 56, 57, 61
 misleading use of, 561, 563
 from stem-and-leaf plots, 545, 546, 571

Modeling
 area, 69, 451
 concrete, 13, 19, 36–37, 43, 86, 135, 140, 179, 199, 251, 258, 278, 329, 335, 379, 393, 404, 409, 426, 441
 creating drawings and models, 258, 409
 decimals, 13, 19, 20, 103, 278, 279
 division, 19, 20, 24, 140, 141, 149
 exercises that use, 17, 23, 25, 42, 43, 47, 62, 64, 65, 71, 78, 85, 90, 93, 94, 114, 116, 143, 145, 147, 163, 164, 172, 184, 193, 198, 202, 204, 208, 219, 224, 225, 231, 234, 239, 241, 255, 262, 263, 276, 277, 282, 287, 288, 293, 297, 301, 303, 318, 319, 320, 321, 326, 327, 343, 370, 403, 413, 417, 431, 432, 464, 500, 501, 521, 522, 582, 583, 593, 619, 620, 622
 formulas, 426
 fractions and mixed numbers, 82, 86, 87, 91, 102, 103, 120, 125, 127, 135, 136, 140, 141, 146, 278, 279, 308
 geometric, 13, 19, 20, 69, 82, 86, 87, 91, 120, 125, 127, 135, 140, 169, 185, 186, 192, 196, 228, 232, 233, 251, 253, 274–275, 279, 324, 325, 336, 342, 350, 380, 393, 400, 401, 404, 414, 415, 421, 426, 441, 443, 451, 498, 499, 519, 520
 graphs, 58
 integers, 31, 32, 36–40, 44, 210

Index

tutoring, 162
utilities, 268
wages, 574
walking, 479
weather, 11, 40, 64–65, 84, 287, 545
weights, 567
windmills, 519
wood, 267
world records, 190
See also Applications; Careers; Math at Work

Reasonableness of solutions, xxxiv–xli, 8, 14, 21, 24, 26, 29, 127, 130, 131, 137, 142, 146, 178, 192, 201, 233, 280, 285, 287, 289, 299, 302, 329, 359, 374, 375, 384, 423, 428, 446, 462
choosing reasonable estimates, 26, 29, 146, 178, 192, 287, 289, 302, 359, 374, 375, 428
See also Estimation; Think It Through

Reasoning
deductive, 9, 15, 24, 49, 63, 80, 115, 146, 163, 175, 192, 223, 249, 269, 302, 319, 369, 398, 431, 466, 481, 496, 527, 558, 575, 604
exercises that use, 6, 17, 19, 23, 24, 30, 33, 34, 41, 46, 50, 71, 89, 99, 108, 114, 122, 135, 138, 144, 168, 173, 183, 190, 198, 199, 207, 208, 212, 213, 218, 231, 235, 247, 261, 276, 282, 292, 308, 333, 339, 342, 344, 348, 352, 357, 363, 376, 383, 387, 416, 419, 423, 425, 426, 436, 460, 474, 476, 489, 500, 502, 536, 537, 541, 542, 548, 556, 558, 563, 564, 574, 585, 588, 590, 595, 596, 597, 602, 607, 608
inductive, 36, 168, 443, 446–447. *See also* Patterns
justifying steps, 5, 9, 14, 21, 149, 152, 194–195, 200–201, 260, 280, 504, 544, 610, 611
logical, 152, 537, 575
making conjectures, 58, 135, 168, 251, 335, 353, 443
making inferences, 242, 289, 309, 359, 360, 438, 496, 558, 566, 587, 596, 604
for multiple-choice questions, 21, 201, 315, 381
proportional, 244–248, 272
unit rates and proportional reasoning, 232–235
validating conclusions, 8, 9, 14, 15, 52, 127, 130, 131, 137, 142, 178, 233, 280, 285, 299, 302, 329, 384, 423, 446, 462
See also Error Analysis; Guided Problem Solving; Problem Solving Strategies

Reciprocals, 141–145, 160, 161

Rectangle
area of, 416
defined, 341
perimeter of, 375, 472, 490

Rectangular prism, 421–422, 424

Reflection, 509, 514–517, 525
defined, 515, 525

graphing, 515, 516, 525
line of, 515

Regular polygons, 340–341, 343, 367

Renaming fractions and mixed numbers, 131

Repeating decimal, 97, 98, 99, 113, 401

Representation. *See* Modeling

Research, 185, 508, 603

Review. *See* Assessment; Extra Practice; Mixed Review; Vocabulary Review

Rhombus, 341, 343

Right angle, 330, 333

Right triangle, 404–408, 429
classifying, 338, 367
defined, 337
finding length of hypotenuse of, 405–408, 429
finding length of legs of, 406, 407, 408

Rise, 498

Root, square, 400–403, 429, 672

Rotation, 519–522, 525
about a point, 519, 520
angle of, 520, 521, 525
center of, 519, 520
clockwise, 519
counterclockwise, 519
defined, 519, 525

Rotational symmetry, 519, 520, 525

Rounding
decimals, 660
estimating by, 4, 6, 8
exercises that use, 2, 62, 120, 122
precision and, 155, 161
whole numbers, 6, 655

Ruler, 155, 156, 157, 260, 262, 263, 397, 427, 624

Rules
function, 452–455, 479
for translations, 511, 512

Run, 498

S

Sales tax, 304, 306, 307

Sample, defined, 550

Sample, random, 549–553

Sample size, 628

Sample space, 591–596, 597, 617

Scale
defined, 259, 267
finding, 260
on graphs, 436–437
of maps, 259, 260, 264, 267
modeling, 260
models, 258, 261

Scale drawing, 259–263
defined, 259, 267
finding scale of, 260, 262
making, 258
using, 259, 262

Scale factor, 256

Scalene triangle, 336, 338, 367

Scatter plot, 567–570, 573
defined, 567, 573
describing trends in, 568, 569, 573
interpreting, 568
making, 567, 569, 570

Scientific calculator, 68, 72

Scientific notation, 106–109, 113
defined, 106, 113
negative exponents in, 110
writing in, 107, 108, 110, 113

Segments, 324–327
constructing congruent, 361, 363, 367
constructing perpendicular bisector, 362, 363, 367
length of, 363

Semicircle, 351

Sequence, 442–445, 478
arithmetic, 442, 444–445, 478
defined, 442
geometric, 442–445, 478
nth term in, 447
value of term in, 447, 448

Sides
congruent, 336
corresponding, 252–253
of triangles, 335

Similar polygons, 251–256, 267
defined, 252, 267
drawing, 256
finding missing measures, 253, 254, 267
indirect measurement, 253, 254, 255, 267
verifying similarity, 251

Simple interest, 468–471, 479

Simplest form
of fraction, 82–85, 113, 118, 226, 272, 586, 587
of ratios, 229, 230, 238, 266, 578

Simulation, 587, 588, 617

Skew lines, 325, 327, 366

Skills Handbook, 654–669
adding and subtracting fractions with like denominators, 666
comparing and ordering whole numbers, 654
dividing a decimal by a whole number, 663
dividing whole numbers, 657
metric units of capacity, 668
metric units of length, 667
metric units of mass, 669
multiplying decimals, 661
multiplying whole numbers, 656
place value and decimals, 658
powers of 10, 664
reading and writing decimals, 659
rounding decimals, 660
rounding whole numbers, 655
zeros in decimal division, 665
zeros in the product, 662

Slide, 509

Slope of a line, 498–502, 525
defined, 498

Index

X _____

x-axis, 486
    reflections, 515–517
x-coordinate, 486, 488

Y _____

y-axis, 486
    reflections, 515–517
y-coordinate, 486, 488

Z _____

Zero(s)
    annexing, in decimal division, 21, 22
    in decimal division, 665
    dividing by, 21
    in product, 662
Zero Property of Multiplication, 15

Acknowledgments

Staff Credits

The people who make up the **Prentice Hall Math** team—representing design services, editorial, editorial services, educational technology, marketing, market research, photo research and art development, production services, publishing processes, and rights & permissions—are listed below. Bold type denotes core team members.

Dan Anderson, Carolyn Artin, Nick Blake, **Stephanie Bradley,** Kyla Brown, Patrick Culleton, Kathleen J. Dempsey, **Frederick Fellows, Suzanne Finn,** Paul Frisoli, Ellen Granter, **Richard Heater,** Betsy Krieble, Lisa LaVallee, Christine Lee, Kendra Lee, Cheryl Mahan, **Carolyn McGuire,** Eve Melnechuk, Terri Mitchell, Jeffrey Paulhus, Mark Roop-Kharasch, Marcy Rose, Rashid Ross, Irene Rubin, Siri Schwartzman, Vicky Shen, **Dennis Slattery,** Elaine Soares, Dan Tanguay, Tiffany Taylor, Mark Tricca, Paula Vergith, Kristin Winters, Helen Young

Additional Credits

Paul Astwood, Sarah J. Aubry, Jonathan Ashford, Peter Chipman, Patty Fagan, Tom Greene, Kevin Keane, Mary Landry, Jon Kier, Dan Pritchard, Sara Shelton, Jewel Simmons, Ted Smykal, Steve Thomas, Michael Torocsik, Maria Torti

TE Design

Susan Gerould/Perspectives

Illustration

Additional Artwork

Rich McMahon; Ted Smykal

Kenneth Batelman: **580;** Joel Dubin: **601;** John Edwards, Inc.: **184, 263, 265, 589;** Das Grup: **593, 594;** Kelly Graphics: **351, 354;** Carla Kiwior: **132, 142;** Brucie Roche: **7, 195, 235, 415, 424, 582;** John Schreiner: **218, 307, 597;** Wilkinson Studios: **423, 613;** JB Woolsey: **233, 253;** XNR Productions, Inc.: **32, 43, 55, 260, 262, 264, 383, 386, 389, 390**

Photography

Front Cover: Paul Frankian/Index Stock Imagery, Inc.
Back Cover: Corbis/Picture Quest

Title page: tl, Bob Daemmrich Photography; **tr,** Williamson Edwards/The Image Bank; **bl,** David Muench; **br,** Bob Daemmrich Photography.

Front matter Pages x, Tom Brakefield/Corbis; **xi,** Jim Craigmyle/Corbis; **xii,** Robert Tyrell; **xiii,** Joe Gemignani/Corbis; **xiv,** Getty Images, Inc; **xv,** Mitch Windham/The Image Works; **xvi,** Roger Ressmeyer/Corbis; **xvii,** Rudi Von Briel/Photo Edit; **xviii,** Jeff Greenberg/PhotoEdit; **xix,** Andersen Ross/Getty Images, Inc; **xx,** David Young-Wolff/PhotoEdit; **xxi,** Andre Jenny/Alamy; **xlviii,** Richard Haynes; **xlix,** Richard Haynes; **l,** Bryan Peterson/Getty Images, Inc.; **lii,** Cindy Charles/PhotoEdit; **liii,** Randall Hyman; **liv,** Jeff Lepore/Photo Researchers, Inc.; **lvi,** Photonica/Getty Images; **lvii,** Brian Bailey/Getty Images, Inc.; **xlviii,** Richard Haynes.

Chapter 1 Pages 3, Art Wolfe/Photo Researchers, Inc; **4,** Tom Brakefield/Corbis; **5,** Russ Lappa; **8,** Mary Kate Denny/Photo Edit; **8 ml,** Richard Haynes; **11 ml,** Gallo Images/Corbis; **11 mr,** Andrew McKim/Masterfile; **14,** Robin Nelson/Photo Edit; **16,** Robert Rathe/Getty Images; **17,** Terry Oakley/Alamy; **18,** Frank Siteman/Monkmeyer; **19,** Richard Haynes; **20,** Spencer Grant/ Photo Edit; **21,** Eyewire/Getty Images, Inc. **23,** Rachel Epstein/ PhotoEdit, **26 tr,** Prentice Hall photo by Jane Latta; **26 mr,** Guy Ryecart/Dorling Kindersley; **26 br,** Dorling Kindersley; **28,** Russ Poole Photography; **28 tl,** Richard Haynes; **28 mr,** Richard Haynes; **31,** Age Fotostock/SuperStock; **32,** Wayne R. Blenduke/ Getty Images; **34,** Reuters NewMedia, Inc./Corbis; **35,** Richard Haynes; **37,** Richard Haynes; **41,** Keith Kent/Peter Arnold, Inc.; **43,** Richard Haynes; **44,** G. Kalt/Zefa/Corbis; **45,** Philip & Karen Smith/SuperStock; **47,** Peter Pinnock/Getty Images, Inc.; **51,** Doug Wilson/Alamy Images, **53,** Richard Haynes; **54 bl,** Clive Boursnel/Dorling Kindersley; **54 br,** Kevin Summers/Getty Images; **55,** Arthur Tilley/Getty Images, Inc.; **56,** Tim Davis/ Getty Images; **57,** Gordon Clayton/Dorling Kindersley; **64 t,** Photo Franca Principe, IMSS; **64–65 b,** Digital Vision/Getty Images, Inc.

Chapter 2 Pages 67, Steve Satushek/Getty Images; **68,** Richard Haynes; **71,** Andrew Syred/Photo Researchers, Inc.; **74,** D. J. Peters/AP/Wide World Photos, **76 ml,** Richard Haynes, **76 br,** Richard Haynes; **78,** G.D.T./Getty Images, Inc.; **79 b,** Richard Haynes; **79 t,** Russ Lappa; **83,** Hans Halberstadt/Corbis; **84,** Rubberball/SuperStock; **86,** Richard Haynes; **87 mr,** A. & J. Visaoe/Peter Arnold, Inc.; **87 bl,** Richard Haynes; **88,** Jim Pickerell, **91,** Associated Press/THE HAWK EYE/AP Wide World; **92,** Tony Savino/The Image Works; **94,** The Image Works; **96,** Spencer Grant/PhotoEdit; **98,** Jeff Greenberg/PhotoEdit; **100,** Janet Foster/Masterfile; **102,** Rhoda Sidney/PhotoEdit; **105,** David Aubrey/Corbis; **106,** Jim Craigmyle/Corbis; **107,** NASA/ Finley Holiday Films; **109,** *FOXTROT* ©1992 Bill Amend. Reprinted with permission of Universal Press Syndicate. All rights reserved; **116 bl,** Jim Corwin/Stock Connection/ PictureQuest; **116 tl,** Dorling Kindersley; **116 tm,** Courtesy of Sony; **116 tr,** Steve Cole/Photodisc/Getty Images, Inc.; **116-117 b,** Abe Rezny/The Image Works.

Chapter 3 Pages 119, Andrew Syred/SPL/Photo Researchers; **121,** Jump Run Productions/Getty Images; **123,** Peter Vanderwarker/Stock Boston; **124,** Richard Haynes; **125,** Richard Haynes; **126 mr,** David Kelly Crow/Photo Edit; **126 bl,** Richard Haynes; **127,** Addison Geary/Stock Boston; **129 ml,** Tom Stewart/Corbis; **129 mr,** John A. Rizzo/Getty Images, Inc.; **130,** Earl Carter/Southeastern Sports Photos; **131,** Marnie Burkhart/ Masterfile; **133,** Tom Stewart/Corbis; **134,** Tom Stewart/Corbis; **135,** Richard Haynes; **136,** Richard Hutchings/PhotoEdit; **138,** Robert Tyrell; **139,** Kwame Zikomo/SuperStock, Inc.; **140,** Richard Haynes; **141,** Richard Haynes; **142,** Pierre Arsenault/ Masterfile; **143 tl,** Richard Haynes; **143,** Richard Haynes; **145,** Douglas Faulkner/Corbis; **149,** Karl Weatherly/PhotoDisc/Getty Images, Inc.; **151,** Gallo Images/Corbis; **155 tl,** David C. Ellis/ Getty Images; **155 tr,** Russ Lappa; **157,** Friedrich Von Horsten/ Animals Animals/Earth Scenes; **164-165 b,** Jose Fuste Raga/ Corbis; **165 mr,** Barbara Magnuson Larry Kimball/Visuals Unlimited; **165 tl,** Rainer Grosskopf/Getty Images, Inc.

Chapter 4 Pages 167, Bruce M. Herman/Photo Researchers, Inc.; **169**, Eddy Lemaistre/For Picture/Corbis; **170**, David Young-Wolff/PhotoEdit; **172**, Francois Gohier/Ardea; **174**, Keren Su/Corbis; **175**, Ariel Skelley/Corbis Stock Market; **177**, Joe Gemignani/Corbis; **180**, Richard Haynes; **181**, Lee Cohen/Getty Images; **182**, Janeart/Getty Images; **183**, Dr. Jeremy Burgess/Photo Researchers, Inc.; **185**, Richard Haynes; **187**, Richard Haynes; **189**, Will Hart; **191**, Prentice Hall; **194**, age fotostock/Superstock; **197**, Stuart Westmorland/Getty Images; **198**, David Young-Wolff/PhotoEdit; **199 t**, Richard Haynes; **200**, Ron Sachs/Corbis; **201**, Alan Thornton/Getty Images, Inc.; **202 tl**, Richard Haynes; **202 mr**, Richard Haynes; **203**, Reuters/Corbis; **204**, Patrick Clark/PhotoDisc/Getty Images, Inc.; **205**, D&J Heaton/Stock Boston; **206**, Russ Lappa; **208 tl**, SuperStock, Inc.; **208 tr**, Michael Newman/PhotoEdit; **210**, Bill Bachmann/Photo Edit **211**, Stephen Simpson/Getty Images; **213**, Kevin R. Morris/Corbis; **214**, Frances Roberts/Alamy; **215**, Jose Luis Pelaez, Inc./Corbis; **217**, Antonio Mo/Getty Images, Inc.; **224 t**, Steve Shott/Dorling Kindersley; **224-225 b**, Ron Kimball/Premium Stock/PictureQuest; **225 mr 1,2,& 3**, Russ Lappa; **225 tl**, Steve Shott/Dorling Kindersley; **225 tr**, Dorling Kindersley.

Chapter 5 Pages 227, Dave G. Houser/Corbis; **228**, Richard Haynes; **229**, AP Photo/Paul Sakuma; **231**, LWA-Dann Tardif/CORBIS; **232**, David Young-Wolff/Photo Edit; **235**, Andy Lyons/Getty Images, Inc.; **236**, BIOS/Peter Arnold, Inc.; **237 t**, Alan Levenson/Getty Images; **237 b**, Ron Kimball/Ron Kimball Stock; **238**, Richard Haynes; **241**, Johnson Space Center/NASA; **246 tl & mr**, Richard Haynes; **247**, Franklin D. Roosevelt Library; **248**, Photodisc Green/Getty Images; **251**, Richard Haynes; **252**, Alaska Stock LLC/Alamy; **255**, Brian Sytnyk/Masterfile; **257**, Richard Haynes; **258**, Richard Haynes; **259**, Getty Images, Inc.; **264**, AP/Wide World Photos; **271 tm**, www.rubberball.com

Chapter 6 Pages 273, Omni Photo Communications; Inc./Index Stock; **276**, Mitsuaki Iwago/Minden Pictures; **278**, Richard Haynes; **280**, Kelly Mooney Photography/Corbis; **281**, Peter Johnson/Corbis; **283**, Hillary Price; **284**, Robin Nelson/Photo Edit; **285**, David Young-Wolff/PhotoEdit; **287**, Tom McHugh/Photo Researchers, Inc.; **288**, Richard Haynes; **290**, Rhoda Sidney/Photo Edit; **291**, Richard Haynes; **293**, UNEP/Rougier/The Image Works; **294**, IML Image Group Ltd./Alamy; **297**, Bob Daemmrich/Stock Boston; **298 tr**, Mitch Windham/The Image Works; **298 bl**, Richard Haynes; **299**, David Young-Wolff/PhotoEdit; **301**, Bob Daemmrich/The Image Works **304**, Bernard Wolf/PhotoEdit; **305 tl**, Adamsmith Productions/Corbis; **305 bl**, Richard Haynes; **307**, Lawrence Migdale/Photo Researchers, Inc.; **310,** Mark Reinstein/The Image Works; **312 tl & mr**, Richard Haynes; **313**, Photo Researchers, Inc.; **320 bgrd, & br**, Courtesy of the U.S. Geological Survey; **321 bl, & ml**, Courtesy of the U.S. Geological Survey; **321 tl**, David Nicholls

Chapter 7 Pages 323, William A. Bake/Corbis; **325**, Rafeal Macia/Photo Researchers, Inc.; **326 mr**, Design by Jean-Charles Guillois and Ines Levy; **326 br**, James Marshall/Corbis; **328 mr**, Kevin Mallet/Dorling Kindersley; **328 tr**, Richard Haynes; **329**, Richard Haynes; **330**, Richard Pasley/Stock Boston; **331**, Richard Haynes; **332 mr & bl**, Richard Haynes; **333**, William Taufic/Corbis; **334**, Spencer Grant/PhotoEdit; **335**, Richard Haynes; **336**, Russ Lappa; **339**, Paul Hermansen/Getty Images,

Inc.; **340**, *Composition A*, 1920 Oil on canvas, 35 1/2 x 35 7/8 inches. © 2006 Mondrian/Holtzman Trust c/o HCR International, Warrenton, VA; **342**, Bill Aron/PhotoEdit; **343 tl**, Max Alexander/DK Picture Library; **343 tr**, Felicia Martinez/PhotoEdit; **343 br**, Paul Trummer/Getty Images, Inc.; **343 bl**, Cavagnaro/Visuals Unlimited; **344**, 1995 by NEA, Inc. Thaves 6–13; **345**, Peter Beck/Corbis; **346**, Roger Ressmeyer/Corbis; **347**, 2004 AFP/Getty Images; **350**, Spencer Grant/PhotoEdit; **351**, Lawrence Migdale; **353**, James L. Amos/Corbis; **354**, Richard Haynes; **355**, NASA; **357**, Spencer Grant/Photo Edit; **361**, Andreas Pollok/Getty Images; **362**, Courtesy of Wellesley College Library, Special Collections, photo by George McLean; **370 bl**, Professional Miniature Golf Association; **370 tr**, Jack Hollingsworth/Getty Images, Inc.; **370-371** Richard Hamilton Smith/Corbis; **371 tr**, SW Productions/Getty Images, Inc.

Chapter 8 Pages 373, Michael Grecco/Stock Boston; **374**, Getty Images; **375**, Jacques Descloitres, MODIS Rapid Response Team, NASA/GSFC; **379**, Richard Haynes; **380**, Janis Daemmrich/Daemmrich Photography; **380 bl**, Richard Haynes; **381**, Rudi Von Briel/Photo Edit; **384**, Bob Daemmrich/The Image Works; **387**, U.S. Coast Guard; **388**, Photo by Randy Varga; **389**, Buddy Mays/Corbis; **390 tl & br**, Richard Haynes; **392**, C Squared Studios/Getty Images, Inc.; **393**, Richard Haynes; **395**, Larry Lilac/Alamy; **397**, Lawrence Migdal/Stock Boston; **400**, Myrleen Ferguson Cate/PhotoEdit; **403**, *FOXTROT* ©1992 Bill Amend. Reprinted with permission of Universal Press Syndicate. All rights reserved. **406**, Jeff Greenberg/PhotoEdit; **408**, Michael J. Howell/Stock Boston; **409 mr & bm**, Russ Lappa; **409 tr**, Richard Haynes; **409 bl**, Russ Lappa; **410**, David Parker/Photo Researchers, Inc.; **413**, Davies & Starr/Getty Images, Inc.; **413**, John Lei/Stock Boston; **413**, Spike Mafford/Getty Images, Inc.; **416**, Richard Haynes; **418**, Amy Etra/PhotoEdit; **420**, Richard Haynes; **421 mr**, George & Monserrate Schwartz/Alamy; **421**, Richard Haynes; **432 tl**, Chris Brown/Stock Boston, Inc./PictureQuest; **432-433 m**, T.J. Florian/PictureQuest; **433 mr**, Digital Vision; **433 tm**, Phil Kember/Index Stock Imagery/PictureQuest

Chapter 9 Pages 435, Charles Bush; **438**, George Shelley/Masterfile; **440**, Bob Daemmrich/Stock Boston; **441 bl**, Russ Lappa; **441 bm**, Russ Lappa; **441 br**, Russ Lappa; **441 tr**, Richard Haynes; **442**, Hal Horwitz/Corbis; **445**, Kaz Chiba/Getty Images; **446**, SuperStock; **449 ml**, Cheryl Hogue/Visuals Unlimited; **449 mr**, Russ Lappa; **450**, Chris Marona/Photo Researchers, Inc.; **455**, Michael Newman/PhotoEdit; **456**, Royalty Free/Corbis; **457**, Mark Bernett/Stock Boston; **459**, Bettmann/Corbis; **461**, Bob Daemmrich/The Image Works; **462**, Jeff Greenberg/PhotoEdit; **464**, Lowe Art Museum, University of Miami/SuperStock, Inc.; **466**, Russ Lappa; **468 mr**, Ariel Skelley/Corbis; **468 bl**, Richard Haynes; **470**, Superstock/Alamy; **472**, AP/Wide World Photos; **473 mr & br**, Richard Haynes; **473 tl**, Richard Haynes; **475**, Richard Hutchings/Photo Researchers, Inc.; **482 ml**, Harold Wilion/Index Stock Imagery/PictureQuest; **482-483 m**, Neil Fletcher/Dorling Kindersley; **483 tm**, Ruth A. Adams/Index Stock Imagery/PictureQuest

Chapter 10 Pages 485, NASA/Masterfile; **487**, David R. Frazier/The Image Works; **489**, John R. Bracegirdle/Getty Images, Inc.; **491**, Dave Nagel/Getty Images, Inc.; **492**, Richard Haynes; **493**, Andersen Ross/Getty Images, Inc.; **494**, Lynda Richardson/

Corbis; **498**, AP Wide World Photos; 499, Corbis; **500 ml**, Peter Guttman/Corbis; **500 mr**, Adam Jones/Photo Researchers, Inc.; **501**, Prentice Hall; **503**, Richard Haynes; **504**, Colorsport; **505 ml, tl, & br**, Richard Haynes; **506**, Getty Images; **507**, Steve Fitchett/Getty Images, Inc.; **508**, Richard Haynes; **510**, Victoria & Albert Museum, London/Art Resource, NY; **513**, George Hall/Corbis; **514 br**, Charles Kennard/Stock Boston; 514 bl, Jerome Wexler/Photo Researchers, Inc.; **514 mr**, Nuridsany et Perennou/Photo Researchers, Inc.; **517**, Sturgis McKeever/Photo Researchers, Inc.; **519**, Jonathan Nourok/Photo Edit; **519 br**, Foto World/Getty Images, Inc.; **528–529 all**, LUCASFILM LTD. *Star Wars: Episode II—Attack of the Clones* © 2002 Lucasfilm Ltd. & TM. All rights reserved. Used under authorization. Unauthorized duplication is a violation of applicable law. No internet use.

Chapter 11 Pages 531, John Hickey/The Buffalo News; **532**, Jose Luis Pelaez, Inc./Corbis; **534 tr & ml**, Richard Haynes; **535**, Dennis MacDonald/PhotoEdit; **537**, Siede Preis/Getty Images, Inc.; **538**, Bill Aron/Photo Edit; **544**, David Young-Wolff/ PhotoEdit; **546**, Jeff Greenberg/PhotoEdit; **550**, Andy King/ Reuters/Landov; **552**, Anton Vengo/SuperStock, Inc.; **553**, Karen Preuss/The Image Works; **554**, Jim Brandenburg/ Minden Pictures; **556**, Amos Nachuom/Corbis; **560**, Tony Freeman/ PhotoEdit; **562**, Patricia Brabant/Getty Images, Inc.; **565**, Michael Newman/PhotoEdit; **567**, Richard Haynes; **568**, David Weintraub/Photo Researchers, Inc.; **576 tr**, Randy Ury/Corbis; **576–577**, Jeff Maloney/Getty Images, Inc.; **577 tm**, Philip Gatward/Dorling Kindersley

Chapter 12 Pages 579, Pictor International, Ltd./PictureQuest; **580**, Jim Cummins/Getty Images; **581**, Richard Haynes; **583**, Andre Jenny/Alamy; **584**, Prentice Hall; **585**, Richard Haynes; **586**, Andy Sacks/Getty Images, Inc.; **586**, Richard Haynes; **587**, Paul Barton/Corbis; **589**, David Young-Wolff/PhotoEdit; **591**, Burke/Triolo Productions/Foodpix; **592**, Hughes Martin/Corbis; **595**, TRBPhoto/Getty Images, Inc.; **596**, Bob Daemmrich/The Image Works; **598**, Emely/Zefa/Corbis; **600 tr & ml**, Richard Haynes; **602**, Comstock/Alamy; **603**, Richard Haynes; **606**, Getty Images, Inc.; **607**, Robert Laberge/Getty Images, Inc.; **609**, Joseph Sohm; ChromoSohm Inc./Corbis; **610**, Todd Warnock/ Getty Images; **611**, David Hiller/Getty Images; **613**, Russ Lappa; **622 tr**, Ken Chernus/Getty Images, Inc.; **622–623 b**, Larry Dale Gordon/Getty Images, Inc.; **623 br**, Tony Bee/photolibrary/ PictureQuest